THE BOOK OF ENOCH

Together with a Reprint of the GREEK FRAGMENTS

(1912)

Translated from the Editor's Ethiopic Text. Contents: Canonicity; Greek, Latin & Ethiopic Versions; Elements of 1 Enoch; Influence on Jewish Literature; Hebrew Book of Enoch; Theology; Parables; Heavenly Luminaries; Dream Visions.

TRANSLATED BY
R.H. Charles

ISBN 1-56459-523-4

Kessinger Publishing's Rare Reprints
Thousands of Scarce and Hard-to-Find Books!

We kindly invite you to view our extensive catalog list at:
http://www.kessinger.net

TO

THE WARDEN AND FELLOWS

OF MERTON COLLEGE

PREFACE

This is not so much a second edition as a new book. A brief comparison of the first edition and the present work will make this clear even to the cursory reader. Alike in the translation and in the commentary it forms a vast advance on its predecessor. I cannot claim to be satisfied with it even as it stands, and yet twenty additional years spent in Apocalyptic and Biblical studies have not, I would fain hope, been fruitless with regard to the present work.

The translation in the first edition was made from Dillmann's edition of the Ethiopic text, which was based on five MSS. With a view to this translation the present editor emended and revised Dillmann's text in accordance with nine hitherto uncollated Ethiopic MSS. in the British Museum, and the Greek and Latin fragments which had just come to light, but notwithstanding every care he felt his work in this respect to be of a wholly provisional character. From the date of the publication of the first edition in 1893 he steadily made preparation for an edition of the Ethiopic text and of the Greek and Latin fragments. This text, which is exhaustive of existing textual materials in these languages, was published by the University Press in 1906, and from this text the present translation is made. A new and revolutionary feature in the translation is due to the editor's discovery of the poetical structure of a considerable portion of the work. I call it revolutionary; for such it proves to be in respect of the critical problems of the text. By its means the lost original of the text is not infrequently recovered, phrases and clauses recognized as obvious interpolations, and not a few lines restored to their original context, whose claims to a place in the text were hitherto ignored on the ground of the weakness of their textual attestation.

During the past eighteen years the criticism of the book has made undoubted headway, and that, I am glad to say, mainly in the direction defined in the first edition. The idea of a *Grundschrift*, which was accepted by most of the chief scholars in this field till its appearance, and to which I strove and not in vain to give the *coup de grâce*, is now universally abandoned. The critical advance made in the present volume is not of a revolutionary character, but consists rather in a more detailed application of the principles of criticism pursued in the first edition.

In my first edition I said that a knowledge of 1 Enoch was indispensable to N.T. students. The further study of Apocalyptic and Biblical literature, Jewish and Christian, in the score of years that have since elapsed, has convinced me still more fully of this fact. And I might add here that to the O.T. student it is likewise indispensable, if we would understand many of the problems underlying O.T. prophecy. To the biblical scholar and to the student of Jewish and Christian theology 1 Enoch is the most important Jewish work written between 200 B.C. and 100 A.D. For a short account of the book the reader should consult the Introduction, § 1.

I cannot help expressing here my deep regret that Jewish scholars are still so backward in recognizing the value of this literature for their own history. Apocalyptic is the true child of Prophecy, and became its true representative to the Jews from the unhappy moment that the Law won an absolute autocracy in Judaism, and made the utterance of God-sent prophetic men impossible except through the medium of Pseudepigraphs, some of which, like Daniel, gained an entrance despite the Law into the O.T. Canon. It is true that eminent Jewish scholars in America and elsewhere have in part recognized the value of Apocalyptic literature, but, as a whole, Orthodox Judaism still confesses and still champions the one-sided Judaism, which came into being after the Fall of Jerusalem in 70 A.D., a Judaism lopped in the main of its spiritual and prophetic side and given over all but wholly to a legalistic conception of religion. It is not strange that since that disastrous period Judaism became to a great extent a barren faith, and lost its leadership in the spiritual things of the world.

I cannot close this Preface without recording my deep obligations to the officials of the University Press for the skill, care and expedition with which they have carried this work through; and likewise acknowledging the very helpful service rendered to me by a promising scholar, the Rev. A. L. Davies, in the correction of proofs, the verification of references, and at times the acquisition of fresh materials.

24 BARDWELL ROAD, OXFORD.
June 1, 1912.

CONTENTS

	PAGE
GENERAL INTRODUCTION	ix–cx
§ 1. Short Account of the Book	ix–xii
§ 2. The Title	xii–xiii
§ 3. Its Canonicity	xiii–xiv
§ 4. The Greek Versions. Editions of these Versions .	xiv–xvi
§ 5. The Relations of the G^g and G^e to each other and to E (the Ethiopic Version)	xvii–xix
§ 6. The Latin Version and Quotations	xix–xx
§ 7. The Ethiopic Version	xx–xxi
§ 8. Ethiopic MSS. Relation of the Ethiopic MSS. .	xxi–xxvii
§ 9. Editions of the Ethiopic Version	xxvii–xxix
§ 10. Translations	xxix–xxx
§ 11. Critical Inquiries	xxx–xlvi
§ 12. The Different Elements in 1 Enoch . . .	xlvi–lii
§ 13. Characteristics and Dates of the Different Elements .	lii–lvi
§ 14. The Poetical Element in 1 Enoch	lvi
§ 15. Original Language of Chapters 6-36—Aramaic; of Chapters 1-5, 37-104—Hebrew	lvii–lxx
§ 16. The Influence of 1 Enoch on Jewish Literature .	lxx–lxxix
§ 17. The Hebrew Book of Enoch	lxxix–lxxxi
§ 18. The Influence of 1 Enoch on Patristic Literature .	lxxxi–xcv
§ 19. The Influence of 1 Enoch on the New Testament .	xcv–ciii
§ 20. Theology	ciii–cx
THE BOOK OF ENOCH.—SPECIAL INTRODUCTIONS, TRANSLATION, CRITICAL AND EXEGETICAL NOTES . .	1–272
SECTION I (chapters i–xxxvi)	1–63
INTRODUCTION.—A. *Critical Structure and Dates.* B. *Relation of this Section to* (a) 72-82; (b) 83-90; (c) 91-104. C. *The Problem and its Solution*	1–4
TRANSLATION AND CRITICAL AND EXEGETICAL NOTES . .	4–63
SECTION II.—THE PARABLES (chapters xxxvii–lxxi) . . .	64–146
INTRODUCTION.—A. *Critical Structure.* B. *Relation of 37-71 to the rest of the Book.* C. *The Date.* D. *The Problem and its Solution*	64–68
TRANSLATION AND CRITICAL AND EXEGETICAL NOTES . .	69–146
SECTION III.—THE BOOK OF THE COURSES OF THE HEAVENLY LUMINARIES (chapters lxxii–lxxxii)	147–173
INTRODUCTION.—A. *Its Critical Structure and Object.* B. *Its Independence of* 1-36. C. *Its Calendar and the Knowledge therein implied*	147–150
TRANSLATION AND CRITICAL AND EXEGETICAL NOTES . .	151–173

Contents

	PAGE
SECTION IV.—THE DREAM-VISIONS (chapters lxxxiii–xc)	179–217
INTRODUCTION.—A. *Critical Structure.* B. *Relation of this Section to* (a) 1–36; (b) 91–104. C. *The Date.* D. *The Problem and its Solution*	179–182
TRANSLATION AND CRITICAL AND EXEGETICAL NOTES	182–217
SECTION V (chapters xci–civ)	218–272
INTRODUCTION.—A. *Critical Structure.* B. *Relation of* 91–104 *to* (a) 1–36; (b) 83–90. C. *Authorship and Date.* D. *The Problem and its Solution*	218–223
TRANSLATION AND CRITICAL AND EXEGETICAL NOTES	224–272
APPENDIX I.—THE GIZEH GREEK FRAGMENT (i–xxxii) AND THE GREEK FRAGMENTS PRESERVED IN SYNCELLUS' CHRONOGRAPHIA	273–305
APPENDIX II.—THE SON OF MAN; ITS MEANING IN JEWISH APOCALYPTIC AND THE NEW TESTAMENT	306–309
INDEX I.—PASSAGES AND PHRASES CLOSELY PARALLEL OR CONNECTED WITH 1 ENOCH	311–314
INDEX II.—NAMES AND SUBJECTS	315–331

THE BOOK OF ENOCH
i.e. 1 ENOCH

INTRODUCTION

§ 1. Short Account of the Book.

It is seldom that authors attain to the immortality which they hope for, and it is still more seldom that anonymous authors achieve this distinction. And yet it is just such a distinction that the authors of the Book of Enoch have achieved. That such should be ultimately his lot was the deep-rooted conviction of one of this literary circle. He looked forward (104^{11-12}) to the time when his writings would be translated into various languages, and become to the righteous 'a cause of joy and uprightness and much wisdom'. This hope was to a large degree realized in the centuries immediately preceding and following the Christian era, when the currency of these apocalyptic writings was very widespread, because they almost alone represented the advance of the higher theology in Judaism, which culminated in Christianity.[1] But our book contained much of a questionable character, and from the fourth century of our era onward it fell into discredit; and under the ban of such authorities as Hilary, Jerome, and Augustine, it gradually passed out of circulation, and became lost to the knowledge of Western Christendom till over a century ago, when an Ethiopic version of the work was found in Abyssinia by Bruce, who brought home three MSS. of it, from one of which Laurence made the first modern translation

---

[1] Nearly all the writers of the New Testament were familiar with it, and were more or less influenced by it in thought and diction. It is quoted as a genuine production of Enoch by St. Jude, and as Scripture by St. Barnabas. The authors of the Book of Jubilees, the Apocalypse of Baruch, and 4 Ezra, laid it under contribution. With the earlier Fathers and Apologists it had all the weight of a canonical book.

of Enoch. It was not, however, till recent years that the Book of Enoch and similar works have begun to come into their own owing to their immeasurable value as being practically the only historical memorials of the religious development of Judaism from 200 B.C. to 100 A.D., and particularly of the development of that side of Judaism, to which historically Christendom in large measure owes its existence.

The Book of Enoch is for the history of theological development the most important pseudepigraph of the first two centuries B.C. Some of its authors—and there were many—belonged to the true succession of the prophets, and it was simply owing to the evil character of the period, in which their lot was cast, that these enthusiasts and mystics, exhibiting on occasions the inspiration of the O.T. prophets, were obliged to issue their works under the aegis of some ancient name. The Law which claimed to be the highest and final word from God could tolerate no fresh message from God, and so, when men were moved by the Spirit of God to make known their visions relating to the past, the present, and the future, and to proclaim the higher ethical truths they had won, they could not do so openly, but were forced to resort to pseudonymous publication.

To describe in short compass the Book of Enoch is impossible. It comes from many writers and almost as many periods. It touches upon every subject that could have arisen in the ancient schools of the prophets, but naturally it deals with these subjects in an advanced stage of development. Nearly every religious idea appears in a variety of forms, and, if these are studied in relation to their contexts and dates, we cannot fail to observe that in the age to which the Enoch literature belongs there is movement everywhere, and nowhere dogmatic fixity and finality. And though at times the movement may be reactionary, yet the general trend is onward and upward. In fact the history of the development of the higher theology during the two centuries before the Christian era could not be written without the Book of Enoch.

From what has been already said it is clear that no unity of time, authorship, or teaching is to be looked for. Indeed, certain considerable portions of the book belonged originally not to the Enoch literature at all, but to an earlier work, i.e. the Book of Noah, which probably exhibited in some degree the syncretism of the work into which it was subsequently incorporated. This Book of Noah clearly embraced chapters 6-11, 54^7-55^2, 60, 65-69^{25}, 106-107.[1]

As regards the Enoch elements, the oldest portions of them are likewise pre-Maccabean, i.e. 12-36, and probably 90^{1-10} 91^{12-17}, i.e. the Apocalypse of Weeks. The Dream Visions, i.e. 83-90, were in all probability written when Judas the Maccabee was still warring, 165-161 B.C., 72-82 before 110 B.C., the Parables, 37-71 and 91-104, 105-64 B.C.

The authors of all the sections belong to the Chasids or their successors the Pharisees.

Conflicting views are advanced on the Messiah, the Messianic kingdom, the origin of sin, Sheol, the final judgement, the resurrection, and the nature of the future life. There is an elaborate angelology and demonology, and much space is devoted to the calendar and the heavenly bodies and their movements. Babylonian influences are here manifest and in a slight degree Greek.

The Book of Enoch, like the Book of Daniel, was written originally partly in Aramaic and partly in Hebrew. From an Aramaic original is derived 6-36, and possibly 83-90, while the rest of the book comes from a Hebrew original. To determine these questions categorically is a task of no little difficulty, seeing that for four-fifths of the text we have only a translation of a translation, and that such close affinities exist between Hebrew and Aramaic. For the resemblances between the two languages are so great that frequently retranslation from the Ethiopic into either is sufficient to explain corruptions in the former. There has accordingly been great divergence of opinion on this question, but in the opinion of the present writer, who

---

[1] Portions have been preserved in Jubilees 7^{20-39} 10^{1-15}, but the date of this Noachic literature is at latest pre-Maccabean.

has spent considerable time on the problem, the balance of evidence is decidedly in favour of the view above stated.

In the course of his studies it suddenly dawned upon the writer that much of the text was originally written in verse. This discovery has frequently proved helpful in the criticism of difficult passages, and the recovery of the original in a multitude of cases.

§ 2. The Title.

Our book appears under various titles, which may be briefly enumerated as follows:

1°. *Enoch.* Jude 14 ἐπροφήτευσεν ... ἕβδομος ἀπὸ Ἀδὰμ Ἐνὼχ λέγων.

Ep. Barn. iv. 3 ὡς Ἐνὼχ λέγει.

Clem. Alex. *Eclog. Proph.* (Dindorf, iii. 456) ὁ Δανιὴλ λέγει ὁμοδοξῶν τῷ Ἐνώχ: also in iii. 474.

Origen, *In Ioannem* vi. 25 ὡς ἐν τῷ Ἐνὼχ γέγραπται: *Contra Celsum* v. 54 τῶν ἐν τῷ Ἐνὼχ γεγραμμένων.

Tertullian, *De Cultu Fem.* ii. 10 'Ut Enoch refert'; *De Idol.* iv 'Enoch praedicens'; xv 'Spiritus ... praececinit per ... Enoch'.

Anatolius of Laodicaea (cited by Eus. *H. E.* vii. 32. 19 τὰ ἐν τῷ Ἐνὼχ μαθήματα).

2°. *The Books of Enoch.* This is probably the oldest title. The fifth Section of the book itself opens with the words: 92¹ 'The book written by Enoch'. 108¹ begins: 'Another book which Enoch wrote.' In 82¹ Enoch says to Methuselah: 'All these things I am recounting to thee ... and given thee books concerning all these: so preserve ... the books from thy father's hand.' 14¹ 'The book of the words of righteousness'. The third Section, i.e. 72¹, begins, 'The book of the courses of the luminaries'. These passages imply a plurality of books.

But though apparently the oldest title, it has not the oldest independent attestation. It is found in the following works:

T. Jud. xviii. 1 (β A S¹) ἐν βίβλοις Ἐνὼχ τοῦ δικαίου.

T. Lev. x. 5 (A) = καθὼς γέγραπται ἐν βίβλοις Ἐνώχ.

Origen, *Contra Celsum*, v. 54 τὰ ἐπιγεγραμμένα τοῦ Ἐνὼχ βιβλία: *In Num. Homil.* xxviii. 2 'In libellis qui appellantur Enoch'.

Pistis Sophia (ed. Schwartze, p. 245) 'Ea in secundo libro Ieu, quae scripsit Enoch'.

Syncellus (*Chronographia*, ed. Dind.), i. p. 20 ἐκ τοῦ πρώτου βιβλίου τοῦ Ἐνώχ. The same phrase recurs in i. p. 21, 47. Cf. i. 42 ἐκ τοῦ πρώτου λόγου Ἐνώχ. Here and in the preceding work the division of Enoch into books is clearly recognized. There were five such divisions or books; see § 6.

3°. *Book of Enoch*. This title is found in:

T. Lev. x. 5 (*a, d e g*) καθὼς περιέχει ἡ (> *a b f*) βίβλος Ἐνὼχ τοῦ δικαίου.

Origen, *De Princ.* i. 3. 3 'In Enoch libro': iv. 35 'in libro suo Enoch ita ait'.

Hilary, *Comment. in Ps.* cxxxii. 3 'Fertur id de quo etiam nescio cuius liber exstat'.

Jerome, *De Viris illustr.* iv 'De libro Enoch qui apocryphus est'.

Syncellus, *op. cit.* i. 60 ὡς ἐν τῇ βίβλῳ αὐτοῦ Ἐνὼχ φέρεται. But this title may refer merely to one of the books of Enoch, and so come under 2°.

3°. *Words of Enoch*. This title has the oldest external attestation. Jub. 21¹⁰ 'For thus I have found it written in the books of my forefathers and in the words of Enoch, and in the words of Noah'.

T. Benj. ix. 1 ἀπὸ λογίων (= λόγων β–*d*) Ἐνὼχ τοῦ δικαίου. This title finds some justification in 1 Enoch 1¹ 'Words of the blessing of Enoch'; 14¹ 'book of the words of righteousness'.

4°. *Writing of Enoch*:

T. Lev. xiv. 1 (β A) ἔγνων ἀπὸ γραφῆς Ἐνώχ. See also in T. Sim. v. 4, T. Naph. iv. 1.

Tertullian, *De Cultu Fem.* i. 3 'Scio scripturam Enoch ... cum Enoch eadem scriptura etiam de domino praedicarit'.

§ 3. Its Canonicity.

The citations of Enoch by the Testaments of the Twelve Patriarchs and by the Book of Jubilees show that at the close of the second century B.C., and during the first century B.C., this book was regarded in certain circles as inspired. When we come down to the first century A.D., we find that it is recognized as Scripture by Jude. See under § 2, 1°. In the next century this recognition is given amply in the Ep. Barnabas xvi. 5 λέγει γὰρ ἡ γραφή; by Athenagoras, *Legatio pro Christianis* 24 ἃ τοῖς προφήταις ἐκπεφώνηται (referring to Enoch); in the third century by Clem. Alex. *Eclog. Prophet.* ii, see § 2, 1°; by Irenaeus iv. 6. 12 'Enoch . . . placens Deo . . . legatione ad angelos fungebatur'; by Tertullian, *De Cultu Fem.* i. 3, *De Idol.* xv, see § 2, 1°; by Zosimus of Panopolis, quoted in Syncellus (Dind. i. 24) τοῦτο οὖν ἔφασαν αἱ ἀρχαῖαι καὶ αἱ θεῖαι γραφαί, ὅτι ἄγγελοί τινες ἐπεθύμησαν τῶν γυναικῶν. After the third century the Book of Enoch fell into discredit and gradually passed out of circulation.

§ 4. THE GREEK VERSIONS. EDITIONS OF THESE VERSIONS.

The Greek Versions have only in part been preserved. Chapters $1-32^6$ and 19^3-21^9 in a duplicate form were discovered in 1886–1887 at Akhmîm by the Mission Archéologique Française at Cairo, and published by M. Bouriant in 1892. These are designated as G^g, and G^{g1} and G^{g2} in the case of the duplicate passage. Large fragments have been preserved in Syncellus, namely $6-10^{14}$. 15^8-16^1, and 8^4-9^4 in a duplicate form. These are designated as G^s and G^{s1}, G^{s2} in the case of the duplicate passage.

The chief literature on these fragments is as follows:—

Bouriant, *Fragments grecs du livre d'Énoch. Mémoires publiés par les membres de la Mission archéologique française au Caire*, tom. ix, pp. 91–136, 1892. This is praiseworthy as a first edition, but the text is disfigured by many errors.

—— *L'Évangile et l'Apocalypse de Pierre avec le texte grec du livre d'Énoch. Texte publié en fac-similé par l'héliogravure d'après les photographies du manuscrit de Gizeh.* Paris, 1893.

Dillmann, *Sitzungsberichte d. kgl. Preuss. Akademie d. Wissenschaften zu Berlin*, 1892, li–liii, pp. 1039–1054, 1079–1092.

Introduction

These studies are of course good, and several of this scholar's suggestions are excellent. In his comparison of the Ethiopic and Greek Versions he had the benefit of having collations of $q\,t\,u$ before him. These gave him no inconsiderable advantage in dealing with the problems before him, though his article takes cognizance of only a limited number of readings where these MSS. furnish a superior text.

Lods, *Le Livre d'Hénoch, Fragments grecs découverts à Akhmîm, publiés avec les variantes du texte Éthiopien, traduits et annotés.* Paris, 1892. Lods' contribution is learned, scholarly, and judicious, but as he had the misfortune to base his work on the corrupt text published by Dillmann in 1851, a large portion of his conclusions was vitiated from the outset.

Charles, *The Book of Enoch*, pp. 318-370. Oxford, 1893. In this work I attempted an exhaustive comparison of the Greek and Ethiopic texts, and carried the criticism of the materials several stages beyond previous scholars in this department.

Swete, *The Old Testament in Greek*, vol. III.

Radermacher, *Das Buch Henoch, herausgegeben . . . von J. Flemming und L. Radermacher*, pp. 18-60, 113-114. Leipzig, 1901. This text, on the whole, is well edited and forms an advance on preceding editions. But, unless I am greatly mistaken, Dr. Radermacher is not a Semitic scholar. This deficiency in his equipment proved a sore handicap in the task he undertook. How is a purely classical scholar to edit a Greek text which is Greek in vocabulary, but largely Semitic in idiom? To show that our text is of this character it will be sufficient to adduce the following passages: 22^9 οὗ ἡ πηγὴ τοῦ ὕδατος ἐν αὐτῷ (אשר .... בו) = 'in which there is the spring of water'. 17^1 ἐν ᾧ οἱ ὄντες ἐκεῖ γίγνονται (אשר. .... שׁ) = 'where the dwellers become'. Here, it is true, ἐκεῖ could be taken with οἱ ὄντες. 32^3 οὗ ἐσθίουσιν ἁγίου τοῦ καρποῦ αὐτοῦ (אשר .... פריו) = 'whose holy fruit they eat'. The editor's failure to recognize this idiom in 16^1 has led him to emend the text in such a way as to obliterate wholly its original form. The unemended text runs: ἀπὸ ἡμέρας . . . . θανάτου ἀφ' ὧν τὰ πνεύματα ἐκπορευόμενα ἐκ τῆς ψυχῆς τῆς σαρκὸς αὐτῶν.[1] This Semitic construction is supported by E though in a slightly corrupted form. Hence it must be preserved, though as I pointed out in 1893, there is according to E the loss of τῶν γιγάντων before ἀφ' ὧν. This very phrase, moreover, τῶν γιγάντων is found in G^g, though this version inserts after it a gloss (?) containing the names of the three orders of giants as they are given in the Targum of Jonathan on Gen. 6$^{1-4}$.

The text and notes are accurately edited, but there are some errors. In v. 6 Radermacher reads οἱ ἀμίαντοι as an emendation of the corrupt reading which he says is αμα | τοι and not αμαρτητοι, as Bouriant and Lods stated. Bouriant and Lods were certainly wrong, and Dillmann's edition and mine, which were necessarily based on the work of these scholars, shared in their error. The autotype reproduction of the text was not published till after the issue of these editions. But if Bouriant and Lods deciphered the MS. wrongly, so also has Radermacher. It reads αμαρ|τοι. The ρ is partially obliterated, but it is unmistakable in the photographic reproduction of the MS. Hence we might possibly emend αμαρτοι into ἀναμάρτητοι, but certainly not into ἀμίαντοι. Notwithstanding, this forms a serviceable edition of the Greek.

Another fragment is found in a Vatican Greek MS., No. 1809, written in tachygraphic characters. This was published by Mai, *Patrum Nova Bibliotheca*, tom. ii, and deciphered by Gildemeister in the *ZDMG.*, 1855, pp. 621-624, and studied afresh by von Gebhardt in Merx' *Archiv*, ii. 243, 1872. Besides the above, references to or Greek quotations explicitly or implicitly from Enoch are found in the *Ep. of Barnabas* (see iv. 3; xvi. 4, 6); Justin Martyr, *Apol.* ii. 5; Athenagoras in his Πρεσβεία, x; Clement Alex., *Eclogae Prophet.* iii. 456 (ed. Dindorf); iii. 474; *Strom.* iii. 9; Origen, *Contra Celsum*, v. 52, 54; *In Ioannem*, vi. 25 (Lommatzsch, i. 241); *Clementine Homilies*, viii. 12. Since these last afford but slight help in correcting the text, we shall do no more here than refer to Lawlor's article on this subject in the *Journal of Philology*, xxv. 164-225, 1897.

---

[1] I have given the idiom in Hebrew, though the original was in Aramaic.

§ 5. The Relations of the G^s and G^g to each other and to E (the Ethiopic Version).

(a) *G^s more original than G^g.* These two fragments are closely related and yet exhibit marks of independence. They are closely related, and probably go back to the same Greek translation of the Aramaic text, since they present in so many passages identically the same text. On the other hand G^s has in several passages a different and undoubtedly better order of text. Thus G^s rightly places 7^{3-5} of G^g (or rather its equivalent of 7^{3-5}) after 8^3 of G^g. For manifestly $7^{1, 2}$ 8^{1-3} precede 7^{3-5}. Thus it alone preserves the original order. The angels went in to the daughters of men, who bare to them three classes of giants. And the angels taught their women sorceries and incantations ($7^{1, 2}$). Then follows a detailed account of the art, which each of the leading twenty angels taught mankind. And after this the giants turned against men and began to devour their flesh (G^s 8^{1-3} G^g 8^{1-3} 7^{3-5}). It will be observed that in 8^3 G^g is very defective compared with G^s in the list of the offices of the various angels. The additional elements in G^s here could not have been written by a Greek, for in every instance the office constitutes when translated into Aramaic a play on the name of the angel who discharges the office. Similarly in 6^7 the order of the names of the angels is different and G^s is here preferable to G^g E.

Again, 8^4 of G^s has preserved in all probability a more original text than G^g E. For it is natural that the substance of the prayer of men as they were slain by the giants should be given when it is first referred to in 8^4. Here, indeed, G^s presents a duplicate text, and both texts give the prayer in question. G^g E, on the other hand, do not give the words of the prayer till 9^3, when the angels are presenting it before God. G^s in Semitic fashion gives the prayer *in extenso* here also. Again the additional clauses ($\pi o \rho \epsilon \acute{u} o \nu$ $\kappa \tau \lambda$.) in G^s $10^{2, 4}$ belong most probably to the original work but have been lost in G^g E, see note on 10^2. The same is true of the addition in G^s 9^9 with its peculiar diction, as is clear from a comparison of $10^{9, 15}$.

Finally G^s preserves several right readings over against G^g E. Thus δῆσον in 10^{11} where G^g E corruptly read δήλωσον, κατακριθῇ in 10^{14} where G^g E read κατακαυσθῇ. Cp. also 10^7.

(b) *Relations of G^s and G^g to E.* Even the most superficial study makes it clear that E and G^g are more closely related than E and G^s or G^s and G^g. Indeed the evidence makes it clear that *E was translated from a MS. which was also the parent or ancestor of G^g*. This follows from the fact that *the same corruptions* appear in G^g E over against true readings in G^s where this exists. Thus they both give impossible readings in 10^7 †ἐπάταξαν (G^s εἶπον); 10^{11} δήλωσον (G^s δῆσον); 10^{14} †κατακαυσθῇ (G^s κατακριθῇ); 14^8 †ἐθορύβαζον (a mistranslation of the Aramaic original) G^g; 14^{18} †οροs (G^g. E = ὁπόs) (corrupt for ὅρασις ?); 15^9 †ἀνωτέρων (G^s ἀνθρώπων); 18^5 †βαστάζοντας ἐν νεφέλῃ; 22^4 †ἐποίησαν for ἐποιήθησαν; 25^5 †εἰς ζωήν; 28^2 †ἀπὸ τῶν σπερμάτων. In 9^6 all the authorities are corrupt, but G^g E agree closely.

On the other hand *E preserves certain original readings lost by G^g and vice versa*. Thus E G^s rightly add αὐτοῖς after ἐγεννήθησαν in 6^1 and read βασιλεὺς τῶν βασιλευόντων in 9^4 where G^g reads β. τῶν αἰώνων, and πάντων τὴν ἐξουσίαν in 9^5 where G^g reads πᾶσαν τ. ἐξουσίαν, and attest ἐν ταῖς θηλείαις in 9^8 and εἰς ἀλλήλους ἐξ αὐτῶν εἰς αὐτούς in 10^9, which G^g in both cases omits. Moreover, in 9^{11} the corruption in E = τὰ εἰς αὐτούς (for ἐᾷς αὐτούς so G^s) is easy of correction, whereas G^g offers the corrupt αιας. In the following passages *G^g omits clauses and passages preserved by E*. Thus it omits by hmt. clauses in $9^{1, 5}$ 10^{16} 12^3 14^8 15^2 $18^{3, 5, 11}$, and without any such intelligible ground 2^3, all 3 and 4 except six words, words and clauses in $6^{1, 5}$ 9^8 $10^{10, 19, 20}$ 14^{14} $15^{4, 8}$ 16^1 19^1 $22^{5, 8}$ $24^{1, 2}$ 27^1. On the other hand *E omits words and clauses preserved by G^g* in $1^{1, 9}$ $5^{1, 3}$ $10^{1, 2}$ 13^7 14^{25} 15^{11} 20^8 $22^{2, 5}$ 26^1.

Naturally G^g and E have severally developed corruptions which it is generally possible to emend in either case by the help of the other.

In the following passages E presupposes ὁμοῦ μετά for ὁμοῦνται in 5^6; τὰ μετὰ αὐτά for μέταλλα in 8^1; ἀνάγω for ἀναγνῶ in 13^4;

Introduction

μυστηρίου for μυρίων in 18^{16}; ὡς εἰρηναῖαι for εἰς σειρῆνας in 19^2; λαῷ for χάῳ in 20^5; κοῖλοι for καλοί in $22^{2,\,3}$. Corruptions of G^s will be found in the following passages: $1^{2,\,3,\,5,\,8,\,9}$ 5^1 6^3 $9^{4,\,6}$ 10^{19} 13^1 $14^{6,\,8,\,13,\,15,\,18,\,19}$ $15^{8,\,9}$ 16^3 $17^{3,\,7}$ $18^{4,\,7,\,11}$ 21^{10} $22^{5,\,6,\,9}$ 23^2 24^3 26^2 31^3.

(c) From the above facts it follows that G^g and E *spring from a common ancestor which we may designate x, and that this x and G^s proceed ultimately from the same original, the first Greek translation of the Book of Enoch*.[1] Hence the genealogy of the above documents might be represented as follows:—

Original Greek Translation from the Semitic

§ 6. THE LATIN VERSION AND QUOTATIONS.

The Latin Fragment, which constitutes a very imperfect reproduction of 106^{1-18}, was discovered in 1893 in the British Museum by Dr. James, the present Provost of King's College, Cambridge, and most kindly placed at my service for publication in my edition of 1 *Enoch* in 1893. In the same year he issued it in the Cambridge Texts and Studies II, No. 3, *Apocrypha Anecdota*, pp. 146–150.

The text has suffered from additions, omissions, and corruptions, and is very seldom a literal rendering of the original for many words together. Notwithstanding, it makes some contribution to the formation of a better text of 106.

This MS. further may point to a Latin translation, or at least to a partially completed Latin translation of Enoch; for (1) occurring in the midst of original Latin treatises it appears to have been found in Latin by the collector or scribe of these

---

[1] This conclusion hardly seems adequate to explain all the phenomena mentioned on pp. xvii–xix. These postulate not only the occurrence of duplicate renderings in the Greek translation, but most probably also the occurrence of variants in the Hebrew original.

treatises. (2) It has suffered much in the course of tradition, and may, therefore, go back to a date when the Book of Enoch was not reprobated generally, and when a Latin translation would have been acceptable. (3) It does not show signs of being an excerpt from a collection of excerpts, such as we find in the Greek fragment of Enoch, 89^{42-49}; but standing as it does without any introductory note or explanation, it looks as if it had been drawn directly from at least a larger Latin fragment of Enoch.

It is possible that the absurd statement with which the fragment opens—'[Cum esset Lamech annorum tricentorum quinquaginta] natus est ei filius'—originally referred to Methuselah, who was 355 years old when Noah was born according to the LXX Chronology. E speaks here of Methuselah taking a wife for his son Lamech and of a son being born to him.

Latin Quotations. These have been collected most fully by Dr. Lawlor in his article in the *Journal of Classical Philology*, xxv. 164–225.

§ 7. THE ETHIOPIC VERSION.

The Ethiopic Version has been preserved in twenty-nine MSS. of which fifteen are to be found in England, eight in France, four in Germany, one in Italy, and one in America. Of these MSS. there are only three of which my knowledge is indirect and slight, but not yet too slight to enable me to estimate their value and their affinities with the other MSS. These MSS. are p and z, $_1z$. Of these z indeed was most kindly lent to the Bodleian Library for my use, but unhappily I was absent part of the time of its sojourn there, and whilst I was present the officials of the Bodleian did not notify me of its arrival. $_1z$ is of no account as it is merely an exact transcript of b. Next as regards p, this MS. formerly belonged to Lord Crawford, and was lent by him to the editor of the German edition of the Ethiopic text of Enoch which appeared in 1901, but since that date this MS. passed into the hands of a lady, who refused to lend it or any other MS. in her possession to the Bodleian

Library for the use of English editors. Of the remaining MSS I have directly examined twenty-two, i. e. $g_1 g m q t u$, $a b f h i k l n o$, and $s u v w y_1 a_1 b$. Of these I photographed thirteen, i.e. $g_1 g m q t u$, $f h i k l n o$. Five others, i. e. $a b y_1 a_1 b$, I had no need to photograph, as the owners of $_1 a_1 b$ most kindly put these MSS. at my service for the space of two years, while $a b y$ were always at hand for consultation in the Bodleian, to which y had been lent for that purpose by the Munich Library. Of the Abbadian MSS. $r s v w$ I made collations on a number of test passages while at Abbadia. These readings are appended in foot-notes on these MSS. in the following list, and are sufficient to show the affinities of these MSS. amongst MSS. of the second class. Finally, as regards $c d e x$ I have used Dillmann's collation of $c d e$ and a photograph of x which I procured from the Vatican. Thus for the construction of the present text I have had at my service photographs of fourteen MSS. $g_1 g m q t u$, the constant use of the five MSS. $a b y_1 a_1 b$, Dillmann's collations of $c d e$, Flemming's collation of p (which I have used sparingly)—in all twenty-three MSS. Four other MSS. $r s v w$ I have collated sufficiently to determine their character. Of the remaining MS. z (for $_1 z$ may be ignored as a transcript of b) it is enough that we have Flemming's assurance that it is closely related to $a b c d e$.

The division of Enoch into chapters was made apparently in the sixteenth century. The division into 108 chapters was made by Dillmann without MSS. authority, but as it has been followed by all subsequent scholars it is here adopted for the sake of convenience. The above division is indeed found in one MS., i.e. h, but this MS. was unknown to Dillmann when he made his text. Moreover, the chapters in h vary frequently in length from those in Dillmann's text.

§ 8. Ethiopic MSS.

The full list of the MSS. is as follows :—

a. Bodley, No. 4. Large quarto. 40 foll. 3 cols. 105 chapters. Latter half of 18th cent. Enoch only.[1]

---

[1] Laurence issued a transcript of this MS. in 1838.

- b. Bodley, No. 5. Large quarto. 141 foll. 3 cols. 18th cent. (?). Enoch (98 chapters), Job, Isaiah, 12 Minor Prophets, Proverbs, Wisdom, Ecclesiastes, Canticles, Daniel.

- c. Frankfort MS. Rüpp. II. 1. 34 × 30 cm. 181 foll. 3 cols. 18th cent. In several hands. Enoch (98 chapters), Job, Octateuch.

- d. Curzon MS. Quarto. 91 foll. 2 cols. Enoch (102 chapters), Job, Daniel, 4 Ezra, Sirach.

- e. Curzon MS. Small quarto. 101 foll. 2 cols. Marginal notes from another hand. Enoch (98 chapters?), Samuel, Kings, and Apocryphal book.

- f. British Museum. Add. 24185 (Wright's Catalogue, 1877, No. 5). 2 cols. of 23 lines. 19th cent. Enoch only. 106 chapters.

- g. Brit. Mus. Orient. 485 (Wright, No. 6). 190 foll. 23 × 19 cm. 2 cols. of 23 or 24 lines. First half of 16th cent. Enoch (without division into chapters), Book of Jubilees. On foll. 168^a–177^a a duplicate of chapters 97^{6b}–108^{10} is inserted from another MS. akin to g. See next MS.

- $_1g$. This MS. consists only of 97^{6b}–108^{10}, and is found in foll. 168^a–177^a of g. It is inserted between the last word and the last but one of 91^5. It is written by the same scribe, but the text though belonging to the best type differs from g.

- h. Brit. Mus. Orient. 484 (Wright, No. 7). 3 cols. of 50 or 51 lines. 18th cent. Enoch (108 chapters), Octateuch, Jeremiah, Daniel, Ezekiel, 1–4 Ezra, Tobit, Judith, Esther, Sirach.

- i. Brit. Mus. Orient. 486 (Wright, No. 8). 3 cols. of 29 lines. 18th cent. Chapters 1–60^{13a} missing. Nos. of remaining chapters erased. Enoch, Samuel, Kings, Jeremiah, Sirach.

- k. Brit. Mus. Orient. 490 (Wright, No. 12). 3 cols. of 30 lines. 18th cent. Enoch (107 chapters), Job, Daniel, 1 Ezra, Isaiah, 12 Minor Prophets.

- l. Brit. Mus. 24990 (Wright, No. 13). 3 cols. of 31 lines. 18th cent. Enoch (divided into chapters, but no numbers supplied), Job, Books ascribed to Solomon, Isaiah, 12 Minor Prophets, Daniel.

- m. Brit. Mus. Orient. 491 (Wright, No. 15). 219 foll. 40 × 32 cm. 3 cols. of 27 lines. 18th cent. Enoch (without division into chapters), Job, 12 Minor Prophets, Tobit, Judith, Esther, Maccabees.

Introduction   xxiii

n. Brit. Mus. Orient. 492 (Wright, No. 16). 3 cols. of 30 lines. 18th cent. Enoch (87 chapters), Books ascribed to Solomon, Jeremiah, 1 Ezra, Canticles, Sirach, Judith, Esther, Tobit.

o. Brit. Mus. Orient. 499 (Wright, No. 23). 3 cols. of 31 lines. 18th cent. Sirach, Daniel, Enoch (106 chapters), Isaiah, 12 Minor Prophets.

p. Formerly in the possession of Lord Crawford—now in the Rylands Collection. 67 foll. 39 × 33 cm. 3 cols. 17th cent. Enoch and other books.

q. Berlin MS. Peterm. II. Nachtr. No. 29 (Dillmann's Cat. 1). 167 foll. 17 × 14 cm. 2 cols. of 13 to 14 lines. 16th cent. Without division into chapters. Enoch only.

r. Abbadianus 16 (vid. *Cat. raison. de mss. éthiop. appartenant à A. d'Abbadie*, Paris, 1859). 19th cent. Enoch (77 chapters) and other works. This is a poor MS., but it exhibits a few good readings.[1]

s. Abbadianus 30. 18th cent. Enoch and other works. This is a poor MS., but has some notably good readings.[1]

t. Abbadianus 35. 40 × 35 cm. 3 cols. of 38 to 39 lines. 17th cent. There are many erasures and corrections and marginal notes. The latter belong to the later type of text, and are designated as t^2. The division into chapters is marked in the margin on the first few folios. Enoch, Job, Samuel I and II, Kings, Chronicles, Books ascribed to Solomon, Prophets, Sirach, 1–4 Ezra, Tobit, Judith, Esther.

u. Abbadianus 55. 191 foll. 51 × 39 cm. 3 cols. of 48 to 50 lines. Possibly as early as the 15th cent. Enoch (without division into chapters) and other works. Text of Enoch much abbreviated after chapter 83.

v. Abbadianus 99. 70 foll. 23 × 17 cm. 2 cols. 19th cent. Copy made for M. d'Abbadie from a MS. in high estimation among the native scholars. This MS. has all the bad characteristics of the later type of text, but has some excellent readings. Enoch only.[1]

w. Abbadianus 197. 157 foll. 26 × 23 cm. 3 cols. of 29 lines. 17th or 18th cent. Enoch (98 chapters) and other works.[2]

---

[1] For further descriptions see my Ethiopic Text, Introd. p. xx.
[2] See my Ethiopic Text, p. xxi.

x. Vatican MS. 71 (cf. Mai, *Script. veterum nova collectio, Romae*, 1831, T. v. 2, p. 100). 27 foll. 3 cols. of 32 lines. 17th cent. Enoch only. 98 chapters.

y. Munich MS. 30. 61 foll. 25 × 15 cm. 2 cols. of 20 to 28 lines. 17th cent. Division into chapters only at the beginning. Enoch only.

z. Paris MS. 50 (see Zotenberg's Cat.). 17th cent. Enoch (division into chapters only at the beginning) and other works.

$_1z$. Paris MS. 49. 18th cent. Copy of *b*.

$_1a$. Garrett MS. 17 × 12 cm. 2 cols. of 22 lines. 19th or end of 18th cent. Enoch only.

$_1b$. Westenholz MS. 71 foll., of which first and last two are empty. 2 cols. of 24 lines. 18th cent. 106 chapters. Enoch only.

Relations of the Ethiopic MSS.

(*a*) *Two forms of text, α, β, of which β is late and secondary.* There are two forms of the Ethiopic text. The first is represented by $g \, _1g \, m \, q \, t \, u$ (and in some degree by *n*), which we shall henceforth designate by α, and the second, which owes its origin to the labours of native scholars of the sixteenth and seventeenth centuries, by all the remaining MSS., i.e. β. The result of these labours has been on the whole disastrous; for these scholars had neither the knowledge of the subject-matter nor yet critical materials to guide them as to the form of the text. Hence in nearly every instance where they have departed from the original unrevised text they have done so to the detriment of the book. But it is not to be inferred from the above that α always represents one type of text and β another type opposed to the former; for the attestation of neither group is wholly uniform, as each group is divided within itself. This statement holds true in a much greater degree of α. Indeed, the cases are comparatively few where α differs as a whole from β. Fifty readings out of fifty-one which any editor must adopt will have the support of one MS. singly as *g, m, q, t, u*, or of groups such as $g \, m$, $g \, q$, $q \, t$, $g \, u$, $g \, m \, _1 q$, $g \, m \, t$, $g \, m \, u$, &c., and the fifty-first time of the undivided a. For instances of the latter see 1^9 (note 23), 8^1 (note 34), 10^3 (note 36), 10^{13} (note 28), 10^{17} (note 7), 10^{22} (note 48), 15^5 (note 24).[1] Moreover, when the attestation of a is divided, the individual or group of a attesting the right reading will often have the support of β or of groups within β. The above facts serve to prove that *the recension was not the work of a few years, but was rather a process which culminated in such a text as we find in β, but particularly in the MS. v.*

(*b*) *β or groups in β sometimes preserve the original texts.* Again it is noteworthy that in a limited number of cases β preserves the original text where a is secondary.[2]

(*c*) *The character and affinities of the chief MSS.*

g. Of the MSS. of a, g is decidedly the best all-round MS. This does not mean that it has more unique and right readings than any other MS. of the older type of text, but that when all the good points of the various MSS. are summed up, g comes out an easy first. In the first thirty-two chapters g alone attests the right reading in 6^4 (note 37),[1] 17^3 (note 27), 18^7 (note 33), 21^5 (note 8), 28^3 (note 11). In 89^{42} (note 4) it has only the support of n, the best of the second class MSS. This MS. has been made the basis, so far as any single MS. can, of my text. It exhibits much strange orthography and bad grammar, and many corruptions. Notwithstanding it is by far the best representative we have of the ancient text. It was this MS. together with m that I used when emending Dillmann's text for my translation and commentary which appeared in 1893.

$_1g$. This MS., which has already been described, shows certain idiosyncrasies in 103^{9-15}, where it uses the first person over against the third in the other MSS. Outside this chapter it agrees in turn with g, m, q, t, u or with combinations of these or with one or more of these combined with β, but it is most nearly related to g.

m. This MS. is in some respects the weakest of the older

---

[1] The references enclosed in brackets are to the critical notes in my edition of the Ethiopic text, 1906.

[2] See further my Ethiopic Text, p. xxii.

group. It attaches itself so closely to g that we must assume its having come under its influence. This fact becomes of importance when we come to chapters 97^{6b}–108^{10}, where we have both g and $_1g$. In the vast majority of its unique readings $_1g$ is unaccompanied by m. Yet somehow m has been influenced by the readings both of g and $_1g$. In 10^2 (note 33)[1] and 17^4 (note 36) it alone attests the primitive text, in 7^3 (note 9) alone with f, and in 15^{11} (note 21) with $b\,x\,y$.

q. Though teeming with every form of error incident to the transmission of a text in the way of additions, corruptions, and omissions, this MS. contains a larger number of unique original readings than any other used in our text. Thus it alone preserves the original text in 9^8 (note 21),[1] 10^{11} (note 16), 14^1 (note 39), 21^2 (note 24), 22^9 (note 25), 24^2 (note 41), 26^3 (note 33), 27^4 (note 47), 32^4 (note 31). It approximates more closely to $g\,_1g\,m$ than to $t\,u$.

t. This is a most interesting MS.,[2] as it gives the older type of reading in the text and the later either over erasures or above the line or in the margin, with the rejected words in the text bracketed. The corrector has not done his work thoroughly. Accordingly many of the older readings remain untouched. The work of erasing has been so frequently perfunctory that it is generally possible to decipher the original text. Moreover, in some cases the correction represents a return to the older text. Cf. 1^6 (note 5).[1] As $g\,_1g\,m$ are closely connected, so are t and u. t is the least original of the MSS. of the first class. Thus it is hardly ever right alone. For one instance in the first thirty-two chapters see 10^{10} (note 3).

---

[1] The references enclosed in brackets are to the critical notes in my edition of the Ethiopic text, 1906.

[2] This MS. is notable also from the fact that for the Books of Samuel and Kings it alone exhibits a third type of text diverging from the two types of text in circulation in Abyssinia. These were the first and primitive type of text and the later or Vulgate. Where this MS. diverges from these two classes of text it repeatedly agrees with the Hebrew (Massoretic) text. Subsequently a corrector worked over this MS. and erased readings belonging to the first class, as well as those peculiar to this MS. which were derived from the Hebrew, and substituted readings of the second or Vulgate type.

u. This MS. would form a good third to *g* and *q* but that it is so imperfect after chapter 83, for nearly one-seventh of the entire book is omitted in the course of 83–108. These omissions are made in the most capricious way. Sometimes words, sometimes phrases, sometimes whole sentences and paragraphs are excised to the entire destruction of the sense. Notwithstanding as *u* is a valuable MS. I have most faithfully recorded all its omissions and changes. In chapters 1–32 it alone preserves the true text in 3 (note 23),[1] 4 (note 33), 21^7 (note 40).

n. Of MSS. of the second class *n* is by far the best. Indeed, though in the main embodying the second type of text, it attests more unique and original readings in chapters 1–32 than *m* or *t* or *u*. Thus it stands alone in giving the original text in 9^{11} (note 15),[1] 10^3 (note 37), 10^7 (note 21), 22^9 (note 29) (?). Alone of MSS. of the second class it gives along with various MSS. of the first class the true text as in 1^3 (note 18),[1] 14^{21} (note 10), 25^7 (note 19), 89^{42} (note 4), &c. Thus *n* exhibits the characteristics of both types of text.

§ 9. Editions of the Ethiopic Version.

Laurence, *Libri Enoch Versio Aethiopica*. Oxoniae, 1838. This text was issued simply as a transcript of *a*, one of the MSS. brought to Europe by Bruce, the great Abyssinian traveller, in 1773. The transcription is not very accurate in the early chapters, though the errors are as a rule easy to correct. In chapters 5–10 there are ten; most of these have passed over into Dillmann's *Apparatus Criticus*, and from Dillmann's to Flemming's. As the text advances it becomes more accurate, so that I found its citation by Dillmann to be sufficiently trustworthy for use in the present edition.

Dillmann, *Liber Henoch, Aethiopice, ad quinque codicum fidem editus, cum variis lectionibus*. Lipsiae, 1851. This edition was based on five MSS., *a b c d e*. No further work on the Ethiopic

---

[1] The references enclosed in brackets are to the critical notes in my edition of the Ethiopic text, 1906.

text appeared till 1892, when Dillmann (*Sitzungsberichte d. kgl. Preuss. Akad. d. Wiss. zu Berlin*, 1892, li–liii, pp. 1039–1054, 1079–1092) published some variants from three MSS. on the first thirty-two chapters of Enoch in connexion with his edition of the fragmentary Greek Version.

Charles, *The Book of Enoch translated from Professor Dillmann's Ethiopic Text emended and revised in accordance with hitherto uncollated MSS. and with the Gizeh and other Greek and Latin Fragments.* Oxford, 1893. This translation was based on a drastic revision of Dillmann's text. Ten new MSS., which belong to the British Museum, were used, three of them, $g_1 g\, m$, being of primary importance, and seven, $f\, h\, i\, k\, l\, n\, o$, being of only secondary. Of these MSS. I collated $m, f\, h\, i\, k\, l\, n\, o$ on about three hundred passages; but $g_1 g$ I collated throughout, on the whole accurately, but defectively, as I now find, in a relatively small number of passages.

Flemming, *Das Buch Henoch: Aethiopischer Text herausgegeben von Joh. Flemming* (= *Texte und Untersuchungen*, Neue Folge, VII. i). Leipzig, 1902. Dr. Flemming's text is based on fifteen MSS., $a\, b\, c\, d\, e\, g_1 g\, m\, p\, q\, t\, u\, v\, w\, y$. Of these six belong to the first class, $g_1 g\, m\, q\, t\, u$, and the rest to the second class. This editor has been at no little pains in the preparation of his text. Thus he has himself collated $g\, m\, p\, q\, y$. His knowledge of $t\, u$ he owes to photographs taken by Professor Meyer in France, and of $v\, w$ to collations of the same scholar. It was a fatal error on Dr. Flemming's part that he did not photograph $g\, m\, q$, or, at all events, revise his collations of them.

Flemming's text naturally constitutes an immeasurable advance on that of Dillmann, and a considerable advance on Dillmann's text as emended in my commentary in 1893. With the help of the three new first-class MSS., $q\, t\, u$, this editor was able to point out a few passages where I followed mere idiosyncrasies of g, and also some others where I preferred the less trustworthy of the two texts $g_1 g$ in chapters 97^{8b}–108^{10}.

On the whole, Flemming's text is good, as might be expected from so excellent an Ethiopic scholar, and several of his suggestions have been accepted in the present edition. On close examination, however, Flemming's edition proves unsatisfactory from its frequent inaccuracy in the collation of the MSS. generally, and its inadequate collation of the first-class MSS. In my review of this edition in the *American Journal of Theology*, pp. 689–703, 1903, I have summed up its serious shortcomings under the following heads: (i) *Inaccurate and defective collation of the MSS.*; (ii) *The adoption of inferior readings into the text where the MSS. evidence for the true text is incontrovertible.* Flemming's treatment of the great Berlin MS. q on chapters 10–32 will exemplify his method in dealing with the other MSS. In six passages in these chapters q alone amongst the Ethiopic MSS. preserves the true text of E, as is proved by G. Yet in two of them, 21^2 (note 24),[1] 24^2 (note 41), q is not collated at all, and in the remaining four, 10^{11} (note 16), 14^1 (note 39), 22^9 (note 25), 32^4 (note 31), the reading of q is relegated to the notes, and the wrong reading adopted. In 10^7 (note 21) q practically gives the original text (which is preserved by n alone), but the corrupt text is adopted by this editor. (iii) *Corrupt passages are left in the text without any attempt to emend them or even to call attention to their viciousness.* (iv) *Divergencies between G and E are left unexplained.* (v) *Practically no use is made of the Semitic background for purposes of emendation.* Notwithstanding the above shortcomings, Dr. Flemming's edition is deserving of the gratitude of Orientalists, as it constitutes a vast advance on that of Dillmann, and forms on the whole a serviceable work for students generally.

Charles, *The Ethiopic Version of the Book of Enoch, edited from twenty-three MSS. together with the fragmentary Greek and Latin Versions*, 1906.

§ 10. Translations.

Laurence, *The Book of Enoch, an apocryphal production, now first translated from an Ethiopic MS. in the Bodleian Library*, Oxford, 1821.

---

[1] The references enclosed in brackets are to the critical notes in my edition of the Ethiopic text, 1906.

HOFFMANN (A.G.), *Das Buch Henoch in vollständiger Übersetzung mit fortlaufendem Commentar, ausführlicher Einleitung und erläuternden Excursen*, 2 vols., Jena, 1833–1838.

DILLMANN, *Das Buch Henoch übersetzt und erklärt*, Leipzig, 1853. (See below under § 11, Critical Inquiries.)

SCHODDE, *The Book of Enoch translated with Introduction and Notes*, Andover, 1882.

CHARLES, *The Book of Enoch translated from Dillmann's Ethiopic Text, emended and revised in accordance with hitherto uncollated Ethiopic MSS. and with the Gizeh and other Greek and Latin Fragments*, Oxford, 1893.

BEER, in Kautzsch's *Die Apokryphen und Pseudepigraphen des Alten Testaments*, Tübingen, 1900, ii. 236–310.

FLEMMING and RADERMACHER, *Das Buch Henoch herausgegeben im Auftrage der Kirchenväter-Commission der Königlich Preussischen Akademie der Wissenschaften*, Leipzig, 1901.

MARTIN, *Le Livre d'Hénoch traduit sur le texte éthiopien*, Paris, 1906.

§ 11. CRITICAL INQUIRIES.

I had intended to give a critical history of all the work done on Enoch since 1850, and had collected almost sufficient materials for that purpose, when I found that my space would not permit of such a large addition to the book. I shall therefore content myself with enumerating these inquiries and adding occasional notes.

LÜCKE, *Einleitung in die Offenbarung des Johannes* (2nd ed. 1852), pp. 89–144: 1071–1073. Lücke regards the book as consisting of two parts; the first embraces 1–35 71–105, written at the beginning of the Maccabaean revolt (p. 142), or, according to his later view, in the reign of J. Hyrcanus (p. 1072); the second consists of the Parables and was written in the early years of Herod the Great (p. 142). 59^{7-14} and $64–67^1$ are interpolations of an uncertain date. In his first edition Lücke maintained the Christian authorship of the whole book.

HOFMANN (J. Chr. K.), 'Ueber die Entstehungszeit des Buch Henoch' (*Zeitschr. D. M. G.* vi. 1852, pp. 87-91); *Schriftbeweis* (2nd ed.), i. 420-423; *Die heil. Schrift N. T.'s zusammenhängend untersucht*, vii. 2, pp. 205 sqq. Hofmann regards Enoch as the work of a Christian writer of the second century A. D. His chief contribution to the understanding of Enoch is his correct interpretation of the seventy shepherds in 89-90.

DILLMANN, *Das Buch Henoch übersetzt und erklärt*, Leipzig, 1853. This edition at once displaced the two that preceded it, corrected their many ungrammatical renderings, and furnished an excellent translation of a text based on five MSS. So much, however, has been done in the criticism of Enoch since 1853 that the need of a new edition was imperatively needed alike in respect of the text, translation, interpretation, and criticism of the book. As for the translation some of the renderings are grammatically impossible; and as regards his interpretation of the book, this has been pressed and strained in order to support the critical views which he then held but which he has long since abandoned. His critical views indeed have undergone many changes, but these undoubtedly are in the right direction.

In his edition of 1853 Dillmann insisted that the book proceeded from one author, with the exception of certain historical additions, 6-16 91^{12-17} 93 106-107, and of certain Noachic interpolations, 54^7-55^2 60 $65-69^{25}$, and also of 20 70 75^5 82^{9-20} 108.

In 1860 in Herzog's *R.-E.*, ed. 1, vol. xii. 308-310, and in 1871 in Schenkel's *Bibel-Lex.* iii. 10-13, he recognized the separate authorship of 37-71 and asserted with Ewald its priority to the rest of the book.

In 1883 in Herzog's *R.-E.*, ed. 2, vol. xii. 350-352 he abandons his original standpoint so far as to describe the Book of Enoch as a mere 'combination of the Enoch and Noah writings', and concedes that 37-71 are later than the rest of the book. His final analysis is as follows. (1) 1-36 72-105, with the exception of certain interpolations, form the groundwork and were composed in the time of J. Hyrcanus. (2) 37-71, together probably with 17-19, were written at latest before 64 B.C. (3) The Noachic fragments 6^{3-8} 8^{1-3} 9^7 $10^{1, 11}$ 20 $39^{1, 2a}$ $54^{7}-55^2$ 60 $65-69^{25}$ 106-107. (4) 108.

See also *Zeitschr. D. M. G.*, 1861, pp. 126-131, for a criticism by Dillmann of Volkmar's theory.

JELLINEK, *Zeitschr. D. M. G.*, 1853, p. 249.

GILDEMEISTER, *Zeitschr. D. M. G.*, 1855, pp. 621-624, gives the Greek fragment of Enoch from the Codex Vaticanus (Cod. Gr. 1809) and discusses the relative merits of the Greek and Ethiopic versions.

EWALD, *Abhandlung über des äthiopischen Buches Henokh Entstehung, Sinn und Zusammensetzung*, 1855; *History of Israel*, v. 345-349 (translated from the German). It was the merit of Ewald first to discern that Enoch was composed of several originally independent books. It is, in fact, as he declares, 'the precipitate of a literature once very active which revolved . . . round Enoch' (*Hist.* v. 349). Though this view was at once assailed by Köstlin and nearly every other critic since, its truth can no longer be denied, and Holtzmann's declaration that 'the so-called groundwork (i. e. 1-37 72-105) is composed of a whole series of sections, some of Pharisaic and others of Essene origin' (*Theol. Literaturzeitung*, 1890, p. 497), was a notable sign of the return to Ewald's view. But though future criticism must confirm Ewald's general judgement of the book, it will just as surely reject his detailed analysis of its parts. His scheme is—

(1) Book I, 37-71 (with the exception of certain interpolations), circ. 144 B.C.

(2) Book II, 1-16 81^{1-4} 84 91-105, circ. 135 B.C.

(3) Book III, 20-36 72-90 106-107, circ. 128 B.C.; 108 later.

(4) Book IV, the Noah book. 6^{3-8} 8^{1-3} 9^7 $10^{1-3, 11, 22b}$ 17-19 54^7-55^2 $60^{1-10, 24, 25}$ $64-69^{16}$. Somewhat later than the former.

(5) Finally the editing, compressing, and enlarging of the former books into one vol.

WEISSE, *Die Evangelien-Frage*, 1856, pp. 214–224. Weisse agrees with Hofmann and Philippi in maintaining a Christian authorship of the book, but his advocacy of this view springs from the dogmatic principle that the entire idea of Christianity was in its pure originality derived from the self-consciousness of Christ.

KÖSTLIN, 'Ueber die Entstehung des Buchs Henoch' (*Theol. Jahrb.*, 1856, pp. 240–279, 370–386). Köstlin, as we have already remarked, contended against Ewald that the book of Enoch did not arise through the editing of independent works, but that by far the larger part of Enoch was the work of one author which through subsequent accretions became the present book. Though this view must be speedily abandoned, it must be confessed that the articles in which it is advocated are masterly performances, and possess a permanent value for the student of Enoch.

HILGENFELD, *Die jüdische Apokalyptik*, 1857, pp. 91–184. This work, like that of Köstlin, is of lasting worth and indispensable in the study of Enoch. We cannot, however, say so much for the conclusions arrived at. Many of these are, in fact, demonstrably wrong. According to Hilgenfeld, the groundwork consists of 1–16 20–36 72–105 written not later than 98 B.C. The later additions, i.e. 17–19 37–71 106–108 are the work of a Christian Gnostic about the time between Saturninus and Marcion. There are no Noachic interpolations.

There is no occasion to enter on the, for the most part, barren polemic between Hilgenfeld and Volkmar on the interpretation and date of Enoch, to which we owe the following writings of Hilgenfeld:—'Die jüdische Apokalyptik und die neuesten Forschungen' (*Zeitschr. f. wissenschaftl. Theol.*, iii. 1860, pp. 319–334): 'Die Entstehungszeit des ursprünglichen Buchs Henoch' (*Z. f. w. Theol.*, iv. 1861, pp. 212–222): 'Noch ein Wort über das Buch Henoch' (*Z. f. w. Theol.*, v. 1862, pp. 216–221). In *Z. f. w. Theol.*, xv. 1872, pp. 584–587, there is a rejoinder to Gebhardt (see below).

VOLKMAR, 'Beiträge zur Erklärung des Buches Henoch' (*Zeitschr. D. M. G.*, xiv. 1860, pp. 87–134, 296): 'Einige Bemerkungen über Apokalyptik' (*Zeitschr. f. w. Theol.*, iv. 1861, pp. 111–136): 'Ueber die katholischen Briefe und Henoch' (iv. 1861, pp. 422–436; v. 1862, pp. 46–75). As Hilgenfeld reckoned the periods of the Seventy Shepherds at seven years each, starting from 588 B.C., and thus arrived at 98 B.C., Volkmar started from the same anterior limit and reckoned each period at ten years. He thus found the entire rule of the shepherds to last 700 years or, through certain refinements, peculiarly Volkmarian, 720 years, and so arrived at the year of Barcochab's rebellion A.D. 132—a year which has exercised a strange fascination over him and has been fatal to his reputation as a critic. Thus Enoch was written 132 B.C. It was the work of a disciple of Akiba, and was designed to announce the final victory of Barcochab. Volkmar restated his theory in an essay: Eine Neutestamentliche Entdeckung, Zürich, 1862. His views have received more attention than they deserved through the rejoinders of Hilgenfeld, Dillmann, Langen, Sieffert, Gebhardt, Drummond, and Stanton.

GEIGER, *Jüdische Zeitschr. f. Wissensch. und Leben*, 1864–1865, pp. 196–204. This article deals mainly with the Calendar in Enoch. I have adopted one of his suggestions in 10^4.

LANGEN, *Das Judenthum in Palästina*, 1866, pp. 35–64. Langen regards Enoch as an early but highly composite work put together in its present form about 160 B.C. (pp. 36, 64), and emanating from orthodox and patriotic Judaism as a protest against heathen religion and philosophy.

SIEFFERT, *De apocryphi libri Henochi origine et argumento*, Regimonti, 1867. Sieffert (p. 3) takes the groundwork to be 1–16 20–36 72–82 91–105, written by a Chasid in the age of Simon the Maccabee (pp. 11–13): 83–90 is a later addition about the year 108 B.C., and 17–19 37–71 106–108 are of Essene origin and composed before 64 B.C. (pp. 27–29).

HOLTZMANN, *Geschichte des Volkes Israel*, 1867, vol. ii, pp. 201, 202.

HALÉVY, 'Recherches sur la langue de la rédaction primitive du livre d'Énoch' (*Journal Asiatique*, 1867, pp. 352–395). This most interesting essay sought to prove that Enoch was originally written in Hebrew. Unhappily the writer lost much time over passages which better MSS. show to be mere corruptions of the text. I have given several of the most probable of Halévy's suggestions in my Notes.

PHILIPPI, *Das Buch Henoch, sein Zeitalter und sein Verhältniss zum Judasbriefe*, Stuttg. 1868. This writer agrees with Hofmann, Weisse and Volkmar, in regarding the book as post-Christian. He thinks it was written in Greek by one author, a Christian, about A.D. 100. It is notable that all the four writers, who assign a post-Christian origin to the book, have done so for dogmatic reasons.

WITTICHEN, *Die Idee des Menschen*, 1868, pp. 63–71; *Die Idee des Reiches Gottes*, 1872, pp. 118–133, 145–150. He sees the primitive work in 1–5 17–19 21^1–54^6 55^3–59^3 61–64 69^{26-29} 71^1–82^8 83^1–$91^{11, 18, 19}$ 92 94–105; while he discovers later additions in 6–16 93 91^{12-17} 106–107; still later additions in 20 54^7–55^2 60 65^1–69^{25} 70 82^{9-20}, and the latest in 108.[1]

GEBHARDT, 'Die 70 Hirten des Buches Henoch und ihre Deutungen mit besonderer Rücksicht auf die Barkochba-Hypothese' (Merx' *Archiv für wissenschaftl. Erforschung des A. T.* 1872, vol. ii. Heft ii. pp. 163–246). In this most trenchant criticism of the different explanations of chaps. 89–90 the writer carefully refrains from advancing any theory of his own. Nay more, he holds it impossible with our present text to arrive at a true interpretation of the author's meaning. But this writer's despair of a true interpretation is over-hasty and his condemnation of the text is unwarrantable.

ANGER, *Vorlesungen über die Geschichte der Messianischen Idee*, 1873, pp. 83–84.

VERNES, *Histoire des Idées Messianiques*, 1874, pp. 66–117, 264–271. These sections are composed mainly of a French

---

[1] The above details regarding Wittichen are due to Martin.

translation of Dillmann's German version. Vernes thinks that the earliest part of Enoch was written in Aramaic by a contemporary of J. Hyrcanus; and that the Parables spring from a Christian and Gnostic circle about the close of the first century A.D. (pp. 264 sqq.).

KUENEN, *Religion of Israel*, 1874–1875, iii. 265, 266 (translated from the Dutch Edition of 1869–70).

TIDEMAN, 'De Apocalypse van Henoch en het Essenisme' (*Theol. Tijdschrift*, 1875, pp. 261–296). Tideman regards the book as proceeding from different authors living at different periods. His analysis is as follows:—

(1) The oldest book: 1–16 20–36 72–82 93 91^{12-19} 92 94–105, from the hand of a Pharisee in the early times of the Maccabees 153–135 B.C.

(2) The second book: 83–91^{10}, from an Essene writer who added it to the older book 134–106 B.C.

(3) The Apocalypse of Noah: 17–19 41^{3-9} $43^{1, 2}$ 44 54^7–55^2 59–60 65–69^{25} 70 106–107, from an author versed in Jewish Gnosticism A.D. 80.

(4) The Parables (with the exception of the Noachic interpolations), written by a Christian in the days of Domitian or Trajan, when the Christians were persecuted and the Romans were at war with the Parthians, A.D. 90–100.

(5) Chapter 108 by the final editor of the book, a Christian Gnostic of the type of Saturninus, A.D. 125.

Christian interpolations are found in 90^{38} 105.

Tideman thinks that we have in the Parables a combination of the thought that the Messiah is to be a man in the clouds (Daniel), and of the doctrine that he was to proceed from the community, 1 En. $90^{37, 38}$.

DRUMMOND, *The Jewish Messiah*, 1877, pp. 17–73. Drummond gives a concise and able review of the work of former critics on Enoch. He rightly approves and further enforces Hofmann's interpretation of the seventy shepherds as angels. He agrees with the limits assigned by Tideman to the oldest book in Enoch; but concludes, against Hilgenfeld and Tideman, that the Parables could not *entirely* be the work of a Christian; for if they were such, there would undoubtedly have been some reference to the crucified and risen Christ such as we find in Test. Levi $4^{1,\,4}$. The difficulties of the case are met, he believes, by supposing that a Christian Apocalypse has been worked into the tissue of an earlier Jewish production, and that all the Messiah passages are due to the former. His chief arguments are: (i) the title 'son of a woman' could not have been applied by a pre-Christian Jew to a supernatural Messiah; (ii) a consistent text is possible by an omission of the Messiah passages, a text also which answers to the title placed at the beginning of each Parable; (iii) the closing chap. 71 confirms this view where in the description of a Theophany there is no mention of the Messiah and the title 'Son of Man' is applied to Enoch; (iv) the Book of Jubilees, though using Enoch extensively, does not cite the Messiah passages.

Of these arguments the only one that can still be maintained with any show of reason is (ii), and this in itself will have no weight if we bear in mind the want of logical sequence and the frequent redundancy characteristic of Semitic writings generally and of Jewish apocalypses in particular. Moreover, in no instance that I am aware of does any superscription in Enoch give an exact account of the chapters it introduces.

HAUSRATH, *Neutestamentliche Zeitgeschichte*, Erster Theil, 3rd ed., 1879, pp. 185–189, 191–193. The oldest book, 1–36 72–105, is referred to the time of J. Hyrcanus. The Parables, with the exception of the Noachic interpolations, were probably composed in the reign of Herod the Great. Hausrath thinks that the Messiah-passages may have won somewhat of a Christian colouring in the process of translation from Hebrew to Greek and Greek to Ethiopic by Christian hands.

LIPSIUS, art. 'Enoch' in Smith and Wace's *Dictionary of Christian Biography*, vol. ii, 1880, pp. 124–128. (1) The oldest book dealt with the Heavenly Luminaries, 17–19 21–36 72–79 82, in which Enoch appears as a teacher of such higher wisdom. This, however, is an unhappy synthesis; for the demonic doctrine of 17–19 connects it peculiarly with the Noachic interpolations, while its Greek colouring as strongly disconnects it with the ultra-Jewish 72–79 82. (2) In the second book, 1–16 80–81 83–105, which never existed independently but only as an expansion of the former, Enoch is represented as a preacher of righteousness. This book belongs to the reign of J. Hyrcanus. (3) The Parables, written under the later Maccabeans or the Herods. (4) Noachic interpolations 54^7–55^2 60^{7-25} 65–68^1 and probably $10^{1-3,\,22b}$ 41^{2-9} 43–44 59 $69^{2,\,3}$ 106–107. Other interpolations and additions 20 108.

This article forms a valuable contribution to the criticism of Enoch, and I welcome it all the more gladly as I arrived at many of its results before I was acquainted with it.

WESTCOTT, *Introduction to the study of the Gospels*, 1881, 6th ed., pp. 99–109; *Gospel of St. John*, 1882, p. 34. In the former work this writer recognizes the probability of the different sections of the book as proceeding from different authors, yet he essays the impossible task of moulding their conflicting features into one consistent whole. In the latter work Dr. Westcott asserts that the title in Enoch is 'A Son of Man'; but wrongly; for it is as definitely 'The Son of Man' as the language and sense can make it. The being so named, further, is superhuman, and not merely human as Dr. Westcott states.

SCHODDE. *The Book of Enoch translated with Introduction and Notes*, Andover, 1882. The introduction is interesting and the account of the bibliography though incomplete is helpful, but the arrangement of the text and notes in this edition is most inconvenient. The translation is made from Dillmann's Ethiopic text. But the work as a whole is unsatisfactory. All Dillmann's slips and inaccuracies, with one or two exceptions, are perpetuated. Dr. Schodde's analysis of 2 Enoch is:—

i. The groundwork 1-36 72-105, before the death of Judas Maccabaeus.

ii. The Parables 37-71, between 37-4 B.C.

iii. Noachic interpolations 54^{7}-55^{2} 60 65-69^{25} 106-107.

He thinks it probable that 20 70 75^{5} 82^{9-20} 93^{11-14} are also interpolations.

WIESELER, 'Ueber die Form des jüdischen Jahres um die Zeit Jesu' (*Beiträge zur richtigen Würdigung der Evangelien*, 1869). We have here an interesting and valuable discussion of the Calendar in Enoch.

'Zur Abfassungszeit des Buchs Henoch' (*Zeitschr. D. M. G.*, 1882, pp. 185-193). Wieseler assigns the Parables no less than the rest of the book to the reign of J. Hyrcanus.

SCHÜRER, *A History of the Jewish People in the Time of Jesus Christ* (translated from the second and Revised Edition of the German), vol. iii, div. ii, pp. 54-73, 1886. This is a most judicious statement of the results already attained by criticism. In accordance with these Schürer divides the book into three parts: (1) 'the original writing' 1-36 72-105, written in the reign of J. Hyrcanus; (2) the Parables, written in the time of Herod the Great; (3) the Noachian Fragments, 54^{7}-55^{2} 60 65-69^{25}, and probably 106-107. 108 is a later addition. He is careful, however, to remind us that the 'original writing is composed of very heterogeneous elements'. While he rightly dismisses as idle all attempts to introduce chronological exactness into the interpretation of the Seventy Shepherds, he thinks there can be no doubt as to where the different periods are intended to begin and end. It was Schürer who was the first to recognize the validity of Hoffmann's interpretation of the Shepherds and to give it currency. This article concludes with a very full list of patristic passages referring to Enoch and with an excellent bibliography of the literature. In his third edition, 1898, pp. 192-209, he maintains the same position.

STANTON, *The Jewish and the Christian Messiah*, 1886, pp.

44-64, 139-140, 142, 153, 170-175, 286, 305, 311-315, 332, 335, 347.

The analysis of the book given in Schürer is adopted also here. Dr. Stanton agrees likewise with the generality of critics in assigning the first part, i.e. 1-36 72-105, to the reign of J. Hyrcanus. The Parables must, he thinks, be ascribed to a Jewish Christian or to a Jew influenced by Christian ideas. The fragments of a lost Apocalypse of Noah are probably $39^{1, 2a}$ 54^7-55^2 60 $65-69^{25}$.

REUSS, *Gesch. der heil. Schriften des A. T.'s*, §§ 498-500.

HOLTZMANN, *Einleitung in das N. T.*, 1886, 109, 110.

FRIEDLIEB, *Das Leben Jesu Christi des Erlösers*, 1887, pp. 126-151. Friedlieb divides the book thus: 1-36 37-64 70-71 72-82, the original work by one and the same author, composed between 141 and 130 B.C. 65-69 are by a second writer; 83-105 by a third, writing between 129 and 125 B.C. The two appendices 106-107 and 108 are perhaps by the final editor.[1]

HOLTZMANN (OSKAR), in Stade's *Geschichte des Volkes Israel*, ii. 1888, pp. 416-429, and 483-490. He resumes, but with more success, the principle laid down by Ewald. He sees in 1 Enoch a whole literature made up of independent fragments which, however, form a complete whole though often mutilated in their existing condition. He distinguishes thus not merely the five constituent books, but even their subdivisions as sections of varied origin. In Book I, for instance, he reckons four sections: (i) 1-5, Introduction, of the date of the early Maccabees. (ii) 6-11, Two narratives, of the same date. (iii) 12-16. (iv) 17-36, Enoch's journey to the hidden places of the earth. This last section contains various accounts dealing with the same theme, and some fragments about the revolution of the stars are interpolated in it. He separates also the Apocalypse of Weeks in Book V. It is earlier than 20 B.C. The rest of that book goes back to the time of the struggle between the Pharisees on one side and the Sadducees and Hasmonaeans on the other,

---

[1] The above details are due to Martin.

with some Christian insertions at the end. The whole work ends with an appendix containing a Noachic fragment 106–107, and a later addition 108. These views on the whole were on the right lines, but did not meet with immediate acceptance.[1]

PFLEIDERER, *Das Urchristenthum*, 1887, pp. 310–318. This writer accepts the traditional view with regard to the groundwork, and approves of Drummond's theory as to the origin of the Messiah-passages in the Parables. This theory he seeks further to substantiate, but without success.

BALDENSPERGER, *Das Selbstbewusstsein Jesu*, 1888, pp. 7–16. This writer assents to the traditional view and date of the groundwork. The Parables he assigns to the years immediately following on the death of Herod the Great. He believes there are many references to the Romans in the Parables, and that Augustus and Herod are designed under the phrase 'the kings and the mighty'.

SALMON, *Introduction to the N. T.*, 4th ed., 1889, pp. 527, 528.

PETER, *Le Livre d'Hénoch. Ses Idées Messianiques et son Eschatologie*, Genève, 1890. This is an interesting little treatise, but by no means free from blemishes. The Parables are pre-Christian, and the traditional view and date of the groundwork are here reproduced.

DEANE, *The Pseudepigrapha*, 1891, pp. 49–94. This is a praiseworthy attempt to popularize a knowledge of these works. The writer assigns the traditional groundwork to the years 153–130 B.C., and regards the Parables as written a few years later. Many of this writer's statements on the theology and influence of 1 Enoch are to be taken with extreme caution.

THOMSON, *Books that influenced our Lord and His Apostles*, 1891, pp. 95, 103, 108, 225–248, 389–411. Mr. Thomson's analysis is as follows:—

---

[1] The above details are due to Martin.

(1) Book of the Parables and the Book of the Weeks, 37–71 91^{12}–99, written about the year 210 B.C.

(2) Noachic Fragments, 60 65–69^{24}.

(3) Book of the Fall of the Angels and of the Luminaries, 1–36 72–91^{11} 100–107, written not later than 160 B.C.

(4) 108.

Mr. Thomson's chief ground for regarding 37–71 as the oldest Section is derived from the presence of the Noachic interpolations. As he believes that these interpolations are confined to this Section, he infers that 37–71 is therefore the oldest and that 1–36 72–91 were not yet in existence. Even if Mr. Thomson were right in his facts, quite another conclusion would be possible. But this writer's premises are without foundation. Interpolations are found in every section in Enoch and numerously in the sections which Mr. Thomson regards as free from them. It cannot be said that this book contributes much to the better interpretation of Enoch, and this is all the more to be deplored as its author obviously possesses abundant ability for the task.

CHEYNE, *Origin of the Psalter*, 1891, pp. 22, 375, 412–414, 423–424, 448–449, and about fifty references besides. 'Possible Zoroastrian Influences on the Religion of Israel,' *Expository Times*, 1891, p. 207. Dr. Cheyne accepts provisionally the traditional division of Enoch into the groundwork, Parables and Noachic fragments, and regards the Parables as pre-Christian. He deals mainly with the dogmatic teaching of the book and its place in the development of Jewish religious thought, and points to the Essene and Zoroastrian elements which have found a place in it.

DE FAYE, *Les Apocalypses juives*, Paris, 1892, pp. 28–33, 205–216.

LODS, *Le Livre d'Hénoch*, 1892, reckons in the original work 1–16 (with certain Noachic interpolations in 6–8) 21 36 72–82 90^{1-11} 94–105.[1]

---

[1] The above details are due to Martin.

Introduction xliii

CHARLES. *The Book of Enoch, translated from Professor Dillmann's Ethiopic Text, emended and revised in accordance with hitherto uncollated Ethiopic MSS. and with the Gizeh and other Greek and Latin Fragments*, Oxford, 1893.

CLEMEN, *Theologische Studien und Kritiken*, 1898, pp. 211-227, 'Die Zusammensetzung des Buches Henoch.' He emphasizes the varied traditions represented by the different portions of the book. These twelve traditions the 'author of the book' either found committed to writing or he collected them from oral transmission. The earliest go back to 167 B.C., the latest to 64 B.C. These traditions are (1) 1-5, (2) 6-11, (3) 12-16, (4) 17-19, (5) 20 (?)-36, (6) 37-69, with some interpolations, (7) 70-71, (8) 72^1-$91^{10,\ 18}$ et sqq. (?), (9) 92 93 91^{12-17} 94-105, (10) 106-107, (11) 108, (12) the Noachic fragments 54^7-55^2 60 65^1-69^{25}. The author found already existing in a written form (9) (11) (12), probably (3), and perhaps even (6). Clemen lays great stress on the changes of person as betraying the composite character of the work.[1]

BEER, 'Das Buch Henoch' (*Die Apokryphen und Pseudepigraphen des A. T., Kautzsch*, vol. ii, 1900, pp. 224-230). Beer thus divides the work:—

(1) 1-5, a work complete in itself and yet forming an introduction in the form of an apologia to the whole book.

(2) 6-11 comprise two different traditions interwoven. The burden of the former is the revelation of mysteries, and the judgement by the Flood: that of the latter is the fall of the angels, their punishment, and the wickedness of the giants. The blending together of the two traditions was made easier by the fact that they both alike dealt with the leading astray of the angels by the daughters of men. This fragment, thus surviving in two mutilated groups, has been drawn from a larger cycle of legends which grew up around the name of Noah. The two groups might be distinguished as follows (*a*): 6^{2b-8} 7^{3-6} 8^4 $9^{1-5,\ 9-11}$ 10^4-11^2 and (*b*) 7^{1b} 8^{1-3} 9^{6-8} 10^{1-3}.

---

[1] The above details are due to Martin.

(3) 12–16. These chapters had originally nothing to do with 6–11. They spring from the Enoch cycle, whereas 6–11 spring from the Noah cycle.

(4) 17–36 likewise belong to the Enoch cycle, and contain two accounts which narrate the same journey in different words, 17–19 and 20–36. Possibly, however, 20 was composed after the other chapters. This Section cannot be shown to depend directly on 12–16 or 6–11.

(5) 37–71. This Book, dealing with the Messiah, is nearer to the ruling idea of chapter 1, which centres round the Messianic account of the last times. The Book is not a single homogeneous work in its present form, as it contains Noachic interpolations and other distinct documents. Thus in 40^2 we have 'the angel who went with me', while in 40^8 we have 'the angel of peace'; the Messiah bears the name of the 'Elect One' in 45 and 49, but that of 'the Son of Man' in 46 and 48^{2-7}. Parallel with the use of these names is the title of the two angels who are commissioned to interpret the visions. For instance, the 'angel who went with me' explains that of the Son of Man, 46^2; the 'angel of peace' explains that of the Elect One, 52^5. Beer questions whether these two names and two angels do not suggest two different texts in the Parables. There is the same doubt as to the authenticity of the passages dealing with physical phenomena which are inserted in this Section. These chapters, though like 17–36 betraying a duplicate origin, are not the continuation of those chapters. 37 begins anew and introduces Enoch as a hitherto unknown person. The physical secrets are common to 33–36 and the Parables, but the title 'Lord of Spirits' is peculiar to the latter. 6–11 do not even mention Enoch's name, while 1–5 and 12–16 recount not visions, but an actual journey of Enoch. These chapters therefore are all of distinct origin from 37–71.

(6) 70 and 71 belong to an independent tradition, for in 71^{14} Enoch is identified with the Son of Man. This Section is, however, connected with the Parables, as the Messiah is here also, in 70^1, called the Son of Man, but not with 12–16, as 71

would be merely a useless repetition of 14—a description of God's habitation.

(7) 72–82. Chapter 80 gives us the somewhat artificial connexion by which 'the writer' has joined on this treatise on the stars to a book on the Messianic kingdom: the fair order described in 72–82 will change in the days of the sinners. This Section has not come down to us in its original condition. 76–77 deal with the winds, the points of the compass, &c., though these subjects have not been promised in 72^4. Moreover, 79^{1-6} and 82^{1-6} each form a conclusion: 82^{9-20} is incomplete, and ought to come before 79. Despite the partial resemblance in the subject, especially in regard to the second source of 17–36 (=21–36), 72–82 is not, at least in its original form, by the same author as 21–36. For instance, the function of Uriel in 72^1 agrees with that in 20^2 21^5; but Uriel writes for Enoch, 33^4, while Enoch writes himself, 74^2.

(8) 83–108. This part is quite in harmony with the subject proposed in 1^1. Beer reckons in this Section six fragments more or less distinct: first, 83–84; second, 85–90; third, the Apocalypse of Weeks, 92 93^{1-14} 91^{12-17}; fourth, the admonitions, $91^{1-11,\ 17,\ 18}$ 94–105; fifth, 106–107; sixth, 108. The Messiah occurs in $90^{37,\ 38}$, but not at all in 1–36 or 72–82. This Messiah, sprung from Abraham, is not the Messiah of the Parables, who is a heavenly, pre-existent being.

Finally, Beer thus assigns the various passages to their different sources: A, from the Enoch cycle, (1) 1–5, (2) 12–16, (3) 17–19 (4) 20–26, (5) 37–69, (6) 70–71, (7) 72–82, (8) 83–84, (9) 85–90, (10) 92 93^{1-14} 91^{12-17}, (11) 91^{1-11} 94–105, (12) 108. Of these (5) and (7) may be subdivided, as above. B, from the Noah cycle, (13) 6–11, (14) $39^{1,\ 2a}$ 54^7–55^2 60 65–69^{25}, (15) 106 107.

MARTIN, *Le Livre d'Hénoch traduit sur le texte éthiopien*, 1906. This scholar (see pp. lxxxviii–xcvii) designates the Book of Enoch as a mosaic composed of nine or ten distinct works or traditions emanating from the Enoch cycle. These are 1° 1–5; 2° 6–16 20–36, before 166 B.C.; 3° 17–19, before 166 B.C.; 4° 37–69, 95–78 B.C.; 5° 70–71; 6° 72–82, before 135 B.C.;

7° 83–90, 166–161 B.C.; 8° 91–105, 95–78 B.C.; 9° 93 91$^{12-17}$, before 170 A.D.; 10° 108, before 64 B.C.

A certain number of strange elements have been incorporated into most of the above works: 1° various fragments, 41$^{3-8}$ 43$^{1-2}$ 44 59 60$^{7-10, 11-23, 24, 25}$ 69^{23} 77 81 89^{31b} 90^{15} 91^{11} 105^{2a}; perhaps also 52^4 68^1—from the Enoch cycle (with the exception of 105^{2a}): 2° fragments from the Noah cycle, 10$^{1-3}$ 39^{1-2a} 54^7–55^2 60^{1-c} 65–69^{25} 106 sq.

There are many ingenious suggestions in Professor Martin's Commentary, some of which I have adopted with due recognition.

§ 12. The different Elements in the Book of Enoch.

The Book of Enoch was intended by its final editor to consist of five Sections, like the Pentateuch, the Psalms, Proverbs, Sirach, and many other Jewish works (see p. lxiv). These consist of 1–36 37–71 72–82 83–90 91–108. Behind this apparently artificial division lies a real difference as to authorship, system of thought, and date. When I edited my first edition of Enoch in 1893 it was necessary for me to go at great length into the differentiae marking these divisions, since the accepted criticism of the day regarded 1–36 72–104 as forming the groundwork, and proceeding from one and the same author. Since that date this impossible hypothesis has vanished from the field of criticism. My task here is, therefore, no longer of a polemical nature, but simply to determine so far as possible the extent, character, and date of the various independent writings embodied in this work. The various Sections will now be dealt with in the order of their occurrence.

Fragments of the Book of Noah. But before we enter on the criticism of the various elements in the book, we should observe first of all that it contains fragments of an earlier work—entitled the Book of Noah. Of the existence of this book we know independently from the Book of Jubilees, 10^{13} 21^{10}, and later sources. But even if we had possessed no independent reference to such a book, we could have had no doubt as to its existence; for the contents of chapters 60 65–69^{25} prove conclusively that

Introduction xlvii

they are from this source; also 106–107. Furthermore, 6–11[1] are derived from the same work. These latter chapters never refer to Enoch, but to Noah. Moreover, where the author of Jubilees in 7^{20-25} describes the laws laid down by Noah for his children, and Noah's accounts of the evils that had brought the Flood upon the earth, he borrows not only the ideas, but at times the very phraseology of these chapters. Finally, we may observe that chapters 88–89[1] presuppose a minute acquaintance with chapter 10. 54^7–55^2 probably belong to the same source. *The Noachic fragments preserved in this book are thus:* 6–11 54–55^2 60 65–69^{25} 106–107.

These facts throw some light on the strange vicissitudes to which even the traditional legends were subject. Thus it would appear that the Noah saga is older than the Enoch, and that the latter was built up on the débris of the former.

Having now disposed of the earlier materials utilized by the writers of the different Sections of Enoch, we shall now proceed to deal with the five Sections or Books in the order of their occurrence.

SECTION I. 1–36. We have already seen that 6–11 belonged originally to the Book of Noah; 12–16, on the other hand, are a vision or visions of Enoch in which he intercedes on behalf of Azazel and the Watchers. These visions are preserved in a fragmentary form, and not in their original order—a fact which is most probably due to the editor of the whole work, since the same dislocation of the text recurs in 78–80 and 91–93. The original order of 12–16 was, so far as the present fragmentary text goes: 14^1 ... 13^{1-2} 13^3 12^3 13^{4-10} 14^2–16^2 12^{4-6} || 16^{3-4}. 12^{1-2} is an editorial introduction.

This portion of our text began obviously with the words: 14^1 'The book of the words of righteousness, and of the reprimand

---

[1] Even these chapters are composite; for they are a conflation of two distinct cycles of myths relating respectively to Semjaza and Azazel (see later under the text, pp. 13–14 notes), and this conflation was anterior to the date of the Dream Visions, which presuppose the existence of these chapters in their present form, or at all events of chapter 10.

of the eternal Watchers.' Then came a request on the part of Azazel that Enoch should intercede for him. This request was acceded to on the part of Enoch, who in a vision received God's judgement on Azazel. But both the request and the vision are lost. In 13^{1-2}, however, the answer to Azazel's request is given in the divine doom announced by Enoch. Next Enoch is besought by the Watchers to intercede for them, 13^3 12^3 13^{4-7}. Thereupon Enoch has a vision regarding them, 13^8, which he recounts to them, 13^{9-10} 14^2-16^2. Finally the Section closes with the message of doom, which Enoch is bidden to take to the Watchers, 16^{3-4}. Of 16^{3-4} there is a doublet, 12^{4-6}, which is more original than 16^{3-4}.

17–19 stand by themselves, exhibiting, as they do, strong traces of Greek influences in their description of the underworld, and yet showing a close affinity to 20–36, since 18^{6-9} is a doublet of 24^{1-3}, 18^{11} of 21^{7-10}, 18^{12-16} of 21^{1-6}; 19^2, moreover, reflects the same view as 10^{14}.

20–36 come apparently from one and the same author: the functions ascribed to the archangels in 20 are tolerably borne out in 21–36. But since only four of the seven archangels mentioned in 20 are dealt with in 21–36, it is possible that a considerable passage was early lost.

1–5 now call for treatment. These chapters are connected in phraseology with every section of the book save 72–82. (See p. 2 sq.) Thus the phrase 'he took up his parable', 1^2, suggests a connexion with 37–71, but this may be a mere coincidence, since the writer is here consciously influenced by Num. 23–24, where the phrase recurs several times. These chapters, moreover, appear to be of composite origin. 2–5 seem to be a unity. But I see no satisfactory solution of the problem.

To sum up. 1–36 may be analysed into the following independent elements, 1–5 6–11 12–16 17–19 20–36. When the Book of Jubilees was written we shall see that 6–36 had already been put together.

SECTION II. 37–71. As all critics are now agreed that the Parables are distinct in origin from the rest of the book, I will

Introduction

simply refer the reader here to p. 65 sq., for some of the grounds for this conclusion.

37–71 have been handed down in a fragmentary condition, and many of the problems they suggest can only be tentatively solved or merely stated.

37–71 consist in the main of three Parables, 38–44 45–57 58–69. These are introduced by 37 and concluded by 70, which describes Enoch's final translation in terms of that of Elijah. 71, which contains two visions received in his lifetime, belongs to one of the three Parables. We have already seen that 54^7–55^2 60 65–69^{25} are interpolated from the ancient Book of Noah.

Behind the Parables there appear to lie two sources, as Beer suggested though he did not work out his suggestion. The one was the 'Son of Man' source, in which the angelic interpreter was 'the angel who went with me': i.e. 40^{3-7} 46–48^7 52^{3-4} 61^{3-4} 62^2–63 69^{26-29} 70–71, and the other 'the Elect One' source, in which the angelic interpreter was 'the angel of peace': i.e. 38–39 $40^{1-2,\,8-10}$ $41^{1-2,\,9}$ 45 48^{8-10} 50–$52^{1-2,\,5-9}$ 53–54^6 55^3–57 $61^{1-2,\,5-13}$ 62^1. See pp. 64–65.

SECTION III. 72–82. Chapter 72 introduces a scientific treatise. In this treatise the writer attempts to bring the many utterances in the O.T. regarding physical phenomena into one system. The sole aim of his book is to give the laws of the heavenly bodies, and this object he pursues undeviatingly to 79^1, where it is said that his treatise is finished. Through all these chapters there is not a single ethical reference. The author's interest is scientific, and, like the author of Jubilees in 6^{32-36}, he upholds the accuracy of the sun and stars as dividers of time, 74^{12}. And this order is inflexible and will not change till the new creation, 72^1. But in 80^{2-8} the interest is ethical and nothing else, and though it recognizes an order of nature, this order is more conspicuous in its breach than in its observance. 80^{2-8} appears then to be an addition. Nor, again, can 81 belong to 72–82. Whereas the blessing of 72–79 82 is for the man who knows the right reckoning of the years, the blessing of 81^4

is for the man 'who dies in righteousness'. 81 is of the nature of a mosaic and may come from the hand of the editor of the complete Enoch. Finally 82 stood originally before 79^6 'Such is the . . . sketch of every luminary which Uriel . . . showed unto me'. After the long disquisition on the stars in 82, the first words in 79^1 come in most appropriately: 'I have shown thee everything, *and the law of all the stars of the heaven is completed.*' If 82 did not precede, these words could not be justified. For like dislocations cf. 12–16 91–93.

Thus the original order of this Section was: 72–78 82 79. For a full discussion of this Section, and its independence of 1–36 and the knowledge it implies of the Calendar, see pp. 147–150.

Section IV. 83–90. This is the most complete and self-consistent of all the Sections, and has suffered least from the hand of the interpolator. For passages that have suffered in the course of transmission see 90^{19}, which I have restored before 90^{14}: also 89^{48}. In 90, vv. 13–15 are a doublet of vv. 16–18.

83–90 is of different authorship from 6–36. (1) The descent of the Watchers in 86^{1-3} differs from that in 6. (2) The throne of judgement is in Palestine in 90^{20-26}, but in the N.W. in the midst of the Seven Mountains in 18^8 25^3. (3) The scene of the kingdom in 83–90 is the New Jerusalem set up by God Himself: in 1–36 it is Jerusalem and the earth *unchanged* though purified, $10^{18,\,20}$. (4) 83–90 are only visions assigned to Enoch's earlier and unwedded life: 6–36 are accounts of actual bodily translations and are assigned to his later life. If these two Sections were from one and the same author, and that an ascetic, exactly the converse would have been the case. For other grounds see p. 179 sq.

Identity of authorship appears, therefore, to be impossible; but the similarities in phraseology and idea (see *loc. cit.*) prove that one of the authors had the work of the other before him. Of the two Sections there is no room for doubt that 83–90 is the later.

Section V. 91–104. *Critical Structure.* This Section is in

the main complete and self-consistent. It has, however, suffered at the hands of the editor of the entire work in the way of direct interpolation and of severe dislocations of the text. We have already seen his handiwork in the case of 12-16 and 78-82. The dislocations of the text are a remarkable feature in this Section, and I cannot see any adequate explanation. The editor incorporated an earlier work—the Apocalypse of Weeks—into his text, 93^{1-10} 91^{12-17}, the former part dealing with the first seven weeks of the world's history and the latter with the last three. Taken together these form an independent whole. But this is not all. Since this Section is of different authorship from the other Sections of the book it is obvious that it began originally with 92^1, 'Written by Enoch the scribe,' &c. On 92 follows $91^{1-10, 18-19}$ as a natural sequel, where Enoch summons his children to receive his parting words. Then comes the Apocalypse of Weeks: 93^{1-10} 91^{12-17}. Thus the original order of the book is 92 $91^{1-10, 18-19}$ 93^{1-10} 91^{12-17} 94.

Relation to 6-36. At first sight the evidence for the unity of authorship of these two Sections is very great. They have many phrases in common. In each there are references to the law, to the eating of blood, and to the regularity of nature. There is no hint of a Messiah in either. There are other resemblances, but they are seeming and not real. On the other hand, in 6-36 the Messianic kingdom is eternal, in 91-104 it is temporary, if the Apocalypse of Weeks is taken to be a constituent part of 91-104. In the former the final judgement is held before the establishment of the kingdom, 10^{12} 16^1, in the latter at the close of the temporary kingdom (93^{1-10} 91^{1-10}). Whereas the resurrection in 6-36 is a resuscitation to a temporary blessedness, 10^{17} 25^5, in the latter it is not to the temporary kingdom spoken of in $91^{13, 14}$ 96^8, but to one of eternal blessedness subsequent to the final judgement, $100^{4, 5}$. Whereas the resurrection in 6-36 is a resuscitation in a physical body, in 91-104 it is a resurrection in a spiritual body, $92^{3, 4}$ $104^{2, 6}$. In the latter there is a resurrection of the righteous only: not so in the former. For other grounds see p. 219 sq.

Relation to 83-90. In 91-104 the Messianic kingdom is temporary in duration, but not so in 83-90: in the former the final judgement is consummated at the close of the kingdom, in the latter at its beginning. In 91-104 there is a resurrection of the righteous only; in 83-90 of the righteous and the apostate Jews. The kingdom to which the righteous rise in 91-104 is not the temporary kingdom on the earth but the new heaven, but in 83-90 it is the Messianic kingdom on the earth.

105. This chapter appears to be an independent fragment.

106-107. These chapters have already been dealt with as part of the Book of Noah.

108. This chapter forms an Appendix to the entire work, added not by the editor but by a subsequent writer to confirm the righteous in the face of repeated disappointment in their expectations.

§ 13. CHARACTERISTICS AND DATES OF THE DIFFERENT ELEMENTS.

I will here deal with these elements in the order of their age.

Book of Noah. This book was, as we have seen already, laid under contribution by the author of the Book of Jubilees and by the general editor of Enoch. Part of it is embodied in 6-36, and this part is presupposed as already existing by 83-90. Now, since 83-90 cannot be later than 161 B.C., it follows that we have here the *terminus ad quem* of this work.

6-36. Since 6-16 23-36 were known to the author of the Book of Jubilees (see my edition, p. lxix), this Section must have been written before the latter half of the second century B.C. Since, further, 83-90, written before 161 B.C., show a minute acquaintance with 10, the date of 6-11 must be put back to the first third of that century. Many other points in 83-90 (see p. 179) point to the acquaintance of the author of 83-90 with 6-36. Again, since 6-36 makes no reference to the persecution of Antiochus, the *terminus ad quem* is thus fixed at 170 B.C. The fact that 6-36 was written in Aramaic is in favour of pre-Maccabean date; for when once a nation recovers, or is trying to recover, its independence, we know from history that it seeks to revive its national language.

83–90. The fourth and last of the four periods into which 83–90 divides history between the destruction of Jerusalem and the establishment of the Messianic kingdom began about 200 B.C. (see pp. 180 sq., 206 sqq.), and marks the transition of supremacy over Israel from the Graeco-Egyptians to the Graeco-Syrians, as well as the rise of the Chasids. The Chasids, symbolized by the lambs that are borne by the white sheep, 90^6, are already an organized party in the Maccabean revolt. But certain of these lambs became horned, i.e. the Maccabean family, and the great horn is Judas Maccabaeus, 90^9. As this great horn is still warring at the close of the rule of the shepherds, 90^{16}, this Section must have been written before the death of Judas, 161 B.C.

93^{1-10} 91^{12-17}. This—the Apocalypse of Weeks—may have been written before the Maccabean revolt. There is no reference in it to the persecution of Antiochus. But the date is wholly doubtful.

72–82. This Section is referred to in Jubilees $4^{17, 21}$, where the author tells how Enoch wrote a book of the order of the months, the seasons of the years, and the rule of the sun. Hence the *terminus ad quem* is 110 B.C. or thereabouts.

91–104. In 83–90 the Maccabees were the religious champions of the nation and the friends of the Chasidim. Here they are leagued with the Sadducees and are the foes of the Pharisaic party. This Section was written, therefore, after 109 B.C., when (?) the breach between John Hyrcanus and the Pharisees took place. But a later date must be assumed according to the literal interpretation of $103^{14, 15}$, where the rulers are said to uphold the Sadducean oppressors and to share in the murder of the righteous. This charge is not justified before 95 B.C. As for the later limit, the Herodian princes cannot be the rulers here mentioned; for the Sadducees were irrevocably opposed to these as aliens and usurpers. The date, therefore, may be either 95–79 B.C. or 70–64 B.C., during which periods the Pharisees were oppressed by both rulers and Sadducees. In my edition of Jubilees, pp. lxix–lxxi, I have given various grounds for regarding 91–104 as dependent on Jubilees.

37–71. From a full review of the evidence, which is given and discussed in the notes on 38^5, it appears that the kings and the mighty so often denounced in the Parables are the later Maccabean princes and their Sadducean supporters—the later Maccabean princes, on the one hand, and not the earlier; for the blood of the righteous was not shed, as the writer complains ($47^{1, 2, 4}$), before 95 B.C.: the later Maccabean princes, on the other hand, and not the Herodians; for (1) the Sadducees were not supporters of the latter, and (2) Rome was not as yet known to the writer as one of the great world-powers—a fact which necessitates an earlier date than 64 B.C., when Rome interposed authoritatively in the affairs of Judaea. Thus the date of the Parables could not have been earlier than 94 B.C. or later than 64 B.C. But it is possible to define the date more precisely. As the Pharisees enjoyed unbroken power and prosperity under Alexandra 79–70 B.C., the Parables must be assigned either to the years 94–79 or 70–64.

The varying relations in which the Maccabees stand to the Chasid or Pharisaic party are faithfully reflected in the books of Enoch. In 83–90 the Maccabees are the leaders of the righteous, and their efforts form the prelude to the Messianic kingdom. In 91–104 they are no longer regarded as the chiefs and friends of the Chasids, and yet they have not become their open foes. They are, however, the secret abettors of their Sadducean oppressors. But when we turn to the Parables the scene is wholly changed. The Maccabeans are now the open and declared enemies of the Pharisees and add to their other guilt the slaying of the righteous.

It is still more instructive to observe the conceptions regarding the Messiah to which the writers of these books were led by the events of their times. In 83–90 we have the Messiah coming forth from the bosom of the community. He is a man only, but yet a glorified man and superior to the community from which he springs. So far as he is a man only, he may be regarded as the prophetic Messiah as opposed to the Apocalyptic Messiah of the Parables: and yet he is not truly the prophetic Messiah; for he has absolutely no function to perform, and he does not appear till the world's history is finally closed. Accordingly his presence here must be accounted for purely through literary reminiscence, and the hope of the Messiah must be regarded as practically dead at this period. The writer felt no need of such a personality so long as the nation had such a chief as Judas Maccabaeus. It was very different fifty years or more later, when the fondest enthusiasts could no longer look to the Asmonaeans for any help or stay in the time of their distress. Accordingly the writer of 91–104 refers only once to the recreant chiefs of the nation as secret upholders of the enemies of the righteous, and directs the thoughts of his readers no longer to a religious monarchy but to a religious commonwealth or restored theocracy established by the righteous themselves, and owning no head but God alone. This Messianic kingdom, further, which was without a Messiah, was to have only a temporary continuance, and heaven was to be the true and final abode of the righteous. Once more, as we turn to a somewhat later book, we find in the Parables that the irremediable degradation and open hostility of the Maccabees have caused the hopes and aspirations of religious thinkers to take various directions. Of these some returned to a fresh study of the Old Testament, and revived, as in the Psalms of Solomon, the expectation of a prophetic Messiah, sprung from the house and lineage of David. Others followed the bold and original thinker of this period, who, starting from a suggestive phrase in Daniel, conceived the Messiah as the supernatural Son of Man, who, possessing divine prerogatives, should destroy the wicked, and justify the righteous, and vindicate a transformed heaven and earth as their habitation for everlasting. For some account of the Messiah of the Parables we must refer the reader to the notes on 46^3 and 38^2.

The teaching of the Parables stands throughout in clear contrast to that of 91–104. Whilst in the latter there is no

Messiah, in the former the conception of the Messiah plays a more important rôle than had ever yet been assigned to him. In the former, again, there was only a resurrection of the righteous; in the latter a resurrection of all Israelites. In the former the Messianic kingdom was only temporary; in the latter it was of everlasting continuance. In the former the final judgement was held at the close of the Messianic kingdom; in the latter at its beginning. In the former there was a resurrection of the spirit only, in the latter of the body also.

§ 14. The Poetical Element in 1 Enoch.

In the course of editing the Ethiopic text of 1 Enoch I was fortunate enough to discover that no small proportion of it was written originally in verse. But the full extent of the poetical element was not recognized till the completion of the present edition. This discovery not only adds to the interest of the book, but also illuminates many a dark passage, suggests the right connexions of wrongly disjoined clauses, and forms an admirable instrument of criticism generally. Our recognition of this fact enables us to recognize the genuineness of verses which had hitherto been regarded as interpolations, and to excise others which were often in themselves unmeaning or at variance with their contexts. The very first chapter is the best witness in these respects. There we find that 1^{3b-9} consists of nine stanzas of three lines each. E had lost two of the lines of stanza seven, but happily these had been preserved by G^g. Again, in 5^{4-9} we have eight stanzas of four lines each. The order of the lines has been disarranged as will be seen in 5^{6-7}, but here the parallelism enables us to effect their restoration. Ch. 51 would without a recognition of the poetical character be in many respects inexplicable. In other passages it enables us to recognize certain lines as dittographs: cf. 59^{6d} 71^{3c} 80^{7c} 82^{2b} 94^{7d}.

Introduction

§ 15. Original Language of Chapters VI-XXXVI— Aramaic; of I-V, XXXVII-CIV—Hebrew.

That 1 Enoch was originally written in a Semitic language is now universally admitted. But what that language is is still, as regards portions of the book, a question of dispute. In the past, Murray, Jellinek, Hilgenfeld, Halévy, Goldschmidt, Charles (formerly), Littmann, and Martin have advocated a Hebrew original, while at various times an Aramaic original has been maintained by De Sacy, Lévi, Eerdmans, Schmidt, Lietzmann, Wellhausen, and Praetorius. Ewald, Dillmann, Lods, Flemming could not come to a decision between Hebrew and Aramaic. But of the above scholars only three have really grappled with the subject, i. e. Halévy, Charles, and Schmidt, and three different theses are advanced by them. While Halévy maintains a Hebrew original, and Schmidt an Aramaic, the present writer, as a result of his studies in editing the Ethiopic text and the translation and commentary based upon it, is convinced that neither view can be established, but that each appears to be true in part.[1] In other words, like the Book of Daniel, part of 1 Enoch was written originally in Aramaic and part in Hebrew. The proofs of this thesis amount in certain Sections almost to demonstration: in the case of others only to a high probability. The results of the present study of this problem tend to show that chapters 6-36 were originally written in Aramaic, and 37-104, and probably 1-5, in Hebrew.

Chapters 1-5. Probably from a Hebrew original. These chapters, as we have shown elsewhere, do not come from the same author or period as 6-36.

1^1. In E the text = ἐξᾶραι πάντας τοὺς πονηρούς whereas G^g has ἐξᾶραι πάντας τοὺς ἐχθρούς. The former, as the context shows, as well as Pss. Sol. 4^9 (see note on p. 4 of the Commentary), is original, the latter not. Now the former = כל־הרשעים, the latter = כל־הצרים, a corruption of the former. The same corruption is found in the LXX of Prov. 20^{22}. Since E and G^g are in the main derived from the same Greek translation, this fact, unless due to a sheer blunder

---

[1] This view was first advanced in my edition of the Ethiopic text, pp. xxvii-xxxiii.

of a copyist, points to the presence of alternative readings in the margin of the Hebrew archetype, which were reproduced by the Greek translator. Other facts point in the same direction: see note on 5⁹ᵇ below.

1⁹. In 'He cometh with ten thousands of His holy ones' the text reproduces the Massoretic of Deut. 33² in reading אָתָא = ἔρχεται, whereas the three Targums, the Syriac and Vulgate read אִתֵּה = μετ' αὐτοῦ. Here the LXX diverges wholly. The reading אתא is recognized as original. The writer of 1–5 therefore used the Hebrew text and presumably wrote in Hebrew.

5⁶ᵇ. ἐν ὑμῖν καταράσονται πάντες οἱ καταρώμενοι = בכם יקללו כל־המקללים is, so far as I am aware, a Hebrew idiom, and not an Aramaic. See note on p. 12.

5⁹ᵇ. Here Gᵍ reads ἁμάρτωσιν, but E = κριθήσονται = יאשמו (cf. Prov. 30¹⁰ Isa. 24⁶ Jer. 2³, &c.). The parallelism shows that Gᵍ is right. Here, as in 1¹ above, we can explain the double rendering by assuming that one of these readings stood in the text and the other in the margin.

Since none of the evidence favours an Aramaic original, and whatever linguistic evidence there is makes for a Hebrew, we may provisionally conclude in favour of the latter.

Chapters 6–36. The evidence in favour of an Aramaic original of these chapters is practically conclusive.

(a) *Aramaic words transliterated in the Greek or Ethiopic.* Amongst the many Semitic words transliterated in these versions the following are Aramaic and Aramaic only: in Gᵍ φουκά, 18⁸, i.e. פיכא, μανδοβαρά, 28¹, and βαβδηρά, 29¹, i.e. מדברא. Another Aramaic form is χερουβίν, 14¹¹, ¹⁸ 20⁷, but this form is indecisive as it is found not infrequently in the LXX. In E manzerân¹ for manzerîn, 10⁹, i.e. ממזרין; 'alwâ, 31² (see note *in loc.*) = אהלא. The Hebrew form is אהלים.

Other transliterations are βάτους, 10¹⁹, i.e. בת, which is both Hebrew and Aramaic: χαλβάνη, 31¹, i.e. חלבנה Hebrew or חלבונא Aramaic. On the other hand there are two Hebrew words transliterated: thus σαρράν, 31¹ = צֳרִי, which is not found in Aramaic but which is rendered in Aramaic by קטף: and γῆ, 27² = גיא = 'valley', which is a pure Hebrew word, the Aramaic being חילא.

---

¹ Here Gᵍ has μαζηρέους and cannot account for E. Hence E here, as in 1¹ 5⁹ᵇ above, presupposes another reading than that in Gᵍ, this reading being in the text or margin of the Greek translation.

These last two cases are somewhat strange, but, since ניא is here used as a proper name, its use in an Aramaic document may be justified.

(b) *Aramaic constructions*. In 19² we have the peculiar Greek αἱ γυναῖκες αὐτῶν τῶν παραβάντων ἀγγέλων. This is a literal reproduction of the Aramaic idiom נשיהון די מלאביא די חטו. The same construction recurs in E 9⁸ which = συνεκοιμήθησαν μετ' αὐτῶν μετὰ τῶν θηλειῶν = שכיבו עמהון עם נשיא. Here G^g, it is true, has omitted μετὰ τῶν θηλειῶν. This omission was probably due to the unintelligibility of the construction to a Greek scribe. G^a, however, preserves the missing clause but wrongly connects it with the following verb—this change being due no doubt to an attempt to normalize the Greek. Thus G^a reads συνεκοιμήθησαν μετ' αὐτῶν καὶ ἐν ταῖς θηλείαις ἐμιάνθησαν. Here the καί should be restored after θηλείαις. In 6⁸ we have a third instance of this idiom, though in a corrupt form: οὗτοί εἰσιν ἀρχαὶ αὐτῶν τῶν δεκά(δων) = ראשיהון דעסריתא. This Aramaic idiom has found its way into the O.T. as in Cant. 3⁷.

(c) *Some of the proper names with which paronomasias are connected postulate an Aramaic original*. Thus in G⁹ 8³ we have ὁ δὲ τρίτος ἐδίδαξε τὰ σημεῖα τῆς γῆς. Now the ὁ τρίτος in 6⁷ is Ἀρακιήλ = ארקיאל, where ארק is Aramaic for 'earth'. Thus this angel naturally taught the signs of the earth: ארקיאל יאליף אתי ארקא. Again in G^a 8³ we have ὁ δὲ εἰκοστὸς ἐδίδαξε τὰ σημεῖα τῆς σελήνης, where ὁ εἰκοστός according to G⁹ 6⁷ is Σαριήλ = סהריאל. Here סהר is Aramaic for 'moon'. Again in 8³ the ὁ ὄγδοος in ὁ ὄγδοος ἐδίδαξε ἀεροσκοπίαν is in G^g 6⁷ Ἐζεκιήλ (G^a Ζακιήλ) = שחקיאל. שחק (= ἀήρ), it is true, is Hebrew as well as Aramaic.

In 13⁷ it is said that 'the angels were mourning in Abilene', i.e. אבלין באבילין. In G⁹ 6⁷ the play on Hermon is possible both in Aramaic and Hebrew (see note *in loc.*), but the play on Jared in the same verse is only possible in Hebrew. Whence we may infer that this paronomasia originated in Hebrew and is only reproduced in this Aramaic document. Finally in E G^a 10⁷ the command is given to Raphael: ἴασαι τὴν γῆν = רפי הארעא, in which there is an obvious play on Raphael's name. But though Nöldeke states that 'רפא ist gemeinsemitisch' (*ZDMG*, 1886, xl. 723, quoted by Schmidt), it is not found in the Targums and later rabbinical literature. Here, therefore, the play may be due to a pre-existing Hebrew document or myth, just as we are obliged to make the same presupposition in the case of 'Jared' above.

(*d*) *Text restored through retranslation into Aramaic.* In this Section there are many corrupt passages, as might be expected, which can be restored through retranslation either into Aramaic or Hebrew, owing to the close affinities of these languages. This may be the case in 9^4 מלכיא (i. e. τῶν βασιλέων E) corrupt for עלמיא = τῶν αἰώνων, or מלכים for עלמים: similarly in 10^7 ἐπάταξαν E G^g = אבדו, which is both Hebrew and Aramaic, and corrupt for אמרו = εἶπον G^s.[1] In 10^{17} τὰ σάββατα αὐτῶν = שַׁבַּתְהֹן, wrongly vocalized for שְׁבַתְהֹן, or = שְׁבָתָם corrupt for שַׁבָּתָם. 14^8 κατεσπούδαζον καὶ †ἐθορύβαζον†. Here the second verb is impossible. The clause in Aramaic = יוחון ויבהלון. Now the pael יבהלון = θορυβάζειν, ταράσσειν, or συνταράσσειν in Dan. $4^{2, 16}$ $5^{9, 10}$ $7^{15, 28}$, and is rendered by Theodotion by the latter two verbs. On the other hand, the LXX renders the same Aramaic verb by κατασπεύδειν in 4^{16} 5^6. Thus the translator of the LXX, who, as we know from the rest of his translation of the Aramaic section of Daniel, was very familiar with Aramaic, assigns to the pael of the Aramaic verb the same meaning as the piel and hiphil of the Hebrew בהל. Hence we may assume that the pael in Aramaic could mean κατασπεύδειν or θορυβάζειν. Thus we could explain ἐθορύβαζον as a mistranslation in this context of יבהלון. It is also possible that the two verbs are alternative renderings of one and the same verb in the Aramaic. This would have been possible also if the original had been Hebrew; for יבהלו pointed as a piel would mean κατεσπούδαζον and ἐθορύβαζον as a niphal. In 13^2 $15^{4, 11}$ 29^2 also the text can be restored by either language. (See notes *in loc.*)

But there are other passages that apparently defy restoration save through retranslation into Aramaic. In 9^{10} ἀνέβη ὁ στεναγμὸς αὐτῶν καὶ οὐ δύναται †ἐξελθεῖν†, the ἐξελθεῖν is meaningless, but by retranslation we discover the origin of the corruption. ἐξελθεῖν = למנפק corrupt for למפסק = 'cease'. The lamentations 'cannot *cease* because of the lawless deeds which are wrought on the earth'.

In 10^7 (where see note) the variations of the versions can be explained through the Aramaic, where E has twice 'earth' (= γῆ), G^g has once γῆ and once πληγή, and G^s πληγή both times. The variations could, of course, have originated in G, but γῆ and πληγή can be readily accounted for as renderings of ארעה, which, punctuated as אַרְעָא = γῆ, and as אַרְעָא = πληγή.

---

[1] Here again the two readings in the Greek versions can be best explained by variants in the margin of the Semitic original. See foot-note under (*a*) above and the paragraphs on 14^8 (*ad fin.*), 17^7.

In 17^7 E = τὰ ὄρη τῶν γνόφων = טורי קבלא. The phrase was derived most probably from Jer. 13^{16} הרי נשף. But G^g reads ἀνέμους τῶν γνόφων = רוחי קבלא. Here, as we have seen several times already, the Greek translator appears to have found טורי in the text and רוחי in the margin (or vice versa), and to have rendered both, one of which was preserved by G^g and the other by the Greek ancestor of E.

In 18^2 the text ἴδον τοὺς τέσσαρας ἀνέμους τὴν γῆν βαστάζοντας καὶ τὸ στερέωμα (G^g E) is quite impossible. The winds do not bear the earth. By retranslation into Aramaic we see that τὴν γῆν arose in the Aramaic through a dittography. The clause = חזית רוחיא ארבע ארעא מסוברין, where ארעא is a dittograph of ארבע. The winds bear the firmament, not the earth.

In 28^2 πλήρης δένδρων καὶ ἀπὸ τῶν σπερμάτων. It would be absurd to speak of a plain as being 'full of trees and seeds'. Here ἀπὸ τῶν σπερμάτων = ומזרעין, corrupt for ונטעונין (cf. Dan. $1^{12, 16}$; Mishna, Kil. ii. 2; iii. 2) = καὶ τῶν φυτευμάτων. Or the wrong phrase may be due to a wrong punctuation of the Aramaic word by the Greek translator. See note *in loc.*

In 31^3 ὅταν τρίβωσιν refer to certain fragrant trees mentioned in the preceding verse. These trees yielded a fragrant odour when burnt. (See note *in loc.*) Hence I assume that ידקקון (= τρίβωσιν) is corrupt for ידלקון = καύσωσιν.

Chapters 37–71 from a Hebrew original. In support of this view Halévy (*op. cit.* pp. 364 sqq.) criticized over a dozen of passages from the Parables and the interpolations with a view to showing that the meaning of the text could not be recovered unless by retranslation from a Hebrew original. Unhappily Halévy based his work on the corrupt text of Dillmann, and most of his conclusions have thereby been invalidated. Some, however, are of permanent value. On the other hand Schmidt (*O. T. and Semitic Studies*, ii. 336–43) strongly contests this view, and maintains the hypothesis of an Aramaic original. I have studied carefully his ingenious essay, but this study has served to confirm me in the belief in a Hebrew original, which I assumed in my edition of 1893, and supported by arguments in my text of 1908. The preparation of my new edition has served to bring fresh evidence on this question to light.

First of all I will give (*a*) *a list of passages which can be restored on the hypothesis of either a Hebrew or an Aramaic original;*

(b) *passages which are believed to presuppose an Aramaic only*; and
(c) *passages which postulate a Hebrew original.*

(a) *Passages which can be restored on the hypothesis of a Hebrew or an Aramaic original.* 37⁴ 'Till the present day such wisdom has never been given by the Lord of Spirits'. Here the Ethiopic has 'ĕmqĕdma = ἐκ προσώπου or ἔμπροσθεν = מִלִּפְנֵי, 'from before,' or practically 'by', as I have rendered it. This late use of מלפני is found in Esther 1¹⁹ 4⁸ 1 Chron. 29¹². The same idiom is found in Aramaic, i.e. מן־קדם: cf. Dan. 6²⁷ (∥ 3²⁹ מִן־). The same idiom recurs in 65¹⁰, and possibly in 48 ², ³, ⁶.

40⁹. The play on the names of Raphael and Gabriel is found in Hebrew; it is possible in Aramaic in the case of Gabriel, but a play on Raphael has never been found in Aramaic. In fact, רפא is not found in the Targums.

45³. 'Shall **try** their works.' For 'try' the text reads 'choose'. Now, as I pointed out in 1906, this = יבחר, corrupt for יבחן: or, if the original had been Aramaic, we had to suppose that the translator followed the wrong meaning of יבחר. Schmidt accepts the latter supposition.

46⁴ᵇ. 'Shall †raise up† the kings ... from their seats.' A dittograph of this verse reappears in 46⁵ᵃ 'shall put down the kings from their thrones'. Here 'raise up' = יטול is corrupt for יַפִּיל = 'put down'. This restoration is possible either in Hebrew or Aramaic.

54¹⁰. 'And **when**.' Here the text reads 'and because', but the context requires 'when'. The wrong rendering can be explained either from Hebrew or Aramaic (see note *in loc.*).

55³. In my note I have restored the text by means of Hebrew: but it is possible also through Aramaic, since מן־קדם can also mean 'because of'.

65¹¹. See note *in loc.*

66². Here the text reads 'hands' הידים or ידיא corrupt for המים or ימיא.

68². Text reads 'provokes me' = יארגזוני or ירגזוני.

69¹. As in 68².

69⁴. The corruption can be explained either by Hebrew or Aramaic.

69¹³. *Task.* Here 'number' = מנין (or מנינא as Schmidt points out) which seems corrupt for ענין (or ענינא) = 'task'.

71¹. Same corruption as in 69⁴.

(b) *Phrases and passages which are adduced by Schmidt in support of an Aramaic original.* Some of these have been dealt with already under (*a*), i.e. 37⁴ 40⁹ 45³ 65¹¹ 68² 69¹³, in which cases Schmidt suggests that the corrupt passages in question can be best explained by an Aramaic original, though possible also by a Hebrew original. His suggestions on 51³ 41⁵ are unnecessary, as the corruptions are native to E, and that on 52⁹, as we shall see later, is untenable, and his transformation of 38² ' whose elect works hang upon the Lord of Spirits ' into ' whose worship has been rendered solely to the Lord of Spirits ' is wholly uncalled for, since there is no difficulty in the phrase which recurs twice in 40⁵ 46⁸, and has a parallel in Judith 8²⁴. The plurals Sûrâfên, Kirûbên, Afnin in 61¹⁰ 71⁷ are certainly Aramaic in form, but σεραφείν which occurs only twice in the O.T., i.e. in Isa. 6²,⁶, appears both times in the oldest MSS. of the ℵ A of the LXX in this form, in Isa. 6² and in B in 6⁶. The Aramaic form χερουβείν is often found in the LXX. Hence this evidence for an Aramaic original is without weight.

But ' the most convincing evidence . . . of an Aramaic original is furnished by the Ethiopic translations of the term "Son of Man". They are walda sab'ĕ 46²,³,⁴ 48² 60¹⁰ : walda b'ĕsî 62⁵ 69²⁹ᵃ,ᵇ 71¹⁴ : and walda 'eguâla 'ĕmaḥejâw 62⁷,⁹,¹⁴ 63¹¹ 69²⁶,²⁷ 70¹ 71¹⁷ . . . . Of these the last is the most peculiar. Literally it means "the son of the offspring of the mother of the living" . . . and is a rendering of οἱ ἄνθρωποι, οἱ υἱοὶ τῶν ἀνθρώπων and especially of υἱὸς ἀνθρώπου.' Schmidt then proceeds to emphasize the importance of these different renderings in the Parables, whereas in the N.T. it is the last that is uniformly used as a rendering of ὁ υἱὸς τοῦ ἀνθρώπου, and observes : ' before 62 he uses no other term than walda sab'ĕ, the equivalent of the Aramaic בר נשא. Later he employs four times the phrase walda bĕ'sî which corresponds to the Aramaic ברה דגברא. . . . This title is found in the Palestinian Lectionary, the Curetonian Fragments, and the Sinaitic text.' From the above evidence Schmidt concludes that, if the translator had ' a Greek text before him in which the N.T. title ὁ υἱὸς τοῦ ἀνθρώπου was uniformly used ', it would be scarcely conceivable that he would have used three distinct Ethiopic expressions to render it, and ' these of such a nature as to correspond exactly to the three different Aramaic terms '. He holds, therefore, that ' the conclusion seems inevitable that he translated directly from the Aramaic. . . . General considerations strengthen this conclusion. If the Parables of Enoch were translated from a Greek text one would certainly expect to find somewhere a quotation from it or a reference to it in early Christian literature '. But Schmidt can find none.

The last argument I will answer first. The reader has only to refer to the list of parallels between the N.T. books and the Parables on pp. xcv sqq. in order to learn that the Parables did influence, and that directly, the writers of the N.T. Further, Tertullian's words, when discussing the authenticity of 1 Enoch, cannot be adequately explained, unless as bearing on passages in the Parables referring to the Son of Man: 'Cum Enoch eadem scriptura etiam de domino praedicarit, a nobis quidem nihil omnino reiiciendum est quod pertineat ad nos. ... A Iudaeis potest iam videri propterea reiecta, sicut et cetera fere *quae Christum sonant*' (*De Cultu Fem.* 1³). The Noah Apocalypse, moreover, which is interpolated in the Parables, is referred to in Origen, *Contra Celsum* 5⁵² (i.e. τοὺς ἀγγέλους) γενέσθαι κακούς, καὶ κολάζεσθαι δεσμοῖς ὑποβληθέντας ἐν γῇ ὅθεν καὶ τὰς θερμὰς πηγὰς εἶναι τὰ ἐκείνων δάκρυα (1 En. 67⁶, ¹¹, ¹²). This evidence necessitates the existence of a Greek Version of the Parables.

Let us turn now to the next argument. The Ethiopic must have been made direct from the Aramaic because of the three forms in which the title 'Son of Man' is given in the Ethiopic, since these, according to Schmidt, correspond exactly to the three forms in Aramaic. But here I must join issue. We have, unless I have failed wholly in this study, seen that the evidence adduced by Schmidt for an Aramaic original is quite inconclusive, and that on the contrary the evidence so far points, though not conclusively, to a Hebrew original. For this conclusion other evidence will be adduced later. We are not, therefore, predisposed to accept such an extraordinary thesis as that the Ethiopic must have been made directly from the Aramaic. Before dealing directly with the titles in question we might point to two facts which render this thesis not merely improbable, but incredible. 1°. No known Ethiopic version has been made directly from the Aramaic. 2°. The Book of Enoch, by its artificial division into five books, like the five books of the Pentateuch, the five books of the Psalms, the five Megilloth, the five books in Proverbs, in Sirach, the five divisions in the Pirke Aboth, and the five books of the Maccabean wars by Jason of Cyrene (see Hawkins², *Horae Synopticae*, p. 164), was after its kind a carefully edited work in which the fragments of a literature were put together with just as much fitness and insight as that of the Proverbs or the Pirke Aboth. This fivefold division was thus a well-known Jewish device, and, since according to the use of the book made by the N.T. writers it existed in its completed form in the first half of the first century A.D., if not nearly a century earlier, we cannot understand how an Ethiopic translator in the sixth or seventh century A.D. could have used the Greek version for the four books of Enoch, 1-36 72-82 83-90 90-108, and an Aramaic for the fifth, i.e. the Parables, 37-71. It is very probable that the entire book was translated early in the first century of the Christian era into Greek. That the Semitic original was early lost is to be inferred from the fact that no evidence of any kind testifies to its existence after the birth of Christianity, whereas multitudinous evidence attests the existence of the Greek version.

We may, therefore, safely relegate to the limbo of impossibilities the hypothesis that chapters 37-71 of the Ethiopic version were translated directly from the Aramaic.

We have now to consider what Schmidt terms 'the most convincing evidence of an Aramaic original', i.e. the Ethiopic translations of the term 'Son of Man'. The Ethiopic translation was made, as we have just seen, from the Greek. Hence whatever explanation we give of the three forms must be justified by a Greek retranslation. This fact at once discounts any attempt to find a Greek prototype for 'ĕguâla 'ĕmaḥĕjâw 'offspring of the mother of the living'. This Ethiopic phrase is used indifferently as a rendering of ἄνθρωπος, υἱὸς ἀνθρώπου, ἄνθρωποι, υἱοὶ ἀνθρώπων, ἀνήρ. And the full form walda 'ĕguâla 'ĕmaḥĕjâw = υἱὸς ἀνθρώπου in Dan. 7^{13} Ps. 79^{18}, in Ezekiel about ninety times, Rev. 1^{13} 14^{14}, and in the Gospels always = ὁ υἱὸς τοῦ ἀνθρώπου. In itself the Ethiopic phrase can mean 'son of man' or 'the Son of Man'. But if the translator wished to make it clear that the latter title was used, he could do so by prefixing a demonstrative pronoun as a rendering of the Greek article ὁ. This is done in every instance in the Parables save three. In the course of eight verses in 89^{42-9} the Greek article is so rendered eleven times.

Let us now examine the other two titles walda sab'ĕ and walda b'ĕsi. sab'ĕ distinctively = ἄνθρωπος (though in a few cases it = ἀνήρ). Thus walda sab'ĕ = υἱὸς ἀνθρώπου. It can also = ὁ υἱὸς τοῦ ἀνθρώπου, but to make this unmistakable the translator could prefix the demonstrative pronoun as the equivalent of ὁ.

Next comes walda b'ĕsi. b'ĕsi = ἀνήρ generally, but as Dillmann (*Lex.* 519) puts it, it stands *creberrime* for ἄνθρωπος. In fact in the Ethiopic Version of our book it is used as a rendering of ἄνθρωπος in 1^2 15^1. If more of the Greek version had survived we should no doubt find many other instances.

The result of the above examination comes to this. The above three renderings do not presuppose three different forms in the Greek. They most probably presuppose merely one, i.e. ὁ υἱὸς τοῦ ἀνθρώπου, but walda b'ĕsî may presuppose ὁ υἱὸς τοῦ ἀνδρός. But I think the latter improbable. In 62⁵ 69²⁹ (bis) 71¹⁴ bĕ'sî may be a rendering of ἀνθρώπου as in 1² 15¹.

This change of rendering may seem surprising, but we have a perfect parallel in the Curetonian and Sinaitic versions of the Syriac N. T.¹ Thus whereas in the Peshitto b'reh dĕ-našâ (ברה דאנשא) occurs uniformly as a rendering of ὁ υἱὸς τοῦ ἀνθρώπου, in the Curetonian version we have b'reh de-gabrâ (ברה דגברא) in Luke 7³⁴ 9²⁶ 22⁴⁸, and in the Sinaitic version b'reh de-gabrâ in Mark 8³⁸ Luke 7³⁴ John 13³¹, and elsewhere in both these versions b'reh de-našâ. In the Palestinian Lectionary there is still another way of rendering the phrase, but this does not concern us here. We have, however, learnt from these versions that differences in the manner of rendering the title 'Son of Man' in these versions does not imply any difference in the original Greek. Similarly we conclude that the three renderings of this title in the Parables do not presuppose corresponding variations in the Greek, but are due to the translator.

If, then, these variations in the Parables are due to the translator or translators it follows that these translators were Aramaic-speaking Jews, since the phrases walda b'ĕsî and walda sab'ĕ are respectively equivalents of b'reh de-gabrâ and b'reh dĕ-našâ.²

On the above grounds we conclude that ὁ υἱὸς τοῦ ἀνθρώπου stood in all cases in the Greek version of the Parables.³ That this Greek *phrase* represents the Hebrew בן־האדם, we shall further conclude from the evidence given in the next section.

(c) Passages which postulate a Hebrew original.

39⁷ᵇ. 'The righteous ... shall †be strong† (*a–m*: 'be beautiful†' *m, β*) as fiery lights.' Neither reading is satisfactory. *a–m* = יחזקו which may be corrupt for יִזְהָרוּ = 'shine': cf. Dan. 12³ .. יזהרו ככוכבים.

46⁷. 'These are they who †judge† the stars of heaven.' Here, as I have shown, the text appears to be based on Dan. 8¹⁰, and should be read (see my note *in loc.*) as follows:—

---

¹ See Schmidt in *Encyclc. Bibl.* iv. 4714.

² The Aramaisms in the Ethiopic version of the O. T. are probably due to Aramaean missionaries.

³ There is just a possibility that two forms stood in the Greek version, i.e. ὁ υἱὸς τοῦ ἀνθρώπου and ὁ υἱὸς τοῦ ἀνδρός, and that these were due to the translators, who in this case also would be Aramaic-speaking Jews, but this is highly improbable.

'These are they who raise their hands against the Most High,
And cast down the stars of heaven,
And tread them upon the earth.'

Thus 'judge' = ידינו which the context shows to be corrupt for ירדו = 'cast down'.

47⁴ᵇ. 'Because the number of the righteous **had been offered**.' As the context shows (see my note *in loc.*) these words mean that the number of the righteous, i.e. the martyrs, is complete: cf. Rev. 6¹⁰, ¹¹. Now *a* reads qarĕba = ἤγγικε = קָרַב, which in Mishnaic Hebrew = 'has been offered'. This meaning is not found in the qal of this verb in Aramaic.

52⁹. 'All these things shall be [denied and] destroyed from the surface of the earth.' Here there were two alternative Greek renderings of יִבָּחֲדוּ. One was originally in the text, and the other in the argin, but subsequently both were incorporated into the text. Or the dittograph was native to the Hebrew, i.e. יבחשו and יבחדו. Schmidt attempts to explain the corruption from an Aramaic basis by assuming that יתרמאן stood in the original, and that this received the two renderings in the text. But רמא does not mean 'to destroy'. Moreover, the Ethiopic word kĕhĕda here, which means 'to deny', occurs again in 45¹ 46⁷ 48¹⁰, in which three passages Schmidt says it goes back to the Aramaic כפר. Thus his proposal is satisfactory in no respect.

60⁶. I have followed *u* in the text, but the parallelism is in favour of regarding the text as corrupt in the word 'worship'. This word is wholly unsatisfactory. It = ישתחוו, which may be corrupt (or יְשַׁחֲתוּ = 'pervert' or 'corrupt'). Thus we recover an excellent parallelism:—

'For those who corrupt the righteous law,
And for those who deny the righteous judgement,
And for those who take His name in vain.'

65¹⁰ᵃ. 'Their judgement has been determined upon and shall not **be withheld** by me for ever.'

For 'withheld' the text reads λογισθήσεται or ἀριθμηθήσεται. The Ethiopic word can mean either. The former rendering (as in 52⁸ᵈ) is generally followed here. It is, however, unsatisfactory. The true reading, as I pointed out in my text, can be recovered by retranslation into Hebrew. οὐ λογισθήσεται = לא יחשב, corrupt for לא יֵחָשֵׂךְ = 'shall not be withheld'. Here Schmidt follows the other possible meaning of the Ethiopic word ἀριθμηθήσεται = יתמנא—a corruption of יתמנע.

65¹⁰ʰ. 'Because of the **sorceries** which they have searched out and learnt, the earth and those who dwell upon it shall be destroyed.' Instead of 'sorceries' the Ethiopic reads 'months' = חדשים, which Halévy rightly recognized as a corruption of חרשים = 'sorceries'. It is true that on an exceptional occasion Aramaic-speaking Jews used חדשיא instead of their own word ירחיא. Hence the evidence for a Hebrew original is slightly weakened here.

The text of this passage as known to Halévy and originally to myself was corrupt, and Schmidt rightly objected to this text even when emended as follows: 'because of the sorceries which they have searched out and (through which) they know that the earth ... will be destroyed.' Schmidt observes that it 'is a strange idea that the terrible judgement of the flood would come because men had succeeded in discovering that the earth with its inhabitants would be destroyed'. This observation is just, but the remedy lies in the MSS. *g t u*, which omit the 'that'. The omission of this word restores the meaning of the whole verse. See note on p. 131.

From the above evidence we infer a Hebrew original. As in the Hebrew chapters of Daniel, so here there were possibly many Aramaisms.

Chapters 72–82. From a Hebrew original.

76¹, ¹⁴. Here the word in the text 'winds' = רוחות, which should have been rendered 'quarters'. This restoration is possible both in Hebrew and Aramaic.

77¹. In this verse there is a play on the four quarters of the earth. It is possible to recover this play by retranslation into either Hebrew or Aramaic in the case of the 'east' and 'north': קֶדֶם or קִדּוּם and צָפוֹן or צפן.

But this is not so in the case of the 'south' and 'west'. As regards the first the text reads 'the south, because the Most High will descend there, yea there ... will He ... descend' = דָּרוֹם כִּי יֵרַד רָם. This is possible only in Hebrew.

77². 'And the west quarter is named (lit. 'its name') diminished because there all the luminaries wane.' הרוח המערבית שמו אחרון כי שם יאחרו כל־המאורות.

78¹. Of the two names of the sun which are transliterated, though corruptly, in this verse, one is Hebrew and not Aramaic; i.e. Orjares = אוֹר חֶרֶס. The other, Tômâs cf. = תָּמַהּ, is Hebrew and Aramaic; but if it is corrupt from חמה, as Halévy conjectures, it is Hebrew.

Introduction

78². Of the four names of the moon which are here transliterated, three are Hebrew only, Asônjâ, i. e. אִישׁוֹן, Eblâ, i. e. לְבָנָה, and Benâsê, i. e. בֶּן־כֶּסֶה.

80⁵. See note *in loc.*

82¹⁰. See note *in loc.*

82¹⁵. 'Tam'âini and Sun.' These two names are one, i. e. שֶׁמֶשׁ תֵּימָנִי. This is Hebrew, and not Aramaic.

Chapters 83–90. From a Hebrew (or Aramaic?) original.

89⁴⁴. The emendation suggested here is possible both in Hebrew and Aramaic.

90¹³ᵃ, ¹⁶ᵃ. In the duplicate version which we have of these verses, 'shepherds' in 90¹³ corresponds to 'ravens' in 90¹⁶. The latter is right. The corruption can be explained from a Hebrew background, רֹעִים, corrupt for עֹרְבִים, or from an Aramaic רעין, corrupt for עורבין.

90¹³ᵇ, ¹⁶ᵇ. In the former 'cried to' corresponds to 'were gathered together' in the latter. Now the former = ἔκραζον = יִזְעֲקוּ or יִצְעֲקוּ, and the latter יָזְעֲקוּ or יָצְעֲקוּ in Hebrew. But this explanation is impossible in Aramaic; for though זעק and צעק occur in the sense of 'to cry', no mood of this verb is used in the sense of 'to assemble'. For this word they use כנש.

90¹⁸. **covered them.** The Ethiopic expression here is not good Ethiopic, but reproduces the Greek ἐκάλυψεν ἐπ' αὐτούς, which in turn is a literal rendering of כסה עליהם (Hebrew), or עליהון כסי) or חפא) in Aramaic.

90²⁷. 'I saw those sheep †burning and their bones burning†.' This clause is obviously corrupt. In 'bones' there appears to be a mistranslation of the late Hebrew עצם or the Aramaic גרם, which literally mean 'bone' or 'bones', but which when compounded with a suffix = 'self' or 'selves'. The participle is then a doublet. Hence we have ואראה הצאן הזאת עצמה בערת = 'I saw those very sheep burning'. This is possible also in Aramaic.

90³⁸. 'The first among them became the **lamb**.' 'The lamb' = הטלה, which was corrupted into המלה, as Goldschmidt has pointed out, whence the corruption in the Ethiopic text 'the word'. This explanation is possible also in Aramaic.

Chapters 91–104. From a Hebrew original.

93⁵. Text reads 'after him' = אחריו, which I take to be corrupt for אחיתו = 'his posterity'.

93⁸ᵇ. The Ethiopic has a peculiar form, and = ἀσεβήσουσιν καρδίαι πάντων ἀπὸ τῆς σοφίας, which is pure Hebrew = ירשע לבב כלם מחכמה. Cf. Ps. 18²² רשעתי מאלהי.

95¹ᵃ. 'Oh that mine eyes were [a cloud of] waters.' The bracketed word is either an intrusion and = ענן, a dittograph of עני = 'eyes', or ענן is corrupt for עין = 'fount', the corruption being due to the occurrence of the phrase 'cloud of waters' in 95¹ᶜ. Hence 'Oh that mine eyes were a fount of waters'. This is possible also in Aramaic.

96⁵.   'Who devour the finest of the wheat
            And drink **wine in large bowls**.'

For the emended phrase E has here the extraordinary words 'strength of the root of the fountain' = ἰσχὺν ῥίζης πηγῆς = כח עיקר עין, corrupt for בְּמִזְרְקֵי יָיִן (Amos 6⁶). See my note *in loc*.

96⁶ᵃ. **From every fountain.** E reads 'at every time' = בכל-עת, corrupt for מכל-עין.

97⁸ᵇ⁻⁹. We have here a remarkable series of rhyming verses which arise on retranslation into Hebrew.

8ᵇ.	עֹשֶׁר עָשָׁרוּ	9.	תעשה שחשבטו
	ורכוש לָט		כי כסף אסף אספנו
8ᶜ.	וכל קנינו	9ᵈ.	ורבים אדרי בתינו
	אשר אונו	9ᶜ.	ומלאים כמים אוצרינו

98⁴ᵃᵇ. See note *in loc*.

99⁶. Here E = εἰς ἡμέραν αἵματος ἀδιαλείπτου, but in Tertullian (*De Idol.* iv) the phrase appears as 'in diem sanguinis *perditionis*' = εἰς ἡμέραν αἵματος ἀπωλείας = ליום דם לאיד, where לאיד is corrupt for לעד = ἀδιαλείπτου.

99¹⁶. E (gβ) reads 'the spirit of His indignation' = רוח אפו, corrupt for חרון אפו = 'His fierce indignation'.

100⁶ᵃ. See note *in loc*.

101⁴. E reads 'kings' = מלכי, corrupt for מלחי, 'sailors.' This is also possible in Aramaic.

§ 16. THE INFLUENCE OF 1 ENOCH ON JEWISH LITERATURE.

In the Book of Jubilees, written before 105 B.C., 1 Enoch is largely drawn upon, as may be seen from the following parallel passages and phrases:—

Jubilees	*1 Enoch*
1¹¹ 'sacrifice . . . to demons'.	19¹ 'sacrificing to demons as gods'.
	89⁵¹⁻⁵³

Jubilees	1 Enoch
1^6 'the plant of uprightness'. Cf. 16^{26}.	10^{16} 'the plant of righteousness and truth'.
	93^2 'the plant of uprightness'. Cf. $93^{5,\,10}$: also 84^6.
2^6 'until I descend and dwell with them'.	25^3 'the Lord of Glory ... when He shall come down to visit the earth'.
2^9 'angel of the presence'.	$40^{2,\,3}$ 'four presences'.
2^9 'the heavens shall be renewed ... the powers of the heaven ... the luminaries be renewed'.	91^{16} 'a new heaven shall appear, and all the powers of the heavens shall give sevenfold light'.
2^2 'the spirit of the winds'.	60^{12}.
'the spirit of snow'.	^{18} 'the spirit of the snow'.
'the spirit of hail'.	^{21} 'the spirit of the rain.'
'the spirit of hoar-frost'.	^{17} 'the spirit of the hoar-frost'.
'the angels of the voices and of the thunder and of the lightning'.	$^{13-15}$ 'the thunder—lightning-peals—the spirit'.
2^4.	$54^{7,\,8}$.
3^{10} 'the heavenly tablets', and *passim*.	$81^{1,\,2}$ 93^2 103^2 'the heavenly tablets'.
4^3.	22^{5-7}.
^{15} 'Jared; for in his days the angels of the Lord descended on the earth'.	6^6 (the angels) 'descended in the days of Jared'.
'the Watchers'. Cf. 10^5.	1^5 12^{2-4} 'the Watchers'.
^{17} 'the first ... who learnt writing'.	12^3 'Enoch the scribe'.
'who wrote down the signs of heaven, &c.'	$72-82$.
^{19} 'what was and what will be, he saw in a vision of his sleep ... until the day of judgement'.	$83-90$. The Dream-Visions.
'placed the testimony on earth for all the children of men and for their generations'.	1^2 37^{2-4} 92^1 104^{11-13}.
^{20} 'he took to himself a wife, and her name was Edni'.	85^3 'Before I took ... Edna'.

Jubilees	1 Enoch
^{21} 'he was with the angels of God these six jubilees of years'.	$12^{1,\,2}$ 'he was hidden … and his activities had to do with the Watchers, &c.'
'and they showed, &c.'	23–36.
'the rule of the sun'.	82^{13-20}.
^{22} 'testified to the Watchers'.	12^{3-6} 13^{1-12} 14^{4-7} 15^2 sqq.
'who had sinned with the daughters of men'. Cf. 5^1.	6^2 7^1 9^8 10^{11} 12^4 $15^{3,\,4}$.
'unite themselves, so as to be defiled with the daughters of men'.	10^{11} 'united themselves with women so as to have defiled themselves with them'. Cf. $15^{3,\,4}$.
^{23} 'we conducted him into the Garden of Eden'.	50^8 '… the garden where the elect and righteous dwell where my grandfather was taken up, the seventh from Adam'. Cf. 70^{1-3}.
'there he writes down the condemnation, &c.'	12^4 15^1 'scribe of righteousness'.
^{26} 'the Mount of the East' (one of the four places of the Lord on earth).	$18^{7,\,8}$ 'as for those towards the east; … the middle one reached to heaven like the throne of God'. Cf. 24^3 25^3.
5^1 'they bare unto them sons, and they were giants'.	7^2 'they bare great giants'. Cf. $15^{3,\,8}$.
^{2} 'all of them corrupted their ways and their orders, and they began to devour each other'. Cf. 7^{24}.	7^5 'they began to sin against birds and beasts … and to devour one another's flesh'.
^{6} 'He bade us to bind them in the depths of the earth'. Cf. 5^{10} 10^7.	10^{12} 'bind them fast in the valleys (*emended*) of the earth'.
^{7} Destruction of the angels' children by the sword.	10^9 $14^{5,\,6}$.
^{9} 'that each should slay his neighbour'.	10^9 'that they may destroy each other in battle'. Cf. 10^{12} 88^1.
^{10} 'and their fathers were witnesses (of their destruction), and after this they were bound	10^{12} 'and when their sons have slain one another, and they have seen the destruction of

Jubilees	1 Enoch
in the depths of the earth for ever, until the day of the great condemnation when judgement is executed, &c.'	their beloved ones, bind them fast for seventy generations in the valleys of the earth till the day of their judgement and of their consummation, till the judgement that is for ever and ever is consummated '.
	12^6 ' the murder of their beloved ones shall† they see '. Cf. 14^6.
11, 12 ' He destroyed all ... and He made ... a new and righteous nature. &c.'	$10^{15, 16}$ ' destroy all ... and let the plant of righteousness and truth appear, &c.'
^{24} ' seven flood-gates of heaven '.	89^2 ' heaven ... a lofty roof with seven water torrents thereon '.
^{25} ' the fountains of the deep also sent up waters '.	89^3 ' fountains were opened on the surface of that great enclosure, &c.'
^{29} ' the fountains of the great deep were closed and the floodgates of heaven were restrained; and ... all the mouths of the abysses of the earth were opened, and the water began to descend into the deep below '. Cf. 6^{26}.	89^7 ' those water torrents were removed from that high roof and the chasms of the earth were levelled up and other abysses were opened. ^{8} Then the water began to run down into these, &c.'
$6^{23, 29-32}$ A year of 364 days, four being intercalary days.	$75^{1, 2}$ $82^{4, 6, 11}$.
$^{32-38}$ Warning against the use of any other calendar.	82^{4-7}.
7^{21} The deluge due to the Watchers' sin.	10^2.
The Watchers' sin. Cf. 4^{22}.	7^1, &c.
' against the law of their ordinances '.	15^{3-7}.
' they made the beginning of uncleanness '.	8^2 ' there arose much godlessness and they committed fornication '.
	9^6 ' hath taught all unrighteousness on earth '.
	10^8 ' ... to him ascribe all sin '.

Jubilees	1 Enoch
^{22} The Giants, the Nâphil, the Eljô.	7^1 (*Syncellus's Greek Version*) The Giants, Nephilim, the Eliud.
'they devoured one another'. Cf. 5^9.	87^1 'devour each other'. Cf. $10^{9, 12}$ 88^1.
^{23} 'shed much blood ... the earth was filled with iniquity'.	9^1 'much blood being shed ... all lawlessness being wrought upon the earth'.
^{24} 'they sinned, &c.' (*emended*).	7^5.
^{25} 'into Sheol shall they go, and into the place of condemnation shall they descend, and into the darkness'. Cf. 22^{22}.	$103^{7, 8}$ 'their souls shall be made to descend into Sheol ... and into darkness ... and a burning flame where there is grievous judgement ...'.
^{30} 'the seventh in his generation'.	60^8 'the seventh from Adam'.
	93^3 'the seventh in the first week'.
'whilst still living he testified to his son, &c.'	$93^{1, 2}$.
8^{12} 'the middle of the earth' (Shem's lot).	26^1 'the middle of the earth' (Palestine).
^{22} 'the mountains of fire'.	Cf. 18^{6-9} 24^{1-3}.
10^1 'the unclean demons began to lead astray ... and destroy them'. Cf. 11^5.	15^8 'the giants shall be called evil spirits ...'.
	11 '... afflict, oppress, destroy, attack, do battle'. Cf. 16^1.
	19^1 'their (the angels') spirits assuming many different forms are defiling mankind and will lead them astray into sacrificing to demons as gods'.
'hold them fast in the place of condemnation'.	19^1 'here shall they stand till the day of the great judgement'.
^{12} 'we explained to Noah the medicines ... how he might heal'.	10^7 'heal the earth which the angels have corrupted, &c.'
12^2 'what help and profit have we from those idols'.	99^7 '... shall get no manner of help from them'.
^{4} 'who causes the rain and the dew to descend on the earth'.	101^2 'withholds the rain and the dew from descending on the earth'.

Introduction   lxxv

Jubilees	*1 Enoch*
15^{32} 'But over Israel He did not appoint any angel or spirit for He alone is their ruler'. This contradicts 1 En. 89^{59}.	89^{59} 'and He called seventy shepherds and cast those sheep to them, &c.'
'He will require them at the hands of His angels, &c.'	$90^{17,\,22}$.
16^{26} 'plant of righteousness'. Cf. 21.	10^{16} 'plant of righteousness'. Cf. $93^{2,\,5}$.
22^{17} 'worship evil spirits'.	99^{7} 'worship impure spirits and demons'.
22 'For they will descend into Sheol, &c.' See 7^{29} above.	$103^{7,\,8}$.
$23^{16\,sqq.}$ Rise of the Chasids.	90^{6-7}.
$^{23-24}$ Attack of the (?) Syrians.	90^{8-11}.
$^{27-29}$ A future time of peace and joy and plenty, with long life.	$5^{7}\ 10^{17}$; also 91–104 *passim*.
^{31} 'their spirits will have much joy' (though 'their bones will rest in the earth').	103^{3} 'all goodness and joy and glory are ... written down for the spirits of them, &c.'
	103^{4} 'and the spirits ... shall live and rejoice ... and their spirits shall not perish'.
30^{22} 'the book of life'. Cf. 36^{10}.	47^{3} 'the books of the living'.
$32^{18,\,19}$ Jacob's seed rule and judge.	$95^{3}\ 96^{1}$ The righteous rule and judge.
35^{17} 'the guardian of Jacob'.	20^{5} 'Michael ... set over the best part of mankind' [+ 'over the people'. *Eth.*]
36^{10} 'the day of turbulence and execration and indignation and anger'.	39^{2} 'books of zeal and wrath, and books of disquiet and expulsion'.
'the book of life'. Cf. 30^{22}.	47^{3} 'the books of the living'.
37^{20} 'the boar' (Esau speaks in reference to himself).	$89^{12,\,42,\,49,\,66}$ 'wild boar', 'wild boars' (= Edom).

In the *Testaments of the Twelve Patriarchs*, written between 137 and 105 (possibly 109–107) B.C., there are nine direct references to a book of Enoch:—

T. Lev. 10⁵ 'the house which the Lord shall choose... as is contained in the book of Enoch the righteous'.	1 En. 89⁵⁰ 'the house for the Lord'.
16¹ 'I have learned (in the book of Enoch β Aᵝ S)... for seventy weeks'.	89⁵⁹ sqq.
14¹ 'I have learned (from the writing of Enoch β Aᵝ S¹) &c.'	91⁶,⁷.
T. Dan. 5⁶ T. Sim. 5⁴ T. Jud. 18¹ (β) T. Zeb. 3⁴ (β) T. Naph. 4¹ T. Benj. 9¹, 10⁶	cannot be traced directly to any passage in 1 Enoch. In T. Zeb. 3⁴ there is a slip, 'Enoch' being written for 'Moses' in βS¹, or else a scribe has changed the reference to Moses as being an anachronism on the lips of Zebulon.

There are also passages in the *Testaments* which are more or less closely parallel to 1 Enoch, e. g. :—

T. Reub. 5⁶,⁷ The Watchers, the women and the giants.	1 En. 6–9².
T. Lev. 3⁴ 'the Great Glory' (α β Aᵝ S).	14²⁰ 102³.
T. Lev. 16² 'make void the law and set at naught... by evil perverseness'.	99², ¹⁴ 104⁹, ¹⁰.
18⁵ (see note on 1 En. 51⁴).	51⁴.
T. Naph. 3⁵ 'the Watchers changed the order of their nature'.	6–9².

1 Enoch was probably used by the author of the *Assumption of Moses*, written between A.D. 7 and 30. Cf. :—

Ass. Mos.	1 Enoch
4⁸ 'sad and lamenting because they will not be able to offer sacrifices to the Lord of their fathers'.	89⁷³ 'they began to place a table... but all the bread on it was polluted and not pure'.
10³,⁴ 'He will go forth from His holy habitation'.	1³ 'will come forth from His dwelling'.

Introduction

Ass. Mos.	1 Enoch
10^4 'And the earth shall tremble: to its confines shall it be shaken: And the high mountains shall be made low, and the hills shall be shaken and fall'.	$1^{5,6}$ '... unto the ends of the earth: ^{6} And the high mountains shall be shaken and the high hills ... made low'.

2 Baruch (for date see Introd. to my *Apoc. Bar.* § 7, pp. lvii and lxiv) has many affinities with 1 Enoch both in diction and in thought, and is manifestly dependent on it.

2 Baruch	1 Enoch
10^6.	38^2.
10^8 Sirens.	19^2 Sirens.
13^8 'The judgement of the Lofty One who has no respect of persons'.	63^8 'His judgements have no respect of persons'.
21^{23} 'treasuries of souls'.	100^5.
24^1 'the books shall be opened in which are written the sins of all those who have sinned'.	90^{20} 'he took the sealed books and opened those books'.
29^4 A later form of the myth of Behemoth and Leviathan which is found first in En. 60^{7-9}.	$60^{7-9, 24}$.
29^5 'The earth also shall yield its fruit ten thousandfold'.	10^{19} 'each measure shall bear a thousand'.
32^6 'renew His creation'.	45^4.
35^2 'O that mine eyes were springs, and mine eyelids a fount of tears'.	95^1 'Oh that mine eyes were [a cloud of] waters that I might weep over you and pour down my tears as a cloud †of† waters'.
48^9 'The spheres ... in their orders'.	2^1 'The luminaries ... rise and set in order'.
50^2.	51^1.
51^3 'who have planted in their heart the root of wisdom' (cf. 59^7).	10^{16} 'the plant of righteousness'.
51^{10} 'they shall be made like unto the angels, and be made equal to the stars'.	$104^{2,4}$ 'shine as the lights of heaven ... have great joy as the angels'. Cf. 69^{11}.

2 Baruch	1 Enoch
54^2 'for Whom nothing is too hard'.	84^3 'nothing is too hard for Thee'.
55^3 Remiel.	20^7 Ramiel (*Greek*).
56^6 'when he (Adam) transgressed, untimely death came into being'.	69^{11} 'men were created exactly like the angels—and death ... could not have taken hold of them'.
56^{10-13} 'even to the angels became he a danger. For, moreover, at that time, when he was created, they enjoyed liberty. And some of them descended and mingled with the women. And then those who did so were tormented in chains'.	6–10.
59^2 'the eternal law'.	99^2 'the eternal law'.
$59^{5,\,8}$.	$18^{11}\ 21^{7-10}\ 40^{11,\,12}\ 47^5$.
^{10} Gehenna.	$27^{2,\,3}\ 54\ 62^{12}\ 90^{26,\,27}$.
'the station of vengeance'.	$18^{12-16}\ 19\ 21\ 22^{10-13}\ 54^{1-6}\ 90^{24-27}$.
68^4.	$89^{73,\,74}$.

The dependence of this book on 1 Enoch is still more evident if we may regard it as proceeding from one author; for it reproduces in the main the conceptions of 1 En. 91–104 save that it expects a Messiah. Thus in this Apocalypse of Baruch the Messianic Kingdom is only of temporary duration. The Messiah reigns till sin is at an end $74^{2,\,3}$. During his reign the earth yields ten thousandfold, and there are no premature deaths. At the close of this period the Messiah returns to heaven and the resurrection ensues 50–51^6. The righteous are then transformed and made like the angels $51^{5,\,10}$.

The author of 4 Ezra, writing between A.D. 81–96, has made a not infrequent use of 1 Enoch, and this mainly of the Parables.

4 Ezra	1 Enoch
6^{49-52} takes up and develops further the myth found in En. 60^{7-9}.	60^{7-9} Leviathan and Behemoth.

4 Ezra	1 Enoch
7³²,³³ 'Et terra reddet qui in ea dormiunt, et pulvis qui in eo silentio habitant, et promptuaria reddent quae eis commendatae sunt animae. Et revelabitur Altissimus super sedem iudicii'.	51¹,³ 'And in those days shall the earth also give back that which has been entrusted to it, And Sheol also shall give back that which it has received, And hell shall give back that which it owes . . . And the Elect One shall in those days sit on My throne'.
7³⁷ 'Et dicet tunc Altissimus ad excitatas gentes: videte et intellegite quem negastis, vel cui non servistis vel cuius diligentias sprevistis'.	62¹ 'thus the Lord commanded . . . those who dwell on the earth, and said: "Open your eyes and lift up your horns if ye are able to recognize the Elect One"'.
	60⁶ 'Who worship not the righteous law and . . . who deny the righteous judgement and . . . who take His name in vain'.
7³⁶ 'Clibanus gehennae ostendetur, et contra eum iocunditatis paradisus'.	48⁹,¹⁰ 27³.
7⁷⁵ 'incipies creaturam renovare'.	72¹.
7⁸⁵,⁹⁵. A development of 1 En. 100⁵.	100⁵.
7¹²⁵. 'Super stellas fulgebunt facies eorum'. Cf. 7⁹⁷.	104² 'ye shall shine as the lights of heaven'.
'. . . nostrae autem facies super tenebras nigrae'.	62¹⁰ 'darkness shall grow deeper on their faces'.

From the second century A.D. onwards all knowledge of 1 Enoch vanishes from Jewish literature with the exception of a few references that are given by Jellinek in the *Zeitschr. D.M.G.*, 1853, p. 249.

§ 17. THE HEBREW BOOK OF ENOCH.

The Hebrew Book of Enoch, ספר חנוך, of which a complete but unedited MS. exists in the Bodleian Library, is a work which must be dated later than the Book of the Secrets of Enoch (or 2 Enoch), as it continually betrays its dependence on that work. A printed edition of the book is given by Jellinek, *Bet ha-Midrasch*, 1873, v. 170-190, but in an incomplete form. It describes the ascent into heaven of Rabbi Ishmael, who receives a series of revelations from Meṭaṭron, who relates in chaps. 3-5 7-16 (cf. 1 En. 14^8 70^2) that he is Enoch the son of Jared, translated to heaven in a chariot of fire at the time of the Deluge, to bear eternal witness against his sinful contemporaries (1 En. 5^{4-6} 14^{1-7}). He had there been instructed by the Angel of Wisdom in all wisdom and knowledge, and all the mysteries of creation (1 En. 93^{10} 63^{11-21}), of heaven and earth, of past and future things, and of the world to come. In chap. 6 it is said that Adam and his generation beheld the heavenly glory, until in the time of Enoch 'Aza and Azael led men to idolatry'. Cf. 'in the days of Jared' (1 En. 6^6)—'Azazel' (1 En. 8^1 10^4 13^1)—'the angels ... spirits shall lead them astray into sacrificing to demons as gods' (1 En. 19^1).

Chaps. 18-22 (not in Jellinek's edition) describe the seven heavens with their hosts of angels, and the courses of the sun, moon, and stars (1 En. 72-82). In chap. 23 Meṭaṭron describes the fragrant odours and perfumes wafted into paradise to the pious and just, for whom paradise and the tree of life are prepared as an eternal inheritance (1 En. 24^4-25^7). In 24-26 he describes the chariot of God, and the many-eyed, radiant, God-praising Ophannim and Seraphim (1 En. 61^{10} 71^7). The latter burn the accusations continually brought by Satan against Israel (1 En. 40^{3-7}). In 27 he tells of a heavenly registrar and keeper of the archives (cf. 1 En. $89^{61-64, 70, 76}$ 98^{6-8} 104^7). Chaps. 35-40 relate how the heavenly hosts pass into God's presence to praise and glorify Him with the song, 'Holy, Holy, Holy is the Lord Sabaoth,' and how at that the Ophannim, Cherubim, Chayyoth, and Seraphim prostrate themselves (cf. 1 En. 39^{10-13} 61^{10-12}). In 41-47 Meṭaṭron shows Ishmael the repositories of the rain, snow, hail, thunder and lightning (cf. 1 En. 60^{11-21}), the spirits of those angels who were punished, and whose bodies were turned to great fiery mountains (1 En. 18$^{11-16, 21}$), the places of punishment (cf. 1 En. 18^{14} 19^1 21^7 27$^{1-3}$, &c.); Metatron next shows all past and future ages from Adam to the end of time, including the Messiah ben David and his age, and the wars of Gog and Magog (1 En. 56^5-57^2), and other events of the Messianic era. In the last chap., 48, he shows Ishmael the glorious future Jerusalem (1 En. 89^{22}), where the souls of the righteous stand praying for its advent upon earth (1 En. 97$^{3, 5}$ 99$^{3, 16}$ 104^3).

The date of this work cannot be later than the time of the completion of the Babylonian Talmud. An apocalyptic fragment (dealt with in *Jewish Encyc.* i. 678, 679), apparently written under the immediate impression of the Hadrianic persecution, seems to supply the link which connects 2 Enoch with this Neo-Hebrew Book of Enoch, which itself must be dated earlier than Talmud *Berachoth* 7 a which quotes from it.[1]

§ 18. The Influence of Enoch on Patristic Literature.

Epistle of Barnabus (soon after 70 A.D.).

4^3 τὸ τέλειον σκάνδαλον ἤγγικεν περὶ οὗ γέγραπται, ὡς Ἐνὼχ λέγει.

Not in our Enoch.

16^5 λέγει γὰρ ἡ γραφή· καὶ ἔσται ἐπ' ἐσχάτων τῶν ἡμερῶν καὶ παραδώσει κύριος τὰ πρόβατα τῆς νομῆς καὶ τὴν μάνδραν καὶ τὸν πύργον αὐτῶν εἰς καταφθοράν.

1 En. 89^{56} 'He forsook that their house and their tower and gave them (those sheep) all into the hands of the lions, to ... devour them'. ^{66} ... devoured ... those sheep ... and they burnt that tower and demolished that house'.

16^4.

91^{13}.

Apocalypse of Peter (early in second century) (ed. Robinson and James, 1892).

^{2} τοὺς πεινῶντας καὶ διψῶντας καὶ θλιβομένους, καὶ ἐν τούτῳ

108$^{7-9}$ 'those who have afflicted their bodies, &c.'

---

[1] This account is based on that given in *Jewish Encyc.* i. 676-679.

τῷ βίῳ τοὺς ψυχὰς ἑαυτῶν δοκιμάζοντας.	
3 Description of the 'two righteous brethren'.	106², ¹⁰ 'body whiter than snow, &c.' See notes *in loc*.
5 ... γῆν ... ἀρωμάτων πλήρη καὶ φυτῶν εὐανθῶν καὶ ἀφθάρτων καὶ καρπὸν εὐλογημένον φερόντων.	24³ 25⁴ Fragrant.
μιᾷ φωνῇ τὸν Κύριον θεὸν ἀνευφήμουν.	61⁹⁻¹² 'one voice ... bless, &c.'
οἱ δὲ οἰκήτορες τοῦ τόπου ἐκείνου ἐνδεδυμένοι ἦσαν ἔνδυμα ἀγγέλων φωτινῶν.	108¹² 'in shining light'.
6 οἱ κολαζόμενοι ... σκοτινὸν εἶχον αὐτῶν τὸ ἔνδυμα κατὰ τὸν ἀέρα τοῦ τόπου.	62¹⁰, ¹⁵, ¹⁶.
οἱ κολάζοντες ἄγγελοι. Cf. 8 ἄγγελοι βασανισταί.	53³ 56¹ 62¹¹ 63¹ 66¹ · the angels of punishment'.
7 πῦρ φλεγόμενον.	10¹³ 90²⁴ 98³ 108⁵.
οἱ βλασφημοῦντες ... τὴν ὁδὸν τῆς δικαιοσύνης. Cf. ¹³.	27² 'utter ... unseemly words, &c.' Cf. 108⁶.
	91¹⁸ 94¹ 'the paths of righteousness'.
15 οἱ πλουτοῦντες καὶ τῷ πλοίτῳ αὐτῶν πεποιθότες ... ἀλλ' ἀμελήσαντες τῆς ἐντολῆς τοῦ θεοῦ.	63¹⁰ 94⁸⁻¹¹ 96⁴⁻⁸ 97⁸⁻¹⁰.
Justin Martyr (died between A.D. 163 and 167), *Apol.* ii. 5 οἱ δὲ ἄγγελοι ... γυναικῶν μίξεσιν ἡττήθησαν καὶ παῖδας ἐτέκνωσαν, οἵ εἰσιν οἱ λεγόμενοι δαίμονες καὶ εἰς ἀνθρώπους φόνους, πολέμους, μοιχείας καὶ πᾶσαν κακίαν ἔσπειραν. Cf. i. 5.	9⁵⁻⁹ 15⁸, ⁹.
Tatian (flor. A.D. 160), *Oratio adv. Graecos* 8 ὑπόθεσις δὲ αὐτοῖς τῆς ἀποστασίας οἱ ἄνθρωποι γίνονται. διάγραμμα γὰρ αὐτοῖς ἀστροθεσίας ἀναδείξαντες ...	8³ 'astrology'.
20. μετῳκίσθησαν οἱ δαίμονες ... καὶ οἱ μὲν ἀπ' οὐρανοῦ κατεβλήθησαν.	6⁶ · who descended', 15⁸, ⁹.
Athenagoras (about A.D. 170), *Legatio pro Christianis*, 24 'De angelis et gigantibus', regards Enoch, though he does not name him,	

as a true prophet ἴστε δὲ μηδὲν ἡμᾶς ἀμάρτυρον
λέγειν, ἃ δὲ τοῖς προφήταις ἐκπεφώνηται, μηνύειν.
ἐκεῖνοι μέν, εἰς ἐπιθυμίαν πεσόντες, παρθένων ...
ἐκ μὲν οὖν τῶν περὶ τὰς παρθένους ἐχόντων οἱ
καλούμενοι ἐγεννήθησαν γίγαντες. 25. οὗτοι
τοίνυν οἱ ἄγγελοι οἱ ἐκπεσόντες τῶν οὐρανῶν περὶ
τὸν ἀέρα ἔχοντες καὶ τὴν γῆν, οὐκέτι εἰς τὰ
ὑπερουράνια ὑπερκύψαι δυνάμενοι· καὶ αἱ τῶν
γιγάντων ψυχαί, οἳ περὶ τὸν κόσμον εἰσὶ πλανώ-
μενοι δαίμονες.   6 7 13^5 14^5 15^{8-10}.

Minucius Felix (second century), *Octavius*, xxvi   8 15^{3-12} 16^1 19^1.
'Isti igitur spiritus, posteaquam simplici-
tatem substantiae suae, onusti et immersi
vitiis, perdiderunt, ad solatium calamitatis
suae non desinunt perditi iam perdere ... et
alienati a Deo, inductis pravis religionibus a
Deo segregare. Eos spiritus daemonas esse
poetae sciunt, philosophi disserunt, Socrates
novit... Magi quoque... quicquid miraculi
ludunt, per daemonas faciunt.'

Irenaeus (ob. circa A.D. 202).

i. 10. 1 (ed. Stieren). Πνεῦμα ἅγιον, τὸ διὰ τῶν   1 En. $10^{13, 14}$.
προφητῶν κεκηρυχός ... κρίσιν δικαίαν ἐν τοῖς
πᾶσι ποιήσηται (sc. Χριστὸς Ἰησοῦς)· τὰ μὲν
πνευματικὰ τῆς πονηρίας, καὶ ἀγγέλους παρα-
βεβηκότας, καὶ ἐν ἀποστασίᾳ γεγονότας, καὶ τοῖς
ἀσεβεῖς καὶ ἀδίκους καὶ ἀνόμους καὶ βλασφήμοις 5^4, &c.
τῶν ἀνθρώπων εἰς τὸ αἰώνιον πῦρ πέμψῃ.

i. 15. 6 (a quotation from a 'divine elder and 8^3 'enchantments
preacher of the truth'):   ... astrology'.
Εἰδωλοποιέ, Μάρκε, καὶ τερατοσκόπε,
Ἀστρολογικῆς ἔμπειρε καὶ μαγικῆς τέχνης,
Δι' ὧν κρατύνεις τῆς πλάνης τὰ διδάγματα,
Σημεῖα δεικνὺς τοῖς ὑπὸ σοῦ πλανωμένοις,
Ἀποστατικῆς δυνάμεως ἐγχειρήματα
Ἅ σοι χορηγεῖ σὸς πατὴρ Σατᾶν ἀεί,
Δι' ἀγγελικῆς δυνάμεως Ἀζαζὴλ ποιεῖν, 8^1 'Azazel taught
Ἔχων σε πρόδρομον ἀντιθέου πανουργίας.   men, &c.'

iv. 16. 2. 'Sed et Enoch, ... cum esset homo, $12^{4, 6}$ 13 14^{3-7} 15
legatione ad angelos fungebatur et translatus   16.
est et conservatur usque nunc testis iudicii

Dei, quoniam angeli quidam transgressi deciderunt in terram in iudicium.'

iv. 36. 4. 'Et temporibus Noe diluvium inducens, uti exstingueret pessimum genus eorum qui tunc erant hominum, qui iam fructificare Deo non poterant, cum angeli transgressores commixti fuissent eis.' 10^2 'a deluge is about to come upon the whole earth, &c.' 9^8 'slept with the women'.

v. 28. 2. 'Et non est mirandum, si daemoniis et apostaticis spiritibus ministrantibus ei, per eos faciat signa, in quibus seducat habitantes super terram.' Cf. Tert. *De Idol.* iv. 99^7 'impure spirits and demons'. 19^1 'lead (mankind) astray, &c.'

Tertullian, writing between 197 and 223, regards Enoch as Scripture, *Apol.* xxii. Cf. 1 En. $15^{8,\,9}$.

(Quoted in note on $15^{8,\,9}$.)

De Cultu Femin. i. 2. 8^{1-3}.

(Quoted in note on 8^1.)

i. 3. 'Scio scripturam Enoch quae hunc ordinem angelis dedit, non recipi a quibusdam, quia nec in armarium Iudaicum admittitur. Opinor, non putaverunt illum ante cataclysmum editam post eum casum orbis omnium rerum abolitorem salvam esse potuisse.' But Tertullian proceeds to show that this was possible: 'cum Enoch filio suo Matusalae nihil aliud mandaverit quam ut notitiam eorum posteris suis traderet.' He then pronounces the singular critical canon: 'cum Enoch eadem scriptura etiam de domino praedicarit, a nobis quidem nihil omnino reiiciendum est quod pertineat ad nos. . . . A Iudaeis potest iam videri propterea reiecta, sicut et cetera fere quae Christum sonant. . . . Eo accedit quod Enoch apud Iudam apostolum testimonium possidet.'

ii. 10 (quoted in note on 8^1). 8^1

De Idol. iv. 19^1 $99^{6,\,7}$

(Quoted in notes on 19^1 and $99^{6,\,7}$.)

De Idol. ix. *De Virg. Veland.* vii 'Si enim propter angelos, scilicet quos legimus a Deo et caelo excidisse ob concupiscentiam feminarum, &c.' $6\ 14^5$.

Clement of Alexandria (circa A.D. 150–210) *Eclogae Prophet.* (ed. Dindorf).

iii. 456 (quoted in note on 19³).	19³.
iii. 474 (quoted in note on 8², ³).	8², ³.
Strom. (ed. Dindorf), iii. 9 (quoted in note on 16³).	8¹⁻³ 16⁷.
Bardesanes (?) (154–222). *Book of the Laws of Countries*. 'If the angels likewise had not been possessed of personal freedom they would not have consorted with the daughters of men and sinned and fallen from their places.	6, &c.
Julius Africanus (ob. circ. 237) *Chronographia*. Πλήθους ἀνθρώπων γενομένου ἐπὶ τῆς γῆς ἄγγελοι τοῦ οὐρανοῦ θυγατράσιν ἀνθρώπων συνῆλθον. Ἐν ἐνίοις ἀντιγράφοις εὗρον, 'οἱ υἱοὶ τοῦ Θεοῦ....' Εἰ δὲ ἐπ' ἀγγέλων νοοῖτο ἔχειν τούτους, τοὺς περὶ μαγείας καὶ γοητείας, ἔτι δὲ ἀριθμῶν κινήσεως, τῶν μετεώρων ταῖς γυναιξὶ τὴν γνῶσιν παραδεδωκέναι, ἀφ' ὧν ἐποίησαν τοὺς παῖδας τοὺς γίγαντας, δι' οὓς τῆς κακίας ἐπιγενομένης, &c.	7¹ 8, &c.

Origen (185–254) does not regard Enoch as inspired, and yet he does not wholly reject it. Cf. *Contra Celsum*, v. 52. Celsus argues that other ἄγγελοι descended to the earth before Christ: ἐλθεῖν γὰρ καὶ ἄλλους λέγουσι πολλάκις καὶ ὁμοῦ γε ἑξήκοντα ἢ ἑβδομήκοντα· οὓς δὴ γενέσθαι κακοὺς καὶ κολάζεσθαι δεσμοῖς ὑποβληθέντας ἐν γῇ· ὅθεν καὶ τὰς θερμὰς πηγὰς εἶναι τὰ ἐκείνων δάκρυα. In a lengthy rejoinder Origen remarks, v. 54 ἐν ταῖς ἐκκλησίαις οὐ πάνυ φέρεται ὡς θεῖα τὰ ἐπιγεγραμμένα τοῦ Ἐνὼχ βιβλία (cf. 1 En. 6 10¹¹⁻¹² 67⁶⁻⁷). That Origen was undecided as to the value to be attached to Enoch is clearer from the following passages. *In Ioannem*, vi. 25 (Lommatzsch, i. 241) ὡς ἐν τῷ Ἐνὼχ γέγραπται, εἴ τῳ φίλον παραδέχεσθαι ὡς ἅγιον τὸ βιβλίον. *In Num. Homil.* xxviii. 2 (Lommatzsch, x. 366) 'De quibus quidem nominibus plurima in libellis, qui appellantur Enoch, secreta continentur, et arcana: sed quia libelli ipsi non videntur apud Hebraeos in auctoritate haberi, interim nunc ea quae ibi nominantur ad exemplum vocare differamus'. *De Princip.* i. 3. 3 (Lommatzsch, xxi. 73) 'Sed et in Enoch libro his similia describuntur'; iv. 35 (Lommatzsch, xxi. 476), quoted on 19³.

In the vision of Perpetua in *Acta SS. Perpet. et Felic.* (early in third century) vii, viii (ed. Robinson, pp. 72 sqq.), we have a remarkable parallel:

vii. After prayer for Dinocrates she sees the place once gloomy now bright, and one drawing water from the pool incessantly. ... 'Then I understood that he was translated from punishment.'	1 En. 22. The divisions for the souls of the dead. ^{9} 'this division has been made for the spirits of the righteous in which there is the bright spring of water'.
xii. 'the house built of light'.	14^{9-17}.

Pseudo-Tertullian, Five Books against Marcion, iii. ch. ii (Migne, ii. 1070). A summary of Enoch's life is given in which occur the words: 'Sacrilegum genus ut fugeret crudele gigantum.'

Commodianus (flor. 250 A.D.), *Instructiones* (ed. Migne, P.L. v. 203, 204), i. 3:

'(Deus) Visitari voluit terram ab angelis istam	(cf Jub. 4^{15}.)
Legitima cuius spreverunt illi dimissi:	
Tanta fuit forma feminarum, quae flecteret illos.	$6^{1,\,2}$.
Ut coinquinati non possent caelo redire,	14^5.
Rebelles ex illo contra Deum verba misere.	$1^9\ 13^2$.
Altissimus inde sententiam misit in illis	$10^{4\,\mathrm{sq.}}\ 12\,\mathrm{sq.}$
De semine quorum gigantes nati feruntur.	7^2.
Ab ipsis in terra artes prolatae fuere,	
Et tingere lanas docuerunt et quaeque geruntur,	8^1.
Mortales et illi mortuos simulacro ponebant.	19^1.
Omnipotens autem, quod essent de semine pravo,	
Non censuit illos recipi defunctos e morte.	
Unde modo vagi subvertunt corpora multa:	15^c.
Maxime quos hodie colitis et deos oratis.	19^1.

Carmen Apologeticum (1011):

'Stellae cadunt caeli, iudicantur astra nobiscum.'	18^{13-16}.

Cyprian (flor. 250 A.D.), *De Hab. Virg.* 14 (Hartel, i, p. 197):

Neque Deus ... tinguere ... docuit ... lapillis aut margaritis ... conspiciatur id desuper quod diabolus invenit ... quae omnia peccatores et apostatae angeli suis artibus prodiderunt, quando ad terrena contagia devoluti a caelesti vigore recesserunt illi et oculos	8^1 &c.

circumducto nigrore fucare et genas mendacio ruboris inficere. . . .'

Pseudo-Cyprian (third century), *Ad Novatianum* (ed. Hartel, *Cyprian*, iii, p. 67)—a citation of 1 En. 1⁹: 'ecce venit cum multis milibus nuntiorum suorum facere iudicium de omnibus et perdere omnes impios et arguere omnem carnem de omnibus factis impiorum quae fecerunt impie et de omnibus verbis impiis quae de Deo locuti sunt peccatores.'

1⁹.

Hippolytus (flor. 220 A.D.), *Or. adv. Graecos* (ed. Bunsen, *Analecta Ante-Nicaena*, i. 393):

καὶ οὗτος μὲν ὁ περὶ δαιμόνων τόπος. Περὶ δὲ Ἅιδου, ἐν ᾧ συνέχονται ψυχαὶ δικαίων τε καὶ ἀδίκων, ἀναγκαῖον εἰπεῖν. Ὁ Ἅιδης τόπος ἐστὶν ἐν τῇ κτίσει ἀκατασκεύαστος. χωρίον ὑπόγειον, ἐν ᾧ φῶς κόσμου οὐκ ἐπιλάμπει.

1 En. 22³ 'all the souls of the children of men'.

21¹ 'where things were chaotic'.

Anatolius appointed Bishop of Laodicea in 269. Quoted in Euseb. *Hist. Eccl.* vii. 32. 19 τοῦ δὲ τὸν πρῶτον παρ' Ἑβραίοις μῆνα περὶ ἰσημερίαν εἶναι, παραστατικὰ καὶ τὰ ἐν τῷ Ἐνὼχ μαθήματα.

Zosimus of Panopolis (third century), quoted in *Syncellus* (Dindorf, i, 1829, p. 24):

τοῦτο οὖν ἔφασαν αἱ ἀρχαῖαι καὶ αἱ θεῖαι γραφαί, ὅτι ἄγγελοί τινες ἐπεθύμησαν τῶν γυναικῶν, καὶ κατελθόντες ἐδίδαξαν αὐτὰς πάντα τὰ τῆς φύσεως ἔργα. ὧν χάριν, φησί, προσκρούσαντες ἔξω τοῦ οὐρανοῦ ἔμειναν, ὅτι πάντα τὰ πονηρὰ καὶ μηδὲν ὠφελοῦντα τὴν ψυχὴν, ἐδίδαξαν τοὺς ἀνθρώπους. ἐξ αὐτῶν φάσκουσιν αἱ αὐταὶ γραφαὶ καὶ τοὺς γίγαντας γεγενῆσθαι.

1 En. 6 7. 8.

Clementine Homilies (written perhaps in the fourth century):

viii. 12-18: The angels before their fall descended to the earth (cf. Jub. 4¹⁵) and πρὸς πᾶσαν ἑαυτοὺς μετέβαλον φύσιν, ἅτε θειωδεστέρας ὄντες οὐσίας,

1 En. 19¹ After the angels' fall—'their spirits assuming many different forms'.

καὶ ῥᾳδίως πρὸς πάντα μετατρέπεσθαι δυνάμενοι. καὶ ἐγίνοντο λίθος τίμιος, &c. . . .	8¹ 'all kinds of costly stones'. 6¹, ² 7¹.
κρατούμενοι, εἰς γυναικῶν μίξιν ὤλισθον· αἷς συμπλακέντες. . . . σαρκὸς γὰρ αὐτοὶ δεσμοῖς πεπεδημένοι κατέχονται, καὶ ἰσχυρῶς δέδενται. οὗ ἕνεκεν εἰς οὐρανοὺς ἀνελθεῖν οὐκέτι ἐδυνήθησαν.	10⁴ 13¹ 14⁵. 14⁵ 'You shall not ascend into heaven unto all eternity'. 7¹ 'they began to go in unto them . . . . and they taught them, &c.'
Μετὰ γὰρ συνουσίαν ὃ τὸ πρῶτον ἐγίνοντο ἀπαιτηθέντες, καὶ παρασχεῖν μηκέτι δυνηθέντες διὰ τὸ ἄλλο τι μετὰ μιασμὸν αὐτοὺς ποιῆσαι μὴ δύνασθαι, ἀρέσκειν τε ταῖς ἐρωμέναις βουλόμενοι, ἀνθ' ἑαυτῶν τοὺς τῆς γῆς μυελοὺς ὑπέδειξαν. λέγω δὲ τὰ ἐκ μετάλλων ἄνθη, χρυσόν, χαλκόν, ἄργυρον, σίδηρον, καὶ τὰ ὅμοια, σὺν τοῖς τιμωτάτοις ἅπασιν λίθοις. σὺν τούτοις δὲ τοῖς μαγευθεῖσιν λίθοις καὶ τὰς τέχνας τῶν πρὸς ἕκαστα πραγμάτων παρέδοσαν, καὶ μαγείας ὑπέδειξαν, καὶ ἀστρονομίαν ἐδίδαξαν, δυνάμεις τε ῥιζῶν, καὶ ὅσα ποτὲ ὑπὸ ἀνθρωπίνης ἐννοίας εὑρεθῆναι ἀδύνατον· ἔτι δὲ χρυσοῦ καὶ ἀργύρου καὶ τῶν ὁμοίων χύσιν, τάς τε τῶν ἐσθήτων ποικίλας βαφάς. καὶ πάνθ' ἁπλῶς ὅσαπερ πρὸς κόσμον καὶ τέρψεώς ἐστι γυναικῶν, τῶν ἐν σαρκὶ δεθέντων δαιμόνων ἐστὶν εὑρήματα. ἐκ δὲ τῆς νόθου μίξεως αὐτῶν, ἄνθρωποι ἐγένοντο νόθοι . . . οὓς . . . γίγαντας ὠνόμασαν . . . πρὸς τὴν ἑαυτῶν πλησμονὴν τὸν κόσμον οὐκ ἔχοντες αὐτάρκη . . . τῶν δὲ ἀλόγων ζώων τότε ἐπιλιπόντων, οἱ νόθοι ἄνθρωποι καὶ ἀνθρωπίνων σαρκῶν ἐγεύ-	8¹ 'metals and the art of working them . . . all kinds of costly stones'. 7¹ 'charms and enchantments'. 8³ 'enchantments . . . astrology'. 7¹ 'the cutting of roots'. 8¹ 'bracelets . . . ornaments . . . and all colouring tinctures'. 7² &c. 7³ '**And when** men could no longer sustain them. ⁴ The giants turned against them and devoured mankind. ⁵ And they began to sin against birds

Introduction   lxxxix

σαντο. . . .	and beasts . . . and to devour one another's flesh '.
Ἐπεὶ οὖν αἱ τῶν τεθνεώτων γιγάντων ψυχαί, . . . ὡς καινὸν γένος, καινῷ καὶ τῷ ὀνόματι προσηγορεύθησαν	$15^8\ 16^1$.
. . . ἐξεπέμφθη γὰρ αὐτοῖς ὑπὸ τοῦ θεοῦ ἄγγελός τις, τὴν αὐτοῦ βουλὴν μηνύων, καὶ λέγων.	15^2.
Τάδε δοκεῖ . . . a reference to Jub. 4^{22} not 1 Enoch.	

There is a parallel but independent passage in the *Clementine Recognitions* (put together in the fourth century). Both the Homilies and the Recognitions are alike indebted for their main ideas to 1 Enoch.

Clem. Recog. iv. 26, 27 (ed. Cotelier, i, p. 543):

'unde colendi idola exordium mundo huic . . .	1 En. 19^1.
Angeli quidam, relicto proprii ordinis cursu,	$15^{3,\ 6,\ 7}$.
hominum favere vitiis coepere, et libidini eorum . . .	
illorum opera, suis magis voluptatibus morem	$7^1\ 8^3$, &c.
gererent: quique . . . docuerunt homines quod daemones artibus quibusdam obedire mortalibus, id est, magicis invocationibus possent; ac . . . totum	
mundum, subtracto pietatis lumine, impietatis fumo	8^2.
repleverunt. Pro his et aliis nonnullis caussis (cf. Jub. 7^{21}) diluvium mundo introductum est . . .'	$10^2\ 106^{13-15}$.

Lactantius (flor. 320), *Instit.* (Migne, *P. L.* vi. 330–332; Brandt and Laubmann, i, pp. 162 sqq.), gives quite a long passage which for its main features is indebted to 1 Enoch.

Instit. ii. 14 'Deus . . . misit angelos ad tutelam cultumque generis humani: quibus . . .	(Jub. 4^{15}.)
praecepit, ante omnia, ne terrae contagione maculati substantiae coelestis amitterent dignitatem. . . . Itaque illos	14^{5-7}.
cum hominibus commorantes dominator ille terrae . . . ad	69^4 'Jeqôn . . . who led astray all the sons of God . . . through the daughters of men'.

vitia pellexit, et mulierum congressibus inquinavit. 7^1.
Tum in caelum ob peccata quibus se immerserant 14^5.
non recepti ceciderunt in terram. Sic eos diabolus 54^6.
ex angelis Dei suos fecit satellites ac ministros.
Qui autem sunt ex his procreati, quia neque angeli
neque homines fuerunt, sed mediam quandam
naturam gerentes, non sunt ad inferos recepti, $15^{8-11}\ 16^1$.
sicut in caelum parentes eorum. Ita duo genera
daemonum facta sunt, unum caeleste, alterum
terrenum. Hi sunt immundi spiritus malorum,
quae geruntur, auctores, quorum idem diabolus est 54^6, &c.
princeps. ... Quod idcirco dictum est, quoniam
custodes eos humano generi Deus miserat: sed et
ipsi, cum sint perditores hominum, custodes tamen
se videri volunt, ut ipsi colantur, et Deus non 19^1.
colatur. ... Magorum quoque ars omnis ac potentia
horum adspirationibus constat, a quibus invocati,
visus hominum praestigiis obcaecantibus fallunt.
... Hi, ut dico, spiritus contaminati ac perditi per
omnem terram vagantur, et in solacium perditionis $15^{8-11}\ 16^1$.
suae perdendis hominibus operantur. ... Hos in
suis penetralibus consecrant, his cotidie vina pro-
fundunt, et, scientes, daemonas venerantur, quasi
terrestres deos. ... 15. ... ex caelestibus de-
pravatos, terrenos esse coepisse. ... 16. ... Eorum
inventa sunt astrologia et haruspicina ... et ars
magica. ... Hi sunt qui fingere imagines et simu-
lacra docuerunt. ... Sed eos magi ... veris suis
nominibus cient, illis caelestibus, quae in litteris
sanctis leguntur, &c.'

Inst. iv. 27, v. 18. Idol-worship due to demons who 1 En. 19^1, &c.
    were condemned to everlasting fire.

vii. 7. The abode of the dead. 22.

vii. 16. In the last days 'nec terra homini dabit 80^2.
    fructum ... Luna ... meatus extraordinarios pera-
    get ... Tunc annus breviabitur'.

vii. 19. The slaughter of the wicked by the just $90^{19}\ 91^{12}$.
    when the sword has descended from heaven.
    The special judgement of the princes and tyrants. 54 63.
    The judgement 'in the middle of the earth'. 90^{26}.

vii. 24. In the millennium 'qui erunt in corporibus

vivi non morientur, sed per eosdem mille annos infinitam multitudinem generabunt ... Terra vero aperiet fecunditatem suam et uberrimas fruges sua sponte generabit, rupes montium melle sudabunt, per rivos vina decurrent, &c.' 10^{17} sq.

vii. 26. All the wicked 'shall be burnt for ever in the sight of the angels and righteous'.   1 En. 48^9.

Priscillian (ob. 380), *De Fide et de Apocryphis* (Schepss, 1889, p. 44), apparently did not know 1 Enoch, but urges from the example of 'Jude' and 'Paul' (Ep. Hebr. 11^5) that it is admissible to cite non-canonical works, as they both refer to Enoch.

Cassianus (360–435), *Collatio* VIII. xxi '... illa opinio vulgi, qua credunt angelos vel maleficia vel diversas artes hominibus tradidisse'.   1 En. 8^1.

Thenceforward the book fails to secure a single favourable notice. *Hilary*, who died 368 A.D., writes in his *Comment. in Ps.* cxxxii. 3 'Fertur id de quo etiam nescio cuius liber extat, quod angeli concupiscentes filias hominum, cum de caelo descenderent, in hunc montem Hermon maxime convenerant excelsum'. Chrysostom (346–407) does not indeed mention Enoch, but declares that the story of the angels and the daughters of men rests on a false exegesis, *Homil. in Gen.* vi. 1, and is a blasphemous fable.

Jerome (346–420) regards Enoch as apocryphal. *De Viris Illustr.* iv 'Iudas frater Iacobi parvam, quae de septem catholicis est, epistolam reliquit. Et quia de libro Enoch, qui apocryphus est, in ea assumit testimonia a plerisque reiicitur: tamen auctoritatem vetustate iam et usu meruit et inter sanctas computatur'. *Comment. in Ps.* cxxxii. 3 'Legimus in quodam libro apocrypho, eo tempore, quo descendebant filii dei ad filias hominum, descendisse illos in montem Hermon, et ibi iniisse pactum quomodo venirent ad filias hominum et sibi eas sociarent. Manifestissimus liber est et inter apocryphos computatur'. *Comment. in Epist. ad Titum,* i. 12 'Qui autem putant totum librum debere sequi eum, qui libri parte usus sit, videntur mihi et apocryphum Enochi, de quo Apostolus Iudas in Epistola sua testimonium posuit, inter ecclesiae scripturas recipere'.

Augustine (354–429) pronounces strongly against Enoch. *De Civ. Dei*, xv. 23. 4 'Scripsisse quidem nonnulla divina Enoch illum septimum ab Adam, negare non possumus, cum hoc in Epistola canonica Iudas Apostolus dicat. Sed non frustra non sunt in eo canone Scripturarum . . . Unde illa quae sub eius nomine proferuntur et continent istas de gigantibus fabulas, quod non habuerint homines patres, recte a prudentibus iudicantur non ipsius esse credenda'. Cp. also *De Civ. Dei*, xviii. 38.

Enoch is finally condemned in explicit terms in *Constit. Apostol.* vi. 16 καὶ ἐν τοῖς παλαιοῖς δέ τινες συνέγραψαν βιβλία ἀπόκρυφα Μωσέως καὶ Ἐνὼχ καὶ Ἀδάμ, Ἡσαίου τε καὶ Δαβὶδ καὶ Ἠλία καὶ τῶν τριῶν πατριαρχῶν, φθοροποιὰ καὶ τῆς ἀληθείας ἐχθρά· τοιαῦτα καὶ νῦν ἐπενόησαν οἱ δυσώνυμοι, διαβάλλοντες δημιουργίαν, γάμον, πρόνοιαν, τεκνογονίαν, νόμον, προφήτας.

Under the ban of such authorities the book of Enoch gradually passed out of circulation and knowledge in the Western Church, and with the exception of 6–9⁴ 8⁴–10¹⁴ 15⁸–16¹ and another fragment which are preserved by *Syncellus* in his *Chronography*, pp. 20–23; 42–47 (ed. Dind. 1829), it was lost to Western Christendom till the present century. Syncellus adds that the book of Enoch runs counter in some respects to the tradition of the Church, and is untrustworthy through the interpolations of Jews and heretics: καὶ ταῦτα μὲν ἐκ τοῦ πρώτου βιβλίου Ἐνὼχ περὶ τῶν ἐγρηγόρων, εἰ καὶ μὴ τελείως χρὴ προσέχειν ἀποκρύφοις μάλιστα τοὺς ἁπλουστέρους, διά τε τὸ περιττά τινα καὶ ἀτριβῆ τῆς ἐκκλησιαστικῆς παραδόσεως ἔχειν καὶ διὰ τὸ νενοθεῦσθαι αὐτὰ ὑπὸ Ἰουδαίων καὶ αἱρετικῶν (ed. Dindorf, pp. 47, 48).

There are also parallels in Gnostic and Apocryphal Literature to 1 Enoch.

In the Gnostic work, *Pistis Sophia*, composed in Egypt in the third century, we find two apparent references to Enoch.

Pistis Sophia (ed. Schwartze, 1851–1853, p. 245):	
'Invenietis ea in secundo libro Ieu, quae scripsit Enoch, quum	1 En. 32³ 'the Garden of Righteousness . . . the tree of

Introduction

loquerer cum eo ex arbore cognitionis et ex arbore vitae in παραδείσῳ Adami. (Translated from the Coptic.)

(p. 25) 'μυστήρια — quae portarant desuper ἄγγελοι peccatores, quorum (μυστηρίων) sunt μαγία'.

knowledge'. 6 'thy father old ..., &c.'

7¹ 8³.

In the Gnostic *Acts of Thomas* 1 Enoch may be referred to in the words of the Dragon :—

ch. xxxii (Tisch. *Acta Apostolorum Apocrypha*, p. 218):

ἐγώ εἰμι ὁ τοὺς ἀγγέλους ἄνωθεν κάτω ῥίψας καὶ ἐν ταῖς ἐπιθυμίαις τῶν γυναικῶν αὐτοὺς καταδήσας, ἵνα γηγενεῖς παῖδες ἐξ αὐτῶν γένωνται, &c.

6⁶ 'they descended, &c.'; 86³ 'many stars descend and cast themselves down from heaven, &c.'

7², ⁴, &c., 'giants'.

The *Acts of 'the Disputation of Archelaus with Manes'* (written perhaps at the beginning of the fourth century).

ch. xxxii (Routh, *Reliquiae*, iv, p. 211):

'Angelorum quidam, mandato Dei non subditi, voluntati eius restiterunt, et aliquis quidem de caelo, tanquam fulgur ignis, cecidit super terram, alii vero infelicitate hominum filiabus admixti, a dracone afflicti, ignis aeterni poenam suscipere meruerunt'.

86¹ 'a star fell from heaven'. ³ 'many stars descend and cast themselves down from heaven'. 7¹ 'they began to go in unto them'. 15³ 18¹¹, ¹².

The Narrative of Joseph of Arimathea (date uncertain) has an unexpected parallel to 1 Enoch.

iii. 3 (Tisch. *Evangelia Apocrypha*, 2nd ed., Lipsiae, 1876, p. 465): The dying thief addresses Christ in the following words:

μὴ ἐν ἐξετάσει σου ποιήσεις τὰ

100¹⁰, ¹² 'from the angels He

ἄστρα ἐλθεῖν κατ' ἐμοῦ ἢ τὴν σελήνην, ὅταν μέλλῃς κρῖναι πᾶσαν τὴν οἰκουμένην, ὅτι ἐν νυκτὶ ἔπραττον τὰς κακάς μου βουλάς· μὴ κινήσεις τὸν ἥλιον ... οὐδὲν γὰρ ἀφέσεως ἁμαρτιῶν δῶρον δύναμαί σοι παρασχεῖν.	will inquire as to your deeds in heaven, from the sun and from the moon and from the stars in reference to your sins ... And now give presents to the rain that it be not withheld, &c.'

The Apocalypse of Paul has a similar but not identical idea.

4 sqq. (Tisch., *Apocal. Apocr.*, p. 36).	$100^{10,12}$.
The sun, and also the moon and the stars, come to the Lord and ask leave to punish men for their sins. As the sun sets πάντες οἱ ἄγγελοι ἔρχονται πρὸς τὸν θεὸν προσκυνῆσαι αὐτῷ, καὶ προσάγουσιν τὰ ἔργα τῶν ἀνθρώπων ἑκάστου ὅ τι ἔπραξεν, &c.	

In the Book of Adam and Eve we have references to 1 Enoch as well as to 2 Enoch, and a definite rejection of its teaching.

2^{xx} (ed. Malan, 1882).	
'Enoch to whom many wonders happened and who also wrote a celebrated book'.	
3^1 'Certain wise men of old wrote concerning them (the giants) and say in their books, that angels came down from heaven and mingled with the daughters of Cain, who bare unto them these giants. But those err in what they say.... They were children of Seth'.	6–10.
2^{13} 'Jared continued to teach his children eighty years; but after that they began to go down from the Holy Mountain ... and to mix with the children of Cain'. Genun had	6^6 'who descended in the days of Jared'.

taught the children of Cain to make musical instruments and induced them to commit all kinds of wickedness, and finally 'took iron and with it made weapons of war'. 'Satan taught him (Genun) to make dyeing-stuffs for garments of divers patterns, and made him to understand how to dye crimson and purple and what not'. . . . 'Ye shall not come up hither again for ever.'	8^1. 8^1. 14^5.
2^5 'the middle of the earth' (= Jerusalem). Cf. 2^{21} $3^{13, 14}$ 4^3.	26^1 90^{26}.
2^{22} 'the mansions of the righteous and of the chosen'.	39^4 'the mansions of the holy and the resting-places of the righteous'. $6, 7$ 'the righteous and the elect'.

For further treatment of the subject see H. J. Lawlor's article in the *Journal of Philology*, vol. xxv, pp. 164-225, to which I express my indebtedness.

§ 19. THE INFLUENCE OF 1 ENOCH ON THE NEW TESTAMENT.

The influence of 1 Enoch on the New Testament has been greater than that of all the other apocryphal and pseudepigraphal books taken together. The evidence for this conclusion may for the sake of convenience be arranged under two heads. (A) A series of passages of the New Testament which either in phraseology or idea directly depend on or are illustrative of passages in 1 Enoch. (B) Doctrines in 1 Enoch which had an undoubted share in moulding the corresponding New Testament doctrines.

(A) We will begin with the General Epistles. I quote from the Revised Version when a more accurate rendering is desirable.

New Testament	*1 Enoch*
(a) St. Jude ^{4} 'Denying our only Master and Lord Jesus Christ.	48^{10} 'Denied the Lord of Spirits and His anointed'. Cf. 38^2 41^2.

New Testament	1 Enoch
6 'The angels which left their own abode'.	12^4 'the Watchers ... who have left the high heaven, &c.'
'reserved ... great day'.	10^{4-6} $^{11,\,12}$ 'Bind ... darkness ... judgement'.
13 'Wandering stars'.	18^{15} $21^{2,\,3,\,6}$.
14 'The seventh from Adam'.	60^8 'The seventh from Adam'.
14, 15 A direct quotation from	1^9. Cf. 5^4 27^2.
1 St. Peter $3^{19,\,20}$.	$10^{4,\,5,\,12,\,13}$ 19^1 20^1.
2 St. Peter 2^4.	$10^{4-6,\,12,\,13}$ 12^5 13^2.
3^{13} 'A new heaven and a new earth'.	$45^{4,\,5}$ 72^1 91^{16}.
1 St. John 1^7 'Walk in the light'.	92^4 'The righteous ... shall walk in eternal light'.

[The contrast between light and darkness in St. John's Epistles repeatedly enforced in 1 Enoch. See 38^4 (note).]

2^1 'Jesus Christ the righteous'.	53^6 'The Righteous and Elect One'.
2^8 'The darkness is past and the true light already shineth'.	58^5 'It has become bright as the sun upon earth, and the darkness is past'.
2^{15} 'Love not the world, nor the things which are in the world'.	108^8 'loved ... nor any of the good things which are in the world'. Cf. 48^7.
3^2 'We shall be like Him'.	$90^{37,\,38}$.
St. James 1^8 'Double-minded man'.	91^4 'A double heart'. See note.
5^{1-6} Woes against the rich.	94^{8-11}; also 46^7 63^{10} 96^{4-8} 97^{8-10}.

(*b*) *Book of Revelation.*—The writer or writers of this book are steeped in Jewish apocalyptic literature.

Rev. 1^4 'Seven spirits which are before His throne'. Cf. 4^5; also 'the seven angels' 8^2.	90^{21} 'those men the seven first white ones'. Cf. Tobit 12^{15}.
2^7 'To him that overcometh will I give to eat of the tree of life': also $22^{2,\,14}$ ('the right to the tree of life') ^{19}.	25^{4-6} Only the elect, the righteous and holy, in the Messianic kingdom are allowed to eat of the tree of life.

Introduction

New Testament	1 Enoch
3^5 'Clothed in white raiment'.	90^{31} 'Clothed in white'.
^{10} 'Them that dwell upon the earth'.	37^5 'Those that dwell on the earth'.

[This phrase has always a bad sense in Revelation with the exception of 14^6. Cf. 6^{10} 8^{13} 11^{10} $13^{8, 14}$ 17^8, and that in this respect Revelation follows the use of this phrase in the Noachic interpolations, see 1 En. 37^5 (note).]

3^{12} 'The New Jerusalem'.	90^{29} 'A new house'.
3^{17} 'I am rich and increased with goods'.	97^8 'We have become rich with riches and have possessions, &c.'
^{20} 'I will come unto him and sup with him'.	62^{14} 'and with that Son of Man shall they (the righteous) eat, and lie down, and rise up for ever and ever'.
^{21} 'Sit with Me on My throne'. Cf. 20^4.	108^{12} 'I will seat each on the throne of his honour'.
4^6 'Round about the throne were four living creatures'.	40^2 'On the four sides of the Lord of Spirits I saw four presences'.
4^8 'they rest not ... saying'.	39^{13} 'who sleep not ... and say'.
5^{11}.	14^{23} 40^1 71^8.
6^{10} 'How long, O Master, the holy and true, dost thou not judge and avenge our blood on them that dwell on the earth?'	47^2 'that the prayer of the righteous may not be in vain before the Lord of Spirits, That judgement may be done unto them, And that they may not have to suffer for ever'. Cf. 97^{3-5} $99^{3, 16}$ 104^3: also 22^{5-7} where the soul of a righteous man in Hades prays for vengeance.
$6^{15, 16}$ Compare the fear of 'the kings of the earth, and the princes, and the chief captains, and the rich, and the strong' when they see 'the face of him that sitteth on the throne'.	$62^{3, 5}$ 'the kings, and the mighty, and the exalted ... shall be terrified ... And pain shall seize them, When they see that Son of Man sitting on the throne of his glory'.
7^1 The four angels of the winds.	69^{22} 'The spirits ... of the winds'.

New Testament	1 Enoch
15 'He that sitteth on the throne shall dwell among them'.	45⁴ 'I will cause Mine Elect One to dwell among them'.
17 'Shall guide them unto fountains of waters of life'.	48¹ 'fountain of righteousness … fountains of wisdom'.
8³,⁴ Angel with golden censer of incense offers it with the prayers of the saints before God. In 5⁸ the elders do so also.	This intercession of the angels is found frequently in 1 Enoch, 9¹⁻³,¹¹ 15² 40⁷ 47² 99³.
9¹ 'I saw a star from heaven fallen unto the earth'.	86¹ 'And I saw … and behold a star fell from heaven'.
14—15.	66¹.
20 'Repented not of the works of their hands that they should not worship demons, and the idols of gold, and of silver, and of brass, and of stone, and of wood'.	99⁷ 'who worship stones and graven images of gold, and silver, and wood, (and stone) and clay, and those who worship impure spirits and demons'.
10⁵⁻⁷.	16¹.
12¹⁰ 'The accuser of our brethren is cast down'.	40⁷ 'fending off the Satans and forbidding them to come … to accuse them who dwell on the earth'.
13¹⁴ 'Deceiveth them that dwell on the earth'.	54⁶ 'Leading astray those who dwell on the earth'. Cf. 67⁷.
14⁹,¹⁰. The worshippers of the beast are to be 'tormented with fire and brimstone in the presence of the holy angels, and in the presence of the lamb'.	48⁹ The unrighteous 'burn before the face of the holy … sink before the face of the righteous'.
10 'Holy angels'.	passim: e.g. 71¹.
13 'Blessed are the dead, &c.'	81⁴.
20 'Blood came out of the winepress even unto the horses' bridles'.	100³ 'The horse shall walk up to the breast in the blood of sinners'.
16⁵ 'Angel of the waters'.	60¹⁶ 'the spirit of the sea'.
17¹⁴ 'Lord of lords and King of kings'.	9⁴ 'Lord of lords … King of kings'.
20¹² 'And the books were opened' and 'another book was opened which is the book of life'.	90²⁰ 'took the sealed books and opened those books'. 47³ 'The books of the living'.

New Testament	1 Enoch
[13] 'The sea gave up the dead which were in it, and death and Hades gave up the dead which were in them'.	51^1 'in those days shall the earth also give back that which has been entrusted to it, and Sheol also shall give back that which it has received, and hell shall give back that which it owes'. Cf. 61^5.

20^{11-15}. The last judgement is held after the temporary Messianic kingdom ($20^{4,5}$), just as in 1 En. 91–104. There is, however, no resurrection in the temporary Messianic kingdom of 1 Enoch as there is in Revelation.

[15] 'Cast into the lake of fire'.	90^{26} 'Cast into this fiery abyss'.

$21^{1,2}$. We have here a new heaven and a new earth, and a new Jerusalem coming down from heaven: yet in $22^{14,15}$ all classes of sinners are said to be without the gates of the city. But if there were a new earth this would be impossible. This contradiction may have arisen from combining the divergent Messianic conceptions which appear in 1 Enoch. Cf. $45^{4,5}$ 90^{29}.

22^3 'no more curse'.	25^6 'no sorrow or plague or torment or calamity'.

(c) We shall next deal with the *Epistles of St. Paul*. This Apostle, as we know, borrowed both phraseology and ideas from many quarters: from the Greek poets; from the apocryphal writings, as the Book of Wisdom; from the lost Revelation of Elias—1 Cor. 2^9 according to Origen, and Eph. 5^{14} according to Epiphanius. We shall find that he was well acquainted with and used 1 Enoch.

Rom. 8^{34} 'Neither angels, nor principalities, nor powers'.	61^{10} 'angels of power and ... angels of principalities'.
9^5 'God blessed for ever'.	77^1 'He who is blessed for ever'.
1 Cor. 6^{11} 'Justified in the name of the Lord Jesus'.	48^7 'in his (i.e. the Messiah's) name they are saved'.

1 Cor. 11^{10}. Tertullian, *C. Marc.* v. 8; *de Virg. Veland.* 7, explains this verse through a reference to the bad angels spoken of in 1 Enoch who would be incited to wantonness by unveiled women.

2 Cor. 4^6 'To give the light of the knowledge of the glory of God in the face of Jesus Christ'.	38^4 'The Lord of Spirits has caused His light to appear on the face of the holy, righteous, and elect'.

New Testament	1 Enoch
5$^{2-4}$.	62$^{15-16}$.
11^{31} 'He who is blessed for ever'.	77^1 'He who is blessed for ever'.
Gal. 1^4 'This present evil world'.	48^7 'this world of unrighteousness'.
Eph. 1^{21} 'Above all principality and power'.	61^{10} 'angels of power and ... angels of principalities'.
^{9} 'According to His good pleasure'.	49^4 'according to His good pleasure'.
5^8 'Children of light.'	108^{11} 'the generation of light'.
Phil. 2^{10} 'At the name of Jesus every knee should bow'.	48^5 'shall fall down and worship before Him' (i.e. the Messiah).
Col. 1^{16} 'Principalities and powers'.	61^{10} 'angels of powers and ... angels of principalities'.
2^3 'In whom are hid all the treasures of wisdom and knowledge'.	46^3 'the Son of man ... who reveals all the treasures of that which is hidden'.
1 Thess. 5^3 'Then sudden destruction cometh upon them as upon a woman with child'.	62^4 'Then shall pain come upon them as on a woman in travail'.

Both these passages refer to the sudden appearing of the Messiah.

5^5 'Sons of light'.	108^{11} 'the generation of light'.
2 Thess. 1^7 'The angels of His power'.	61^{10} 'the angels of power'.
1 Tim. 1^9 'Law is not made for a righteous man but for the lawless', &c.	93^4 'a law shall be made for the sinners'.
1^{15} 'Worthy of all acceptation' (cf. 4^9).	94^1 'worthy of acceptation'.
5^{21} 'The elect angels'.	39^1 'elect and holy children ... from the high heaven'.
6^{15} 'King of Kings and Lord of Lords'.	9^4 'Lord of Lords ... King of Kings'.
^{16} 'Dwelling in the light which no man can approach unto, whom no man hath seen'.	14^{21} 'None of the angels could enter and could behold His face by reason of the magnificence and glory'.

(d) *Epistle to the Hebrews.* This Epistle was possibly written by Barnabas. As we have seen above (p. lxxxi) this writer cites 1 Enoch as Scripture in the Epistle which goes by his name.

Introduction

New Testament	1 Enoch
Hebrews 4^{13} 'There is no creature that is not manifest in His sight: but all things are naked and laid open before the eyes of Him with whom we have to do'.	9^5 'all things are naked and open in Thy sight, and Thou seest all things, and nothing can hide itself from Thee'.
11^5 'Enoch was translated... for before his translation he had this testimony that he pleased God'.	The parallel passage must, it seems, depend on the Enoch book where Enoch is always accounted an example of righteousness and therefore translated. Cf. 15^1 &c. In Sirach 44^{16} Enoch is translated indeed, but is cited as an example of repentance. Philo, *De Abrahamo*, speaks of the former evil life of Enoch.
11^{10} 'The city which hath foundations whose builder and maker is God' (cf. 13^{14}).	90^{29} God Himself builds the New Jerusalem.
12^9 'Father of spirits'.	'Lord of Spirits', 37^2 and *passim* in Parables.
^{22} 'The heavenly Jerusalem'.	90^{29}.

(e) Acts of the Apostles.

3^{14} 'The Righteous One', i.e. Christ. Cf. also 7^{52} 22^{14}.	53^6 'the Righteous and Elect One' (i.e. the Messiah).
4^{12} 'There is none other name under heaven... whereby we must be saved'.	48^7 'in His (i.e. the Messiah's) name they are saved'.
10^4 'Thy prayers... are gone up for a memorial before God'.	99^3 'raise your prayers as a memorial ... before the Most High'.
17^{31} 'He will judge the world in righteousness by the man whom He hath ordained'.	41^9 'He appoints a judge for them all and he judges them all before Him'.

(f) The Gospels.

St. John 2^{16} The temple is called 'God's house', but owing to	89^{51} Temple = 'house' of 'the Lord of the sheep'. But in

New Testament	1 Enoch
sin of Israel 'your house', i.e. merely house of Israel in St. Luke 13¹⁵ and parallels.	89⁵⁶ owing to sin of Israel it is said 'He forsook that their house'.
5²² 'He hath committed all judgement unto the Son'.	69²⁷ 'the sum of judgement was given unto the Son of Man'.
²⁷ 'He gave him authority to execute judgement because he is the Son of Man'.	
8¹².	48⁴.
12³⁶ 'Sons of light'.	108¹¹ 'the generation of light'.
14² 'Many mansions'.	39⁴ 'dwelling-places of the holy and the resting-place of the righteous'. Cf. 39⁷ 48¹, &c.
St. Luke 1⁵² 'He hath put down princes from their thrones'.	46⁴ 'shall †raise up† (Read 'put down') the kings ... from their seats'.
9³⁵ 'This is My Son, the Elect One'. So Greek ὁ ἐκλελεγμένος.	40⁵ 'the Elect One', i.e. the Messiah. Cf. 45³, ⁴ ('Mine Elect One'); 49², ⁴, &c.
13³⁵ See on St. John 2¹⁶.	
16⁸ 'Sons of the light'.	108¹¹ 'the generation of light'.
16⁹ 'Mammon of unrighteousness'.	63¹⁰ 'unrighteous gains'.
18⁷ 'Shall not God avenge His elect which cry to Him day and night, and He is longsuffering over them'. Cf. 2 Pet. 3⁹; Sir. 32¹⁸.	47¹, ² 'the prayer of the righteous ... that judgement may be done unto them and that they may not have to suffer for ever'.
21²⁸ 'Your redemption draweth nigh'.	51² 'the day has drawn nigh that they should be saved'.
23³⁵ 'The Christ of God, the Elect One', ὁ ἐκλεκτός.	40⁵ 'The Elect One'.
St. Matthew 5²², ²⁹, ³⁰ 10²⁸ where Gehenna is the place of final punishment.	27² 90²⁶, ²⁷ where Gehenna first definitely appears as hell.
8²⁹.	16¹.
13⁴².	98³.
19²⁸ 'When the Son of Man shall sit on the throne of His glory'.	62⁵ 'When they see that Son of Man sitting on the throne of his glory'.

New Testament	1 Enoch
19²⁸ 'Ye also shall sit on twelve thrones'.	108¹² 'I will seat each on the throne of his honour'.
19²⁹ 'Inherit eternal life'.	40⁹ 'inherit eternal life'.
21¹³ 23³⁸. See St. John 2¹⁴.	89⁵⁶.} 89⁵⁴.}
25⁴¹ 'Prepared for the devil and his angels'.	54⁴,⁵ 'chains . . . prepared for the hosts of Azazel'.
26²⁴ 'It had been good for that man if he had not been born'.	38² 'It had been good for them if they had not been born'.
28¹⁸ 'All authority hath been given to Me in heaven and on earth'.	62⁶ '(the Son of man) who rules over all'.
St. Mark 11¹⁷. See St. John 2⁶.	89⁵⁴.

§ 20. THEOLOGY.

The books or sections of Enoch were written by orthodox Jews, who belonged to the apocalyptic or prophetic side of Judaism, and by Judaism is here meant, not the one-sided legalistic Judaism that posed as the sole and orthodox Judaism after the fall of Jerusalem in 70 A.D., but the larger and more comprehensive Judaism that preceded it. This larger Judaism embraced both the prophetic and the legalistic elements. No religion can make progress without both elements, and, if progress in spiritual development is to be realized, the prophetic element is absolutely indispensable.

Most Jewish writers have ascribed the Book of Enoch and kindred literature to the Essenes. But this is indefensible. For the Essenes, if we are to accept the account of Josephus, *Bell. Iud.* ii. 8. 2; *Ant.* xviii. 1. 5; Philo, ii. 633–634 Ἐσσαίων οὐδεὶς ἄγεται γυναῖκα; and Pliny, *Hist. Nat.* v. 17 (see Schürer³, ii. 568); Hippolytus, *Refutatio omnium Haeres.* ix. 18–28, entirely condemned marriage. Now so far is this from being the case in 1 Enoch, that not only is no word said against marriage in any of the sections, but marriage is glorified and fruitful wedlock in 6–36 as having its place in the Messianic kingdom. When later this kingdom became wholly of a spiritual nature, as in 91–104 or 37–71, marriage could no longer be considered as a part of the Messianic blessedness. Again, whereas the Essenes objected to animal sacrifice, no such objection is taken either in 1 or 2 Enoch In the former in 89^{50} the temple sacrifices are referred to with complete approval in the words 'and they offered a full table before Him'. In 89^{73} the sacrifices are said to be 'polluted', but no condemnation of sacrifice in itself is here implied. The writer uses no stronger words than Mal. 1^7, 'Ye offer polluted bread upon Mine altar.' In 2 Enoch 59^{2-3} the spiritual value of animal sacrifice is clearly expressed. Furthermore, not a word is said on behalf of certain characteristic beliefs of Essenism—such as the necessity of bathing before meals and at other times, the duty of having all things in common and of having common meals, the rejection of anointing the body, the claim that all were free and that none should be slaves.

The teaching of our books on the chief doctrines of Judaism will now be given under the following heads.

Origin of evil. Moral evil is not brought into causal connexion with the transgression of Adam save in one passage, i.e. 69^{11} (Book of Noah), where it is stated that man was created originally righteous and immortal, but that death got power over him through sin.[1] This thought is not worked out or even touched upon in the other sections. Throughout 6–36 moral evil is traced to the lust of the Watchers 6–7, 15, and the revelations of Azazel 9^6 10^8. The origin of evil is thus carried back into the spiritual world. But even when the Watchers were judged and imprisoned and their children destroyed, the evil set in movement by them was not at an end; for the disembodied spirits of their children became demons $15^{8,\,9,\,11}$ 16^1 (cf. 99^7), who were to work moral ruin on the earth without hindrance till the final judgement 16^1. 6–36, here, develops the view propounded in Gen. 6^{1-3} that evil originated in the angelic world: and the same view is implied in 83–90. The origin of evil is

---

[1] In this same source 69^6 it is said that the Satan Gadreel seduced Eve: cf. 4 Macc. $18^{7\,81}$.

carried back one stage further in 37–71. Sin, as affecting mankind at large, did not originate with the Watchers, but with the Satans, 40^7, who appear to belong to a counter kingdom of evil ruled by a chief called Satan 53^3. They existed as evil agencies before the fall of the Watchers; for the guilt of the latter consisted in their becoming subject to Satan, and so subsequently leading mankind astray 54^6.

Angelology. The angelology appears in our book in a very developed form. The subject is too large to enter on here. The reader can consult the Index. We might, however, shortly remark that the seven archangels 20^{1-8} 81^5 $87^{2,3}$ 88^1 $90^{21, 22}$ form the highest order, their names being given in 20^7. In 40 only four of these are mentioned as the angels of the presence. Then come the Cherubim, Seraphim, Ophannim, the angel of peace, angels of principalities and powers, Watchers, angels of punishment.

Demonology. Two classes can be clearly distinguished here. (*a*) The fallen Watchers or the angels who kept not their first estate 6 15^3 69^{2-3} 86 106^{13-14}. These are referred to in Jude 6 and 1 Pet. 2^4. From the time of their first judgement anterior to the Deluge they were kept imprisoned in darkness. They were subject to Satan 54^6. (*b*) The demons $15^{8, 9, 11}$ 16^1 19 99^7. The demons are, according to 16^1, the spirits which went forth from the souls of the giants, who were the children of the fallen angels and the daughters of men. These demons were to work moral ruin on the earth without hindrance till the final judgement as disembodied spirits.

So in the N.T. the demons are disembodied spirits, Matt. 12^{43-45} Luke 11^{24-26}. They are not punished till the final judgement. This is clearly the explanation of Matt. 8^{29}, 'Art thou come hither to torment us *before the time?*' They are subject to Satan, Matt. 12^{24-28}.

Soul and Spirit. On this very complex problem see my *Eschatology*, 231–233.

Salvation by works and yet by grace.

The moral ideal is summed up in terms of righteousness and

uprightness. The Son of Man is himself the ideally righteous one 46³:—

> 'This is the Son of Man who hath righteousness
> With whom dwelleth righteousness ...
> And whose lot hath the pre-eminence before the Lord of Spirits in uprightness for ever.'

Man's duty is to 'love righteousness and walk therein' 94¹. Cf. 91¹⁹. The freedom of the will is assumed, and two ways are set before man for his choice, 'the ways of righteousness and the ways of violence' 91¹⁸ 94³. Though the writer of 91-104 acknowledges the activity of the demonic world 99⁷ (cf. 100⁴), yet he maintains that it is in man's power to attain to righteousness and that a man's sin is of his own devising, and attacks in unmeasured terms the immoral view that sin is something original and unavoidable, 98⁴ᶜᵈᵉ:—

> 'Even so sin has not been sent upon the earth,
> But man of himself has created it,
> And under a great curse shall they fall who commit it.'

On the other hand, the writer of 37-71 is conscious of the need of a spiritual dynamic. Thus he very frequently calls the righteous 'the elect'—a phrase found only four times outside 37-71 in this book. Yet there is no determinism. All righteous living is the outcome of dependence on God. Thus he speaks of 'the faithful who hang upon the name of the Lord of Spirits' 46⁸ᵇ, 'the elect ones who hang upon the Lord of Spirits' 40⁵, and of 'the righteous whose elect works hang upon the Lord of Spirits' 38²ᵇ. Their works are thus wrought in conscious fellowship with God. And when by sin they fall from such fellowship, they are forgiven on repentance 40⁹.[1] These works, moreover, shall be tested at the judgement 45³ᵇ, they shall be weighed in the balance 41¹ 61⁸ᶜ. But this idea is not incompatible with divine grace. But progress is not limited to this world. In the Messianic kingdom they will seek the light and find righteousness, and they will have peace 58⁴ᵃᵇ, and their life

---

[1] The Gentiles also can repent and turn to God 50²,³.

will be a constant progress from light to light and righteousness to righteousness—which is the heritage that has been preserved for them by the Messiah $58^{5, 6}$.

Retribution, national and individual. The problem of combining both these types of retribution had been partly solved in the O.T. With the new solution of the problem of national retribution we shall deal under the title 'the Kingdom'. But the more difficult of the two problems had to do with the individual. Earthly prosperity is no mark of the divine favour, but only a source of delusion to those who experience it. In 91-104 the writer denies Ezekiel's doctrine that a man's earthly condition corresponds to his moral desert. The wicked often enjoy unbroken prosperity in this life 102^{6-11} $103^{5d, 6b}$, and die in honour 103^{6c}, and the righteous fare ill 102^{5b}, and die in darkness and tribulation $102^{7a, 11}$. But the righteous are bidden to be of good cheer, though their life on earth be only such as sinners deserved, and their latter end be full of grief; for in the next life the balance will be redressed, and 'all goodness and joy and glory are prepared for them and written down for the spirits of those who have died in righteousness' 103^3. 'The angels remember' them 'for good before the glory of the Great One' 104^1, for though aforetime they were 'put to shame through ill and affliction', they shall in due time 'shine as the lights of heaven' and 'the portals of heaven shall be opened' to them 104^2, and they 'shall become companions of the hosts of heaven' 104^6. And as for the wicked their recompense is awaiting them; for they shall 'descend into Sheol . . . and into darkness and chains and a burning flame where there is grievous judgement' shall their spirits enter for all the generations of the world $103^{7, 8}$.

We cannot leave this subject without confessing 'how nobly its author maintains the cause of goodness in the face of triumphant evil, how unhesitatingly he concedes that this world gives its best to the unrighteous and the sinner, and that godliness can find no stay or encouragement therein. Yet though the lot of the latter is thus one of contumely and rebuke and shame, the righteous are not for a moment to regret their high calling, but to be steadfast and hopeful; for the day of their glorification is at hand. It is a noble work, yet falls ... short of what was noblest in the past. It never reminds the faithful, as do some of the psalmists, that present life and communion with God more than outweigh every temporal blessing' (see my *Eschatology, Hebrew, Jewish, and Christian*, p. 212).

On the teaching of 6–36 see pp. 3 sq., 222; and on that of 37–71 see pp. 67 sq.

The Kingdom. On this subject the teaching of our book is most revolutionary. In 6–36 it presents a picture of the kingdom of the O.T. prophetic type of a very sensuous character. The Kingdom of God was to be established on the earth, as it is, though purified, with Jerusalem as its centre, the righteous were to live patriarchal lives and have a thousand children each, and God was to come down and dwell with men.

91–104. A great gulf divides as a whole the eschatology of this section from 6–36 and that of the O.T. The hope of an eternal Messianic kingdom on the present earth is now absolutely and finally abandoned. The hopes of the faithful were lifted bodily out of their old materialistic environment that hampered every advance, and were established in a spiritual region of illimitable horizons, and thus the possibility was achieved of endless development in every direction. The way was thus made possible for the rise of Christianity.[1]

---

[1] The incident recorded in Matt. 22$^{23-33}$ Mark 12$^{18-27}$ Luke 20$^{27-38}$ can hardly be understood apart from Enoch. When the Sadducees said, 'Whose wife shall she be of them? for the seven had her to wife,' they are arguing from the sensuous conception of the Messianic kingdom—no doubt the popular one—given in 1 Enoch 1-36, according to which its members, including the risen righteous, were to enjoy every good thing of earth and have each a thousand children. They thought therefore to place Jesus on the horns of a dilemma, and oblige Him to confess either that there was no resurrection or else that polygamy or polyandry would be practised in the coming kingdom. But the dilemma proves invalid: and the conception of the future life portrayed in our Lord's reply tallies almost exactly in thought and partially in word with that described in 91-104, according to which there is to be a resurrection indeed, but a resurrection of the spirit, and the risen

This transference of the hopes of the faithful to a spiritual and eternal kingdom necessitated the recasting of many other theological beliefs. There was still a Messianic kingdom on earth looked forward to but it was to be of merely temporary duration—from the eighth to the tenth world week, 91^{12-17}. On this change of conception two others perforce followed. The resurrection and the final judgement could not initiate a temporary Messianic kingdom, but were of necessity adjourned to its close.

The Messiah. There are two very different conceptions of the Messiah in 1 Enoch. In 83–90 he is represented as the head of the Messianic community out of which he proceeds, but he has no special rôle to fulfil.

But in the Parables (37–71) the case is very different. Four titles applied for the first time in literature to the personal Messiah are afterwards reproduced in the N.T.—'the Christ', 'the Righteous One', 'the Elect One', and 'the Son of Man'.

'The Christ' or 'the Anointed One', variously applied in the O.T., is for the first time associated in 48^{10} 52^4 with the Messiah.

'The Righteous One.' This title, which occurs in Acts 3^{14} 7^{52} 22^{14}, first appears in 38^2 53^6.

'The Elect One.' This title, likewise appearing first in 40^5 45^{3-4} 49^2, ^{4} $51^{3,\,5a}$, &c., passes over into the N.T.—Luke 9^{35} 23^{35}.

'The Son of Man.' This definite title (see notes on $46^{2,\,3}$) is found first in the Parables, and is historically the source of the N.T. designation. See Appendix II on this title.

Conversion of the Gentiles. The conversion of the Gentiles is looked for in four Sections of our book, i.e. 10^{21} $90^{30,\,33}$ 91^{14} 50^2.

Judgement. Where the eternal Messianic kingdom on earth is expected as in 1–36, the final judgement naturally precedes it, but where, as in 91–104, only a temporary Messianic kingdom is

---

righteous are to rejoice 'as the angels of heaven' (104^4 Matt. 22^{30} Mark 12^{25}), being 'companions of the hosts of heaven', 104^6.

expected, the final judgement naturally takes place at its close. In the Parables (37–71), where the kingdom is at once eternal and embraces earth and heaven, it is initiated by the final judgement.

Sheol. This word bears several different meanings in our text, see note on 63^{10}; also my *Eschatology*, 184–188, 236–237. In 91–104 Sheol—or rather a part of it—has for the first time become an abode of fire, so far as the wicked are concerned, and become identical with Gehenna, 98^3 99^{11} 103^7 sqq. Another part of Sheol is the intermediate abode of the righteous, $102^{5,\ 11}$ (cf. 100^5).

The Resurrection. In 6–36 the resurrection is to an earthly Messianic kingdom of eternal duration, and the resurrection is of both soul (or spirit) and body. The body is a physical body. The same holds true of 83–90. In 37–71 the resurrection is to a spiritual kingdom, in which the righteous are clothed with a spiritual body—'garments of life', 'garments of glory', 62^{16}. In 91–104 there is only a resurrection of the spirit: see notes on 22^{13} 51^1 61^5 90^{33} 91^{10} 100^5. In this last Section only the righteous attain to the resurrection.

THE BOOK OF ENOCH

ABBREVIATIONS, BRACKETS, AND SYMBOLS SPECIALLY USED IN THE TRANSLATION OF 1 ENOCH

a, b, c, d, &c., denote the Ethiopic MSS.

a denotes the earlier Ethiopic MSS., i.e. $g_1 g\, m\, q\, t\, u$.

β denotes the later Ethiopic MSS., i.e. $a\, b\, c\, d$, &c. (i.e. from a to $z\, a\, b$, with the exception of the earlier MSS.).

$a-g$ denotes all the MSS. of the a class but g, and so on.

$\beta-abc$ denotes all the MSS. of the β class but a, b. and c, and so on.

E denotes the Ethiopic Version.

G^s denotes the fragments of the Greek Version preserved in Syncellus: in the case of 8^b-9^b there are two forms of the text, $G^{s1}\, G^{s2}$.

G^g denotes the large fragment of the Greek Version discovered at Akhmim, and deposited in the Gizeh Museum, Cairo.

The following brackets are used in the translation of 1 Enoch:

⌈ ⌉. The use of these brackets means that the words so enclosed are found in G^g but not in E.

⌈ ⌉. The use of these brackets means that the words so enclosed are found in E but not in G^g or G^s.

⟨ ⟩. The use of these brackets means that the words so enclosed are restored.

[ ]. The use of these brackets means that the words so enclosed are interpolations.

( ). The use of these brackets means that the words so enclosed are supplied by the editor.

The use of thick type denotes that the words so printed are emended.

THE BOOK OF ENOCH

SECTION I

(CHAPTERS I—XXXVI)

INTRODUCTION

A. *Critical Structure and Dates.* B. *Relation of this Section to* (a) 72–82; (b) 83–90; (c) 91–104. C. *The Problem and its Solution.*

A. Critical Structure and Dates. This Section is of composite structure and from many hands. We shall consider 1–5 last of all. First of all 6–11 stand apart from the rest. These chapters belonged originally to the Book of Noah, many fragments of which are found throughout this book. They never refer to Enoch but only to Noah, 10^1. Since this Section was known to the author of the Book of Jubilees it must have been written before the last quarter of the second century B.C. But since we see that $88-89^1$ presupposes a minute acquaintance with 10, and since 83–90 were written before the death of Judas the Maccabee in 161, the date of 6–11 must be put back to the first third of the second century B.C. Again, since these chapters and 12–36 make no reference to the persecution of Antiochus, the *terminus ad quem* is thus fixed at 170 B.C. The fact that 4–36 were written in Aramaic is also in favour of a pre-Maccabean date; for when once a nation recovers, or even when it is trying to recover, its independence, we know from history that it seeks to revive its national language, in case it had lost it. Jubilees and the Testaments of the XII Patriarchs which were composed about 107 B.C. were written in Hebrew, as we might expect. Later we shall see grounds for regarding 83–90 and other sections of Enoch as having been written in Hebrew.

12–16 next call for consideration. These chapters preserve in a fragmentary and dislocated form a vision or visions of Enoch. The original order, as I have shown on pp. 27, 28, was 14^1: some verses lost: 13^{1-3} 12^3 13^{4-10} 14^2-16^2 12^{4-6} (of which 16^{3-4} is a doublet). 12^{1-2} is merely an editorial addition. Similar dislocations of the text will be found in 79–82 and 91–93. Since 12–16 were known to the author of the Book of Jubilees and were written in Aramaic they were probably pre-Maccabean. In these chapters the transcendence of God is pictured in an extreme degree. He dwells in heaven in a crystal palace of fire, into which not even an angel may enter, 14^{9-23}, whereas in 6–11, 20–36 the old Hebrew standpoint is fairly preserved. The Messianic Kingdom will be established on earth, and all sin vanish, 10^{17-22}; the chambers of blessing in heaven will be opened, 11^1; Jerusalem will be the centre of the Messianic Kingdom, 25^5, and God Himself will come down to visit the earth with blessing and will sit on His throne on earth, 25^3; men will enjoy patriarchal lives and die in happy old age, 10^7 25^6.

17–19 stand by themselves, exhibiting, as they do, strong traces of Greek influence in the adoption of Greek conceptions of the underworld (cf. 17^5 sqq.)—a thing that a Chasid could not have done after the Maccabean revolt. And yet, though these chapters betray Greek influences, they attest their close relationship with 20–36; for 18^{6-9} is a doublet of 24^{1-3}, 18^{11} of 21^{7-10}, 18^{12-16} of 21^{1-6}, and 19^2 of 10^{14}.

20–36 springs apparently from one and the same hand. The connexion of 20 with 21–36 is loose it is true, and yet the functions ascribed to the Archangels in 20 are tolerably borne out in 21–36. These chapters also were known to the author of the Book of Jubilees. They were written in Aramaic. Their date, therefore, is most probably pre-Maccabean.

Only 1–5 have now to be dealt with. It is difficult to say anything definite regarding them. They look like an introduction to the entire book written by the final editor. Their phraseology connects them with every Section of the book but 72–82. Thus the phrases 'the Holy One', 1^2, 'the elect', 1^3, 'the Holy Great One', 1^3, 'the eternal God' (or 'the God of the world'), 1^4, 'the Watchers', 1^5, 'the righteous', 1^8, 'His holy ones', 1^9, 'proud and hard words', 5^4, 'hard-hearted', 5^4, 'Ye shall find no peace', 5^4, are found in some cases in every Section of the book, and in all cases in one or more. In 5^9 the righteous look forward to a Messianic Kingdom on earth, in which they should enjoy patriarchal lives in blessedness and peace.

There is one passage which helps us to determine the *terminus a quo*. In 5^9 the words

> '*They shall complete the number of the days of their life*
> *And their lives shall be increased in peace*
> *And the years of their joy shall be multiplied*'

are most probably derived from Jub. 23$^{27, 29}$:

> 'And the days shall begin to grow many and increase amongst the children of men
>
> ... And all their days they shall complete and live in peace and joy.'

The *terminus ad quem* cannot be definitely determined. It is possible that there is some connexion between 1–5 and Wisdom. Thus the resemblance in word and thought between 5^7 καὶ τοῖς ἐκλεκτοῖς ἔσται φῶς καὶ χάρις καὶ εἰρήνη and 1^8 καὶ ἐπὶ τοὺς ἐκλεκτοὺς ἔσται συντήρησις καὶ ἐπ' αὐτοὺς γενήσεται ἔλεος and Wisd. 4^{15}

> ὅτι χάρις καὶ ἔλεος ἐν τοῖς ἐκλεκτοῖς αὐτοῦ
> καὶ ἐπισκοπὴ ἐν τοῖς ὁσίοις (ἐκλεκτοῖς A) αὐτοῦ

can hardly be accidental. Since 1–5 is derived from a Semitic original, the borrowing, if there is any, would naturally be on the part of Wisdom. The date of Wisdom is disputed. It is earlier than Philo at all events. Pss. Sol. 4^9 presuppose 1$^{1\,b}$ (see note).

B. (*a*) **Relation of 1–36 to 72–82.** These two Sections come from different authors; see Special Introd. to 72–82. (*b*) **Relation of 1–36 to 83–90.** These two Sections are of distinct authorship. The former, with the exception of chapters 1–5, is older, and was known in part to the author of the latter; see Special Introd. to 83–90. (*c*) **Relation of 1–36 to 91–104.** These two Sections are likewise independent; but the author of the latter was acquainted with 1–36 or some form of it; see Special Introd. to 91–104.

C. **The Problem and its Solution.** Under this heading I treat for convenience sake 1–36 as the work of a single writer. The author essays to justify the ways of God. The righteous will not always suffer, and the wicked will not always prosper, 1^1. The limits thereto are set by death, 22, and by great world judgements. But the cure of the world's corruption can only be understood by apprehending its cause, and this cause is to be traced to the lust of the fallen Watchers for the daughters of men. Original sin stands not in the following of Adam—whose sin seems limited in its effects to himself, 32^6—but in the evil engendered through the Watchers, 9$^{6,\,9,\,10}$ 10^8. Hence the Watchers, their companions and children were destroyed, 10$^{4-10,\,12}$; and their condemnation and confinement form the prelude to the first world judgement, of which the Deluge forms the completion, 10$^{1-3}$. But though only the righteous survived the Deluge, sin still prevailed in the world through the demons—the spirits which had gone forth from the slaughtered children of the Watchers and the daughters of men, and all manner of corruption was wrought through them, 16¹, as they escape punishment till the final judgement. But the recompense of character is not withheld till the last judgement; there is a foretaste of the final doom immediately after death, 22. In the second and last judgement on Sinai, 1⁴, the Watchers, the demons, and godless, 10¹³ 16¹, and all classes of Israel, with one exception, receive their final award, 1⁹. To make this possible, this judgement is preceded by a General Resurrection of Israel, 22. The fallen angels are transferred from their preliminary to their final place of punishment, 10⁶, ¹³⁻¹⁵. A final end is now made of sin on the earth, and the earth cleansed, 10¹⁵, ¹⁶, ²⁰⁻²²; the wicked are cast into Gehenna, and their punishment is a spectacle for the righteous to behold, 27²; the Messianic kingdom is established, with Jerusalem and Palestine as its centre, 25⁵—there is no Messiah, and God abides with men, 25³; all the Gentiles will become righteous and worship God, 10²¹; the righteous are allowed to eat of the tree of life, 25⁴⁻⁶, and thereby enjoy patriarchal lives, 5³ 25⁶, each begetting 1.000 children, 10¹⁷, and enjoying unlimited material blessings, 5⁷ 10¹⁸, ¹⁹ 11².

As to what becomes of the righteous, after the second death, there is no hint in this fragmentary Section. There is much celestial, terrestrial, and subterrestrial geography in 17-19, 21-36.

I-V. *Parable of Enoch on the Future Lot of the Wicked and the Righteous.*

I. 1. The words of the blessing of Enoch, wherewith he blessed the elect ⌜and⌝ righteous, who will be living in the day of tribulation, when all the wicked ⌜and godless⌝ are to be removed.   **2.** And he took up his parable and said—Enoch a righteous man, whose eyes were opened by God, saw the vision

---

I. 1. The blessing of Enoch. Cf. Deut. 33¹, 'the blessing of Moses.' **The elect and righteous.** This designation is found also in 38², ³, ⁴ 39⁶, ⁷ 48¹ 58¹, ³ 61¹³ 62¹², ¹³, ¹⁵ 70³. **All the wicked.** Here G^s reads πάντας τοὺς ἐχθρούς = כל־הצרים corrupt for בל־הרעים. Hence E is right here. The same corruption is attested by the LXX in Prov. 20²². This passage appears to have been known by the author of the Pss. Sol. 4⁹ τὸ κρίμα τοῦ θεοῦ αὐτῶν ἐν τῷ ἐξαίρεσθαι ἁμαρτωλοὺς ἀπὸ προσώπου δικαίου. **Removed.** + 'And the righteous shall be saved' G^s. **2. Saw.** G^s 'had' corrupt. The corruption might have arisen in G: i.e. ἔχων corrupt for ὁρῶν. The phrase 'saw the vision' is taken from Num. 24⁴ of the Holy One in the heavens, ⌜which⌝ the angels showed me, and from them I heard everything, and from them I understood as I saw, but not for this generation, but for a remote one which is for to come. 3. Concerning the elect I said, and took up my parable concerning them:

The Holy Great One will come forth from His dwelling,
4. And the eternal God will tread upon the earth, (even) on Mount Sinai,

מחזה שדי יחזה. **The Holy One.** For this and similar designations of God see 1³. The change from the third to the first person in this verse is of frequent occurrence in this book: cf. 12¹⁻³ 37¹,² 70¹⁻³ 71⁵ 92¹. **Which the angels showed me.** G⁵ reads corruptly 'he showed me', and adds καὶ ἁγιολόγων ἁγίαν ἤκουσα ἐγώ. **And from them.** G⁵ 'and when (ὡς) from them'. **As I saw.** So G⁵ θεωρῶν. E probably implies the same text. mut²β read 'what I saw' and gqt '(that) I should see'. **To come.** + 'do I speak' G⁵ (ἐγὼ λαλῶ em. by Swete from ἐγὼ ἄλλο). **3. The elect.** This designation belongs mainly to the Parables. It is found in 1⁸ 5⁷ 25⁵ 40⁵ 41² 48¹,⁹ 51⁵ 56⁶,⁸ 58³ 61⁴,¹² 62⁷,⁸,¹¹ 93². Before 'concerning' G inserts 'and'. **My.** So G⁵. >E. **3ᵇ–9.** A poem consisting of tristicha. The discovery of this structure is helpful in the restoration of the text. See specially Stanzas 1 and 7. **The Holy Great One.** G⁵ prefixes 'and'. E reads here and always 'the Holy and Great One', but G⁵ seems to preserve the original here as in 10¹ 14¹ where it recurs. This title is found in the following passages: 10¹ 14¹ 25³ 84¹ 92² 97⁶ 98⁶ 104⁹. God is designated simply as 'the Holy One', 1² 93¹¹, and as 'the Great One', 14² 103⁴ 104¹ (twice). **Come forth from His dwelling.** Cf. Mic. 1³ יֵצֵא מִמְּקוֹמוֹ, Is. 26²¹. Assumptio Moysis 10³. **4. The eternal God**

= אֱלֹהֵי הָעוֹלָם, ὁ θεὸς τοῦ αἰῶνος. Cf. Gen. 21³³, אֵל עוֹלָם, Is. 40²⁸, ὁ αἰώνιος θεός, Rom. 16²⁶. Ass. Moysis 10¹⁷ Deus aeternus. This could also be translated 'God of the world' as I have shown below, but I have here with Dalman (*The Words of Jesus*, 163 sqq., Eng. Transl.) adopted the former rendering. Thus in 25³,⁵,⁷ 27³ we have ὁ βασιλεὺς τοῦ αἰῶνος in the Greek where E renders ὁ βασιλεὺς ὁ αἰώνιος, cf. Jer. 10¹⁰ מֶלֶךְ עוֹלָם: in 12³ ὁ βασιλεὺς τῶν αἰώνων (so 1 Tim. 1¹⁷) (where E = ὁ βασ. τοῦ αἰῶνος): in 9⁴ (G⁵) ὁ βασ. τῶν †αἰώνων, for αἰώνων there stood βασιλέων in the original as in G¹,² E: in 9⁴ ὁ κύριος τῶν αἰώνων (G³¹) (where E = ὁ κύριος τῶν † βασιλέων, the corruption originating in the Aramaic (here G⁹,¹² om.)). With ὁ κύρ. τῶν αἰώνων compare 22¹⁴ κυριεύων τοῦ αἰῶνος. In 9⁴ we have θεὸς τῶν αἰώνων in G⁹¹, where G¹² has θεὸς τῶν ἀνθρώπων. Here αἰώνων was wrongly read as αὐτῶν. This idea of time comes out clearly in 5¹ καὶ ζῇ εἰς πάντας τοὺς αἰῶνας, where E has ὁ ζῶν for καὶ ζῇ. With this we might compare Dan. 12⁷ חַי הָעוֹלָם (Aram. חַי עָלְמָא Dan. 4³¹). Dalman (*op. cit.* 164), however, thinks it probable that עוֹלָם, when united with the article in the Book of Enoch, does not merely represent the adjective 'eternal'. מֶלֶךְ עוֹלָם means 'eternal king'; מֶלֶךְ הָעוֹלָם is 'the king who

[And appear from His camp]
And appear in the strength of His might from the heaven
⌜of heavens⌝.

5. And all shall be smitten with fear,
And the Watchers shall quake,
And great fear and trembling shall seize them unto the
ends of the earth.

6. And the high mountains shall be shaken,
And the high hills shall be made low,

as ruler controls the immeasurable duration of the world'. Against this view we might set the fact that E renders ὁ βασιλεὺς τοῦ αἰῶνος as ὁ βασιλεὺς ὁ αἰώνιος (see above), and that in 15³ in G⁵ τοῦ αἰῶνος can only mean 'eternal' in τὸν οὐρανὸν τὸν ὑψηλὸν ... τοῦ αἰῶνος. But the words which I have rendered 'the eternal God' could also be rendered 'God of the world': cf. 58⁴ 81¹⁰ 82⁷ 84²: also 12³ 81³. **Will tread upon the earth.** So G. From Mic. 1³ ‏ודרך על ...ארץ‎. Here for ἐπὶ τὴν γῆν E reads corruptly ἐκεῖθεν. Sinai, whence the Law was given, will likewise be the place of future judgement. Cf. Deut. 33² Ps. 68¹⁷. **[And appear from His camp].** So G⁵. This I have bracketed as an addition. It is against the parallelism. It is also against the sense. In 3ᵇ it is already said that 'the Holy One will come forth from His dwelling', and the writer has gone on to speak of God's advent on Sinai. E, it is true, reads 'And appear with His hosts'. But if G⁵ originally read ἐν τῇ παρεμβολῇ it is wholly improbable that a scribe would change it into ἐκ τῆς παρεμβολῆς against the context. **5–9.** Dln. thinks that we have in 5–9 a description combining the two great judgements; but everything from verse 4 to end is perfectly applicable to the final judgement. Yet cf. 83⁷. **5. The Watchers.** These are the עירין first mentioned in Dan. 4¹⁰, ¹⁴, ²⁰ (in Hebrew text) 2 Enoch 18¹. This name belongs to the fallen angels here and in 10⁹, ¹⁵ 12⁴ 13¹⁰ 14¹, ³ 15² 16¹, ² 91¹⁵. In 12², ³ 20¹ 39¹², ¹³ 40² 61¹² 71⁷ it designates the archangels. **And the Watchers shall quake.** So E. But G⁵ has here 'And the watchers shall †believe' (i.e. πιστεύσουσιν). This change seems due to the scribe who added the following words:

'And they shall sing hidden things in the ends of the (word omitted)
And all the ends of the earth shall be shaken.'

The scribe seems to have been thinking of 2 Enoch 18 where the singing of the Watchers is mentioned. But the text of E is right and gives a sense which accords perfectly with 10¹³⁻¹⁴. **Fear and trembling.** So E. G⁵ trans. 'trembling and fear'. The order of E is probably original. Cf. Job 4¹⁴ Ps. 2¹¹ Mk. 5³³ 2 Cor. 7¹⁵ Eph. 6⁸. Yet the order here in G⁵ recurs in G⁵ in 13³. **6.** Cf. Judges 5⁵ Ps. 97⁵ Is. 64¹, ³ Mic. 1⁴ Hab. 3⁶ Judith 16¹⁵ Assumpt. Moyseos 10⁴. **Shaken.** + 'shall fall and be dissolved' G⁵ (πεσοῦνται καὶ διαλυθήσονται). But this addition of G⁵ is against the parallelism. **Made low.** + 'so that the mountains shall waste away' G⁵ (τοῦ δια(ρ)ρυῆναι ὄρη). Another impossible interpolation.

And shall melt like wax before the flame.

7. And the earth shall be ⌈wholly⌉ rent in sunder,
And all that is upon the earth shall perish,
And there shall be a judgement upon all (men).

8. But with the righteous He will make peace,
And will protect the elect,
And mercy shall be upon them.

And they shall all belong to God,
And they shall be prospered,
And they shall ⌈all⌉ be blessed.

⌈And He will help them all⌉,
And light shall appear unto them,
⌈And He will make peace with them⌉.

9. And behold! He cometh with ten thousands of ⌈His⌉ holy ones

Hills... melt like wax. From Ps. 97⁵. Before the flame. G⁵ reads 'before the fire in the flame'. The idea of the destruction of the world by fire may be here hinted at as in Sibyl. Or. 3⁸⁴, ⁶⁰, ⁷², ⁸⁴⁻⁸⁷ 4¹⁷³ sqq. 5²¹¹ sqq. 2 Pet. 3⁷, ¹⁰ Life of Adam 49³ sq., but it is unlikely. The text does not go beyond Mic. 1⁴ Nah. 1⁶ Ps. 97⁵ 104³². 7. 'Wholly'. So G⁵ σχίσμα [ραγάδι]. σχίσμα and ραγάς appear to be duplicate renderings of the same Hebrew word. διασχισθήσεται ... σχίσμα a Hebrew construction. 8. Make peace with. Cf. 1 Macc. 6⁴⁹, ⁵⁸ for the phrase μετὰ ... εἰρήνην ποιήσει. On the idea cf. 5⁴ of the text. See 5⁴ note. The righteous. This designation is found in all parts of the book: 1⁷, ⁸ 5⁶ 25⁴ 38³ 39⁴ 43⁴ 47¹, ², ⁴ 48¹, ⁷, ⁹ 50² 53⁷ 56⁷ 58³, ⁵ 60² 61³ 62³ 82⁴ 94³, ¹¹ 95³, ⁷ 96¹, ⁸ 97¹, ³, ⁵ 98¹²⁻¹⁴ 99³ 100⁵ ⁷, ¹⁰ 102⁴, ¹⁰ 103¹ 104¹, ⁴, ¹², ¹³. With the righteous. There is a dittography in E here. Will protect, &c. So E. This is probably a free rendering of G⁵ ἐπὶ τοὺς ἐκλεκτοὺς ἔσται συντήρησις. Wisdom 4¹⁵ may here be dependent on our text: καὶ ἐπισκοπὴ ἐν τοῖς ἐκλεκτοῖς αὐτοῦ. After συντήρησις G⁵ adds καὶ εἰρήνη. All belong to God. Ps. 100³ Jer. 31¹, ⁹ Hos. 1⁹, ¹⁰ &c. They shall be prospered. G⁵ reads τὴν † εὐδοκίαν δώσει αὐτοῖς, where εὐδοκίαν is corrupt for εὐοδίαν—a corruption found also in Sir. 43²⁶. Here again the active construction in G⁵ is probably right. ⌈All⌉ be blessed. G⁵ reads 'He will bless them all'. ⌈And He will help them⌉. So G⁵ καὶ πάντων ἀντιλήμψεται. Here there is an obvious dittograph in G⁵; for it adds καὶ βοηθήσει ἡμῖν. This line is omitted in E quite wrongly. In fact E preserves only the second line of this stanza Light shall appear unto them (G⁵). E reads 'light (+ 'of God' a–g, β–o) shall shine upon them'. Cf. 38⁴. ⌈And He will make peace with them⌉ (G⁵). E om. but the tristich requires it. 9. This verse is composed of two tristichs.

To execute judgement upon all,
And to destroy ⌜all⌝ the ungodly:

And to convict all flesh
Of all the works ⌜of their ungodliness⌝ which they have
 ungodly committed,
⌜And of all the hard things which⌝ ungodly sinners ⌜have
 spoken⌝ against Him.

II. 1. Observe ye every thing that takes place in the heaven,

And behold. So E. G⁵ reads ὅτι corrupt for ἰδού. So Jude ἰδοὺ ἦλθεν Κύριος ἐν ἁγίαις μυριάσιν αὐτοῦ: Ps. Cypr. *Ad Novatianum* (Hartel's *Cyprian* iii. 67) 'Ecce venit cum multis milibus nuntiorum suorum': Ps. Vigilius (Migne lxii, col. 363) 'Ecce veniet Dominus in millibus'. Cometh with ten thousands of ⌜His⌝ holy ones. From Deut. 33² וְאָתָא מֵרִבְבֹת קֹדֶשׁ. Since the LXX here renders σὺν μυριάσιν Καδής our author has followed the M.T. The ⌜His⌝ is found G⁵, Jude, and Ps. Cyprian. As Zahn pointed out, the above passage from Ps. Cyprian is derived directly from our text, and not from it indirectly through Jude. This entire verse has been quoted by Jude 14, 15 in a compressed form, who in the same passage draws upon 5⁴ 27² 60⁸. Ten thousands of ⌜His⌝ holy ones. Cf. Deut. 33² Dan. 7¹⁰. The angels are so called in 12² 14²³ 39⁵ 47² 57² 60⁴ 61⁸, ¹⁰, ¹² 65¹² 69¹³ 81⁵ 103² 106¹⁹, as already in Job 5¹ 15¹⁵ Zech. 14⁵ Dan. 4¹³ 8¹³. They are called 'holy angels' in 20¹⁻⁷ 21⁵, ⁹ 22³ 24⁶ 27² 32⁶ 71⁸ 93². 'Holy ones of heaven': 9³. For other designations see 6² (note). All the ungodly. The 'all' is corrupt in E, but recoverable by an easy emendation. Which they have ungodly committed (G⁵). Here E is corrupt, reading warasajû for zarase'û. ⌜All the hard things which⌝ ... ⌜have spoken⌝ (G⁵). The text of G⁵ here presents a dittograph. σκληρῶν ὧν ἐλάλησαν λόγων καὶ περὶ πάντων ὧν κατελάλησαν.

II. The author in 2–5³ emphasizes the order and regularity that prevail in the world of nature in contrast to the disorder that prevails in the world of man. This was a favourite theme with Jewish writers. The noble words of Hooker (*Ecclesiastical Polity*, i. 16. 8) express the view of these old writers: 'Of Law there can be no less acknowledged than that ... her voice is the harmony of the world: all things in heaven and earth do her homage, the very least as feeling her care, the greatest as not exempted from her power.' In Sir. 43 we have the glorification of the sun, moon, stars, the rainbow, clouds, snow, lightning, thunder, dew, and other natural phenomena. The moon is especially glorified since the Jewish feasts were celebrated in accordance with the moon's phases. This last is, of course, a view in which the author of 72–82 would not have agreed, since he held that the only true divider of time was the sun. In Sir. 16²⁶⁻²⁹ there is a nearer approximation to our text, though there is no sure ground for recognizing it as a source of it. Sirach runs:—

27. ἐκόσμησεν εἰς αἰῶνα τὰ ἔργα αὐτοῦ,
  καὶ τὰς ἀρχὰς αὐτῶν εἰς γενεὰς
  αὐτῶν ...

how they do not change their orbits, ⌜and⌝ the luminaries which are in the heaven, how they all rise and set in order each in its season, and transgress not against their appointed order. 2. Behold ye the earth, and give heed to the things which take place upon it from first to last, ⌜how steadfast they are⌝, how ⌜none of the things upon earth⌝ change, ⌜but⌝ all the works of God appear ⌜to you⌝. 3. Behold the summer and the winter, ⌜how the whole earth is filled with water, and clouds and dew and rain lie upon it⌝.

καὶ οὐκ ἐξέλιπον ἀπὸ τῶν ἔργων αὐτῶν

2 3. ἕκαστος τὸν πλησίον αὐτοῦ οὐκ ἔθλιψεν,
καὶ ἕως αἰῶνος οὐκ ἀπειθήσουσιν τοῦ ῥήματος αὐτοῦ.

The next work that calls for consideration here is the T. Naplit. 2⁹ οὕτως οὖν ἔστωσαν, τέκνα μου, πάντα τὰ ἔργα ὑμῶν ἐν τάξει εἰς ἀγαθὸν ἐν φόβῳ θεοῦ, καὶ μηδὲν ἄτακτον ποιήσητε ἐν καταφρονήσει, μηδὲ ἔξω καιροῦ αὐτοῦ. 3², ³ ὁ ἥλιος καὶ ἡ σελήνη καὶ οἱ ἀστέρες οὐκ ἀλλοιοῦσιν τὴν τάξιν αὐτῶν· οὕτω καὶ ὑμεῖς μὴ ἀλλοιώσητε νόμον θεοῦ ἐν ἀταξίᾳ τῶν πράξεων ὑμῶν. 3. ἔθνη πλανηθέντα καὶ ἀφέντα Κύριον ἠλλοίωσαν τὴν τάξιν αὐτῶν. These passages may have been before our writer. From works that preceded our book we now pass to works which were written later. The earliest of these is the Pss. Sol. 18¹²⁻¹⁴.

2. ὁ διατάξας ἐν πορείᾳ φωστῆρας εἰς καιροὺς ὡρῶν ἀφ᾽ ἡμερῶν εἰς ἡμέρας,
καὶ οὐ παρέβησαν ἀπὸ ὁδοῦ ἧς ἐνετείλω αὐτοῖς.

3. ἐν φόβῳ θεοῦ ἡ ὁδὸς αὐτῶν καθ᾽ ἑκάστην ἡμέραν,
ἀφ᾽ ἧς ἡμέρας ἔκτισεν αὐτοὺς ὁ θεὸς καὶ ἕως αἰῶνος,

4. καὶ οὐκ ἐπλανήθησαν ἀφ᾽ ἧς ἡμέρας ἔκτισεν αὐτούς·
ἀπὸ γενεῶν ἀρχαίων οὐκ ἀπέστησαν ἀπὸ ὁδοῦ αὐτῶν,
εἰ μὴ ὁ θεὸς ἐνετείλατο αὐτοῖς ἐν ἐπιταγῇ δούλων αὐτῶν.

The next writer who deals with the same subject is the author of 1 Apoc. Bar. 48², ¹⁰.

'Thou instructest created things in the understanding of Thee,
And Thou makest wise the spheres so as to minister in their orders.
Armies innumerable stand before Thee,
And minister in their orders quietly at thy nod.'

In Clement's *Ep. ad Cor.* 20 the same theme is dealt with at length in dependence mainly on the sources already mentioned. 1. Observe (G⁵), and so E by a change of a vowel. Season. + 'and for (or 'in') their own festivals they appear' G⁵. 2. The Hebrews divided the year into two seasons, קַיִץ embracing Spring and Summer, and חֹרֶף embracing Autumn and Winter. Gen. 8²² Is. 18⁶ Zech. 14⁸. ⌜How steadfast they are⌝. G⁵ reads ὡς εἰσιν φθαρτά. But φθαρτά is impossible in this context. The object of the writer is to praise the works of nature. Hence φθαρτά is corrupt. Possibly it is a rendering of נבלים (as in Is. 24⁴) corrupt for נְכֹנִים = 'steadfast'. Hence render: 'how steadfast they are.' How ⌜none of the things upon earth⌝, &c. E reads 'how none of the works of God change in appearing'.

III. Observe and see how (in the winter) all the trees ⌜seem as though they had withered and shed all their leaves, except fourteen trees, which do not lose their foliage but retain the old foliage from two to three years till the new comes.

IV. And again, observe ye the days of summer how the sun is above the earth over against it. And you seek shade and shelter by reason of the heat of the sun, and the earth also burns with glowing heat, and so you cannot tread on the earth, or on a rock by reason of its heat.

V. 1. Observe ye⌝ how the trees cover themselves with green leaves and bear fruit: wherefore give ye heed ⌜and know⌝ with regard to all ⌜His works⌝, and recognize how He that liveth for ever hath made them so.

2. And ⌜all⌝ His works go on ⌜thus⌝ from year to year ⌜for ever⌝, and all the tasks ⌜which⌝ they accomplish for Him, and ⌜their tasks⌝ change not, but according as ⌜God⌝ hath ordained so is it done.

3. And behold how the sea and the rivers in like manner accomplish ⌜and change not⌝ their tasks ⌜from His commandments⌝.

III. In the Geoponica 11¹ fourteen evergreen trees are mentioned. Δένδρα ἀειθαλῆ ἐστι, μηδέποτε φυλλορροοῦντα ἐν τῷ χειμῶνι ιδ'· φοῖνιξ, κίτριον, στρόβιλος, δάφνη, ἐλαία, κυπάρισσος, κερατέα, πίτυς, πρῖνος, πύξος, μυρσίνη, κέδρος, ἰτέα, καὶ ἄρκευθος. The twelve trees enumerated in Jub. 21¹² as fitting for use on the altar have nothing to do with this list; for they are not all evergreen. Nor have those referred to in T. Lev. 9¹² (see my edition of the text of the *Test. XII Patr.*, pp. 248 sq. for a full discussion of the twelve trees which are mentioned in Jub. 21¹², and the Aramaic and Greek fragments of a still older work). 1. In G⁵ 3¹ᵇ-5¹ᵃ has been lost through homoeoteleuton.

V. 1. The trees ... bear fruit. G⁵ reads 'the green leaves on them cover the trees and all their fruit is for honour and glory'. He that liveth (cf. Sir. 18¹) ... them so. Here I have emended gabarkemmū la'ĕlūntū kuĕllōmū into gabrōmū la'ĕlūntū kamāhū in accordance with G⁵. G⁵ = 'the living God hath made them so and He liveth for ever'. Here there is a manifest dittograph. 2. ⌜All⌝ His works. E adds qedmēhū = 'before Him'. This seems corrupt for kamāhū = 'thus' (οὕτως in G⁵) or for kuĕllōmū = 'all'. The tasks which they accomplish for Him. So G⁵ πάντα ὅσα ἀποτελοῦσιν αὐτῷ τὰ ἔργα. Here τὰ ἔργα does not mean 'the works' as in the beginning of the verse, but the 'offices' or 'tasks' discharged by them as the next sentence—καὶ οὐκ ἀλλοιοῦνται αὐτῶν τὰ ἔργα—proves, and likewise the clause

4. But ye—ye have not been steadfast, nor done the commandments of the Lord,
But ye have turned away and spoken proud and hard words
With your impure mouths against His greatness.
Oh, ye hard-hearted, ye shall find no peace.

5. Therefore shall ye execrate your days,
And the years of your life shall perish,
And ⌜the years of your destruction⌝ shall be multiplied in eternal execration,
And ye shall find no mercy.

6 a. In those days ye shall make your names an eternal execration unto all the righteous,

καὶ οὐκ ἀλλοιοῦσιν αὐτῶν τὰ ἔργα in ver. 3. But E omits ὅσα before ἀποτελοῦσιν and αὐτῶν τὰ ἔργα, and renders 'all His works serve Him and change not'. God. > G⁸. **4. Of the Lord.** G⁸ reads 'His'. **Spoken.** The charge of blasphemy is frequent in 91-104. Cf. 91⁷, ¹¹ 94⁹ 96⁷ 100⁹. **Proud and hard words.** Cf. 27² 101³. From these passages the close of St. Jude 15 is drawn. Cf. Ps. 12⁴ Dan. 7⁸, ¹¹, ²⁰ Rev. 13⁶. **His greatness.** G⁸ adds a gloss 'for ye have spoken (κατελαλήσατε) with your lies'. **Hard-hearted.** Cf. 98¹¹ 100⁵ 'obstinate of heart'. **Ye shall find no peace.** This phrase occurs in Sects. 1-36 and 91-104 only: 1⁸ 5⁴ 12⁵ 13¹ 16⁴ 94⁶ 98¹¹, ¹⁵ 99¹³ 101³ 102³ 103⁸. It is derived from Is. 48²² 57²¹. **5. Therefore.** All MSS. of E but q prefix 'and'. **Shall perish** (G⁸ ἀπολεῖται). E tahagu̇elū (= 'ye shall destroy') corrupt for jahagu̇elū = ἀπολεῖται. **Mercy.** + καὶ εἰρήνη G⁸. **6-7** I have been obliged to rearrange the text of these verses, which is certainly in disorder. Thus in v. 6 there are ten lines, one of which—the eighth (6 h)—καὶ αὐτοὶ κληρονομήσουσιν τὴν γῆν is a doublet of 7 b. Strangely enough this line is repeated in an impossible place in v. 8. Now when we excise this line we have in vv. 6-7 the following arrangement: a tristich, a tetrastich, a distich, and a tristich. This of course cannot be right. Removing the tetrastich from consideration, 6 d e f g, which is right, we have a tristich, a distich, and a tristich. Now the first tristich deals with the curse that will befall sinners in many forms. A fourth line is wanting that deals with the same subject. There are actually two suitable, either the last line of v. 6 ἀλλὰ ἐπὶ πάντας ὑμᾶς καταλύσει κατάρα or the last line of v. 7 ὑμῖν δὲ τοῖς ἀσεβέσιν ἔσται κατάρα. But 6 j follows closely on 6 i; hence we have found the missing line of the first stanza in 7 c. Thus we have two complete tetrastichs in v. 6, i.e. 6 a b c, 7 c, and 6 d e f g. It is now obvious that the remaining distich in v. 6 belongs to the distich in v. 7, and thus the stanza in v. 7 is completed. **6. Ye shall make your names** (where E = δώσετε

    b. And by you shall ⌜all⌝ who curse, curse.
    c. ⌜And all⌝ the sinners ⌜and godless⌝ shall imprecate by you,
7*c.* And for you the godless there shall be a curse.

6*d.* ⌜And all the . . . shall rejoice,
  e. And there shall be forgiveness of sins,
  f. And every mercy and peace and forbearance:
  g. There shall be salvation unto them, a goodly light.

  i. And for all of you sinners there shall be no salvation,
  j. But on you all shall abide a curse⌝.
7*a.* But for the elect there shall be light and grace and peace,
  b. And they shall inherit the earth.

τὰ ὀνόματα ὑμῶν). G^g reads 'your names shall be' (ἔσται). But, since the phrase is clearly from Is. 65^{15} והנחתם שמכם לשבעה לבחירי, ἔσται may be corrupt for δώσετε. But if we compare Is. 65^{15}, on which this line was modelled, it is probable that instead of תתנו (= δώσετε) there stood originally in the text תַּנִּיחוּ (= καταλείψετε), as in Is. For in the preceding verse it is said that their life would prematurely come to an end, and so here it is added that they would leave as a kind of inheritance their name to be used in formulas of cursing, i. e. as an example of one cursed. This is the meaning of the next two difficult lines, where G^g is to be followed. And by you shall ⌜all⌝ who curse, curse. So G^g καὶ ἐν ὑμῖν καταράσονται πάντες οἱ καταρώμενοι. E = 'and you shall the sinners curse'. G^g is clearly right and reflects a Hebrew idiom. All who curse will introduce the names of these sinners into their formulas of cursing as instances of persons wholly accursed. The text = בכם יקללו כל־המקללים. ⌜And all⌝ the sinners ⌜and godless⌝ shall imprecate by you. So G^g since E is corrupt. Here again we have the same idiom as in the preceding line. ἐν ὑμῖν ὁμοῦνται = בכם ישבעו. This idiom is found in Ps. 102^9 מהוללי בי נשבעו: 'they who are mad against me swear by me.' See also Is. 65^{16} and Jer. 29^{22}, 'And of them shall a curse (קללה) be taken by all the captives of Judah . . . saying: the Lord make thee like Zedekiah . . . whom the king of Babylon roasted in the fire.' And all the . . . shall rejoice. The MS. reads οἱ αμαρτοι. What does this corrupt form stand for? It may be corrupt for οἱ (ἀν)αμάρ(τη)τοι, a bad rendering of המטהרים = 'those cleansed' or 'purified'. The piel and hithpael of טהר in this sense means purification from ceremonial and ritual uncleanness in the O.T., whereas the context requires spiritual cleansing. **Forgiveness of sins.** This forgiveness will fit them for the sinless life spoken of in v. 9. But for the Watchers there is no forgiveness 12^5. 7. G^g τοῖς ἐκλεκτοῖς ἔσται φῶς καὶ χάρις καὶ εἰρήνη. Has this influenced Wisd. 4^{15} χάρις καὶ ἔλεος τοῖς ἐκλεκτοῖς αὐτοῦ? **Grace.** So G χάρις. E = χηρά. **They shall inherit the earth.** From

8. And then there shall be bestowed upon the elect wisdom,
And they shall all live and never again sin,
Either through ungodliness or through pride:
But they who are wise shall be humble.

9. And they shall not again transgress,
Nor shall they sin all the days of their life,
Nor shall they die of (the divine) anger or wrath,
But they shall complete the number of the days of their life.

And their lives shall be increased in peace,
And the years of their joy shall be multiplied,
In eternal gladness and peace,
All the days of their life.

VI–XI. *The Fall of the Angels: the Demoralisation of Mankind: the Intercession of the Angels on behalf of Mankind. The Dooms pronounced by God on the Angels: the Messianic Kingdom (a Noah fragment).*

VI. 1. And it came to pass when the children of men had multiplied that in those days were born unto them beautiful and

Ps. 37^{11}. 8. And. > G^g. Wisdom: see 42^{1,3}. + φῶς καὶ χάρις, καὶ αὐτοὶ κληρονομήσουσιν τὴν γῆν. τότε δοθήσεται πᾶσιν τοῖς ἐκλεκτοῖς G^g. Here φῶς ... γῆν is a doublet from v. 7, and τότε ... ἐκλεκτοῖς a doublet of the first line of this verse. They who are wise, &c. Here G^g gives 'And there shall be light in the enlightened man and in the man of knowledge understanding'. This line does not seem to be original. 9. Cf. Is. 35^{10} 51^{11} 65^{20}: text 25^4 note. Sin. So G^g ἁμάρτωσιν. But E = κριθήσονται = יאשמו (cf. Prov. 30^{10} Is. 24^6 Jer. 2^3, &c. The word means 'reum iudicare' in Arabic). But this is not the meaning of the word here. The parallelism requires us to follow the other meaning of this word as given in G^g. (The divine) anger or wrath. G^g reads ὀργῇ θυμοῦ, 'the anger of (the divine) wrath', which may be right. Cf. Is. 42^{25}, &c. They shall complete ... in peace, And the years of their joy. Expanded from Jub. 23^{29}(?). Increased ... multiplied. The words recall the familiar phrase in Gen. 1^{22,28} 8^{17} Jer. 23^3 'Increase and multiply'. But the increase is a spiritual increase and not a materialistic, as in Joy ... gladness. Cf. Is. 35^{10}.

VI–XI. The abruptness with which 6–11 are introduced is quite in keeping with the fragmentary and composite nature of the rest of the Section. As Dillmann (Herzog, R. E.^{3} xii. 352) has already seen, 6$^{3-8}$ 8$^{1-3}$ 9^7 10^{11} belong to a Semjaza cycle of myths; for in these passages Semjaza is represented as chief and Azazel tenth in command: as also in 69^2. Elsewhere in Enoch Azazel is chief and Semjaza is not mentioned. Again 10$^{1-3}$ belongs to an Apocalypse of Noah, many fragments of which are comely daughters.   2. And the angels, the children of the

found in Enoch. Another fragment of this Apocalypse is preserved by Syncellus in the Greek; but to this there is no corresponding text in the Ethiopic. But these myths were already combined in their present form, when 88-89¹ were written. But not only does 10¹⁻³ belong to the Book of Noah but 6-11 as a whole. These never refer to Enoch but to Noah 10¹. Moreover, when the author of Jubilees is clearly drawing on the Book of Noah, his subject matter 7²¹⁻²⁵ agrees closely with that of these chapters in Enoch (see Charles's edition of Jubilees, pp. lxxi sq., 61, 264). 12-16 on the other hand belong to the Book of Enoch. And comely (E G^g). > G^a.

VI. 2. Children of the heaven. Cf. 13⁸ 14³ 39¹. See 15¹⁻⁷. Cf. 'Sons of the holy angels', 71¹. The entire myth of the angels and the daughters of men in Enoch springs originally from Gen. 6¹⁻⁴, where it is said that 'the sons of God came in to the daughters of men'. These words are not to be taken as expressing alliances between the Sethites and the Cainites, but as belonging to a very early myth, possibly of Persian origin, to the effect that demons had corrupted the earth before the coming of Zoroaster and had allied themselves with women. See Delitzsch, *Neuer Commentar über d. Genesis*, 1887, pp. 146-8. Bousset, *Rel. d. Jud.*³ 382, 560; Gunkel, *Genesis* 56. The LXX originally rendered the words 'sons of God' by ἄγγελοι τοῦ Θεοῦ, and this rendering is found in Philo, *de Gigantibus*, Eusebius, Augustine, and Ambrose. This view of Gen. 6¹⁻⁴ was held by most of the early fathers. That this was the original meaning of Gen. 6¹⁻⁴ Is. 24²¹ is now generally admitted. For a history of the interpretation of this passage in Jewish and Christian writers see my edition of Jubilees 4¹⁵ note. On the myths regarding the intercourse of angels with the daughters of men, see Grünbaum in *ZDMG*. xxxi. 225 ff. (Referred to by Delitzsch.) For statements of later writers either depending directly on this account in Enoch or harmonizing with it, cf. T. Reuben 5⁶; Napth. 3⁵; Jub. 4¹³ 5¹ sq.; Joseph. *Ant*. i. 3. 1; Philo, *de Gigantibus*; 2 Enoch 7, 18; Jude 6; 2 Pet. 2⁴; Justin Martyr, *Apol*. i. 5; Ps. Clemens, *Hom*. viii. 13; Clem. Alex. *Strom*. v. 1. 10; Tert. *De Virg. Veland*. vii; *Adv. Marc*. v. 18; *De Idol*. ix; Lact. *Instit*. ii. 15; Commodian. *Instruct*. i. 3. In the *De Civ. Dei* xv. 23, Augustine combats this view, and denies the inspiration of Enoch, which is upheld by Tertullian. I append here a fragment of the Book of Noah, relating not to the fallen angels but to mankind. It may have belonged to it. Fragment of the Book of Noah which Syncellus states was derived ἐκ τοῦ πρώτου βιβλίου Ἐνώχ. 'And again: "from the mountain on which they swore and bound themselves by common imprecations, [that] cold shall not depart from it for ever, nor snow nor hoar-frost, and dew shall not descend on it except it descend on it for a curse, until the great day of judgement. In that season (time) it shall be consumed and brought low and shall be burnt up and melt as wax before fire; so shall it be burnt up by reason of all the works thereof. And now I say to you, sons of men, great wrath is upon you, upon your sons, and this wrath shall not cease from you until the time of the slaughter of your sons. And your beloved ones shall perish and your honoured ones shall die from off all the earth; for all the days of their life from henceforth shall not be more than an hundred and twenty years. And think not that they may yet live for more years. For there is not for them

[Sect. I] *Chapter VI. 2-6* 15

heaven, saw and lusted after them, and said to one another: 'Come, let us choose us wives from among the children of men and beget us children.' 3. And Semjâzâ, who was their leader, said unto them: 'I fear ye will not indeed agree to do this deed, and I alone shall have to pay the penalty of a great sin.' 4. And they all answered him and said: 'Let us all swear an oath, and all bind ourselves by mutual imprecations not to abandon this plan but to do this thing.' 5. Then sware they all together and bound themselves by mutual imprecations upon it. 6. And they were in all two hundred; who descended ⌈in

any way of escape from this time by reason of the wrath, wherewith the king of all the ages is wroth with you. Imagine not that you will escape these things." And these (words) are from the first book of Enoch concerning the watchers.' Saw and > G^s. 4. And said (E G^g). > G^s. This thing. We must with G^s omit méker (= 'plan') as a gloss on 'thing' in E. Its presence makes the text ungrammatical. 6. And they were in all G^s ἦσαν δὲ οὗτοι. Who descended ... on Mount Hermon. I have here followed G^s οἱ καταβάντες ἐν ταῖς ἡμέραις Ἰάρεδ εἰς τὴν κορυφὴν τοῦ Ἑρμονιεὶμ ὄρους. The Ethiopic text reads: 'and they descended on Ardis which is the summit of Mt. Hermon.' The name Ardis, otherwise unknown, is to be explained with Dillmann as a compression of Ἰάρεδ εἰς, the translator not having found ἐν ταῖς ἡμέραις in his text. Halévy in the *Journal Asiatique*, Avril-Mai 1867, pp. 356-7, reproduces this verse in Hebrew, whereby we see at a glance why the angels descended in the days of Jared—from ירד to descend, and why it was that they bound themselves by mutual oaths on Hermon—from חָרַם a curse.

וַיֵּרְדוּ בִּימֵי יָרֶד עַל רֹאשׁ הַר חֶרְמוֹן
וַיִּקְרְאוּ לָהָר חֶרְמוֹן כִּי בוֹ נִשְׁבְּעוּ וְהֶחֱרִימוּ
בֵּינֵיהֶם׃

Cf. Book of Jubilees 4^{15}: 'Jared; for in his days the angels of the Lord descended on the earth.' This play on Jared shows that the idea originated in Hebrew. It cannot be reproduced in Aramaic, which does not possess the root ירד. The play on Hermon is possible not only in Hebrew (see above) but also in Aramaic אחרימו ... חרמון. Cf. Hilary, *Comm. in Pss.* 132^3 'Hermon autem mons est in Phoenice, cuius interpretatio anathema est. Fertur id de quo etiam nescio cuius liber exstat, quod angeli concupiscentes filias hominum, cum de caelo descenderent, in hunc montem Hermon maxime convenerant excelsum.' The reasons for the descent of the angels in the Book of Jubilees differ from those given in this chapter. In 4^{15} and 5$^{1\,sqq.}$ of that book it is stated that the watchers were sent to the earth by God 'to instruct the children of men to do judgement and uprightness', and that when so doing they began to lust after the daughters of men. This form of the myth seems to be followed in Test. Reuben 5^6. In Enoch the angels are said to have descended through their lust for the daughters of men, and the same reason is given in *Jalkut Shim.* Beresh. 44. See Weber, *Jüd. Theologie* 253. Against this and other statements of Enoch there is an implicit polemic in the Book the days¹ of Jared on the summit of Mount Hermon, and they called it Mount Hermon, because they had sworn and bound themselves by mutual imprecations upon it. 7. And these are the names of their leaders: Sêmîazâz, their leader, Arâkîba, Râmêêl, Kôkabiêl, Tâmiêl, Râmiêl, Dânêl, Êzêqêêl, Barâqîjâl, Asâêl, Armârôs, Batârêl, Anânêl, Zaqîêl, Samsâpêêl, Satarêl, Tûrêl, Jômjâêl, Sariêl. 8. These are their chiefs of tens.

of Jubilees. In later tradition (Eisenmenger, *Entdeckt. Jud.* ii. 387) the reason that Azazel could not return to heaven was that he had outstayed the limit of time assigned to angelic visitants to earth—seven days. In the Targ. Jon. on Gen. 6³ Shamchazai and Uziel (i.e. Azazel) are mentioned in connexion with this myth. 7. This list is incomplete. A name has been lost after Tûrêl. **Semîazâz**. Derivation doubtful. Possibly from שמעזז 'mighty name' or שמחזאי. **Râmêêl**. This is probably corrupt for Arakiêl—'Αρακιήλ as in G⁸. Now in G⁸ 8³ where it is speaking of 'Αρακιήλ we have ὁ δὲ τρίτος ἐδίδαξεν τὰ σημεῖα τῆς γῆς. Thus 'Αρακιήλ = ארקיאל where ארק = 'earth'. Thus we see that the duties of the angel are reflected in his name. This is frequent in Judaism. Arakiêl is mentioned as unfallen in *Sib. Or.* 2²¹⁵⁻¹⁷. **Kôkabiêl** = כוכביאל = 'star of God'. **Tâmiêl** = תומיאל = 'the perfection of God'. **Râmiêl**. See 1 Apoc. Bar. 55³, *Sib. Or.* 2²¹⁵⁻¹⁷. **Dânêl**, i.e. Δανειήλ G⁸ דניאל. **Êzêqêêl**. Since G⁸ 8³ writes ὁ δὲ ὄγδοος ἐδίδαξεν ἀεροσκοπίαν, this word comes from שחקיאל. שחק is rendered by ἀήρ in 2 Kings 22¹² Ps. 18¹¹ (Beer). Here again the name and functions of the angel are connected. **Barâqîjal** = ברקיאל = 'lightning of God'. **Armârôs**. This is the form in E, but G⁸ gives Φαρμαρός and G⁸ 'Αρεαρώς. Since G⁸ 8³ writes in reference to this angel ἐδίδαξεν . . . ἐπαοιδάς . . . καὶ ἐπαοιδῶν λυτήριον the word may go back to חבר = 'an incantation', 'spell'. If so Armârôs or 'Αρεαρώς would be corruptions of Abaros or something similar. **Anânêl** = ענניאל. **Samsâpêêl**. The word should be 'Shamshiel'. Since G⁸ 8³ describes the functions of this angel as ὁ δὲ ἕβδομος ἐδίδαξε τὰ σημεῖα τοῦ ἡλίου the name is from שמש, i.e. שמשיאל = 'sun of God'. On Shamash the sun god see *K.A.T.*³ 367-370. **Tûrêl** = טוריאל = 'rock of God'. **Jômjâêl** = יומיאל = 'day of God'. **Sariêl**. E reads corruptly 'Arâzjâl. This name recurs as Esdrêêl in 8³. Since in G⁸ 8³ this angel ἐδίδαξε τὰ σημεῖα τῆς σελήνης, these forms are corrupt for Sariel as in G⁸ (G⁸ 'Ατριήλ but in 8³ Σεριήλ) Σαριήλ = סהריאל where סהר = 'moon'. See *K.A.T.*³ 367. **Chiefs of tens** = ἀρχαὶ τῶν δεκάδων. G⁸ reads ἀρχαὶ αὐτῶν οἱ δέκα, which points to the Aramaic construction ראשיהון דעסריתא = ἀρχαὶ αὐτῶν τῶν δεκάδων. In 19² αἱ γυναῖκες αὐτῶν τῶν . . . ἀγγέλων there is again the same Aramaic idiom.

APPENDIX ON VI. 7.

The three lists of the fallen angels given above in E 6², G Syn., and G Giz. go back to one and the same original. In E 69² the same list reappears. In the process of transmission, however, many corruptions and transpositions of the text

Sect. I] *Chapter VI. 7-8* 17

have occurred. In the main the same order is observed in 6^7 69^2 and G^s. But a very different order is presented by G^g. As Lods (106-7) has observed the names in G were from the third onward written in four columns. These were read from left to right by E and G^s, but from top to bottom of each column by G^g. Within G^s and G^g certain transpositions have occurred. These will be made clear by the following Table:—

	(1)	(2)	(3)	(4)
E 69^2	1. Samjâzâ	2. Artâqifâ	3. †Armên	4. Kôkabêl
E 6^7	1. Samlazâz	2. Arâkiba	3. †Ramêêl	4. Kôkabîêl
G^s	1. Σεμιαζᾶς	2. Ἀτηρκούφ	3. Ἀραακιήλ	4. Χωβαβιήλ
G^g	1. Σεμιαζά	2. Ἀραθάκ	3. †Κιμβρά	9. †Χωχαριήλ (8^3 Χωχιήλ)

	(5)	(6)	(7)	(8)	(9)
	5. †Tûrâêl	6. Rûmjâl	7. Dûnjâl	8. †Nêqâêl	9. Barâqêl
	5. Tâmlêl	6. Râmlêl	7. Dânêl	8. Êzêkêêl	9. Barâqîjâl
	5. †Ὀραμμαμή	6. Ῥαμιήλ	G^s wanting	8. Ζακιήλ	9. Βαλκιήλ
	14. Ταμιήλ	13. Ῥαμιήλ	5. Δανειήλ	10. Ἐζεκιήλ (8^3 Σαθιήλ)	15. Βαρακιήλ (and in 8^3)

	(10)	(11)	(12)	(14)
	10. Azâzêl	11. Armârôs	12. Batarjâl	14. Hanânêl
	10. Asâêl	11. Armârûs	12. Batarêl	13. Anânêl
	10. Ἀζαλζήλ (8^1 Ἀζαήλ)	11. Φαρμαρύς	12. Ἀμαριήλ	13. Ἀναγημάς
	19. Ἀσεάλ	6. Ἀρεαρώς (8^3 Ἀρμαρώς)	11. Βατριήλ	16. Ἀνανθρά

	(15)	(16)	(17)	(18)
	15. Tûrêl	16. Simlpêsîêl	17. Jêtrêl	18. Tûmâêl
	14. Zaqlêl	15. Samsapêêl	16. Satarêl	wanting
	14. Θαυσαήλ	7. Σαμψίχ	16. Σαριναᾶς	17. Εὐμιήλ
	20. Ῥακειήλ	4. Σαμμανή	12. Σαθιήλ	17. Θανιήλ

	(19)	(20)	(21)	(13)
	19. Tûrêl	20. Rûmâêl	21. †Azâzêl	13. Basasêjal
	17. Tûrêl	19. Jômjâêl	19. †Arâzjal (8^3 Esdrêêl)	wanting
	18. Τυριήλ	19. Ἰουμιήλ	20. Σαριήλ	15. Σαμιήλ
	21. Τουριήλ	8. Ἰωμειήλ	13. Ἀτριήλ (8^3 Σιρσήλ)	7. Σεμιήλ

In the above Table I have followed the order of E 69^2; the names as they appear in that list head each of the twenty-one columns. Next comes the list in E 6^7; then that in G^s, and finally that in G^g. On the left of each name is placed a number which gives its place in its own list. Above each column I have put a number in brackets for convenience in references. Column (13) is placed at the end instead of after (12) since Basasêjal has no parallel in E 6^7 and no certain one in G^s or G^g.

As regards E 69^2, (15) which appears again in (19) is certainly corrupt, also (21) which is a repetition of (10). To (13) we have already referred. Thus the twenty-one names are reduced to nineteen.

Of E 6^7 (18) is wanting: also (13): (15) is hopeless. This list furnishes nineteen names.

Of G^s (7) is wanting, and (15) and (5) are corrupt. This list has twenty names.

Of G^g the list is complete, but (15) is hopeless.

In the above Table the identifications may be regarded as certain in (1), (4), (6), (7-12), (14), (16), (19-20), as probable or possible in (2-3), (5), (17-18), (21), as undeterminable in (13) and (15).

VII. 1. And all the others together with them took unto themselves wives, and each chose for himself one, and they began to go in unto them and to defile themselves with them, and they taught them charms and enchantments, and the cutting of roots, and made them acquainted with plants.   2. And they became pregnant, and they bare great giants, whose height was three thousand ells: 3. Who consumed all the acquisitions of men. And when men could no longer sustain them,   4. The giants turned against them and devoured mankind.   5. And they began to sin against birds, and beasts, and reptiles, and fish, and to devour one another's flesh, and drink the blood.   6. Then the earth laid accusation against the lawless ones.

VIII. 1. And Azâzêl taught men to make swords, and knives, and shields, and breastplates, and made known to them the metals (of the earth) and the art of working them, and bracelets, and

VII. 1. And all ... with them. G^g = 'these and all the rest'. Defile themselves. So G^g. E reads tadammarû (= 'unite themselves') corrupt (?) for jětgammanû = G^g. Charms and enchantments. Cf. Wisd. 12^4 18^{13}; Jos. Ant. viii. 2. 5; Bell. vii. 6. 3. Plants (= βοτάνας G^g). Not 'trees' here. The Ethiopic has both meanings. 2. Bare great giants. For further references see Sir. 16^7 Jub. 7$^{22-23}$ Wisd. 14^6 Tob. 6^{14} 1 Bar. 3^{26} 3 Macc. 2^4. The text in EG^g is defective here, and must be made good from G^s, which gives: 'And they bare unto them three kinds: first great giants, and the giants †begat the Naphilim, and to the Naphilim were† born the Eliûd, and they grew according to their greatness.' That these classes of giants were mentioned here is presupposed by 86^4 and 88^2 of our text. Moreover Jub. 7$^{21-22}$ is based on this passage: 'The watchers took unto themselves wives ... and they begat sons (the giants), the Naphidim (and the Eljô), and they were all alike, and they devoured one another, and the giants slew the Naphil, and the Naphil slew the Eljô, and the Eljô mankind.' In 7^{24} Jub. quotes the greater part of 8^3 of our text of EG^g. Hence since G^s omits 7^3, ^{4b}, ^{5a}, ^{6} (7^{4b}, ^{5b} are inserted after 8^3) and EG^g omit portions of 7^2, both texts are here defective. The three classes of giants go back to Gen. 6^4. The γίγαντες = גִּבֹּרִים, the Ναφηλείμ = נְפִלִים, and the Ἐλιούδ = אַנְשֵׁי הַשֵּׁם. I have obelized 'begat' (ἐτέκνωσαν) as corrupt. ἐτέκνωσαν may be corrupt for ἔτεινον: cf Jub. 7^{21} above. Or the corruption may have arisen in the Aramaic: ἐτέκνωσαν = מוֹלִדִין corrupt for מוֹבְדִין = 'destroyed'. 3. And when (ὡς δὲ G^g). E = ὥστε corrupt for ὡς δέ. 5. Blood. The eating of blood with the Jews was a great crime, Gen. 9^4 Acts 15^{20} Book of Jubilees 7^{28}, ^{29} 21^6, ^{18}, below 98^{11}.

VIII. 1. Azâzêl. The origin of this word is unknown. See Encyc. Bib. in loc. Breastplates. + διδάγματα ἀγγέλων G^g. The metals of the earth. So G^s. E twice deals with this phrase. First, here it gives only τὰ μετ' αὐτά

Sect. I]   *Chapters VII. 1—VIII. 3*   19

ornaments, and the use of antimony, and the beautifying of the eyelids, and all kinds of costly stones, and all colouring tinctures. 2. And there arose much godlessness, and they committed fornication, and they were led astray, and became corrupt in all their ways.   3. Semjâzâ taught enchantments, and root-cuttings, 'Armârôs the resolving of enchantments, Barâqîjâl (taught) astrology, Kôkabêl the constellations, Ezêqêêl the knowledge

corrupt for τὰ μέταλλα, and then at the end of the verse tauláta, a transliteration of τὰ μέταλλα, and appends τῆς γῆς. Hence the above rendering is to be followed. G⁵ reads only τὰ †μεγάλα. With our text cf. Tertullian, *De Cultu Fem.* i. 2 'Metallorum opera nudaverunt'. **Antimony.** This mineral is referred to in the following excerpt from Tert. *De Cultu Fem.* i. 2, in which he lays under contribution this and the preceding chapter: 'Herbarum ingenia traduxerant et incantationum vires provulgaverant et omnem curiositatem usque ad stellarum interpretationem designaverant, proprie et quasi peculiariter feminis instrumentum istud muliebris gloriae contulerunt, lumina lapillorum quibus monilia variantur et circulos ex auro quibus brachia artantur —et illum ipsum nigrum pulverem quo oculorum exordia producuntur': and in ii. 10: 'Quodsi iidem angeli qui et materias eiusmodi et illecebras detexerunt, auri dico et lapidum illustrium, et operas eorum tradiderunt, et iam ipsum calliblepharum—tincturas—docuerunt, ut Enoch refert.' Cf. T. Reub. 5⁴: also Is. 3¹⁶⁻²⁴ for the ornaments of women. 2. **Godlessness.** + 'upon the earth' G¹. **And they committed ... astray.** > G². 3. G² gives this verse as follows. 'First Azazel—the tenth of the leaders—taught (men) to make swords and breastplates and every kind of warlike arms, and the metals of the earth and the gold, how they were to work them and make them ornaments for the women, and the silver. And he showed

them the art of using antimony (l. στιβίζειν for στίλβειν) and beautifying the face, and precious stones and colouring tinctures. And the children of men made (them) for themselves and their daughters and transgressed and led astray the holy ones.' This last sentence is alien to the Book of Noah, and belongs rather to the Book of Jubilees and the Testaments. The latter books represent the daughters of men as seducing the angels by their ornaments, &c., whereas the older books declare that such arts were first introduced by the fallen angels. Cf. Clem. Alex. *Eclog. Proph.* (ed. Dindorf, iii. 474) ἤδη δὲ καὶ 'Ενώχ φησιν τοὺς παραβάντας ἀγγέλους διδάξαι τοὺς ἀνθρώπους ἀστρονομίαν καὶ μαντικὴν καὶ τὰς ἄλλας τέχνας. **Semjâzâ** (G⁵). E corruptly reads Amlzârâ—an internal Ethiopic corruption. **Armârôs.** On 6⁷ I have suggested that this word is corrupt, and was originally derived from חֶבֶר on the ground of what follows. His function was ἐπαοιδῶν λυτήριον. An allied phrase is found in Dan. 5¹² מִשְׁרָא קִטְרִין (= λύειν συνδέσμους Theod.) 'the resolving of spells'. In 95⁴ below we have 'anathemas that cannot be resolved'. Here the word חרם is referred to. **Barâqîjâl ... Kôkabêl.** See notes on 6⁷. **Ezêqêêl the knowledge of the clouds.** E is here very corrupt. Though it gives Ezêqêêl rightly in 6⁷, here it reads 'Tamiel'. G⁵ is also corrupt—Σαθήλ corrupt for Ζακιήλ, as in 6⁷, or 'Εζεκιήλ Again G⁵ E have ἀστεροσκοπίαν, which, of the clouds, ⟨Araqiêl the signs of the earth, Shamsiêl the signs of the sun⟩, and Sariêl the course of the moon. 4. And as men perished, they cried, and their cry went up to heaven. ...

IX. 1. And then Michael, Uriel, Raphael, and Gabriel looked down from heaven and saw much blood being shed upon the earth, and all lawlessness being wrought upon the earth. 2. And they said one to another: 'The earth made †without inhabitant cries the voice of their crying† up to the gates of heaven. 3. ⌜And now to you, the holy ones of heaven⌝, the souls of men make their suit, saying, "Bring our cause before the Most High".' 4. And they said to the Lord of the ages: 'Lord of lords, God of gods, King of kings ⟨and God of the ages⟩, the throne of Thy glory (standeth) unto all the generations of the ages, and Thy name holy and glorious and blessed unto all the ages! 5. Thou hast made all things, and power over all things hast Thou: and all things are naked and open in Thy

---

as I have already pointed out in 6⁷ (which see), is corrupt for ἀεροσκοπίαν (so G⁸). ⟨Araqiêl ... sun⟩ supplied from G⁸, save that for ὁ τρίτος and ὁ ἕβδομος I have given the names these numbers represent. **Sariêl.** E = Esdrêêl corrupt: G⁸ Σεριή(λ). See note on 6⁷ on this word. **4. And** (E G⁸¹). G⁸² reads τότε, G⁸ οὖν. **They cried, and their cry went up to heaven** (E) = ἐβόησαν καὶ ἀνέβη ἡ βοὴ αὐτῶν εἰς τὸν οὐρανόν. G⁸ om. ἐβόησαν καί. G⁸¹² reads ἐβόησαν εἰς τὸν οὐρανόν. Our text, therefore, may be a conflation of these two readings: yet cf. 9¹⁰. **To heaven.** + 'saying, Bring our cause before the Most High and our destruction before the Great Glory, before the Lord of all the lords in greatness' G⁸². Cf. G⁸¹. This fragment most probably preserves part of the original text: cf. 9³,⁵. The cry of men is not inarticulate, but a prayer for justice.
IX. 1. And then (E). G⁸ 'then'. + 'the four great archangels hearing' G⁸¹,². **Michael, &c.** See 40² note on the four archangels. **Looked down from heaven** = אוֹדִיקוּ מִשְׁמַיָּא. An echo of Ps. 14². **2. The earth †made without inhabitant... heaven** (E). G⁸ reads 'the voice of them that cry upon the earth to the gates of heaven'. G⁸¹,² omit. On 'made without inhabitant' cf. 67² 84⁶ T. Napth. 3⁶. **3.** On the intercession of angels see ver. 10 note, and my note on T. Lev. 3⁵, where the chief passages on this subject from 200 B.C. to 100 A.D. are dealt with. **And now ... heaven** (E). Lost in G⁸¹,² through hmt. **Holy ones.** See 1⁹ note. **Most High.** See 99³ note. **4. Lord of the ages** (G⁸¹). > G⁸². E = κυρίῳ τῶν βασιλέων, where τ. βασιλέων = מלכיא corrupt for עלמיא = τῶν αἰώνων. **Lord of lords, God of gods.** So in Deut. 10¹⁷. The prayer of the angels is fuller in G⁸, and still more in 84⁴,³ **Of kings** (E G⁸¹,²). G⁸ reads τῶν αἰώνων = עלמיא corrupt for מלכיא. ⟨**God of the ages.**⟩ Restored from G⁸¹,². In G⁸² ἀνθρώπων, i. e. אנשן is corrupt for αἰώνων. **5. Power over all things** (E G⁸). G⁸

sight, and all things Thou seest, and nothing can hide itself from Thee. 6. Thou seest what Azâzêl hath done, who hath taught all unrighteousness on earth and revealed the eternal secrets which were (preserved) in heaven, which men were striving to learn: 7. And Semjâzâ, to whom Thou hast given authority to bear rule over his associates. 8. And they have gone to the daughters of men upon the earth, and have slept with the women, and have defiled themselves, and revealed to them all kinds of sins. 9. And the women have borne giants, and the whole earth has thereby been filled with blood and unrighteousness. 10. And now, behold, the souls of those who have died are crying and making their suit to the gates of heaven, and their lamentations have ascended: and cannot cease

= 'all power'. And nothing can hide itself from Thee. 6. Thou seest. Lost in G^g through hmt. 6. Revealed the eternal secrets which were... learn. So G^{g}¹ with the correction of ἔγνωσαν into γνῶναι (cf. G^g εἰδέναι); for it is untranslatable as it stands. E is very corrupt: 'the eternal secrets which are wrought in the heaven mankind knows' (q). But G^{gs} show that 'ĕlla jetgabarû should be emended into 'ĕlla jetgĕbarû (= ἃ ἐπιτηδεύουσιν) and transposed after 'in the heaven'. Next 'a'ĕmara (q) (= ἔγνω) should be emended into 'a'ĕmrō = γνῶναι or εἰδέναι. Thus E agrees with G^g when ἔγνωσαν in the latter is corrected as above suggested. G^g = 'revealed to the world the things that are (preserved) in heaven. And the children of men are practising his (Azazel's) practices in order to know the mysteries'. 7. ⟨And.⟩ Supplied from G^g. 8, 9. Cf. Justin, Apol. ii. 5 Οἱ δὲ ἄγγελοι—γυναικῶν μίξεσιν ἡττήθησαν καὶ παῖδας ἐτέκνωσαν, οἵ εἰσιν οἱ λεγόμενοι δαίμονες—καὶ εἰς ἀνθρώπους φόνους, πολέμους, μοιχείας—καὶ πᾶσαν κακίαν ἔσπειραν. 8. With the women. Here E = μετ' αὐτῶν μετὰ τῶν θηλειῶν

—the literal rendering of an Aramaic idiom = עִם נְשַׁיָּא עֲמְהֵין = 'with the women'. G^g not understanding this idiom divided the phrase into two parts, and connected them with different verbs συνεκοιμήθησαν μετ' αὐτῶν καὶ ἐν ταῖς θηλείαις ἐμιάνθησαν. G^s omitted the latter half of the phrase and read αὐταῖς after συνεκοιμήθησαν. All kinds of sins. + 'and have taught them to make hate-producing charms' (G^s). But as Martin suggests μίσητρα is possibly corrupt for μυσητίαν. Hence 'taught them to practise lewdness'. 9. Giants. G^s reads τιτᾶνας, G^g γίγαντας. 10-11. The intercession of the angels on man's behalf, which appears in this chapter and is found also in 15² 40⁶ 47² 99³,¹⁵ 104¹, is an O.T. doctrine; cf. Job 5¹ 33²³ Zech. 1¹². It was evidently a popular doctrine. Cf. Tobit 12¹² Ἐγὼ προσήγαγον τὸ μνημόσυνον τῆς προσευχῆς ὑμῶν ἐνώπιον τοῦ ἁγίου (contrast Acts 10⁴); also 12¹⁵ ἐγώ εἰμι Ῥαφαήλ εἷς ἐκ τῶν ἑπτὰ ἁγίων ἀγγέλων οἱ προσαναφέρουσι τὰς προσευχὰς τῶν ἁγίων: Rev. 8³, Test. Levi 3⁵: also 5⁴,⁷ ἐγώ εἰμι ὁ ἄγγελος ὁ παραιτούμενος τὸ γένος Ἰσραήλ. 10. Cease. EG^{ss}

because of the lawless deeds which are wrought on the earth.
11. And Thou knowest all things before they come to pass, and
Thou seest these things and Thou dost suffer them, and Thou
dost not say to us what we are to do to them in regard to these.'

X. 1. Then said the Most High, the Holy and Great One
spake, and sent Uriel to the son of Lamech, and said to him:
2. '⟨Go to Noah and⟩ tell him in my name "Hide thyself!", and
reveal to him the end that is approaching: that the whole earth
will be destroyed, and a deluge is about to come upon the whole
earth, and will destroy all that is on it.   3. And now instruct
him that he may escape and his seed may be preserved for all the
generations of the world.'   4. And again the Lord said to

read ἐξελθεῖν = למנפק corrupt for למפסק = 'cease'. The lamentations must keep ascending to heaven without ceasing because of the deeds of violence on earth.   11. Seest (G^g). E 'knowest'. Dost suffer them (G^g). E = τὰ εἰς αὐτούς corrupt for ἑὰς αὐτούς.

X. 1. Said. So G^g. E. om. The Holy and Great One (E). G^g 'And the Great Holy One'.   Uriel (G^g). G^g Ἰστραήλ. E is corrupt.   2. ⟨Go to Noah and.⟩ Restored from G^g πορεύου πρὸς τὸν Νῶε καὶ. This phrase belonged to the original, though already lost in the archetype of E. It belongs to the original, for each new command issued to the angels begins with the word 'go'. Cf. G^g 10^4, ^{9}, ^{11}. 3. And now (E). G^g 'and'. > G^g. G^g is here much fuller: 'Instruct the righteous (man) what he is to do, (even) the son of Lamech, and he will preserve his soul unto life and escape through the world, and from him will be planted a plant, and it will be established throughout all the generations of the world.' Of the world. n, G^g. > E-n.   4. Azazel is punished in a place by himself. In his case as in that of his followers the place of punishment is in the valleys of the earth in the Noah sections of the book, but in the genuine Enoch beyond the earth.   Azazel as the chief offender and leader is first punished. The preliminary punishment of Azazel is described in vv. 4, 5: the final one in ver. 6. Azazel was conceived as chained in the wilderness into which the scapegoat was led. The Jerusalem Targum (Ps. Jonathan) on Leviticus says that the goat was sent to die in a hard and rough place in the wilderness of jagged rocks, i.e. Beth Chaduda. The passage in Ps. Jon. on Lev. 16$^{7-22}$ is as follows: ויפטור ביד גבר... למהך למדברא רצוק דהוא בית הדורי... ויפטור נברא ית צפירא כמדברא רצוק ויסוק צפירא על טווריא דבית הדורי.   'And they will send it by the hand of a man... that it may go into the precipitous desert, which is Beth Chadure... and the man will send the goat into the precipitous wilderness, and the goat will ascend the mountains of Beth Chadure.' In the Mishna (Joma 6^8) we find this word written חדודי 'Chadûdê'. This Beth Chaduda was three miles (Joma 6^8), or according to another account, twelve miles from Jerusalem. This is clearly the Dudael mentioned in this

Raphael: 'Bind Azâzêl hand and foot, and cast him into the darkness: and make an opening in the desert, which is in Dûdâél, and cast him therein. 5. And place upon him rough and jagged rocks, and cover him with darkness, and let him abide there for ever, and cover his face that he may not see light. 6. And on the day of the great judgement he shall be cast into the fire. 7. And heal the earth which the angels have corrupted, and proclaim the healing of the earth, that they may heal the plague, and that all the children of men may not perish through all the secret things that the Watchers have disclosed and have taught their sons. 8. And the whole earth has been corrupted through the works that were taught by Azâzêl: to him ascribe all sin.' 9. And to Gabriel said the Lord:

verse, and it is thus a definite locality in the neighbourhood of Jerusalem. See Geiger in the *Jüdische Zeitschrift f. Wissenschaft und Leben* 1864, pp. 196-204. Cf. Lev. 16¹⁰, ²². Again the Lord (E). > G⁵. To Raphael. + 'go Raphael and' (G⁸). G⁸ is probably right here. 5. **Place upon him.** The Greek gives ὑπόθες αὐτῷ, but this is probably a slip for ἐπίθες αὐτῷ. Cf. 54⁶. **For ever.** Like εἰς τὸν αἰῶνα, of which the Ethiopic text is an exact rendering, this phrase has no definite meaning in itself. It may denote according to the context an unending period: or a period of seventy generations, as here; cf. ver. 12; or a period of five hundred years, as in ver. 10. 6. **Day of the great judgement.** So G⁵. E reads 'great day of judgement'. See 45² (note). This judgement inaugurates the final punishment of the angels. The fire: see 18¹¹ 19 21⁷⁻¹⁰. 7. The command given to Raphael is such as his name suggests from רפא 'to heal'. Cf. Tob. 3¹⁷ 12¹⁴. **Heal the earth** (E G⁸). G⁵ 'the earth shall be healed'. **Healing of the earth** (E G⁵). G⁸ 'healing of the plague'. **They may heal the plague** (G⁸⁵). E (i.e. *gins*), 'one may heal the earth'. The rest of the MSS. of E = 'I may heal', &c. We should observe here that in these two clauses E has both times *medir* = γῆ, G⁸ has both times πληγή, and G⁵ has first γῆ and then πληγή. Two explanations are possible. Either πληγή was original in both cases, and G⁵ represents the first stage in the corruption and E the second. Or the variations in G arose from two possible renderings of ארעא, which punctuated as אַרְעָא = γῆ and as אַרְעָא = πληγή. **Have disclosed.** E G⁵ have here ἐπάταξαν = אבה corrupt for אמר = εἶπον which we find in G⁸. Cf. ἐμηνύσατε in 16³. For an analogous corruption see 2 Chron. 22¹⁰. Bouriant's conjecture—ἐπέταξαν—which I formerly followed is impossible. 8. All sin is here ascribed to the fallen angels. The works that were taught (G⁸ τοῖς ἔργοις τῆς διδασκαλίας). E 'the teaching of the works'. 9, 10. The destruction of the giants through Gabriel. The account here is followed closely by the Book of Jubilees 5⁶⁻¹¹. The giants slay each other in the presence of their parents; cf. 14⁶. The latter are then bound in the abysses of the

'Proceed against the bastards and the reprobates, and against the children of fornication: and destroy [the children of fornication and] the children of the Watchers from amongst men: [and cause them to go forth]: send them one against the other that they may destroy each other in battle: for length of days shall they not have. 10. And no request that they (i.e. their fathers) make of thee shall be granted unto their fathers on their behalf; for they hope to live an eternal life, and that each one of them will live five hundred years.' 11. And the Lord said unto Michael: 'Go, bind Semjâzâ and his associates who have united themselves with women so as to have defiled themselves with them in all their uncleanness. 12. And, when their sons have slain one another, and they have seen the destruction of their beloved ones, bind them fast for seventy generations in the valleys of the earth, till the day of their

earth, and their power of hurting the earth is at an end; cf. 14⁶. But this is not so with the spirits of the giants. They enjoy an impunity in wrong-doing till the final judgement: see 15¹¹–16¹. 9. [The children of fornication and.] > G^g. This is a dittograph from the preceding clause in E. It is against the context also. 'The children of the Watchers' is sufficient: this phrase includes the three classes in the preceding clause. [And cause them to go forth.] A duplicate rendering in E of πέμψον. One against the other (E G^s). > G^g. That they may destroy each other in battle (E). This is not a paraphrastic rendering of G^g ἐν πολέμῳ, since G^s has ἐν πολέμῳ καὶ ἐν ἀπωλείᾳ. The original was probably קרב מותא = 'a deadly war' or 'a war of extermination'. Cf. Jub. 5⁹. 10. An eternal life = 500 years. Touching the prayer of the angels cf. 12⁶ 13⁴⁻⁶ 14⁷. 11. The Lord (E). > G^g. Bind (i.e. δῆσον G^s). G^g E read δήλωσον, a corruption native to G^g; for the original acc. μιγέντας remains unchanged, though of course δήλωσον would require μιγεῖσι. United themselves . . . defiled themselves with them. Quoted verbally in Jub. 4²². 12. Their sons. So G^g οἱ υἱοὶ αὐτῶν. E reads 'all these sons', but kuellû = 'all' is an internal corruption for 'ĕllû = οἱ here. Slain one another. Cf. 12⁶ 14⁶ Jub. 5⁹. Valleys (νάπας G^g). E reads 'hills'. νάπαι is used as a rendering of גבעה in Is. 40¹² Ezek. 6³. This fact and the influence of the Greek myth of the Titans may explain how the Ethiopic translator attached this meaning to t. That νάπαι means valleys in this passage is beyond the possibility of doubt. In 67⁴ also this valley (not valleys) in which the fallen angels are cast is dealt with at length. Jub. 5¹⁰, which is here dependent on our text, writes: 'After this they were bound in the depths of the earth for ever until the day of the great condemnation.' This verse is referred to by St. Jude 6: ἀγγέλους τε τοὺς μὴ τηρήσαντας τὴν ἑαυτῶν ἀρχὴν ἀλλὰ ἀπολιπόντας τὸ ἴδιον οἰκητήριον εἰς κρίσιν μεγάλης ἡμέρας . . . ὑπὸ ζόφον τετήρηκεν.

judgement and of their consummation, till the judgement that is for ever and ever is consummated.   13. In those days they shall be led off to the abyss of fire: ⟨and⟩ to the torment and the prison in which they shall be confined for ever.   14. And whosoever shall be condemned and destroyed will from thenceforth be bound together with them to the end of all generations.   15. And destroy all the spirits of the reprobate and the children of the Watchers, because they have wronged mankind.   16. Destroy all wrong from the face of the earth and let every evil work come to an end: and let the plant of righteousness and truth appear: ⌜and it shall prove a blessing: the works of righteousness and truth⌝ shall be planted in truth and joy for evermore.

17. And then shall all the righteous escape,
    And shall live till they beget thousands of children,
    And all the days of their youth and their old age shall they
        complete in peace.

18. And then shall the whole earth be tilled in righteousness,

13. The final place of punishment for the angels as for Azazel, 10^6. **Abyss of fire.** This is the λίμνη τοῦ πυρός of Rev. 20^{10}, $^{14-15}$ which was prepared for the devil and his angels, Matt. 25^{41}, as here $10^{6, 13}$. Cf. 18^{11} 19 21^{7-10} 90^{24}. **In which they** (E^s). E^a reads 'and they'. The absence of the relative here in E_s is due to an Ethiopic idiom.   14. See 19^2. **Condemned** (G^s). G^g E read καταχαυσθῇ corrupt for καταστρφῇ. **All generations** (E). G^g 'the generation', G^s 'their generation'.   15. The writer is still describing the duties of Gabriel, i.e. the destruction of the giants and the imprisonment of the fallen Watchers, as we see from 10^9, ^{10}. This verse is therefore out of place. Possibly it belongs after 10^{10}. Thus 10^{1-3} refers to Uriel, 10^{4-8} to Raphael, 10^9, ^{10}, ^{15} to Gabriel, and 10^{11-13} to Michael. **And 1°** (E). $> G^s$.   16. **Plant of righteousness**, i.e. Israel. Israel springs from a seed that 'is sown' by God, 62^8: hence it is established as 'a plant of the seed for ever', 84^6, is called 'the plant of uprightness', 93^2, 'the plant of righteousness', 93^5, 'the eternal plant of righteousness', 93^{10}, and finally 'the plant of righteous judgement', 93^8. **Righteousness and truth.** After these words G^s omits through hmt. καὶ ἔσται εὐλογία· τὰ ἔργα τῆς δικαιοσύνης καὶ τῆς ἀληθείας, which are preserved by E.   17. The writer has here gone over wholly to a description of the Messianic times. The picture is a very sensuous one. **Their old age:** cf. $25^{5, 6}$ (note). Here G^s E have τὰ σάββατα αὐτῶν = שַׁבַּתָּם in which the word is wrongly vocalized for שִׂבָתָם = τὸ γῆρας αὐτῶν. The error could also be explained in Hebrew. See Wellhausen, *Skizzen*, vi. 241, 260. **18, 19.** The future is depicted after O. T. prophecy. Cf. Amos $9^{13, 14}$ Hos. $2^{22, 23}$ Jer. 31^5 Is. 25^6 Ezek. 28^{26} $34^{26, 27}$.

and shall all be planted with trees and be full of blessing. 19. And all desirable trees shall be planted on it, and they shall plant vines on it: and the vine which they plant thereon shall yield wine in abundance, and as for all the seed which is sown thereon each measure (of it) shall bear a thousand, and each measure of olives shall yield ten presses of oil. 20. And cleanse thou the earth from all oppression, and from all unrighteousness, and from all sin, and from all godlessness: and all the uncleanness that is wrought upon the earth destroy from off the earth. 21. ⌜And all the children of men shall become righteous⌝, and all nations shall offer adoration and shall praise Me, and all shall worship Me. 22. And the earth shall be cleansed from all defilement, and from all sin, and from all punishment, and from all torment, and I will never again send (them) upon it from generation to generation and for ever.

XI. 1. And in those days I will open the store chambers of blessing which are in the heaven, so as to send them down ⌜upon the earth⌝ over the work and labour of the children of men. 2. And truth and peace shall be associated together throughout all the days of the world and throughout all the generations of men.'

18. Shall all be planted with trees (E). G^g 'and a tree shall be planted in it'. Is this 'the plant of righteousness' of v. 16? The sequel, however, points to the former. The 'all' in E, i. e. kuĕlantāhā, may be corrupt for balū'elēhā = ἐν αὐτῇ (G^g). 19. And all ... be planted (E). G^g is corrupt: 'and all the trees of the earth shall rejoice, shall be planted' (τῆς γῆς ἀγαλλιάσονται φυτευθήσεται). Wine in abundance (E). G^g 'pitchers of wine'. As for all the seed ... presses of oil (E = πᾶς ὁ σπόρος ὁ σπαρεὶς ἐν αὐτῇ ἕκαστον μέτρον ποιήσει χιλιάδας καὶ ἕκαστον μέτρον ἐλαίας κτλ.). G^g is corrupt and defective: χιλιάδας καὶ σπόρου ποιήσει καθ' ἕκαστον μέτρον ἐλαίας. Each measure shall bear, &c. Cf. the chiliastic expectations in 2 Bar. 29^5 and Iren. adv. Haer. v. 33, and contrast Is. 5^{10}. 20. Oppression (E). G^g 'impurity'. All 4° (E). > G^g. From off the earth. 21. And all the children of men shall become righteous (E). > G^g. The conversion of the Gentiles. Cf. 90^{30} (note) 91^{14}. 22. The earth (E). G^g 'all the earth'. From all 4° (E). > G^g. Upon it (E). G^g 'upon them'.

XI. 1. This chapter concludes an account of the Messianic kingdom. Cf. Deut. 28^{12}. Upon the earth (E). > G^g. 2. Cf. 85^{10} Is. 32^{17}. Truth and peace shall be associated together (so G^g E save that E reads 'peace and truth'). Cf. Ps. 85^{11}. Of men (G^g). E = αἰώνων, a corruption of ἀντων = ἀνθρώπων.

XII-XVI. *Dream Vision of Enoch: his intercession for Azázêl and the fallen Angels: and his announcement to them of their first and final doom.*

XII. 1. Before these things Enoch was hidden, and no one of the children of men knew where he was hidden, and where he

XII-XVI. Vision of Enoch, in which he intercedes on behalf of Azazel and the Watchers. The pronouncement of their doom by God, which Enoch announces to them. The vision or rather visions are preserved only in a fragmentary condition, and not in their original order—a fact which is in part due to our editor, as we shall find elsewhere, as in chapters 78-80 and 91-94. The doom pronounced on Azazel and the fallen angels in 10 has not yet been executed; for Enoch is asked to intercede on their behalf. The order of the original visions was as follows: Enoch was asked to intercede for Azazel. This Section is lost, but its presence in the original vision is implied in 13^{1-2}, in which he announces the result of his mission on Azazel's behalf and pronounces his doom. Next the Watchers besought him to intercede on their behalf, 13^3 12^3 13^{4-7}. Enoch has a fresh vision, 13^8. When he awakes from it he proceeds to the Watchers and recounts it to them, 13^{9-10}. The vision is related at length, and all that God said relating to the Watchers, their original condition, their sin and their doom, 14^2-16^2. Finally, the section closes with the message of doom which Enoch is bidden to take to the Watchers, 16^{3-4}. But this message appears in a duplicate form in 12^{4-6}. The latter is more original since it reflects the discourse of God to Enoch in his vision. This repetition is thoroughly Semitic. I will here write out 12^{4-6}, printing the words which are based on 14^2-16^2 in black type. 12^4 εἰπὲ τοῖς ἐγρηγόροις τοῦ οὐρανοῦ (14^3) οἵτινες, ἀπολιπόντες τὸν οὐρανὸν τὸν ὑψηλόν, τὸ ἁγίασμα τῆς στάσεως τοῦ αἰῶνος, μετὰ τῶν γυναικῶν ἐμιάνθησαν, καὶ ὥσπερ οἱ υἱοὶ τῆς γῆς ποιοῦσιν, οὕτως καὶ αὐτοὶ ποιοῦσιν, καὶ ἔλαβον ἑαυτοῖς γυναῖκας (15^3)· ἀφανισμὸν μέγαν †κατηφανίσατε† τὴν γῆν. 5. καὶ οὐκ ἔσται ὑμῖν εἰρήνη οὔτε ἄφεσις (16^4). 6. καὶ περὶ ὧν χαίρουσιν τῶν υἱῶν αὐτῶν, τὸν φόνον τῶν ἀγαπητῶν αὐτῶν ὄψονται (14^6 10^{12}), καὶ ἐπὶ τῇ ἀπωλείᾳ τῶν υἱῶν αὐτῶν στενάξουσιν καὶ δεηθήσονται (10^{10}), εἰς τὸν αἰῶνα, καὶ οὐκ ἔσται αὐτοῖς εἰς ἔλεον καὶ εἰρήνην (16^4). The original order therefore of this section was, so far as the present fragmentary text goes: 14^1 ... 13^{1-2} 13^3 12^3 13^{4-10} 14^2-16^2 12^{4-6} ‖ 16^{3-4}. 12^{1-2} is an editorial introduction. It is remarkable that whereas *the angels intercede* in the Noah section *on behalf of man*, in this Enoch section *a man intercedes on behalf of the fallen angels*. In the Noah fragment (68^{2-3}) the angels are troubled over the doom of the Watchers, but they are afraid to approach God on their behalf.

XII. 1-2. An introduction from the final editor. See preceding note. 1. Before these things, i.e. before the intercession of the angels on behalf of mankind and God's judgement on the watchers, 9-10. Was hidden (E). G^s 'was taken'—ἐλήμφθη. This is the Ethiopic way of rendering μετέθηκεν (= לקח) in Gen. 5^{24}: cf. $71^{1,5}$ in our text. It is possible that the editor intends the reader to understand that abode, and what had become of him. 2. And his activities had to do with the Watchers, and his days were with the holy ones.

3. And I Enoch was blessing the Lord of majesty and the King of the ages, and lo! the Watchers called me—Enoch the scribe—and said to me: 4. 'Enoch, thou scribe of righteousness, go, †declare† to the Watchers of the heaven who have left the high heaven, the holy eternal place, and have defiled themselves with women, and have done as the children of earth do, and have taken unto themselves wives: "Ye have wrought

Enoch at this date had already been translated; but, if so, this was not the meaning of the vision he has incorporated; for Enoch is still living: his final translation from earth has not yet fallen out; for as a man he writes the petition for the angels, 13^4: receives a vision in sleep and is transported in spirit unto heaven, 14^2: speaks with a tongue of flesh, 14^2: and is terrified, like a mortal man, at the presence of God, 14^{24}. Furthermore, the next verse (12^7) was apparently before the author of Jub. 4^{21}, who states that Enoch spent six jubilees of years (i.e. 294) with the angels, being instructed in the things of heaven and earth, and that afterwards he was taken from amongst the children of men. 2. His activities. Here E reads 'all his activities', but kuĕllû = 'all' is a corruption of 'ĕllû = τά as frequently. For 'his' G^g corruptly reads 'their'. His days. E corruptly prefixes 'in'. 3. This verse, which contains the request of the Watchers that Enoch should intercede for them, should be read after 13^3. See note on xii–xvi. Of majesty (G^g). So E (i.e. $q\beta$) by changing the vocalization of one letter. Otherwise E = 'great', 'majestic'. King of the ages. This title occurs also in G^g 9^4, where however it is corrupt. Watchers. + 'of the Holy Great One', G^g. The scribe: cf. 92^1. Enoch is further called 'the scribe of righteousness', 12^4 15^1, because he is himself a righteous man, 15^1 71^{14-16}, and declares the righteous judgement that is coming, 13^{10} $14^1,^3$ 81^6 82^1, &c. The idea of a heavenly 'scribe' is derived in the main from the Babylonian Nabû. He is the man (in Ezek. $9^{2\ sqq.}$) clad in linen with writer's inkhorn by his side. He is accompanied by six other men. These go back to the seven gods of the planets. In later Jewish writings this office is fulfilled by Michael in 1 Enoch $89^{61\ sqq.}$, by Enoch in 1 Enoch $12^{3\ sq.}$ 15^1 92^1, and by Vretil, an archangel, in 2 Enoch $22^{11\ sq.}$. The same function was discharged in the ancient Egyptian religion by the god Thoth. See Zimmern in K.A.T.^{3} 404 sqq. 4–6. These verses form in reality the close of the Section chs. 2–16. See introduction to this section, p. 27. 4. Declare (E). Read with G^g 'and say'. Cf. 16^4, where 'say' is preserved in the duplicate account. Have left, &c. Cf. 15^3, which contains most of this verse. ἀπολιπόντες is used in the same connexion in Jude 6. The holy eternal place (E). All MSS. but g insert 'and' before 'eternal'. G^g 'the holiness of the eternal place'. Ye have wrought (G^g). This is better than E = 'and they have wrought'. These words begin God's message to the Watchers. This reading is supported by the fact that both in G^g and E the great destruction on the earth: 5. And ye shall have no peace nor forgiveness of sin: and inasmuch as †they† delight themselves in †their† children, 6. The murder of †their† beloved ones shall †they† see, and over the destruction of †their† children shall †they† lament, and shall make supplication unto eternity, but mercy and peace shall ye not attain."'

XIII. 1. And Enoch went and said: 'Azâzêl, thou shalt have no peace: a severe sentence has gone forth against thee to put thee in bonds: 2. And thou shalt not have toleration nor †request† granted to thee, because of the unrighteousness which thou hast taught, and because of all the works of godlessness and unrighteousness and sin which thou hast shown to men.' 3. Then I went and spoke to them all together, and they were all afraid, and fear and trembling seized them. 4. And they besought me to draw up a petition for them that they might find forgiveness, and to read their petition in the presence of the Lord of heaven. 5. For from thenceforward they could not speak (with Him) nor lift up their eyes to heaven for shame of their sins for which they had been condemned. 6. Then

next verse, which is clearly part of the message, begins with 'and', and therefore presupposes something preceding. **5. And ye shall** (G^g). E read 'and they shall'. **No peace.** Cf. 5^4 16^4. **Forgiveness.** Contrast 5^6. **They delight.** For 'they' and 'their', obelized in this clause and the following verse, read 'ye' and 'your'. **6.** Cf. 14^6 10$^{10, 12}$.

XIII. 1-2. Message of doom to Azazel. This should have been preceded by an account of Enoch's intercession to God for Azazel and the divine reply, but these are lost. See introductory note, p. 27. **Went and said** (E). G^g reads εἶπεν πορεύου. Perhaps the two forms already existed in the Aramaic — אמר אזיל (so G^g) and אזל ואמר (E) — the corrupt form in the text and the true in the margin, and being reproduced in the archetype of G E, were followed respectively by G^g and the Greek archetype of E. **Thou shalt have no peace.** Cf. 16^4 5^4. **In bonds.** Cf. 10^4. **2. Toleration** (G^g ἀνοχή). E 'relaxation', 'quiet'. **Request** (G^g E). Here ἐρώτησις seems corrupt. We should expect at least 'thy request'. Perhaps שאלא (= ἐρώτησις) was corrupt for שלא = 'rest'. **3. Together** (E). > G^g and α. **Fear and trembling** (E). ∽ G^g. Cf. 1^5. **4. Read** (G^g ἀναγνῶ). E = ἀνάγω, 'take up.' **5.** Cf. the Apology of Athenagoras: xxv. 1 οὗτοι οἱ ἄγγελοι οἱ ἐκπεσόντες τῶν οὐρανῶν ... οὐκέτι εἰς τὰ ὑπερουράνια ὑπερκύψαι δυνάμενοι. **Of their sins for which they had been condemned** (E). G^g 'of those things in regard to which they had sinned and been condemned'

I wrote out their petition, and the prayer †in regard to their spirits and their deeds individually and in regard to their requests

(περὶ ὧν ἡμαρτήκεισαν καὶ κατεκρίθησαν).
6. Spirits. + And their deeds individually (E). [And.] Though in G⁵ E, it should be bracketed. The passage †in regard to their spirits ... length † is clearly corrupt. First of all 'length' is corrupt. μακρότης stands in G⁵ and nûḫat in E is an exact rendering of it, and cannot in any case mean 'patientia'—the meaning assigned in this solitary case to it in Dillmann's Lexicon. The Ethiopic can only = μακρότης. From the conjunction of the words ἄφεσις καὶ μακρότης (G⁵ E) it is clear that μακρότης here represents אוריכותא, and that after it there stood originally either דיומא or דרוחא : in the former case we should have the familiar phrase 'length of days' (Heb. ארך ימים): in the latter 'forbearance' (Heb. ארך אפים). Which of these two restorations is right we cannot decide before a study of the context. Does the phrase μακρότης ... refer to the Watchers or to their children? If to the Watchers, then obviously the phrase must mean 'forbearance', since they could not supplicate for 'length of days' 'on behalf of their spirits'. That 'forgiveness' (ἄφεσις) refers to the Watchers is clear from 12⁶ 13⁴. If then 'forgiveness and forbearance' have to do with the Watchers only, then the clause in E, 'and their works individually and,' as well as the καί in G⁵ before περὶ ὧν must be excised. We should then have 'in regard to their spirits in regard to which they besought forgiveness and forbearance'. But this is not satisfactory. The Watchers were deeply concerned for their children (cf. 12⁶ 10¹² 14⁶ where they are called τῶν ἀγαπητῶν αὐτῶν) (cf. 10¹²), and prayed earnestly on their behalf, 12⁶, and hoped that they would live each 500 years, 10¹⁰. Hence it is highly improbable that there should be here no mention of their sons but only of themselves. Now if originally there had been a reference in this passage to the sons of the Watchers, the phrase behind μακρότης would probably refer to them as the word ἄφεσις referred to the Watchers themselves, as we have seen above. And that there was such a double request—for themselves and for their children—is shown by 14⁷. Hence we should read here μακρότης ἡμερῶν. The Watchers prayed that their sons might have 'length of days'. If we turn to 10⁹ we shall actually find this phrase where God declares regarding the sons of the Watchers: μακρότης γὰρ ἡμερῶν οὐκ ἔστιν αὐτῶν. The concluding clause therefore should run: 'in regard to whom they besought forgiveness and length of days.' In the words preceding this clause, therefore, we should find a reference to the Watchers themselves and to their sons. The reference to the former must lie in 'in regard to their (i.e. their own) spirits'. Possibly τῶν πνευμάτων αὐτῶν is an inaccurate rendering of נפשותידן = 'themselves'. Hence 'in regard to themselves'. But in G⁵ there is no trace of a phrase referring to their sons. Some trace of this lost phrase may survive—in fact does survive—in E, which, translated word for word = καὶ ἑκάστου ἔργου αὐτῶν. Possibly this may be a corruption of τῶν ἑκάστου ἀγαπητῶν. Or E may be corrupt for ba'ěnta wělûdômû = περὶ τῶν υἱῶν αὐτῶν. In any case (cf. 14⁷) there was here a reference to the sons of the Watchers. Hence the passage is probably to be read as follows : ' in regard to themselves and the beloved ones of each and in regard to their requests that they should have forgiveness and length (of days). Irenaeus iv. 16. 2 (Stieren's ed.) refers to this

that they should have forgiveness and length†.   7. And I went off and sat down at the waters of Dan, in the land of Dan, to the south of the west of Hermon: I read their petition till I fell asleep.   8. And behold a dream came to me, and visions fell down upon me, and I saw visions of chastisement, ⌜and a voice came bidding (me)⌝ to tell it to the sons of heaven, and reprimand them.   9. And when I awaked, I came unto them, and they were all sitting gathered together, weeping in 'Abelsjâil, which is between Lebanon and Sênesêr, with their faces covered.   10. And I recounted before them all the visions which I had seen in sleep, and I began to speak the words of righteousness, and to reprimand the heavenly Watchers.

XIV. 1. The book of the words of righteousness, and of the reprimand of the eternal Watchers in accordance with the command of the Holy Great One in that vision.   2. I saw in my sleep what I will now say with a tongue of flesh and with the breath of my mouth: which the Great One has given to men to

passage: 'Enoch ... cum esset homo, legatione ad angelos fungebatur et translatus est et conservatur usque nunc testis iudicii Dei, quoniam angeli quidam transgressi deciderunt in terram in iudicium.'   7. **Waters of Dan.** This river is one of the tributaries of the Jordan, and is called 'the little Jordan' in Jos. *Ant.* v. 3. 1; viii. 8. 4. This place—from דין 'to judge'—is chosen because its name is significant of the subject the writer is dealing with, i. e. the judgement of the angels. **South of the west of Hermon.** G⁸ reads 'south of Hermon of the west'. **I read.** gmq prefix 'and'.   8. **To tell ... and reprimand** (E). G⁸ = 'Tell ... to reprimand'. **Sons of heaven.** See 6² note.   9. 'Abelsjâil is probably a corruption of 'Αβειλήνη, a town in the Antilibanus, which could be loosely described as lying between Lebanon and Senir, i. e. Hermon. There was a play of words in the original. The angels were mourning (אָבְלִין) in Abilene (אֲבִילִין). **Sênesêr**, i. e. Senir, a name of Hermon (Deut. 3⁹) or a part of it, Cant. 4⁸.   10. **Before them.** G⁸ transposes before 'and'. **Recounted** (ἀνήγγειλα G⁸). E = 'spake'. **And to reprimand** (E). G⁸ = 'reprimanding'. In 1 Cor. 6³ St. Paul speaks of Christians as having hereafter to judge the angels.

XIV. 1. This verse gives the title of the section 12-16. On the original order see note on p. 27. **The book of the words.** So q G⁸. In q the demonstrative, i. e. the article, has been prefixed to the word 'book'. The other MSS. of E = 'this book is the word'. **Holy Great One** (G⁸). E 'Holy and Great One'.   XIV. 2— XVI. 2. *The Vision.*   2. **And with the breath of my mouth.** So G⁸, save that it omits 'and'. E differs, but by a slight emendation in accordance with G⁸ and 84¹ we arrive at this reading.

converse therewith and understand with the heart. 3. As He has created and given ⌜to man the power of understanding the word of wisdom, so hath He created me also and given⌝ me the power of reprimanding the Watchers, the children of heaven. 4. I wrote out your petition, and in my vision it appeared thus, that your petition will not be granted unto you ⌜throughout all the days of eternity, and that judgement has been finally passed upon you: yea (your petition) will not be granted unto you⌝. 5. And from henceforth you shall not ascend into heaven unto all eternity, and ⌜in bonds⌝ of the earth the decree has gone forth to bind you for all the days of the world. 6. And (that) previously you shall have seen the destruction of your beloved sons and ye shall have no pleasure in them, but they shall fall before you by the sword. 7. And your petition on their behalf shall not be granted, nor yet on your own: even though you weep and pray and speak all the words contained in the writing

To ... understand with the heart (E = νοῆσαι καρδίᾳ). G^g νοήσει καρδίας = 'with understanding of the heart'. 3. As (E = ὡς). G^g = ὅς. To man the power of understanding the word of wisdom, so hath He created me also and given (E). > G^g through hmt. 4. Thus, that ... unto you. G^g is defective: 'this and neither was your petition accepted'. 5. In bonds of the earth (so G^g ἐν τοῖς δεσμοῖς τῆς γῆς). This is a peculiar expression. E has simply 'on the earth'. Perhaps we should read δεσμοῖς ἐν τῇ γῇ. Cf. Origen (c. Celsum v. 52) κολάζεσθαι δεσμοῖς ὑποβληθέντας ἐν γῇ, and Jude 6 εἰς κρίσιν μεγάλης ἡμέρας δεσμοῖς ἀϊδίοις ὑπὸ ζόφον τετήρηκεν. On the other hand, if τῆς γῆς is original, then possibly the error arose in the Aramaic. ἐν τ. δεσμοῖς τ. γῆς = באסורי ארעה corrupt for כאסירי ארעה = 'as prisoners of (i.e. 'on') the earth'. Cf. Lam. 3³⁴ where the phrase occurs. 6. Cf. 10⁹ 12⁶. Ye shall have no pleasure in them (G^g).

Here ὄνησις has the meaning of ἀπόλαυσις as in the poet Philemon: γένοιτό σοι τέκνων ὄνησις, ὥσπερ καὶ δίκαιον (see Schleusner in loc.): a clause which gives exactly the same sense as that in our text. Cf. ὀνίνημι, Sir. 30³, where the Syriac renders by חדי. The same idea is expressed in our text with regard to the sons of the watchers in 12⁶ περὶ ὧν χαίρουσιν τῶν υἱῶν αὐτῶν. E here gives a free rendering 'ye shall not possess them', i.e. so as to delight in them. Previous translators—myself included—wrongly took ὄνησις as meaning 'profit' here; but 12⁶ is decisive. 7. The twofold petition of the watchers on their own behalf and that of their sons. Cf. 13⁶ note. And speak all the words. So G^g καὶ μὴν λαλοῦντες πᾶν ῥῆμα, where I have emended μή into μήν. The converse change of μή into μήν is found in G^g 10⁷. If, however, the negative is original, καὶ μὴ λαλοῦντες may be corrupt for καὶ μὴ λαχόντες or λαβόντες = ולא מקבלין, which should be taken as the apodosis

Sect. I] **Chapter XIV. 3-14** 33

which I have written. 8. And the vision was shown to me thus: Behold, in the vision clouds invited me and a mist summoned me, and the course of the stars and the lightnings sped and hastened me, and the winds in the vision caused me to fly and lifted me upward, and bore me into heaven. 9. And I went in till I drew nigh to a wall which is built of crystals and surrounded by tongues of fire: and it began to affright me. 10. And I went into the tongues of fire and drew nigh to a large house which was built of crystals: and the walls of the house were like a tesselated floor (made) of crystals, and its groundwork was of crystal. 11. Its ceiling was like the path of the stars and the lightnings, and between them were fiery cherubim, and their heaven was (clear as) water. 12. A flaming fire surrounded the walls, and its portals blazed with fire. 13. And I entered into that house, and it was hot as fire and cold as ice: there were no delights of life therein: fear covered me, and trembling gat hold upon me. 14. And as I quaked and trembled, I fell upon my face. And I beheld a vision,

'ye are not to be granted a single request in the writing', &c. 8. The vision (E). G^g 'in the vision'. Sped (E). G^g reads κατεσπούδαζον. Hastened. G^g E have here ἐθορύβαζον = יִבָּהֵל. In this context the translator should have rendered it by ἐτάχυνον. בהל has these two meanings both in Hebrew and Aramaic. In Daniel, conversely, בהל is several times rendered by κατασπεύδω in the LXX when it ought to have been rendered by θορυβάζω or συνταράσσω. Cf. 4⁵ 5⁶, &c. Here Dillmann's Lexicon and all previous translations should be corrected accordingly. Caused me to fly (E = ἀνεπτέρωσαν). But G^g has ἐξεπέτασαν, which E apparently confused with ἐξέπτησαν, and derived it from ἐκπέταμαι, to which it ascribed an active meaning. The same wrong meaning is attached by the Ethiopic translator to ἐξεπέτασε in Prov. 13¹⁶.

On the whole I am inclined to regard ἐξεπέτασαν here as a corruption of ἐξεπέρασαν (so Lods). The idea may be derived from Num. 11³¹ πνεῦμα ἐξῆλθεν παρὰ Κυρίου καὶ ἐξεπέρασεν. Lifted me upward (G^g). E = 'hastened me', and connects 'upward' with the next clause. 9-13. Enoch is carried up into heaven and passes within the outer wall that surrounds the πρόναος or forecourt of the palace of God. 10. Of crystals ¹⁰ = ἐν λίθοις χαλάζης. Cf. Is. 30³⁰ אַבְנֵי בָרָד. Of crystals ²⁰ (E). G^g καὶ πᾶσαι ἦσαν ἐκ χιόνος. 13. Delights = τρυφή. G^g has τροφή. The words are frequently confused; cf. Gen. 49²⁰. On the other hand τρυφή is used of Sheol in Sir. 14¹⁶ οὐκ ἔστιν ἐν ᾅδου ζητῆσαι τρυφήν (בשאול לבקש תענוג). Cf. also Erubin 54ᵃ, 'Do good to thyself; for there is no luxury (תענוג) in Sheol.' 14. Cf. 60³ 71¹¹ Ezek. 1²⁸ Dan. 8¹⁷, ¹⁸, &c.

15. And lo! there was a second house, greater than the former, and the entire portal stood open before me, and it was built of flames of fire.   16. And in every respect it so excelled in splendour and magnificence and extent that I cannot describe to you its splendour and its extent.   17. And its floor was of fire, and above it were lightnings and the path of the stars, and its ceiling also was flaming fire.   18. And I looked and saw ⌜therein⌝ a lofty throne: its appearance was as crystal, and the wheels thereof as the shining sun, and there was the vision of cherubim.   19. And from underneath the throne came streams of flaming fire so that I could not look thereon.   20. And the Great Glory sat thereon, and His raiment shone more brightly than the sun and was whiter than any snow.   21. None of the angels could enter and could behold His face by reason of the magnificence and glory, and no flesh could behold Him.   22. The flaming fire was round about Him, and a great fire stood before Him, and none around could draw nigh Him: ten thousand times ten thousand (stood) before Him, yet He needed

15. Enoch approaches the palace of God but does not enter, as no mortal may behold God. As the doors are open, he can describe what is within. There was a second house ... before me and. So E. G^g seems corrupt ἄλλην θύραν ἀνεῳγμένην κατέναντί μου καὶ ὁ οἶκος μείζων τούτου καὶ ὅλος.   16. It so excelled ... that I cannot describe, &c. Cf. Targ. Jon. on Ezek. 1^{27}, 'the appearance of glory such as the eye cannot see and there was no power to look thereon.'   18. In this and the following verses the writer draws upon Is. 6 Ezek. 1 10 Dan. 7$^{9, 10}$. This passage (vv. 18–22) is used by the author of 71$^{5-8}$.   Therein. > G^g.   A lofty throne. On a throne in heaven cf. 1 Kings 22^{19} Is. 6^1 Ezek. 1^{26} Dan. 7^9 Ass. Mos. 4^2 Test. Lev. 5^1 Rev. 4^2 sqq. The wheels thereof as the shining sun (E). G^g τροχὸς ὡς ἡλίου λάμποντος. The expression goes back to Dan. 7^9 גלגלוהי נור דלק = τροχοὶ αὐτοῦ πῦρ καιόμενον.   Vision of cherubim. G^g reads ὄρος, corrupt possibly for ὅρασις. E = ὀπός (from ὄψ) 'the voice'.   19. Cf. Dan. 7^{10}.   Streams of flaming fire (E). G^g 'flaming streams of fire'.   20. The Great Glory. Cf. 102^3 T. Lev. 3^4. Whiter, &c. On the brightness that surrounds the throne cf. Ps. 104^2 Dan. 7^9 Jam. 1^{17} Rev. 4^3. See K.A.T.^{3} 353.   21. Enter. + 'into this house', G^g. By reason of the magnificence and glory (G^g). E = 'of the Magnificent and Glorious One'; but it is probably corrupt.   22. Could draw nigh. Cf. 3 Macc. 2^{15} 1 Tim. 6^{16}. Ten thousand times, &c., Dan. 7^{10}. He needed no counsellor. Cf. Sir. 42^{21} οὐδὲ προσεδεήθη οὐδενὸς συμβούλου = לא צריך לכל מבין. So E by a slight change. As it stands it = 'He needed no counsel'. Here, since G^g has

no counsellor.   23. And the most holy ones who were nigh to Him did not leave by night nor depart from Him.   24. And until then I had been prostrate on my face, trembling: and the Lord called me with His own mouth, and said to me: 'Come hither, Enoch, and hear my word.'   25. ⌈And one of the holy ones came to me and waked me⌉, and He made me rise up and approach the door: and I bowed my face downwards.

XV. 1. And He answered and said to me, and I heard His voice: 'Fear not, Enoch, thou righteous man and scribe of righteousness: approach hither and hear my voice.   2. And go, say to ⌈the Watchers of heaven⌉, who have sent thee to intercede ⌈for them: "You should intercede⌉ for men, and not men for you: 3. Wherefore have ye left the high, holy, and eternal heaven, and lain with women, and defiled yourselves with the daughters of men and taken to yourselves wives, and done like the children of earth, and begotten giants (as your) sons.   4. And though ye were holy, spiritual, living the eternal life, you have defiled yourselves with the blood of women, and have begotten (children) with the blood of flesh, and, as the children of men, have lusted

---

πᾶς λόγος αὐτοῦ ἔργον, it is probable that the two texts are both defective and complementary. At all events 2 Enoch 33⁴ has: 'My wisdom is My counsellor, and. My word is reality,' and seems dependent on the present passage.   23. The most holy ones. So G^g. E^a has 'the holiness of the holy ones'.   24. Prostrate (G^g). E = περίβλημα, but is internally corrupt for περιβεβλημένος. With 'prostrate on my face, trembling' cf. Dan. 8^{17} 'I was affrighted and fell on my face': 2 Enoch 21² 'I was afraid and fell on my face': Luke 24⁵.   Hear my word (G^g). E 'to My holy word' reading ἅγιον for ἄκουσον.   25. Bowed (G^g). E reads 'ëneṣer (= 'I looked') corrupt for 'aṣànĕn = 'bowed'.

XV. 1. And ²⁰ G^g. > E. Scribe of righteousness. See 12³.   2. And go, say (E). G^g 'go and say'. The Watchers of heaven. > G^g.   For them: You should intercede. > G^g through hmt. Cf. 9¹⁰ note.   3. Cf. 12⁴ Jude 6.   4–7. For man as mortal and dwelling upon the earth wedlock is appointed that so the race may continue to exist: but for the angels who are immortal and dwell in the heaven such commingling is contrary to their nature and involves pollution and guilt.   4. Spiritual, living the eternal life (E). G^g 'and spirits, living, eternal'. Here E appears to be right. 'Living' by itself would be meaningless as qualifying 'spirits'. Cf. ver. 6. αἰώνια is simply a rendering of לְעֹלָם, which latter world is to be connected with חיין before it as in E. With the blood ¹⁰ (G^g). E badība (= 'with') corrupt for badama = G^g.   As the children of men. G^g E read ἐν αἵματι ἀνθρώπων = בדם אנשׁ corrupt for בִּבְנֵי נָשָׁא = ὥσπερ after flesh and blood as those ⌜also⌝ do who die and perish. 5. Therefore have I given them wives also that they might impregnate them, and beget children by them, that thus nothing might be wanting to them on earth.   6. But you were ⌜formerly⌝ spiritual, living the eternal life, and immortal for all generations of the world.   7. And therefore I have not appointed wives for you; for as for the spiritual ones of the heaven, in heaven is their dwelling.   8. And now, the giants, who are produced from the spirits and flesh, shall be called evil spirits upon the earth, and on the earth shall be their dwelling.   9. Evil spirits have proceeded from their bodies; because they are born from men, ⌜and⌝ from the holy watchers is their beginning and primal origin; ⌜they shall be evil spirits on earth, and⌝ evil spirits shall they be called.   [10. As for the spirits of heaven, in heaven shall be their dwelling, but as for the spirits of the earth which were born upon the earth, on the earth shall be their dwelling.]   11. And the spirits of the giants afflict, oppress,

υἱοὶ τῶν ἀνθρώπων. Cf. ὥσπερ υἱοὶ τῆς γῆς in the preceding verse. ἐπεθυμήσατε cannot be construed with ἐν τῷ αἵματι unless it represents some Semitic idiom as ב נצא. If it could, it would mean bloodthirstiness, an idea quite foreign to the context. And lusted after. + 'and done' E.   5. Nothing ... to them. E^{gts} read balā'elēbōn (= ἐν αὐταῖς)—corrupt for kuĕllū lōmū (as Flemming suggests) = τῶν αὐτοῖς. 6. Spiritual, living the eternal life (E). G^s as in v. 4. And immortal (G^s). E with the exception of m omits 'and'.   8, 9. The union of angels and the daughters of men will give birth to a new order of beings, i.e. giants, and from these giants when they die will proceed evil spirits, i.e. demons, and these will have the earth for their habitation. Observe that the evil activities of these demons are not restrained or forbidden as those of their parents, for the latter were thrown into chains immediately on the death of the giants, their children.   8. From the spirits (E^{st} G^{as}). All other MSS. of E = 'from the body'. On these verses cf. Justin. Apol. xxii, quoted in the note on 9^{8, 9} Tertull. Apol. xxii 'Quomodo de angelis quibusdam sua sponte corruptis corruptior gens daemonum evaserit ... apud litteras sanctas ordo cognoscitur'. In Lact. Instit. ii. 15, the demons are regarded purely as wicked angels. Shall be called evil spirits (E G^s). G^s defective and corrupt πνεύματα ἰσχυρά. 9. From men (G^s). G^s E 'from those above'. Beginning (E). G^{as} read ἡ ἀρχὴ τῆς κτίσεως αὐτῶν. They shall be ... earth (E G^s). > G^s.   10. Of the earth (E). G^s 'on the earth'. G^s omits v. 10. This verse is merely a repetition of phrases found in verses 7, 8.   11. Afflict. G^s E read νεφέλας = ענני, a corruption probably of מעני = 'afflict'. G^s reads νεμόμενα = 'laying waste'. Beer takes νεμόμενα in the sense of destroy, attack, do battle, and work destruction on the earth, and cause trouble: they take no food, ⌈but nevertheless hunger⌉ and thirst, and cause offences.   12. And these spirits shall rise up against the children of men and against the women, because they have proceeded ⌈from them⌉.

XVI. 1. From the days of the slaughter and destruction and death ⌈of the giants⌉, from the souls of whose flesh the spirits, having gone forth, shall destroy without incurring judgement —thus shall they destroy until the day of the consummation, the great ⌈judgement⌉ in which the age shall be consummated, over the Watchers and the godless, yea, shall be wholly consummated."   2. And now as to the Watchers who have sent thee to intercede for them, who had been ⌈aforetime⌉ in heaven, (say to them):   3. "You have been in heaven, but ⌈all⌉ the mysteries had not yet been revealed to you, and you knew worthless ones, and these in the hardness of your hearts you

'pasturing' = רעין, a corruption of רעצין, 'laying waste,' which itself was corrupted into ענני = νεφέλας. Cause trouble (E). G^{g2} δρόμους ποιοῦντα where perhaps δρόμους is corrupt for τρόμους.   ⌈But nevertheless hunger⌉ (G^{g1}). Beer quotes Wellhausen, *Reste Arab. Heidenthums*^{2}, 149 sq., to the effect that the Jinns suffer from a devouring hunger and yet cannot eat. Instead of ἀσιτοῦντα, λιμάττοντα would be better. G^{g} adds καὶ φάσματα ποιοῦντα—possibly rightly.   Cause offences G^{g2}. E is internally corrupt, but by an easy emendation of Dillmann's = G^{g2}.   Against the women (E). G^{g2} = 'of the women'.

XVI. 1. The demons will not be punished till the final judgement. This doctrine likewise appears in the Book of Jubilees 10$^{5-11}$, and in the N.T. Cf. Matt. 8^{29}, 'Art Thou come hither to torment us *before the time*?'   Of the giants (E G^{g}). > G^{g2}. +Ναφηλείμ, οἱ ἰσχυροὶ τῆς γῆς, οἱ μεγάλοι ὀνομαστοί G^{g2}. These are derived from Gen. 6^{4}. Ναφη-

λείμ is a transliteration of נפלים, and is thus a doublet of τῶν γιγάντων preceding, οἱ ἰσχ. τῆς γῆς is an expansion of הגברים, and οἱ μεγ. ὀνομαστοί of אנשי השם. A different nomenclature is given in G^{g} 7^{2} (see note in loc.), but that passage is derived from a Noah Apocalypse.   From the souls of whose flesh (E^{emg} G^{g}). Here *emy* in E alone preserve the true reading. though 'ĕmnafsät must be changed into 'ĕmnafsäta. *g* reads 'ĕmnafseta, which is an early corruption of the latter. All the rest are still further corrupt. We have here a Semitic idiom which shows itself clearly in G^{g} ἀφ' ὧν ... ἐκ τῆς ψυχῆς τῆς σαρκὸς αὐτῶν = די מנפש בסרהן = 'from the souls of whose flesh'.   2. Aforetime (E). > G^{g2}. 3. This statement is the basis of Clem. Alex. *Strom.* ed. Dindorf, iii. 9 οἱ ἄγγελοι ἐκεῖνοι οἱ τὸν ἄνω κλῆρον εἰληχότες, κατολισθήσαντες εἰς ἡδονάς, ἐξεῖπον τὰ ἀπόρρητα ταῖς γυναιξὶν ὅσα τε εἰς γνῶσιν αὐτῶν ἀφῖκτο. E wrongly inserts 'and now' at the beginning of have made known to the women, and through these mysteries women and men work much evil on earth." 4. Say to them therefore: "You have no peace."'

XVII–XXXVI. *Enoch's Journeys through the Earth and Sheol.*

XVII–XIX. *The First Journey.*

XVII. 1. And they took ⌜and brought⌝ me to a place in which those who were there were like flaming fire, and when they wished, they appeared as men. 2. And they brought me to the place of darkness, and to a mountain the point of whose summit reached to heaven. 3. And I saw the places of the luminaries ⌜and the treasuries of the stars⌝ and of the thunder, ⌜and⌝ in the uttermost depths, where were a fiery bow and arrows and their quiver, ⌜and a fiery sword⌝ and all the lightnings. 4. And they took me to the living waters, and to the fire of the

---

this verse. ⌜All⌝ (G^g). > E. 4. No peace: see 5^4 (note).

XVII–XIX. These chapters are certainly foreign to the rest of this section. They are full of Greek elements. We have references in 17^{5,6} to the Pyriphlegethon, Styx, Acheron and Cocytus: in 17$^{5, 7, 8}$ 18^{10}, to the Ocean Stream: in 17^6 to Hades in the west. Again, 18$^{6-9}$ is a duplicate account of 24$^{1-3}$; 18$^{12-16}$ a duplicate account of 21$^{1-6}$, and 18^{11} of 21$^{7-10}$, though in the last case there are important divergencies. Again, according to 15^{12}-16 an end was set to the destructive agencies of the fallen angels by their imprisonment (cf. 10$^{11-14}$ 14^5), whereas according to 19^1 the spirits of the fallen angels are represented as seducing mankind to sacrifice to demons. Notwithstanding these chapters belong to the Enoch tradition.

XVII. 1. ⌜And brought⌝. Supplied from G^g. On the power of assuming different forms cf. 19^1 2 Cor. 11^{14}. 2. Of darkness (G^g ζοφώδη). E = γνοφώδη taking γνόφος in the sense of 'whirlwind' or 'tempest' as in Job 27^{20} (LXX). On the idea in E cf. Job 37^9. The point of whose summit (E). G^g 'whose summit'. 3. Places of the luminaries. These may be the 'chambers of the luminaries'; cf. 41^5. ⌜And the treasuries of the stars⌝. Supplied from G^g Of the thunder. Cf. 41^3 44 59 60$^{13-15}$ and notes. In the uttermost depths = εἰς τὰ ἄκρα βάθη. So I emend E which = εἰς τὰ ἄκρα ἐν τῷ βάθει αὐτοῦ (?). G^g reads εἰς τὰ ἀεροβάθη, 'in the depths of air.' Fiery bow—the bow with which the lightnings are shot; cf. Ps. 7^{12} Hab. 3^9 Lam. 2^4 3^{12}. Arrows, i. e. the lightnings; cf. Ps. 18^{14} 77$^{17, 18}$. Their quiver. Cf. Lam. 3^{13}. And a fiery sword (E). >G^g. Cf. Ps. 7^{12} Deut. 32^{41}. 4. Took (E). G^g 'brought'. Living waters. So G^g and superscription in *g*. All other MSS. of E read 'waters of life'. Cf. 'fountain of life' in Ps. 36^9 Prov. 10^{11} 13^{14} 14^{27} 16^{22} Rev. 22^{17}. The expression 'water of life' is found in the Babylonian myths. In the

Sect. I]   *Chapters XVI. 4—XVIII. 2*   39

west, which receives every setting of the sun.   5. And I came to a river of fire in which the fire flows like water and discharges itself into the great sea towards the west.   6. I saw the great rivers and came to the great ⌜river and to the great⌝ darkness, and went to the place where no flesh walks.   7. I saw the mountains of the darkness of winter and the place whence all the waters of the deep flow.   8. I saw the mouths of all the rivers of the earth and the mouth of the deep.

XVIII. 1. I saw the treasuries of all the winds; I saw how He had furnished with them the whole creation and the firm foundations of the earth.   2. And I saw the corner-stone of the earth: I saw the four winds which bear [the earth and] the

Adapa Myth it is parallel to the 'bread of life', while in the Descent of Ishtar, Ishtar is sprinkled with it before she leaves the lower world. See *K.A.T.³* 524 sq., 562.   **Fire of the west**: see 23 (notes).   **Which receives every setting of the sun**. Blau, in the *Jewish Encyc.* v. 582, explains this fire in the west to be Gehenna. He says the sun receives its fire from it, and he quotes Baba Bathra 84ᵃ. But this is quite wrong. Gehenna is not in the west in Enoch, and the passage in the Talmud merely says that the sun is red in the evening because it passes the gate of Gehenna, just as it is red in the morning because it passes the roses of the Garden of Eden.   **Receives** (E). Gˢ παρέχον.   **5. River of fire**. The Πυριφλεγέθων.   **Great sea**. Ὠκεανός or the Great Ocean Stream.   **Towards the west** (E). Gˢ 'of the west'.   **6. I saw** (Gˢ). E 'and I saw'.   **The great rivers**. Styx, Acheron, and Cocytus.   **River and to the great**. Supplied from Gˢ.   **No flesh** (Gˢ). E 'all flesh'.   **7. I saw** (Gˢ). E 'and I saw'. This omission of the copula is more in keeping with Aramaic idiom.   **The mountains of the darkness** (E) = τὰ ὄρη τῶν γνόφων—a phrase that is most probably derived from Jer. 13¹⁶ הָרֵי נָשֶׁף where the Targ. Jon. has טוּרֵי קְבַל. In the original then we should have had טורי קבלא. But in the text before the translator טורי was corrupted into רוחי, whence Gˢ has τοὺς ἀνέμους. We must suppose that the true reading was inserted in the margin and was reproduced as such in the Greek. Hence E.   **The mountains** are probably those which the Babylonian Cosmogony represents as standing at the ends of the earth in the neighbourhood of the 'springs of the great deep', which are referred to in the next line.   **8. I saw** (Gˢ). E 'and I saw'. See note on v. 7.   **Mouths of, &c.**, i. e. Oceanus.

XVIII. **1. I saw** (Gˢ). E 'and I saw'. So also in the next sentence.   **Treasuries of all the winds**: see 41⁴ (note) 60¹¹, ¹²; also 34–36.   **Foundations of the earth**. A frequent phrase in the O.T. Cf. 2 Sam. 22¹⁶ Job 38⁴ Ps. 18¹⁵ 82⁵, &c.   **I saw** ²⁰ (Gˢ). E 'and I saw'.   **2. The cornerstone**: Job 38⁶.   **I saw** ²⁰ (Gˢ). E 'and I saw'.   **The four winds which bear [the earth and] the firmament**. Gˢ E have τοὺς τέσσαρας ἀνέμους τὴν γῆν βαστάζοντας καὶ τὸ στερέωμα. Gunkel, *Zum religionsgesch. Verständnis*, firmament of the heaven. 3. ⌜And I saw how the winds stretch out the vaults of heaven⌝, and have their station between heaven and earth: ⌜these are the pillars of the heaven⌝. 4. I saw the winds of heaven which turn and bring the circumference of the sun and all the stars to their setting. 5. I saw the winds on the earth carrying the clouds: I saw ⌜the paths of the angels: I saw⌝ at the end of the earth the firmament of the heaven above. 6. And I proceeded and saw a place which burns day and night, where there are seven mountains of magnificent stones, three towards the east, and three towards the south. 7. And as for those towards the east ⟨one⟩ was of

p. 46 (n. 6) proposes to read τῆς γῆς instead of τὴν γῆν, and to omit καί. Hence 'the four winds of the earth bearing the firmament'. But the τῆς γῆς or τὴν γῆν seems wholly wrong here. It could have arisen in the Aramaic through a dittograph. Thus ἰδον τοὺς τέσσαρας ἀνέμους τὴν γῆν βαστάζοντας = חדת רוחיא ארבע ארעא מסובן where ארעא is a dittograph of ארבע. Hence 'the four winds which bear the firmament'. 3. And I saw ... heaven (E). > G^g through hmt. These are ... heaven (E). > G^g through hmt. Pillars of the heaven. The expression is from Job 26^{11}, but the idea in the text is not biblical nor Babylonian. 4. I saw (G^g). E 'and I saw'. Turn and bring, &c. Cf. 72^5 73^2. Bring ... to ... setting (E) = δύνοντας in an active sense. G^g has διανεύοντας, which Dillmann emends into δινεύοντας, 'whirling,' but this idea is already conveyed by στρέφοντας. Swete proposes διανύοντας; but this would require τρόχον, whereas the context requires τροχόν (cf. 73^2). 5. Carrying the clouds (t, β), but G^g gmqu read ἐν τῇ νεφέλῃ. An explanation of the difficulties suggested in Job 36^{29} 37^{16}. The paths of the angels: I saw (E). > G^g through hmt. At the end of the earth the firmament, &c.

The ends of the firmament of heaven rest on the ends of the earth; cf. 33^2; the vault of heaven is supported by the winds, 18^2,^{3}. 6-9. This is another version of what is recounted in 24$^{1-3}$. 6. And saw a place G^g: i.e. καὶ εἶδον τόπον for which E corruptly reads εἰς τὸν νότον. The seven mountains are in the NW. Cf. 77$^{3-4}$ 70^3. Indeed the closing words of this verse imply that these mountains are in the NW.—three extending towards the south and three towards the east from the NW. corner where the seventh stands. Seven mountains. These mountains, as I have shown in the note preceding, are in the NW. They and the Garden lie in the same quarter, the Garden to the east of the seven mountains, 32$^{1-2}$: according to 70^3 the Garden lies in the NW., and so apparently in 77^3. These mountains are bounded by flaming mountain ridges 24^1 (18^9). In 24$^{1-3}$ the seven mountains are as here in the NW., while the verses that follow 24^4 sqq. refer in some way to the Garden; for they speak of the tree of life. Again, it is worth observing that in 77^3 the seas of waters are said to adjoin the Garden. The same idea underlies 60$^{22-23}$. The Jewish ideas on these matters might be represented therefore thus:—

coloured stone, and one of pearl, and one of jacinth, and those towards the south of red stone. 8. But the middle one reached to heaven like the throne of God, of alabaster, and the summit of the throne was of sapphire. 9. And I saw a flaming fire. And beyond these mountains 10. Is a region the end of the

```
                                    N
The Great Mountain: Three Mountains: Garden of Righteousness: Seas of Waters

Three
Mountains

W                                                                        E
```

With the above sketch, which represents the views of all the Sections of Enoch, it is difficult to reconcile the statement in 60⁸, where a waste wilderness named Dendáin is said to lie to the east of the Garden. See note on 32¹. This idea of the seven mountains seems to be originally derived from Babylonian sources, and had ultimately to do with the seven planet gods, the sevenfold division of the heaven and the like division of the earth, six-sevenths land and one-seventh sea, 4 Ezra 6⁴², the seven great rivers and seven great islands, 1 Enoch 77⁵,⁸. See *K.A.T.*³ 615–619. With the mountains in our text those mentioned in 52² 77⁴ may originally have been connected. Three¹⁰ (E). > G⁸. 7. Jacinth (?) E = λάσεως. This may be corrupt for λάσπιδος (= ישפה) 'jasper'. But since τaθev is the reading of G⁸, the Ethiopic translator probably found merely a corrupt form which suggested some derivative of λᾶσθαι as λατικοῦ. This word taken in conjunction with τaθev might point to ὑακίνθου or ἰανθίνου as Diels suggests. Beer takes it to be a transliteration of פטדה 'topaz'. Where the ideas of the various stones are drawn from cannot be said with certainty. Cf. Ezek. 28¹³; *K.A.T.*³ 619, 624. The difficulty of determining this is enhanced by the difficulty of identifying the stones in question. 8. Like the throne of God. In 25³ it is declared to be the throne of God. This mountain of God, which as we have seen was conceived to be in the NW., is already referred to in Is. 14¹³, where it is said to be in the N. The throne of God in Ezekiel 1²⁶ which is borne of cherubim comes from the N., as appears from 1⁴; cf. Job 37²². This throne is 'the holy mountain of God' in Ezek. 28¹⁴,¹⁶, where 'stones of fire' are associated with the mountain of God, as in our text 18⁹ 24¹. Indeed in Ezek. 28¹³⁻¹⁴ the Garden or Paradise and the Mountain of God are already associated as in Enoch, or identified. Alabaster. G⁸ φουκα, i.e. נופך. Sapphire. Ezek. 1²⁶. 9. And beyond these (G⁸ κἀ(πέ)κεινα τῶν . . . τούτων). E corrupt καὶ ἃ ἐπὶ ἐκεῖνων τῶν ὀρέων, for kuëllû is corrupt for 'ëllû, but attests the same text. The statement in 24¹ would lead us to connect this clause with what precedes, but the καί is against it. Hence I have combined it with the next verse. But the former may be right. The seven mountains are encircled with fire—according to 24¹ by a mountain range of fire. In the translation I always follow G⁸ in the case of ἐπέκεινα as it great earth: there the heavens were completed. 11. And I saw a deep abyss, with columns ⌜of heavenly fire, and among them I saw columns⌝ of fire fall, which were beyond measure alike towards the height and towards the depth. 12. And beyond that abyss I saw a place which had no firmament of the heaven above, and no firmly founded earth beneath it: there was no water upon it, and no birds, but it was a waste and horrible place. 13. I saw there seven stars like great burning mountains, and to me, when I inquired regarding them, 14. The angel said: 'This place is the end of heaven and earth: this has become a prison for the stars and the host of heaven. 15. And the stars which roll over the fire are they which have transgressed the commandment of the Lord in the beginning of their rising, because they did not come forth at their appointed times. 16. And He was wroth with them, and bound them till the time when their guilt should be consummated (even) ⌜for ten thousand years⌝.'

XIX. 1. And Uriel said to me: 'Here shall stand the angels who have connected themselves with women, and their spirits assuming many different forms are defiling mankind and shall lead them astray into sacrificing to demons ⌜as gods⌝, (here shall

is always misrendered in E; cf. 18^{12} 24^2 $30^{1,3}$ 31^2. 10. The same idea as in 18^5 33^2. 11. This may be the final place of punishment for the fallen angels. If so, cf. 10^6, ^{13} 18^{11} 21^{7-10} 90^{24}. Of heavenly fire; cf. Gen. 19^{24} Ps. 11^6 Ezek. 38^{22}. > τοῦ πυρὸς τοῦ οὐρανοῦ καὶ ἴδον ἐν αὐτοῖς στύλους through hmt. G^s. Height... depth (E). ∞ G^s. 12–16. This place of punishment for the disobedient stars is again described in 21^{1-6}. It is already occupied. 13–16. The stars are really personified as animate beings. 13. And to me, when I inquired regarding them (περὶ ὧν πυνθανομένῳ μοι G^s). E corrupt = καὶ ὡς πνεύματα πυνθανόμενά μου. 14. Host of heaven, צבא השמים; cf. 1 Kings 22^{19}, but specially Is. 24^{21}. 15. The Lord (G^s). E 'God'. The stars are regarded as conscious beings and are accordingly punished. The ἀστέρες πλανῆται of Jude 13 recall this verse. Rising. +ὅτι τόπος ἔξω τοῦ οὐρανοῦ κενός ἐστιν G^s—a gloss on the last clause of ver. 12. 16. Ten thousand years (G^s ἐνιαυτῶν μυρίων). E corrupt = ἐνιαυτῷ μυστηρίου. Cf. 21^6.

XIX. See introductory note on xvii–xix, p. 38. 1. Sacrificing to demons; cf. Deut. 32^{17} Ps. 106^{37} Bar. 4^7. This passage and 99^7 are probably the source of Tertullian, De Idol. iv 'Henoch praedicens omnia elementa, omnem mundi censum, quae caelo, quae mari, quae terra continentur, in idolatriam versuros daemonas et spiritus desertorum angelorum, ut pro Deo adverthey stand), till ⌜the day of⌝ the great judgement in which they shall be judged till they are made an end of. 2. And the women also of the angels who went astray shall become sirens.' 3. And I, Enoch, alone saw the vision, the ends of all things: and no man shall see as I have seen.

XX. *Names and Functions of the Seven Archangels.*

XX. 1. And these are the names of the holy angels who watch. 2. Uriel, one of the holy angels, who is over the world and over Tartarus. 3. Raphael, one of the holy angels, who is over the spirits of men. 4. Raguel, one of the holy angels who †takes vengeance on† the world of the luminaries. 5. Michael, one of the holy angels, to wit, he that is set over the best part of mankind ⌜and⌝ over chaos. 6. Sara-

sus Deum consecrarentur.' As gods (E). > G^s. Day of the great judgement: see 45^2 (note). The day of (E). > G^s. 2. The women will be subjected to the same punishment as the fallen angels; cf. 10^{13}. The women ... of the angels. G^s reproduces here literally an Aramaic idiom. αἱ γυναῖκες αὐτῶν τῶν παραβάντων ἀγγέλων = נשיהון די מלאכיא די חטו. E is corrupt, reading 'ashitôn (ymtu, β), which should be emended into lasehûtàn = G^s. Sirens (G^s εἰς σειρῆνας). E = ὡς εἰρηναῖαι, a corruption of G^s. σειρήν is a rendering in the LXX of ענה in Mic. 1^8 Jer. 27 (50)^{39}; cf. Is. 13^{21}, and of תן in Job 30^{29}, Is. 34^{13}, &c. 3. The ends of all things. Quoted by Clemens Alex. *Eclog. Proph.* (Dind. iii. 456) ὁ Δανιὴλ λέγει ὁμοδοξῶν τῷ Ἐνὼχ τῷ εἰρηκότι 'καὶ εἶδον τὰς ὕλας πάσας', and by Origen, *De Princ.* iv. 35 'scriptum namque est in eodem libello dicente Enoch "universas materias perspexi"'.

XX. Of the seven archangels given in this chapter, only four—Uriel, Raphael, Raguel, and Michael—are mentioned as acting in 21-36. In the original probably all were men-

tioned. Cf. 81^5. 1. This verse is defective in G$^{s\,1,\,2}$. The latter omits it, while the former reads simply 'angels of the powers'. But part of the verse is preserved in ver. 8 in both, i.e. ὀνόματα ζ ἀρχαγγέλων. Who watch: see 12^2 (note). 2. The province assigned to Uriel serves to explain such passages as 19 21$^{5,\,9}$ 27^2 33$^{3,\,4}$. Cf. his rôle as overseer of the world in 72 sqq.; 4 Ezra 4^1. Tartarus (G$^{s\,1,\,2}$). E = τρόμου corrupt. 3. Raphael: see 10$^{4,\,7}$. The definition here given is vague, but suits admirably in 22$^{3,\,6}$. In 32^6, however, Raphael discharges duties which according to 20^7 should belong to Gabriel. 4. Raguel. There seems to be no connexion between the name of the angel and the duty assigned to him. Cf. 23^4. †Takes vengeance on†. See note on 23^4. Of the luminaries (G$^{s\,1,\,2}$). E 'and on the luminaries'. 5. Michael is the guardian angel of Israel: so in Dan. 10$^{13,\,21}$ 12^1, and likewise universally: see Weber, *Jüd. Theol.* 170: according to this verse Michael is the right speaker in 24-27, where he instructs Enoch on the blessings that are to befall the chosen people. And over chaos qâêl, one of the holy angels, who is set over the spirits, who sin in the spirit.   7. Gabriel, one of the holy angels, who is over Paradise and the serpents and the Cherubim.   8. Remiel, one of the holy angels, whom God set over those who rise.

XXI–XXXVI. *The Second Journey of Enoch.*
XXI. *Preliminary and final place of punishment of the fallen angels (stars).*

XXI. 1. And I proceeded to where things were chaotic.   2. And I saw there something horrible: I saw neither a heaven above nor a firmly founded earth, but a place chaotic and horrible. 3. And there I saw seven stars of the heaven bound together in it, like great mountains and burning with fire.   4. Then I said: 'For what sin are they bound, and on what account have they been cast in hither?'   5. Then said Uriel, one of the holy angels, who was with me, and was chief over them, and said: 'Enoch, why dost thou ask, and why art thou eager for

($G^{s\,1,\,2}$). Ἐπὶ τῷ λαῷ.   6. **Saraqâêl** (E). $G^{s\,1,\,2}$ Sariel   **Spirits.** + 'of mankind' E.   7. Gabriel should be the speaker in 32 according to this verse.   8. This verse is preserved only in $G^{s\,2}$, but it is genuine as is shown by the preservation of the number ἑπτά in $G^{s\,1,\,2}$. Here $G^{s\,1,\,2}$ add 'seven names of archangels'.   **Remiel.** Cf. 2 Bar. 55³ 4 Ezra 4³⁶ Sibyl. 2²¹⁵ Apoc. El. 10⁵⁻¹¹.

XXI. 1–6. This place of preliminary punishment of the disobedient stars has been already described in 18¹²⁻¹⁶. There is no material difference between the two accounts.   1. Origen. (*De Princ.* iv. 35) has cited this verse: 'Ambulavi usque ad imperfectum.'   2. **Chaotic.** So $G^{s\,1,\,2}$: so also E by the emendation of zakōna into za'akō (Flemming).   3. **Together** (E). $G^{s\,1,\,2}$ read instead καὶ ἐρ(ρ)ιμμένους, 'and cast down'.   5. **And was chief over them** ($G^{s\,1,\,2}$). In E all MSS. but g read 'he was chief over me'. g reads 'and was chief over me'. To be emended as in 24⁶ 72¹ 74².   **Why art thou eager for the truth?** ($G^{s\,1,\,2}$—περὶ τίνος τὴν ἀλήθειαν φιλοσπουδεῖς;). G is clearly here a rendering of אִצְבָּא יַצִּיבָא. This is the actual phrase in Dan. 7¹⁶ יַצִּיבָא אִבְעֵה, where both the LXX and Theod. have τὴν ἀκρίβειαν ἐζήτουν. A modified form of the phrase recurs in 25¹ διὰ τί θέλεις τὴν ἀλήθειαν μαθεῖν; = לְיַצְּבָא אִצְבָּא—which construction occurs also in Dan. 7¹⁹, i.e. צְבִית לְיַצָּבָא where the LXX rightly has ἤθελον ἐξακριβάσασθαι, and Theod. less accurately ἐζήτουν ἀκριβῶς. Now that we have determined the Aramaic and Greek renderings, we turn to E. First of all in 21⁵ E = περὶ τίνος ἀκριβῶς καὶ φιλοσπουδεῖς ('about whom inquirest thou accurately and art eager?'), and in 25¹ διὰ τί ἀκριβῶς μαθεῖν ('wherefore dost thou inquire accurately to learn?'). Now if E had the text of G^s before him such renderings would be extraordinary; for E can quite easily and the truth? 6. These are of the number of the stars ⌜of heaven⌝ which have transgressed the commandment of the Lord, and are bound here till ten thousand years, the time entailed by their sins, are consummated.' 7. And from thence I went to another place, which was still more horrible than the former, and I saw a horrible thing: a great fire there which burnt and blazed, and the place was cleft as far as the abyss, being full of great descending columns of fire: neither its extent or magnitude could I see, nor could I conjecture. 8. Then I said: 'How fearful is the place and how terrible to look upon!' 9. Then Uriel answered me, one of the holy angels who was with me, and said unto me: 'Enoch, why hast thou such fear and affright?' And I answered: 'Because of this fearful place, and because of the spectacle of the pain.' 10. And he said ⌜unto me⌝: 'This place is the prison of the angels, and here they will be imprisoned for ever.'

rightly translate ἀλήθεια: see 10^{16} 11^2 15^1 or ἀληθινός 15^1 27^2. Hence we must conclude that in 21^5 he had περὶ τίνος τὴν ἀκρίβειαν φιλοσπουδεῖς, and in 25^1 διὰ τί θέλεις τὴν ἀκρίβειαν μαθεῖν. This is the rendering in the Ethiopic version of Dan. 7^{16}. In fact tajaqqa (in 21^5 25^1) and its derivations are never, so far as I can discover, used as renderings of ἀλήθεια. Our translator therefore had τὴν ἀκρίβειαν before him and had a difficulty in rendering it exactly, though other Ethiopic translators had not. 6. Of heaven ($G^{g 1, 2}$). > E. Ten thousand years ($G^{g 1, 2}$). This period was assigned as one of punishment among the Greeks for sinful souls. See Dieterich, *Nekyia*, 113 sq., 156. But compare Rohde, *Psyche*², ii. 179. E reads 'âlam = 'age' corrupt for 'âm = ἔτη. The time entailed by their sins ($G^{g 1, 2}$ τὸν χρόνον τῶν ἁμαρτημάτων αὐτῶν). This is clearer than E 'the number of the days entailed by their sins'. 7–10. This is the final place of punishment for the fallen angels. It is distinct from that in 18^{12-16} 19^{1-2} 21^{1-6}, where the seven stars are already undergoing punishment in the preliminary place of punishment. This final place of punishment is again mentioned in 10^6 18^{11} 54^6 90^{24-25}. In it the fallen angels and the faithless angelic rulers are punished for evermore. 7. Conjecture (m $G^{g 1, 2}$). All other MSS. give corruptions of 'ajjĕnō. Before this rare word all MSS. add a gloss naṣĕrō = 'to look upon'. 8. The place. Here, as frequently, E renders the Greek article by a demonstrative, 'this place.' Terrible. So $G^{g 1, 2}$ δεινός. E = ὀδυνηρός. 9. Uriel (E). > $G^{g 1, 2}$. Was with me. Seventeen MSS., including four out of the best five, add here 'and (> some MSS.) he answered me'. This I have emended into 'and I answered', and added it after 'affright', where it occurs in $G^{g 1, 2}$ but is lost in E. The spectacle of the pain (E, where again before 'pain' there is the demonstrative for the Greek article. G^g τῆς προσόψεως τῆς δεινῆς = 'the terrible spectacle'. 10. Unto me (E). > G^g. For ever. Here G^g

Sheol or the Underworld.

XXII. 1. And thence I went to another place, and he showed me in the west ⌜another⌝ great and high mountain [and] of hard rock.

E

2. And there was in it †four†

G^g

2. And there were †four†

has a dittograph, μέχρι ενος (i.e. αἰῶνος) εἰς τὸν αἰῶνα.

XXII. This chapter contains a very detailed description of Sheol or Hades. According to this writer Sheol is situated in the far west according to Babylonian (*K.A.T.*³ 636), Greek, and Egyptian ideas, and in this respect the writer runs counter to the views of the Hebrews who placed Sheol in the underworld. In all the other sections of the book the Hebrew conception prevails. This is the most ancient account of the doctrine of Sheol from the Pharisaic or Chasid standpoint, but clearly this doctrine cannot have leaped into life fullgrown as it appears here, but must already have passed through several stages of development. Hades is no longer here, as in the O.T., a place mainly of a semi-conscious state of existence where the only distinctions that prevailed were social and not moral; but has already become essentially a place of conscious existence, where everything is determined by moral distinctions and moral distinctions alone. See 63¹⁰ for the history of this doctrine, and my *Eschatology*, pp. 426-7, for an enumeration of the various stages of development through which this conception passed. So far as we may infer from 1–36, the doctrine of this chapter must be limited to Israelites and their progenitors from Adam, just as only Israelites are taken account of in Dan. 12. 1. [And.] Bracketed as an intrusion in E. Not in G⁵. 2. †Four†. There are four divisions, according to the text of this verse, in

Hades: two for the righteous, vv. 5-9, and two for the wicked, vv. 10-13. But I cannot help regarding the text as here corrupt. In 22⁸⁻⁹ in G⁵ Enoch asks the angel about all the hollow places, and the angel replies: 'These *three*,' &c. In E, however, owing to the mention of four places in 22², the scribe was conscious of a contradiction in the text, and accordingly added 'regarding it and' before the words 'regarding all the hollow places'. This addition referred presumably to the fourth place *of which there is no description in the text*. If we examine the chapter further, our conviction as to the corruption of the numbers of the places grows in strength. In 22³⁻⁴ Enoch asks and is told the object of Sheol. In 22⁸⁻⁹ᵃ he asks and is told the object of the separation of the three chambers in Sheol. What follows is a detailed account of these chambers: the first for the righteous, 22⁹ᵇ, the second for sinners who have not met with retribution in this life, 22¹⁰⁻¹¹, and the third for those who have, 22¹²⁻¹³. All this is clear and consecutive. But the writer wished to introduce into this passage the idea, which is in some form common to all the sections of the book, that the souls of the righteous, who had fallen at the hands of sinners, claimed retribution in the spirit-world. Hence, after asking the object of Sheol, he turns aside for a moment to deal with the martyred righteous, and with a graphic touch draws the attention of the angel to a spirit that was demanding the vengeance of heaven on him

Sect. 1]   Chapter XXII. 1-4   47

E
hollow places, deep and wide and very smooth. †How† smooth are the hollow places and deep and dark to look at.

G^g
hollow places in it, deep and very smooth: †three† of them were dark and one bright and there was a fountain of water in its midst. And I said: '†How† smooth are these hollow places, and deep and dark to view.'

3. Then Raphael answered, one of the holy angels who was with me, and said unto me: 'These hollow places have been created for this very purpose, that the spirits of the souls of the dead should assemble therein, yea that all the souls of the children of men should assemble here.   4. And these places have been made to receive them till the day of their judgement and till their appointed period [till the period appointed], till the great judgement (comes) upon them.'

---

that wronged him, and asks: 'Whose spirit is this?' Abel stands here for a class—22$^{6-7}$—whose abode in Sheol is no doubt along with the rest of the righteous, 25^{9a}. Hence we conclude that there were originally only three places in Sheol mentioned in this chapter.   †Four† ... †three†. Read 'Three ... two'. See preceding note. Hollow. Twice in E the text = καλοί corrupt for κοῖλοι.   †How†. Since the angel, in reply, gives the object of Sheol, 'how' cannot be right: we expect 'why', 'wherefore', or 'for what purpose'. Hence, I suggest that מה (= πῶς) was corrupt for למה. Hence read 'for what purpose are these hollow places smooth and deep and dark to view?'   Hollow places (G^g = κοιλώματα). E = κυκλώματα, a corruption. Dark to view. This statement comes in strangely after that made in the preceding sentence that there was 'one bright'.   3-4. The object with which Sheol was made a place of assemblage for all the departed.   3. Hollow (G^g κοῖλοι). E = καλοί, corrupt. Have been created (E). G ἐκρίθησαν corrupt for ἐκτίσθησαν.   Spirits of the souls of the dead (G^g E^{ag}). Other MSS. corrupt.   4. Have been made. G^g E = ἐποίησαν corrupt for ἐποιήθησαν. To receive them (G^g εἰς ἐπισύνσχεσιν αὐτῶν—of which E is a free rendering). This seems to be the equivalent of the 'promptuaria' for departed souls in 4 Ezra 4^{35} 7^{35}, which are called 'habitacula' in 7^{85}. See our text 100^{4,5} note.   [Till the period appointed.] A dittograph.   5-7. These verses have hitherto been supposed to give a description of the first division of Sheol for righteous souls which in their life met with persecution and suffered a violent and undeserved death. These cry continually to God for vengeance on those who wronged them. In the time of the author many of the Chasidim must have perished in this way. This idea of

E

5. I saw the spirits of the children of men who were dead, and their voice went forth to heaven and made suit. 6. Then I asked Raphael the angel who was with me, and I said unto him: 'This spirit—whose is it whose voice goeth forth and maketh suit?'

Gᵍ

5. I saw ⟨the spirit of⟩ a dead man making suit, and his voice went forth to heaven and made suit. 6. And I asked Raphael the angel who was with me, and I said unto him: 'This spirit which maketh suit, whose is it, whose voice goeth forth and maketh suit to heaven?'

7. And he answered me saying: 'This is the spirit which went forth from Abel, whom his brother Cain slew, and he makes his suit against him till his seed is destroyed from the face of the earth, and his seed is annihilated from amongst the seed of men.'

E

8. Then I asked regarding it, and regarding all the **hollow places**: 'Why is one separated from the other?'

Gᵍ

8. Then I asked regarding all the **hollow places**: 'Why is one separated from the other?'

---

the righteous or of the angels crying for vengeance on the wicked is in some form common to all the Sections of this book. Cf. 9¹⁻³, 10, 11 22⁵⁻⁸ 47¹, ³ 89⁷⁶ 97³, ⁵ 99³, ¹⁶ 104³. Cf. Rev. 6¹⁰ 4 Ezra 4³⁶. *But these verses contain no description of a division in Sheol, but only an account of a soul demanding vengeance.* **5. Spirits of the children of men who were dead** (E). Gᵍ is defective and corrupt ἀνθρώπους νεκροὺς ἐντυγχάνοντος. Possibly vv. 5-6 refer only to a single spirit. To this ἐντυγχάνοντος points, and also ἡ φωνὴ αὐτοῦ in the next clause in Gᵍ. If this is right, as I have concluded above, there were only three places in all: the first for the righteous martyrs, 22⁵⁻⁷, and other righteous, 22⁹ᵇ, the second for sinners who had escaped punishment in life, 21¹⁰⁻¹¹, and the third for the sinners who had suffered in their life, 22¹²⁻¹³. This view derives support from 22⁹, 'The three places.' The text of 22² has been emended accordingly. **6-7.** Abel's spirit cries for the destruction of the seed of Cain. **6. Whose voice**: οὗ ... ἡ φωνὴ αὐτοῦ = קָלֶה ... דִּי. **7. Answered.** + 'and said to me' E, a doublet of the following word 'saying'. **8.** Enoch asks with what object was Sheol divided into three parts? His question deals not with three-fourths of Sheol but with all of it. περὶ τῶν κοιλωμάτων πάντων. **Hollow places.** E = κριμάτων, and Gᵍ κυκλωμάτων, both corrupt

[Sect. I]   *Chapter XXII. 5-11*   49

E

9. And he answered me and said unto me: 'These three have been made that the spirits of the dead might be separated. And such a division has been made (for) the spirits of the righteous, in which there is the bright spring of water. 10. And such has been made for sinners when they die and are buried in the earth and judgement has not been executed on them in their lifetime. 11. Here their spirits shall be set apart in this great pain till the great day of judgement and punishment and

G^g

9. And he answered me saying: 'These three have been made that the spirits of the dead might be separated. And this division has been made for the spirits of the righteous, in which there is the bright spring of water. 10. And this has been made for sinners when they die and are buried in the earth and judgement has not been executed upon them in their lifetime. 11. Here their spirits shall be set apart in this great pain, till the great day of judgement, scourgings, and torments of the accursed

---

for κοιλωμάτων.   9. The first division is for the souls of the righteous—both those who have been martyred and those who have not. **Spirits.** In E only n reads 'spirits', the rest give 'souls'. But the word nafs in E frequently means spirit as in 15¹² 69¹² 99⁷, as well as in verses 11, 12, 13 of this chapter. Hence I have rendered it 'spirit' in such cases. **In which.** Here G⁸ has οὗ ... ἐν αὐτῷ = בָהּ ... יִד. **The bright spring of water.** In E for 'bright' the text gives 'brightness' or 'light'. In the underworld, souls, according to the Greek Cults, Jewish, Hellenistic, and Christian literature, suffered from thirst: see Dieterich, *Nekyia*, 97 sqq. In the Greek Hades there was a spring of forgetfulness on the left, while on the right was the spring of memory—the cool water —ψυχρὸν ὕδωρ, by the drinking of which consciousness and memory were quickened, the first condition of the full

or blessed life. See Rohde, *Psyche*, ii. 2. 310, 390-391. The expression 'water of life' is found in Babylonian literature in the Adapa Myth and the Descent of Ishtar, *K.A.T.*³ 523 sqq. **10-11.** The second division is for those sinners who lived prosperously and escaped punishment in life, and finally attained to honourable burial. According to Hebrew and Greek ideas the privation of funeral rites was a great calamity, and involved, at least according to ancient ideas, inevitable suffering for the departed soul.   **10.** **And this.** In E bakama kamāhū is corrupt for wakamāhū = καὶ οὗτος. Here οὗτως is corrupt for οὗτος the demonstrative. The angel points to each division as he describes it. I have introduced this emendation into my translation of G⁵ in verses 9, 10, 12, 13. **11. Great pain.** Cf. 103⁷,⁸ Luke 16²³⁻²⁵. **Great day of judgement.** Cf. 45² n. **The accursed.** Here τῶν

E

torment of those who †curse† for ever, and retribution for their spirits. There He shall bind them for ever. 12. And such a division has been made for the spirits of those who make their suit, who make disclosures concerning their destruction, when they were slain in the days of the sinners. 13. Such has been made for the spirits of men who were not righteous but sinners, who were complete in transgression, and of the transgressors they shall be companions: but their spirits shall not be slain in the day of judgement nor shall they be raised from thence.' 14. Then

G^g

for ever, so that (there may be) retribution for their spirits. There He shall bind them for ever. 12. And this division has been made for the spirits of those who make their suit, who make disclosures concerning their destruction, when they were slain in the days of the sinners. 13. And this has been made for the spirits of men who shall not be righteous but sinners, who are godless, and of the lawless they shall be companions: but their spirits shall not be punished in the day of judgement nor shall they be raised from thence.' 14. Then I blessed the Lord of Glory and said: 'Blessed

---

κατηραμένων, which E takes actively, is to be taken passively as in Wisd. 12^{11} 2 Kings 9^{34} Matt. 25^{41}. So that (there may be) retribution = ἐν' ἀνταπόδοσις. Emended by Radermacher. 12–13. The third division is for sinners who suffered in this life, and therefore incur a less penalty in Sheol. For them Sheol is an everlasting place of punishment, since they are not raised from it to be delivered over to a severer condemnation at the final judgement. 12. These sinners demand vengeance on those that did violence to them in life, just as the righteous in the first division demanded justice against those that had destroyed them. 13. Companions. So also E—kamahōmû.

Their spirits. + 'because those who suffer affliction here are punished less', G^g—a gloss. Shall not be punished (G^g). Here E has 'shall not be slain = ἀναιρεθήσονται or φονευθήσονται. The same word is found in 99^{11} 108^3 in the same connexion. Cf. Matt. 10^{28}. Nor shall they be raised. The resurrection here implied is of Israel only: so the entire Section 1–36 would lead us to infer. Otherwise this declaration of a General Resurrection is solitary and unique in pre-Christian Jewish Apocrypha. 14. After each fresh revelation Enoch generally bursts forth into a doxology. Cf. 25^7 27^5 36^4 39$^{9-12}$ 48^{10} 81^3 83^{11} 84 90^{40}. These doxologies have, as a rule, a close connexion in

| E | G^g |

<table>
<tr><td>I blessed the Lord of glory and said: 'Blessed be my Lord, the Lord of righteousness, who ruleth for ever.'</td><td>art Thou, Lord of righteousness, who rulest over the world.'</td></tr>
</table>

XXIII. *The Fire that deals with the Luminaries of Heaven.*

XXIII. 1. From thence I went to another place to the west of the ends of the earth. 2. And I saw a ⌜burning⌝ fire which ran without resting, and paused not from its course day or night but (ran) regularly. 3. And I asked saying: 'What is this which rests not?' 4. Then Raguel, one of the holy angels who was with me, answered me ⌜and said unto me⌝: 'This course ⌜of fire⌝ ⌜which thou hast seen⌝ is the fire in the west which †persecutes† all the luminaries of heaven.'

XXIV—XXV. *The Seven Mountains in the North-West and the Tree of Life.*

XXIV. 1. ⌜And from thence I went to another place of the

thought with their respective contexts. Lord of glory: see 25³ (note). Lord of righteousness; cf. 90⁴⁰ 106³.

XXIII. 1, 2. Enoch still remains in the west, but proceeds to another quarter of the west where there is a restless river of fire. 17⁴ appears to deal with the same subject. **1. West of the ends** (G⁸). E. = 'west, to the ends'. **2. Burning** (E). > G⁸. **But (ran) regularly** (E). G⁸ ἅμα (corrupt for ἀλλὰ) διαμένον. **4. And said unto me** (E). > G⁸. **Of fire** (G⁸). > E. Unless we take coaznl (= 'and this is') as a corruption of coä 'ěj = 'of fire' (Flemming). But it may = τό before πρὸς δυσμάς. **Which thou hast seen** (E). > G⁸. **Persecutes** (G⁸ ἐκδιώκον). The text is highly doubtful. E certainly supports ἐκδιώκον though it is corrupt: that is, it reads jěnaděd (= 'burns') corrupt for jěsaděd = 'persecutes'. But in 20⁴, where the functions of Raguel are described, it is said that he 'takes vengeance on the world of the luminaries', i.e. ἐκδικῶν. These verbs are confused elsewhere; cf. Sir. 39³⁰. Both passages clearly embody the same idea. Raguel 'takes vengeance on the world of the luminaries' in 20⁴ and 'persecutes all the luminaries of heaven' in 23⁴. The idea of 'taking vengeance on' or 'persecuting' *all* the luminaries is inconceivable, and since the object in both passages is the same, the corruption lies in the verb. ἐκδιώκον is probably secondary to ἐκδικῶν. The latter = פָּרַד, which means either 'to requite in a good or bad sense' or 'to take vengeance on'. Hence I suggest that the meaning 'requite' should be restored here, and in 20⁴.

XXIV. Enoch has been in the extreme west in 23: now he goes to the NW. First he sees a mountain range of fire and then the seven great mountains, one of which is the throne of God. **1. And from thence ... of the earth** (E). > G⁸. **Day and**

earth⌐, and he showed me a mountain range of fire which burnt ⌐day and⌐ night. 2. And I went beyond it and saw seven magnificent mountains all differing each from the other, and the stones (thereof) were magnificent and beautiful, magnificent as a whole, of glorious appearance and fair exterior: ⌐three towards⌐ the east, ⌐one⌐ founded on the other, and three towards the south, ⌐one⌐ upon the other, and deep rough ravines, no one of which joined with any other. 3. And the seventh mountain was in the midst of these, and it excelled them in height, resembling the seat of a throne: and fragrant trees encircled the throne. 4. And amongst them was a tree such as I had never yet smelt, neither was any amongst them nor were others like it: it had a fragrance beyond all fragrance, and its leaves and blooms and wood wither not for ever: and its fruit ⌐is beautiful, and its fruit⌐ resembles the dates of a palm. 5. Then I said: '⌐How⌐ beautiful is this tree, and fragrant, and its leaves are fair, and its blooms ⌐very⌐ delightful in appearance.' 6. Then answered Michael, one of the holy ⌐and honoured⌐ angels who was with me, and was their leader.

XXV. 1. And he said unto me: 'Enoch, why dost thou ask me regarding the fragrance of the tree, and ⌐why⌐ dost thou wish to learn the truth?' 2. Then I answered him ⌐saying⌐:

(E). > G^g. 2. **Beyond it** (ἐπέκεινα αὐτῶν). E 'towards it'—always wrong in its rendering of this word; cf. 18^9 note. **Differing each from the other**, i.e. of seven different precious stones. **And beautiful** (E). G^g 'in beauty'. **Three towards** ^{1o} (E). >G^g. **One** $^{1o, 2o}$ (E). >G^g. **Rough** (G^g τραχεῖαι). E = σκολιαί. 3. **Excelled them in height** (ho,b nŏḥŏmŭ G^g, save that G^g om. 'them'). All other MSS. of E read nŭḥŏmŭ = 'their height'. **Resembling** (G^g and E by emending sa jĕtmăsalŭ into zajĕtmăsal). **Fragrant** (E = εὐώδη. G^g εὐειδῆ, 'of goodly appearance'—corrupt; cf. 24$^{4, 5}$ 25^5). 4. **The tree described here is the tree of life**; cf. 25$^{4-6}$. **Neither was any amongst them** (E). G^g = 'and no one else had enjoyed (ηὐφράνθη) them'. **Is beautiful, and its fruit** (E). > G^g through hmt. 5. **How** (G^g. > E). **Fragrant** (G^g εὐώδες. E = εὐειδές). **Its blooms** (G^g). E reads fěrěhū corrupt for şĕgěhū = G^g. **Very** (E. >G^g). 6. **Michael, the patron angel of Israel**, is in charge of these special treasures of the Messianic kingdom. And yet, according to 20^7, we should expect Gabriel here. **And honoured** (E. > G^g).

XXV. 1. **Ask.** + 'and why didst thou marvel' G^g. **Why** ^{2o} (G^g). > E. **Wish to learn the truth** (G^g). E = ἀκριβῶς μαθεῖν = 'inquire accurately to learn'. See note on 21^5. 2. **Then I.**

'I wish to know about everything, but especially about this tree.'
3. And he answered saying: 'This high mountain ⌜which thou hast seen⌝, whose summit is like the throne of God, is His throne, where the Holy Great One, the Lord of Glory, the Eternal King, will sit, when He shall come down to visit the earth with goodness. 4. And as for this fragrant tree no mortal is permitted to touch it till the great judgement, when He shall take vengeance on all and bring (everything) to its consummation for ever. It shall then be given to the righteous and holy. 5. Its fruit shall be for food to the elect: it shall be transplanted to the holy place, to the temple of the Lord, the Eternal King.
6. Then shall they rejoice with joy and be glad.

+ 'Enoch' a–η, β against G^g, η. Saying (E). > G^g. 3. On this mountain see note on 18^8. This mountain is the middle one of the seven in 18$^{6-9}$ 24$^{1-3}$. Which thou hast seen (E). > G^g. The Holy Great One ... Glory (E). G^g 'the great Lord, the Holy One of Glory'. Holy Great One: see 1^3 (note). Lord of Glory; cf. 22^{14} (25^7) 27$^{3, 5}$ 36^4 40^3 63^2 83^8. Eternal King; cf. vv. 5, 7; 27^3; only found in 1–36. When He shall come down, &c. This mountain, as we have seen in 18^6 note, is in the NW. In 77^1 it is said that God will descend in the south. 4. Then (G^g). E = τόδε corrupt for τότε. Holy (G^g ὁσίοις. E = 'humble'; cf. 108^7). 4, 5. This tree is the tree of life. By the eating of this tree after the final judgement men are endowed with long life—not eternal life; cf. 5^9 10^{17} 25^6. Cf. 2 Bar. 73$^{2, 3, 6, 7}$ 74. The writer of 1–36 has not risen to the conception of an eternal life of blessedness for the righteous, and so has not advanced a single step beyond the conceptions found in Is. 65 66. This materialistic conception of the tree of life based on Gen. 2^9 3^{22}, and here published afresh, gained afterwards a wide currency in Jewish and Christian literature though mainly with a symbolical meaning; cf. Rev. 2^7 22$^{2, 14}$ 4 Ezra 8^{52}. 5. Its fruit ... to the elect. G^g reads ὁ καρπὸς αὐτοῦ τοῖς ἐκλεκτοῖς † εἰς ζωήν † εἰς βοράν. The writer had before him Ezek. 47^{12} והיו פריו למאכל. εἰς ζωήν = לחיא, which I take to be corrupt for להוא = ἔσται. Thus the original possibly ran ואנבה לבחדיא להוא למבל. E is here very corrupt = ἐκ τοῦ καρποῦ αὐτοῦ δοθήσεται τοῖς ἐκλεκτοῖς ζωή, καὶ εἰς βορρᾶν. Transplanted to (G^g μεταφυτευθήσεται ἐν). The μετά reflects probably a separate verb in the original. The tree of life, which, according to the Massoretic Text, stood along with the tree of knowledge in the earthly Garden of Eden was, according to our text, removed to the Garden of Righteousness in the NW., whence it was subsequently to be transplanted to the holy place. The holy place, i.e. Jerusalem. We cannot tell whether the author intended here the New Jerusalem which, according to 90^{29}, was to be set up by God Himself. It is, at all events, a Jerusalem cleansed from all impurity, and that is probably all that the author meant. 6. In this verse I have followed G^g. E differs only in

And into the holy place shall they enter;
And its fragrance shall be in their bones,
And they shall live a long life on earth,
Such as thy fathers lived:
And in their days shall no ⌜sorrow or⌝ plague
Or torment or calamity touch them.'

7. Then blessed I the God of Glory, the Eternal King, who hath prepared such things for the righteous, and hath created them and promised to give to them.

Jerusalem and the Mountains, Ravines, and Streams.

XXVI. 1. And I went from thence to the middle of the earth, and I saw a blessed place ⌜in which there were trees⌝ with branches abiding and blooming [of a dismembered tree].

the second and third lines, where it reads
'Into the holy place shall they enter
($m\iota u$, β–$o_1 b$),
Its fragrance shall be in their bones.'
But gq, $o_1 b$ read wajābaw'ū = 'and they shall draw the fragrance thereof into their bones', instead of jĕbaw'ū = 'shall enter'. If this reading were right ἐν τοῖς ὀστέοις αὐτῶν would = בגרמיהן = 'into themselves'. Then we should have
'Then shall they rejoice with joy,
And be glad in the holy place:
And they shall draw the fragrance thereof into themselves
And they shall live', &c.
The eating of this tree imparts life; cf. Test. Lev. 18¹¹: its fruit fills and heals the righteous, 4 Ezra 7¹²³; cf. 8⁵² Rev. 2⁷ 22⁴. Since the word used here is ὀσμαὶ αὐτοῦ, Beer thinks there may be an echo of this idea in 2 Cor. 2¹⁶ ὀσμὴ ἐκ ζωῆς εἰς ζωήν. No sorrow or plague. Cf. Is. 65¹⁹, ²⁰. Touch. Cf. in this sense Job 1¹¹ 2⁵ 1 Chron. 16²², &c. With βάσανοι ... οὐχ ἅψονται αὐτῶν cf. Wisd. 3¹ οὐ μὴ ἅψηται αὐτῶν βάσανος which seems a quotation. βάσανος = כיבא.
7. On the doxology cf. 22¹⁴ n. Who.

So G⁵ ὅς. E = ὡς = 'because'. Created them (G⁵). E 'created such things'.

XXVI. Enoch visits Jerusalem and its vicinity. 1. The middle of the earth. The writer regards Jerusalem as the centre of the earth; cf. Ezek. 38¹² 5⁵ טבור. In the Book of Jubilees, 8¹², ¹⁹ it is called the navel or ὀμφαλός of the earth, just as Delphi was regarded amongst the Greeks. This idea reappears in the Talmud—Joma 54ᵇ Sanh. 37ᵃ. See Weber, *Jüd. Theol.* 208. In En. 90²⁶ Gehenna is in the middle of the earth. Blessed place. All MSS. of E except η read 'blessed planted place' against G⁵; cf. 27¹ 89⁴⁰ Dan. 11¹⁶, ⁴¹, ⁴⁵. In which there were trees. So G⁵, but lost in E owing to hmt.: i.e. esaw zabōtū fell out after zabōtū. Or it may have been omitted by the translator owing to the final phrase. Of a dismembered tree. This phrase can only be interpreted of Israel. If it is original, then 'in which there were trees' cannot be original, and the text may refer to the participation of the righteous descendants of Israel in the Messianic Kingdom in Palestine.

2. And there I saw a holy mountain, ⌜and⌝ underneath the mountain to the east there was a stream and it flowed towards the south.   3. And I saw towards the east another mountain higher than this, and between them a deep and narrow ravine: in it also ran a stream ⌜underneath⌝ the mountain.   4. And to the west thereof there was another mountain, lower than the former and of small elevation, and a ravine ⌜deep and dry⌝ between them: and another deep and dry ravine was at the extremities of the three ⌜mountains⌝.   5. And all the ravines were deep ⌜and narrow⌝, (being formed) of hard rock, and trees were not planted upon them.   6. And I marvelled ⌜at the rocks, and I marvelled⌝ at the ravine, yea, I marvelled very much.

The Purpose of the Accursed Valley.

XXVII. 1. Then said I: 'For what object is this blessed land, which is entirely filled with trees, and this accursed valley

Since, however, the trees here spoken of are again referred to in 27¹ γῆ ... πλήρης δένδρων, we conclude that the clause 'in which there were trees' is original and that 'of a dismembered tree' is a disturbing gloss, which introduces symbolical meanings into a non-metaphorical passage.   Abiding. G^s E μενούσας = קימי. Cf. Jer. Targ. on Gen 3²² קיים כאילן חייא.   2. A holy mountain, i.e. Zion.   And ²⁰. So E. > G^s.   A stream, i.e. the brook of Siloah.   Flowed (E = τὴν ῥύσιν εἶχεν). G^s corruptly reads δύσιν.   3. Another mountain, i.e. the Mount of Olives.   Between them (E). G^s 'between it'.   Ravine, i.e. the valley of the Kedron or of Jehoshaphat.   A stream, i.e. the brook Kedron.   Underneath (G^s).   E 'towards' or perhaps 'alongside'.   4. Another mountain, i.e. the Mount of Offence.   A ravine, i.e. the valley of Hinnom at the point where the three mountains meet.   Deep and dry (G^s).   E 'underneath it'.   Mountains (G^s). > E.   Description is accurate.

5. And narrow (E). > G^s.   6. The valley of Hinnom.   At the rocks, and I marvelled E. > G^s through hmt.

XXVII. 1. Then (E). G^s 'and'. Blessed land.   See 26¹ n.   And this accursed valley between (E). G^s = 'and (why is) this valley accursed'. But G^s has probably lost ἡ before κεκατηραμένη and E is right.   The valley of Hinnom or Gehenna had three meanings in the O.T. 1° It was used merely in a topographical sense as the boundary between Judah and Benjamin, Jos. 15³ 18¹⁶. 2° It was used in a religious significance as implying a place of idolatrous and inhuman sacrifices. Cf. 2 Kings 16³ 2 Chron. 28³ Jer. 7³¹, &c. 3° It signified the place of punishment for rebellious and apostate Jews in the presence of the righteous; cf. Is. 66²⁴ (50¹¹) Jer. 7³² Dan. 12². In Apocalyptic the idea underwent further development. 1° Thus it was conceived as a place of corporal and spiritual punishment for apostate Jews in the presence of the righteous for ever; cf. 27², ³ 90²⁶, ²⁷.

⌜between?⌝ 2. ⌜Then Uriel, one of the holy angels who was with me, answered and said: 'This⌝ accursed valley is for those who are accursed for ever: here shall all ⌜the accursed⌝ be gathered together who utter with their lips against the Lord unseemly words and of His glory speak hard things.

| E | G^g |

Here shall they be gathered together, and here shall be their place of judgement. 3. In the last days there shall be upon them the spectacle of righteous judgement in the presence of the righteous for ever: here shall the merciful

Here shall they be gathered together, and here shall be the place of their habitation. 3. In the last times, in the days of the true judgement in the presence of the righteous for ever: here shall the godly

In 37-70 there appears to be a modification of this idea; for though the punishment is everlasting, only its initial stages were to be executed in the presence of the righteous. On the expiration of these the wicked were to be swept for ever from the presence of the righteous; cf. 48⁹ (note) 62¹², ¹³. 2° A place of spiritual punishment only, for apostate Jews in the presence of the righteous. This new development is attested in 91-104; cf. 98³ 'their spirits shall be cast into a furnace of fire': also 103⁸. From 99¹¹ 103⁷, ⁸ it is clear that to this writer Gehenna and Sheol have become equivalent terms. Cf. also 100⁹ 108⁶, the latter passage being from a different hand. On Sheol see note on 56⁸, and on the question generally my Art. on 'Gehenna' in Hastings, B. D., whence these statements are drawn. In the N. T. (Matt. 5²⁹, ³⁰ 10²⁸ 18⁹ 23¹⁵, &c.) and in 4 Ezra 7³⁶⁻³⁸ Gehenna is no longer the place of punishment of unrighteous Jews but of the wicked generally. In later Judaism the conception underwent a further change. Gehenna was regarded

as the Purgatory of faithless Jews who were afterwards to be admitted into Paradise, but the place of eternal perdition for the Gentiles; cf. Weber, Jüd. Theol. 341 sq. 2. Then Uriel... said: 'This (E). > G^g. Valley. G^g has here γῆ which is a transliteration of גַּיְא, as in Neh. 11³⁵ Ezek. 32⁵ in the LXX. It is transliterated as γί in 2 Chron. 28³ Ezek. 39¹⁵, as γαί in Jos. 18¹⁶ Ezek. 39¹¹. The accursed (G^g). > E. Utter unseemly words. See 5⁴ note. Gehenna is the final abode of godless Israelites. Place of their habitation (οἰκητήριον αὐτῶν G^g). E reads mĕkuĕnânihômû = 'place of their judgement', which may be a corruption of makânômû = οἰκητήριον αὐτῶν. But the corruption may have arisen in the Greek, i. e. οἰκητήριον may have been corrupted into κριτήριον. 2-3. Accordingly as we follow G^g or E the text differs somewhat. In the days (G^g ἐν ταῖς ἡμέραις). Here E reads ἔσται αὐτοῖς εἰς τὴν ὅρασιν (or ἡ ὅρασις). This introduces the idea which reappears in 48⁹ 62¹². See note on 27¹. The godly = εὐσεβεῖς

Sect. I]   *Chapters XXVII. 2—XXVIII. 3*   57

E

bless the Lord of Glory, the Eternal King.

G^g

bless the Lord of Glory, the Eternal King.

4. In the days of judgement over the former, they shall bless Him for the mercy in accordance with which He has assigned them (their lot).'   5. Then I blessed the Lord of Glory and set forth His ⌜glory⌝ and lauded Him gloriously.

XXVIII—XXXIII. *Further Journey to the East.*

XXVIII. 1. And thence I went ⌜towards the east⌝, into the midst ⌜of the mountain range⌝ of the desert, and I saw a wilderness and it was solitary, full of trees and plants.   2. ⌜And⌝ water gushed forth from above.   3. Rushing like a copious watercourse [which flowed] towards the north-west it caused clouds and dew to ascend on every side.

emended from ἀσεβεῖς. Here E reads maḥārjān, which may be corrupt for mehūrān = 'those who have obtained mercy'. Lord of Glory. Cf. 25³. Eternal King. Cf. 25³. 5. His ⌜glory⌝ (G^g). E om. 'glory' perhaps owing to its occurrence just before. Lauded (G^g ὕμνησα). E reads zakarkū = 'remembered', corrupt for zamarkū = ὕμνησα.

XXVIII. 1. Dillmann takes the plain here referred to to be that of the Jordan, and the mountain range of the desert to be the rocky region which separates this plain from Jerusalem. According to Ezek. 47⁸,¹² this desert should one day be well watered and covered with trees.   1. Towards the East (E). > G^g. Of the mountain range (E). > G^g. And plants. Here both G^g and E read καὶ (> E) ἀπὸ τῶν σπερμάτων. In no case can σπερμάτων be right in its literal meaning. The difficulty can be explained from a corruption in the Aramaic or from a faulty rendering by the Greek translator. In the former case καὶ ἀπὸ τ. σπερμάτων = וּמִזְרָעִין corrupt for חוֹרְשִׁין (cf. Dan. 1¹²,¹⁶, Mishna, *Kil.* ii. 2; iii. 2) = καὶ τῶν φυτευμάτων. Or the Greek translator may here have found וּמִזְרָעִין, which he should have read as וּמִזְדָּרְעִין = καὶ ἀπὸ τ. φυτευμάτων, but which he read as וּמִזְרָעִין = καὶ ἀπὸ τ. σπερμάτων. Theodotion gives the same misrendering in Dan. 1¹²,¹⁶.   2. And (E). > G^g.   3. Rushing (G^g φερόμενον). E = φαινόμενον corrupt for φαιρόμενον, i.e. φερόμενον. Which flowed. Bracketed as an addition in E. It caused...to ascend (G^g ἀνάγει). E = καὶ ἀνάγεται, but by the change of a vowel point we recover ἀνάγει. Owing to this internal corruption E reads ὕδωρ καὶ δρόσος. Clouds. G^g E read ὕδωρ. But water is the subject of the verb, and in no case can it be said that water 'ascends'. Besides, δρόσον shows that we require here some such word as 'mist' or 'cloud' or 'vapour'. Now the exact phrase we need is found in Ps. 135⁷ Jer. 10¹³ 51¹⁶ מַעֲלֶה נְשִׂאִים, which the LXX in each case renders

XXIX. 1. And thence I went to another place in the desert, and approached to the east of this mountain range. 2. And ⌜there⌝ I saw aromatic trees exhaling the fragrance of frankincense and myrrh, and the trees also were similar to the almond tree.

XXX. 1. And beyond these, I went afar to the east, and I saw another place, a valley (full) of water. 2. And ⌜therein there was⌝ a tree, the colour (?) of fragrant trees such as the mastic. 3. And on the sides of those valleys I saw fragrant cinnamon. And beyond these I proceeded to the east.

XXXI. 1. And I saw other mountains, and amongst them were ⌜groves of⌝ trees, and there flowed forth from them nectar, which is named sarara and galbanum. 2. And beyond these mountains I saw another mountain ⌜to the east of the ends of the earth⌝, ⌜whereon were aloe trees⌝, and all the trees were full

by ἀνάγειν νεφέλας and the Targums by מסיק עננין. Hence I assume that מים (= ὕδωρ) is here a primitive corruption of עננין = 'clouds'. The word 'clouds' is to be taken in the sense of 'mist', for so Onkelos renders אֵד = 'mist' in Gen. 2⁶.

XXIX. 1. And thence. These words E had by a slip transposed before †'water' (i.e. 'clouds') in the preceding verse. G⁸ reads ἔτι ἐκεῖθεν. 2. **There** (E). > G⁸. **Aromatic trees.** G⁸ E read κρίσεως δένδρα. κρίσεως = דדינא which, as Praetorius and Beer have recognized, is corrupt for דרחא. Hence we should have here εὐώδη instead of κρίσεως. **Exhaling** (G⁸). E = πλέον corrupt for πνέοντα (G⁸). **Frankincense and myrrh.** לבונה ומור. **Almond tree** (G⁸ καρύαις). E omits unless we suppose kuaskuas, which occurs without any sense in the preceding line after πνέοντα, to be a corrupt transliteration of καρύαις = שָׁקֵד.

XXX. 1. Beyond (G⁸ ἐπέκεινα). Here, as elsewhere, E is unable to render this word correctly. See 18⁹ note. **Went** (G⁸ ᾠχόμην). E has here dabra (= ὄρη) which seems to be a corrupt remnant of qarabkû = ᾠχόμην. Cf. 29¹ 30³. **Afar** (G⁸). E 'not afar'. **Another.** +'great' G⁸. **Water.** +'like that which fails not' E—a gloss? 2. **Therein there was a tree** (G⁸). E = 'I saw a beautiful tree'. **The colour** (G⁸ χρόα). E = ὅμοιον — the same in sense. For χρόα Radermacher conjectures χλόᾳ. 3. **Fragrant cinnamon.** G⁸ E have here the strange phrase κινάμωμον ἀρωμάτων, which is a rendering of קנמן־בשם. See Exod. 30²³. **Beyond.** E misrenders here: see 18⁹ note.

XXXI. 1. Groves of (G⁸). > E. **Nectar** = נְקַטָר. E prefixes 'as it were'. **Sarara** (E). G⁸ σαρράν = a transliteration of צֳרִי a kind of balsam. **Galbanum** = χαλβάνη = חלבנה. 2. **Beyond.** E misrenders. Cf. 18⁹ note. **To the east of the ends of the earth** (G⁸). > E. **Whereon were aloe trees** (E). > G⁸. Observe that G⁸ and E are complementary. The former gives the habitat of the trees—the furthest east—but not their name. E omits the habitat but supplies the name.

of stacte, being like almond trees. 3. And when one burnt it, it smelt sweeter than any fragrant odour.

E

XXXII. 1. And after these fragrant odours, as I looked towards the north over the mountains I saw seven mountains full of choice nard and fragrant trees and cinnamon and pepper.

G^g

XXXII. 1. To the north-east I beheld seven mountains full of choice nard and mastic and cinnamon and pepper.

The aloe mentioned here is not 'the common bitter aloes used in medicine to which alone the name is given in classical writers', nor yet what is commonly known as the American aloe; but 'the modern eagle wood, a precious wood exported from South-Eastern Asia, which yields a fragrant odour when burnt' (*Encyc. Bib.* i. 120-121). In Hebrew its form is אהלים (Num. 24^6 Prov. 7^{17}) or אהלות (Ps. 45^9 Cant. 4^{14}—in the last passage א in the LXX and Aquila render it by ἀλόη. In Aramaic the form is אֲהָלָא. All (G^g). E reads 'ĕlkû corrupt for kuĕllû = 'all'. Of stacte. I have with much hesitation emended ἐξ αὐτῆς in G^g into στακτῆς. E is very corrupt = στερεός, which is transposed after almond trees. 3. Burnt. G^g has τρίβωσιν: E = λάβωσιν, but jĕnaś'ewô may be corrupt for jĕḥasjĕwô = τρίβωσιν. If my identification of this tree in the note on ver. 2 is right, we should expect καύσωσιν here, as eagle wood exhales fragrant odours when burnt. Now τρίβωσιν = ידקקה (Pael) corrupt for ידלקן = καύσωσιν, 'burnt'. It. G^g reads διό, which may be corrupt for αὐτό. E = τὸν καρπόν. Smelt sweeter (G^g). E = 'was better'.

XXXII. The Earthly Garden of Eden and the Tree of Knowledge. 1.

G^g has lost 'and after these odours' by hmt., and reads 'To the NE. I saw seven mountains'. This statement that the seven mountains are in the NE. creates some difficulty, if the text is correct. And that the text of G^g is correct seems to follow from the statement in ver. 2 'far towards the east' in both G^g and E. This being so, it seems necessary to conclude that the Garden of Righteousness in 70^3 77^3 in the NW. is distinct from the primitive earthly Garden of Righteousness or Eden in the NE., and that the seven mountains mentioned here in connexion with the Garden of Righteousness in 31$^{1-2}$ are distinct from those mentioned in 18^6 24^2 sqq. For the Garden of Righteousness and the Seven Mountains, one of which is the throne of God, are situated in the NW. The tree of knowledge is in the earthly Garden of Righteousness in the NE., 32$^{3-6}$, and the tree of life among the Seven Mountains, 24^2-25^6, in the NW. Again, it is noteworthy that whereas the Garden of Righteousness in 61^{12} 60$^{8, 23}$ 65^2 70^3 77^3 is the abode of the departed righteous, the earthly Garden of Righteousness seems not to be. A special division in Sheol is assigned to the souls of the righteous in 22^9. The earthly Garden of Eden, if the above conclusion is right,

2. And thence I went over the summits of ⌜all⌝ these mountains, far towards the east ⌜of the earth⌝, and passed above the Erythraean sea, and went far from it, and passed over ⌜the angel⌝ Zotîêl.

E

3. And I came to the Garden of Righteousness, and saw beyond those trees many large trees growing there and of goodly fragrance, large, very beautiful and glorious, and the tree of wisdom whereof they eat and know great wisdom.

G^g

3. And I came to the Garden of Righteousness, and from afar off trees more numerous than these trees and great—††two†† trees there, very great, beautiful, and glorious, and magnificent, and the tree of knowledge, whose holy fruit they eat and know great wisdom.

---

has no further connexion with the destinies of mankind according to the Book of Enoch. The above conclusions appear tenable, although in Gen. 2^8 the Garden of Eden is said to be in the East, while in 3^{24} it is implied that it lies in the West, and in 2$^{10-14}$ in the North. See Gunkel, *Genesis*^{3} 26. These variations in Genesis are due to different sources. **2. All** (G^g). > E. **Of the earth** (G^g). > E. **Erythraean sea.** The Persian and Indian oceans: cf. 77$^{6, 7}$. **Went** (G^g). E reads κὸνκῦ corrupt for hòrkū = G^g. **Far from it** (E = ἀπὸ τούτου μακράν). G^g reads ἐπ' Ἄκρων, καὶ ἀπὸ τούτου = 'towards Akron and from this'. **The angel** (E). > G^g. **3. Beyond.** So E, which so renders μακρόθεν and wrongly takes it as governing the following words in the genitive. **Growing** (E = φυόμενα). G^g reads δύω μέν, but this reading is certainly corrupt. If δύω μέν were original, then τὸ δένδρον τῆς ζωῆς would have to be inserted before καὶ τὸ δένδρον τῆς φρονήσεως. But the tree of life, according to 24^3-25, is in the neighbourhood of the chief of the Seven Mountains in the NW. See notes 32^1 25^5 18^9. The passages from the Zohar quoted by Lawrence, and subsequently adduced by Lods and Lawlor in support of δύω μέν cannot, therefore, bear on our text; but may be derived ultimately from 2 Enoch, and in part from Gen. 3. These passages are (Lawrence, p. xxix) from vol. i, Parasha בראשית, p. 37^b, ed. Mont. et Amstel.: 'Sanctus et Benedictus sustulit eum (Enochum) ex mundo, ut ipsi serviret ... Ex eo inde tempore liber tradebatur, qui Enochi dictus est. In hora qua Deus eum sustulit, ostendebat ei *omnia repositoria suprema*, ostendebat ei *arborem vitae medio in horto, folia eius atque ramos.*' Again (vol. ii, Parasha בשלח, p. 55^a): 'In Enochi libro narratur, Sanctum et Benedictum, cum ascendere eum iusserit et *omnia ei superiorum et inferiorum regnorum repositoria* ostenderit monstrasse quoque *arborem vitae* et arborem de qua Adamus praeceptum recepit.' These passages refer to 2 Enoch. The italicized words *omnia repositoria suprema* refer to Paradise and Hell, which are described

4. ⌜That tree is in height like the fir, and its leaves are⌝ like (those of) the Carob tree: and its fruit is like the clusters of the vine, very beautiful: and the fragrance of the tree penetrates afar. 5. Then I said: '⌜How⌝ beautiful is the tree, and how attractive is its look!' 6. Then Raphael, the holy angel who was with me, answered me ⌜and said⌝: 'This is the tree of wisdom, of which thy father old (in years) and thy aged mother, who were before thee, have eaten, and they learnt wisdom and their eyes were opened, and they knew that they were naked and they were driven out of the garden.'

XXXIII. 1. And from thence I went to the ends of the earth and saw there great beasts, and each differed from the other; and (I saw) birds also differing in appearance and beauty and voice, the one differing from the other. 2. And to the east of those beasts I saw the ends of the earth whereon the heaven rests, and the portals of the heaven open. 3. And I saw how the stars of heaven come forth, and I counted the

in 2 Enoch 8-10. The next italicized words—*arborem vitae medio in horto*—may be taken directly from 8³ of the same book or from Gen. 2⁹, while the phrase *arborem de qua Adamus praeceptum recepit* might possibly refer to 1 Enoch 32³⁻⁶, but much more likely to Gen. 2¹⁷. Whose holy fruit = οὗ ... τοῦ καρποῦ αὐτοῦ—an Aramaic idiom פִּרְיָה ... דְּ. 4. That tree ... its leaves are. So G^s. > E through hmt. Like the clusters of the vine. According to certain Rabbinic authorities the tree of which Adam ate was the vine: cf. Sanh. 70ᵃ אילן שאכל ממנו אדם הראשון גפן. See also Ber. 40ᵃ. The fragrance of the tree penetrates afar. So E in q. gmu add asyndetically after 'penetrates' as a variant (?) 'proceeds', while tβ subsequently connect the two verbs. G^s reads 'its fragrance penetrates afar from the tree'. 5. Then (G^s). E 'and'. Τότε occurs frequently in 6-32, i.e. 9¹ 10¹, ¹⁸ 11² 13⁵, ⁶ 21⁴, ⁵, ⁸ 22⁵, ⁸, ¹⁴ 23⁴ 24⁶, ⁸ 25⁶, ⁷ 27⁵

32⁵, ⁶. This is an Aramaic feature. E in a few cases fails to preserve it. How (G^s ὡς). > E as in 24⁸. The tree (G^s). E reads 'this tree'; but here, as frequently, E renders the Greek article by a demonstrative pronoun. And how. All MSS. of E except *q* add 'beautiful and' against G^s and *q*. 6. Adam and Eve seem to be still living. Hence, if 10¹ belongs to this section originally, the writer adopted the Samaritan chronology. See 65² (note). Observe that Adam's sin is not regarded as the cause of man's fall and destruction in the deluge. Then (G^s). E 'and'. See note on 32⁵. Raphael. We should, according to 20⁷, expect Gabriel here. And said (E). > G^s. Of which. G^s breaks off with ἐξ οὗ ἔφαγεν ὁ πατήρ σου.

XXXIII. 2. Whereon the heaven rests. See 18⁵ note. 3. The portals of the stars here mentioned are described at length in 72-82. If we are to regard the two accounts as in the portals out of which they proceed, and wrote down all their outlets, of each individual star by itself, according to their number and their names, their courses and their positions, and their times and their months, as Uriel the holy angel who was with me showed me. 4. He showed all things to me and wrote them down for me: also their names he wrote for me, and their laws and their companies.

Enoch's Journey to the North.

XXXIV. 1. And from thence I went towards the north to the ends of the earth, and there I saw a great and glorious device at the ends of the whole earth. 2. And here I saw three portals of heaven open in the heaven: through each of them proceed north winds: when they blow there is cold, hail, frost, snow, dew, and rain. 3. And out of one portal they blow for good: but when they blow through the other two portals, †it is with violence and affliction on the earth, and they blow with violence.†

XXXV. And from thence I went towards the west to the ends of the earth, and saw there three portals of the heaven open such as I had seen in the †east†, the same number of portals, and the same number of outlets.

The Journey to the South.

XXXVI. 1. And from thence I went to the south to the ends of the earth, and saw there three open portals of the heaven: and thence there come dew, rain, †and wind†. 2. And

---

main consistent, the portals of the stars are also those of the sun and moon, 72³. 4. This verse conflicts with the preceding. There Enoch writes down the various statements: here Uriel. Companies or 'companions'. So a. β reads 'functions'.

XXXIV. Cf. 76. 1. Device (a-m), mt²β read 'wonder'. 2. And. > q. North winds (bamangala mas'ĕ gm, β). This ought to be the meaning, but it is questionable whether the Ethiopic will admit of it. The text of t¹t²u is practically the same. q (bamā'ĕkala mas'ĕ) = 'winds through the north'. 3. They blow (a-m, chĕln₁a). mt², ablefox₁b 'it blows'. It is ... violence. Probably corrupt for 'they blow with violence and there is affliction on the earth'.

XXXV. The †east†. Read 'the north'., Otherwise and preferably we should transpose this chapter after 36³.

XXXVI. 1. Come. Here a-q, β

from thence I went to the east to the ends of the heaven, and saw here the three eastern portals of heaven open and small portals above them. 3. Through each of these small portals pass the stars of heaven and run their course to the west on the path which is shown to them. 4. And as often as I saw I blessed always the Lord of Glory, and I continued to bless the Lord of Glory who has wrought great and glorious wonders, to show the greatness of His work to the angels and to spirits and to men, that they might praise His work and all His creation: that they might see the work of His might and praise the great work of His hands and bless Him for ever.

add 'the south wind', but this cannot be right, and here again, as several times before, we must follow q in omitting this phrase. The fact also that tu, $abcklx_1a$ omit the following 'and' points in the same direction. u emends 'the south wind' into 'from the south'. †And wind†. As Martin remarks these words are meaningless here. The text seems imperfect. Possibly there stood (cf. 34², originally something like: 'And from thence came the south winds, and when they blow there is dew and rain'. 4. To spirits and to men (yqu^1 though reading nafāsāt (-sātā x). Other MSS. 'to the spirits of men'. The work of His might. q reads 'the might of His work'.

SECTION II

(CHAPTERS XXXVII—LXXI)

THE PARABLES. INTRODUCTION

A. *Critical Structure.* B. *Relation of 37-71 to the rest of the Book.* C. *Date.* D. *The Problem and its Solution.*

A. This Section is in a fragmentary condition, and many of the critical questions connected with it can only be tentatively solved or merely stated. It consists in the main of three Parables—38–44, 45–57, 58–69. These are introduced by 37 and concluded by 70 which records Enoch's final translation. 71 appears to be out of place, and belongs to one of the three Parables. The two visions recorded in it were witnessed in Enoch's lifetime. See notes *in loc.* There are many interpolations. 60 $65-69^{25}$ are confessedly from the Book of Noah. $39^{1-2a}\ 54^{7}-55^{2}$ are probably from the same work. These interpolations are adapted by their editor to their adjoining contexts in Enoch. This he does by borrowing characteristic terms, such as 'Lord of Spirits', 'Head of Days', to which, however, either through ignorance or of set intention he generally gives a new connotation: see Notes for details.

There now remain the following chapters and verses: $37-41^2$ 42 $45-54^6\ 55^3-58\ 62-63\ 69^{26}-71$. But these passages can hardly have been derived from the same hand originally. There are traces of a composite origin. Beer, in Kautzsch's *Apok. und Pseudep.* ii. 227, has drawn attention to the fact that behind the Parables there appear to lie two distinct sources—one dealing with the Elect One ($40^5\ 45^3\ 49^{2,\ 4}\ 51^{3,\ 5}\ 52^{6,\ 9}\ 53^6\ 55^4\ 61^{5,\ 8,\ 10}\ 62^1$) and the other with the Son of Man ($46^{2,\ 3,\ 4}\ 48^2\ 62^{7,\ 9,\ 14}\ 63^{11}\ 69^{26,\ 27,\ 29}\ 70^1\ 71^{17}$), and that in the former the *angelus interpres* was designated 'the angel of peace who went with me' and in the latter 'the angel who went with me' (see 40^2 note). This observation is just, and even with the present text it is possible, I think, to distinguish these sources, though Beer has not attempted it. But these two sources do not account for the whole of the Parables. In 71 there are two distinct visions, 71^{1-4} and 71^{5-17}, where the *angelus interpres* is Michael and not either of the former angels, unless we identify him with one of them, which is indeed possible: see my edition of the *Test. XII Patriarchs*, pp. 39–40. Whence 42 is drawn is a difficulty. But returning to the two sources above-mentioned, we might assign to the 'Son of Man' source and the angelic interpreter—'the angel who went with me.'

40^{3-7}.
$46-48^{7}$.
52^{3-4}.
61^{3-4}.
$62^{2}-63$.
69^{26-29}.
$70-71$.

And to the source dealing with the Elect One and the angelic interpreter—'the angel of peace.'

$38-39$.
$40^{1-2, 8-10}$.
$41^{1-2, 9}$.
45.
48^{8-10}.
$50-52^{1-2, 5-9}$.
$53-54^{6}$.
$55^{3}-57$.
$61^{1-2, 5-13}$.
62^{1}.

The above analysis of the sources can of course only be provisional until the Greek version of the original is recovered. The second source differs from the former in recognizing the judgement of the sword, 38^{5}, 48^{8-10}, and the attack of the hostile Gentiles on Jerusalem, 56, the progressive conversion of the Gentiles who had no part in oppressing Israel, 50^{2-4}, and the triumphant return of the Dispersion, 57. $55^{3}-57^{3a}$ looks like an independent source adapted to a new context. There is no hint of the judgement of the sword in the first source.

These two sources had much material in common. 52^{1-2} apparently belonged to both in some form. The Elect One and the Son of Man alike judge the kings and the mighty, and the same attributes are to a great extent ascribed to each, save that of pre-existence, which, as it happens, is attributed only to the Son of Man, 48^{2} sqq.

B. **Relation of 37–71 to the rest of the book.** As all critics are now agreed that the Parables are distinct in origin from the rest of the book, there is no occasion for treating exhaustively the grounds for this conclusion. Accordingly, we shall give here only a few of the chief characteristics which differentiate this Section from all the other Sections of the book. (*a*) **Names of God found only in 37-71.** 'Lord of Spirits' (passim); 'Head of Days' (46^2); 'Lord of the mighty' (63^2); 'Lord of the rich' (63^2); 'Lord of wisdom' (63^2). (*b*) **Angelology.** The four chief angels in 37-71 are Michael, Raphael, Gabriel, and Phanuel. Phanuel is not mentioned elsewhere in the book, which gives Uriel instead. In 14^{11} God is surrounded by Cherubim; but in 61^{10} 71^6 by Cherubim, Seraphim, and Ophannim, angels of power, and angels of principalities. The angel of peace (40^8) is also peculiar to the Parables. (*c*) **Demonology.** In the other Sections of the book the sins of the angels consisted in their lusting after the daughters of men (6-8), but in 54^6 in their becoming subjects of Satan. In 37-71 an evil spirit-world is presupposed from the beginning, but not in the rest of the book. Satan and the Satans, 40^7 53^3 54^6, are not even mentioned in the other Sections. These have access to heaven, 40^7, whereas in the other Sections only good angels have access there. The angels of punishment also are found for the first time in 37-71. (*d*) **The Messianic doctrine** in 37-71 is unique, not only as regards the other Sections of Enoch, but also in Jewish literature as a whole. The Messiah pre-exists, 48^2 (note), from the beginning: he sits on the throne of God, 51^3, and possesses universal dominion, 62^6; all judgement is committed unto him, 69^{27}, and he slays the wicked by the word of his mouth, 62^2. Turning to the other Sections we find that there is no Messiah in 1-36 and in 91-104, while in 83-90 the Messiah is evidently human and possesses none of the great attributes belonging to the Messiah of the Parables. (*e*) **The scene of the Messianic kingdom** in 1-36 is Jerusalem and the earth purified from sin; in 83-90, a heavenly Jerusalem set up by God Himself; in 91-104, Jerusalem and the earth as they are; but in 37-70, a new heaven and a new earth, $45^{4,\ 5}$ (note). Again, the **duration of the Messianic kingdom** in 1-36 is eternal, but the life of its members limited. The duration of the Messianic kingdom in 83-90 is eternal, and the life of its members eternal (?). The duration of the Messianic kingdom in 91-104 is limited, and the life of its members limited. (In 91-104 the real interest centres, not in the Messianic kingdom, but in the future spiritual life of the righteous.) But the duration of the Messianic kingdom in 37-71 is eternal, and the life of its members eternal.

C. Date. From a full review of the evidence, which is given and discussed in the notes on 38^5, it appears that the kings and the mighty so often denounced in the Parables are the later Maccabean princes and their Sadducean supporters — the later Maccabean princes, on the one hand, and not the earlier; for the blood of the righteous was not shed, as the writer complains ($47^{1, 2, 4}$), before 95 B.C.: the later Maccabean princes, on the other hand, and not the Herodians; for (1) the Sadducees were not supporters of the latter, and (2) Rome was not as yet known to the writer as one of the great world-powers—a fact which necessitates an earlier date than 64 B.C., when Rome interposed authoritatively in the affairs of Judaea. Thus the date of the Parables could not have been earlier than 94 B.C. or later than 64 B.C. But it is possible to define the date more precisely. As the Pharisees enjoyed unbroken power and prosperity under Alexandra 79-70 B.C., the Parables must be assigned either to the years 94-79 or 70-64. Finally, if we consider that 56^5-57^{3a} is an interpolation, and that this passage must have been written before 64 B.C., the Parables might reasonably be referred to the years 94-79. See also Gen. Introd.

D. The Problem and its Solution. Seeing that God is a just God, how comes it that wickedness is throned in high places and that righteousness is oppressed? Is there no end to the prosperity and power of unbelieving rulers, and no recompense of reward for the suffering righteous? The author (in the genuine portions) finds the answer in a comprehensive view of the world's history: only by tracing evil to its source can the present wrongness of things be understood, and only by pursuing the world's history to its final issues can its present inequalities be justified. The author has no interest save for the moral and spiritual worlds, and this is manifest even in the divine names 'Lord of Spirits', 'Head of Days', 'Most High'. Whole hierarchies of angelic beings appear in 61^{10-12}. His view is strongly apocalyptic, and follows closely in the wake of Daniel. The origin of sin is traced one stage further back than in 1-36. The first authors of sin were the Satans, the adversaries of man, 40^7 (note). The Watchers fell through becoming subject to these, and leading mankind astray, 54^6. Punishment was at once meted out to the Watchers, and they were confined in a deep abyss, 54^5, to await the final judgement, 54^6 55^4 64. In the meantime sin flourishes in the world: sinners deny the name of the Lord of Spirits, 38^2 41^2, and of His Anointed, 48^{10}; the kings and the mighty of the earth trust in their sceptre and glory, 63^7, and oppress the elect of the children of God, 62^{11}. But the prayer of the righteous ascends, and their blood goes up before the Lord of Spirits crying for vengeance, 47^1; and the angels unite in the prayer of the righteous, 47^2. But the oppression of the kings and the mighty will not continue for ever: suddenly the Head of Days will appear and with Him the Son of Man, $46^{2, 3, 4}$ 48^2, to execute judgement upon all alike—on the righteous and wicked, on angel and on man. And to this end there will be a Resurrection of all Israel, 51^1 61^5; the books of the living will be opened, 47^3; all judgement will be committed unto the Son of Man, 41^9 69^{27}; the Son of Man will possess universal dominion, 62^6, and sit on the throne of his glory, $62^{3, 5}$ $69^{27, 29}$, which is likewise God's throne, 47^3 51^3. He will judge the holy angels, 61^8, and the fallen angels, 55^4, the righteous upon earth, 62^3, and the sinners, 62^2; but particularly those who oppress his saints, the kings and the mighty and those who possess the earth, $48^{5, 8-9}$ 53^3 $62^{3, 11}$. All are judged according to their deeds, for their deeds are weighed in the balance, 41^1. The fallen angels are cast into a fiery furnace, 54^4; the kings and the mighty confess their sins, and pray for forgiveness, but in vain, 63; and are given into the hands of the righteous, 38^5; and their destruction will furnish a spectacle to the righteous as they burn and vanish for ever out of sight, $48^{9, 10}$ 62^{12}; to be tortured in Gehenna by the angels of punishment, 53^{3-5} $54^{1, 2}$. The remaining sinners and godless will be driven from off the face of the earth, 38^3 41^2 45^6. The Son of Man will slay them with the word of his mouth, 62^2. Sin and wrongdoing will be banished from the earth, 49^2; and heaven and earth will be transformed, $45^{4, 5}$; and the righteous and elect will have their mansions therein, 39^5 41^2. And the light of the Lord of Spirits will shine upon them, 38^4; they will live in the light of eternal life, 58^3. The Elect One will dwell amongst them, 45^4; and they will eat and lie down and rise up with him for ever and ever, 62^{14}. They will be clad in garments of life, $62^{15, 16}$; and shine as fiery lights, 39^7. And they will seek after light and find righteousness and peace with the Lord of Spirits, 58^4; and grow in knowledge and righteousness, 58^5.

THE PARABLES.

XXXVII. 1. The second vision which he saw, the vision of wisdom—which Enoch the son of Jared, the son of Mahalalel, the son of Cainan, the son of Enos, the son of Seth, the son of Adam, saw.   2. And this is the beginning of the words of wisdom which I lifted up my voice to speak and say to those which dwell on earth: Hear, ye men of old time, and see, ye that come after, the words of the Holy One which I will speak before the Lord of Spirits.   3. It were better to declare (them only) to the men of old time, but even from those that come after we will not withhold the beginning of wisdom.   4. Till the present day such wisdom has never been given by the Lord of Spirits as I have received according to my insight, according to the good pleasure of the Lord of Spirits by whom the lot of

XXXVII. 1. The genealogy with which this Section begins agrees with many other characteristics of the Parables in marking it out as an independent work. The *second vision*. Apparently the first vision is that referred to in 1^2 'the vision of the Holy One in the heavens'.   2. *Beginning*. The Ethiopic word here and in the next verse could be rendered 'sum'. The phrase may = ראש החכמה. But in Prov. 9^{10} it is תחלת חכמה. And *say* ($m, \beta-dy_1n$). $a-m, dy_1n$ read 'say'. *Men of old time*. These would embrace Cainan, Mahalalel, and Jared, according to the LXX chronology, which is followed in the Similitudes. See 54^7 (note) 70^4 (note). *Words of the Holy One* (gml, fv_1b). Other MSS. 'holy words'. *Lord of Spirits*. This expression occurs in 2 Macc. 3^{24} ὁ τῶν πνευμάτων ... δυνάστης and nowhere else in contemporary or earlier writings that I am aware of. The way is prepared for it in Num. 16^{22} 27^{16} 'the God of the Spirits of all flesh'. Cf. also Heb. 12^9 'the Father of Spirits'. The phrase 'Lord of Spirits' is found in 37^4 (twice) 38^2 (twice), $^{4, 6}$ $39^{2, 7}$ (twice), $^{8, 9}$ (twice), ^{12} $40^{1, 2, 4, 5, 6, 7, 10}$ 41^2 (twice), $^{6, 7}$ 43^4 (twice) $45^{1, 2}$ 46^3 (twice), $^{6, 7, 8}$ $47^{1, 2}$ (twice), ^{4} $48^{2, 3, 5, 7}$ (twice), ^{10} (twice) 49^2 ^{4} 50^2 ^{3} (twice), ^{5} 51^3 $52^{4, 9}$ 53^6 $54^{6, 7}$ 55^3 ^{4} 57^2 $58^{4, 6}$ (twice) $59^{1, 2}$ $60^{6, 8, 24, 25}$ (twice) $61^{3, 5, 8, 9}$ (thrice), $^{11, 13}$ (twice) $62^{2, 10, 12, 14, 16}$ (twice) $63^{1, 2}$ (twice), $^{7, 12}$ (twice) $65^{9, 11}$ 66^2 67^8, ^{9} 68^4 (twice) 69^{24} (twice), ^{29} 70^1 $71^{2, 17}$. We find it in all 104 times, and 28 of these at least in the Interpolations. In the genuine portions it stands in the closest connexion with the character of its context; cf. 39^{12} 40^{1-10} 46^{3-8}, &c.; but in the Interpolations this appropriateness is wanting; cf. $41^{6, 7}$ $59^{1, 2}$ where only things of the natural world are in question. This leads to the conjecture that this title was introduced into these Interpolations when they were incorporated in the Parables, with a view of adapting them to their new contexts.   3. *To the men of old time*. Here for 'ĕllû I have read la'ĕlla. For construction cf. 95^7.   4. Cf. 2 Enoch 47^2 'There have been many books from the beginning of Creation ... but none shall make things known to you like my writings'. See also our text $93^{10\,sqq.}$ *By* ^{10}, i.e. 'ĕmqĕdma eternal life has been given to me. 5. Now three parables were imparted to me, and I lifted up my voice and recounted them to those that dwell on the earth.

XXXVIII—XLIV. The First Parable.

XXXVIII. *The Coming Judgement of the Wicked.*

1. The first Parable.
 When the congregation of the righteous shall appear,
 And sinners shall be judged for their sins,
 And shall be driven from the face of the earth:

2. And when the Righteous One shall appear before the eyes of the righteous,
 Whose elect works hang upon the Lord of Spirits,

מלפני = Eternal life. Cf. Dan. 12^2. חיי עולם 5. Parables = παραβολαί = משלים. The word has already occurred in 1^2. It is used pretty much in the same sense here as in Num. 32^{7,18} Job 27^1, and means merely an elaborate discourse, whether in the form of a vision, prophecy, or poem. His object is generally parenetic. Those that dwell on the earth. This phrase (except in 46^7 and 70^1, where it is merely geographical) is used in a good ethical sense in the genuine portions of this section. Cf. 37^2 40^{6,7} 48^5. So Rev. 14^6. But in the Interpolations it calls up different associations: these are bad in 54^9 55^1 60^5 65^{6,12} 66^1 67^8, and either doubtful or merely geographical in 43^4 53^1 54^6 55^2 67^7 69^1. We should observe that this phrase has an evil significance in Revelation, except in 14^6. Cf. 3^{10} 6^{10} 8^{13} 11^{10} (twice) 13^{8,14} 17^8.

XXXVIII. The time of requital is coming. When the kingdom of the righteous appears, and the light of the Lord of Spirits shines on the face of the righteous and elect, where will be the future habitation of the sinners and the godless? 1. Congregation of the righteous. This phrase, which is peculiar to the Parables, is explained by a comparison of 38^3 53^6 62^8. Its equivalent occurs in Ps. 149^1 'congregation of the saints' קהל חסידים, or rather in Ps. 1^5 עדת צדיקים, 74^2 עדתך = LXX τῆς συναγωγῆς σου 111^1. Cf. Pss. Sol. 17^{18} συναγωγὰς ὁσίων. Driven from the face of the earth. This form of punishment is elsewhere mentioned in 1^1 38^3 41^2 48^{9,10} 53^2. 2. The Righteous One (ṣādĕq *m* β). *a–m* read ṣĕdĕq 'righteousness'. Though less well attested the former is preferable. Almost the same connexion of thought is found in 53^6. The Messiah is variously named: 'the Righteous and Elect One,' 53^6; 'the Elect One of righteousness and of faith,' 39^6; 'the Elect One,' 40^5 45^3 49^{2,4} 51^{3,5} 52^{6,9} 53^6 55^4 61^{5,8,10} 62^1; 'The Messiah,' 48^{10} 52^4. For other designations see note on 46^3. Observe that as the members of the kingdom are 'the righteous', so the Messiah is 'the Righteous One'; cf. 'The Elect', 'The Elect One'. Works. *q* reads 'hope and works'. Hang upon the Lord of Spirits. Cf. 40^5 46^8. With this expression cf. Judith 8^{24} ἐξ ἡμῶν κρέμαται

And light shall appear to the righteous and the elect who dwell on the earth,

Where then will be the dwelling of the sinners,
And where the resting-place of those who have denied the Lord of Spirits?
It had been good for them if they had not been born.

3. When the secrets of the righteous shall be revealed and the sinners judged,
And the godless driven from the presence of the righteous and elect,

4. From that time those that possess the earth shall no longer be powerful and exalted:

And they shall not be able to behold the face of the holy,
For the Lord of Spirits has caused His light to appear

ἡ ψυχὴ αὐτῶν. Perhaps תלה or תלא stood in the original. Light shall appear. Cf. Is. 9² 60¹. Denied the Lord of Spirits. For 'denied' q reads 'outraged'. This charge is frequently brought against the sinners: it is in fact 'the very head and front of their offending'. Cf. 41² 45² 46⁷ 46¹⁰ 63⁷. Cf. St. Jude 4. They deny likewise the heavenly world, 45¹; the Messiah, 48¹⁰; the spirit of God, 67¹⁰; the righteous judgement, 60⁶. The righteous on the other hand believe in the name of the Lord, 43⁴. Observe that this phrase is taken over into the Interpolations, 67⁹, ¹⁰. It had been good for them, &c. A familiar Jewish expression = טוֹטַב היה לו Wajikra R. 26 (quoted by Edersheim, Life... of Jesus the Messiah, ii. 120). Cf. 2 Par. 16⁶ 4 Ezra 4¹² 2 Enoch 41² St. Matt. 26²⁴. 3. When the secrets of the righteous shall be revealed. The blessings in store for the righteous, the heritage of faith, are still hidden, 58⁵; but they will one day be revealed. The Messiah himself is hidden with the Lord of Spirits, 62⁷. Cf. Mark 4¹¹. And the sinners (q). Other MSS. om. 'and' and make this clause the apodosis 'the sinners shall be judged'. But the parallelism supports q, and we have seen, where the Greek is preserved, that q is not infrequently right when standing alone. 4. The supremacy and oppression of the earth's rulers and great ones are speedily drawing to a close. This is the constant theme of the Parables, 46⁴⁻⁸ 48⁸⁻¹⁰ 53⁵ 62¹⁻¹² 63, and has been taken over into the Interpolations, 67⁸⁻¹³; and this is one of the leading characteristics which distinguish 37-69 from 91-104. With the rulers of the earth as such the latter Section has practically no concern. From that time. The MSS. prefix 'and' which I take to be the word introducing the apodosis. Has caused His light to appear. I have emended tar'ĕja = 'is seen' into 'ar'aja = 'has caused to appear'. This emendation is required by the fact that 'the Lord of Spirits' is in the nom. in a, d, and 'His light' in the acc. in q. $β$-d reads 'the light of the Lord of Spirits is seen'. This light is at once spiritual and physical: the nearness of God's presence

On the face of the holy, righteous, and elect.

5. Then shall the kings and the mighty perish

transfigures the countenance and person of His saints. Light in all its forms is the blessing of the kingdom. The righteous will have light, and joy, and peace, 5^7, and the light of God shining upon them, 1^8. In the Parables the heaven will be transformed into an eternal light, 45^4; and light will appear unto the righteous, 38^2; and the light of days will abide upon them, 50^1; they will abide in the light of the sun and in the light of eternal life, 58^3; their faces will be illuminated with the light of the Lord of Spirits, 38^4; and they will seek after light and find righteousness, and the light of truth will be mighty for evermore, 58^{3-6}. This idea is still further developed in 91–108. The righteous belong to the generation of light, 108^{11}; and will be clad in light, 108^{12}; and will walk in eternal light, 92^4; and will be resplendent and shine as the lights of heaven for evermore, 108^{12} 104^2. The holy, righteous, and elect. So $a, def klny_1 a$. $abcoprz_1 b$ read 'the holy and righteous and elect'. The latter has the support of 48^1 where it recurs. 5. Then (q). Other MSS. 'and then'. The kings and the mighty (a). $t^2 \beta$ 'the mighty kings'. Cf. $62^{1, 3, 6, 9}$ $63^{1, 2, 12}$ $67^{8, 12}$. These designations are practically synonymous in the Parables. The phrase 'mighty kings' which appears often in Dillmann's text is without the support of the best MSS. except in 55^4, and there I feel we must regard the text as corrupt, and read 'the kings and the mighty'. This better text removes, as we shall find, at least one formidable difficulty in the interpretation. Who then are these kings and mighty ones? The facts taken together point decidedly to unbelieving native rulers and Sadducees. They have denied the Lord and his Anointed, 48^{10}; and a heavenly world, 45^1; they persecute the houses of His congregations, i.e. the Theocratic community, 46^8; and they are an offence thereto, an offence on the removal of which the Theocratic ideal will be realized, 53^6; they do not acknowledge from whom their power is derived, 46^5; but trust in their riches, 46^7; and place their hope in their sceptre and glory, 63^7; they have made the righteous their servants, 46^7; and outraged God's children, 62^{11}; and shed their blood, $47^{1, 2}$. Accordingly they will have to stand before the Messiah whom they have denied, when He judges the angels, 61^8 55^4; and the righteous, $62^3 (\beta)$; and the sinners, 62^2; and they will be terrified, 62^5; and fall down and worship the Messiah, 62^9; and acknowledge the righteousness of their judgement, 63^9; and pray for a respite in order to repent, 63^1; and express their thanksgiving of faith, 63^8; but their prayer will not be heard, and the Lord of Spirits, 62^{12}, and the righteous, 48^9, will execute judgement upon them, and their destruction will form a spectacle over which the righteous will rejoice, 62^{12}; and they will be delivered over to the angels of punishment, 62^{11}; and will descend into the tortures of hell, 63^{10}. Only one statement seems to point to heathen rulers, i.e. 'their faith is in the gods which they have made with their hands', 46^7. But this is only a strong expression for the heathen or Sadducean attitude of the Maccabean princes and their supporters, and with it we might aptly compare Pss. Sol. 1^8 8^{14} 17^{17}, wherein the same persons are charged with surpassing the heathen in idolatries. There is a like exaggeration of the

And be given into the hands of the righteous and holy.

wickedness of the Sadducees in 99⁷ 104⁹. The kings and the mighty in the text, therefore, are native rulers and Sadducees. We thus agree with Köstlin, *Theol. Jahrb.* 1856, 268 sqq., and Dillmann, Herzog, *R. E.* xii. 352, in identifying these princes with the last of the decaying Asmonean dynasty. The Herodian dynasty was not supported by the Sadducees, and thus may be left out of consideration. Further, as there are no references to Rome in the Parables, it cannot as yet have made its power to be felt in Palestine; and the Parables, therefore, must have been written before 64 B.C., when Rome interposed in favour of Aristobulus II. Baldensperger, *Das Selbstbewusstsein Jesu* (p. 12), indeed, tries to show that there are references to the Roman power; but his main contention, that the falling Asmoneans could hardly be designated as 'mighty kings', is already answered on critical grounds: the phrase 'mighty kings' does not belong to the true text. The lower limit is thus 64 B.C., and the higher may be reasonably fixed at 94. The differences between the Maccabees and the Pharisees, which had already grown important under John Hyrcanus with his Sadducean policy, were further developed under Aristobulus I, and in the early years of Alex. Jannaeus were intensified into an irreconcilable antagonism. This antagonism *first* issued in bloodshed about 95 B.C., when 6,000 Pharisees were put to death because they insulted Alex. Jannaeus for failing to comply with their views on ritual. This fact explains the writer's demand for vengeance for the murder of the righteous, 47¹,²,⁴. Subsequent years only embittered the strife between the Pharisees and the Asmonean head of the Sadducees, and provoked a civil war in which 50,000 Jews fell. Weary of the struggle, Jannaeus asked the Pharisees to name their conditions of peace: their answer was laconic and irreconcilable, 'Thy death'; but in the subsequent strife they were for the time crushed into impotence. Owing to the multitudes of Pharisees slain by Jannaeus, he came to be called 'the slayer of the pious'. With the accession of Alexandra 79, however, the Pharisees became masters of the nation, and peace prevailed till 70, when again the nation was rent in twain and plunged into devastating and bloody wars, through the fraternal strife of Hyrcanus II and Aristobulus II. To a devout Pharisee the Maccabees with their Saddacean and Hellenic principles might well appear as enemies of the Theocratic community during the years 94-79 or 70-64. To one or other of these periods, therefore, we assign the composition of the Parables. Perish and. $>q$. Be given into the hands of the righteous. This phrase would seem to indicate the period of the sword, when the righteous were themselves to slay the wicked. But this would be unsuitable here: the judgement is catastrophic and forensic. The Son of Man is judge, and his judgements are executed by the angels of punishment, 41² 62¹¹. This phrase recurs in 48⁹; but there the context requires us to understand the casting of the kings into Gehenna. In 50², where we again find this idea unmistakably, the difficulty is obviated by the fact that 50 is most probably an interpolation. Either, then, we have here an inconsistent feature introduced by the original writer, or else the phrase is only to be taken in a general sense, as expressing the triumph of the righteous. Righteous and holy. This designation of the members of the kingdom is found also in 48¹,⁴,⁷

6. And thenceforward none shall seek for themselves mercy
from the Lord of Spirits:
For their life is at an end.

The Abode of the Righteous and of the Elect One: the Praises of the Blessed.

XXXIX. [1. And it †shall come to pass in those days that elect and holy children † will descend from the high heaven, and their seed † will become one with the children of men. 2. And in those days Enoch received books of zeal and wrath, and books of disquiet and expulsion.]

And mercy shall not be accorded to them, saith the Lord of
Spirits.

3. And in those days a whirlwind carried me off from the
earth,
And set me down at the end of the heavens.

4. And there I saw another vision, the dwelling-places of the
holy,

$51^2 (65^{12})$. 6. **Thenceforward.** q reads 'there'. **Seek for themselves** ($a, cov_1 b$). Other MSS. 'seek'. The 'for themselves' could also be translated 'for them'; but the dative here is clearly the Hebrew *dativus ethicus*.

XXXIX. 1-2^a. This passage is obviously an interpolation. It has nothing to do with its present context and appears to be a fragment of the older book of Enoch, such as we find in chapters 6-36. Here manifestly 39^{2b} 'And mercy shall not be accorded to them, saith the Lord of Spirits' should follow immediately on 38^6. This interpolation refers to the descent of the Watchers to unite themselves with the daughters of men.

XXXIX. 1. And it shall come to pass. Here and in the rest of this verse we should have past and not future tenses. This may be due to the interpolator who made these changes in order to adapt it to the time of the adjoining context. **Elect and holy children...from the high heaven.** For 'elect and holy' q reads 'holy and elect'. For the idea cf. 106^{13} 'Some from the heights of heaven'. For the epithet 'elect' cf. 1 Tim. 5^{21} 'the elect angels'. Schodde compares Tob. 8^{15}. **2. Enoch received books of zeal,** &c. As we shall find later, sometimes an angel dictates to Enoch, at others the angel himself writes the book and commits it to Enoch. **Zeal and wrath.** q trans. **3. Carried me off.** This seems to be recounted as a real translation of Enoch, as in 52^1; cf. 2 Kings 2^{11}, and not as a mere incident in a dream, as in $14^{8, 9}$. **4. Dwelling-places.** This could be rendered 'dwellings' or 'abiding-places': see $39^{7, 8}$ 41^2 2 Enoch 61^2 John 14^2. The vision here (39^{4-12}) set forth is prophetic, but there are many difficulties in the interpretation which we can surmount only by bearing in mind that

And the resting-places of the righteous.

5. Here mine eyes saw their dwellings with His righteous angels,
And their resting-places with the holy.

And they petitioned and interceded and prayed for the children of men,
And righteousness flowed before them as water,

And mercy like dew upon the earth:
Thus it is amongst them for ever and ever.

6 *a*. And in that place mine eyes saw the Elect One of righteousness and of faith,

7 *a*. And I saw his dwelling-place under the wings of the Lord of Spirits.

6 *b*. And righteousness shall prevail in his days,
And the righteous and elect shall be without number before Him for ever and ever.

7 *b*. And all the righteous and elect before Him shall be †strong† as fiery lights,.

what we have here to deal with is a vision of the future Messianic kingdom, and that we must not press the details; for in this, as in visions frequently, there is no exact observance of the unities of time and place. No one individual period is indicated; for the fact that the Messiah is surrounded by all His righteous and elect ones shows that the history of the world is closed, and the final judgement already passed; yet this is impossible, as the angels are still praying on behalf of men. Nor from this chapter, taken by itself, can we argue as to the locality indicated by the vision. At first sight it seems to be heaven, as the Messiah and the righteous are under the wings of the Lord of Spirits; yet this is impossible, as the history of mankind is not yet consummated, and the Messiah appears only to carry out its consummation. The chief inference that we can legitimately draw is that the Messianic community will one day be composed of both angels and men, under the rule of the Messiah and the immediate protection of the Lord of Spirits. 5. His righteous angels (*a*). β 'the angels'. Righteousness flowed... as water. Cf. Amos 5^{24}. See also 49^1 97^9. 6-7. The text is slightly confused. By placing 7^a before 6^b I think I have recovered the original. 6. That place (*a–m*). *m*, *t*^{2}β 'those days'. The Elect One (*a–q*). *q*, β–*az* 'the place of the elect'. See note on 38^2. 'Elect One' = בָּחִיר. Cf. Is. 41^8, ^{9} 42^1 Luke 23^{35}. 7^a. His dwelling-place (*gm*). *qtuβ* 'their dwelling-place'. 6^b. In his days (*a*). *t*^{2}β 'in their days'. 7^b. Be †strong† (jĕthĕjalû *a–m*). *mt*^{2}β–*a* jetlahajû = 'be beautiful', not 'shine' as it has hitherto been taken. The latter is probably a correction of the former. *a–m* = יחזקו, which may be corrupt for יזהרו = 'shine'. Thus 'the righteous

And their mouth shall be full of blessing,
And their lips extol the name of the Lord of Spirits,
And righteousness before Him shall never fail,
[And uprightness shall never fail before Him].

8. There I wished to dwell,
And my spirit longed for that dwelling-place:
And there heretofore hath been my portion,
For so has it been established concerning me before the Lord of Spirits.

9. In those days I praised and extolled the name of the Lord of Spirits with blessings and praises, because He hath destined me for blessing and glory according to the good pleasure of the Lord of Spirits. 10. For a long time my eyes regarded that place, and I blessed Him and praised Him, saying: 'Blessed is He, and may He be blessed from the beginning and for evermore. 11. And before Him there is no ceasing. He knows before the world was created what is for ever and what will be from generation unto generation. 12. Those who sleep not bless Thee: they stand before Thy glory and bless, praise, and extol, saying: "Holy, holy, holy, is the Lord of Spirits: He filleth the earth with spirits."' 13. And here my eyes saw all those who sleep not: they stand before Him and bless and say: 'Blessed be Thou, and blessed be the name of the Lord for ever and

... shall shine as fiery lights', i.e. the stars; cf. Dan. 12³. This restoration is not possible in Aramaic. And uprightness, &c. Bracketed as a doublet of the preceding line. *abdux₁a*—very second rate MSS.—omit it. 8. Enoch predestined to a place in the kingdom. And there (*g, n*). Other MSS. 'there'. 9. The good pleasure of the Lord. In 37⁴ and here the free grace of God is brought forward, but not exclusively; for, like a true Pharisee, man's part in salvation is emphasized in 37⁴ 'according to my insight'. 11. Before Him there is no ceasing. Past, present, and future are before Him. 12.

Those who sleep not: cf. 39¹³ 40² 61¹². This designation is taken over into the Interpolations, 71⁷. In the note on 1⁵ I have identified them with the 'Watchers'. Holy, holy, holy, is the Lord of Spirits. The change in the trisagion, Is. 6³, is in keeping with the character of the entire section. 13. All + *q* 'the wakeful ones'. 13—XL. Enoch next sees all the chief angels and thousands of thousands of angels who stood before the throne of God, and recounts this, not as a prophetic vision, but as an actual experience. 14. The change of face here is not to be understood as a transfiguration, as in Ascensio Isaiae 7²⁵:

ever.' 14. And my face was changed; for I could no longer behold.

The Four Archangels.

XL. 1. And after that I saw thousands of thousands and ten thousand times ten thousand, I saw a multitude beyond number and reckoning, who stood before the Lord of Spirits. 2. And on the four sides of the Lord of Spirits I saw four presences, different from those that sleep not, and I learnt their names: for the angel who went with me made known to me their names, and showed me all the hidden things.

3. And I heard the voices of those four presences as they uttered praises before the Lord of glory. 4. The first voice blesses the Lord of Spirits for ever and ever. 5. And the

Enoch is '*blinded* by excess of light'. For (a). $t^a\beta$–e 'till'.

XL. 1. **Thousands of thousands and ten thousand times ten thousand.** This phrase is taken over exactly into the Interpolations, 60¹ 71⁸, though the phrase was of course a current one, owing to Dan. 7¹⁰. Cf. Rev. 5¹¹. 2. There are higher angels than those that sleep not: these are the four angels of the presence—מַלְאֲכֵי הַפָּנִים—so called from Is. 63⁹. Their names here are Michael, Raphael, Gabriel, and Phanuel; and the same list is carried over into the Interpolations, 71⁹. In later Judaism we find Uriel instead of Phanuel. In 9¹ the names of the four chiefs are Michael, Gabriel, Uriel, and Raphael. In 20 there are seven chief angels enumerated: Uriel, Raphael, Raguel, Michael, Saraqael, Gabriel, and Remiel. Thus, Michael, Raphael, and Gabriel belong in common to 20 and 40, but the functions respectively assigned them in these chapters are irreconcilable. In 90²¹ there is a reference to seven chief angels: in 81⁵ 90³² three angels are mentioned who were charged with the escort of Enoch: in 87²,³ we find again four. It would be a mere waste of time to attempt to reconcile the angelology of these various passages. On Angelology see Schwab, *Vocabulaire de l'Angélologie*, 1897, supplement, 1899; *Jewish Encyclopaedia*, i. 583-597; Weber², *Jüd. Theol.* 1897. **That sleep not** (a–m). $t^a\beta$ 'that stand'. **The angel who went with me.** This angel is similarly named in 43³ 46² 52³,⁴ 61³, whereas we have the 'angel of peace' in 40⁸ 52⁵ 53⁴ 54⁴ 56², and 'the angel' in 61² 64². There is generally a certain fitness in the designation 'angel of peace' in the contexts, where it occurs in contrast to the wicked angels and the angels of punishment. This designation has also been taken over into the Interpolations, 60²⁴; it is already found in the T. Dan. 6⁸ T. Ash. 6⁶ T. Benj. 6¹. The origin of the phrase is probably to be traced to Is. 33⁷, as that verse was, according to Jerome, understood of the angels, and מַלְאֲכֵי שָׁלוֹם would in that case = 'angels of peace'. Cf. Rosenmüller's *Scholia in loc.* 4. **The first presence, Michael,** has for his task the praise of the Lord of Spirits, as his name indicates, מִיכָאֵל. In ver. 9 he is 'the merciful and long-suffering'. 5. **The second presence is Raphael,** who second voice I heard blessing the Elect One and the elect ones who hang upon the Lord of Spirits. 6. And the third voice I heard pray and intercede for those who dwell on the earth and supplicate in the name of the Lord of Spirits. 7. And I heard the fourth voice fending off the Satans and forbidding them to come before the Lord of Spirits to accuse them who dwell on the earth. 8. After that I asked the angel of peace who went with me, who showed me everything that is hidden: 'Who are these four presences which I have seen and whose

praises the Elect and the elect ones. Conformably to his name (from רפא, to heal) he is appointed to heal the wounds and ills of men (ver. 9): cf. Tobit 12^{14} 'God sent me (Raphael) *to heal thee*'; and 3^{17} 'Raphael was sent to heal them both'. In Rabbinic writings he was the power that presided over medicine; cf. Eisenmeng. *Entd. Jud.* ii. 380. See also 10^7 20^3. The Elect One. This designation of the Messiah comes from Is. 42^1. Its later use seems to be confined to the Parables (see 38^2) and St. Luke 9^{35} οὗτός ἐστιν ὁ υἱός μου ὁ ἐκλελεγμένος = 'the Elect One' (W. and H.). This, the correct text, has been preserved in the Ethiopic N.T.: St. Luke 23^{35} 'the Christ of God the Elect One'. And the elect ones. *q* 'of the elect ones'. 6. The third presence is Gabriel, whose task is that of intercession on behalf of the inhabiters of the earth. Cf. Test. Lev. 3^5 'In it are the archangels who minister and make propitiation to the Lord for all the sins of the righteous'. As the hero or strong one of God (גבר and אל) he is naturally set over all the powers (ver. 9). Pray and intercede . . . supplicate. These verbs are in the plural in all MSS. but *d*. Those who dwell, &c.: see 37^5. 7. The fourth is Phanuel, who is set over the repentance and hope of the inheritors of eternal life (ver. 9). He prevents the Satans from appearing before the Lord of Spirits to accuse men. The Satans appear here for the first time in Enoch, 40^7. They seem to belong to a counter kingdom of evil, ruled by a chief called Satan, 53^3. They existed as evil agencies before the fall of the Watchers; for the guilt of the latter consisted in becoming subject to Satan, 54^6. This view harmonizes exactly with that of Gen. 3^1 combined with 6$^{1-4}$. These Satans had the right of access into heaven, 40^7 (cf. Job 1^6 Zech. 3)—a privilege denied to the Watchers, 13^5 14^5. Their functions were threefold: they tempted to evil, 69$^{4, 6}$; they accused the dwellers upon earth, 40^7; they punished the condemned. In this last character they are technically called 'angels of punishment', 53^3 56^1 62^{11} 63^1; this designation has been taken over into the Interpolations: cf. 66^1 (note). The Talmud (cf. Weber, *Jüd. Theol.* 251-254) does not draw this clear line of demarcation between the Satans and the fallen angels, but rather confuses their attributes just as in ch. 69. For the close connexion between the Demonology of Enoch and the N.T. see Gen. Introduction. 8. Angel of peace. See note on ver. 2: also Test. Dan. 6^5 note T. Ash. 6^6 Test. Benj. 6^1. Hidden. +*abcdex* 'and I said unto him'.

words I have heard and written down?' 9. And he said to me: 'This first is Michael, the merciful and long-suffering: and the second, who is set over all the diseases and all the wounds of the children of men, is Raphael: and the third, who is set over all the powers, is Gabriel: and the fourth, who is set over the repentance unto hope of those who inherit eternal life, is named Phanuel.' 10. And these are the four angels of the Lord of Spirits and the four voices I heard in those days.

XLI. 1. And after that I saw all the secrets of the heavens, and how the kingdom is divided, and how the actions of men are weighed in the balance. 2. And there I saw the mansions of the elect and the mansions of the holy, and mine eyes saw there all the sinners being driven from thence which deny the name of the Lord of Spirits, and being dragged off: and they could not abide because of the punishment which proceeds from the Lord of Spirits.

9. **Michael** (a). β 'the holy Michael'. **Gabriel** (a). β 'the holy Gabriel'. **Repentance unto hope** (a–q, dghklno vwy). q 'repentance unto repentance', abcex 'repentance and hope'. Our text = τῆς μετανοίας εἰς ἐλπίδα. Cf. Acts 11¹⁸ μετάνοιαν εἰς ζωήν 2 Cor. 7¹⁰ μετάνοιαν εἰς σωτηρίαν. **Is named** (a). β 'is'. 10. **Lord of Spirits** (a). β 'the Most High God'.

XLI. 1. **The kingdom is divided.** What 'the kingdom' means here is doubtful. Dillmann takes it to mean the Messianic kingdom; Schodde, the kingdom of this world. Can it refer to the division of heaven into seven parts? **The actions of men are weighed**: cf. 61⁸. The idea is derived from the O.T., where Job (31⁶) prays to be weighed in an even balance, and the spirits of men are weighed by God, Prov. 16² 21² 24¹², and the wicked are found wanting, Ps. 62⁹ Dan. 5²⁷ Pss. Sol. 5⁶. In Enoch, as in the O.T., this idea is not incompatible with the doctrine of divine grace; but in the Talmud it is absolutely materialized, and man's salvation depends on a literal preponderance of his good deeds over his bad ones: see Weber, *Jüd. Theol.* 279–284. This weighing of man's deeds goes on daily (idem 283). But as the results of such judgements were necessarily unknown, there could not fail to be much uneasiness, and to allay this the doctrine of Abraham's meritorious righteousness was in due time developed, in virtue of which all natural descendants of Abraham through Jacob became entitled to salvation (Weber, 292–297). This doctrine, though as yet unknown in Enoch, was a popular belief in N.T. times; cf. Matt. 3⁹. **2. And**¹ᵃ (q). > a–qβ. **The sinners being driven from thence**: see 38¹. **Deny the name of the Lord of Spirits**: see 38². **3–8.** These verses are, it is obvious, alien in spirit and position to the context; they belong in character and detail to 43¹,² 44 59 69¹³⁻²⁵: see 43. They may, however, belong to the Parables, since

XLI. 3-9. *Astronomical Secrets.*

3. And there mine eyes saw the secrets of the lightning and of the thunder, and the secrets of the winds, how they are divided to blow over the earth, and the secrets of the clouds and dew, and there I saw from whence they proceed in that place and from whence they saturate the dusty earth. 4. And there I saw closed chambers out of which the winds are divided, the chamber of the hail and winds, the chamber of the mist, and of the clouds, and the cloud thereof hovers over the earth from the beginning of the world. 5. And I saw the chambers of the sun and moon, whence they proceed and whither they come again, and their glorious return, and how one is superior to the other, and their stately orbit, and how they do not leave their orbit, and they add nothing to their orbit and they take nothing from it, and they keep faith with each other, in accordance with the oath

---

Jewish mystics were interested in these questions. 3. The lightning and thunder are treated of repeatedly: see 17³ 43¹⁻² 44 59 60¹³⁻¹⁵; cf. Job 38²⁴, ²⁵, ³⁵. The secrets of the winds. On the manifold functions of the winds in Enoch see 18¹⁻⁵ 34–36 77. Dusty earth (gf¹α). mt²β 'dust of the earth'. 4. And there (mqtB). gu 'there'. The chamber of the..winds..mist.. clouds, &c. These conceptions rest on the poetical fancies of Job 38²². The writers in Enoch conceive all the natural powers, as thunder and lightning, rain, hail, dew, sun and moon, &c., as dwelling in their respective chambers. And winds (ahov₁b). β–hov₁b 'and'. And of the clouds (qtu¹β–a). > gu³. The cloud thereof, i. e. the cloud of mist. Have we here a reference to Gen. 1² or to 2⁶ (Beer)? 5. For the teaching of Enoch on the sun and moon see 72⁵. Their glorious return, i. e. from west to east on the other side of the firmament, or, according to 72⁵, round by way of the north. The perfect regularity with which the sun and moon traverse their orbits is here emphasized, as in 74¹² is that of the sun and stars. Yet in 80⁴ it is said that the moon will become irregular. We shall find, however, that 80 is an interpolation. The oath. A certain degree of consciousness seems to be attributed to the sun, moon, and stars. The sun and moon are subject only to God, 41⁶; they give thanks and praise, and rest not; for to them thanksgiving is rest, 41⁷; cf. 69²⁴. God calls the stars by name and they answer, 43¹; they keep faith with each other, 43²; they are weighed, as men, in a righteous balance, 43³; the disobedient stars are punished, 18¹³⁻¹⁶. In 72–79 various functions regarding the division of time are assigned to them. In the Persian religion the stars were regarded as embodied existences divided into troops, each under its own leader, Herzog², R. E. xi. 235. This theory would suit 82⁹⁻²⁰ perfectly. It must be confessed, however, that the conception by which they are bound together. 6. And first the sun goes forth and traverses his path according to the commandment of the Lord of Spirits, and mighty is His name for ever and ever. 7. And after that I saw the hidden and the visible path of the moon, and she accomplishes the course of her path in that place by day and by night—the one holding a position opposite to the other before the Lord of Spirits.

And they give thanks and praise and rest not;
For unto them is their thanksgiving rest.

8. For the sun changes oft for a blessing or a curse,
And the course of the path of the moon is light to the righteous,
And darkness to the sinners in the name of the Lord,
Who made a separation between the light and the darkness,
And divided the spirits of men,
And strengthened the spirits of the righteous,
In the name of His righteousness.

9. For no angel hinders and no power is able to hinder; for He appoints a judge for them all and he judges them all before Him.

The Dwelling-places of Wisdom and of Unrighteousness.

XLII. 1. Wisdom found no place where she might dwell;

varies. **By which they are bound together.** So k alone reading zaḥabĕrŭ—probably a fortunate conjecture. Very early the original reading zaḥabĕrŭ was corrupted into zaḥadarŭ (a, eh^2o_1b), and later into zanabarŭ ($abcdfhlnx_1a$). Hence there is no need to assume a corruption in the Greek or Hebrew. **6. Traverses.** q, c 'returns'. **7. Hidden...path of the moon**, i.e. when the moon is invisible: see 73–74. **Before.** + mt^1u 'the glory of'. **8. The sun** (a, py). $m, t^2\beta$-py read 'the shining sun'. **Divided the spirits of men.** There seems to be an actual predestination here spoken of. This division into children of light and darkness is in the past: the spirits of the righteous are strengthened in the present. **9. No angel hinders and no power** ($mq, t^3u\beta$-y). gt^1, y read 'neither angel nor power'. **He appoints a judge for them all.** Here I follow g in reading 'He appoints', and $_1a$ in taking 'a judge' in the acc. The rest of the MSS. read 'the judge sees them all'. It would also be possible to render the latter reading: 'the Judge of all sees'. The text is uncertain. If the reading adopted in the translation is right the judge appointed is the Messiah. This verse is to be read directly after 41^2; cf. Acts 17^{31}.

XLII. As has been already recognized, this chapter is a fragment, and out

Then a dwelling-place was assigned her in the heavens.

2. Wisdom went forth to make her dwelling among the children of men,

And found no dwelling-place:

Wisdom returned to her place,
And took her seat among the angels.

3. And unrighteousness went forth from her chambers:
Whom she sought not she found,
And dwelt with them,

As rain in a desert
And dew on a thirsty land.

XLIII—XLIV. *Astronomical Secrets.*

XLIII. 1. And I saw other lightnings and the stars of heaven, and I saw how He called them all by their names and they hearkened unto Him. 2. And I saw how they are weighed in a righteous balance according to their proportions of light: (I saw) the width of their spaces and the day of their appearing, and how their revolution produces lightning: and (I saw) their revolution

of connexion with its present context: where in the present book of Enoch it should stand, I do not know. 1, 2. The praise of wisdom was a favourite theme. Wisdom was regarded as having her dwelling-place in heaven, 84³ Job 28¹²⁻¹⁴, ²⁰⁻²⁴ Baruch 3²⁹ Sir. 24⁴; and as coming to earth and desiring to make her abode with men, Prov. 1²⁰ sqq. 8 9¹⁻¹⁰ Sir. 24⁷; but as men refused to receive her, cf. 1 En. 94⁵, she returned to heaven. But in the Messianic times she will return, and will be poured out as water in abundance, 49¹; and the thirsty will drink to the full of wisdom, 48¹; she will be bestowed on the elect, 5⁸ 91¹⁰; cf. 2 Bar. 44¹⁴ 4 Ezra 8⁵²; and the spirit of Wisdom will abide in the Messiah the Elect One, 49³. We are reminded in some measure here of the Prologue of St. John. Went forth (a, β-abcdefgi). abcex 'came'. 3. The

different welcome which the wicked give to unrighteousness intensifies their guilt in respect to wisdom. They received not wisdom when she came unto them; but they took home unto themselves unrighteousness though she sought them not.

XLIII, XLIV. These chapters belong to the same class as 41³⁻⁹. Though in my first edition I treated these sections on natural phenomena as interpolations I no longer do so. Their presence, however, frequently deranges the context. On the other hand we see from Job, Sirach, and Wisdom that the wise in Israel were interested alike in ethical and cosmic questions.

XLIII. 1. Called them all by their names: cf. Ps. 147⁴ Is. 40²⁶ Bar. 3³⁴. 2. Weighed in a righteous balance. On the conscious existence attributed to the stars see 41⁵. How their revolution pro-according to the number of the angels, and (how) they keep faith with each other. 3. And I asked the angel who went with me who showed me what was hidden: 'What are these?' 4. And he said to me: 'The Lord of Spirits hath showed thee their parabolic meaning (lit. 'their parable'): these are the names of the holy who dwell on the earth and believe in the name of the Lord of Spirits for ever and ever.'

XLIV. Also another phenomenon I saw in regard to the lightnings: how some of the stars arise and become lightnings and cannot part with their new form.

XLV—LVII. The Second Parable.

The Lot of the Apostates: the New Heaven and the New Earth.

XLV. 1. And this is the Second Parable concerning those who deny the name of the dwelling of the holy ones and the Lord of Spirits.

2. And into the heaven they shall not ascend,
And on the earth they shall not come:
Such shall be the lot of the sinners

duces lightning ($gyt^1\{mu\}$). $t^2\beta$ 'and revolution: how one flash of lightning produces another'. 3. The angel who went with me who showed me what was hidden: cf. 46^2. Taken over into the Interpolations, 60^{11}. 3, 4. There is some mysterious connexion between the stars and the holy, whereby the stars represent the holy; cf. Dan. 8^{10}. Does it mean that the holy will be as numerous as the stars? or as bright as the stars? cf. 104^2 Dan. 12^3 Matt. 13^{43}. There was a close connexion between the stars and the angels in the O. T.; cf. Job 38^7, where the morning stars are undoubtedly angels; cf. also Deut. 4^{19}. 4. Holy (a). β 'righteous'. Believe in the name: cf. 39^6 'the Elect One... of *faith*'; 58^5 'the inheritance of *faith*'; 61^4 'the measures given to *faith*'; 61^{11} 'in the spirit of *faith*'.

Contrast the *denial* of sinners, 38^2.

XLIV. The reference here is to shooting stars, ἀστέρες διαθέοντες, Arist. *Meteor.* i. 4. Lightning in general is produced by the quick movement of the stars, 43^2; but some of the stars at times are transformed wholly into lightning.

XLV. 1. It is idle to expect an accurate description of the contents of the Parable from the opening verse or superscription. We find none such in $38^{1, 2}$; nor yet in $58^{1, 2}$. For a summary of the thought of the Parables see pp. 67–68. Those who deny the name of the dwelling: see 38^2 (note). The Lord of Spirits (a). β 'of the Lord of Spirits'. 2. And ^{10} (a–t). > t, β. On the earth they shall not come. The earth will be transformed (ver. 5) and be thenceforth the abode of the righteous only.

Who have denied the name of the Lord of Spirits,
Who are thus preserved for the day of suffering and tribulation.

3. On that day Mine Elect One shall sit on the throne of glory
And shall try their works,
And their places of rest shall be innumerable.
And their souls shall grow strong within them when they see Mine elect ones,
And those who have called upon My glorious name:
4. Then will I cause Mine Elect One to dwell among them.

Denied the name of the Lord of Spirits: see 38^2 (note). **Day of suffering and tribulation.** The final judgement is variously named—'that great day,' 54^6; 'day of ... judgement,' 22^4 100^4; 'day of ... judgement and ... consummation,' 10^{12}; 'day of the consummation,' 16^1; 'the great judgement,' 16^1 19^1 22^4 25^4; 'day of the great judgement,' 10^6 19^1 84^4 94^9 98^{10} 99^{15} 104^5; 'great day of judgement,' 22^{11}; 'judgement which is for ever,' 104^5; 'great judgement which is for ever,' 91^{15}; 'judgement that is for ever and ever,' 10^{12}; 'day of tribulation,' 1^1 96^2; 'day of tribulation and pain,' 55^3; 'day of tribulation and great shame,' 98^{10}; 'day of suffering and tribulation,' 45^2 63^8; 'day of affliction,' 48^{10} 50^2; 'day of anguish and affliction,' 48^8; 'day of destruction,' 98^{10}; 'day of slaughter,' 94^9; 'day of unceasing bloodshed,' 99^6; 'day of darkness,' 94^9; 'day of unrighteousness,' 97^1. As the same phrase is applied to quite different events it is necessary to observe that— (1) The Deluge or first world judgement is referred to in $10^{4,\,5,\,12\,b}$ 54^5 $^{7-10}$ 91^5 93^4. (2) Final world judgement *at the beginning of the Messianic kingdom*, $10^{6\,12\,c}$ 16^1 19^1 $22^{4,\,11}$ 25^4 45^2 54^6 55^4 90^{20-27}. (3) Judgement of the sword *at the beginning of the Messianic kingdom*, when the righteous slay the wicked, 50^2 90^{19} 91^{12} 95^7 96^1 98^{12}. (4) Final world judgement *at the close of the Messianic kingdom*, 94^9 98^{10} 100^4 103^8 104^5. In 48^{8-10} there seems to be a combination of (2) and (3), and in 99^9 99^{15} of (3) and (4). **3. Mine Elect One** (a–m). m, $t^3\beta$ 'the Elect One': see 40^5. **On the throne of glory.** The Elect One will sit on the throne of his glory, 45^3 55^4 $62^{3,\,5}$; as Son of Man, he will sit on the throne of his glory, $69^{27,\,29}$; being placed thereon by the Lord of Spirits, 61^8 62^2; and his throne is likewise the throne of the Head of Days, 47^3 51^3. The Elect One sits on his throne to judge; for all judgement has been committed unto him, 69^{27}. **Try.** Text reads jahari (= choose) = יבחר corrupt for יבחן. If the original were Aramaic we should only have to suppose that the translator followed the wrong meaning of יבחר. **Places of rest.** This is not the same word as is used in 39^4; but may be rendered similarly, as it is the Ethiopic rendering of mansio, μονή. **Souls** (a). β 'spirits'. But as we have seen in ch. 22 the Ethiopic words are often interchangeable. **Elect ones** (a–m, $dekln wy^2 \mu$). m, $abcfhoxy^1$ 'Elect One'. **Glorious** (a). $t^3\beta$ 'holy and glorious'. **4. Mine Elect**

And I will transform the heaven and make it an eternal blessing and light,

5. And I will transform the earth and make it a blessing:

    And I will cause Mine elect ones to dwell upon it:
    But the sinners and evil-doers shall not set foot thereon.

6. For I have provided and satisfied with peace My righteous ones
    And have caused them to dwell before Me:

    But for the sinners there is judgement impending with Me,
    So that I shall destroy them from the face of the earth.

The Head of Days and the Son of Man.

XLVI. 1. And there I saw One who had a head of days,
    And His head was white like wool,
    And with Him was another being whose countenance had the appearance of a man,
    And his face was full of graciousness, like one of the holy angels.

One (*mt*, β-*cn*). *gqu, cy*² 'Mine elect ones'. 4, 5. After the judgement the Messianic kingdom is established and its scene will be a transformed heaven, 45⁴ 51⁴; and earth, 41² 45⁵; its members will be angels, 39⁴ (note), and men; and the Elect One will abide amongst them. This idea of the transformation of the world was derived directly from Is. 65¹⁷ and 66²², and probably originally from Zoroastrianism: see Cheyne's *Origin of the Psalter*, 404, 405. It is found elsewhere in Enoch in 72¹ 91¹⁶. In Isaiah this idea is only adopted eclectically; for it is incompatible with other facts in the context, i.e. 65²⁰, &c.; but in Enoch it is accepted in its entire significance as logically involving the immortal blessedness of man; cf. 2 Bar. 32⁶ 57² 4 Ezra 7⁷⁵. 6. Destroy them from the face of the earth. Cf. 69²⁷.

XLVI. 1. In this and the following chapters Daniel 7 has been laid under contribution, and from it have been drawn directly the expressions 'Head of Days', and 'Son of Man'. The former means in Daniel the Everlasting, and seems to do so here likewise: r'ĕsa mawā'ĕl = 'the sum of days'. Hence the first line = 'And there I saw the Everlasting'. It is of course awkward that the word 'head' occurs in the next line in a literal sense. The phrase 'Head of Days' is found in Enoch in 46² 47³ 48², and has been carried over into the Interpolations, 55¹ 60². The original writer uses this expression of Daniel with much appropriateness in connexion with the supernatural Son of Man and the question of final judgement; in fact the two expressions are correlative: observe the question, 'Why he went with the Head of Days?' but this technical appropriateness is wanting in the Interpolations. Another being ... like one of the holy angels: cf. 1 Sam. 29⁹

2. And I asked the angel who went with me and showed me all the hidden things, concerning that Son of Man, who he was,

Acts 6¹⁵. **2. The angel.** MSS. wrongly read 'one of the angels'. See note on 40². **That Son of Man.** There are some difficulties connected with this expression in Enoch, as it has there three different Ethiopic renderings, = *filius hominis*, 46², ³, ⁴ 48², *filius viri*, 62⁵ 69²⁹ 71¹⁴, and *filius prolis matris viventium*, 62⁷, ⁹, ¹⁴ 63¹¹ 69²⁶, ²⁷ 70¹ 71¹⁷; and these are the greater as the Ethiopic translator can only have had one and the same phrase before him, i.e. ὁ υἱὸς τοῦ ἀνθρώπου. For the LXX invariably uses υἱὸς ἀνθρώπου as a rendering of בן אדם and בר אנש, and exact Greek equivalents of the Ethiopic expressions are hardly conceivable. Are we then to suppose that these variations existed in the Hebrew, and accordingly postulate on the part of the Ethiopic translators a direct acquaintance with an Hebrew MS. (similarly, as Nöldeke, *Encyc. Brit.* xxi. 654, in the case of the Ethiopic Bible, postulates the presence of Aramaic teachers in order to explain the fact that certain religious conceptions are there expressed by Aramaic words)? These suppositions are not necessary. There is no strict uniformity of rendering in the Ethiopic Bible. υἱὸς ἀνθρώπου is rendered by 'proles matris viventium' in Num. 23¹⁹ Ps. 8⁴ 144³ 146³ (in the last two instances, two distinct Hebrew expressions are used); but by 'filius prolis matris viventium' in Ps. 80¹⁷. This latter rendering is practically the authorized one in the Ethiopic as it is found throughout Ezekiel, in Dan. 7¹³, and universally in the N. T. Again ብእሲ = *vir* is frequently used where we should expect ሰብእ = *homo*, and vice versa. Hence *filius viri* and *filius hominis* in the Ethiopic text may be synonymous and the variation may be due to the carelessness of the translator. Of such carelessness there are many instances in Enoch. In 89¹ we find ብእሲ where we should have በግዕ as it is correctly in vv. 9 and 36. Again, in 89⁴⁵ we have twice the rendering 'sheep' where according to the context and the Greek it should be 'lamb'. Accordingly we hold that these variations were confined to the Ethiopic version, and this conclusion is confirmed by the fact that *filius viri*, 69²⁹, does not imply one born of man without the mediation of a mother as some have supposed; for the same phrase, as the text stands at present, is applied to Enoch in 71¹⁴, and is therefore the equivalent of *filius hominis* in 46³, &c. We have above remarked that the expression in the Greek version of Enoch appears to have been ὁ υἱὸς τοῦ ἀνθρώπου, and not υἱὸς ἀνθρώπου, for in Enoch it is the distinct designation of the personal Messiah. In 48¹⁰ 52⁴ he is styled the 'Messiah'. It will be observed that the demonstrative precedes the title 'Son of Man' in our text, as it does in every instance of its occurrence save in 62⁷. Wellhausen presses home the fact that the use of the demonstrative before the expression 'Son of Man' proves conclusively that 'Son of Man' cannot be a Messianic title; for that such a phrase as 'this Messiah' or 'that Messiah' is an impossibility. Since such importance is attached to the presence or absence of the demonstratives, it is well to point out that in all probability the demonstratives are here translations of the Greek article. In the earlier chapters, where the Greek version is preserved, we find that 'this' (= zĕ or zentû) is a rendering of the Greek article in 25¹ 27² 28² 32⁵, and

Chapter XLVI. 2-3

and whence he was, (and) why he went with the Head of Days?
3. And he answered and said unto me:
This is the Son of Man who hath righteousness,

'that' (= w'ětû) in 13^{10} 14^{10}: 'those' (= 'ĕlkû) in 10^{9}. In 89^{42-49}, where the Greek version also survives, we find that 'that' (= zekû or zektû or w'ětû), though occurring twelve times in these verses, is eleven times a rendering of the Greek article. Every Ethiopic scholar is aware of this fact, and attention is rightly drawn to it in Dillmann's Ethiopic Lexicon under each of the above demonstratives. Moreover we can show in the Parables in three passages undeniable instances of such renderings, i.e. in 52^{5} 62^{10} and 71^{13}, where w'ětû precedes respectively the phrases 'Angel of peace', 'Lord of Spirits', and 'Head of Days'. No Jew could say 'that God'. Now turning from the above general evidence to the passages themselves we find that in two, i.e. 46^{3} and 71^{14}, w'ětû serves as the copula—a frequent usage in Ethiopic, and in these passages it cannot rightly be taken otherwise. Thus there are three passages where the demonstrative is wanting, i.e. 62^{7}, as we have already observed, and these two, 46^{3} 71^{14}. These facts, combined with the usage of our translator in rendering the Greek article, as we have shown above, makes it probable in the highest degree that zekû and zentû stand for the article and nothing more in $46^{2, 4}$ 48^{2} $62^{9, 14}$ 63^{11}, and that similarly w'ětû in $69^{26, 29 \text{ (bis)}}$ 70^{1} 71^{17} is a rendering of the article. For the relation between the title 'Son of Man' in Enoch and in the N. T. see Appendix on 'the Son of Man'.
3. The Son of Man. Here the w'ětû (= 'that') that precedes this title is a copula as in 71^{14}. See preceding note. The Messiah is conceived in the Parables as (1) the Judge of the world, (2) the Revealer of all things, (3) the Messianic Champion and Ruler of the righteous. (1) As judge, he possesses (a) righteousness, (b) wisdom, and (c) power (Pss. 45^{4-8} 72 Is. 11^{3-5} Jer. $23^{5, 6}$). (a) He is the Righteous One in an extraordinary sense, 38^{2} (see note) 53^{6}; he possesses righteousness, and it dwells with him, 46^{3}, and on the ground of his essential righteousness, 46^{3}, has he been chosen no less than according to God's good pleasure, 49^{4}. (b) Wisdom, which could find no dwelling-place on earth, 42, dwells in him and the spirit of Him who giveth knowledge, 49^{3}; and the secrets of wisdom stream forth from his mouth, 51^{3}, and wisdom is poured out like water before him, 49^{1}. (c) In him abides the spirit of power, 49^{3}, and he possesses universal dominion, 62^{6}. (2) He is the revealer of all things. His appearance will be the signal for the revelation of good and the unmasking of evil; will bring to light everything that is hidden, alike the invisible world of righteousness and the hidden world of sin, 46^{3} $49^{2, 4}$; and will recall to life those that have perished on land and sea, and those that are in Sheol and hell, 51^{1} 61^{5}. Evil when once unmasked will vanish from his presence, 49^{2}. Hence all judgement has been committed unto him, 69^{27}, and he will sit on the throne of his glory, 45^{3} (see note), and all men and angels will be judged before him, 51^{2} 55^{4} 61^{8} $62^{2, 3}$, and no lying utterance will be possible before him, 49^{4} 62^{3}, and by the mere word of his mouth will he slay the ungodly, 62^{2}. (3) He is the Messianic champion and ruler of the righteous. He is the stay of the righteous, 48^{4}, and has already

With whom dwelleth righteousness,
And who revealeth all the treasures of that which is hidden,
Because the Lord of Spirits hath chosen him,
And whose lot hath the pre-eminence before the Lord of Spirits in uprightness for ever.

4. And this Son of Man whom thou hast seen
Shall †raise up† the kings and the mighty from their seats,
[And the strong from their thrones]
And shall loosen the reins of the strong,
And break the teeth of the sinners;

5. [And he shall put down the kings from their thrones and kingdoms]
Because they do not extol and praise Him,

been revealed to them, 62⁷; he is the avenger of their life, 48⁷, the preserver of their inheritance, 48⁷; he will vindicate the earth as their possession for ever, 51⁵, and establish the community of the righteous in unhindered prosperity, 53⁶ 62⁸; their faces will shine with joy, 51⁵, and they will be vestured with life, 62¹⁵, and be resplendent with light, 39⁷, and he will abide in closest communion with them for ever, 62¹⁴, in the immediate presence of the Lord of Spirits, 39⁷, and his glory is for ever and ever, and his might unto all generations, 49². Who hath righteousness. On the Messiah as the possessor of righteousness cf. Is. 9⁶⁻⁷ 11³ ᵃᵖᵖ· Jer. 23⁵ Zech. 9⁹ Pss. Sol. 17²⁵, ²⁸, ²⁹, ³¹, ⁴², ⁴⁶ 18⁸. Hath chosen him. Hence he is called 'the Elect One': see 38² (note) 40⁴ (note). Whose lot hath the pre-eminence (aefh¹k). t²β–efh¹k read 'whose lot hath surpassed everything', cf. Heb. 1⁴. 4. This = the Greek article. See note on 46². Shall †raise up†. The verb is here obviously corrupt. The clause 'shall raise up the kings ... from their thrones' and 46⁵ ᵃ 'shall put down the kings from their thrones' are dittographs. One or other is corrupt and one or other is an intrusion. The parallelism seems to be in favour of 46⁴ ᵇ being retained, though the verb gives the wrong sense, whereas the right sense 'shall put down' is obviously preserved in 46⁵ ᵃ. It is hard to explain with any confidence the origin of this error. Possibly יָרִים stood in the original, which could mean either 'shall raise up' or 'shall remove, destroy'. The present context could admit only of the latter meaning. Or we might take the former verb as = יִטֹּל—a corruption of יַפִּיל—'shall cast down,' seeing that in 46⁵ ᵃ the same verb in the Ethiopic for 'shall put down' is given. 'Shall put down the countenance' = יַפִּיל פָּנִים. Cf. 48⁸. In any case we should read 'shall put down the kings', &c. It is possible that Is. 14⁹ 'it hath raised up from their thrones all the kings of the nations' may have led to the above misrendering or corruption. With the restored text we might compare such expressions as Sir. 10¹⁴ θρόνους ἀρχόντων καθεῖλεν ὁ κύριος, Wisd. 5²³ περιτρέψει θρόνους δυναστῶν. The clause in Luke 1⁵² καθεῖλε δυνάστας ἀπὸ θρόνων seems to be an echo of our text. Break the teeth of the sinners. From

[Sect. II]   *Chapter XLVI. 4-7*

> Nor humbly acknowledge whence the kingdom was bestowed
>   upon them.
>
> 6. And he shall put down the countenance of the strong,
>   And shall fill them with shame.
>
> And darkness shall be their dwelling,
> And worms shall be their bed,
>
> And they shall have no hope of rising from their beds,
> Because they do not extol the name of the Lord of Spirits.
>
> 7. And these are they who †judge† the stars of heaven,
>   [And raise their hands against the Most High],
>   †And tread upon the earth and dwell upon it†.
>
> And all their deeds manifest unrighteousness,

Ps. 37 58⁶.   **5. Acknowledge whence the kingdom,** &c. Cf. Wisd. 6²⁻³ ἐναντιώσασθε οἱ κρατοῦντες πλήθους ... ὅτι ἐδόθη παρὰ τοῦ κυρίου ἡ κράτησις ὑμῖν, Rom. 13¹.   **6. Worms shall be their bed.** Cf. Is. 14¹¹. In 2 Macc. 9⁵,⁹ it is said that Antiochus Epiphanes died of the disease here referred to. But the expression is best taken figuratively of the destruction awaiting the oppressors of the righteous; cf. Is. 66²⁴ Judith 16¹⁷ Sir. 7¹⁷ Mark 9⁴⁸. **Worms ... their bed ... Because they do not extol.** Cf. Acts 12²³ for a like connexion of thought.   **7.** This verse seems very corrupt. It is clearly an echo of Dan. 8¹⁰, where it is said of Antiochus Epiphanes: 'And (the little horn) waxed great, even to the host of heaven; and some of the host and of the stars it cast down to the ground and trod upon them.' Here also the stars stand for the righteous, and the verb 'tread' recalls 'trod' in Daniel, and the parallel suggests that 'tread' had the same meaning in Enoch that it had in Daniel. In other words we should find it stated that the oppressors 'tread down the righteous' and not that they 'tread the earth'. Thus 46⁷ᶜ connects immediately with 46⁷ᵃ. In other words 47⁷ᵇ is either displaced or interpolated. That it is the latter I conclude, since we require here, not a tristich, but a distich like the immediate stanzas before and after, and since the divine designation 'Most High' does not occur elsewhere in the Parables. I have obelized 'judge'. It = ידינו, which may be corrupt for יורדו (or יפילו as in Dan. 8¹⁰) = 'cast down'. This brings our text into line with Dan. 8¹⁰ᵇ. Finally, 'and dwell upon the earth' may be a wrong gloss on the preceding words; for this clause, which has always good ethical associations in the Parables (37² note), has here a bad ethical sense. But probably a corruption inheres in 'and dwell upon it': i.e. וישבו בה corrupt for יושביה = 'those who dwell upon it.' As for what remains, 'and they tread upon the earth,' a glance at Dan. 8¹⁰ shows that an accusative referring to the righteous has here been lost: 'and tread to the earth those who dwell upon it.' Thus this stanza should run:—

> 'And these are they who cast down
>   the stars of heaven,
> And tread to the earth those who
>   dwell upon it.'

Manifest. a–q, *defḥkly*₁a. > q₁b. t² abcox 'and manifest'. All MSS. but

And their power rests upon their riches,

And their faith is in the †gods† which they have made with their hands,

And they deny the name of the Lord of Spirits,

8. And they persecute the houses of His congregations,

And the faithful who hang upon the name of the Lord of Spirits.

The Prayer of the Righteous for Vengeance and their Joy at its Coming.

XLVII. 1. And in those days shall have ascended the prayer of the righteous.

And the blood of the righteous from the earth before the Lord of Spirits.

2. In those days the holy ones who dwell above in the heavens Shall unite with one voice

And supplicate and pray [and praise,

---

qu, en₁h make a dittographic addition here: *gu* add 'and all their works are unrighteousness'; *t, abcdfhklox₁a* 'their works are unrighteousness'. Their power rests upon their riches. Perhaps חילם = 'their power' was a corruption of תהלתם = 'their glorying'. Cf. 94⁸ where 'the rich trust in their riches'. Their faith is in the gods, &c. This is a strange expression for the idolatrous tendencies of the Sadducean court. But אלילים (= 'gods') may be corrupt for מעללים = 'deeds'. Hence 'deeds which they have wrought', &c. For a discussion of the verse see 38⁵ note. 8. Persecute (gt). *mqu, β* read 'are driven forth'. The houses (gmt¹u). *q, t³β* read 'from the houses'. Cf. 53⁶.

XLVII. 1. The blood of the righteous. 'The righteous' is here a collective in the singular, though in the preceding phrase 'the prayer of the righteous' it is in the plural. The same juxtaposition of cases is found in 47⁴. Cf. 91¹⁰ 'the righteous one shall arise from sleep and wisdom . . . be given unto them'. Moreover, we find in the next verse 'the blood of the righteous ones'. The first of the Maccabees to shed the blood of the righteous was Alexander Jannaeus, 95 B.C. (see 38⁵ note).   2. On the intercession of angels see 15² note. Cf. Rev. 6¹⁰ for a like prayer for vengeance. See 97⁸ note. The text is uncertain. I have bracketed 'and praise . . . Lord of Spirits', since the context points not to thanksgiving but to prayer on behalf of the martyrs. Moreover, the words that follow 'And that the prayer of the righteous', &c. depend directly on 'supplicate and pray' as their object. Furthermore, the MSS. are divided on the text of 47²ᵃ. For 'unite' (*gtu, β*) *mq* read 'dwell', and for 'dwell' (*a–m, β*) *m* reads 'unite'. Finally, *q, dy* omit the 'and' beginning the next line. In the words 'unite' and 'dwell' there is only a difference of one letter in the Ethiopic. It is just possible that they may be doublets, and that the text stood originally 'In those days the holy

And give thanks and bless the name of the Lord of Spirits]
On behalf of the blood of the righteous which has been shed,
And that the prayer of the righteous may not be in vain before the Lord of Spirits,
That judgement may be done unto them,
And that they may not have to suffer for ever.

3. In those days I saw the Head of Days when He seated himself upon the throne of His glory,
And the books of the living were opened before Him:

ones who dwell above in the heavens shall with one voice supplicate and pray'. **3. Books of the living.** The idea underlying this phrase is to be traced to the O.T. (1) There the book of life (or its equivalents Exod. 32^{32} $^{sq.}$ 'God's book', Ps. 69^{28} 'book of the living') was a register of the citizens of the Theocratic community. To have one's name written in the book of life implied the privilege of participating in the *temporal* blessings of the Theocracy, Is. 4^3, while to be blotted out of this book, Exod. 32^{32} Ps. 69^{28}, meant exclusion therefrom. In the O.T. this expression was originally confined to *temporal* blessings only, but in Dan. 12^1 it is transformed through the influence of the new conception of the kingdom, and distinctly refers to an immortality of blessedness. It has the same meaning in our text. A further reference to it is to be found in 104^1. The phrase again appears in the Book of Jubilees 30^{20} $^{sqq.}$ in contrast with 'the book of those that shall be destroyed', but in the O.T. sense. 'The holy books' in 108^3 (103^3?), cf. also 108^7, have practically the same meaning. In the N.T. the phrase is of frequent occurrence, Phil. 4^3 Rev. 3^5 13^8 17^8 20$^{12, 15}$ 21^{27} 22^{19}, and the idea in Luke 10^{20} Heb. 12^{23} 'written in heaven'. For later instances of its use see Pastor Hermae, *Vis.* i. 3, 2 (see Harnack *in loc.*); Sim. ii. 9; Mand. viii. 6; 1 Clem. xlv. 8.

There is no idea of absolute predestination involved in this conception. The same thought, i.e. the inscription of the name in the book of life, underlies the words 'the memorial of the righteous shall be before the face of the Great One unto all the generations of the world', 103^4. Contrast Pss. Sol. 13^{10} 'the memorial of the wicked shall no more be found'. (2) Books of remembrance of good and evil deeds. For those wherein good deeds were recorded see Ps. 56^8 Mal. 3^{16} Book of Jubilees 30^{22}; wherein evil deeds were recorded, Is. 65^6 1 En. 81^4 89$^{61-64}$, 68, 70, 71, 76, 77 90^{17}, 20 98^7, 8 104^7 2 Bar. 24^1; wherein good and evil deeds were recorded, Dan. 7^{10} Rev. 20^{12} Asc. Is. 9^{22}. (3) The heavenly tablets = πλάκες τοῦ οὐρανοῦ in Test. XII Patriarchs. The conception underlying this phrase is to be traced partly to Ps. 139^{16} Exod. 25^9, 40 26^{30}, where we find the idea that there exist in heaven divine archetypes of certain things on earth; partly to Dan. 10^{21}, where a book of God's plans is referred to, but most of all to the growing determinism of thought, for which this phrase stands as a concrete expression. In Apocryphal literature historical events are not depicted according to the manifold variety of life, but are methodically arranged under artificial categories of measure, number, weight, Wisdom 11^{20} 4 Ezra 4$^{36, 37}$. The conception is not a hard and fixed one: in Enoch and

And all His host which is in heaven above and His counsellors stood before Him,

4. And the hearts of the holy were filled with joy;

Because the number of the righteous had been offered,
And the prayer of the righteous had been heard,
And the blood of the righteous been required before the Lord of Spirits.

Test. XII Patriarchs it wavers between an absolute determinism and prediction pure and simple: whereas in Jubilees in addition to these significations, it implies at times little more than a contemporary heavenly record of events. In Enoch the idea is mainly predestinarian, the 'heavenly tables' record all the deeds of men to the remotest generations, 81$^{1, 2}$; and the entire history of the earth, 93$^{1-3}$; and all the unrighteousness that will arise, 106^{19} 107^{1}; as well as all the blessings in store for the righteous, 103$^{2, 3}$. They are likewise called the Book of the Angels, 103^{2}; for they are designed also for the perusal of the angels, 108^{7}, that they may know the future recompenses of the righteous and the wicked. In Test. XII Patriarchs Levi 5^4 Asher 7^5 (β) the idea is predictive; in Asher 2^{10} it concerns a question of Levitical law. In Jubilees the use of the phrase is very loose, the heavenly tables are the statute book of the Theocracy, or a mere contemporary record, or else are predictive or determinative. The heavenly tables record (1) Laws Levitical and criminal, in some instances previously observed in heaven, in others, established for the first time on earth: Feast of weeks, 6$^{17-18}$; Tabernacles, 16$^{16-29}$; Passover, 49; 'the Festival of the Lord,' 18$^{18-19}$; Ceremonial cleanness, 3$^{8-44}$; Circumcision, 15^{25}; the Sabbath, 50$^{6-13}$; tithes, 32^2, $^{8, 9, 10-15}$; marriage of elder daughter, 28^6; destruction of him who gives his daughter to a Gentile, 30^8; of the murderer, 4^5; of the incestuous person, 33^{10} (ordained because of Reuben); of the seed of Lot, 16^9; of the Philistines, 24^{33}. (2) Merely a contemporary event: the slaughter of the Shechemites, 30$^{9 \text{ sqq.}}$; the institution of the 'Festival of the Lord', 18$^{18-19}$; the showing of the Seven Tables to Jacob, 32^{22}; Isaac's blessing of Levi and Judah, 31^{32}; the naming of Abraham, 19^9; and of Levi, 30^{20}, as friends of God. (3) Predictions: of the judgement of all creation, 5^{13}; of the Messianic kingdom, 23$^{30-32}$; of the recording of the faithful as friends of God and the transgressors as haters, 30$^{21-22}$. *All His host.* God as the Jehovah of Hosts in His manifestations is generally so accompanied; cf. 1^4, ^{9} 60^1, ^{4} 71$^{9-13}$. According to the Parables it is the Messiah that judges. 4. *The number of the righteous* (מ ṣādĕq). Other MSS. read 'righteousness' (ṣĕdĕq). *Been offered.* '*a* reads qarĕba = ἤγγικε = קָרַב, which in Mishnaic and late Hebrew = 'had been offered' as well as 'had drawn nigh'. The latter meaning is inappropriate; for the judgement is already begun. The text means that the number of the righteous, i.e. the martyrs, is complete. The martyrs were regarded as offerings to God. Cf. Rev. 6$^{10, 11}$, and my note *in loc.* For qarĕba β reads baṣeḥa = 'has come'.

The Fount of Righteousness: the Son of Man—the Stay of the Righteous: Judgement of the Kings and the Mighty.

XLVIII. 1. And in that place I saw the fountain of righteousness
Which was inexhaustible:
And around it were many fountains of wisdom;
And all the thirsty drank of them,
And were filled with wisdom,
And their dwellings were with the righteous and holy and elect.

2. And at that hour that Son of Man was named
In the presence of the Lord of Spirits,
And his name before the Head of Days.

3. Yea, before the sun and the signs were created,
Before the stars of the heaven were made,
His name was named before the Lord of Spirits.

4. He shall be a staff to the righteous whereon to stay themselves and not fall,
And he shall be the light of the Gentiles,
And the hope of those who are troubled of heart.

5. All who dwell on earth shall fall down and worship before him,

XLVIII. 1. And (gt, β). > $gmк$. Place: see 46¹. Fountains of wisdom: see 42^b, ² (note). Cf. Is. 55¹ sqq. 2. At that hour, i.e. when Enoch was beholding these visions. That Son of Man was named. The pre-existence of the Son of Man is plainly taught in the Parables. He (not his name) has been chosen and hidden in God's presence from before creation and unto eternity, 48³, ⁶; the Most High has preserved him and revealed him to the elect, 46¹⁻² 62⁷; his glory is for ever and ever, 49²; when Enoch was translated the Son of Man was already abiding with the Lord of Spirits, 70¹. This actual pre-existence of the Son of Man is in keeping with his other supernatural attributes of universal dominion, 62⁶, and unlimited judicial authority, 69²⁷. This idea of pre-existence is found also in 4 Ezra 12³², 13²⁶. Cf. Schürer, II. ii. 159–162 (Eng. Trans.), who agrees with the view above followed. 3. The signs. These are the signs of the Zodiac, מזרות, Job 38³². See also 8³ 72¹³, ¹⁹. 4. Righteous. + 'and to the holy' β. Whereon to stay themselves. Cf. 61³ where the same phrase recurs. The light of the Gentiles. Is. 42⁶ 49⁶ Luke 2³². The hope of those who are troubled of heart. Cf. Is. 61^b, ² 'The Lord hath anointed me . . . to bind up the broken-hearted' (נשברי לב). 5. All . . . shall fall down . . . before him. Even those who denied him, 62⁶, ⁹ 63 90⁵⁷

And will praise and bless and celebrate with song the Lord of Spirits.

6. And for this reason hath he been chosen and hidden before Him,

Before the creation of the world and for evermore.

7. And the wisdom of the Lord of Spirits hath revealed him to the holy and righteous;

For he hath preserved the lot of the righteous;

Because they have hated and despised this world of unrighteousness,

And have hated all its works and ways in the name of the Lord of Spirits:

For in his name they are saved,

And according to his good pleasure hath it been in regard to their life.

8. In these days downcast in countenance shall the kings of the earth have become,

And the strong who possess the land because of the works of their hands;

For on the day of their anguish and affliction they shall not (be able to) save themselves,

9. And I will give them over into the hands of Mine elect:

Phil. 2¹⁰. Praise and bless (a–η). ση, β. The Lord (a–m). m, β 'the name of the Lord'. 6. And (η, β). > a–q. For this reason, i.e. that given in vv. 4, 5. Hidden. Cf. 4 Ezra 13⁵². Before Him. > q. For evermore. + q, abcdLxy₁a 'before Him'. 7. Revealed him, i.e. through O.T. prophecy. Holy and righteous (gmq, β–l). tu, l 'righteous and holy'. Preserved the lot of the righteous. The Messiah is the stay of the righteous, and the guardian and surety of the inheritance that awaits them. Hated and despised this world: cf. 108⁸, ⁹, ¹⁰ Gal. 1⁴. In his name they are saved. A frequent N.T. expression; cf. 1 Cor. 6¹¹ Acts 4¹². According to his good pleasure ... life (g). mtu, β–owy₁b 'he is the avenger of their life': owy₁b 'his good pleasure hath been for their life'. η is corrupt. The difference lies between bafaqādū (g) and faqādē (mtu). Cf. 62¹¹ on the latter reading. גאל, 'avenger', is a name in later Judaism for the Messiah. See Weber, pp. 359, 362. 8. Day of their anguish: see 45³ note. 9. Give them over into the hands, &c. Cf. 38⁵

> As straw in the fire so shall they burn before the face of the holy:
> As lead in the water shall they sink before the face of the righteous,
> And no trace of them shall any more be found.

10. And on the day of their affliction there shall be rest on the earth,
> And before them they shall fall and not rise again:
> And there shall be no one to take them with his hands and raise them:
> For they have denied the Lord of Spirits and His Anointed.
> The name of the Lord of Spirits be blessed.

note. **As straw in the fire.** Exod. 15⁷ Is. 5²⁴ Obadiah 18 Mal. 4¹. **Before the face of the holy** (*gqtu*). β 'before...righteous'. The reference here is to Gehenna; cf. 27², ³ 90²⁶, ²⁷; but in the Parables Gehenna undergoes transformation. In 27², ³ 90²⁶, ²⁷ the sufferings of the wicked form an ever-present spectacle to the righteous. Cf. 4 Ezra 7⁸⁶ 'Apparebit lacus tormenti, et contra illum erit locus requietionis: clibanus gehennae ostendetur, et contra eum iocunditatis paradisus'. But in the Parables, where heaven and earth are transformed on the advent of the Messiah, this spectacle is only a temporary one, and Gehenna and its victims vanish for ever from the sight of the righteous, 48⁹ 62¹², ¹³. Cf. Rev. 20¹⁴. **As lead in water.** Exod. 15¹⁰. **Before the face of the righteous** (a). β 'before...holy'. 10. **Rest.** Cf. 53⁷. **And** (> η) **before them** (a). β 'and before him'. **Fall and not rise again**: cf. ver. 4 for the opposite; cf. also Ps. 36¹². **The Lord...and His Anointed**: cf. Ps. 2². The term 'Messiah' or 'Anointed One' was applicable to any one specially commissioned by God to a religious or Theocratic function: hence to David and his successors, and even to a Gentile prince—Cyrus (Is. 45¹); to the Jewish high-priest—'the anointed priest', Lev. 4³, ⁵, ¹⁶ 6²²; to the Servant of Jehovah, Is. 61¹. In the Psalms the title generally refers to the reigning king or to the Davidic king as such, yet its ideal aspect is never lost sight of. When the historical kingship came to an end, the idea still remained, and was kept prominent through the liturgical use of the Psalms. Its imperfect realization in the kings of the past made Israel look forward to the true Messianic king in whom it should be perfectly embodied. But the term is never used technically in this sense in the O.T. In this technical sense it is first found in the Parables, 48¹⁰ 52⁴, and a decade or so later in Pss. Sol. 17³⁶ 18⁶, ⁸. For its later occurrences see 4 Ezra 7²⁹ 12³² 2 Bar. 29³ 30¹ 39⁷ 40¹ 70⁹ 72², and N.T. *passim*. See Cheyne, *Origin of the Psalter*, 338–339; Art. on the Messiah, *Encyc. Bib.* iii. 3057 sqq. On the question generally cf. Schürer, *Div.* ii, vol. ii. 120–187.

The Power and Wisdom of the Elect One.

XLIX. 1. For wisdom is poured out like water,
And glory faileth not before him for evermore.

2. For he is mighty in all the secrets of righteousness,
And unrighteousness shall disappear as a shadow,
And have no continuance;
Because the Elect One standeth before the Lord of Spirits,
And his glory is for ever and ever,
And his might unto all generations.

3. And in him dwells the spirit of wisdom,
And the spirit which gives insight,
And the spirit of understanding and of might,
And the spirit of those who have fallen asleep in righteousness.

4. And he shall judge the secret things,
And none shall be able to utter a lying word before him;
For he is the Elect One before the Lord of Spirits according to His good pleasure.

XLIX. That the Messiah will thus deal with the mighty ones of the earth is clear from his nature and attributes. 1. **Wisdom is poured out like water**: cf. Is. 11^9. Wisdom here = the knowledge and fear of God. Cf. 39^5. **Glory faileth not**, &c. The Messiah is the object of endless glorification. 2. **Mighty in all the secrets of righteousness.** On the revealing and manifesting power of the Messiah see 46^3 (note). **Disappear as a shadow, And have no continuance.** The phraseology is borrowed from Job 14^2. The word translated 'continuance' is formed from the verb translated 'standeth': unrighteousness will have no standing ground because the Elect One standeth. **Glory is for ever and ever**, &c.: cf. Is. 9$^{6, 7}$ Mic. 5^2. 3. Further endowments of the Messiah after Is. 11^2. **The spirit of wisdom**: cf. 51^3. **The spirit which gives insight** (ηητυ). m, β 'the spirit of Him who gives insight'. **The spirit of those who have fallen**, &c. The eschatological hopes of all the faithful in the past are realized in him. 4. **Judge the secret things**: cf. ver. 2 and 43^3 note. **A lying word.** Falsehood will be impossible in his presence; cf. 62^3 67^9. **For he is the Elect One.** For these very purposes has he been chosen; cf. 45^5.

The Glorification and Victory of the Righteous: the Repentance of the Gentiles.

L. 1. And in those days a change shall take place for the holy and elect,

And the light of days shall abide upon them,

And glory and honour shall turn to the holy,

2. On the day of affliction on which evil shall have been treasured up against the sinners.

And the righteous shall be victorious in the name of the Lord of Spirits:

And He will cause the others to witness (this)

That they may repent

L. It is very hard to decide on the character of this chapter. It seems to be an interpolation: if it is original, the writer is inconsistent with himself, and the incongruous details were due to literary reminiscence. These details belong to the same sphere of thought as 83–90 and 91–104, where the judgement of the sword forms the prelude to the Messianic kingdom, which is gradually established and attended by the conversion of the heathen $90^{30, 33}$ 91^{14}, and ultimately followed by the final judgement. And yet there is an echo of this judgement of the sword in 48^9. On the other hand 37–71 are strongly eschatological and catastrophic in character, and the kingdom is ushered in by the sudden appearing of the Son of Man, who inaugurates his reign by the two tremendous acts of the resurrection and the final judgement. This judgement is summary and forensic, 62^3. There is no place of repentance; cf. 62–63. God's mercy is shown in His dealings with the righteous, 61^{13}. All sinners are forthwith driven from off the earth: heaven and earth are transformed and become the habitation of the righteous. Hence there is no room for the period of the sword, or for the progressive conversion of the heathen. The writer has not taken into account the destiny of the latter, save indirectly in teaching a general judgement. These verses, then, may be a later addition made with the purpose of filling up a gap in the Parables. On the other hand there are greater inconsistencies in the Parables and other apocalyptic writings. 1. The night of oppression will give place to the sunshine of glory and honour for the righteous with the advent of the Messianic kingdom; cf. $58^{4, 6}$. Observe that there is no mention of the Messiah in vv. 1–4, nor yet of the kings and mighty ones, both of which facts tend to confirm the conclusion we have above arrived at. Holy and elect: cf. 62^8. 2. The period of the sword when the righteous slay the wicked is here referred to; cf. $90^{19, 34}$ 91^{12}. On the day (a). β 'and on the day'. Day of affliction: cf. 48^{10} 45^2 (note). On which ($gmt. > qu, \beta$) evil (g wrongly in acc.) shall have been treasured up (gq; 'shall be treasured up' β–fy; 'is treasured up' ut^2). Cause the others... that they may repent: cf. $90^{30, 33, 34}$ 91^{14}. 3. The Gentiles who repent

And forgo the works of their hands.

3. They shall have no honour through the name of the Lord of Spirits,
   Yet through His name shall they be saved,
   And the Lord of Spirits will have compassion on them,
   For His compassion is great.

4. And He is righteous also in His judgement,
   And in the presence of His glory unrighteousness also shall not maintain itself:
   At His judgement the unrepentant shall perish before Him.

5. And from henceforth I will have no mercy on them, saith the Lord of Spirits.

The Resurrection of the Dead, and the Separation by the Judge of the Righteous and the Wicked.

LI. 1. And in those days shall the earth also give back that which has been entrusted to it,

will be saved as by fire. They will not have the abundant entering in of the Jews. Through the name of (a). $t^3\beta$ 'before'. 4, 5. When the hour of the final judgement arrives, the season of mercy for the Gentiles is past for ever. Note the affinities of thought between 50^{3-5} and 60^5, ^{25}. Cf. 4 Ezra 7^{33} 2 Bar. 85^{12}. Observe that the final judgement here is not at the beginning of the Messianic reign as in the Parables, but apparently at its close, as in 91-104. In 4 Ezra and 2 Bar., where the Messianic kingdom is of temporary duration, and brought to a close by the final judgement, a period of repentance is rightly spoken of. Cf. 2 Bar. 85^{12} 4 Ezra 7^{34}.

LI. 1. The resurrection here is a resurrection of all Israel but not of the Gentiles. 51^1 would indeed seem to point to the latter, and this all the more so, as 4 Ezra 7^{32} and 7^{37} which are evidently based on it, and on 1 En. 60^6, are applied to a general resurrection. But the whole history of Jewish thought points in an opposite direction. As we shall see below, no Jewish books except the T. Benj. 10^{6-8} and 4 Ezra teach indubitably the doctrine of a general resurrection. Individual utterances to the contrary in the Talmud will be noticed below. On the question generally see Cheyne, *Origin of the Psalter*, 381-452; 'Possible Zoroastrian Influences on the Religion of Israel,' *Expository Times*, 1891, pp. 224-228, 248-253; Eisenmenger, *Entdecktes Judenthum*, ii. 819, 820-949; Weber, *Jüd. Theol.* 367-371, 390-398; Schulz, *A. T. liche Theologie*, 4te Aufl. 753-768; Herzog, *R. E.*³ Art. 'Unsterblichkeit', vol. xvi. 189-195; Hamburger, *R. E.* ii. 98 sqq. (Art. 'Belebung der Todten'); Edersheim, *Life and Times of Jesus*, ii. 397-403; Stade, *Über d. A. T. lichen Vorstellungen von dem Zustande nach dem Tode*, 1877; Castelli, 'Future Life in Rabbinic Literature,' Art. in *Jewish Quarterly Review*, July, 1889, pp. 314-352; Montefiore, 'Doctrine of Divine

And Sheol also shall give back that which it has received,

Retribution in O.T.,' Oct. 1890, 1-12; Charles, *Eschatology, Hebrew, Jewish, and Christian*, 1899 (see Index). The various forms in which the Jewish doctrine of the resurrection appeared are: (1) a resurrection of all Israelites. This doctrine is first taught in Dan. 12^2; but, though so powerfully attested, it did not become the prevailing belief. It is the accepted faith in 1 En. 1-36 (with the exception of one class of sinners in 22^{13}) 37-70 83-90 Ps. 65 (title) in LXX 2 Macc. 7$^{9, 14, 23, 29, 36}$ 12$^{43, 44}$ compared with 6^{26} 2 Bar. 30 50-51^6. (2) A resurrection of the righteous Israelites. In post-Exilic Is. 25^8 26^{19} Pss. 16$^{10, 11}$ 17^{15} 49^{15} 73$^{24-27}$ (cf. Cheyne, *Origin of the Psalter*, 406-408) Job 14$^{13-15}$ 19$^{26, 27}$ 1 En. 91-104 Pss. Sol. 3^{16} 13^9 14^7 15^{15}; Josephus, *Ant*. xviii. 1. 3; *Bell. Jud*. ii. 8. 14. That the resurrection was the sole prerogative of righteous Israelites, became the accepted doctrine in Talmudic theology: Weber, *Jüd. Theol.* 390-391. Individual voices, however, are not wanting, who asserted the resurrection of pious Gentiles, Eisenmenger, *Entdecktes Judenthum*, 908, 909: indeed, that of all the Gentiles, with some few exceptions, but only to die again, *op. cit.* 908-910; Weber, 391. Even imperfect Israelites could attain to this resurrection of life after purgation in Gehenna, Weber, 391. (3) A resurrection of all mankind, 4 Ezra 7$^{32, 37}$ Test. XII Patriarch. Benj. 10$^{6-8}$. Concurrently with the above forms of doctrine, other Jews believed only in the immortality of the soul: Wisd. 3$^{1\,sqq.}$ 4^7 5^{16} 8^{20} compared with 9^{15} 15^8 Jub. 23^{30}. 1. The earth also ... received. So g save that for mâhdantâ (q, β) = 'that which has been entrusted to it' it substitutes a gloss = 'those who are treasured up in it'. tu are defective: 'Sheol shall give back that which has been entrusted to it, that which it has received.' β has a conflate text based partly on the original of g and on tu: 'the earth shall give back that which has been entrusted to it, and Sheol shall give back that which has been entrusted to it, that which it has received.' Cf. 4 Ezra 7^{32} 'Et terra reddet qui in ea dormiunt, et pulvis qui in eo silentio habitant, et prumptuaria reddent quae eis commendatae sunt animae'. Our text is quoted in the Ps. Philo *Liber bibl. Antiquitatum*, an old Jewish work written originally in Hebrew soon after A.D. 70 but preserved only in Latin. It was printed thrice in the sixteenth century. See *Encyc. Brit*.^{11} ii. 178. The earth gives up the *body* just as Sheol and Abaddon give up the *soul*. They are both reunited at the resurrection. The raising of both was subsequently justified in Sanh. 91^a (Lev. R. iv) on the ground that the soul and body could respectively plead their innocence on the day of judgement in that neither had sinned without the other. The fable of the lame man who helped the blind in robbing an orchard is here given, and as it is shown that justice can be achieved only by punishing the lame and blind together, 'so God brings the soul and puts it in the body and punishes them both together' (מביא נשמה וזרקה בגוף הן אותם באחד). In 91-104 the resurrection is that of the spirit only. Sheol and hell (haguel = ἀπώλεια = אבדון) are here used in their new sense of the Intermediate State. For some of the chief changes in the meaning of Sheol see 63^{10} note. Sheol and Abaddon are here apparently distinguished. Is Sheol the intermediate place for the righteous and Abaddon for the wicked? Or is Sheol for the righteous and the ordinary sinners, and Abaddon for only the apostates and the worst sinners? Some such idea

And hell shall give back that which it owes.

5 *a*. For in those days the Elect One shall arise,

2. And he shall choose the righteous and holy from among them:
For the day has drawn nigh that they should be saved.

3. And the Elect One shall in those days sit on My throne,
And his mouth shall pour forth all the secrets of wisdom and counsel:
For the Lord of Spirits hath given (them) to him and hath glorified him.

4. And in those days shall the mountains leap like rams,
And the hills also shall skip like lambs satisfied with milk,
And the faces of [all] the angels in heaven shall be lighted up with joy.

---

seems to underlie the separate mention of the two places. They are seemingly distinguished even in Job 26⁶ (28²²). 2–5. These verses seem to be disarranged. The judge is simply mentioned as 'he' in ver. 2, and is not particularized as 'the Elect One' sitting on God's throne till ver. 3. Hence it would seem at first sight that we should transpose ver. 3 before ver. 2. But there appears to be a better solution of the difficulty. ver. 2 has only two lines and ver. 5 four. This fact suggests that the missing line of ver. 2 is to be found in ver. 5. This idea gains confirmation when we observe that when 5ᵃ is restored before ver. 2, the first line of each of the first four stanzas begins with the phrase 'in those days', and the removal of 5ᵃ brings ver. 4 and 5ᵇᶜᵈ into a harmony of form and subject. Chapter 51, then, is found to consist of five stanzas of three lines each. 5ᵃ. Shall arise, i. e. come forward, appear. 2. The day has drawn nigh, &c. Cf. Luke 21²⁸. 3. The Messiah is the embodiment of wisdom, 49³, and in this wisdom shall the members of his kingdom share, 48¹

61⁷, ¹¹. Cf. 42² note. The Elect One (*gmu, β*). *qt*¹ 'Mine Elect One'. My throne (*a*). *t*²*β* 'His throne'. His mouth shall pour . . . counsel. Emended. *q, β* read 'all the secrets of wisdom shall go forth from the counsel of his mouth'. But since *a–q* put 'all the secrets' in the acc. and *gu* insert 'and' after 'wisdom', I have read jăwad'ĕ (for jĕwad'ĕ) = 'shall pour forth' and omitted 'from' before 'counsel'. 4. The mountains leap, &c., i. e. with joy; cf. Ps. 114⁴, ⁶. And the faces of [all] the angels . . . shall be lighted up with joy. There are two ways of taking the original text which is preserved in *gqtu*, the oldest MSS. malā'ĕkt = 'angels' can either be taken as the subject of the verb according to *gtu* and gaṣŏmū as an accusative of limitation: '[all] the angels shall be lighted up as to their faces with joy,' or better 'angels' can be taken as a *nominativus pendens* resumed in the suffix in gaṣŏmū. Hence 'the faces of [all] the angels shall', &c. The text of *m* also would admit of this rendering. The text of *q* is different but gives the same sense. It reads lakuĕllū

5 *b*. And the earth shall rejoice,
   c. And the righteous shall dwell upon it,
   d. And the elect shall walk thereon.

The Seven Metal Mountains and the Elect One.

LII. 1. And after those days in that place where I had seen all the visions of that which is hidden—for I had been carried off in a whirlwind and they had borne me towards the west—

malā'ĕkt, 'of all the angels,' and can only therefore be translated as follows: 'the faces of [all] the angels.' In this verse we have the compound future jĕkawnû...jĕbarhû = 'shall be lighted up' as in 10^{21}. Finally, the word 'all' is unnecessary. kuĕllû (= 'all') I take as a corruption of 'ĕllû—a corruption that has occurred in the earlier chapters where the Greek exists, and 'ĕllû is simply a translation of the Greek article as very frequently in this book. In my former edition, with all other translators, I rendered this: 'they shall all be angels in heaven: their faces shall be lighted up with joy' (β). The later MSS. β certainly admit of this translation, but it is wanting in sense. Who are the 'all'? Hence the idea that the righteous shall become like the angels is not found in this passage.
5. The earth rejoices, for it is transformed, 45^5, and has at last become the inheritance of the righteous as anciently promised; cf. Ps. 37$^{3, 9, 11, 29, 34}$. Walk (η). *mtu* read 'go', β 'go and walk'. *g* supports β, but 5^{bc} and all of 5^d but the last word are written over an erasure.

LII. This obscure chapter seems to symbolize the various future kingdoms of the world, and to be founded on Dan. 2$^{31-45}$. These kingdoms of material force, symbolized by iron and brass and silver and gold and clay, will be as the chaff of summer threshing-floors before the kingdom of the Messiah, Dan. 2^{35}; they will be broken to pieces and consumed, Dan. 2^{44}. So here the various world powers represented by these mountains of iron and copper and silver and gold, &c., will melt as wax before the fire in the presence of the Messiah, 52^6, and be destroyed from off the face of the earth, 52^9, and no earthly might will avail in that day, 52$^{7, 8}$. Observe that the idea of symbolizing the world powers by mountains is drawn from the same section of Daniel. In Dan. 2^{35} the Messianic kingdom is symbolized by a mountain. But this chapter seems to be composed of two independent documents. In 52$^{1-4}$ the mountains serve to exalt the dominion of the Messiah, whereas in 52$^{6-9}$ they are destroyed before his presence. Again, we remark that the question Enoch puts in 52^3 receives two independent answers, one from the angel who went with him in 52^4 and the other from the angel of peace in 52$^{5 sqq.}$. In the Introduction to the Parables, p. 64 sq., I have shown—following a suggestion of Beer—that there are two sources in the Parables, and this chapter furnishes very clear evidence in this direction. 52$^{1-2}$ is common to both sources, 52$^{3-4}$ to the Son of Man source, and 52$^{5-9}$ to the source dealing with the Elect One. Thus we have the explanation of the divergence between 52$^{3-4}$ and 52$^{5-9}$.
1. In that place, i.e. in heaven where he had seen all the preceding visions. It is idle to attempt to get an exact idea of Enoch's movements. In 39^3 he was carried off by a whirlwind to the

2. There mine eyes saw all the secret things of heaven that shall be, a mountain of iron, and a mountain of copper, and a mountain of silver, and a mountain of gold, and a mountain of soft metal, and a mountain of lead.

3. And I asked the angel who went with me, saying, 'What things are these which I have seen in secret?' 4. And he said unto me: 'All these things which thou hast seen shall serve the dominion of His Anointed that he may be potent and mighty on the earth.'

5. And that angel of peace answered, saying unto me: 'Wait a little and there shall be revealed unto thee all the secret things, which surround the Lord of Spirits.

ends of the heaven: here he is borne to the west. 2. There ought to be seven mountains mentioned here. The six that are mentioned in this verse and in 52⁶ consist of iron, copper, silver, gold, soft metal, lead. Now if we turn to 67⁴, where these mountains are again referred to but the nature of only five of them specified, we find that these five are of gold, silver, iron, soft metal, tin. It is not improbable, therefore, that the seventh mountain, the mention of which has been lost from the text, consisted of 'tin'. This conclusion receives support from the following considerations. In 52⁷⁻⁸ there is a fresh enumeration of metals, which though not referring directly to the metal mountains yet does so indirectly. In this list the following metals are given: gold, silver, iron, bronze, tin, lead. Here again we find the missing metal 'tin', though a fresh metal 'bronze' is also mentioned. This 'bronze' may be the same as the 'copper' in the other list. So much for our text. Now for a myth indirectly connected with it. In Origen's *Contra Celsum*, vi. 22, there is a description of a ladder with seven gates from the mysteries of Mithras. The first gate consists of lead (μόλυβδος) and is assigned to Saturn, the second of tin (κασσίτερος), which is assigned to Venus on the ground of its splendour and softness (τὸ φαιδρόν τε καὶ μαλακὸν τοῦ κασσιτέρου), the third of copper (χαλκός) assigned to Jupiter, the fourth of iron (σίδηρος) assigned to Mercury, the fifth of a mixture of metals (κεραστὸν νόμισμα) assigned to Mars, the sixth of silver (ἄργυρον) assigned to the Moon, and the seventh of gold (χρυσός) assigned to the Sun. The metals in this passage and in our text are evidently the same. The question now arises with which of these seven metals is the 'soft metal' in our text to be identified? If the word we have rendered 'tin' is rightly translated, then possibly it should be identified with the κεραστὸν νόμισμα. On the other hand Celsus's description of 'tin' as being 'soft' might point to another conclusion. Owing to the difficulty of identifying the ancient metals we must leave this question undecided. See *K. A. T.*³ 618, note 4. Shall be. + 'upon the earth' (q, t², β). Lead 52⁶ 65⁷, ⁸ 67⁴, ⁶. 3–4. From the Son of Man source. See note at beginning of chapter. 5. That angel. Here w'ĕtû (= that) is merely a translation of the Greek article. Wait a little. + 'and thou shalt see' β. Surround the Lord of

6. And these mountains which thine eyes have seen,
    The mountain of iron, and the mountain of copper, and the mountain of silver,
    And the mountain of gold, and the mountain of soft metal, and the mountain of lead,
    All these shall be in the presence of the Elect One,
    As wax before the fire,
    And like the water which streams down from above [upon those mountains],
    And they shall become powerless before his feet.
7. And it shall come to pass in those days that none shall be saved,
    Either by gold or by silver,
    And none be able to escape.
8. And there shall be no iron for war,
    Nor shall one clothe oneself with a breastplate.
    Bronze shall be of no service,
    And tin [shall be of no service and] shall not be esteemed,
    And lead shall not be desired.
9. And all these things shall be [denied and] destroyed from the surface of the earth,
    When the Elect One shall appear before the face of the Lord of Spirits.'

Spirits (a–m). m, t²β 'the Lord of Spirits has established'. **6. As wax before the fire.** Cf. 1⁶ Ps. 97⁵ Mic. 1⁴. **Like the water which streams down,** Mic. 1⁴. MSS. add here 'upon those mountains'. The thought of this verse recurs in 53⁷. **7.** From Zeph. 1¹⁸ 'Neither their silver nor their gold shall be able to deliver them'. Cf. Is. 13¹⁷. **8. Nor shall one clothe oneself with a breastplate (or 'coat of mail').** I have here read wa'ljelabĕs with q instead of wa'llĕbĕs with gt, efhn₁a₁b or wa'llebsa with mu, abcklox = 'nor garment for a breastplate'. I have omitted la before der'a with u, though the construction with la should be possible. Otherwise with u, β render 'garment for a coat of mail' (or 'breastplate'). In a–s there is a dittograph: 'nor garment ('nor shall one clothe oneself' q) for war nor garment for a breastplate' (or 'coat of mail'). **Shall be of no service and.** Bracketed as a dittograph from the preceding line. q omits 'and shall not be esteemed'. **9. Be [denied and] destroyed.** We have here two alternative renderings of יָבְחֲרוּ such as ἀπαρνηθήσονται and ἀφανισθήσονται. One was originally in the text and the other in the margin, but subsequently both were incorporated into the text. Schmidt, who advocates an Aramaic original, proposes רמא; but this verb means 'to cast down' and 'to deceive'—senses which do not explain our text.

The Valley of Judgement: the Angels of Punishment: the Communities of the Elect One.

LIII. 1. There mine eyes saw a deep valley with open mouths, and all who dwell on the earth and sea and islands shall bring to him gifts and presents and tokens of homage, but that deep valley shall not become full.

2. And their hands commit lawless deeds,
 And the sinners devour all whom they lawlessly oppress:
 Yet the sinners shall be destroyed before the face of the Lord of Spirits,
 And they shall be banished from off the face of His earth,
 And they shall perish for ever and ever.

3. For I saw all the angels of punishment abiding (there) and

---

LIII. 1. The deep valley here is that of Jehoshaphat, where, according to Joel 3², ¹², God was to assemble and judge the Gentiles. The valley of Jehoshaphat (Joel 3², ¹²) is rendered in Theodotion by the phrase τὴν χώραν τῆς κρίσεως and by the Targ. Jon. מישר פלגות דינא (= 'the plain of the decision of judgement'). According to the Midrash Mishle, 68ᵈ, God will judge the whole world in this valley. (Weber, *Jüd. Theol.* 395.) Since the fourth cent. this valley has generally been identified with that of the Kidron. But many scholars are of opinion that it was not originally a geographical designation. In the Midrash Tillim, viii (Neubauer, *Geog.*, p. 51) it is stated that no such valley exists (אין עמק ששמו יהושפט). See *Encyc. Bib.* ii. 2353. All those who dwell upon earth will bring gifts and presents to the Messiah to win a favourable judgement; but these will be of no avail (cf. 52⁷). The idea of the nations and the rich men of the earth bringing gifts to the Messiah is a favourite one in the Talmud, Weber (386–387). There (a–q). g, β 'and there'. Deep valley with open mouths (mqlu, β–א). g 'open and deep-mouthed valley'. 2. Sinners devour all whom they lawlessly oppress. So I render this line, emending jĕṣămĕwû into jĕṣămawû. That this is the meaning of the text appears to follow from the last words of this chapter, 53⁷, 'the oppression of sinners.' The verb 'oppress', ṣămawa, is formed from the noun ṣăma, used in 53⁷. If we do not emend, the sense is poor and needs supplementing: 'sinners lawlessly devour all that they (? who) produce.' Banished from off the face of His earth: see 38¹ (note). And they shall · perish. All MSS. insert a negative: if it is retained the text must be rendered: 'And they shall not cease.' 3. Angels of punishment: see 40⁷ (note). These angels apparently prepare the chains and fetters for the kings and the mighty in the valley of Jehoshaphat where the kings are to be judged. The chains for the fallen angels are forged in Gehenna, 54³⁻⁶. The kings are then taken and cast into Gehenna, 54². Abiding (mql (gu) preparing all the instruments of Satan. 4. And I asked the angel of peace who went with me: 'For whom are they preparing these instruments?' 5. And he said unto me: 'They prepare these for the kings and the mighty of this earth, that they may thereby be destroyed.

6. And after this the Righteous and Elect One shall cause the house of his congregation to appear: henceforth they shall be no more hindered in the name of the Lord of Spirits.

7. And these mountains shall not stand as the earth before his righteousness,

But the hills shall be as a fountain of water,

And the righteous shall have rest from the oppression of sinners.'

LIV. 1. And I looked and turned to another part of the earth, and saw there a deep valley with burning fire. 2. And they brought the kings and the mighty, and began to cast them into this deep valley. 3. And there mine eyes saw how they made these their instruments, iron chains of immeasurable weight. 4. And I asked the angel of peace who went with me, saying:

$aehk$). $bcdflsopxy_1a_1b$ = 'going'.
5. Prepare (β). > a. These. > qu, nx. This earth. Here 'this' is probably for the Greek article. 6. House of his congregation: cf. 62^8 see 38^1 (note). The houses of his congregations are the synagogues; cf. Ps. 74^8. 7. These mountains ... the hills. There is a return here to the figurative language of 52. The mountains and the hills are symbols of the world powers as personated in the kings and the mighty. Before the Messiah's righteousness, the mountains (i.e. the kings) will not be like the earth which abideth for ever, Ps. 78^{69} Eccles. 1^4; and the hills (i.e. the mighty) shall be as a fount of water, Is. 64^3; cf. 52^6. The earth's great ones will become strengthless and vanish at the presence of the Messiah. His righteousness ($a-q$). q, $t^2\beta-n$ 'His face'.

LIV. In 53 the writer described the scene of the judgement and the fetters that were being prepared to bind the kings on their condemnation. Here he speaks of Gehenna into which the kings are cast: they are punished in the sight of the righteous; cf. 62^{12}. The fallen angels are cast into a furnace of fire. The idea of the fallen angels and kings being judged together is to be traced to Is. $24^{21, 22}$. 1. To another part of the earth. The writer now turns from the valley of Jehoshaphat on the north-east of Jerusalem to the valley of Hinnom lying to the south of it. A deep valley: see 48^9 (note). This valley seems to be that spoken of in $56^{3, 4}$. 2. This > q, $bcdxy$. 3-5. The pre-Messianic judgement of

'For whom are these chains being prepared?' 5. And he said unto me: 'These are being prepared for the hosts of Azâzêl, so that they may take them and cast them into the abyss of complete condemnation, and they shall cover their jaws with rough stones as the Lord of Spirits commanded.

6. And Michael, and Gabriel, and Raphael, and Phanuel shall take hold of them on that great day, and cast them on that day into the burning furnace, that the Lord of Spirits may take vengeance on them for their unrighteousness in becoming subject to Satan and leading astray those who dwell on the earth.'

LIV. 7—LV. 2. *Noachic Fragment on the first World Judgement.*

7. And in those days shall punishment come from the Lord of Spirits, and He will open all the chambers of waters which are

---

the watchers in ver. 5 is that described at length in 10–16. **4. Chains.** $m, \beta-dn$ read 'chains of instruments'; qt 'chains and instruments'. I have omitted this addition with n. **5. Abyss.** Cf. 10^4. The abyss of complete condemnation is not Gehenna but only the preliminary place of punishment; cf. 10^5, ^{12}. We are not told by whom the chains are forged for the fallen angels, nor yet who are the agents who execute the first judgement upon them. Chains are also made for the kings and the mighty, 53^5. **And they shall cover.** q reads 'to cover'. **6. The final judgement upon the watchers. On that great day**: see 45^2 (note). Observe that in the Parables the guilt of the watchers originated in their becoming subjects of Satan: see 40^7 (note): Book of Jubilees, $10^{8\,\text{sqq.}}$. **And** ^{50}. $> q$, *abcde*. **Cast them** (tu, β). $> gmq$. **Furnace** $(a-q)$. q, y 'fire'; $\beta-y$ 'furnace of fire'; cf. 10^6 18^{11} 21^{7-10} $90^{24,25}$. This is to be distinguished from Gehenna. **7—LV. 2.** This digression on the first world-judgement is a Noachic fragment. The Book of Noah is mentioned in the Book of Jubilees, 10^{13} 21^{10}. These fragments, 39^1, ^{2a} 54^7–55^2 60 65–69^{25}, deal mainly with the Deluge. They are to be regarded as interpolations on the following grounds out of many: (1) They always disturb the context in which they occur. (2) They profess to be a revelation of Noah, 60^{7-11}, ^{24}, ^{25} 65–68^1. (3) Such a definite date as is given in 60^1 is unknown in the Parables. (4) The demonology is different: the Satans and the fallen angels which are carefully distinguished in the Parables are confused in the additions, 69. The chief, moreover, of the fallen angels in the Parables is Azazel; in the additions, Semjaza. (5) The interpolator seeks to adapt his additions to their new contexts, and accordingly incorporates in them many terms and phrases from the Parables, such as 'angel of peace', 60^{24}, see 40^2 (note); 'none shall utter an idle word,' 67^9, see 49^4 (note); 'denied the Lord of Spirits,' $67^{8, 10}$, see 38^2 (note); 'the angel who went with me and showed me what was hidden,' 60^{11}, see 43^3 (note); *but observe that in such borrowings he misuses technical terms and phrases, either* above the heavens, and of the fountains which are beneath the earth. 8. And all the waters shall be joined with the waters: that which is above the heavens is the masculine, and the water which is beneath the earth is the feminine. 9. And they shall destroy all who dwell on the earth and those who dwell under the ends of the heaven. 10. And when they have recognized

through ignorance or of set purpose. Cf. 'Lord of Spirits', see 37^2 (note); 'Head of Days,' 55^1, see 46^1 (note); 'angels of punishment,' 40^7 66^1 (note); 'Son of Man,' 60^{10} (note); 'those who dwell on the earth,' 51^9 37^5 (note). (6) The interpolator misunderstands the Parables, and combines absolutely alien elements; cf. 'the burning valley in the metal mountains in the west'—an illegitimate combination of 52^1, ^{7} and 54^1. (7) Finally, the Parables follow the LXX chronology; the interpolations follow the Samaritan. Thus in 61^{12} Enoch speaks of the elect as being already in Paradise, and in 70^4 on his translation he finds his forefathers already there. This could be the case only according to the LXX reckoning; for according to the Samaritan all his forefathers survived him, and, according to the Hebrew, all except Adam. The interpolations follow the Samaritan reckoning: see 65^2 (note). The object of the interpolator is clear. Although the final world judgement is treated at length, there are only the briefest references to the first. It was to supply this defect in the Parables that an existing Apocalypse of Noah was laid under contribution. 7. Above the heavens. All MSS. but $_1b$ add 'and in addition to the fountains which are beneath the heavens'—an addition which originated in a dittograph of the following clause. According to early Semitic views there were only waters above the heavens and below the earth. 8. We have here a fragment of Babylonian cosmology. According to the Babylonians water was the primeval element or elements; for there the waters were distinguished as Apsu and Tiamat—in other words as the male and female elements. From the mingling of these two arose the gods: see $K.A.T.^3$, p. 492 sq.; Hastings, *Encyc. of Religion*, ii. 314; Jastrow, *Religion of Babylonia*, 411 sqq. Traces of this myth are found in Jer. Berakh. ix. 2 'the upper water is male and the lower water is female' (המים העליונים זכרים והתחתונים נקבות). A protest against accepting water as the primitive element is found in Chag. 14^b on the part of Rabbi Aqiba. This religious and philosophical idea is stated in Jer. Chag. ii. 1 'Originally the world consisted of water in water' (בתחלה היה העולם מים במים). 9. All who dwell on the earth: see 37^5 note. 10. And ^{10}. > q. When. tu, ew read ba'ĕntaza = 'inasmuch as' = διότι, gmq, $t^?\beta$-ew ba'ĕntaz = 'on this account', διὰ τοῦτο. Here διότι = כי or באשר. Thus the sentence = διότι ἔγνωσαν ... καὶ (= the vaw of the apodosis in Hebrew) ἐν τούτοις (or τούτῳ) = ובאלה ... כי ידעו. Here the Greek translator should have rendered כי by ἐπεί and not by διότι. The same confusion could arise in the case of Aramaic; for ארי = either διότι or ἐπεί. As regards the sense of the passage, we find that the kings and the mighty in $63^{4\ sqq.}$ come to acknowledge their guilt before their destruction. But it is possible that the their unrighteousness which they have wrought on the earth, then by these shall they perish.'

LV. 1. And after that the Head of Days repented and said: 'In vain have I destroyed all who dwell on the earth.' 2. And He sware by His great name: 'Henceforth I will not do so to all who dwell on the earth, and I will set a sign in the heaven: and this shall be a pledge of good faith between Me and them for ever, so long as heaven is above the earth. And this is in accordance with My command.

LV. 3—LVI. 4. *Final Judgement of Azazel, the Watchers and their children.*

3. When I have desired to take hold of them by the hand of the angels on the day of tribulation and pain **because of this**, I will cause My chastisement and My wrath to abide upon them, saith God, the Lord of Spirits. 4. Ye †mighty kings† who dwell on the earth, ye shall have to behold Mine Elect One, how he sits on the throne of glory and judges Azâzêl, and all his associates, and all his hosts in the name of the Lord of Spirits.'

LVI. 1. And I saw there the hosts of the angels of punishment going, and they held scourges and chains of iron and bronze.

---

reading of gmq, $t^2\beta$–ew is right and that we should render: 'And owing to this they will recognize ... and by this (i.e. the deluge) shall they perish.'

LV. 1. The Head of Days: see 46^1 (note). We have here a good illustration of the method by which the interpolator seeks to assimilate his additions by incorporating technical terms from the main text. **Repented**: cf. Gen. 8^{21}. **2. So** (q, $t^2\beta$–x). > gmt^1u, x. **This is in accordance with My command** (gt). m reads 'this is My command', q (ungrammatical) 'this command is according to My desire', u, $t^2\beta$ 'after this according to My command'. The last reading would perhaps connect best with what follows. **3.** This verse connects immediately with 54^6. **Day of tribulation and pain**: see 45^2 (note). **Because of this**. Text = ἔμπροσθεν τούτου, a mistranslation of מפני זאת. **I will cause ... to abide** a–qu. q, β–d '(My chastisement) shall abide'. **Chastisement ... wrath** (a). ⌒ β. **4.** The kings have to witness the judgement passed on the angels: if Azazel and his hosts are judged and condemned by the Messiah, how much more likely will they! The text should almost certainly be 'Ye kings and mighty': see 38^5 (note), 62^6. **Of glory** (a–q). q, β 'of My glory'.

LVI. 1–4. These verses refer to the watchers and their children the demons. The term 'beloved' is specially used of the demons in regard to their parents in 1–36: see 10^{12} 14^6. **1. They**

2. And I asked the angel of peace who went with me, saying: 'To whom are these who hold the scourges going?' 3. And he said unto me: 'To their elect and beloved ones that they may be cast into the chasm of the abyss of the valley.

4. And then that valley shall be filled with their elect and beloved,
> And the days of their lives shall be at an end,
> And the days of their leading astray shall not thenceforward be reckoned.

LVI. 5–8. *Last struggle of heathen Powers against Israel.*

5. And in those days the angels shall return
> And hurl themselves to the east upon the Parthians and Medes:

held (*gq*, β). > *mtu*. Scourges and (*g*). > *qt*, β. *wu* read 'and'. 2. These who (*g*, *t³*). *mqt¹u* read 'these', β-*n* 'who'. Scourges (*g*). > *a-g*, β. 3. Chasm of. > *q*. 4. And¹⁰. > *q*. Not thenceforward be reckoned, i.e. be at an end. 5—LVII. 3ᵃ. We have here another section of the 'Elect One' source (see Introd. p. 65), or rather a fresh source partially adapted to the 'Elect One' source. It depicts the last struggle of the heathen powers against the Messianic kingdom established in Jerusalem. Such a conception is quite in place in 83–90 91–104, but is difficult to reconcile with the ruling ideas in 37–70. A Messiah who was only a man with his seat at Jerusalem might well be conceived of as assailed by the Gentile powers. But this is impossible in the case of a superhuman Messiah, who, possessing universal dominion and attended by legions of angels, holds universal assize, and, supported by the actual presence of the Almighty, destroys all his enemies with the breath of his mouth. Hence this section forms a harsh break in the context. Moreover, the Parables deal only in general terms: no names are mentioned as here, nor is any definite information given as a means of determining their date or the persons against whom they are directed. Finally, the seat of the kingdom on the Advent of the Messiah will not be Jerusalem merely as is here implied, but a transformed heaven and earth. This section may be dated with some probability. The description is prophetical, and is merely a reproduction of the coming strife of Gog and Magog against Israel. The latter names are replaced by those of the Medes and Parthians, who are the only great world powers from whom the interpolator believes great danger may be apprehended. Syria had ceased to be formidable from 100 B.C. onward, and Rome had not intervened in Jewish affairs practically till 64 B.C. The date therefore of this section must be earlier than 64 B.C. If it belonged originally to the Elect One source, then it serves to determine its date. 5. In Ezek. 38[14–17] it is said that God will stir up the Gentiles; but here in keeping with the views of a later time this business is assigned to the angels; cf. Dan. 10[13, 20, 21] 12[1]. Return (*gm¹q*). *m²tu*, β 'assemble'. The Parthians and Medes. These are the chief nations in the league

They shall stir up the kings, so that a spirit of unrest shall come upon them,

And they shall rouse them from their thrones,

That they may break forth as lions from their lairs,

And as hungry wolves among their flocks.

6. And they shall go up and tread under foot the land of His elect ones,

[And the land of His elect ones shall be before them a threshing-floor and a highway]:

7. But the city of my righteous shall be a hindrance to their horses.

And they shall begin to fight among themselves,

And their right hand shall be strong against themselves,

And a man shall not know his brother,

Nor a son his father or his mother,

Till there be no number of the corpses through their slaughter,

And their punishment be not in vain.

8. In those days Sheol shall open its jaws,

And they shall be swallowed up therein,

And their destruction shall be at an end;

Sheol shall devour the sinners in the presence of the elect.'

against Israel. **6. And the land ... a highway**. Bracketed as a dittograph of the preceding line. It makes the stanza too long. Cf. 58⁶⁴. The land of His elect ones, i.e. Palestine. His elect ones ¹⁰ (gqt). mu, β–e 'their elect ones'. Threshing-floor: cf. Is. 21¹⁰. **7. But the attack on Jerusalem** will fail, Zech. 12²,³; and civil strife will break out amongst the invading nations, Ezek. 38²¹ Zech. 14¹³ Hag. 2²², and they will involve each other in common destruction; cf. 100¹⁻³, to which section these ideas rightly belong. But ¹⁰ (tuβ). > gmq. **His brother** (a). β 'his neighbour and his brother'. **No number ... slaughter**. Cf. Nah. 3³. All the MSS. read 'a number ... through their slaughter'. A scribe in t inserts a negative before the verb—which I have followed in my translation. But I suggest that 'ĕmōtōmū (= 'through their slaughter') is corrupt. It = ἐκ θανάτου αὐτῶν = ממותם corrupt for מרבות. Hence 'the number of the corpses be more than myriads'. g omits 'ĕmōtōmū. This and the following line is read by q as follows: 'For their number through their death and chastisement shall be corpses and it shall not be in vain'. **8. In those** (a–q). qβ 'and in those'. **Sheol shall open its jaws.** Cf. Num. 16³¹⁻³³ Is. 5¹⁴. See 63¹⁰. **Shall be at an end** (g). > t, β. q reads 'shall not end', m 'has sunk down', א 'has been destroyed'.

The Return from the Dispersion.

LVII. 1. And it came to pass after this that I saw another host of wagons, and men riding thereon, and coming on the winds from the east, and from the west to the south. 2. And the noise of their wagons was heard, and when this turmoil took place the holy ones from heaven remarked it, and the pillars of the earth were moved from their place, and the sound thereof was heard from the one end of heaven to the other, in one day. 3. And they shall all fall down and worship the Lord of Spirits. And this is the end of the second Parable.

LVIII—LXXI. The Third Parable.

LVIII. *The Blessedness of the Saints.*

LVIII. 1. And I began to speak the third Parable concerning the righteous and elect.

2. Blessed are ye, ye righteous and elect,
For glorious shall be your lot.

3. And the righteous shall be in the light of the sun,
And the elect in the light of eternal life:

LVII. On the destruction of the Gentile invaders, the dispersed of Israel return to Jerusalem from the East and from the West; cf. Is. 27[13] 43[5, 6] 49[12, 22, 23]. 1. And men (a). β 'men'. Coming on the winds. A figure expressing the swiftness of their return. Perhaps for 'on' we should read 'like', the mistake having arisen from a corruption of כ into ב in the Hebrew. From the west. q reads 'to the west'. 2. The noise...was heard (gq, β). *ntu* 'there was the noise'. The pillars of the earth were moved: cf. Hag. 2[6, 7] Joel 3[16]. One end of heaven to the other (a–q). β reads 'the end of the earth to the end of the heaven'.

LVIII. Here begins the third Parable. It is probable that a large part of it has been lost, being displaced to make room for the Noachic fragments. As it stands it embraces 58 61-64 69[26-29]. The introductory words, 'Concerning the righteous and the elect,' in this Parable, as in the other two, are but a very indifferent index to its contents. The Parable as it has reached us, might reasonably be described as 'Concerning the final judgement held by the Son of Man over all created beings, but especially over the great ones of the earth and the final blessedness of the righteous and elect'. 2. Glorious shall be your lot. This lot is preserved for them by the Messiah, 48[7]. 3. Light of the sun: see 38[4] (note). Eternal life: see 37[4] (note): cf. Dan. 12[2] Pss. of Sol. 3[16]. 4. They

> The days of their life shall be unending,
> And the days of the holy without number.

4. And they shall seek the light and find righteousness with the Lord of Spirits:
    There shall be peace to the righteous in the name of the Eternal Lord.

5. And after this it shall be said to the holy in heaven
    That they should seek out the secrets of righteousness, the heritage of faith:
    For it has become bright as the sun upon earth,
    And the darkness is past.

6. And there shall be a light that never endeth,
    And to a limit (lit. 'number') of days they shall not come,
    For the darkness shall first have been destroyed,
    [And the light established before the Lord of Spirits]
    And the light of uprightness established for ever before the Lord of Spirits.

The Lights and the Thunder.

LIX. 1. In those days mine eyes saw the secrets of the lightnings, and of the lights, and the judgements they execute (lit. 'their judgement') : and they lighten for a blessing or a

will through a natural affinity seek after light and righteousness; cf. 38⁴ (note). The Eternal Lord, or 'Lord of the ages'. See 81¹⁰ and note on 1⁵. In 12³ we have 'the king of the ages' or 'the Eternal King'. Cf. 82⁷ 84². **5.** They will be bidden to seek and make their own the hidden recompense of righteousness (cf. 38³), the glorious heritage which has been ordained for them in heaven and preserved for them by the Messiah, 48⁷. This will not be achieved once and for all; but this will be a progress from light to light and from righteousness to righteousness. Heritage of faith: cf. 39⁶ 61⁴, ¹¹. Bright as the sun, &c.: cf. 1 John 1⁵. **6.** That never endeth. The MSS. read za'l jĕthualaquĕ (gmqu) or za'l jĕthuĕlaquĕ = 'that cannot be numbered'. I have emended this into za'ljĕthalaq = 'that never endeth'. And the light established ... Spirits. Bracketed as a dittograph of the following line.

LIX. This chapter is an intrusion, and belongs to the same class as 41³⁻⁸ 43 44. It is probably drawn from a Noah-Apocalypse. **1.** The statements of the writer rest on Job 36³¹ 37⁵, ¹³ 38²⁴⁻²⁷. He wishes to bring out the ethical ends of the thunder and the lightning. In those days (a). β 'and in those days'. Of the lights (a, ev). β-ev 'the lights'. For a blessing or a curse: cf. Job 36³¹ curse as the Lord of Spirits willeth. 2. And there I saw the secrets of the thunder, and how when it resounds above in the heaven, the sound thereof is heard, and he caused me to see the judgements executed on the earth, whether they be for well-being and blessing, or for a curse according to the word of the Lord of Spirits. 3. And after that all the secrets of the lights and lightnings were shown to me, and they lighten for blessing and for satisfying.]

Book of Noah—a Fragment.

Quaking of the Heaven: Behemoth and Leviathan: the Elements.

LX. 1. In the year five hundred, in the seventh month, on the fourteenth day of the month in the life of †Enoch†. In that Parable I saw how a mighty quaking made the heaven of heavens to quake, and the host of the Most High, and the angels, a thousand thousands and ten thousand times ten thousand, were disquieted with a great disquiet. 2. And the Head of Days sat on the throne of His glory, and the angels and the righteous stood around Him.

37^{13}. 2. Cf. 60^{13-15}. He caused me to see ($a-u, cefhkmy$). *abdoec₁a₁b* 'they caused me to see'. Judgements. Text = οἰκήματα 'dwellings' corrupt for κρίματα (or οἰκητήρια corrupt for κριτήρια). On the earth. All MSS. but *u* add 'and the voice of the thunder'. 'Lord of Spirits' incorporated from the adjoining context. 3. Job 38^{24-27}.

LX. This chapter is one of the Noachic fragments. For the grounds on which these are regarded as interpolations see 54^7 (note): also the following notes on $60^{1, 2, 6, 10, 11}$, &c. 1. The year five hundred. This date is drawn from Gen. 5^{32}, and is a date in the life of Noah and not of Enoch as it stands in our text. For Enoch we should read Noah. In the seventh month, on the fourteenth day of the month. This, according to Levitical law, was the eve of the Feast of Tabernacles. In that Parable. This phrase marks a clumsy attempt to connect this chapter with the main context, but betrays the hand of the interpolator. A Parable in Enoch's sense is an account of a vision; but the text requires here the word 'vision'; for the writer says, 'I saw the heaven quaking.' The heaven...to quake. This was a token of the manifestation of divine judgement; cf. $1^{6, 7}$. Host of the Most High...a thousand thousands: cf. 1^9 40^1 $71^{8, 13}$. 2. Head of Days: see 46^1 (note) 54^7 (note). The angels and the righteous. According to this we are to regard God as accompanied by angels and *saints*. The righteous here can have no other meaning. Such a conception of the

3. And a great trembling seized me,
And fear took hold of me,
And my loins gave way,
And dissolved were my reins,
And I fell upon my face.

4. And Michael sent another angel from among the holy ones and he raised me up, and when he had raised me up my spirit returned; for I had not been able to endure the look of this host, and the commotion and the quaking of the heaven. 5. And Michael said unto me: 'Why art thou disquieted with such a vision? Until this day lasted the day of His mercy; and He hath been merciful and long-suffering towards those who dwell on the earth. 6. And when the day, and the power, and the punishment, and the judgement come, which the Lord of Spirits hath prepared for those who worship not the righteous law, and for those who deny the righteous judgement,

---

final Messianic judgement is difficult though possible; but in the case of the first judgement (i. e. the Flood) it is not possible except through misconception. Here again the hand of an ignorant interpolator is disclosed. **3.** Cf. 14¹⁴, ²⁴. **Loins gave way.** Ps. 69²³. Is. 45¹. **Dissolved.** All MSS. but *u*, *dy* add 'and'. This insertion led to the addition of *tamaswa* = 'melted' in β in order to supply a verb to 'reins'. **My reins** (*mq,fnx*). *gtu* β-*fnx* read 'all my being'. **4.** Cf. Dan. 8¹⁷ 10⁹, ¹⁰. **Michael sent another angel.** Michael is the chief archangel: cf. 40⁴, ⁹. The other angel is appointed to a like duty with the angel of peace in the Parables, and is actually so named in 60²⁴. **5. Michael** (*a*). β 'the holy Michael'. **Merciful and long-suffering**: cf. ver. 25 50³, ⁵ 61¹³. **6. Worship not** (*u*). All other MSS. omit the negative. In my edition of 1893 I restored this negative on various grounds when *u* was as yet unknown. If the negative is not original, then the corruption may have originated in the Hebrew. The text = προσκυνοῦσι = יִשְׁתַּחֲוּוּ, which may be corrupt for יְשַׁחֲתוּ = 'pervert', 'destroy'. This gives an excellent sense. **The righteous law.** The text = 'the righteous judgement' = מִשְׁפַּט צֶדֶק, which, as Halévy (*Journ. Asiat.* 367–369, 1867) has shown, can mean either 'the righteous law' or 'the righteous judgement'. This phrase occurs twice in this verse, and I have translated it in the first instance as 'the righteous law', and in the second as 'the righteous judgement'. With the three clauses in this verse we might compare 4 Ezra 7³⁷

'Videte et intellegite quem negastis,
  Vel cui non servistis,
  Vel cuius diligentias sprevistis'.

If the negative is not original, and my conjecture is right, the text would run

'Who corrupt the righteous law
  And deny the righteous judgement',
&c.

and for those who take His name in vain—that day is prepared, for the elect a covenant, but for sinners an inquisition.

25. When the punishment of the Lord of Spirits shall rest upon them, it shall rest in order that the punishment of the Lord of Spirits may not come in vain, and it shall slay the children with their mothers and the children with their fathers. Afterwards the judgement shall take place according to His mercy and His patience.'

7. And on that day were two monsters parted, a female monster named Leviathan, to dwell in the abysses of the ocean over the fountains of the waters.   8. But the male is named Behemoth, who occupied with his breast a waste wilderness named †Dûidâin†, on the east of the garden where the elect and

---

For the elect a covenant. Cf. Dan. 9⁴ 'Who keepeth covenant ... with them that love Him'.   25. I have restored this verse immediately after ver. 6, where, if anywhere, it has some meaning. Immediately preceding it there is a dittograph: 'in order that the punishment of the Lord of Spirits may not be (bcz: 'may not come' e: all other MSS. omit negative and verb) in vain, and may slay the children with their mothers and the children with their fathers.' Again, before the final sentence beginning 'Afterwards', &c., all MSS. insert the following dittograph: 'When the punishment of the Lord of Spirits shall rest upon these.'   7–10. A fragment dealing with certain myths relating to the Creation but not to the Deluge.   7. This strange fancy about Behemoth and Leviathan, which are first mentioned in Job 40 41, is found by Jewish expounders also in Gen. 1²¹ Ps. 50¹⁰ Is. 27¹. For later allusions see 4 Ezra 6⁴⁹⁻⁵² 2 Bar. 29⁴. Here they are represented as huge monsters created on the fifth day of Creation to be the food of the righteous in Messianic times (cf. B. Bathra 74ᵃ). This doctrine does not appear in 1 Enoch. For further information see Weber, *Jüd. Theol.* 202, 389, 402; *Jewish Encyc.* viii. 38; Bousset, *Rel. des Judenthums*, 271. The Talmudic view agrees with that of 4 Ezra and 2 Bar. so far as to make Behemoth food for the righteous. Fountains of the waters: cf. Gen. 7¹¹ Job 38¹⁶ 1 En. 89⁷.   8. †Dûidâin† (*u*). *g* Dûnadâin, *t* Dûndâin, *m,β–eh* Dêndâin, *h* Dêin (?). Probably in the longer forms of the name we have a duplication of the initial letters, and Dain or Dein was the older form of the word. From the statement that the place lies to the east of Eden, it seems clear, as Kohut (*Jewish Encyc.* viii. 39) has pointed out, that the word is corrupt for Naid or Nud; cf. *tu*. This is 'the land of Nod to the east of Eden' (Gen. 4¹⁶). On the east of the garden, i. e. the garden of Eden. The locality of Eden varies in the different sections: see notes on 18⁶ 32², ³ 70²⁻⁴ 77³. Here again the question arises: have we to do here with the earthly garden of righteousness or with the heavenly? or are they after all identical? See note on 32¹. The garden, whichever it is, is apparently empty in righteous dwell, where my grandfather was taken up, the seventh from Adam, the first man whom the Lord of Spirits created. 9. And I besought the other angel that he should show me the might of those monsters, how they were parted on one day and cast, the one into the abysses of the sea, and the other unto the dry land of the wilderness. 10. And he said to me: 'Thou son of man, herein thou dost seek to know what is hidden.'

11. And the other angel who went with me and showed me what was hidden told me, what is first and last in the heaven in the height, and beneath the earth in the depth, and at the ends of the heaven, and on the foundation of the heaven. 12. And the chambers of the winds, and how the winds are

Enoch's time in 32^{3-6}, and the righteous dead are in the West, 22; it is the abode of the righteous and the elect in Enoch's and Noah's times in 61^{12} $60^{8,\ 23}$; the abode of the earliest fathers in Enoch's time, 70^{3-4}; the abode of Enoch and Elijah in Elijah's time, 89^{52}: see 65^2 (note). This passage and the LXX are the oldest testimonies for the translation of Enoch unto Paradise : later this idea made its way into the Latin version of Sir. 44^{16} and the Ethiopic version of Gen. 5^{24}: eight others shared this honour with Enoch according to the Talmud, Weber, 251. Seventh from Adam: cf. 93^3 Jude 14 Book of Jubilees 7^{39}. 7-9, 24. 4 Ezra 6^{49-52} and 2 Bar. 29^4 appear to have drawn on our text. The following citation with references tends to prove this. 4 Ezra 6^{49} 'Et tunc †conservasti (= נצרת corrupt for יצרת : hence read 'creasti') *duo animalia, nomen uni vocasti Behemoth et nomen secundi vocasti Leviathan*' (1 Enoch $60^{7,\ 8}$). 6^{50} '*Et separasti ea ab alterutro* (1 Enoch 60^9), non enim poterat septima pars ubi erat aqua congregata capere ea'. 6^{51} '*Et dedisti Behemoth* unam *partem quae* siccata (1 Enoch $60^{8,\ 9}$) *est tertio die, ut inhabitet* (60^8) *in ea ubi sunt montes mille*': 6^{52} '*Leviathan autem dedisti septimam partem humidam* ($60^{8,\ 9}$): *et servasti ea ut fiant in devorationem* (60^{24}) *quibus vis et quando vis*'. 2 Bar. 29^4 'And *Behemoth* shall be revealed from his place and *Leviathan* shall ascend *from the sea, those two great monsters* (1 Enoch $60^{7,\ 8}$) which I created on the fifth day of creation, and kept until that time; and then they *shall be for food* for all that are left'. 9. The ('that' $q,\ \beta-n$) other angel: see vv. 4, 11. 10. Thou son of man. This use of the phrase is after the manner of Ezekiel, and stands in strong contrast with the main conception of the Son of Man in the Parables, 46^{1-3} (notes). 11. We should expect the answer to the question in ver. 9 to follow here, but it is not given till ver. 24, and a long account (11-23) dealing with physical secrets intervenes. In 60^{24} it is the angel of peace who gives the answer. The other angel who went with me and showed me, &c. Borrowed from 46^2; cf. 43^3. 12. Chambers of the winds: cf. 18^1 41^4. All MSS. but g

divided, and how they are weighed, and (how) the **portals** of the winds are reckoned, each according to the power of the wind, and the power of the lights of the moon, and according to the power that is fitting: and the divisions of the stars according to their names, and how all the divisions are divided.   13. And the thunders according to the places where they fall, and all the divisions that are made among the lightnings that it may lighten, and their host that they may at once obey.   14. For the thunder has †places of rest† (which) are assigned (to it) while it is waiting for its peal; and the thunder and lightning are inseparable, and although not one and undivided, they both go together through the spirit and separate not.   15. For when the lightning lightens, the thunder utters its voice, and the spirit enforces a pause during the peal, and divides equally between them; for the treasury of their peals is like the sand, and each one of them as it peals is held in with a bridle, and turned back by the power of the spirit, and pushed forward according to the many quarters of the earth.   16. And the spirit of the sea is masculine and strong, and according to the might of his strength he draws it back with a rein, and in like manner it is driven forward and disperses amid all the mountains of the earth.

read 'in the chambers', &c. How they are weighed: cf. 41^1 43^2 Job 28^{25}. **Portals.** So Flemming emends anq'eta (a) into 'anàqda. Spirits or angels are appointed to control the various phenomena of nature. This is peculiar to these interpolations, as in other parts of the book the powers of nature are either personified or are regarded as conscious intelligences; cf. 18^{14-16}. The view taken by the interpolator is followed by the Book of Jubilees 2^2, where we find 'angels of the spirit of fire', 'angels of hail', 'angels of hoar-frost', 'angels of thunder', &c., Rev. $7^{1, 2}$ 14^{18} (angel of fire); 19^{17} (angel of the sun); Asc. Is. iv. 18.   **Lights of the moon.** Its various phases.   13. Cf. Job 37^{1-5}.   14. This verse is very unintelligible. Halévy's discussion of this passage (*Journ. Asiat.* 369-372, 1867) is worth consulting. He arrives at the following translation: 'For the thunder has fixed laws in reference to the duration of its peal which is assigned to it: the thunder and the lightning are not separated in a single instance: they both proceed with one accord and separate not. For when the lightning lightens, the thunder utters its voice, and the spirit during its peal makes its arrangements, and divides the time equally between them.'   16. The ebb and flow of the sea explained.   **Disperses amid all the mountains.** With the flow of the sea is connected its subterranean advance into the mountains to nourish

17. And the spirit of the hoar-frost is his own angel, and the spirit of the hail is a good angel. 18. And the spirit of the snow has forsaken (his chamber) on account of his strength—there is a special spirit therein, and that which ascends from it is like smoke, and its name is frost. 19. And the spirit of the mist is not united with them in their chambers, but it has a special chamber; for its course is †glorious† both in light and in darkness, and in winter and in summer, and in its chamber is an angel. 20. And the spirit of the dew has its dwelling at the ends of the heaven, and is connected with the chambers of the rain, and its course is in winter and summer: and its clouds and the clouds of the mist are connected, and the one gives to the other. 21. And when the spirit of the rain goes forth from its chamber, the angels come and open the chamber and lead it out, and when it is diffused over the whole earth it unites with the water on the earth. And whensoever it unites with the water on the earth. . . . 22. For the waters are for those who dwell on the earth; for they are nourishment for the earth from the Most High who is in heaven: therefore there is a measure for the rain, and the angels take it in charge. 23. And these things I saw towards the Garden of the Righteous. 24. And the angel of peace who was with me said to me: 'These two

---

the springs. So Dillmann. 17. Is his own angel, i.e. the hoar-frost has a special angel of its own. Is a good angel. Though hail is often hurtful, it is not in charge of a demon but of a good angel. 19. The mist is to be distinguished from the foregoing phenomena; for it appears in all seasons and by night and day. Is glorious. Text may = כבד. If so it should have been rendered 'is oppressive'. In its chamber is an angel (tu). gmq 'its chamber is an angel': $β-ai$ 'in its chamber is light and its angel'. 20. The dew has its dwelling at the ends of the heaven: this would agree with $34^{1,2}$ 36^1 and 75^5. 21. As the rain is of such importance alike for the ethical and material well-being of man, Job $37^{12, 13}$, its spirit is not independent but subordinated to the angels; cf. Job 28^{26} 38^{25-30}. And ^{1o}. $> gq$. And whensoever... on the earth ($a-q$ (save that x omits 'with the water on the earth'), $bfhiklnx_1a$). $> qacileoy_1b$. The apodosis of this sentence is lost. 22. For ^{1o} ($mt, β-doy_1b$). $> u$. q, doy_1b read 'from the place of'. g a corruption of mt. Observe that the seas and the garden adjoin in 77^{3-4} as here in 60^{23-23}. 23. The Garden of the Righteous: see ver. 8 (note). 24. This verse contains the answer to the question in ver. 9. The appearance of the angel of peace monsters, prepared conformably to the greatness of God, shall feed. . . .

Angels go off to measure Paradise: the Judgement of the Righteous by the Elect One: the Praise of the Elect One and of God.

LXI. 1. And I saw in those days how long cords were given to those angels, and they took to themselves wings and flew, and they went towards the north.

2. And I asked the angel, saying unto him: 'Why have those (angels) taken these cords and gone off?' And he said unto me: 'They have gone to measure.'

3. And the angel who went with me said unto me:

'These shall bring the measures of the righteous,
And the ropes of the righteous to the righteous,
That they may stay themselves on the name of the Lord of Spirits for ever and ever.

4. The elect shall begin to dwell with the elect,

here may be due to the interpolator. Elsewhere this chapter speaks of 'another angel' sent by Michael, 60⁴, ⁹, ¹¹.

LXI. 1. Here the true text of the Parables is resumed, but the opening verses are very difficult. Those angels. q reads 'the two angels'. The angels here referred to may have been definitely named in some preceding part now lost. Wings. In the O.T. the angels are not represented as winged, unless in its latest books; cf. 1 Chron. 21¹⁶. Towards the north, i.e. the north-west; cf. 70³. Paradise is the destination of the angels; cf. 60⁸ (note). 2. The angel, i.e. the angel of peace, who is the *angelus interpres* in the sections dealing with the Elect One: see Introd. p. 64 sq. Cords (a). β 'long cords'. Have gone. > mu, d. To measure, (η)tuβ. gm 'to begin' by a scribal slip. The cords which the angels take with them are for measuring Paradise. See the reference to this in 70³. For this idea of angels with measuring cords see Ezek. 40³, ⁶ Zech. 2¹⁻³. 3–4. Here as ch. 52 there are two sources. These verses belong to the 'Son of Man' source, since the *angelus interpres* is 'the angel who went with me'. See Introd. p. 64 sq. 3. The measures of the righteous represent alike the blessed and their habitation. They are an ideal representation of the community of the righteous, living and departed, and reveal especially the latter; for it matters not by what death these perished; they are alive unto the Lord of Spirits, and will return and stay themselves on the day of his Elect One: these measures are given to faith and strengthen the righteous. To the righteous (gqtu, n). > m, β-n. Stay themselves on. Cf. 48⁴ 61⁵. 4. Sinners will be driven

And those are the measures which shall be given to faith
And which shall strengthen righteousness.

5. And these measures shall reveal all the secrets of the depths of the earth,
And those who have been destroyed by the desert,
And those who have been devoured by the beasts,
And those who have been devoured by the fish of the sea,

That they may return and stay themselves
On the day of the Elect One;
For none shall be destroyed before the Lord of Spirits,
And none can be destroyed.

6. And all who dwell above in the heaven received a command and power and one voice and one light like unto fire.

7. And that One (with) their first words they blessed,
And extolled and lauded with wisdom,
And they were wise in utterance and in the spirit of life.

8. And the Lord of Spirits placed the Elect One on the throne of glory.
And he shall judge all the works of the holy above in the heaven,
And in the balance shall their deeds be weighed.

---

from off the face of the earth; cf. 38¹ (note). **Righteousness** (a). β 'the voice of righteousness'. 5. Only the resurrection of the righteous is here spoken of. In 51¹,² there is an account of the resurrection of all Israel: see note. After the resurrection follows the judgement. **Devoured**¹⁰. q omits next nine words through hmt. Hence it supports gmtu here. **By the beasts** (tu). gm by a scribal error 'by the treasuries'. Flemming, followed by Martin, abandons the text of tu(gm), and gives that of β-n, which reads 'of the sea and by the beasts', and omits the second 'and those who have been devoured'. 6. **All who dwell above in the heaven**, i.e. the angels;

cf. vv. 10 12 47². In 9³ they are called 'the holy ones of heaven'. The angels were commanded to sing praises, and for that purpose one power and one voice are given to them. 7. **That One**. Either the Elect One or the Lord of Spirits. But the translation given above is questionable. For la before w'ětû read ba. Then render 'with their first words they blessed'. This seems right, though no object of the praise is definitely stated. 8. See 45³ (note); cf. Ps. 110¹. **Glory** (a). β 'His glory'. The holy above in the heaven, i.e. the angels; cf. 61⁶ (note). For 'the holy' q reads 'the righteous'. **Shall their deeds be weighed** (mqu, β). g 'they shall

9. And when he shall lift up his countenance
    To judge their secret ways according to the word of the name of the Lord of Spirits,
    And their path according to the way of the righteous judgement of the Lord of Spirits,
    Then shall they all with one voice speak and bless,
    And glorify and extol and sanctify the name of the Lord of Spirits.

10. And He will summon all the host of the heavens, and all the holy ones above, and the host of God, the Cherubin, Seraphin, and Ophannin, and all the angels of power, and all the angels of principalities, and the Elect One, and the other powers on the earth (and) over the water   11. On that day shall raise one voice, and bless and glorify and exalt in the spirit of faith, and in the spirit of wisdom, and in the spirit of patience,

weigh their deeds', t, *abcdefhkl* 'he shall weigh their deeds'. On this matter see 41^1 note.   9. **Their ... ways.** t 'their cause'. **According to the word of the name of the Lord of Spirits.** This clause is evidently parallel with the next, 'according to the way of the righteous judgement of the Lord of Spirits.' We might therefore translate nagara 'command': 'according to the command of the name of the Lord of Spirits.' **Lord of Spirits**^{10} (a). β 'Most High God'. **Sanctify** (a, n). β-n 'praise'. 10. **He will summon**: i.e. God will summon. In my text I took *jeṣēw'ē* as a misrendering of $\beta o \eta \sigma \epsilon \iota$. In that case we should render: 'all the host of the heavens shall cry out.' **Cherubin, Seraphin, and Ophannin**: cf. 14^{11}, ^{18} 20^7 71^7. The Cherubim and Seraphim appear in the O.T. but are carefully distinguished. Schulz, *A. Tliche. Theol.*, p. 617, says that in no instance are the Cherubim to be regarded as angels, but as symbolic figures: they form God's chariot, and are the means of revealing or concealing His presence. But this does not hold of later developments. In the present passage they form an order of angels as they do in Rev. $5^{6\,sqq.}$ 2 Enoch 19^1 20^1. The Seraphim are beings whose special duty was to serve in God's immediate presence. On the nature of these see also Delitzsch on Is. 6^2. The Ophannim (i.e. wheels) are derived from Ezek. 1^{15}. In the Talmud as here they are classed with the Cherubim and Seraphim, Weber, pp. 168, 205. On the angelology of the O.T. see Schulz, *A. Tliche. Theol.* (606-622); *Jewish Encyc. in loc.* **Angels of power, and all the angels of principalities.** These are exactly St. Paul's 'principalities and powers'; cf. Rom. 8^{38} Eph. 1^{21} Col. 1^{16}. **The other powers on the earth**, &c., i.e. the lower angel-powers over nature. 11. **Glorify.** + 'and praise', β. **Exalt.** $> g$. **In the spirit of faith**, &c. These words express the virtues which animate the angels who give praise. The virtues are seven in number; cf.

and in the spirit of mercy, and in the spirit of judgement and of peace, and in the spirit of goodness, and shall all say with one voice: "Blessed is He, and may the name of the Lord of Spirits be blessed for ever and ever."

12. All who sleep not above in heaven shall bless Him:
All the holy ones who are in heaven shall bless him,
And all the elect who dwell in the garden of life:

And every spirit of light who is able to bless, and glorify, and extol, and hallow Thy blessed name,
And all flesh shall beyond measure glorify and bless Thy name for ever and ever.

13. For great is the mercy of the Lord of Spirits, and He is long-suffering,
And all His works and all that He has created
He has revealed to the righteous and elect
In the name of the Lord of Spirits.'

Judgement of the Kings and the Mighty: Blessedness of the Righteous.

LXII. 1. And thus the Lord commanded the kings and the mighty and the exalted, and those who dwell on the earth, and

---

49³. In the spirit of patience (il₁a). Other MSS. (perhaps rightly) 'in patience'. Blessed is He, &c.: cf. 39¹⁰.   12. All who sleep not: see 1⁵ (note). The holy ones (a, bwxy). β-bwxy 'His holy ones'. Garden of life: see 60⁸ (note). The LXX chronology is followed here as in the Parables generally; cf. 54⁷ (note). Spirit of light. A phrase embracing good spirits, human and angelic. This thought (cf. 108¹¹, 'generation of light') is more fully developed in the N.T., 'children of light', Luke 16⁸. Blessed (a). β 'holy'.   13. Mercy: see 60⁵ (note).

LXII. Here we have a lengthened account of the judgement, particularly of the kings and of the mighty. This subject has already been handled shortly, 46⁴⁻⁸ 48⁸⁻¹⁰ 53-54³; but here the actual scene is portrayed. The kings and the mighty will be filled with anguish when they behold the Messiah, and will fall down and worship, and pray for mercy at his hands. But their prayers will be of no avail and they will be carried off by the angels of punishment. The blessedness of the lot of the righteous is then dwelt upon in contrast with the fate of the wicked.   1. The kings and said: 'Open your eyes and lift up your horns if ye are able to recognize the Elect One.'

2. And the Lord of Spirits seated him on the throne of His glory,
   And the spirit of righteousness was poured out upon him,
   And the word of his mouth slays all the sinners,
   And all the unrighteous are destroyed from before his face.

3. And there shall stand up in that day all the kings and the mighty,
   And the exalted and those who hold the earth,
   And they shall see and recognize
   How he sits on the throne of his glory,
   And righteousness is judged before him,
   And no lying word is spoken before him.

4. Then shall pain come upon them as on a woman in travail,
   [And she has pain in bringing forth]
   When her child enters the mouth of the womb,
   And she has pain in bringing forth.

5. And one portion of them shall look on the other,
   And they shall be terrified,
   And they shall be downcast of countenance,
   And pain shall seize them,

the mighty: see 38^5. **Lift up your horns**: cf. Ps. 75^4. **Recognize**, i.e. recognize him to be what he is—the Messiah. The word translated 'recognize' could also be rendered 'comprehend', 'understand'. **2. Seated him.** MSS. read nabara = 'sat' which Dillmann emended into anbarô = 'seated him'. Cf. Is. 11^4. **The word of his mouth.** The judgement is forensic. **All the sinners, and all the unrighteous.** Though the writer is chiefly concerned with the judgement of the kings, the condemnation of the sinners and godless and unrighteous is frequently referred to; cf. $38^{1, 2, 3}$ 41^2 $45^{2, 3, 6}$ [50^2] $53^{2, 7}$ 62^{13} 69^{27}. **From before his face** (a). β 'and from before his face'. **3.** The fact that even the righteous are judged opens up a terrible prospect for the kings and the mighty: cf. 1 Pet. 4^{18}. **Righteousness** (a). β–no $_1b$ 'the righteous in righteousness', no $_1b$ 'the righteous'. **No lying word**: see 49^4 (note). **4.** Cf. Is. 13^8 21^3 26^{17}, &c. [**And she has pain**, &c.] Bracketed as a dittograph of the fourth line. **5. One portion of them shall look on the other.** With this scene cf. Wisdom

When they see that Son of Man
Sitting on the throne of his glory.

6. And the kings and the mighty and all who possess the earth shall bless and glorify and extol him who rules over all, who was hidden.

7. For from the beginning the Son of Man was hidden,
And the Most High preserved him in the presence of His might,
And revealed him to the elect.

8. And the congregation of the elect and holy shall be sown,
And all the elect shall stand before him on that day.

9. And all the kings and the mighty and the exalted and those who rule the earth
Shall fall down before him on their faces,
And worship and set their hope upon that Son of Man,
And petition him and supplicate for mercy at his hands.

10. Nevertheless that Lord of Spirits will so press them
That they shall hastily go forth from His presence,
And their faces shall be filled with shame,
And the darkness shall grow deeper on their faces.

$5^{1 \text{ sqq}}$. This shows that Is. 13^8 was in the mind of the writer. **Son of Man** ($a-m$). m, β 'Son of the woman'. See 46^2 (note). **6**. The kings are now ready to acknowledge and worship the Son of Man, but it is too late. The kings and the mighty ($a-u$). u, β 'the mighty kings'. **Rules over all**: cf. Dan. 7^{14}. **Who was hidden**. This could also be rendered 'that was hidden', i.e. the unseen universe. **6, 7. Hidden**: cf. 48^6. This word occasions a digression and an explanation. Before he appeared to judge he was preserved by the Lord of Spirits and revealed to the elect through the spirit of prophecy, 46^7. By this means the community of the elect was founded (lit. 'sown'), but was not to behold him till the final judgement. The community that is 'sown' is called the 'plant of righteousness'; cf. 10^{16} (note). **7. From the beginning** (mqt, $\beta_{-1}a$). The readings of gu_1a are corruptions of this. **8. Congregation**: cf. 38^1 (note). **Elect and holy** (a). β 'holy and elect'. **9, 10**. The description of the judgement of the kings resumed: they implore mercy, but in vain. **10. Shame and darkness**: cf. 46^6 4 Ezra 7^{55}. **Darkness shall grow deeper, &c.** (gt, $\beta-f$). Nah. 2^{10} 'the

11. And He will deliver them to the angels for punishment,
    To execute vengeance on them because they have oppressed
    His children and His elect.

12. And they shall be a spectacle for the righteous and for His
    elect:
    They shall rejoice over them,
    Because the wrath of the Lord of Spirits resteth upon them,
    And His sword is drunk with their blood.

13. And the righteous and elect shall be saved on that day,
    And they shall never thenceforward see the face of the
    sinners and unrighteous.

14. And the Lord of Spirits will abide over them,
    And with that Son of Man shall they eat
    And lie down and rise up for ever and ever.

15. And the righteous and elect shall have risen from the earth,
    And ceased to be of downcast countenance.

16. And they shall have been clothed with garments of glory,
    And these shall be the garments of life from the Lord of
    Spirits:
    And your garments shall not grow old,
    Nor your glory pass away before the Lord of Spirits.

faces of all of them shall gather darkness' may be the source of our text. **11. He will deliver them to the angels, &c.** I have here accepted an emendation of Flemming. $m\beta$ read 'the angels of punishment shall take them in charge'. Angels for punishment: see 40^7 (note). Cf. 53^3–54^2. **12. Spectacle**: see 48^9 (note). Sword. Used figuratively here; cf. 63^{11}. Drunk: cf. Is. 34^6. **13. Saved**: cf. 48^7. **14.** The kingdom is at last established and God Himself dwells amongst them; cf. Is. $60^{19, 20}$ Zeph. 3^{15-17}: and the Messiah will dwell with them; cf. 45^4 38^2. The kingdom lasts for ever. Eat. β–a^1 read 'abide and eat'. Eat and lie down. From Zeph. 3^{13}. **15.** This verse does not refer to the resurrection but signifies that all the humiliations of the righteous are at an end. **16. Of glory** (a, in). β–in 'of life'. Garments of life (η, β). a–η 'your garments, garments of life'. In a–η the addition seems to be drawn from the next line. From (a–t^1, t^2). β 'with'. On the garments of the blessed cf. 2 Cor. 5^3, ^{4} Rev. $3^{4, 5, 18}$ 4^4 6^{11} $7^9, 13, 14$ 4 Ezra $2^{39, 45}$ Herm. *Sim.* 8^2. See also 1 Enoch 108^{12}. These garments are the spiritual bodies that await the righteous. Cf. 2 Cor. 5^{2-5}. Shall not grow old: cf. Deut. 8^4 29^5.

The unavailing Repentance of the Kings and the Mighty.

LXIII. 1. In those days shall the mighty and the kings who possess the earth implore (Him) to grant them a little respite from His angels of punishment to whom they were delivered, that they might fall down and worship before the Lord of Spirits, and confess their sins before Him. 2. And they shall bless and glorify the Lord of Spirits, and say:

'Blessed is the Lord of Spirits and the Lord of kings,
And the Lord of the mighty and the Lord of the rich,
And the Lord of glory and the Lord of wisdom,

3. And splendid in every secret thing is Thy power from generation to generation,
And Thy glory for ever and ever:

Deep are all Thy secrets and innumerable,
And Thy righteousness is beyond reckoning.

4. We have now learnt that we should glorify
And bless the Lord of kings and Him who is king over all kings.'

5. And they shall say:
'Would that we had rest to glorify and give thanks
And confess our faith before His glory!

LXIII. The writer again returns to the kings and the mighty in order to describe their bitter and unavailing repentance. The description is not an amplification of 62⁵⁻¹², but takes up the history at a later stage after that the kings have appealed in vain to the Messiah and are already in the custody of the angels of punishment. As their appeal to the Messiah has failed, they entreat the angels of punishment, to whom they are delivered, to grant them a respite to worship the Lord of Spirits and confess their sins before Him. This in fact forms an indirect and last despairing appeal to the Lord of Spirits. At the same time it is a justification of God's justice. For a somewhat similar passage cf. Wisdom 5³⁻⁸. 1. The mighty and the kings (*a*). *aehknrw* 'kings', *bcdfilopxy*₁*a*₁*b* 'mighty kings'. His angels (*a–tu*, β). *t*, *q*³ 'the angels'. 2. Their confession acknowledges all that they formerly denied; cf. 46⁶. 3. Cf. 49². Splendid in every secret thing is Thy power (*a–mu*). β 'every secret thing is lighted up and Thy power'. 5. Would that. The Ethiopic here is a rendering of the Hebraism מי יתן, or the Aramaism מן ייהב. Glorify and give thanks. (*a–q*). *y*, β 'glorify Him and thank Him'. β adds 'and bless Him'.

6. And now we long for a little rest but find it not:
We follow hard upon and obtain (it) not:

And light has vanished from before us,
And darkness is our dwelling-place for ever and ever:

7. For we have not believed before Him
Nor glorified the name of the Lord of Spirits, [nor glorified our Lord]

But our hope was in the sceptre of our kingdom,
And in our glory.

8. And in the day of our suffering and tribulation He saves us not,
And we find no respite for confession

That our Lord is true in all His works, and in His judgements and His justice,
And His judgements have no respect of persons.

9. And we pass away from before His face on account of our works,
And all our sins are reckoned up in righteousness.'

10. Now they will say unto themselves: 'Our souls are full of unrighteous gain, but it does not prevent us from descending from the midst thereof into the †burden† of Sheol.'

6. And now (ηβ). a–η 'now'. Follow hard upon ($gt^1\ _1b$ = καταδιώκομεν). > κ, i. mq, $t^2β$-$i\ _1a\ _1b$ 'are driven away'. Obtain (it) not. η omits the following 'and' and reads: 'obtain not light: it has vanished,' &c. Darkness is our dwelling-place: cf. 46⁶. 7. Believed, or 'confessed'. Of Spirits (gη, efv). m 'of lords', tu, β-efc 'of kings'. The following clause is bracketed as a dittograph. Our Lord (a). β 'the Lord in all His work'. Sceptre (ym, io $_1a\ _1b$). tu, fv 'throne', q, dhkln 'sceptre of the throne'. 8. There is no place of repentance when the final judgement has come. Our Lord is true, &c. Cf. Jub. 4²¹. He is 'faithful and He is righteous beyond all and there is no accepting of persons with Him'. In His judgements (a–η). β 'in all His judgements'. 10. Riches avail not to their salvation; cf. 52⁷ 53 Ps. 49⁷⁻¹². Unrighteous gain: cf. Luke 16⁹, ¹¹ Sir. 5⁸. From the midst thereof (gqu). mt, β–b 'from the flame thereof'. Into the †burden†. Kĕbad = βάρος, which the Ethiopic translator may have confused with βάριν as in Pss. 47⁵, ¹² 121⁷ Lam. 2⁵. If this is so, then we should render 'into the stronghold of Sheol'. Though the general sense is clear, the details are uncertain. Perhaps we should read 'into the burden of the flame of Sheol'. Sheol. This word has

11. And after that their faces shall be filled with darkness
And shame before that Son of Man,

borne different meanings at different periods and also different meanings during the same period, owing to the coexistence of different stages in the development of thought. As these different meanings are to be found in Enoch, a short history of the conception will be the best means of explanation. (1) Sheol in the O.T. is the place appointed for all living, Job 30^{23}: from its grasp there is never any possibility of escape, Job 7^9. It is situated beneath the earth, Num. 16^{30}; it is the land of darkness and confusion, Job $10^{21, 22}$; of destruction, forgetfulness, and silence, Pss. $88^{11, 13}$ 94^{17} 115^{17}. Nevertheless the identity of the individual is in some measure preserved, Is. 14^{10} Ezek. 32^{21} 1 Sam. 28^{15} sqq.: but the existence is joyless and has no point of contact with God or human interests, Pss. 6^5 30^9 Is. $38^{11, 18}$. In the conception of Sheol there is no moral or religious element involved; no moral distinctions are observed in it; good and bad fare alike. But the family, national, and social distinctions of the world above are still reproduced, and men are gathered to their fathers or people, Gen. $25^{8, 9}$ 35^{29} Ezek. 32^{17-32}: kings are seated on their thrones even there, Is. $14^{9, 10}$ Ezek. $32^{21, 24}$. Thus the O.T. Sheol does not differ essentially from the Homeric Hades, Odyss. xi. 488, 489. This view of Sheol was the orthodox and prevailing one till the second century B.C.; cf. Sir. 14^{16} $17^{22, 23}$ 30^{17} 1 Bar. 3^{11} Tob. 3^{10} 13^2 1 Enoch 102^{11} (i.e. where Sadducees are introduced as speaking). Individual voices indeed had been raised against it in favour of a religious conception of Sheol, and finally through their advocacy this higher conception gradually won its way into acceptance.

(2) This second and higher conception of Sheol was the product of the same religious thought that gave birth to the doctrine of the Resurrection—the thought that found the answer to its difficulties by carrying the idea of retribution into the life beyond the grave. The old conception thus underwent a double change. Firstly, it became essentially a place where men were treated according to their deserts, with a division for the righteous, and a division for the wicked. And, secondly, from being the unending abode of the departed, it came to be only an intermediate state; cf. En. 22 51^1 102^6 (?) Luke 16^{23} (?). (3) The conception underwent a further change, and no longer signified the intermediate state of the righteous and of the wicked, but came to be used of the abode of the wicked only, either as their preliminary abode, cf. Rev. 1^{18} 6^8 $20^{13, 14}$, or as their final one, En. 63^{10} 99^{11} 103^7. This was probably due to the fact that the Resurrection was limited to the righteous, and thus the souls of the wicked simply remained in Sheol, which thus practically became hell or Gehenna; cf. Pss. Sol. 14^6 15^{11}. In 63^{10} the kings are cast into Sheol, but into Gehenna in 54^{1-2}. That this conception of Sheol appeared in isolated cases in the Persian period, see Cheyne, *Origin of the Psalter*, 381-412. Cf. on the question generally, Oehler, *Theol. des A. T.* i. 253-266; Schulz, *A. Tliche. Theol.* 697-708; Charles, *The Doctrine of a Future Life*, passim. In the Talmud Sheol has become synonymous with Gehenna, Weber, *Jüd. Theol.* 341-342.   11. With darkness: cf. 46^6 62^{10}. Sword. Used figuratively here; cf. 62^{12}. Bousset suggests that this verse is an interpola-

And they shall be driven from his presence,
And the sword shall abide before his face in their midst.

12. Thus spake the Lord of Spirits: 'This is the ordinance and judgement with respect to the mighty and the kings and the exalted and those who possess the earth before the Lord of Spirits.'

Vision of the fallen Angels in the Place of Punishment.

LXIV. 1. And other forms I saw hidden in that place. 2. I heard the voice of the angel saying: 'These are the angels who descended to the earth, and revealed what was hidden to the children of men and seduced the children of men into committing sin.'

Enoch foretells to Noah the Deluge and his own Preservation.

LXV. 1. And in those days Noah saw the earth that it had sunk down and its destruction was nigh. 2. And he arose from thence and went to the ends of the earth, and cried aloud to his grandfather Enoch: and Noah said three times with an

---

tion. If we excise it the whole chapter refers to the judgement of the Lord of Spirits. This verse closely resembles 62^{10}. **12.** Thus $(a-y)$. g 'as', β 'and thus'.

LXIV. A brief digression on the fallen angels whose judgement has already been described in the second Parable, 54^3 sqq. $55^{3,4}$. This chapter, if originally a part of the Parables, as it quite well can be, is in the wrong place here; for 'that place', spoken of as the place of punishment of the angels, cannot be Sheol referred to in 63^{10}. **2. I heard.** m, vx 'and I heard'. **Voice of the angel.** m 'voice of the angels'. **Descended.** $+ t, \beta$ 'from heaven'.

LXV—LXIX. 25. These chapters professedly and in fact belong to a Noah Apocalypse, and have no right to form a part of the text of Enoch. The main reasons for this conclusion are to be found in the note on 54^7. Like the other Noachic interpolations, this interpolation is of a fragmentary nature: it deals mainly with three subjects: (1) 65^1–67^3, the impending Flood and the deliverance of Noah; (2) 67^4–69^1, the punishment of the fallen angels, with a digression on the kings and the mighty; (3) 69^{2-25}, the fall of the angels and the secrets they disclosed.

LXV. 1. Observe that the vision is Noah's. The vision opens here with a subsidence of the earth, as in 60^1 with a quaking of the heavens. **And** (q, β). $> a$–q. **Noah.** t 'I Noah', and in the first person throughout verses 1-2. **2. The ends of the earth.** The entrance to heaven is at the ends of the earth. Cf. 106^8. **Grandfather.** In reality great-grandfather; cf. 60^8.

embittered voice: 'Hear me, hear me, hear me.' 3. And I said unto him: 'Tell me what it is that is falling out on the earth that the earth is in such evil plight and shaken, lest perchance I shall perish with it.' 4. And thereupon there was a great commotion on the earth, and a voice was heard from heaven, and I fell on my face. 5. And Enoch my grandfather came and stood by me, and said unto me: 'Why hast thou cried unto me with a bitter cry and weeping?

6. And a command has gone forth from the presence of the Lord concerning those who dwell on the earth that their ruin is accomplished because they have learnt all the secrets of the angels, and all the violence of the Satans, and all their powers—the most secret ones—and all the power of those who practise sorcery, and the power of witchcraft, and the power of those who make molten images for the whole earth: 7. And how silver is produced from the dust of the earth, and how soft metal originates in the earth. 8. For lead and tin are not produced from the earth like the first: it is a fountain that produces them, and an angel stands therein, and that angel is pre-eminent.' 9. And after that my grandfather Enoch took hold of me by my hand and raised me up, and said unto me: 'Go, for I have asked the Lord of Spirits as touching this commotion on the earth. 10. And He said unto me: "Because of their unrighteousness

---

3. I said (a, r). t^2, β–*iv* 'he said'.
4. A voice. This is the command in ver. 6. Fell on my face. As in 60^5. 6–10ª. The text seems to be in disorder. It would be clearer if 65^{9-10a} followed immediately on 65^5.
6. Because they have learnt all the secrets of the angels, &c.: cf. 7 8 69. Their powers—the most secret ones (*gt*). β–*an* 'their secret powers', *m* 'the powers of their most secret secrets', *qu* 'their powers'. The power of witchcraft: cf. 7^1. The destruction of the earth is ascribed to the corruption wrought through the angels. 8. From the earth. > *q*.

An angel stands ... is pre-eminent. I here read jĕtbadar with *t* = 'is pre-eminent'. Other MSS. jĕbadĕr = *celer est, praecurrit* (and possibly *praecellit* as Dillmann assumes). 9. My hand (*gq*). *mtu*, β 'his hand'. 10. This verse is very corrupt, but it is possible I think to recover the original meaning and text. The present text runs as follows: 'Because of their unrighteousness their judgement has been determined upon, and shall not be reckoned before Me because of the months which they have searched out and learnt that (> *gtu*) the earth and those who dwell upon it shall be their judgement has been determined upon and shall not be withheld by Me for ever. Because of the sorceries which they have searched out and learnt, the earth and those who dwell upon it shall be destroyed." 11. And these—they have no place of repentance for ever, because they have shown them what was hidden, and they are the damned: but as for thee, my son, the Lord of Spirits knows that thou art pure, and guiltless of this reproach concerning the secrets.

12. And He has destined thy name to be among the holy,

destroyed.' Here first of all Halévy has pointed out that the knowledge of the future could hardly have been regarded by the author as criminal. He fixes on 'months' as a corruption = חדשים corrupt for חרשים = 'sorceries' (Is. 3³). But the objection here is that the bulk of the evidence points not to a Hebrew but an Aramaic original. But since Aramaic speaking Jews (Jer. Taanith, iii. 69) sometimes used חרשיא instead of the regular ירחיא, it is possible that חרשיא was here a corruption of חרשיא. But if ירחיא did stand in the original, it may have been a corruption of סתריא 'secrets'. Next, in my Ethiopic Text of 1906, p. 118, I pointed out that 'shall not be reckoned' is wrong. This phrase = ולא יחשב—a corruption for ולא יחשך 'shall not be withheld'. At the same time I pointed out in the same work, p. xxxi, that this restoration was possible through Aramaic. Thus יתמנא = 'shall be numbered' would be a corruption of יתמנע 'shall be withheld'. Subsequently Nathaniel Schmidt, in a reprint from *Old Testament and Semitic Studies in Memory of W. R. Harper*, pp. 338-339, adopted the idea I have above suggested but not that of Halévy. He renders: 'Because of their violence their judgement will be carried out, and will not be withheld by Me, on account of the months during which they will inquire and learn how the earth and its inhabitants are to be destroyed.' Here 'will be reckoned' = יתמנא corrupt for יתמנע 'will be withheld'. So far so good, but the rest is impossible. First 'will be carried out' and 'will inquire and learn' should be in the past. Even had these renderings been right, the sense arrived at is unsatisfactory. The 'months' referred to are those during which Noah preached the coming end of the world and they remained unrepentant. If Professor Schmidt had studied my Text he would have seen that the word 'how' is not admitted into it since three of the best MSS. *gtu* omit it. Bearing this fact in mind, and adopting Halévy's emendation of 'months' and my own of 'shall not be reckoned', we arrive at the translation in our text. The meaning is clear and in keeping with the teaching in the earlier chapters of the book: the world will be destroyed because of the wickedness of the inhabitants and the sorceries (or secret things) they have discovered. 11. Place of repentance. Text = 'return' = Aramaic חִיּוּבָא, which should here be rendered 'repentance'. The restoration is possible also in Hebrew, since תשובה has both meanings. 12. Noah is to be the founder of a

And will preserve thee amongst those who dwell on the earth,
And has destined thy righteous seed both for kingship and for great honours,
And from thy seed shall proceed a fountain of the righteous and holy without number for ever.'

The Angels of the Waters bidden to hold them in Check.

LXVI. 1. And after that he showed me the angels of punishment who are prepared to come and let loose all the powers of the waters which are beneath in the earth in order to bring judgement and destruction on all who [abide and] dwell on the earth. 2. And the Lord of Spirits gave commandment to the angels who were going forth, that they should not cause the waters to rise but should hold them in check; for those angels were over the powers of the waters. 3. And I went away from the presence of Enoch.

God's Promise to Noah: Places of Punishment of the Angels and of the Kings.

LXVII. 1. And in those days the word of God came unto me, and He said unto me: 'Noah, thy lot has come up before Me, a lot without blame, a lot of love and uprightness. 2. And now

---

new and righteous generation. Thy righteous seed (*gmtu(q)*). β 'thy seed in righteousness'. Both for kingship (*q(t)*). β 'both for kings', *gmu* 'both kings' corrupt. Fountain: cf. Deut. 33³³ Ps. 68³⁶.

LXVI. 1. He, i.e. Enoch. Angels of punishment. We have here a new use of this phrase. These angels have to do solely with the second judgement in the Parables, and are employed here only through a misconception as the agents of the Deluge or first judgement, and as angels over the waters; cf. 40⁷ (note) 54⁷. [Abide and.] Bracketed as a dittograph. *q* om. *u, bx* omit ' and dwell '. 2. Cause the waters to rise. The text here reads 'hands' = ידיא corrupt for מיא 'waters'. The angels of the waters are here bidden to pause in order that during the pause the ark may be built 67³. The same idea is found in Rev. 7¹ sqq., where the four angels of the winds are bidden to restrain the winds till the servants of God are sealed in their foreheads. Cf. 2 Bar. 6⁴ sqq. Angels over the powers of the waters: cf. Rev. 16⁵.

LXVII. 1. The character of Noah here is based on Gen. 6⁹. 2. This account differs from 89¹, where it is the angels are making a wooden (building), and when they have completed that task I will place My hand upon it and preserve it, and there shall come forth from it the seed of life, and a change shall set in so that the earth will not remain without inhabitant. 3. And I will make fast thy seed before me for ever and ever, and I will spread abroad those who dwell with thee: it shall not be unfruitful on the face of the earth, but it shall be blessed and multiply on the earth in the name of the Lord.'

4. And He will imprison those angels, who have shown unrighteousness, in that burning valley which my grandfather Enoch had formerly shown to me in the west among the mountains of gold and silver and iron and soft metal and tin. 5. And I saw that valley in which there was a great convulsion and a convulsion of the waters. 6. And when all this took place, from that fiery molten metal and from the convulsion

said that Noah himself makes the ark. **Have completed**. *t*, and *a–t* but in a corrupt form. β 'have gone'. 3. Cf. 65¹². **It shall not be unfruitful** = 'ljĕmakĕn, emended from 'ljĕmakĕr (*a, β–b₁ary₁b*). *b₁ary₁b* omit. Otherwise read 'ljĕmĕkĕrŭ 'they shall not tempt (thy seed)'. But the text is wholly uncertain. **4–LXIX. 1.** This section deals with the punishment of the fallen angels and its significance in regard to the kings and the mighty. It is very confused. Part of the confusion is owing to an original confusion of thought on the part of the writer, and much to the corruptness of the text. The latter is largely obviated by the ascertainment of a better text: see Crit. Notes on vv. 8, 11, 13. As for the former, it has been caused by the writer describing the first judgement in features characteristic of the final, and in identifying localities in the Parables which are absolutely distinct, i. e. the burning valley of Gehenna is placed among the metal mountains, 67⁴, though it is definitely said to lie in another direction, 54¹, in the Parables. It is obvious, therefore, that no weight is to be attached to phrases denoting locality in this section. **4.** After treating of the judgement of mankind through the Deluge, the writer proceeds to describe the judgement of the angels, who were the real cause of man's corruption. The fallen angels are cast into a burning valley—really the Gehenna valley of 54. There is a twofold confusion here. It is not said that the angels in 54 were cast into the valley of Gehenna, but into a 'burning furnace'; and, in the second place, this was the final place of punishment, not the preliminary. But, again, the burning valley is here said to be amongst the metal mountains in the west. This, as we have shown above, is a misleading combination of utterly disparate ideas. **In the west.** The mountains mentioned are in the west according to 52¹ ˢᵠᵠ·. The phrase is no real note of locality. **5, 6.** These verses combine features of the Deluge and of volcanic disturbances. The latter are thereof in that place, there was produced a smell of sulphur, and it was connected with those waters, and that valley of the angels who had led astray (mankind) burned beneath that land. 7. And through its valleys proceed streams of fire, where these angels are punished who had led astray those who dwell upon the earth.

8. But those waters shall in those days serve for the kings and the mighty and the exalted, and those who dwell on the earth, for the healing of the body, but for the punishment of the spirit; now their spirit is full of lust, that they may be punished in their body, for they have denied the Lord of Spirits and see their punishment daily, and yet believe not in His name. 9. And in proportion as the burning of their bodies becomes severe, a corresponding change shall take place in their spirit for ever and ever; for before the Lord of Spirits none shall utter an idle word.   10. For the judgement shall come upon them, because they believe in the lust of their body and deny the Spirit

connected with the punishment of the angels. Burned beneath that land. Not merely the immediate neighbourhood of the Gehenna valley is here designated, but, as Dillmann points out, the adjacent country down to and beyond the Dead Sea. A subterranean fire was believed to exist under the Gehenna valley; cf. 27¹ (note).   8. Those waters shall serve ... for the healing of the body. The hot springs resulted from the meeting of the water and fire underground by which the angels were punished. As an instance of such a hot spring Dillmann mentions Kallirrhoe to the east of the Dead Sea, to which Herod the Great resorted, Jos. *Ant.* xvii. 6. 5; *Bell. Iud.* i. 33. 5. It has been objected that according to the latter passage these waters were sweet and not sulphurous. So far as this objection is valid, it cannot hold against the hot springs of Machaerus, *Bell. Iud.* vii. 6. 3, which were bitter, and in the neighbourhood of which there were sulphur mines. Holtzmann (*Jahrb. f. D. T.* xii. 391) refers to the eruptions of Mount Epomeo in Ischia in 46 and 35 B.C. (quoted by Schodde), but, as we have seen above, there is no need to go to the west for an explanation. In those days. Those of the writer. Healing of the body (gm, br). qtu, $\beta-b$r read 'healing of the soul and body'. For the punishment of the spirit, i.e. in the final judgement. Punished in their body. In Gehenna they will suffer in the body as well as in the spirit. Denied the Lord of Spirits: cf. 38² (note) 54⁷ (note). See their punishment daily. The hot springs are a testimony to the present punishment of the angels: a testimony likewise to the punishment that will befall the kings and the mighty.   9. The punishment will work repentance in the kings, which will be unavailing. An idle word: cf. 49⁴ (note). 10. Deny the Spirit of the Lord.

Chapters LXVII. 7—LXVIII. 2

of the Lord. 11. And those same waters shall undergo a change in those days; for when those angels are punished in these waters, these water-springs shall change their temperature, and when the angels ascend, this water of the springs shall change and become cold. 12. And I heard Michael answering and saying: 'This judgement wherewith the angels are judged is a testimony for the kings and the mighty who possess the earth.' 13. Because these waters of judgement minister to the healing of the body of the kings and the lust of their body; therefore they will not see and will not believe that those waters will change and become a fire which burns for ever.

Michael and Raphael astonied at the Severity of the Judgement.

LXVIII. 1. And after that my grandfather Enoch gave me the teaching of all the secrets in the book and in the Parables which had been given to him, and he put them together for me in the words of the book of the Parables. 2. And on that day Michael answered Raphael and said: 'The power of the spirit transports and makes me to tremble because of the severity of the judgement of the secrets, the judgement of the angels: who

---

This expression is unique in Enoch. 11. Referred to by Origen *C. Celsum* v. 52. See Introd. pp. lxiv, lxxxv. The removal of the angels to another place of punishment is followed by a cooling of the waters. In these waters (*a*). β-ε 'in those days'. 12. Michael (α). β 'the holy Michael'. 13. Kings. Text reads 'angels' = מלאכיא corrupt for מלכיא 'kings'. Lust (*m*). *gytu* 'desire', β-γ 'death'.

LXVIII. 1. According to this verse the Parables already exist as a complete work in the hands of the interpolator. The verse comes from the redactor who combined the Parables and the Noah fragments. The meaning of this chapter is difficult to determine. It has probably to do with the Satans or chiefs of the angels. Words of the book. *g* 'book of the words'. 2. The dialogue between Michael and Raphael is designed to set forth the severity of the judgement over the fallen angels, or rather the Satans. The power of the spirit. This is a strange expression. I suggested in 1893 that it was corrupt for 'the power of my spirit'. Halévy suggests that 'power' = יד which here = 'punishment'. Makes me to tremble. Text reads 'provokes' = יארגזני, which should here have been rendered 'makes me to tremble'. Because of (α-η). *q*, β 'and because of'. Judgement of the secrets. This may mean the judgement on account of the secrets divulged by the angels or Satans. Of can endure the severe judgement which has been executed, and before which they melt away?' 3. And Michael answered again, and said to Raphael: 'Who is he whose heart is not softened concerning it, and whose reins are not troubled by this word of judgement (that) has gone forth upon them because of those who have thus led them out?' 4. And it came to pass when he stood before the Lord of Spirits, Michael said thus to Raphael: 'I will not take their part under the eye of the Lord; for the Lord of Spirits has been angry with them because they do as if they were the Lord. 5. Therefore all that is hidden shall come upon them for ever and ever; for neither angel nor man shall have his portion (in it), but alone they have received their judgement for ever and ever.'

The Names and Functions of the (fallen Angels and) Satans: the secret Oath.

LXIX. 1. And after this judgement they shall terrify and make them to tremble because they have shown this to those who dwell on the earth.

2. And behold the names of those angels [and these are their

---

the angels ($q-\beta$). $> a-q$. Executed. + 'and abides' β. 3. Michael (a). β 'the holy Michael'. So also in ver. 4. Answered. + 'me' gqu. Is not softened (β). a 'is not convicted'. The former looks like an emendation. At the same time a does not give a good sense. Where the Greek exists β is hardly ever right against a, though one or more individual MSS. of β may be. Word of judgement (that) has gone forth (gq). mtu, β 'word: judgement has gone forth'. Upon them because of those who have thus led them out. Dillmann thinks this may mean those angels who are conducted from the preliminary to the final place of punishment. It might perhaps be better to translate as I have done above. In this case we should have the judgement of the Satans who are rigorously punished because they seduced the angels into sin. The words 'They do as if they were like the Lord' favour this interpretation; cf. Is. 14$^{11-13}$. 5. All that is hidden (a). β 'the hidden judgement'.

LXIX. 1. Make them to tremble. Text = 'irritate them' = יארניזהק, which also means 'make them to tremble'. So Schmidt has pointed out, acting on Halévy's suggestion that text = ירניום. 2. I have bracketed the bulk of this verse and all ver. 3 as an intrusion here. These angels are the angels who fell in the time of Jared: whereas those mentioned in 69^4 $^{sqq.}$ are Satans. This list of angels is the same as that in 6^7, but many corruptions have taken place in the text. Ver. 4 follows naturally on the words 'Behold the names of those angels', though names: the first of them is Samjâzâ, the second Artâqîfâ, and the third Armên, the fourth Kôkabêl, the fifth †Tûrâêl†, the sixth Rûmjâl, the seventh Dânjâl, the eighth †Nêqâêl†, the ninth Barâqêl, the tenth Azâzêl, the eleventh Armârôs, the twelfth Batarjâl, the thirteenth †Busasêjal†, the fourteenth Hanânêl, the fifteenth †Tûrêl†, and the sixteenth Sîmâpêsîêl, the seventeenth Jetrêl, the eighteenth Tûmâêl, the nineteenth Tûrêl, the twentieth †Rûmâêl†, the twenty-first †Azâzêl†. 3. And these are the chiefs of their angels and their names, and their chief ones over hundreds and over fifties and over tens.]

4. The name of the first Jeqôn: that is, the one who led astray [all] the sons of God, and brought them down to the earth, and led them astray through the daughters of men. 5. And the second was named Asbeêl: he imparted to the holy sons of God evil counsel, and led them astray so that they defiled their bodies with the daughters of men. 6. And the third was named Gâdreêl: he it is who showed the children of men all the blows of death, and he led astray Eve, and showed [the weapons of death to the sons of men] the shield and the coat of mail, and the sword for battle, and all the weapons of death to the children of men. 7. And from his hand they have proceeded against those who dwell on the earth from that day and for evermore.

---

probably it ran originally 'behold the names of the Satans'. 4. Jeqôn (a-u). β reads Jeqûn. Sons of God. Cf. Job 38⁷. The text reads 'sons of the (+ 'holy' *l, bcdelopyx* ₁a₁b) angels', or (+ 'holy' *l, bcdelopyx*₁a₁b) 'sons of the angels'. Schmidt thinks that this is a mistranslation of בני אלהיא; but, though בן אלהים means 'angel', in the LXX it is never so rendered. בני אלהים is rendered by ἄγγελοι θεοῦ, not by ἄγγελοι alone. Hence, I suppose a corruption of אלהיא into מלאביא. Led them astray, &c. In the Parables the Satans and the fallen angels are carefully distinguished: the latter fall in the days of Jared according to 1-36 and 91-104. In this chapter, however, according to the present text, the functions of these two classes are confused. It is Azazel in 1-36 who is the cause of all the corruption upon earth, and Semjaza in 6³ 8³ 9⁷. Jeqûn = 'the inciter': Asbeêl = עזביאל, 'the deserter from God', or חשביאל, 'the thought of God' (Schmidt). 6. Gâdreêl is evidently a Satan as he led astray Eve. The name עדריאל means in Aramaic 'God is my helper'. In 8¹ the making of weapons of war is ascribed to Azazel. [The weapons of death to the sons of men.] A dittograph from the close of the verse.

8. And the fourth was named Pênêmûe: he taught the children of men the bitter and the sweet, and he taught them all the secrets of their wisdom. 9. And he instructed mankind in writing with ink and paper, and thereby many sinned from eternity to eternity and until this day. 10. For men were not created for such a purpose, to give confirmation to their good faith with pen and ink. 11. For men were created exactly like the angels, to the intent that they should continue pure and righteous, and death, which destroys everything, could not have taken hold of them, but through this their knowledge they are perishing, and through this power †it is consuming me†. 12. And the fifth was named Kâsdejâ: this is he who showed the children of men all the wicked smitings of spirits and demons, and the smitings of the embryo in the womb, that it may pass away, and [the smitings of the soul] the bites of the serpent, and the smitings which befall through the noontide heat, the son of the serpent named Tabâ'ĕt. 13. And this is the task of Kâsbeêl, the chief of the oath which he showed to the holy ones when he dwelt high above in glory, and its name

---

8. **Pênêmûe.** Perhaps, as Halévy suggests, from פנימה, 'the inside'. This Satan taught the secret things of wisdom. **9, 10.** Though the invention of the art of writing is ascribed to an evil spirit, the writer does not seem to condemn it save in so far as it is used as a safeguard against the bad faith of men. **11. Men were created exactly like the angels.** Man was originally righteous and immortal; cf. Book of Wisdom, 1¹³, ¹⁴ 2²³, ²⁴. This is also the doctrine of the Talmud, Weber, *Jüd. Theol.* 215, 216, 222, 248. Man lost his uprightness and immortality through the envy of the devil, Wisdom 2²⁴, through the evil knowledge introduced by the Satans or angels, 1 Enoch 69¹¹, through his own evil act, 98⁴. **Pure and righteous** (a–y). q 'pure and holy', β 'righteous and pure'. **†It is consuming me†.** Perhaps we should read 'they are being consumed'. **12.** Cf. Rosenmüller's *Scholia* on Ps. 91⁵, ⁶, which, according to ancient Jewish interpretation, treated of demonic dangers. **The serpent named Tabâ'ĕt.** I know nothing about this name. Schmidt (*op. cit.* p. 341) rewrites the last clause of 69¹² and the whole of 69¹³. But it is wholly hypothetical and unlikely. Till the Greek version or the Aramaic original is found the passage seems beyond restoration. Schmidt finds that the name of the sixth Satan is Tabâ'ĕt and that of the seventh Ḥakael, fragments of the latter surviving in Biqâ and Akâe. **13.** Cf. 41⁵. I do not pretend to interpret this and many of

Sect. II]   *Chapter LXIX. 8-20*   139

is Bîqâ.   14. This (angel) requested Michael to show him the hidden name, that he might enunciate it in the oath, so that those might quake before that name and oath who revealed all that was in secret to the children of men.   15. And this is the power of this oath, for it is powerful and strong, and he placed this oath Akâe in the hand of Michael.   16. And these are the secrets of this oath . . .

> And they are strong through his oath:
> And the heaven was suspended before the world was created,
> And for ever.

17. And through it the earth was founded upon the water,
    And from the secret recesses of the mountains come beautiful waters,
    From the creation of the world and unto eternity.

18. And through that oath the sea was created,
    And †as its foundation† He set for it the sand against the time of (its) anger,
    And it dare not pass beyond it from the creation of the world unto eternity.

19. And through that oath are the depths made fast,
    And abide and stir not from their place from eternity to eternity.

20. And through that oath the sun and moon complete their course,

---

the following verses. **Task.** The text reads 'number' = בני corrupt for עני = 'task'.   **14. This** (*a*). β 'and this'. **Show him** (*a–q*). β 'show them'. **The hidden name that.** + 'they might enunciate that (+ 'evil and' *m*) hidden name' *mu*: + 'they might see that hidden name and' β.   **16. They are strong** (*ml*, β–*d*). *gqu* 'strengthened'. **Heaven was suspended**: cf. Job 26⁷ for a similar expression regarding the earth.   **17. And through it the earth** (*q, β*). *a–q* 'through it and the earth'. **Earth was founded upon the water**: cf. Pss. 24² 136⁶. **From the secret recesses of the mountains come beautiful waters**: cf. Ps. 104¹⁰, ¹³. **Beautiful waters** (*a–u, aefhikp*). *u, ly₁a* 'waters for the living', *bcx* 'beautiful waters for the living'.   **18. †As its foundation† He set for it the sand, &c.**: cf. Jer. 5²² Job 26¹⁰ Ps. 104⁹, &c. Masharatâ, 'its foundation,' seems corrupt for wasinòtâ, 'to limit it.'   **19. The**

> And deviate not from their ordinance from eternity to eternity.
> 21. And through that oath the stars complete their course,
>   And He calls them by their names,
>   And they answer Him from eternity to eternity.

[22. And in like manner the spirits of the water, and of the winds, and of all zephyrs, and (their) paths from all the quarters of the winds. 23. And there are preserved the voices of the thunder and the light of the lightnings: and there are preserved the chambers of the hail and the chambers of the hoar-frost, and the chambers of the mist, and the chambers of the rain and the dew. 24. And all these believe and give thanks before the Lord of Spirits, and glorify (Him) with all their power, and their food is in every act of thanksgiving: they thank and glorify and extol the name of the Lord of Spirits for ever and ever.]

> 25. And this oath is mighty over them,
>   And through it [they are preserved and] their paths are preserved,
>   And their course is not destroyed.

Close of the Third Parable.

> 26. And there was great joy amongst them,
>   And they blessed and glorified and extolled
>   Because the name of that Son of Man had been revealed unto them.
> 27. And he sat on the throne of his glory,
>   And the sum of judgement was given unto the Son of Man,

---

depths made fast: cf. Prov. 8²⁸. 20. To eternity (gβ). > a–q. 21. Calls them by their names: cf. 43¹ (note). 22–24. An interpolation. Ver. 21 deals with the oath, and this subject is resumed in ver. 25. Ver. 23 seems to be an interpolation within an interpolation. 22. Quarters. So I have rendered ḥebrāta with Flemming. Otherwise 'bands'. 23. Voices of the thunder (a). β 'chambers of the voices of the thunder'. Chambers of the hail, &c.: cf. 60¹¹,¹⁹⁻²¹. 24. Cf. 41⁷ for a similar thought. 26–29. These verses form the conclusion of the third Parable. We have again returned to the chief theme of the third Parable. It is not improbable that the interpolator omitted part of this Parable and replaced it with his own additions. 26. Because the name of that Son of Man had been revealed. This is obscure. Cf. for a different use of the phrase, 48⁷ 62⁷. 27. He, i. e. the Messiah. On the throne of his glory: see 45³ (note). The sum of

And he caused the sinners to pass away and be destroyed
  from off the face of the earth,
And those who have led the world astray.

28. With chains shall they be bound,
And in their assemblage-place of destruction shall they be
  imprisoned,
And all their works vanish from the face of the earth.
29. And from henceforth there shall be nothing corruptible,

For that Son of Man has appeared,
And has seated himself on the throne of his glory,
And all evil shall pass away before his face,
And the word of that Son of Man shall go forth
And be strong before the Lord of Spirits.

This is the third Parable of Enoch.

The final Translation of Enoch.

LXX. 1. And it came to pass after this that his name during his lifetime was raised aloft to that Son of Man and to the Lord of Spirits from amongst those who dwell on the earth. 2. And he was raised aloft on the chariots of the spirit and his name vanished among them. 3. And from that day I was no longer

judgement, i.e. all judgement; cf. St. John 5²² (πᾶσαν τὴν κρίσιν), ²⁷. This meaning of דין is found in Ps. 139¹⁷. The sinners. Though the Parables are directed chiefly against the kings and the mighty ones, the author returns repeatedly to the judgement of sinners in general; cf. 38¹,²,³ 41² 45²,⁵,⁶ [50²] 53²,⁷ 62⁴,¹³. And be destroyed. > η. From off the face of the earth: cf. 38¹ (note). 28. Cf. 53–56. 29. This verse summarizes shortly such a chapter as 49. The word of (nagarū la t, bcehl²nx). a–t, dfikl²opwy₁a₁b 'they shall say to'.

LXX. There is certainly some awkwardness in the author making Enoch describe his own translation; but this in itself forms no valid reason for obelizing the chapter, as in every other respect it is quite in keeping with the thought of the Parables. 1. Son of Man: cf. 46² (note). And to the Lord (gqt). mu, β 'to the Lord'. Those who dwell on the earth: cf. 37⁵ (note). 2. He was raised aloft. t reads 'his name was raised aloft'. Chariots of the spirit: cf. 2 Kings 2¹¹. This is an account of Enoch's translation; cf. 87³,⁴ 89⁵². His name (mqt). gu, β 'the name'. The name here stands for the person. The actual pre-existence of the Son of Man is here supposed; cf. 48² (note).

numbered amongst them; and he set me between the two winds, between the north and the west, where the angels took the cords to measure for me the place for the elect and righteous. 4. And there I saw the first fathers and the righteous who from the beginning dwell in that place.

Two earlier Visions of Enoch.

LXXI. 1. And it came to pass after this that my spirit was translated
And it ascended into the heavens:
And I saw the holy sons of God.

They were stepping on flames of fire:
Their garments were white [and their raiment],
And their faces shone like snow.

---

3. **Numbered** (*gqt*, i). *m*, β-ἰ 'dragged'. **Between the north and the west.** See 18⁶ sqq. (note) 24¹⁻³ (note) 60⁸ (note) 67⁴. **The cords**: cf. 61¹ sqq. 4. Paradise is already peopled with his righteous forefathers. This agrees perfectly with 61¹², which speaks of the elect being already in Paradise.

LXXI. This chapter seems to belong to the Parables, though in the first edition I thought otherwise. A closer study of the text as well as of Appel's *Die Komposition des aethiopischen Henochsbuchs*, 1906, has led me to revise my earlier views. The chapter consists of two visions. In the first 71¹⁻⁴ Enoch was translated in spirit into the heavens, 71¹, where he had a vision of God, 71², and under the guidance of Michael was introduced into the secrets of the spiritual, 71³, and the physical worlds, 71⁴. The second vision consists of 71⁵⁻¹⁷. In this vision it is said afresh that Enoch was translated in spirit into the heaven of heavens, 71⁵, where he has a vision of the house of God surrounded by angels, 71⁵⁻⁸. Amongst these were the four archangels who came in the train of God. Michael accordingly could not be in attendance on Enoch as in the former vision, 71¹⁻⁴. Moreover, the vision of God is described afresh and in different terms, 71¹⁰ sqq. Finally, it is to be observed that both visions belong to the period *before Enoch's final translation to heaven in 70*; for it could not have been the aim of Michael to show to Enoch, 71³, after his final translation, what he had already seen under the guidance of the angel of peace or the other *angelus interpres*. That 71⁵⁻¹⁷ belongs to the same earlier period will become clear as we advance. *First Vision* 71¹⁻⁴. **1. Translated**. The Ethiopic here as always renders 'hidden'. See 12¹ (note). **Holy sons of God**. This is practically the same phrase as in 69⁵; cf. 69⁴ (see note) 'sons of God', and 106⁵ 'sons of the God of heaven'. The expression is to be referred ultimately to בְּנֵי אֱלֹהִים, where the Elohim are interpreted as angels. *bcdoxy₁b* omit 'holy'. [**And**

2. And I saw two streams of fire,
And the light of that fire shone like hyacinth,
And I fell on my face before the Lord of Spirits.

3. And the angel Michael [one of the archangels] seized me by
   my right hand,
And lifted me up and led me forth into all the secrets,
And he showed me all the secrets of righteousness.

4. And he showed me all the secrets of the ends of the heaven,
And all the chambers of all the stars, and all the luminaries,
Whence they proceed before the face of the holy ones.

5. And he translated my spirit into the heaven of heavens,
And I saw there as it were a structure built of crystals,
And between those crystals tongues of living fire.

6. And my spirit saw the girdle which girt that house of fire,
And on its four sides were streams full of living fire,
And they girt that house.

7. And round about were Seraphin, Cherubin, and Ophannin:
And these are they who sleep not
And guard the throne of His glory.

8. And I saw angels who could not be counted,
A thousand thousands, and ten thousand times ten thousand,
Encircling that house,

their raiment]. A duplicate rendering. **2. Streams of fire**: cf. 14^{19} Dan. 7^{10}; also ver. 6 of this chapter. These streams really proceed from beneath the throne. **3. And he showed me all ($> \beta$) the secrets of righteousness.** All the MSS. except *u* insert before this line 'And he showed me all ($> \beta$) the secrets of mercy'. These two lines =

καὶ ἔδειξέ μοι πάντα τὰ μυστήρια τῆς ἐλεημοσύνης
καὶ ἔδειξέ μοι πάντα τὰ μυστήρια τῆς δικαιοσύνης.

These are alternative renderings of והראני כל סודי הצדק. The context requires a tristich. **4.** This parallel treatment of ethical and natural phenomena reminds us of the appearance of such passages as 41$^{3-8}$ 43-44 in the midst of contexts of a wholly ethical character. **5-17.** *The Second Vision.* **5. He translated my spirit** (*a*). The text does not state who translated Enoch. β reads 'a spirit translated him'. **There.** MSS. add 'in the midst of that light' as an explanatory gloss on 'there'. **5, 6.** Cf. 14$^{9-17}$. **6. The girdle** (*a–η*). *q, β* 'a girdle'. **7. Cherubin, Seraphin, and Ophannin**: cf. 61$^{10, 12}$ 39^{13} 40^{2}. **And**$^{3°}$ (*a*). $> \beta$. **8. A**

And Michael, and Raphael, and Gabriel, and Phanuel,
And the holy angels who are above the heavens,
Go in and out of that house.

9. And they came forth from that house,
And Michael and Gabriel, Raphael and Phanuel,
And many holy angels without number.

10. And with them the Head of Days,
His head white and pure as wool,
And His raiment indescribable.

11. And I fell on my face,
And my whole body became relaxed,
And my spirit was transfigured;

And I cried with a loud voice,
. . . with the spirit of power,
And blessed and glorified and extolled.

12. And these blessings which went forth out of my mouth were well pleasing before that Head of Days. 13. And that Head of Days came with Michael and Gabriel, Raphael and Phanuel, thousands and ten thousands of angels without number.

[Lost passage wherein the Son of Man was described as

thousand thousands, &c.: cf. 14^{22} 40^1. **Michael, Gabriel, &c.**: see 40^{4-7}. **Go in and out**. This is not so in 14^{22}. 9. **And** ^{20} (a–t). $> t, \beta$. 10. **The Head of Days**: see 46^1 (note) Dan. 7^9. 11. **And I fell . . . relaxed.** Cf. 60^3. **Spirit was transfigured.** Distinguish this from 39^{14}, and cf. Asc. Is. 7^{25}. **Spirit of power**: cf. 61^{11}. Some word or words seem to have been lost before this phrase. 13. The following verses show, as Appel has pointed out (p. 44), that after the Head of Days the Son of Man was mentioned, and that Enoch asked some question regarding him. This passage has been lost, but the context requires its restoration. In answer to this question of Enoch an angel comes forward and makes answer in ver. 14. But owing to the loss of this passage the text has been changed by some scribe in verses 14, 16 and been made to apply to Enoch instead of to the Son of Man. The scribe, however, has fallen from his rôle in ver. 17 and forgotten to make the necessary changes; for that verse as it stands refers undoubtedly to the Son of Man and not to Enoch: 'There will be length of days with accompanying the Head of Days, and Enoch asked one of the angels (as in 46³) concerning the Son of Man as to who he was.]

14. And he (i.e. the angel) came to me and greeted me with His voice, and said unto me:

> 'This is the Son of Man who is born unto righteousness,
>
> And righteousness abides over him,
>
> And the righteousness of the Head of Days forsakes him not.'

15. And he said unto me:

> 'He proclaims unto thee peace in the name of the world to come;
>
> For from hence has proceeded peace since the creation of the world,
>
> And so shall it be unto thee for ever and for ever and ever.

16. And all shall walk in his ways since righteousness never forsaketh him:

> With him will be their dwelling-places, and with him their heritage,
>
> And they shall not be separated from him for ever and ever and ever.

---

that Son of Man.' 14. Cf. 46³. He (*ymt*). > *u*. *η, β* 'that angel'. This is ... is. Emended as explained in note on ver. 13. Text reads 'Thou art ... art'. Who is born unto righteousness. For 'unto' (*glu, abcfklnz*) *mq, dehiouvy₁a₁b* read 'in'. On this and the next line, wherein the righteousness of the Son of Man is dwelt on, see 46³ (note). Forsakes him not. Text 'forsakes thee not'. See note on ver. 13. 15. This verse rightly applies to Enoch. Proclaims unto thee peace. For the phrase cf. Mic. 3⁵ Zech. 9¹⁰ Is. 57⁷. The world to come. This is apparently the earliest use of this expression = העולם הבא. See Dalman, *Worte Jesu*, 120 sqq.; Stave, *Ueber den Einfluss des Parsismus auf das Judentum*, 201; Mt. 12³² Mk. 10³⁰ Lk. 16³⁰ 20³⁵ Eph. 1²¹ Heb. 6⁶. 16. All. + 'shall be and' (*β-αl₁b*). Throughout the verse I have changed the second person into the third and so restored the verse that it refers, as it did originally, to the Son of Man and not to Enoch. With him ... their dwelling-places. Cf. 39⁴,⁷

17. And so there shall be length of days with that Son of Man,
    And the righteous shall have peace and an upright way
    In the name of the Lord of Spirits for ever and ever.'

17. **Length of days**: i.e. an eternity. **An upright way** (*m*). β 'his upright way'. *gtu* gives the reading of *m* in a corrupt form. All the MSS. add here 'to the righteous'.

Note on 71¹⁴⁻¹⁷. From the above it follows that I do not regard our text as supporting the view which some modern scholars have attached to it, i.e. the elevation of Enoch to the dignity of the Messiah: see Bousset, *Rel. des Judenthums*, 348; Dalman, *Worte Jesu*, 200. The former quotes in this connexion 2 Enoch 22⁸ 67² Targ. Jon. on Gen. 5²⁴; Ps. Clem. *Hom.* xviii. 13; *Recog.* ii. 47.

SECTION III

(CHAPTERS LXXII—LXXXII)

THE BOOK OF THE COURSES OF THE HEAVENLY LUMINARIES. INTRODUCTION

A. *Its Critical Structure and Object.*   B. *Its Independence of 1-36.*
C. *Its Calendar and the Knowledge therein implied.*

A. Critical Structure and Object. Chapter 72 introduces us to a scientific treatise. In this treatise the writer attempts to bring the many utterances in the O.T. regarding physical phenomena into one system, and puts this forward as the genuine and biblical one as opposed to all other systems. The paramount and, indeed, the only aim of this book, according to 72^1, is to give the laws of the heavenly bodies, and this object it pursues undeviatingly from its beginning to 79^1, where it is said that the treatise is finished and all the laws of the heavenly bodies set forth. Through all these chapters there is not a single ethical reference. The author has no other interest save a scientific one coloured by Jewish conceptions and beliefs. Our author, like the author of Jubilees, upholds the accuracy of the sun and stars as dividers of time, 74^{12}: 'The sun and stars bring in all the years exactly, so that they do not advance or delay their position by a single day unto eternity'. And this order is inflexible: there will be no change in it till the new creation, 72^1. So far, then, we have to deal with a complete and purely scientific treatise, in which there is no breach of uniformity till the new creation. But the moment we have done with 79, we pass into a new atmosphere in 80^{2-8}. The whole interest is *ethical and nothing else*: there is, indeed, such a thing as an order of nature, but, owing to the sin of men, this order is more conspicuous in its breach than in its observance, 80^{2-8}, and the moon becomes a false guide and misleader of men, 80^4; and even the sun (80^5 see note) shines in the furthest west at nightfall, but 80^{5a} may be interpolated.

Chapter 80^{2-8}, therefore, is manifestly an addition, made to give an ethical turn to a purely scientific treatise, and so furnish it with some fitness for its present collocation.

Again, it is to be observed that this addition consists of tristichs, and is thus different in form from the rest of 72–82. It can hardly be connected with any of the other writers of our book. The regularity of nature till the day of the new creation is an article of their creed, though in later apocalypses this view is partially abandoned.

Nor, again, can 81 belong to this book. Before entering on this question, however, let us consider 82^{1-8}, which forms, according to most critics, the close of this treatise, vv. 9–20 being regarded as a Noachic interpolation, but wrongly: see 82^9 (note). These verses, 82^{1-8}, manifestly do belong to 72–79. The same formula occurs in 82^1, 'my son Methuselah,' as in 76^{14} and in 79^1 (according to some MSS.). The wisdom dealt with in 82^{1-8} is the same scientific lore as in 72–79. And the blessing of the author of 82^{1-8} is for the man who sins not in calculating the seasons, 82^4.

72–79 and 82 constitute the original Book of the Heavenly Luminaries. But, whereas the blessing of the author of 72–79, 82 is for the man who knows the right reckoning of the years, the blessing of 81^4 is for the man 'who dies in righteousness . . . concerning whom there is no book of unrighteousness written'. These two blessings, in fact, give the keynote of the respective contents of the book of the Heavenly Luminaries and 81, and disclose the motives of their respective authors. This chapter did not, any more than 80, belong to this treatise originally. In fact, we find on examination that it is of the nature of a mosaic, and came probably from the editor of the complete Enoch. The phrase 'those seven holy ones', in 81^5, points to some previous statement apparently; but none such is to be found. The words may be drawn from $90^{21, 22}$. The heavenly tablets in $81^{1, 2}$ may come from 93^2 103^2. The expression 'Lord of the world', 81^{10}, may be suggested by 82^7, 'Lord of the whole creation of the world,' &c.

Again, we observe that $81^{5, 6}$ are written with reference to $82^{1, 2}$ and 91^1. This latter verse introduces the Section beginning in the *present* form of Enoch with 91. We shall see later that 91 does not really form the beginning of the last book of Enoch, but that it has been dislocated from its right position by the author of 81 to serve his editorial purposes.

Finally, with regard to 82, it is evident that it does not stand in its original position. The Book of the Heavenly Luminaries rightly concludes with 79, which closes thus: 'Such is the picture and sketch of every luminary, which Uriel the archangel, who is their leader, showed unto me.' 82 must have preceded this chapter originally, and probably immediately. After the long disquisition on the stars in 82, the first words of 79 would come in most appropriately: 'And now, my son, I have shown thee everything, *and the law of all the stars of the heaven is completed.*' If 82 does not precede, these words have practically no justification in 72–78. The final editor of the whole book was fond of such dislocations. There has been a like rearrangement of 91–93.

B. **Its Independence of 1–36.** (1) In 1^2 the revelation of Enoch is not for the present, but for remote generations: in 93^{10} it is to remain a secret till the seventh week of the world: in 104^{12} it is one day to be disclosed. But in 82^1 the revelations are entrusted to Methuselah to be transmitted to *the generations of the world*. (2) In 33^4 Uriel writes down everything for Enoch, but in $72^1\ 74^2\ 75^3\ 79^{2,\ 6}$ Uriel only shows the celestial phenomena to Enoch, and Enoch himself writes them down, 82^1. (3) The description of the winds coming from different quarters in 34–36 differs from that in 76. (4) The heavenly bodies are partly conscious in 1–36; cf. $18^{12-16}\ 21^{1-6}$; but not so in 72–82. (5) The portals of the stars in 36^2 are described as *small* portals *above* the portals of the winds. As in 72–82 these portals are also those of the sun and moon, they can hardly be called 'small', being each equal to thirty degrees in width. Besides, though described at great length in 72–82, they are never said to be 'above' those of the winds. (6) The river of fire in 23, in which the luminaries set and recruit their exhausted fires, has no point of connexion with 72–82. There is undoubtedly some relationship between the later chapters of 1–36 and 72–82; but it is not that of one and undivided authorship.

C. **Its Calendar and the Knowledge therein implied.** The chronological system of this book is most perplexing. It does not in its present form present a consistent whole, and probably never did. We are not to regard it as anything more than the attempt of an individual to establish an essentially Hebrew calendar over against the heathen calendars in vogue around. In itself this calendar cannot be said to have any value. It is useful, however, as giving us some knowledge of the chronological systems more or less known to the Palestinian Jews. For (1) the writer is acquainted with the signs of the zodiac, but carefully refrains from using them, replacing them by his system of portals. (2) He is acquainted with the spring and autumn equinoxes and the summer and winter solstices. (3) He knows apparently the length of the synodic months (cf. 78$^{15, 16}$), which was not published till the time of Gamaliel II, A.D. 80-115. (4) His attempt to reconcile the lunar year and his peculiar year of 364 days by intercalations, in the third, fifth, and eighth years, furnishes strong presumption that he had the Greek eight-year cycle before him, and the presumption becomes a certainty, when we consider that, whereas every detail in the Greek cycle is absolutely necessary to the end desired, in the Enochian system, on the other hand, though these details are more or less reproduced, they are absolutely idle, as Enoch's system is really a one-year cycle, and the lunar year is reconciled to his solar year of 364 days by the addition of ten days each year: cf. 74$^{13-16}$. (5) He alludes to the seventy-six years' cycle of Calippus, 79^5 (note).

The writer puts forward a year of 364 days, but this he did only through sheer incapacity for appreciating anything better; for he must have been acquainted with the solar year of 365¼ days. His acquaintance with the Greek cycles shows this. Moreover, in 2 Enoch the year of 365¼ days is distinctly taught. It is surprising also that any writer under cloak of Enoch's name should fix upon a year of 364 days, as Enoch was early regarded as the teacher of the solar year of 365 days, owing to the significant duration of his life. And our surprise is not lessened when we consider that all the surrounding nations and peoples—the Egyptians, Persians, Arabs, Cappadocians, Lycians, Bithynians, the inhabitants of Gaza and Ascalon—observed a year of 365 days. But this year was generally a movable year of 365 days exactly, and consequently one in which New Year's day ran through all the days of the year in the course of 1,461 such years, and the festivals continually changed their season. Now the writer of Enoch recommends his year of 364 days especially on the ground that the position of the years is not prematurely advanced or delayed by a single day, 74^{12}. It was, therefore, nothing but his national prejudices, and possibly his stupidity, that prevented him, knowing as he did the Greek systems, from seeing that only a year of 365¼ days could effect such a result. As for Wieseler's theory that the writer held to a year of 364 days with one intercalary day each year, and one every fourth year, there is no evidence for it in the text. The author's reckoning of the year at 364 days may be partly due to his opposition to heathen systems, and partly to the fact that 364 is divisible by seven, and amounts to fifty-two weeks exactly.

The Sun.

LXXII. 1. The Book of the courses of the luminaries of the heaven, the relations of each, according to their classes, their dominion and their seasons, according to their names and places of origin, and according to their months, which Uriel, the holy angel, who was with me, who is their guide, showed me; and he showed me all their laws exactly as they are, and how it is with regard to all the years of the world and unto eternity, till the new creation is accomplished which dureth till eternity. 2. And this is the first law of the luminaries: the luminary the Sun has its rising in the eastern portals of the heaven, and its setting in the western portals of the heaven. 3. And I saw six portals in which the sun rises, and six portals in which the sun sets: and the moon rises and sets in these portals, and the leaders of the stars and those whom they lead: six in the east and six in the west, and all following each other in accurately corresponding order: also many windows to the right and left of these portals.

LXXII. 1. As in the Parables, the superscription of this book is far from accurately describing its contents. Dominion: cf. 75^3 82^{8-20}. Names: cf. $78^{1, 2}$. Places of origin. Probably their places of rising. The new creation: cf. 45^4 $91^{15, 16}$ Is. 65^{17} 66^{22} 2 Peter 3^{13} Rev. 21^1. In the Yasts, xiii. 57-58 (S. B. E. xxiii. 194), similarly, it is stated that 'the stars, the moon, the sun and the endless lights ... move round in their far-revolving circle for ever till they come to the time of the good restoration of the world'. All the laws of the heavenly bodies given in this book are valid till the new creation. 2. This verse introduces an account of the sun in its progress through the signs of the zodiac and the increase and decrease of the days and nights thereby occasioned. Portals. The subject of the portals has already to some extent appeared in 33-36. But observe that, though portals of the winds and portals of the stars are there described, there is no mention of portals of the sun and moon. According to 72-82, the sun, moon, and stars pass through the same portals: can this hold true of 33-36, where the portals of the stars are said to be small and situated above the portals of the wind? Moreover, in 72^6 one of the sun's portals is called 'great'. 3. Portals. These twelve portals go back ultimately to the twelve signs of the zodiac. According to the Babylonian view from which the speculations in the text are derived there were portals on both sides of the heaven in which the sun and moon rose and set. *Creation Epos*, v. 9. See K. A. T.³ 619, 630. In which (a, n). β-n 'from which'. Leaders of the stars: see 75^1 (note). Windows: cf. ver. 7, 75^7. Right and left, i.e.

4. And first there goes forth the great luminary, named the Sun, and his circumference is like the circumference of the heaven, and he is quite filled with illuminating and heating fire.   5. The chariot on which he ascends, the wind drives, and the sun goes down from the heaven and returns through the north in order to reach the east, and is so guided that he comes to the appropriate (lit. 'that') portal and shines in the face of the heaven.   6. In this way he rises in the first month in the great portal, which is the fourth [those six portals in the east].   7. And in that fourth portal from which the sun rises in the first month are twelve window-openings, from which proceed a flame when they are opened in their season.   8. When the sun rises in the heaven, he comes forth through that fourth portal thirty mornings

south and north, according to the familiar Hebrew use.   4. Cf. 41^{5-7}, where the conception seems to be different. His circumference. The sun is clearly circular; cf. 73^2 75^3; also 18^4 78^4. It is doubtful whether he is conceived of as a sphere or merely as a disk. I have translated on the latter supposition.   5. The sun, as also the other heavenly bodies, traverses the heaven in a chariot, 73^2 $75^{3,8}$, driven by the wind, 18^4 73^2. Through the north: cf. 41^5. Is guided. Possibly by an angel. In 2 Enoch several angels precede the sun on his course. In 1-36 the heavenly bodies have a semi-conscious existence; this is not so in 72-82.   6. In the first month. The writer begins his description of the sun's course with the first Hebrew month Abib (cf. Exod. 13^4), the time of the spring equinox. This month, called generally after the Captivity Nisan (cf. Neh. 2^1), was the first month of the ecclesiastical year, and corresponds to our April. The civil year began with Tishri, or October. The great portal. So called in contra-distinction from the 'window-openings' in the next verse. Yet these portals are called 'small' in 36^2.   7. Twelve window-openings. There are twelve such at every portal; cf. 72^3 75^7. The flame is the source of heat; cf. 75^7.   8. The author's system, whereby he seeks to replace the heathen conception of the sun's revolution through the signs of the zodiac by a scheme founded as he believes on the O.T., is as follows. There are six portals in the east through which the sun rises in the course of the year, and six in the west in which he sets. The first portal forms the most southern point of the sun's journey, and the sixth portal the most northern. During the first six months, from the shortest day to the longest, the sun advances from the first portal to the sixth, and conversely, from the longest day to the shortest, he returns from the sixth portal to the first. In each portal the sun rises and sets one month in his journey northwards, and likewise rises and sets for one month in each portal on his return journey. Thus arises the division of the year into twelve in succession, and sets accurately in the fourth portal in the west of the heaven. 9. And during this period the day becomes daily longer and the night nightly shorter to the thirtieth morning. 10. On that day the day is longer than the night by a ninth part, and the day amounts exactly to ten parts and the night to eight parts. 11. And the sun rises from that fourth portal, and sets in the fourth and returns to the fifth portal of the east thirty mornings, and rises from it and sets in the fifth portal. 12. And then the day becomes longer by †two†

months. Moreover, during each month on his journey northwards, the day daily grows longer and the night daily shorter, and this is owing to a daily change of position on the part of the sun within each gate. Of these different positions or stations of the sun there are 364. In this way the author seeks to dispense with the signs of the zodiac. The sun's northward journey from the first to the sixth portal corresponds with his course through the signs Capricornus, Aquarius, Pisces, Aries, Taurus, and Gemini; and the sun's return journey from the sixth to the first portal corresponds with his course through Cancer, Leo, Virgo, Libra, Scorpio, and Sagittarius. Though perfectly acquainted with a year of $365\frac{1}{4}$ days, as we shall see later, the author reckoned it as consisting of 364 days, partly possibly on antiheathen grounds, and partly for the attractive reason that the sum total is divisible by seven, and thus represents 52 sabbaths of days. The author's solar year of 364 days is made up of eight months of 30 days each, and four months of 31 days each—these latter corresponding with the spring and autumn equinoxes and the summer and winter solstices, or, according to the system of our author, with the sun's position in the first, third, fourth, and sixth portals. These four months have each 31 days 'on account of the sign', i.e. that of the equinoxes or the solstices; cf. $72^{13, 19}$. The author's division of the day into eighteen parts is possibly his own device, yet it may rest on traditions derived from northern Asia of the latitude of $49°$, as Krieger supposes, when the longest day is twice as long as the shortest night, as our author states it. 10. On that day $(a-t)$. t, β 'and on that day'. By a ninth part. The MSS. read: 'the day is longer by twice as much than the night'; for kāʿěbata means here 'twice as much' as in $72^{14, 26}$. Hence it is an interpolation. This interpolation further led to the extrusion of tāsʿěta ʿěda = 'the ninth part' from the clause in mt, β. But this last phrase is found in gqu, and gives the sense required by the context. The ninth part = the ninth part of the whole day. During six months the day grows longer and the night shorter each month by $\frac{1}{18}$th. Hence the entire difference each month amounts to $\frac{2}{18}$ths or $\frac{1}{9}$th of a day. Flemming transposes the phrase before 'ělat, making it dependent on kāʿěbata, and renders it 'um das Doppelte eines Neuntels'; but this rendering, which Martin follows, is doubtful grammatically, and even if it were right in grammar it would be wrong in sense. Exactly (a). $> \beta$. 11. In the fourth. + 'portal' $q, \beta-bcdx_1a$. 12. And^{1o}. $>bcllopxy_1a_1b$. † Two †. We should read 'one'.

parts and amounts to eleven parts, and the night becomes shorter and amounts to seven parts. 13. And it returns to the east and enters into the sixth portal, and rises and sets in the sixth portal one and thirty mornings on account of its sign. 14. On that day the day becomes longer than the night, and the day becomes double the night, and the day becomes twelve parts, and the night is shortened and becomes six parts. 15. And the sun mounts up to make the day shorter and the night longer, and the sun returns to the east and enters into the sixth portal, and rises from it and sets thirty mornings. 16. And when thirty mornings are accomplished, the day decreases by exactly one part, and becomes eleven parts, and the night seven. 17. And the sun goes forth from that sixth portal in the west, and goes to the east and rises in the fifth portal for thirty mornings, and sets in the west again in the fifth western portal. 18. On that day the day decreases by †two† parts, and amounts to ten parts and the night to eight parts. 19. And the sun goes forth from that fifth portal and sets in the fifth portal of the west, and rises in the fourth portal for one and thirty mornings on account of its sign, and sets in the west. 20. On that day the day is equalised with the night, [and becomes of equal length], and the night amounts to nine parts and the day to nine parts. 21. And the sun rises from that portal and sets in the west, and returns to the east and rises thirty mornings in the third portal and sets in the west in the third portal. 22. And on that day the night becomes longer than the day, and night becomes longer than night, and day shorter than day till the thirtieth morning, and the night amounts exactly to ten parts and the day to eight parts. 23. And the sun rises from that third portal and sets

---

13. It returns (*a*). β 'the sun returns'. Portal¹⁰. > *a–t*. On account of its sign, i.e. that of the summer solstice; cf. 72¹⁹ 75³ 78⁷. 14. On that day (*a–q*). *q*²β 'and on that day'. 15. Mounts up to start on his return journey to the first portal. 18. For '†two†' read 'one'. The same error occurred in ver. 12. 19. Its sign. + 'in the fourth portal in the east', *a–u*. + 'in the east', *u*. 20. Clause bracketed as a duplicate rendering. 22. And night becomes longer than night (*a–m*). β 'till the thirtieth morning'. Morning (*a·q, efln*). > *q. abcdhikory*

in the third portal in the west and returns to the east, and for thirty mornings rises in the second portal in the east, and in like manner sets in the second portal in the west of the heaven. 24. And on that day the night amounts to eleven parts and the day to seven parts.   25. And the sun rises on that day from that second portal and sets in the west in the second portal, and returns to the east into the first portal for one and thirty mornings, and sets in the first portal in the west of the heaven. 26. And on that day the night becomes longer and amounts to the double of the day: and the night amounts exactly to twelve parts and the day to six.   27. And the sun has (therewith) traversed the divisions of his orbit and turns again on those divisions of his orbit, and enters that portal thirty mornings and sets also in the west opposite to it.   28. And on that night has the night decreased in length by a †ninth† part, and the night has become eleven parts and the day seven parts.   29. And the sun has returned and entered into the second portal in the east, and returns on those his divisions of his orbit for thirty mornings, rising and setting.   30. And on that day the night decreases in length, and the night amounts to ten parts and the day to eight.   31. And on that day the sun rises from that portal, and sets in the west, and returns to the east, and rises in the third portal for one and thirty mornings, and sets in the west of the heaven.   32. On that day the night decreases and amounts to nine parts, and the day to nine parts, and the night is equal to the day and the year is exactly as to its days three hundred and sixty-four.   33. And the length of the day and of the night, and the shortness of the day and of the night arise —through the course of the sun these distinctions are made (lit.

$_1a\,_1b$ 'day'.   25. In the first portal ($\beta-a$). gq 'in it on the first day (!)', m 'in the sixth portal', tu 'on that day'.   27. That portal (m, β). $a-m$ 'all the portals'.   28. On that night (gq, f). $mt, \beta-f$ 'on that day'. A †ninth† part (gqu). > m. $t, \beta-a$ 'one part'. The 'ninth', if original, must be of half the sun; for night and day cannot decrease or increase by more than $\frac{1}{18}$th, as in ver. 16. Perhaps we might emend 'ĕmnûḫâ into 'ĕm a'âlt, and translate 'has the night grown shorter than the day by a ninth part'.   31. That portal ($a-t$). t, β 'that second portal'.

'they are separated'). 34. So it comes that its course becomes daily longer, and its course nightly shorter. 35. And this is the law and the course of the sun, and his return as often as he returns sixty times and rises, i.e. the great luminary which is named the Sun, for ever and ever. 36. And that which (thus) rises is the great luminary, and is so named according to its appearance, according as the Lord commanded. 37. As he rises, so he sets and decreases not, and rests not, but runs day and night, and his light is sevenfold brighter than that of the moon; but as regards size they are both equal.

The Moon and its Phases.

LXXIII. 1. And after this law I saw another law dealing with the smaller luminary, which is named the Moon. 2. And her circumference is like the circumference of the heaven, and her chariot in which she rides is driven by the wind, and light is given to her in (definite) measure. 3. And her rising and setting changes every month: and her days are like the days of the sun, and when her light is uniform (i.e. full) it amounts to the seventh part of the light of the sun. 4. And thus she rises. And her first phase in the east comes forth on the thirtieth

---

35. *As often as he returns sixty times* ($a-m$). m, β 'as often as he returns, he returns sixty times'. *Sixty times.* The sun is one month in each portal on his northward journey, and one month in each portal on his southward: therefore two months in each portal. The author disregards for the time being the extra day in the first, third, fourth, and sixth portals. *The great luminary* (a). β 'the great eternal luminary'. 37. *As he rises, so he sets* (g). mqt 'so he rises and ($+$ 'so' qt) he sets', u 'and so he sets', $\beta-anx$ 'and so he rises and sets'. *Day and night.* $+$ 'in his chariot' t^2, β. *Sevenfold brighter.* Cf. 78^4 73^2. *As regards size . . . equal.* According to Lucretius $5^{564-591}$ the sun, moon, and the stars are about the same size as—possibly a little greater or less than—they appear to us. This view he derived from his master Epicurus, as may be seen from comparing a letter of the latter to Pythocles in Diog. Laer. x. 84-94. But it is not necessary to suppose any dependence on the part of our text, which gives probably the ordinary accepted view.

LXXIII. This and the following chapter treat of the course of the moon. 2. *The heaven* ($a-m$, $bedilo$). m, $aefhknpw$ 'the sun'. 3. *Her rising and setting*, i.e. the place of her rising and setting. *Seventh part of the light of the sun*: cf. 72^{37} 78^4. 4. *Her first phase*, lit. 'her beginning'. The moon on the first day of her reappearance is here the new moon in the popular sense, not the morning: and on that day she becomes visible, and constitutes for you the first phase of the moon on the thirtieth day together with the sun in the portal where the sun rises. 5. And the one half of her goes forth by a seventh part, and her whole circumference is empty, without light, with the exception of one-seventh part of it, (and) the fourteenth part of her light.

new moon strictly so called, which is invisible. Thirtieth morning, i.e. of the solar month. Together with the sun. The sun and moon are still in the same portal on the first day after conjunction, as each portal embraces an extent of 30 degrees, and the moon advances only 13 degrees daily. 5–8. The author's account of the phases of the moon is very hard to follow. His scheme seems to be as follows. The lunar month amounts to 30 days and 29 days alternately. It is divided into two parts: during the first part the moon waxes from new moon to full moon in 14 days when the month is 29 days, and in 15 when the month is 30 days. During the second part the moon wanes from full moon till she disappears, always, it would seem, in 15 days. Again, the author divides the moon into 14 parts, and explains the waxing of the moon by the successive lighting up of each one of the 14 parts by the sun, and the waning by the successive withdrawal of light from the 14 parts till it all disappears. But to proceed more exactly, where there are 15 days from new moon to full moon, the author supposes an additional 28th part; this part only is lighted up on the first day of such a month, whereas $\frac{1}{14}$th part is lighted up each day of the remaining 14 days, till the moon becomes full. The waning, which apparently always takes 15 days, is the reverse of this process. Again, where there are 14 days from new moon to full moon, the moon has at the end of the first day $\frac{1}{14}$th part + $\frac{1}{28}$th part, i.e. $\frac{3}{28}$ths, and takes an additional 14th part of light each of the remaining 13 days. According to the text above followed, vv. 5, 6 suppose the period from new to full moon to be 14 days, whereas ver. 7 supposes this period to be 15 days. 5. In this verse and the next the fractions are *fractions of half the moon*. Thus, $\frac{1}{7}$th of it, i.e. of the half moon = $\frac{1}{14}$th of whole moon, and $\frac{1}{14}$th of half moon = $\frac{1}{28}$th of whole moon: thus, $\frac{2}{28}$ths of whole moon are lighted on the first day of new moon, when there are but 14 days to the full moon. Goes forth. The MSS. read reḥɔq = ἐξέχων, which is used of the rising or appearing of the sun. ἐξέχων might in turn be a rendering of אצי, which is used of the rising of the sun and stars. Flemming obelizes the word and proposes ré'ûj = 'visible'. One-seventh part (*gqlu, abcfiklx₁b*). The rest of the MSS. are corrupt. (And) the fourteenth part (*gqu*). *ml, β* 'of the fourteenth part'. Possibly the 'em (= 'of') is a corruption of the wa (= 'and') which I have supplied. *g* adds 'of half', but unnecessarily, since the fractions are fractions of the half of the moon. 6. Observe when the period from new moon to full moon is 14 days that it is not said that the moon receives $\frac{1}{14}$th part and $\frac{1}{28}$th, but only the former; it seems, therefore, that the moon is supposed to have this $\frac{1}{28}$th to begin with. It is different in the case of the 15-days' period. On the first day of such a period the moon receives $\frac{1}{28}$th part of light. In this

6. And when she receives one-seventh part of the half of her light, her light amounts to one-seventh part and the half thereof. 7. And she sets with the sun, and when the sun rises the moon rises with him and receives the half of one part of light, and in that night in the beginning of her morning [in the commencement of the lunar day] the moon sets with the sun, and is invisible that night with the fourteen parts and the half of one of them. 8. And she rises on that day with exactly a seventh part, and comes forth and recedes from the rising of the sun, and in her remaining days she becomes bright in the (remaining) thirteen parts.

The Lunar Year.

LXXIV. 1. And I saw another course, a law for her, (and) how according to that law she performs her monthly revolution. 2. And all these Uriel, the holy angel who is the leader of them all, showed to me, and their positions, and I wrote down their positions as he showed them to me, and I wrote down their months as they were, and the appearance of their lights till fifteen days were accomplished. 3. In single seventh parts

---

verse there are 14 days to full moon. One-seventh part 2° ($gmqu, d$). t, l 'the thirteenth part', β–$dklo$ 'the fourteenth part'. According to t and the inferior MSS. the parts are fractions of the half moon in the first half of the sentence, and fractions of the whole moon in the second half. Yet Flemming and Martin follow the inferior MSS. herein. 7. Half of one part of light, i.e. $\frac{1}{28}$th. See previous notes, and observe that in this verse the fractions are *fractions of the whole moon*. Fourteen parts ($yu, abcdefhknox_1a$). mqt, il_1b 'thirteen parts'. 7, 8. These verses suppose the case when there are 15 days from new to full moon. On the first day the moon receives $\frac{1}{28}$th part of light, and has advanced to some slight degree out of conjunction, but still practically sets with the sun, and may be said to be invisible. On the second day she receives $\frac{1}{14}$th part of light, and becomes visible to that extent. Thus the $\frac{1}{28}$th part is ignored as being practically invisible. During the remaining 13 days the moon receives daily $\frac{1}{14}$th part of light. 8. Thirteen parts (a, n). β–n 'fourteen parts'.

LXXIV. In this chapter the writer deals shortly with the waxing and waning of the moon, her monthly change of position with regard to the signs and the sun, and the difference between lunar and solar years. 2. Of them all, i.e. the various phases of the moon. Fifteen days, i.e. from a conjunction till full moon or from full moon till a conjunction. 3.

she accomplishes all her light in the east, and in single seventh parts accomplishes all her darkness in the west.   4. And in certain months she alters her settings, and in certain months she pursues her own peculiar course.   5. In two months the moon sets with the sun in those two middle portals the third and the fourth. 6. She goes forth for seven days, and turns about and returns again through the portal where the sun rises, and accomplishes all her light: and she recedes from the sun, and in eight days enters the sixth portal from which the sun goes forth.   7. And when the sun goes forth from the fourth portal she goes forth seven days, until she goes forth from the fifth and turns back again in seven days into the fourth portal and accomplishes all her light: and she recedes and enters into the first portal in eight days.   8. And she returns again in seven days into the fourth portal from which the sun goes forth.   9. Thus I saw their position—how the moons rose and the sun set in those days. 10. And if five years are added together the sun has an overplus of thirty days, and all the days which accrue to it for one of those five years, when they are full, amount to 364 days.

Cf. 73 and 78.   And in single seventh ... darkness. $>a$, an.   4. Her own peculiar course, i.e. a course independent of that of the sun. 5, 6. During two months the moon sets with the sun as new moon and as full moon. When the sun is in Aries and Libra, the new moon and the full moon are in the third and fourth portals. In verse 6 the moon goes forth as it waxes from the third portal through the signs to the first portal in seven days, turns about, and returns to the portal where the sun rises, i.e. the third, in seven or eight days, and there becomes full moon, and proceeds thence through the fourth and fifth to the sixth portal, where she arrives after eight days. Thence the moon returns to the third portal in seven days. 6. And accomplishes. t^2, β 'and in that accomplishes'.   7, 8. The scheme with regard to the fourth portal and the new moon. The moon proceeds to the sixth portal and returns to the fourth in 14 days, and thence to the first portal and back in 15 days. 9. How the moons rose and the sun set ($a-q$). η, β ' according to the order of their moons the sun rising and setting'.   10, 11. The difference between the lunar and the solar year. According to $78^{13,\ 14}$, in a lunar year there are six months of 30 days, and six months of 29 days each—in all 354 days. In a solar year there are twelve months of 30 days each and four intercalary days in the equinoxes and solstices—in all 364 days (cf. $74^{10,\ 12}$ 75^2). Thus the difference between the lunar and the solar year amounts to 10 days. But in ver. 10^a and 11 no account is taken of the intercalary days in the solar year, so that the solar year is reckoned at

11. And the overplus of the sun and of the stars amounts to six days: in 5 years 6 days every year come to 30 days: and the moon falls behind the sun and stars to the number of 30 days. 12. And the sun and the stars bring in all the years exactly, so that they do not advance or delay their position by a single day unto eternity; but complete the years with perfect justice in 364 days. 13. In 3 years there are 1092 days, and in 5 years 1820 days, so that in 8 years there are 2912 days. 14. For the moon alone the days amount in 3 years to 1062 days, and in 5 years she falls 50 days behind: [i. e. to the sum (of 1770) there is to be added (1000 and) 62 days]. 15. And in 5 years there

---

360 days. Thus the difference in this case is six days. 11. The moon (t^2, β). α has preserved the word but in the wrong context; for it has transposed it into the next sentence and made it the subject of 'bring in'. 12. And the sun. So gmt save that they place 'from' before 'the sun'. > y^u, β. And the stars (u). gmt 'and from the stars'. > t^2, β. Here all MSS. add 'and (> n) the moon'. But 'the moon' belonged to ver. 11, see note. This wrong transposition was made by α. β followed α herein, and at the same time preserved the word in its original setting. Our author advocates a solar and sidereal year, as the author of Jubilees 6^{32-34}. For 'and the sun and the stars' t^2, β read 'and the moon', thus representing the moon as the perfect time divider in glaring contradiction with verses 10-11 and Jub. 6^{36}. But complete = ἀλλὰ τελοῦσιν, which was corrupted into ἀλλὰ ἀλλάττουσιν. Whence the Ethiopic text. 13-16. We have here clearly a reference to the eight-year cycle or octaeteris. In this cycle an intercalary month of 30 days was inserted in the third, fifth, and eighth years of the cycle in order to reconcile the lunar and solar years, which were reckoned respectively at 354 and 365½ days. As our author, however, does not reckon the solar year at 365½ days, but at 364, he proceeds to reconcile this solar year of 364 days with the lunar year of 354. Thus (ver. 13) in three such solar years there are 1092 days; in five, 1820 days; in eight, 2912 days; whereas (ver. 14, 15), in three lunar years there are 1062 days; in five, 1770 days; in eight, 2832 days. Thus there is a difference of 80 days between eight solar years of 364 days and eight lunar years. As all these calculations merely amount to saying that his solar year has 10 days more than the lunar, the writer had obviously the eight-year cycle before him; for only thus can we explain the external resemblance of his system to the Greek cycle; cf. Special Introd. p. 150. Unless the author had the Greek eight-year cycle before him and wished to give his own work some semblance of likeness thereto, there was no need to go through all these periods of three, five, and eight years; for they do not in fact contribute a single additional fact, but merely say over and over again that the difference between 364 and 354 days is 10 days. 14. [i. e. to the sum (of 1770) there is to

are 1770 days, so that for the moon the days in 8 years amount to 2832 days.   16. [For in 8 years she falls behind to the amount of 80 days], all the days she falls behind in 8 years are 80. 17. And the year is accurately completed in conformity with their world-stations and the stations of the sun, which rise from the portals through which it (the sun) rises and sets 30 days.

LXXV. 1. And the leaders of the heads of the thousands, who are placed over the whole creation and over all the stars, have also to do with the four intercalary days, being inseparable from their office, according to the reckoning of the year, and these render service on the four days which are not reckoned in the reckoning of the year.   2. And owing to them men go wrong therein, for those luminaries truly render service on the world-stations, one in the first portal, one in the third portal of the heaven, one in the fourth portal, and one in the sixth portal, and the exactness of the year is accomplished through its separate

be added (1000 and) 62 days.] This clause is bracketed as a marginal gloss as Beer and Flemming have recognized. If it belonged to the text at all, it should be found at the close of ver. 15; for it simply states that 2832 (= the days in 8 lunar years) arises from the addition of 1770 (= the days in 5 lunar years) and 1062 (= the days in 3 lunar years). The words ('1000 and') are found only in the margin of c.   16. The bracketed clause and that which follows are duplicate renderings.   17. Their world-stations (a–m). m, β 'their stations'. Are these the *world-stations* referred to in 75^2 in connexion with the intercalary days, which are presided over by the four angels who are heads of thousands? In ver. 12 the stars are mentioned in connexion with the sun. In my first edition I explained it as follows: 'which (i. e. the sun and moon) rise from the portals through which it (i. e. the sun) rises and sets thirty days'. But this is very unsatisfactory.

LXXV. This chapter deals with the intercalary days, the stars, and the sun. 1. The four intercalary days are under the charge of the highest stars, the leaders of the heads of ten thousands. These are not the chiliarchs, as Dillmann supposes (p. 248), but the leaders of the chiliarchs. For further development of this subject see $82^{11, 12}$. These leaders are not angels, as might be supposed, but simply 'luminaries'; cf. ver. 2.   And^{10} (q, β). > a–q. Their office (m). a–m 'its (> q) office', t^2, β 'their position'. The reckoning ^{10} (a). β 'all the reckoning'. Are not reckoned in the reckoning of the year. Apparently the year was popularly reckoned at 360 days; cf. 82^6.   2. Men do not know of these intercalary days, and so reckon wrongly; cf. 82^{4-6}. The exactness of the year (q). g 'in exactness the world', mtu, β 'the three hundred and sixty-four stations. 3. For the signs and the times and the years and the days the angel Uriel showed to me, whom the Lord of glory hath set for ever over all the luminaries of the heaven, in the heaven and in the world, that they should rule on the face of the heaven and be seen on the earth, and be leaders for the day and the night, i. e. the sun, moon, and stars, and all the ministering creatures which make their revolution in all the chariots of the heaven. 4. In like manner twelve doors Uriel showed me, open in the circumference of the sun's chariot in the heaven, through which the rays of the sun break forth: and from them is warmth diffused over the earth, when they are opened at their appointed seasons. 5. [And for the winds and the spirit of the dew† when they are opened, standing open in the heavens at the ends.] 6. As for the twelve portals in the heaven, at the ends of the earth, out of which go forth the sun, moon, and stars, and all the works of heaven in the east and in the west, · 7. There are many windows open to the left and right of them, and one window at

exactness of the world'. In the Ethiopic 'ām = 'year' and 'ālam = 'world'. Is accomplished (gm, β). qtu 'accomplishes', i. e. 'the exactness', &c. 3. Yet these intercalary days are a reality; for Uriel showed them to Enoch; cf. 72^1. Signs, i.e. of the zodiac; cf. $72^{13, 19}$. Lord of glory ($a-q$). q 'Lord of Spirits', $\beta-l$ 'eternal Lord of glory': see 84^2 (note). Chariots of the heaven: cf. 72^5. q reads 'troops of the heaven'. 4. The variation in the amount of heat given by the sun is explained by twelve openings in the disk of the sun through which heat is given forth in proportion to the number of windows opened. Doors Uriel showed me, open ((m)tu, $afhikn$). g 'open'. q 'doors and Uriel showed me'. 5. The first clause of this verse is unintelligible, and the rest of it looks like a dittograph of the last clause in ver. 4, and the first in ver. 6. The second clause follows $a-u$: t^2, β read 'when they are opened in the seasons, standing open', &c. The entire verse is, with Dillmann, Beer, Martin, to be rejected as an intrusion. 6, 7. Adjoining each one of these twelve portals of the sun are twelve windows open to the left and right of them; cf. $72^{3, 7}$. These diffuse warmth over the earth, one being open at a time, and all differing in degree of heating power. 6. This verse begins in a with a dittograph from ver. 4, 'when they are opened'. Cf. ver. 5. β has no such dittograph, but tries to give a meaning to the verse by inserting 'I saw', and changing the words 'twelve portals', which are a *nominativus pendens*, into the acc. But this is manifestly wrong. These portals have been under discussion continually throughout the last three chapters.

its (appointed) season produces warmth, corresponding (as these do) to those doors from which the stars come forth according as He has commanded them, and wherein they set corresponding to their number. 8. And I saw chariots in the heaven, running in the world, above those portals in which revolve the stars that never set. 9. And one is larger than all the rest, and it is that that makes its course through the entire world.

The Twelve Winds and their Portals.

LXXVI. 1. And at the ends of the earth I saw twelve portals open to all the quarters (of the heaven), from which the winds go forth and blow over the earth. 2. Three of them are open on the face (i.e. the east) of the heavens, and three in the west, and three on the right (i.e. the south) of the heaven, and three on the left (i.e. the north). 3. And the three first are those of the east, and three are of †the north, and three [after those on the left] of the south†, and three of the west. 4. Through four of these come winds of blessing and prosperity, and from

To say that Enoch saw them now would be immeasurably inept. 8. Above. + 'and below' *bodflopwry* $_1{}^a {}_1{}^b$. 9. One is larger. This may be the Great Bear.

LXXVI. This chapter gives a detailed account of the twelve portals of the winds and the nature of the winds which issue therefrom. The short account in 33-36 agrees with it. This disquisition on the nature of the winds has as much relation to reality as that on the year of 364 days. 1. The quarters. The text has here 'wind', which is a rendering of רוח = 'quarter of the heaven'. See note on 77¹. 2. This method of designating the four quarters of the earth was usual among the Hebrews; cf. 72³. 3. And 1º. > *gmt*. The order of the winds in this verse is undoubtedly wrong. First of all the clause which I have bracketed is nonsense in any case.

It was added after the transposition. Martin suggests that the words translated 'north' and 'south', i.e. mas'ĕ and 'azēb, should be rendered 'south' and 'north', since these words at one period were confused together. This is quite true, but it can hardly be the case in the Ethiopic version of Enoch, which carefully renders βορρᾶς by mas'ĕ in 28³ 32¹, cf. 70³, &c., &c., and νότος by 'azēb in 18⁶, ⁷. Hence we have simply to transpose the text here in order to recover the original order, i.e. 'And the three first are those of the east, and three are of the south, and three of the north, and three of the west'. This is the order in which the winds are dealt with in the verses that follow. 4. Through four of these portals come beneficial winds, i.e. the middle wind of the three in each quarter: the rest are hurtful. The winds from the four those eight come hurtful winds: when they are sent, they bring destruction on all the earth and on the water upon it, and on all who dwell thereon, and on everything which is in the water and on the land.

5. And the first wind from those portals, called the east wind, comes forth through the first portal which is in the east, inclining towards the south: from it come forth desolation, drought, heat, and destruction. 6. And through the second portal in the middle comes what is fitting, and from it there come rain and fruitfulness and prosperity and dew; and through the third portal which lies toward the north come cold and drought.

7. And after these come forth the south winds through three portals: through the first portal of them inclining to the east comes forth a hot wind. 8. And through the middle portal next to it there come forth fragrant smells, and dew and rain, and prosperity and health. 9. And through the third portal lying to the west come forth dew and rain, locusts and desolation.

10. And after these the north winds: from the seventh portal in the east come dew and rain, locusts and desolation. 11. And from the middle portal come in a direct direction health and rain and dew and prosperity; and through the third portal in the west come cloud and hoar-frost, and snow and rain, and dew and locusts.

---

corners are destructive as in Rev. 7¹ seq. According to our author's scheme there are two destructive winds at each corner of the earth. **5–6.** Winds from the east, i.e. the ESE. wind, the E. and ENE. winds. **6.** What is fitting or 'advantageous' or 'right'. So I render rĕt'ĕ. The same idea recurs in ver. 11, where the word is rĕt'ĕt, but is rendered 'in a direct direction'. Perhaps we should read ret'ĕ in the latter verse also, and render as above. **7–9.** Winds from the south. **7.** The SES. wind. Through the first (*qu*). *gmt*, β read 'the first through the first'. The latter form is not found in the description of any of the winds. **8.** The S. wind. **9.** The SWS. wind. **10.** The NEN. wind. North winds. MSS. add a gloss 'which is named the sea and which came forth'. In the east. *gtu* add 'towards the south', *m*, β–o_1a 'which inclines towards the south', *q* 'south'. **11.** The N. and NWN. winds. Come in a direct direction. Perhaps we should read 'comes what is fitting'. See note on ver. 6. Health and rain and dew (*a*). β 'rain and dew and health'. In the west. MSS. add 'which inclines

12. And after these [four] are the west winds: through the first portal adjoining the north come forth dew and hoar-frost, and cold and snow and frost. 13. And from the middle portal come forth dew and rain, and prosperity and blessing; and through the last portal which adjoins the south come forth drought and desolation, and burning and destruction. 14. And the twelve portals of the four quarters of the heaven are therewith completed, and all their laws and all their plagues and all their benefactions have I shown to thee, my son Methuselah.

The Four Quarters of the World: the Seven Mountains, the Seven Rivers, &c.

LXXVII. 1. And the first quarter is called the east, because it is the first: and the second, the south, because the Most High will descend there, yea, there in quite a special sense will He who is blessed for ever descend. 2. And the west quarter is named the diminished, because there all the luminaries of the heaven wane and go down. 3. And the fourth quarter, named the north, is divided into three parts: the first of them is for the dwelling of men: and the second contains seas of water, and the abysses and forests and rivers, and darkness and clouds; and the third part contains the garden of righteousness.

to the north'—an absurd addition. 12. The WNW. wind. Dew. + 'and rain' β. 13. The W. and WSW. winds. 14. Quarters. MSS. read 'portals', i.e. θυρῶν corrupt for μερῶν, a rendering of רוחות. All ^{2o}. > qu. All ^{3o}. > η, β-fhi. My son Methuselah: cf. 82^1.

LXXVII. 1-3. These verses deal not with the ten winds but with the four quarters. The first quarter is the east, i.e. קֶדֶם, because it is in front or the first, קַדְמוֹנִי. The second the south, דָּרוֹם, 'because the Most High descends there' from יָרַד רָם; cf. 25^3. The west is called the waning quarter, for which probably there stood in the Hebrew אַחֲרוֹן (not existing in Aramaic), which the Greek translator rendered by ὑστερῶν. So Dillmann. The north, צָפוֹן, is divided into three parts: one for men, the second for waters; cf. צָפָה = 'an overflowing': for darkness and cloud, from צָפַן, 'to render invisible'. The third encloses Paradise, from צָפַן, 'to reserve'. Paradise is the recompense *reserved* for the righteous, Ps. 31^{19}; cf. Halévy, *Journal Asiat.* 1867. 1. The first quarter. Here and in verses 2, 3 the text = 'wind', which is a rendering of רוּחַ, which in this context, as in Ezek. 42^{20}, should have been rendered μέρος = 'quarter'. 3. The garden of righteousness: see 60^8 (note) 70^3 (note). 4. The number seven plays a great rôle in this book,

4. I saw seven high mountains, higher than all the mountains which are on the earth: and thence comes forth hoar-frost, and days, seasons, and years pass away. 5. I saw seven rivers on the earth larger than all the rivers: one of them coming from the †west† pours its waters into the Great Sea. 6. And these two come from the north to the sea and pour their waters into the Erythraean Sea in the east. 7. And the remaining four come forth on the side of the north to their own sea, ⟨two of them to⟩ the Erythraean Sea, and two into the Great Sea and discharge themselves there [and some say: into the desert]. 8. Seven great islands I saw in the sea and in the mainland: two in the mainland and five in the Great Sea.

The Sun and Moon: the Waxing and Waning of the Moon.

LXXVIII. 1. And the names of the sun are the following: the first Orjârês, and the second Tômâs. 2. And the moon

and generally in Jewish writers; cf. 18⁶ 24² 32¹ 61¹¹ 72²⁷ 91¹⁶ 93¹⁰. **Seven high mountains.** These appear to have nothing to do with those of 18⁶ 24² 32¹, though originally they are derived from the same source. **Pass.** + 'and go' *q, β*. 5. **Seven** (*β*). > *a*. **One of them coming from the †west†.** This must be the Nile, as Dillmann takes it, but the description 'from the west' cannot be right. Hence I take 'ârab (= west) to be a transliteration of עֲרָבָה, which here means simply 'desert' or 'steppe', and render 'coming from the desert'. Here Aramaic fails to explain the difficulty. **The Great Sea,** i.e. the Mediterranean; cf. Num. 34⁶,⁷. 6. **The Euphrates and Tigris.** **The Erythraean Sea.** A general name for the Arabian, Persian, and Indian seas. 7. **The remaining four,** i.e. the Indus, Ganges, Oxus, and Jaxartes (Dillmann). ⟨**Two of them to.**⟩ These words must be supplied. [**And some say: into the desert.**] This is manifestly a gloss. Such a second view is impossible in a vision. 8. **Two in the mainland and five in the Great Sea** (*bedfilory*₁*a*₁*b*). So also *aehl*s save that they omit 'in the mainland' after 'two'. *a-m* read 'seven, and two in the Red Sea': *m* 'two in the mainland and five in the Red Sea'. The text is wholly uncertain. Perhaps we might compare Jub. 8²⁹ where 'five great islands' are referred to. The sevenfold division of the earth is of Babylonian origin. See *K. A. T.*³ 618. From this source is developed the idea in 4 Ezra 6⁴² where the land is said to be ⅚ths of the earth and the sea ⅐th, the seven high mountains in our text, 77⁴, the seven streams, 77⁵, and the seven islands, 77⁸.

LXXVIII, LXXIX. The relations of the sun and moon are again described, as well as the waxing and the waning of the moon. **LXXVIII. 1. And** ¹⁰ (*a-q, ehl*). > *q, β-ehl*. Halévy points out that the two names of the sun given here correspond to the two has four names: the first name is Asônjâ, the second Eblâ, the third Benâsê, and the fourth Erâe. 3. These are the two great luminaries: their circumference is like the circumference of the heaven, and the size of the circumference of both is alike. 4. In the circumference of the sun there are seven portions of light which are added to it more than to the moon, and in definite measures it is transferred till the seventh portion of the sun is exhausted. 5. And they set and enter the portals of the west, and make their revolution by the north, and come forth through the eastern portals on the face of the heaven. 6. And when the moon rises one-fourteenth part appears in the

seasons of the year in Palestine; cf. 2^3 $3\ 4\ 68^{15}$. Orjârès from אוֹר חֶרֶם is the sun when his power is diminished in the winter season; for חרם or חרשׁ = 'potsherd' as well as 'sun'. The second name חַמָּה in our text, altered into Tomas by change of ḥ and t, denotes the sun when the heat is powerful in the summer, from חמם. 2. Halévy attempts to show that the four names of the moon are connected with its various phases. But this seems improbable. Asônjà from אִישׁוֹן יָהּ where אִישׁוֹן is a diminutive of אִישׁ and יָהּ merely an intensive termination. This is the name of the moon in connexion with its likeness to the human face; cf. ver. 17. Eblâ, corrupted from לְבָנָה = the pale star, denotes, he thinks, the moon in her waning period. Benâsê, from בְּדְבָסָה (i. e. בסה, to cover), is an appropriate name of the moon in the period of conjunction when she is invisible. But in Prov. 7^{20} Ps. 81^4 כֶּסֶה means the full moon as opposed to הַחֹדֶשׁ, 'the new moon'. Erae from יָרֵחַ (i. e. from ירח, 'to cast, dart,' or possibly, as Martin proposes, from ארח, 'to journey,' 'go') is suitable as a designation of the waxing or full moon. 3. Cf. $72^{4,\ 37}$ 73^2. According to Chullin 60^b the sun and moon were originally of the same size, but that God subsequently bade the moon to lessen her size (מעטי את עצמך). The size of the circumference (a). β 'the size'. + 'like the circumference of the heaven' a-u—a repetition from the preceding clause. 4. From 72^{37} and 73^3 we have already learnt that the light of the sun is sevenfold that of the moon: from 73^2 that light is added to the moon in due measure. Here we are further informed that ⅐th of the light of the sun is gradually transferred to the moon, and that this seventh part is wholly transferred when the moon is full. Of the above Semitic words the two names for the sun חֶרֶם and חַמָּה are Hebrew and not Aramaic, while of the four names of the moon לְבָנָה, אִישׁוֹן, and בְּדְבָסָה are Hebrew only. In Aramaic סיהרא is 'moon', and ירח 'month' or 'new moon'. When our translator wishes to render 'new moon' he puts ἄrèq (= חדשׁ) as in 78^{12}. 5. By the north: cf. 72^5. 6-17. These verses give a detailed description of the waxing and waning of the moon, of the length of the months, &c. 6. This case where there are fourteen days from new moon to full moon has already been treated of in $73^{6,\ 6}$ (notes). In this verse the text follows a-u. u is partly untranslatable. β heaven: [the light becomes full in her]: on the fourteenth day she accomplishes her light. 7. And fifteen parts of light are transferred to her till the fifteenth day (when) her light is accomplished, according to the sign of the year, and she becomes fifteen parts, and the moon grows by (the addition of) fourteenth parts. 8. And in her waning (the moon) decreases on the first day to fourteen parts of her light, on the second to thirteen parts of light, on the third to twelve, on the fourth to eleven, on the fifth to ten, on the sixth to nine, on the seventh to eight, on the eighth to seven, on the ninth to six, on the tenth to five, on the eleventh to four, on the twelfth to three, on the thirteenth to two, on the fourteenth to the half of a seventh, and all her remaining light disappears wholly on the fifteenth. 9. And in certain months the month has twenty-nine days and once twenty-eight. 10. And Uriel showed me another law: when light is transferred to the moon, and on which side it is transferred to her by the sun. 11. During all the period during which the moon is growing in her light, she is transferring it to herself when opposite to the sun during fourteen days [her light

reads 'And when the moon rises, she appears in the heaven, and has a fourteenth part of the light, and on the fourteenth day she accomplishes all her light'. [The light becomes full in her] (a–μ). I have bracketed this clause as a duplicate rendering of τὸ φῶς πληροῖ (or τελεῖ), which the translator renders again as 'she accomplishes her light'. 7. This case, where there are fifteen days from new moon to full moon, has already been discussed: see 73$^{7, 8}$ (note). 8. As the moon wanes her light decreases each day by $\frac{1}{14}$th part; on the fifteenth day the remainder, i.e. $\frac{2}{28}$th, vanishes. Half of a seventh (t, β). a–t 'half and to a seventh'. 9. Twenty-nine days: cf. 74$^{10-17}$ 78$^{15-17}$. Once twenty-eight. As we learnt from 74$^{13-16}$ that the author was acquainted with the eight-year cycle of the Greeks, so here, as Wieseler has already pointed out, we find a reference to the seventy-six year cycle of Callippus. The cycle of Callippus is already an emended Metonic cycle. According to the cycle of Meton, to which there is no allusion in Enoch, seven lunar months were intercalated in nineteen lunar years, in the third, fifth, eighth, eleventh, thirteenth, sixteenth, nineteenth, and thus the difference between the solar and lunar years at the end of this cycle was about 7½ hours. Callippus, recognizing this difference, quadrupled the Metonic cycle and deducted one day from the last month of this period of seventy-six years, and thus this month had only twenty-eight days as in our text. 11. The moon waxes over against the sun on the side turned to the sun, i.e. the western side. [Her light is accomplished in the heaven] ^{10}

is accomplished in the heaven], and when she is illumined throughout, her light is accomplished in the heaven. 12. And on the first day she is called the new moon, for on that day the light rises upon her. 13. She becomes full moon exactly on the day when the sun sets in the west, and from the east she rises at night, and the moon shines the whole night through till the sun rises over against her and the moon is seen over against the sun. 14. On the side whence the light of the moon comes forth, there again she wanes till all the light vanishes and all the days of the month are at an end, and her circumference is empty, void of light. 15. And three months she makes of thirty days, and at her time she makes three months of twenty-nine days each, in which she accomplishes her waning in the first period of time, and in the first portal for one hundred and seventy-seven days. 16. And in the time of her going out she appears for three months (of) thirty days each, and for three months she appears (of) twenty-nine each. 17. At night she appears like a man for twenty days each time, and by day she appears like the heaven, and there is nothing else in her save her light.

Recapitulation of several of the Laws.

LXXIX. 1. And now, my son, I have shown thee everything, and the law of all the stars of the heaven is completed. 2. And he showed me all the laws of these for every day, and for every season of bearing rule, and for every year, and for its going

---

(β). Bracketed as a dittograph from the next clause. a reads 'her light is accomplished'. 13. This remark is quite true. She becomes. q, β prefix 'and'. 15. Each half-year has three months of thirty days and three of twenty-nine. And ^{2e} (a). $> \beta$. At her time. $+ gmt$ (and indeed qu originally) 'when she is accomplishing 'her waning'. In the first period of time, i.e. in the first half-year. The author recognizes only two seasons in the year; cf. 3 4 78^1 (note). So often as the moon is in the first portal during the first half-year, she is waning; cf. $79^{2, 4}$. 16. In the time of her going out, i.e. in the second half of the year. 17. Cf. ver. 2 (note).

LXXIX. 1. My son. + 'Methuselah' t, β. The law of all $(a-u)$. u, β 'all the laws of'. 2. Of bearing rule $(a-u)$. β 'for every forth, and for the order prescribed to it every month and every week: 3. And the waning of the moon which takes place in the sixth portal: for in this sixth portal her light is accomplished, and after that there is the beginning of the waning: 4. ⟨And the waning⟩ which takes place in the first portal in its season, till one hundred and seventy-seven days are accomplished: reckoned according to weeks, twenty-five (weeks) and two days. 5. She falls behind the sun and the order of the stars exactly five days in the course of one period, and when this place which thou seest has been traversed. 6. Such is the picture and sketch of every luminary which Uriel the archangel, who is their leader, showed unto me.

LXXX. 1. And in those days the angel Uriel answered and said to me: 'Behold, I have shown thee everything, Enoch, and I have revealed everything to thee that thou shouldest see this sun and this moon, and the leaders of the stars of the heaven and all those who turn them, their tasks and times and departures.

power'. 3, 4. Cf. 78^{15}, but the verse is obscure or corrupt. 3. Of the waning (a). β 'of the month and of the waning'. 4. ⟨And the waning.⟩ Restored. So also Flemming and Martin. 5. She falls behind (a–t). n 'and she falls behind'; t, β–n 'and how she falls behind'. And the order. Here I have emended wa (>mq) baśer'ātā of a, β–bx (= 'and according to the order of') into walaśer'ātā. For this use of la in replacing another preposition in an enumeration—in this instance 'em—see Dillmann's Gramm.^{2} p. 347. Our text here identifies the solar and sidereal years, as in 74^{12}. Exactly five days. Cf. 74$^{10-17}$. The moon falls behind five days in the half-year.

LXXX. For the reasons for regarding this chapter as an interpolation see Introduction to this Book of the Heavenly Luminaries (pp. 147–8). In that Introduction we have already remarked that the moment we have done with 79 we pass into a world of new conceptions, the whole interest of which is ethical and nothing else. There is absolutely no fixity in natural phenomena: their laws and uniformities are always dependent on the moral action of men; cf. 4 Ezra 5$^{1-13}$. This line of thought is quite alien to 72–79. See 2^1 (note). 1. The angel (gmt). > qu, β. I have shown (mq, β). gtu 'I will show'. Leaders of the stars: cf. 72^3 75$^{2, 3}$. Those who turn them. These are probably the winds; cf. 72^5 73^2. And times. + 'and they turn them' gmt. Verses 2–8 are written as tristichs. This fact helps us materially in the criticism of verses 5 and 7. 2.

Chapters LXXIX. 3—LXXX. 5

Perversion of Nature and the heavenly Bodies owing to the Sin of Men.

2. And in the days of the sinners the years shall be shortened,
And their seed shall be tardy on their lands and fields,
And all things on the earth shall alter,

And shall not appear in their time:
And the rain shall be kept back
And the heaven shall withhold (it).

3. And in those times the fruits of the earth shall be backward,
And shall not grow in their time
And the fruits of the trees shall be withheld in their time.

4. And the moon shall alter her order,
And not appear at her time.

5. [And in those days the sun shall be seen and he shall journey in the evening †on the extremity of the great chariot in† the west]

And shall shine more brightly than accords with the order of light.

Cf. Jer. 3³ 5²³. **Shall alter** (β). 'Alter' is here intransitive, but α-u give the transitive tense and t supplies 'its ways'. **Shall withhold** (m, β). gqtu 'shall stand still' (by merely the change of a vowel point). **4.** Cf. for similar ideas Joel 2¹⁰ Amos 8⁹ 4 Ezra 5⁴. **5.** The first two lines of this verse are very corrupt and have been dislocated from their proper context in this chapter. By their removal verses 4-5 form a tristich relating to the moon. These corrupt clauses are probably fragments of a tristich relating to the sun. The Ethiopic reads: 'And in those days the heaven (mq, β: gtu 'in the heaven') shall be seen, and hunger shall come on the extremity of the great chariot to (α-q : q, t²β 'in') the West'. Here Halévy conjectured, and his conjecture is generally accepted, that השמים (= 'the heaven') was corrupt for השמש (= 'the sun'), רעב (= 'hunger') for ערב (= 'evening'). But we must go further. There is no meaning in the phrase 'on the extremity' in connexion with the chariot of the sun. This phrase = בקץ which may be corrupt for מציק = 'causing distress'. Next there is no point in saying 'the sun shall be seen'. This line, moreover, is too short, and the second too long. If we transfer 'in the evening' to the first line we have 'shall be seen in the evening'. The possible corruption here is suggested by 4 Ezra 5⁴ 'relucescet subito sol noctu'. יראה ('shall be seen') may be corrupt for יזרח = 'shall rise'. Thus we arrive at the following:—

'And in those days the sun shall rise in the evening,
And his great chariot journey to the west, causing distress (as it goes).'

With this we might contrast Amos 8⁹

6. And many chiefs of the stars shall transgress the order (prescribed).
And these shall alter their orbits and tasks,
And not appear at the seasons prescribed to them.

7. And the whole order of the stars shall be concealed from the sinners,
And the thoughts of those on the earth shall err concerning them,
[And they shall be altered from all their ways],
Yea, they shall err and take them to be gods.

8. And evil shall be multiplied upon them,
And punishment shall come upon them
So as to destroy all.'

The Heavenly Tablets and the Mission of Enoch.

LXXXI. 1. And he said unto me:
'Observe, Enoch, these heavenly tablets,
And read what is written thereon,
And mark every individual fact.'

2. And I observed the heavenly tablets, and read everything which was written (thereon) and understood everything, and read the book of all the deeds of mankind, and of all the

---

'I will cause the sun to go down at noon'. The above emendations are possible in Hebrew, but not in Aramaic. **6. Chiefs of the stars shall transgress the order (prescribed)** ($q^{eo'}$, and in part by gq, o_1b). Beer conjectured this text, which differs from that of the rest of the MSS. by the vocalization of two consonants. The rest of the MSS. = 'chiefs of the stars of the order shall transgress'. **7. Shall be concealed from the sinners**: cf. 75^2 82^{4-6}. **Those on the earth**. This phrase is used here exactly in the sense in which it appears in the interpolations in the Parables;

see 37^3 (note). [**And they shall be altered ... ways.**] Bracketed as an intrusion: possibly it is a dittograph of ver. 6^b. **Take them to be gods**: cf. 19^1 Acts 7^{42}. **8. All** (a). β ' them all'.

LXXXI. For the reasons for regarding this chapter as an interpolation see Introduction to this Book of the Heavenly Luminaries (p. 148). **1. These heavenly tablets**. For a complete account of this and kindred expressions see 47^3 (note). β-*n* reads 'the writing of the heavenly tablets'. **2. The book of all the deeds** (*mt*). *gu* 'the book, all the deeds': *q*, β 'the children of flesh that shall be upon the earth to the remotest generations. 3. And forthwith I blessed the great Lord, the King of glory for ever, in that He has made all the works of the world,

> And I extolled the Lord because of His patience,
> And blessed Him because of the children of men.

4. And after that I said:
> 'Blessed is the man who dies in righteousness and goodness,
> Concerning whom there is no book of unrighteousness written,
> And against whom no day of judgement shall be found.'

5. And those seven holy ones brought me and placed me on the earth before the door of my house, and said to me: 'Declare everything to thy son Methuselah, and show to all thy children that no flesh is righteous in the sight of the Lord, for He is their Creator. 6. One year we will leave thee with thy son, till thou givest thy (last) commands, that thou mayest teach thy children and record (it) for them, and testify to all thy children; and in the second year they shall take thee from their midst.

---

book and all that was written therein, all the deeds'. 3. Cf. 22¹⁴ for a similar expression of praise. The great Lord (a). β 'the Lord'. The King of glory for ever (a). β–bc 'the eternal King of glory'. Children of men (a, ﬁloy₁a₁b). β–ﬁhilnoy₁a₁b 'children of the world'. 4. See Introd. (p. 148) on the contrast between this blessing and that pronounced by the writer of 72–79. Book of unrighteousness: see 47³ (note). Day of judgement (gniu). q, t²β 'unrighteousness'. Shall be found (a–m). m, t²β 'has been found'. If this clause be taken strictly, it is here taught that there is no judgement for the righteous. 5. Seven holy ones (a). β 'three holy ones'. Cf. 87² 90²¹,²² and 20. No flesh is righteous, &c.: cf. Job 9² Ps. 14¹. Creator: cf. 94¹⁰. 6. Thy son (a). β 'thy sons'. These two verses, vv. 5, 6, may be inserted to serve as an introduction to 91–104. Till. After 'till' (= עַד) the MSS. add 'again' = עוֹד which is here simply a dittograph of the preceding. The word 'again' is meaningless as it stands. Givest thy (last) commands (těʽězěz mt, β–cde). This is the idiomatic meaning of the Hebrew צוה. The reading of g is a corruption of mt. Hence all MSS. but q and three third-rate MSS. support the above text. q = 'comfortest him' (těnâzězô). According to Dillmann cde read těʽězěz = 'growest strong'. But this gives no

7. Let thy heart be strong,
   For the good shall announce righteousness to the good;

   The righteous with the righteous shall rejoice,
   And shall offer congratulation to one another.

8. But the sinners shall die with the sinners,
   And the apostate go down with the apostate.

9. And those who practise righteousness shall die on account of the deeds of men,
   And be taken away on account of the doings of the godless.'

10. And in those days they ceased to speak to me, and I came to my people, blessing the Lord of the world.

Charge given to Enoch: the four Intercalary Days: the Stars which lead the Seasons and the Months.

LXXXII. 1. And now, my son Methuselah, all these things I am recounting to thee and writing down for thee, and I have revealed to thee everything, and given thee books concerning all these: so preserve, my son Methuselah, the books from thy father's hand, and (see) that thou deliver them to the generations of the world.

---

suitable sense. **8. The apostate go down**, i.e. into Gehenna. **9. The righteous die indeed**, yet are they 'gathered' unto the abodes of the blessed. The phrase is borrowed directly from Is. 57¹, where the literal translation runs, 'the righteous is gathered out of the way of or because of the evil' מִפְּנֵי הָרָעָה נֶאֱסַף הַצַּדִּיק: cf. 2 Kings 22²⁰ Book of Wisdom 4⁷⁻¹⁴. The Hebrew verb is used of being 'gathered to one's fathers', Num. 20²⁶. In Ps. 104²⁹ God is said to 'gather' the spirit of animals when they die. **10. Lord of the world** (or 'Eternal Lord' a–q: q, β 'Lord of the ages'); cf. 1³ 12³ 58⁴ 81³ 82⁷ 84².

LXXXII. The conclusion of the Book of the Heavenly Luminaries. **1.** In 33⁴ Uriel writes down everything for Enoch; but in this book, cf. 72¹ 74² 75³ 79²⁻⁶ 82¹, Uriel only shows the hidden things to Enoch, and Enoch writes them down. **For thee.** > *gmt.* **Methuselah.** > *gmq.* **Deliver them to the generations** ('children' *g*) **of the world.** These revelations of Enoch are for all the world from the earliest generations: those in 1–36 are only for the far distant generations; cf. 1². See special Introd. (p. 149). It is evidently this passage that Tertullian refers to in *De Cultu Fem.* i. 3 'Cum Enoch filio suo Matusalae nihil aliud

2. I have given wisdom to thee and to thy children,
[And thy children that shall be to thee],
That they may give it to their children for generations,
This wisdom (namely) that passeth their thought.

3. And those who understand it shall not sleep,
But shall listen with the ear that they may learn this wisdom,
And it shall please those that eat thereof better than good food.

4. Blessed are all the righteous, blessed are all those who walk in the way of righteousness and sin not as the sinners, in the reckoning of all their days in which the sun traverses the heaven, entering into and departing from the portals for thirty days with the heads of thousands of the order of the stars, together with the four which are intercalated which divide the four portions of the year, which lead them and enter with them four days. 5. Owing to them men shall be at fault and not reckon them in the whole reckoning of the year: yea, men shall be at fault, and not recognize them accurately. 6. For they belong to the reckoning of the year and are truly recorded (thereon) for ever, one in the first portal and one in the third, and one in the fourth and one in the sixth, and the year is completed in three hundred and sixty-four days.

mandaverit quam ut notitiam eorum posteris suis traderit'. 2. **Wisdom.** The surpassing wisdom conveyed in these revelations is a frequent theme with the Enoch writers; cf. 37⁴ 92¹ 93¹⁰⁻¹⁴. To thee and to thy children ($mq̈u, β$): cf. Ps. 78⁵,⁶. t reads 'to thy son': g corrupt. As we must infer from these words that Lamech is already born, the writer has followed the Samaritan or Massoretic reckoning: the former would allow of Noah being present. [And thy children ... to thee.] Bracketed as an interpolation. 3. Better than good food: cf. Ps. 19¹⁰. 4. The four intercalary days introduced by four leaders: cf. ver. 11, 75¹,². Blessed are all those ($t, β-y$). > $gu, y. mq$ 'blessed (+ 'moreover' q) are all' (+ 'the righteous' m). Heads of thousands, i.e. the chiliarchs which lead these days. Divide ($qt, β-no\ _1b$). Cf. 82¹¹. $gmu, no\ _1b$ 'are divided'. 5. Cf. 75². Whole reckoning of the year. So with Beer I correct baḥasâba kuĕllû 'âlam (= 'in the reckoning of the whole world') into bakuĕllû ḥasâba 'âmat. 6. On the four intercalary days, and the portals to which they belong, see 75. The year is completed in three hundred, &c. ($β$).

7. And the account thereof is accurate and the recorded reckoning thereof exact; for the luminaries, and months and festivals, and years and days, has Uriel shown and revealed to me, to whom the Lord of the whole creation of the world hath subjected the host of heaven. 8. And he has power over night and day in the heaven to cause the light to give light to men—sun, moon, and stars, and all the powers of the heaven which revolve in their circular chariots. 9. And these are the orders of the stars, which set in their places, and in their seasons and festivals and months.

10. And these are the names of those who lead them, who watch that they enter at their times, in their orders, in their seasons, in their months, in their periods of dominion, and in their positions. 11. Their four leaders who divide the four parts of the year enter first; and after them the twelve leaders of the orders who divide the months; and for the three hundred and sixty (days) there are heads over thousands who divide the days; and for the four intercalary days there are the leaders which sunder the four parts of the year. 12. And these heads over thousands are intercalated between leader and leader, each behind a station, but

a–gmu 'the year of three hundred and sixty-four days is completed'. 7. To whom ... hath subjected. The text *a–q*, *β* reads za'azaza (za'azazô *brefaz*) lita (= 'whom He hath commanded for me') which I have emended into za'azaza lôtû = $\overset{\circ}{q}$ ἐπέταξε. But ἐπέταξε is corrupt for ὑπέταξε. Hence my translation. Uriel is the ruler of the starry world, 72¹. Lord of the whole creation of the world. Here only; cf. 84². 9–20. Dillmann regards these verses as a later addition to the book, but without adequate reason. They are quite in harmony with all that rightly belongs to this section of the book. Moreover, 72¹ promises an account of the stars, and 79¹ declares that the full account has now been given. This would be impossible without 82⁴⁻²⁰. 10. Who watch that they enter. Here the Ethiopic is literally 'who watch and enter'. But the context requires the rendering I have given. Hence it is possible that we have here the survival of the Hebrew idiom of the voluntative with waw. If so, the text would represent something like אֲשֶׁר יִצְרוּ וְיָבֹאוּ. Times. + 'who lead them in their places' (> 'in their places' *u*) *a*. 11. For (> *q*) the three hundred and sixty (days) there are heads (*gqu*). *t, β* 'for the three hundred and sixty-four (days) with the heads'. *m* supports *gqu*, but by a slip omits 'and sixty'. 12. A station. *q, a* read 'his station'. There is no difficulty in the text of *gmqu* which we have followed here.

Sect. III]   **Chapter LXXXII. 7-17**   177

their leaders make the division.   13. And these are the names of the leaders who divide the four parts of the year which are ordained: Mîlkî'êl, Hel'emmêlêk, and Mêl'êjal, and Nûrêl. 14. And the names of those who lead them: Adnâr'êl, and Îjâsûsa'êl, and 'Êlômê'êl—these three follow the leaders of the orders, and there is one that follows the three leaders of the orders which follow those leaders of stations that divide the four parts of the year.

15. In the beginning of the year Melkejâl rises first and rules, who is named †Tam'âinî, and sun† and all the days of his dominion whilst he bears rule are ninety-one days.   16. And these are the signs of the days which are to be seen on earth in the days of his dominion: sweat, and heat, and calms; and all the trees bear fruit, and leaves are produced on all the trees, and the harvest of wheat, and the rose-flowers, and all the flowers which come forth in the field, but the trees of the winter season become withered.   17. And these are the names of the leaders which are under them: Berka'êl, Zèlebs'êl, and another who is added a head of a thousand, called Hilûjâsĕph: and the days of the dominion of this (leader) are at an end.

The twelve leaders of the months divide the months: the chiliarchs divide the 360 days, and the four leaders which divide the year into four parts have charge of the intercalary days.   12. I don't understand this verse. 13. Milkiel from מַלְכִּיאֵל is simply an inversion of Helemmelek from אֱלִימֶלֶךְ as Halévy has shown. Melejal = מלאיאל (Schwab) and Narel = נראל. These four are over the four seasons of the year. Under each of these are three leaders who preside over the three months of each season.   14. This verse seems unintelligible.   15-17. The period from spring to summer = 91 days under the dominion of Melkejal.   15. Of the year (m, β). > a-m. The leader of this period is named 'Tam'âinî' and 'sun'. As Goldschmidt and Beer have pointed out, these two names are one, i.e. שֶׁמֶשׁ תֵּימָנִי = 'the southern sun'. This explanation is not possible through Aramaic.   16. Calms (zàḥn u). a-u, ḥazan, 'anxiety.' Rose-flowers. Not known in the O.T. though the word is found in the A.V. in Is. 35¹ Song of Solomon 2¹. The rose is mentioned in Sir. 24¹⁴ 39¹³ Wisdom 2⁸. But in the first two passages it is probably the oleander that is referred to. The rose in later Hebrew is וֶרֶד and in Aramaic וַרְדָא. Which come forth (a-m). β 'bloom'. > m. 17. The leaders under them, i.e. the leaders of the three months. Berka'êl = ברכיאל: Zèlebs'êl = זלבשאל = 'this is the heart of God' (Schwab). Another who is added ... called

18. The next leader after him is Hêl'emmêlêk, whom one names the shining sun, and all the days of his light are ninety-one days. 19. And these are the signs of (his) days on the earth: glowing heat and dryness, and the trees ripen their fruits and produce all their fruits ripe and ready, and the sheep pair and become pregnant, and all the fruits of the earth are gathered in, and everything that is in the fields, and the winepress: these things take place in the days of his dominion. 20. These are the names, and the orders, and the leaders of those heads of thousands: Gîdâ'ijal, Kê'êl, and Hê'êl, and the name of the head of a thousand which is added to them, Asfâ'êl: and the days of his dominion are at an end.

Hilûjâsêph. There is here a play on the proper name אליוסף ... נוסף. 18–20. The period from summer to autumn. 19. And these are the signs of (his) days (β). *gmt* 'and these are the days of his sign'. *yx* corrupt forms of *gmt*. 20. This verse is confused. The three names are those of the leaders of the three months. The fourth — Asfâ'êl from יוֹסְפְאֵל 'God adds', which is merely an inversion of Hilûjâsêph from אליוסף —is the chiliarch who has to do with the intercalary day under one of the four chief leaders. There is no account of the remaining six months. This may have been omitted by the final redactor.

SECTION IV

(CHAPTERS LXXXIII—XC)

THE DREAM-VISIONS. INTRODUCTION

A. *Critical Structure.* B. *Relation of this Section to* (a) 1–36; (b) 91–104. C. *The Date.* D. *The Problem and its Solution.*

A. Critical Structure. There is no difficulty about the critical structure of this Section. It is the most complete and self-consistent of all the Sections, and has suffered least from the hand of the interpolator. There seems to be only one interpolation, i.e. 90^{14} b. Of dislocations of the text there are two: 89^{48} b should be read after 89^{49}: see 89^{48} Crit. Note; and 90^{19} should be read before 90^{14}: see 90^{13-19} (note). In 90, vv. 13–15 are a doublet of vv. 16–18.

B. (a) Relation of this Section to 6–36. This question can only be determined by giving the points of likeness as well as of divergence. The points of likeness or identity in (1) phraseology, and (2) in ideas, are:—

(1) 'Tongue of flesh,' 84^1 14^2; 'make the earth without inhabitant,' 84^5 9^2; 'Holy and Great One,' 84^1 1^3; 'glorious land' (i.e. Jerusalem or Palestine), 89^{40}, compared with 'blessed land', 27^1. The doxology in 84^2 appears to be a more rhetorical form of that in 9^4. Finally, 88^1–89^1 presupposes 10^{1-12}. See notes *in loc.*

(2) There is, in the main, the same doctrine of the fallen angels: the judgement in both is at the beginning of the Messianic kingdom; Gehenna is found in both, 90^{26} 27^1; the abyss of fire for the fallen angels, 90^{24} 10^6 18^{11} 21^{7-10}; the conversion of the Gentiles, 90^{30} 10^{21}.

There is, practically, nothing that is distinctive in (2)—certainly nothing more than would refer the two Sections to the same school of thought. But the evidence of (1) is of a different nature, and points, when combined with the evidence of (2), to a close connexion between the two Sections either in identity of authorship, or in the acquaintance of one of the authors with the work of the other. That the latter alternative is the true one, we shall find on the following grounds:—(1) In 83^{11} the sun comes forth from the 'windows of the east'; a term that is never used of the sun in 1-36, nor in 72-82: see 83^{11} (note). 'Windows' has a different reference altogether: see 72^3 (note). (2) In 84^4 'the great day of judgement' = Deluge; in 1-36 and 91-104 always = final judgement: see 84^4 (note). (3) The account of the descent of the watchers in 86^{1-3} differs from that in 6. (4) In 90^{19} the period of the sword is an important feature; yet is not alluded to in 1-36. (5) The throne of judgement is in Palestine in 90^{20-26}; whereas the throne on which God will sit when He comes to bless His people in 25^3 is the centre of the Seven Mountains: see 18^8 (note). (6) Appearance of the Messiah emphasized in $90^{37,\ 38}$; not alluded to in 1-36. (7) The scene of the kingdom in 83-90 is the New Jerusalem set up by God Himself; in 1-36 it is Jerusalem and the entire earth *unchanged* though purified, $10^{18,\ 20}$. (8) Life of the members of the Messianic kingdom is apparently unending in 90^{33-38}; but only finite in $10^{17}\ 25^6$. Life is transfigured by the presence of the Messiah in 90^{38} in the New Jerusalem: but in $25^{5,\ 6}$ by the external eating of the tree of life. (9) The picture on 83-90 is developed and spiritual; that in 1-36 is naïve, primitive, and sensuous. (10) 83-90 are only visions assigned to Enoch's earlier and unwedded life; 1-36 are accounts of actual bodily translations and are assigned to his later life. If these two Sections were from the same author and that an ascetic, exactly the converse would have been the case.

On these grounds, therefore, identity of authorship seems impossible; but the similarities in phraseology and idea prove that one of the authors had the work of the other before him. Of the two Sections there is no room for doubt that 83-90 is the later.

(*b*) **Relation of 83-90 to 91-104.** See Special Introd. to 91-104 (pp. 220-221).

C. The Date. The fourth period began about 200 B.C. (see note on 90^{6-17} pp. 206 sqq.) and marks the transition of supremacy over Israel from the Graeco-Egyptians to the Graeco-Syrians, as well as the rise of the Chasids. The Chasids, symbolized by the lambs that are born to the white sheep, 90^6, are already an organized party in the Maccabean revolt, 90^{6-7} (note). The lambs that become horned are the Maccabean family, and the great horn is Judas Maccabeus, 90^9 (note). As this great horn is still warring at the close of the rule of the twelve shepherds, 90^{16}, this Section must have been written before the death of Judas, 161 B.C., possibly before his purification of the temple.

As the fourth period began about 200 B.C., the author of 83–90, writing in the lifetime of Judas Maccabeus, must have expected its close between 140 and 130 B.C.; for, on the analogy of the third period, each shepherd would rule between five and six years. This expectation in connexion with Judas Maccabeus was not unnatural, as his eldest brother, Simon, did not die till 135 B.C.

D. **The Problem and its Solution.** This Section forms in short compass a philosophy of religion from the Jewish standpoint. It is divided into two visions, the former of which deals with the first world-judgement of the deluge, and the latter with the entire history of the world till the final judgement. The writer does not attempt to account for the sin that showed itself in the first generation. In his view, it was not the sin of man, but the sin of the angels who fell (in the days of Jared), that corrupted the earth, 84^4 86–87, and brought upon it the first world-judgement.

In the second vision the interest centres mainly on the calamities that befall Israel from the exile onwards. Why has Israel become a byword among the nations, and the servant of one gentile power after another? Is there no recompense for the righteous nation and the righteous individual? That Israel, indeed, has sinned grievously and deserves to be punished, the author amply acknowledges, but not a punishment so immeasurably transcending its guilt. But these undue severities have not come upon Israel from God's hand: they are the doing of the seventy shepherds into whose care God committed Israel, 89^{59}. These shepherds or angels have proved faithless to their trust, and treacherously destroyed those whom God willed not to destroy; but they have not therein done so with impunity. An account has been taken of all their deeds and of all whom they have wickedly destroyed, 89^{61-64}, and for all their victims there is laid up a recompense of reward, 90^{33}. Moreover, when the outlook is darkest, and the oppression at its worst, a righteous league will be established in Israel, 90^6; and in it there will be a family from which will come forth the deliverer of Israel, i.e. Judas Maccabeus, 90^{9-16}. The Syrians and other enemies of Israel will put forth every effort to destroy him, but in vain; for a great sword will be given to him wherewith to destroy his enemies, 90^{19}. Then all the hostile Gentiles will assemble for their final struggle against Israel, still led by Judas Maccabeus, $90^{13, 16}$; but this, their crowning act of wickedness, will also be the final act in their history and serve as the signal for their immediate judgement. God will appear in person, and the earth open its mouth and swallow them up, 90^{18}. The wicked shepherds will then be judged and the fallen watchers, and cast into an abyss of fire, 90$^{20-25}$. With the condemnation of the Apostates to Gehenna the great assize will close, 90^{26}. Then his New Jerusalem will be set up by God Himself, 90$^{28, 29}$; and the surviving Gentiles will be converted and serve Israel, 90^{30}; and all the Jews dispersed abroad will be gathered together, and all the righteous dead will be raised to take part in the kingdom, 90^{33}. Then the Messiah will appear amongst them, 90^{37}; and all the righteous will be gloriously transformed after his likeness, 90^{38}; and God will rejoice over them.

87-90 were written by a Chasid in support of the Maccabean movement.

LXXXIII—LXXXIV. *First Dream-Vision on the Deluge.*

LXXXIII. 1. And now, my son Methuselah, I will show thee all my visions which I have seen, recounting them before thee. 2. Two visions I saw before I took a wife, and the one was quite unlike the other: the first when I was learning to write: the second before I took thy mother, (when) I saw a terrible vision. And regarding them I prayed to the Lord.   3. I had laid me down in the house of my grandfather Mahalalel, (when) I saw in a vision how the heaven collapsed and was borne off and fell to the earth. 4. And when it fell to the earth I saw how the earth was swallowed up in a great abyss, and mountains were suspended on mountains, and hills sank down on hills, and high trees were rent from their stems, and hurled down and sunk in the abyss. 5. And thereupon a word fell into my mouth, and I lifted up

LXXXIII. 1. My visions (a–t). t, β 'visions'.   2. Before I took a wife, i.e. before I was sixty-five; cf. Gen. 5^{21}. The name of this wife was Edna, 85^3; cf. Book of Jubilees 4^{19}, where these dream-visions are referred to. We should observe that 83-90 are only dreams or dream-visions; whereas in the other Sections of the book Enoch has open intercourse with the angels, and is translated bodily and therein admitted to higher privileges than in mere visions. Yet if 83-90 came from the same hand as the other Sections, the converse should have been the case on *ascetic* grounds, and Enoch should have had his bodily translations to heaven and his intercourse with the angels during his unmarried years, and his dream-visions after he had taken a wife.   3. **Mahalalel**. In text it is Malāl'ēl.   5. **Lifted up** (my (my voice) to cry aloud, and said: 'The earth is destroyed.' 6. And my grandfather Mahalalel waked me as I lay near him, and said unto me: 'Why dost thou cry so, my son, and why dost thou make such lamentation?' 7. And I recounted to him the whole vision which I had seen, and he said unto me: 'A terrible thing hast thou seen, my son, and of grave moment is thy dream-vision as to the secrets of all the sin of the earth: it must sink into the abyss and be destroyed with a great destruction. 8. And now, my son, arise and make petition to the Lord of glory, since thou art a believer, that a remnant may remain on the earth, and that He may not destroy the whole earth. 9. My son, from heaven all this will come upon the earth, and upon the earth there will be great destruction.' 10. After that I arose and prayed and implored and besought, and wrote down my prayer for the generations of the world, and I will show everything to thee, my son Methuselah. 11. And when I had gone forth below and seen the heaven, and the sun rising in the east, and the moon setting in the west, and a few stars, and the whole earth, and everything as †He had known† it in the beginning, then I blessed the Lord of judgement and extolled Him because He had made the sun to go forth from the windows of the east, †and he ascended and rose on the face of the heaven, and set out and kept traversing the path shown unto him.

---

voice) (mqu, β-n). g 'arose'; t, n 'began'. 7. Secrets of all the sin (tu, β, save that tu, b read kuĕllû for kuĕllû). gm 'sin of all the sin'; q 'sin of all'. Perhaps q is right. gm could be explained as a dittograph of q and tu, β as an emendation of gm. 8. Lord of glory. Cf. 25^3 $27^{3,\,5}$ 36^4 40^3 63^2 75^3. And that He may not ... earth (t, β). > a-t through hmt.(?). 10. The prayer may be that given in 84^{2-6}. And besought (a-q). > q, β. My prayer (mt, β). g 'I prayed and'. > qu. 11. The whole earth (gmq, $cdfiloy$ $_1a$ $_1b$). > t, $abehknx$. As †He had known† it. Read 'a'ĕmarkû for 'a'emara, and translate 'as I had known it'. Otherwise it is possible that ἐνόησεν stood before the Ethiopic translator—a corruption of ἐποίησεν (Flemming), or that the Greek translator confused הֵבִין and הֵכִין. In the last case render 'as He had established'. Lord of judgement. Here only. Windows. This term is never used in 1-36 nor in 72-82 of the sun. Portal is the word invariably used in connexion with the sun. For the word 'windows' see 72^3 (note). †And he ascended. This cannot be right. What we require is 'so that he ascended', and so all translators,

LXXXIV. 1. And I lifted up my hands in righteousness and blessed the Holy and Great One, and spake with the breath of my mouth, and with the tongue of flesh, which God has made for the children of the flesh of men, that they should speak therewith, and He gave them breath and a tongue and a mouth that they should speak therewith:

2. 'Blessed be Thou, O Lord, King,
Great and mighty in Thy greatness,
Lord of the whole creation of the heaven,
King of kings and God of the whole world.

And Thy power and kingship and greatness abide for ever and ever,
And throughout all generations Thy dominion:
And all the heavens are Thy throne for ever,
And the whole earth Thy footstool for ever and ever.

3. For Thou hast made and Thou rulest all things,
And nothing is too hard for Thee,
Wisdom departs not from the place of Thy throne,
Nor turns away from Thy presence.

myself included, wrongly rendered the words. Hence I assume here a wrong punctuation of the Hebrew on the part of the Greek translator. Text = καὶ ἀνέβη καὶ ἀνέτειλε = וַיַּעַל וַיִּזְרַח, which should have been read as וַיַּעֲלֶה וְיִזְרַח. Then we should have 'so that he ascended and rose', &c.

LXXXIV. 1. *Enoch's Prayer for his Posterity*. The Holy and Great One: see 1³ note. Tongue of flesh: see 14². Children of the flesh of men (*gmt, abcfhiknx*). *u, delopy* ₁a ₁b 'children of men'; *q* 'children of men of flesh'. 2. Cf. 9⁴ seq. Lord of the whole creation of the heaven. Here only; cf. 82⁷, also 58⁴ (note). King of kings. Also in 9⁴. God of the whole world. Here only; see note on 1³. All the heavens are Thy throne, &c. From Is. 66¹. 3. Nothing is too hard for Thee (= ἀδυνατήσει παρὰ σοὶ οὐδέν). This clause is drawn from Jer. 32¹⁷, ז לא יפלא ממך כל דבר. Here the LXX render οὐ μὴ ἀποκρυβῇ ἀπὸ σοῦ οὐδέν. Cf. Gen. 18¹⁴. After this clause the text adds a dittograph = καὶ οὐδεμία or earlier καὶ οὐδέν. Departs not (*g*). Other MSS. 'departs not from Thee'. From the place of Thy throne, nor turns away. The text = 'nor turns away (*gqm* corrupt here) from her life (> *qu*), (+ from *mq*) Thy throne and'. By the simple transposition of the verb 'nor turns away' the parallelism of the text is restored. Further 'ĕmmanbartä (= 'from her life') has been emended into 'ĕmmĕnbârâta (= 'from the place'). Thus the phrase 'from the place of Thy throne' = ἀπὸ τοῦ τόπου τοῦ θρόνου σοῦ = מִמְּכוֹן כִּסְאֶךָ Ps. 89¹⁵. To re-

> And Thou knowest and seest and hearest everything,
> And there is nothing hidden from Thee [for Thou seest everything].

4. And now the angels of Thy heavens are guilty of trespass,
   And upon the flesh of men abideth Thy wrath until the great day of judgement.

5. And now, O God and Lord and Great King,
   I implore and beseech Thee to fulfil my prayer,
   To leave me a posterity on earth.
   And not to destroy all the flesh of man,
   And make the earth without inhabitant,
   So that there should be an eternal destruction.

6. And now, my Lord, destroy from the earth the flesh which has aroused Thy wrath,
   But the flesh of righteousness and uprightness establish as a plant of the eternal seed,
   And hide not Thy face from the prayer of Thy servant, O Lord.'

LXXXV—XC. *The Second Dream-Vision of Enoch: the History of the World to the Founding of the Messianic Kingdom.*

LXXXV. 1. And after this I saw another dream, and I will show the whole dream to thee, my son. 2. And Enoch lifted

---

turn to the word 'ĕmmanbartâ, which I have emended as above, we should observe that it does not admit of any reasonable rendering in this passage. The word means 'life', 'food', 'condition'. None of these meanings suit the passage. With the above passage we might compare Wisdom 9^4 'Wisdom that sitteth by Thee on Thy throne'. Wisdom is represented in both these passages as the assessor or $πάρεδρος$ of God. The idea is to be traced to Prov. 8^{30} in the LXX version $ἤμην παρ᾽ αὐτῷ$: cf. Sir. 1^1 $μετ᾽ αὐτοῦ ἐστιν εἰς τὸν αἰῶνα$. [For Thou seest everything]. A dittograph from the preceding line. 4. Upon the flesh of men: cf. vv. 1, 5, Job 12^{10}. Great day of judgement. Most MSS. read 'day of the great judgement'. See my text, which follows in part g and in part q; see 45^2 (note). This phrase can refer here only to the Deluge. In 19^1 it refers to the final judgement, and so always in 91–104; cf. 94^9 98^{10} 99^{15} 104^5. 5. Great King. Also in 91^{13}. 6. A plant of the eternal seed: see 10^{16} (note). This idea was a very favourite one; cf. 62^8 $93^{2, 5, 10}$.

LXXXV—XC. The second Dream-vision. In this second vision the up (his voice) and spake to his son Methuselah: 'To thee, my son, will I speak: hear my words—incline thine ear to the dream-vision of thy father. 3. Before I took thy mother Edna, I saw in a vision on my bed, and behold a bull came forth from the earth, and that bull was white; and after it came forth a heifer, and along with this (latter) came forth two bulls, one of them black and the other red. 4. And that black bull gored the red one and pursued him over the earth, and thereupon I could no longer see that red bull. 5. But that black bull grew and that heifer went with him, and I saw that many oxen proceeded from him which resembled and followed him. 6. And that cow, that first one, went from the presence of that first bull in

writer gives a complete history of the world from Adam down to the final judgement and the establishment of the Messianic kingdom. After the example of Ezekiel men are symbolized by animals. The leaders of the chosen race are represented by domestic animals, the patriarchs by bulls, and the faithful of later times by sheep (cf. Ezek. 34$^{5, 6, 8}$ seq.). This difference may be intended to mark the later declension of Israel in faith and righteousness. The Gentiles are symbolized by wild beasts and birds of prey (cf. Ezek. 39^{17}, where the enemies of Israel are symbolized by the birds of the air and the beasts of the field); the fallen watchers by stars; unfallen angels by men. At times the author is obliged to abandon his symbolism, and he is not always consistent in his use of it, as the same symbol varies in meaning. Even the divine name is adapted to the prevailing symbolism. In the main the narrative is based on the O. T., but at times mythical elements from later Jewish exegesis are incorporated.

LXXXV. 2. Cf. Prov. 5^1. 3. Edna: cf. 83^2. I saw in a vision on my bed. Cf. Dan. 4^{10} 'I saw in a vision of my head upon my bed' (also 4^7 7^1). On my bed (η, β). gmt 'of my bed'. u corrupt. Bull. The Ethiopic word is lâhm. This word has various meanings in the following chapters. In the sing. it = bull or heifer; in the plur. it = bulls, or cattle, or cows. The context must determine the sense. The author uses also the unequivocal word sôr, which always means a bull. Ṭâ'wâ = vitulus or vitula in these chapters. Eve is so designated in this verse, i. e. a heifer, to denote her as a virgin. In verse 6 she is called 'a cow'. White is the colour that symbolizes righteousness throughout this vision; cf. 85^8 87^2, &c. Cf. Is. 1^{18} Ps. 51^7 Rev. 7^{14}. Two bulls (g, α). Other MSS. 'other young bulls'. Cain is black, as this colour symbolizes his sin: Abel is red—the colour emblematic of his martyrdom. 4. Bull. So I render ṭâ'wâ when it = vitulus, as in vv. 4, 5, 6. 5. That heifer. The same word is used of Eve in verse 3. This heifer is Cain's wife, and according to the Book of Jubilees 4$^{1, 9}$ his sister, by name Avan. Oxen. This is the rendering of the plural of lâhm, and includes bulls and cows. Him^{30} (η, β). gmt 'them'. 6. Eve seeks Abel.

order to seek that red one, but found him not, and lamented with a great lamentation over him and sought him.   7. And I looked till that first bull came to her and quieted her, and from that time onward she cried no more.   8. And after that she bore another white bull, and after him she bore many bulls and black cows.

9. And I saw in my sleep that white bull likewise grow and become a great white bull, and from him proceeded many white bulls, and they resembled him.   10. And they began to beget many white bulls, which resembled them, one following the other, (even) many.

The Fall of the Angels and the Demoralization of Mankind.

LXXXVI. 1. And again I saw with mine eyes as I slept, and I saw the heaven above, and behold a star fell from heaven, and it arose and eat and pastured amongst those oxen.   2. And after that I saw the large and the black oxen, and behold they all changed their stalls and pastures and their cattle, and began to live with each other.   3. And again I saw in the vision, and looked towards the heaven, and behold I saw many stars descend

Over him (dibêhû *q*). *g* 'with regard to him' (habêhû); *mt*, *β* 'thereupon' (sôbêhâ). According to Jub. 4⁷ 'Adam and Eve mourned for Abel twenty-eight years'. In 'mourning' there is here as in our text a play on the word Abel, though the former is אבל and the latter הבל.   8. **Another white bull** (*mt*, *β*). *gqu* 'a pair of white oxen', i.e. Seth and a sister to be his wife. On the latter see Jub. 4⁸, ¹¹.   **Black cows.** The adjective 'black' belongs probably to the 'bulls' also.   9. **Bull.** Rendering of sôr; see verse 3. This bull is Seth. The descendants of Seth are likewise righteous like their progenitor. **Many** (gmqt). > *β*.

LXXXVI. 1. **A star**, i.e. Azazel. Cf. 88¹ 10⁴ ***. According to Jalkut Shim. Ber. 44 (see Weber, *Jüd. Theol.* 253) Azazel and Shemjaza descended together, but only the former was guilty of sin with the daughters of men. 2. **And after that** (*β*). *mq* 'and these'; *t* 'and in the midst'; *u* 'and'. > *g*.   **To live with each other.** *g* reads jaḥajĕwû = 'to live one to another'; *a–g*, *β* ja'awajewû, 'to lament one to ('with' *β*) another'. The latter reading is not satisfactory. The black bulls did not leave their pastures, &c. simply to engage in lamentation. The time for lamentation does not arrive till verse 6. Thus ja'awajĕwû may be an emendation of *g* jaḥajĕwû. But the construction that follows 'one to another' (*a*) seems impossible. If we read 'to live' we must adopt the *β* text in what follows, i.e. 'with each and cast themselves down from heaven to that first star, and they became bulls amongst those cattle and pastured with them [amongst them]. 4. And I looked at them and saw, and behold they all let out their privy members, like horses, and began to cover the cows of the oxen, and they all became pregnant and bare elephants, camels, and asses. 5. And all the oxen feared them and were affrighted at them, and began to bite with their teeth and to devour, and to gore with their horns. 6. And they began moreover to devour those oxen; and behold all the children of the earth began to tremble and quake before them and to flee from them.

The Advent of the Seven Archangels.

LXXXVII. 1. And again I saw how they began to gore each other and to devour each other, and the earth began to cry aloud. 2. And I raised mine eyes again to heaven, and I saw in the vision, and behold there came forth from heaven beings who were like white men: and four went forth from that place and three with them. 3. And those three that had last come forth grasped me by my hand and took me up, away from the generations of the earth, and raised me up to a lofty place, and showed me a tower raised high above the earth, and all the hills were

---

other'. 3. Fall of the rest of the angels. Became bulls amongst those cattle and pastured with them (a). β 'were amongst those cattle and bulls, pasturing with them'. 4. Elephants, camels, and asses. Symbolizing the three kinds of giants; see 7² (note). 6. The children of the earth. The writer here forgets his rôle, and uses non-symbolical language. From them (gm). > other MSS.

LXXXVII. 1. The conflict of the bulls and giants. 2. And I saw in the vision. > qu. Beings who were like white men, i.e. unfallen angels. As men are represented by animals, the unfallen angels are naturally represented by men. White: cf. 85³. Four (a). β 'one'. Four . . . and three with them. On these seven archangels see 81⁵ 90²¹,²² 20. The three are found again in 90³¹. With them (m). a-m, β 'with him'. 3, 4. If we are to regard this high tower as Paradise, and it seems we must, as according to the universal tradition of later times Enoch was translated thither, we have in 83–90 a conception of its locality and inhabitants differing from any that has preceded; see 60⁸ (note). 3. All the hills were lower (t, β), a-t lower.   4. And one said unto me: "Remain here till thou seest everything that befalls those elephants, camels, and asses, and the stars and the oxen, and all of them."

The Punishment of the Fallen Angels by the Archangels.

LXXXVIII. 1. And I saw one of those four who had come forth first, and he seized that first star which had fallen from the heaven, and bound it hand and foot and cast it into an abyss: now that abyss was narrow and deep, and horrible and dark. 2. And one of them drew a sword, and gave it to those elephants and camels and asses: then they began to smite each other, and the whole earth quaked because of them.   3. And as I was beholding in the vision, lo, one of those four who had come forth stoned (them) from heaven, and gathered and took all the great stars whose privy members were like those of horses, and bound them all hand and foot, and cast them in an abyss of the earth.

'it was built all the hills' (sic).   4. One said ($a-q$. $ceʃhik$). q, $β-ceʃhik$ 'they said'. Oxen and all of them ($a-u$). u, $β$ 'and all the oxen'.

LXXXVIII—LXXXIX. 1. There is a very close connexion between this Section and chapter 10^{1-12}. Thus 88^1, which treats of Azazel, refers to 10^{4-8}, 88^2 (of Gabriel) refers to 10^{9-10}, 88^3 (of Michael) refers to 10^{11-12}, and 89^1 (of Uriel) refers to 10^{1-3}. Thus the text here clearly presupposes chapter 10, but not quite in its present form, as Lawlor, *Journal Philol.*, 1897, pp. 187-189 supposes. For only one leader is here referred to, i.e. Azazel 86^1 88^1, whereas in 10^{11} a second leader is associated with Shemjaza. 1. It is Raphael who here casts Azazel into the desert named Beth Chaduda. See 10^{4-8}.   2. Gabriel deals here with the giant offspring of the angels and the women. Cf. 10^{9-10}. And camels (t, $β$). > $a-l$.   3. Michael deals with the fallen angels. There is no mention here of any leader such as Shemjaza, whom we find specially named in 10^{11}. Cf. 10^{12-13}. *Who had come forth stoned (them) from heaven.* The text seems corrupt. Either emend wagara (= 'stoned') into warada (= 'descended') and read 'who had come forth descended from heaven', or transpose 'from heaven' before 'stoned'; then we have 'who had come forth from heaven (cf. 87^2) stoned'. I should add here that after wagara n adds saifa = 'sword'. The phrase would then be rendered 'hurled a sword'. As regards the number of the verbs 'gathered' and 'took' the MSS. vary. $β$ reads the singular in each case, supported in the former by tu and in the latter by mt.

LXXXIX. 1-9. *The Deluge and the Deliverance of Noah.*

LXXXIX. 1. And one of those four went to that white bull and instructed him in a secret, without his being terrified: he was born a bull and became a man, and built for himself a great vessel and dwelt thereon; and three bulls dwelt with him in that vessel and they were covered in. 2. And again I raised mine eyes towards heaven and saw a lofty roof, with seven water torrents thereon, and those torrents flowed with much water into an enclosure. 3. And I saw again, and behold fountains were opened on the surface of that great enclosure, and that water began to swell and rise upon the surface, and I saw that enclosure till all its surface was covered with water. 4. And the water, the darkness, and mist increased upon it; and as I looked at the height of that water, that water had risen above the height of that enclosure, and was streaming over that enclosure, and it stood upon the earth. 5. And all the cattle of that enclosure were gathered together until I saw how they sank and were swallowed up and perished in that water. 6. But that vessel floated on the water, while all the oxen and elephants and camels and asses sank to the bottom with all the animals, so that I could no longer see them, and they were not able to escape, (but) perished and sank into the depths. 7. And again I saw in the vision till those water torrents were removed from that high roof, and the chasms of the earth were levelled up and

---

LXXXIX. 1-9. The Deluge and the Deliverance of Noah. **1.** Cf. 10¹⁻³, where Uriel visits Noah for the same end. **To that white bull** (*m*₁, *a–m, β* 'those white bulls'. **Without his being terrified** (*gqu*). *mt, β* 'terrified as he was'. In order to build the Ark, Noah is represented as becoming a man. **Three bulls.** Noah's three sons. **Covered in:** cf. Gen. 7¹⁶ 1 En. 67². **2.** As men are symbolized by animals, their place of habitation is naturally called a pen, fold, or enclosure. **Seven:** cf. 77⁴ (note). **3, 4. The Deluge. 3. Saw**¹⁰ (= ré'lkwò *u*). *g* 'er'ejò, *η* r'ĕjò, *t, β* 'ljär'ajò = 'caused it not to be seen'. **6. With all the animals,** i.e. the real animals. **7. The chasms of the earth,** &c. The writer conceived the flood as having been caused by a cleaving of the depths of the earth—cf. Gen. 7¹¹—and the staying of the flood as having been due to a closing or levelling up of these clefts or chasms. Cf. Jub. 6²⁶ 'The mouths of the depths of the abyss ... were closed' and Prayer of Manasses 3 ὁ κλείσας τὴν other abysses were opened.   8. Then the water began to run down into these, till the earth became visible; but that vessel settled on the earth, and the darkness retired and light appeared. 9. But that white bull which had become a man came out of that vessel, and the three bulls with him, and one of those three was white like that bull, and one of them was red as blood, and one black: and that white bull departed from them.

LXXXIX. 10-27. *From the Death of Noah to the Exodus.*

10. And they began to bring forth beasts of the field and birds, so that there arose different genera: lions, tigers, wolves, dogs, hyenas, wild boars, foxes, squirrels, swine, falcons, vultures, kites, eagles, and ravens; and among them was born a white bull.   11. And they began to bite one another; but that white bull which was born amongst them begat a wild ass and a white bull with it, and the wild asses multiplied.   12. But that bull which was born from him begat a black wild boar and a white sheep; and the former begat many boars, but that sheep begat twelve sheep.   13. And when those twelve sheep had grown, they gave up one of them to the asses, and those asses

ἄβυσσον.   9. Noah and his three sons. And one black (β). > a.   That white bull departed from them, i.e. Noah died.   10. The necessities of his subject oblige the author to mar the naturalness of his symbolism. His cattle produce all manner of four-footed beasts and birds of prey. Nearly all these appear later as the enemies of Israel; cf. Ezek. 39¹⁷.   Different genera. Here 'ahzāb means races not merely of man but of all kinds of animals. Flemming has rightly pointed out that hebr here should be written ḥebr, and not ḥebr as Dillmann takes it. 'ĕmkuĕllū ḥĕbr = διάφορα as in Deut. 22⁹.   A white bull, i.e. Abraham. 11. The wild ass is Ishmael, the progenitor of the Arabs or Midianites, who in vv. 13, 16 are called the 'wild asses', which is on the whole an apt designation; cf. Gen. 16¹².   The 'white bull' is Isaac.   The wild asses (ᾱ, *abdiklnax*₁*a*). cefh 'the wild ass'.   12. A black wild boar, i.e. Esau. Later Jewish hatred thus expresses itself in associating Edom with the name of the animal it detested most; cf. vv. 42, 43, 49, 66. In ver. 72 it is used of the Samaritans.   A white sheep, i.e. Jacob. Israel is specially in the symbolic language of the O.T. the sheep of God's pasture, Pss. 74¹ 79¹³ 100³ Jer. 23¹, and hence there is a peculiar fitness in representing the individual who first bore the name as a white sheep. The idea of declension in faith (see p. 186) can hardly attach to this instance of its use.   13. One of them, i.e. Joseph. The asses, the Midianites; cf. vv. 11, again gave up that sheep to the wolves, and that sheep grew up among the wolves. 14. And the Lord brought the eleven sheep to live with it and to pasture with it among the wolves: and they multiplied and became many flocks of sheep. 15. And the wolves began to fear them, and they oppressed them until they destroyed their little ones, and they cast their young into a river of much water: but those sheep began to cry aloud on account of their little ones, and to complain unto their Lord. 16. And a sheep which had been saved from the wolves fled and escaped to the wild asses; and I saw the sheep how they lamented and cried, and besought their Lord with all their might, till that Lord of the sheep descended at the voice of the sheep from a lofty abode, and came to them and pastured them. 17. And He called that sheep which had escaped the wolves, and spake with it concerning the wolves that it should admonish them not to touch the sheep. 18. And the sheep went to the wolves according to the word of the Lord, and another sheep met it and went with it, and the two went and entered together into the assembly of those wolves, and spake with them and admonished them not to touch the sheep from henceforth. 19. And thereupon I saw the wolves, and how they oppressed the sheep exceedingly with all their power; and the sheep cried aloud. 20. And the Lord came to the sheep and they began to smite those wolves: and the wolves began to make lamentation; but the sheep became quiet and forthwith ceased to cry out. 21. And I saw the sheep till they departed from amongst the wolves; but the eyes of the wolves were blinded, and those wolves departed in pursuit of the sheep with all their power. 22. And the Lord of the sheep went with them, as their leader, and all His sheep followed Him: and His face was

---

16. **The wolves**, i. e. the Egyptians—henceforth their standing designation in this vision. 16. **A sheep which had been saved**, i. e. Moses. **Lord of the sheep.** This title is the usual one in this and the following chapters, and occurs about twenty-eight times. 18. **Another sheep**, i.e. Aaron. **Met it** (*a-t*). *t, β-il* 'met that sheep'. **Went and** (*ymy*). > *tu, β*. 20. The plagues of Egypt. **They began** (*a-m*). *m, β* 'He began'. 21–27.

dazzling and glorious and terrible to behold. 23. But the wolves began to pursue those sheep till they reached a sea of water. 24. And that sea was divided, and the water stood on this side and on that before their face, and their Lord led them and placed Himself between them and the wolves. 25. And as those wolves did not yet see the sheep, they proceeded into the midst of that sea, and the wolves followed the sheep, and [those wolves] ran after them into that sea. 26. And when they saw the Lord of the sheep, they turned to flee before His face, but that sea gathered itself together, and became as it had been created, and the water swelled and rose till it covered those wolves. 27. And I saw till all the wolves who pursued those sheep perished and were drowned.

LXXXIX. 28-40. *Israel in the Desert, the Giving of the Law, the Entrance into Palestine.*

28. But the sheep escaped from that water and went forth into a wilderness, where there was no water and no grass; and they began to open their eyes and to see; and I saw the Lord of the sheep pasturing them and giving them water and grass, and that sheep going and leading them. 29. And that sheep ascended to the summit of that lofty rock, and the Lord of the sheep sent it to them. 30. And after that I saw the Lord of the sheep who stood before them, and His appearance was great and terrible and majestic, and all those sheep saw Him and were afraid before His face. 31. And they all feared and trembled because of Him, and they cried to that sheep with them [which

---

The Exodus from Egypt. 22. Glorious and terrible to behold (*gmt*). *qu* 'terrible to behold', β-a 'His appearance was terrible and glorious'. 24. Led them (*u*). Other MSS. 'leading them'. In the latter MSS. we must excise the following 'and'. 28. Began to open their eyes, i.e. to recover their spiritual vision and return to God; cf. 89³², ³³, ⁴¹, ⁴⁴, ⁵⁴ 90⁶, ⁹, ¹⁰,

²⁶, ³³. And to see (*mtu*, β). *gq* 'and they saw'. 29. Moses' ascent of Sinai and return to Israel at God's command, Exod. 19. 30. Great and (*a*). > β-v. 31. That sheep with them, i.e. Aaron. With them (*gmq*). *t*, β 'with him'. [Which was amongst them] (*gu*). Bracketed as a dittograph. *mqt*, β 'to the other sheep which was among

was amongst them]: "We are not able to stand before our Lord or to behold Him." 32. And that sheep which led them again ascended to the summit of that rock, but the sheep began to be blinded and to wander from the way which he had showed them, but that sheep wot not thereof. 33. And the Lord of the sheep was wrathful exceedingly against them, and that sheep discovered it, and went down from the summit of the rock, and came to the sheep, and found the greatest part of them blinded and fallen away. 34. And when they saw it they feared and trembled at its presence, and desired to return to their folds. 35. And that sheep took other sheep with it, and came to those sheep which had fallen away, and began to slay them; and the sheep feared its presence, and thus that sheep brought back those sheep that had fallen away, and they returned to their folds. 36. And I saw in this vision till that sheep became a man and built a house for the Lord of the sheep, and placed all the sheep in that house. 37. And I saw till this sheep which had met that sheep which led them fell asleep: and I saw till all the great sheep perished and little ones arose in their place, and they came to a pasture, and approached a stream of water. 38. Then that sheep, their leader which had become a man, withdrew from them and fell asleep, and all the sheep sought it and cried over it with a great crying. 39. And I saw till they left off crying for that sheep and crossed that stream of water, and there arose the two sheep as leaders in the place of those which had led them and fallen asleep (lit. "had fallen asleep and

('with' *q*) them'. 32. Cf. Exod. 24¹³ ᵇᵉᵍ. 32. Again ascended or 're-turned and ascended'. 33. Fallen away. + 'from His path' β. 34. It, i.e. Moses. Return to their folds, i.e. to abandon their errors. 35. Cf. Exod. 32²⁴⁻²⁹. And³⁰. + 'after that' *t*, β. 36. In this vision (*a*-*u*). β 'there a vision'. That sheep, i.e. Moses becomes a man to build the tabernacle; cf. vv. 1, 9. Placed all the sheep in that house, i.e. made the tabernacle the centre of their worship. 37. Death of Aaron and of all the generation that had gone out of Egypt. That sheep (*t*, β). So *g*, but corrupt. *mu* defective. > *q*. Led them (*a*). β 'led the sheep'. Pasture. The land to the east of Jordan. A stream. The Jordan. 38. Death of Moses; cf. Deut. 34. 39. Two sheep as leaders. Joshua and Caleb. For 'the two' the text reads kuĕllōmū (= 'all') led them"). 40. And I saw till the sheep came to a goodly place, and a pleasant and glorious land, and I saw till those sheep were satisfied; and that house stood amongst them in the pleasant land.

LXXXIX. 41-50. *From the Time of the Judges till the Building of the Temple.*

41. And sometimes their eyes were opened, and sometimes blinded, till another sheep arose and led them and brought them all back, and their eyes were opened.

42. And the dogs and the foxes and the wild boars began to devour those sheep till the Lord of the sheep raised up [another sheep] a ram from

Greek fragment from Vatican MS., published by Mai, *Patrum Nova Bibliotheca*, t. ii, deciphered by Gildemeister in the *ZDMG*, 1855, pp. 621, 622.

Ἐκ τοῦ τοῦ Ἐνὼχ βιβλίου χρῆσις.

42. Καὶ οἱ κύνες ἤρξαντο κατεσθίειν τὰ πρόβατα καὶ οἱ ὕες

which I have emended into kĕl'ĕhŏmū = 'the two'. 40. Palestine; cf. 26¹. Observe that the epithet 'glorious' is used in the same connexion by Dan. 11¹⁶,⁴¹. 41-50. History of the times from the Judges to the building of the Temple. Of vv. 42-49 there is preserved a valuable fragment of the Greek version. This was published by Mai from a Vatican MS. in the *Patrum Nova Bibliotheca*, t. ii. I have given this fragment for purposes of comparison with the English version of the Ethiopic. Amongst other things the reader can observe how frequently the Greek article is translated by the Ethiopic demonstrative. Furthermore, the ἑξῆς which occurs between two verses belonging immediately to each other, i.e. 46, 47, and the φησίν inserted in ver. 47 prove that the collector of these Greek excerpts had not the complete Enoch before him, but drew them from an author who had brought together passages from Enoch and annotated them. So Gildemeister, *Zeitschrift D. M. G.*, 1855, pp. 621 sqq. 41. Periods of religious advance and declension: work of Samuel. 42. The dogs and the foxes and the wild boars. The 'dogs' are, according to vv. 46, 47, the Philistines. The 'foxes' are taken by Dillmann to be the Amalekites, but this interpretation will not suit ver. 55, where the foxes are still notable foes of Israel close on the time of the Exile, whereas the Amalekites practically disappear from history with the reign of David. We shall most probably be right in taking the 'foxes' to mean the Ammonites. From the earliest times down to the wars of the Maccabees the Ammonites were always the unrelenting foes of Israel. This is the view also of the glosser on the Greek Fragment, vv. 42-49. The 'wild boars' are the Edomites; cf. vv. 12, 43, 49, 66. Till the their midst, which led them. 43. And that ram began to butt on either side those dogs, foxes, and wild boars till he had destroyed them †all†. 44. And that sheep whose eyes were opened saw that ram, which was amongst the sheep, till it †forsook its glory† and began to butt those sheep, and trampled upon them, and behaved itself unseemly. 45. And the Lord of the sheep sent the lamb to another lamb and raised it to being a ram and leader of the sheep instead of that ram which had †for-

καὶ οἱ ἀλώπεκες κατήσθιον αὐτά, μέχρι οὗ ἤγειρεν ὁ κύριος τῶν προβάτων κριὸν ἕνα ἐκ τῶν προβάτων. 43. Καὶ ὁ κριὸς οὗτος ἤρξατο κερατίζειν καὶ ἐπιδιώκειν ἐν τοῖς κέρασιν καὶ ἐνετίνασσεν εἰς τοὺς ἀλώπεκας καὶ μετ' αὐτοὺς εἰς τοὺς ὕας καὶ ἀπώλεσεν ὕας πολλοὺς καὶ μετ' αὐτοὺς ... τὸ τοὺς κύνας. 44. Καὶ τὰ πρόβατα ὧν οἱ ὀφθαλμοὶ ἠνοίγησαν ἐθεάσοντο τὸν κριὸν τὸν ἐν τοῖς προβάτοις, ἕως οὗ ἀφῆκεν τὴν ὁδὸν αὐτοῦ καὶ ἤρξατο πορεύεσθαι †ἀνοδίᾳ. 45. Καὶ ὁ κύριος τῶν προβάτων ἀπέστειλεν τὸν ἄρνα τοῦτον ἐπὶ

Lord of the sheep raised up. So *g, n*. This reading is confirmed by the Greek μέχρι οὗ ἤγειρεν ὁ κύριος τῶν προβάτων κριὸν ἕνα. Other MSS. give 'till another sheep, the Lord of the sheep, arose'. The words 'another sheep' are a gloss, and we should render 'raised up a ram from their midst'. **43. Destroyed them †all†.** The Greek text (ἀπώλεσεν πολλούς) is here decidedly better. Saul by no means destroyed them all. **44. That sheep whose eyes were opened.** This phrase as applied to Samuel here cannot be used in the sense of spiritual awakening and return to God which it has elsewhere in this vision; cf. ver. 28 (note). Here it must mean the prophetic gift of insight as in 1². The Greek version certainly escapes this difficulty by applying the phrase in its usual sense to the sheep, and is probably the true text. **Till.** The MSS. = ὡς corrupt for ἕως. **†For**sook its glory†** = ἀφῆκεν τὴν δόξαν αὐτοῦ. For δόξαν the Greek reads ὁδόν. If the suffix αὐτοῦ refers to the subject of the verb, i.e. Saul, then 'forsook his way' can hardly be right. Perhaps דרכו (= ὁδὸν αὐτοῦ) is corrupt for דרך יי in the earlier script, i.e. 'the way of the Lord'. In 89⁵⁴ we have the expression 'the house of the Lord' = בית יי. Hence here and in ver. 45 we should probably read 'the way of the Lord' instead of 'its glory'. **45, 46. David anointed king.** Observe that in ver. 45 the Greek used ἄρνα and not πρόβατον for Samuel and for David so long as the latter is not yet king, where the Ethiopic employs the more general term 'sheep'. Observe further that Solomon previous to his coronation, ver. 48ᵇ, is called 'a little sheep', i.e. a lamb. I have followed the Greek, reading 'the lamb' twice where the Ethiopic has 'the sheep'. **45. That ram.** All MSS. except *d* read saken its glory†. 46. And it went to it and spake to it alone, and raised it to being a ram, and made it the prince and leader of the sheep; but during all these things those dogs oppressed the sheep. 47. And the first ram pursued that second ram, and that second ram arose and fled before it; and I saw till those dogs pulled down the first ram. 48. And that second ram arose and led the [little] sheep. 49. And those sheep grew and multiplied; but all the dogs, and foxes, and wild boars feared and fled before it, and that ram butted and killed the wild beasts, and those

ἄρνα ἕτερον τοῦ στῆσαι αὐτὸν εἰς κριὸν ἐν ἀρχῇ τῶν προβάτων ἀντὶ τοῦ κριοῦ τοῦ ἀφέντος τὴν ὁδὸν αὐτοῦ. 46. Καὶ ἐπορεύθη πρὸς αὐτὸν καὶ ἐλάλησεν αὐτῷ σιγῇ κατὰ μόνας καὶ ἤγειρεν αὐτὸν εἰς κριὸν καὶ εἰς ἄρχοντα καὶ εἰς ἡγούμενον τῶν προβάτων καὶ οἱ κύνες ἐπὶ πᾶσι τούτοις ἔθλιβον τὰ πρόβατα. 47. [Ἑξῆς δὲ τούτοις γέγραπται ὅτι] ὁ κριὸς ὁ πρῶτος τὸν κριὸν τὸν δεύτερον ἐπεδίωκεν καὶ ἔφυγεν ἀπὸ προσώπου αὐτοῦ· εἶτ' ἐθεώρουν, [φησίν], τὸν κριὸν τὸν πρῶτον ἕως οὗ ἔπεσεν ἔμπροσθεν τῶν κυνῶν. 48. Καὶ ὁ κριὸς ὁ δεύτερος ἀναπηδήσας ἀφηγήσατο τῶν προβάτων. 49. Καὶ τὰ πρόβατα ηὐξήθησαν καὶ ἐπληθύνθησαν· καὶ πάντες οἱ

'that sheep'. d 'that ram, sheep' (sic). Greek alone right. 46. During all these things = ἐπὶ πάντων τούτων. But the Greek has the dative = 'in addition to all these things'. 48. Led the sheep. So Greek. Ethiopic MSS. give 'led the little sheep'. But the word 'little' should be omitted, as it is wanting in the Greek, and the expression 'little sheep' is pointless here, and found but once before in ver. 37. It crept into the text from the next line. The rest of the verse, 48ᵇ, I have transposed after ver. 49. Ver. 49 recounts the victories of David; ver. 48ᵇ his death and the accession of Solomon. This passage is wanting in the Greek, but this is so only because the fragment ends with ver. 49, at the close of which these words originally stood. Thus they form a natural transition to the account of the temple. A further and stronger reason for their genuineness is the phrase 'a little sheep' applied to Solomon, previous to his becoming king. This phrase has nothing derogatory in it, but can only be a loose rendering of ἀμνός, 'lamb,' applied also to David previous to his being appointed king, see ver. 45. Evidently the Ethiopic translator did not feel the technical use of the word, as he has obliterated it altogether in ver. 45. Thus, as the technical term is not found in the Ethiopic in this connexion, an Ethiopic interpolator could not have produced this manifest, though imperfect, form of it. 48ᵇ. A little sheep, i. e. lamb; see vv. 45, 46 (note). 49. This is a description of the reign wild beasts had no longer any power among the sheep and robbed them no more of aught. 48ᵇ. And that ram begat many sheep and fell asleep; and a little sheep became ram in its stead, and became prince and leader of those sheep.

κύνες καὶ οἱ ἀλώπεκες ἔφυγον ἀπ' αὐτοῦ καὶ ἐφοβοῦντο αὐτόν.

50. And that house became great and broad, and it was built for those sheep: ⟨and⟩ a tower lofty and great was built on the house for the Lord of the sheep, and that house was low, but the tower was elevated and lofty, and the Lord of the sheep stood on that tower and they offered a full table before Him.

LXXXIX. 51-67. *The Two Kingdoms of Israel and Judah to the Destruction of Jerusalem.*

51. And again I saw those sheep that they again erred and went many ways, and forsook that their house, and the Lord of the sheep called some from amongst the sheep and sent them to the sheep, but the sheep began to slay them. 52. And one of them was saved and was not slain, and it sped away and cried aloud over the sheep; and they sought to slay it, but the Lord of the sheep saved it from the sheep, and brought it up to me,

of David. 50. **That house.** As Dillmann shows by a comparison of vv. 56, 66 sq., 72 sq., and the passage in Test. Levi 10⁵ ὁ γὰρ οἶκος, ὃν ἂν ἐκλέξεται κύριος, Ἰερουσαλὴμ κληθήσεται, καθὼς περιέχει ἡ βίβλος Ἐνὼχ τοῦ δικαίου, this house is Jerusalem and the tower is the temple. **It was built for those sheep: ⟨and⟩ a tower lofty and great was built on the house** (*gmt, ilno* ₁*a*₁*b*, save that *mt, in* insert 'that' before 'house'). β–*ilno* ₁*a*₁*b* 'it was built for those sheep ⟨and⟩ a high tower on the house', *q* 'it was built for those sheep ⟨and⟩ a lofty tower was built'. I have added ⟨and⟩ and yet it is after a fashion found in *m, ilno* ₁*a*₁*b,* for after 'tower' they add 'lofty on that house *and* a tower'— a dittograph of some sort. **A full table,** i. e. offerings and sacrifices. 51-67. Gradual declension of Israel till the destruction of the Temple. 51. **Forsook ... their house.** True only of the Ten Tribes. **That their house** = τὸν οἶκον αὐτῶν. Here, as in ver. 53, the Ethiopic translator renders the art. by a demonstrative. **Called some ... and sent them,** i. e. the prophets. **Slay.** Cf. 1 Kings 18⁴. 52. Escape and translation of Elijah; cf. 1 Kings 19 2 Kings 2¹¹ 1 Enoch 93⁸.

and caused it to dwell there. 53. And many other sheep He sent to those sheep to testify unto them and lament over them. 54. And after that I saw that when they forsook the house of the Lord and His tower they fell away entirely, and their eyes were blinded; and I saw the Lord of the sheep how He wrought much slaughter amongst them in their herds until those sheep invited that slaughter and betrayed His place. 55. And He gave them over into the hands of the lions and tigers, and wolves and hyenas, and into the hand of the foxes, and to all the wild beasts, and those wild beasts began to tear in pieces those sheep. 56. And I saw that He forsook that their house and their tower and gave them all into the hand of the lions, to tear and devour them, into the hand of all the wild beasts. 57. And I began to cry aloud with all my power, and to appeal to the Lord of the sheep, and to represent to Him in regard to the sheep that they were devoured by all the wild beasts. 58. But He remained unmoved, though He saw it, and rejoiced that they were devoured and swallowed and robbed, and left them to be devoured in the hand of all the beasts. 59. And He called seventy

From the sheep (*gm*). Other MSS. 'from the hands of the sheep'. 53, 54. The fruitless activity of the prophets, and the complete apostasy of the nation owing to their abandonment of the Temple. 54. Forsook the house... and His tower. Judah and Benjamin did not forsake Jerusalem and the Temple, but apparently our author treats the Twelve Tribes in their solidarity. Of the Lord. + 'of the sheep' β. Invited that slaughter and betrayed His place, i. e. called in heathen nations to help them and so betrayed Jerusalem. Thus Ahaz hired Tiglath-pilezer, king of Assyria, to help him against Rezin, king of Syria, 2 Kings 16⁷ ⁷⁴⁺. 55. The final fortunes of the two kingdoms and the names of their oppressors. Lions and tigers, i. e. the Assyrians and Babylonians. In vv. 56, 65 (?), where the lions alone are mentioned, the Babylonians are meant. The 'wolves' are the Egyptians; cf. ver. 13. The 'hyenas', Martin suggests, are the Syrians, but they are symbolized by the 'ravens' in 90⁸ ⁹ ¹³: they may be the Ethiopians. 56. This verse describes how God gradually withdrew from the degraded Theocracy and gave Israel defenceless into the hands of its enemies. To ... devour. The prophets use the same figure and phraseology in regard to the destruction of Israel by the heathen; cf. Jer. 12⁹ Is. 56⁹ Ezek. 34⁵ ⁸. Barnabas 16⁵ refers to this verse: λέγει γὰρ ἡ γραφή· καὶ ἔσται ἐπ' ἐσχάτων τῶν ἡμερῶν καὶ παραδώσει κύριος τὰ πρόβατα τῆς νομῆς καὶ τὴν μάνδραν καὶ τὸν πύργον αὐτῶν εἰς καταφθοράν. 57. Lord of the sheep. *gmq* read 'Lord of the lions'. The wild beasts. > *g*. 59. Seventy (β). α 'seven'. The shepherds, and cast those sheep to them that they might pasture them, and He spake to the shepherds and their companions: "Let each individual of you pasture the sheep henceforward, and

seventy shepherds. This is the most vexed question in Enoch. The earliest interpreters took the first thirty-seven shepherds to mean the native kings of Israel and Judah. It was Ewald's merit to point out that this was a conception impossible for a Jew, and that the seventy shepherds must represent so many heathen oppressors of Israel. This interpretation has undergone many forms, but all alike have proved unsatisfactory; cf. Gebhardt's 'Die 70 Hirten des Buches Henoch u. ihre Deutungen' in Merx's *Archiv f. Wissenschaftl. Erforschung*, 1871, pp. 163-246. To Hoffmann, *Schriftbeweis*, i. 422, is due the credit of giving the only possible and satisfactory explanation. This explanation, which has been accepted by Schürer, Drummond, Wieseler, Schodde, Thomson, and Deane, interprets the shepherds as angels and not as men; and that his interpretation is the true one there is no further room for doubt. For (1) the seventy shepherds exist *contemporaneously*, and are summoned *together* before the Lord of the sheep to receive their commission, 89[59]. This could not be said of either native or Gentile rulers. (2) The shepherds are appointed to protect the sheep, 89[75], and to allow only a limited portion of them to be destroyed by the Gentiles. This could not be said of heathen rulers. (3) Jews and Gentiles and their kings also are alike symbolized by animals. Hence the shepherds cannot symbolize men. If not men, they are angels. (4) In the earlier history God was the true shepherd of Israel, but on its apostasy He withdrew from it and committed its pasturing to seventy of His angels. With the growing transcendence of God, His place was naturally taken by angels. (5) The angel who records the doings of the seventy shepherds is simply named 'another', 89[61], in connexion with them, and so naturally belongs to the same category. (6) In the last judgement they are classed with the fallen angels, 90[21-25]. (7) God speaks directly to the shepherds and not through the medium of angels as elsewhere in the book. The idea of the seventy shepherds is used by the author to explain some pressing difficulties in Israel's history. So long as God was the immediate shepherd of Israel, it was not possible for such calamities to befall it as it experienced from the Captivity onwards. Israel, therefore, during the latter period was not shepherded by God but by angels commissioned by Him. But again, though God rightly forsook Israel and committed it to the care of angels, though, further, Israel was rightly punished for its sins, yet the author and the Jews generally believed that they were punished with undue severity, indeed, twofold more grievously than they deserved (Is. 40[2]). How was this to be accounted for? The answer was not far to seek. It was owing to the faithlessness with which the angels discharged their trust. Had they only fulfilled their commission, the Gentiles could not have made havoc of Israel and apostate Jews only could have been cut off. There may be some distant connexion between the seventy angels here and the seventy guardian angels of the Gentile nations; cf. Weber, 170 sq. The theory of the everything that I shall command you that do ye. 60. And I will deliver them over unto you duly numbered, and tell you which of them are to be destroyed—and them destroy ye." And He gave over unto them those sheep. 61. And He called another and spake unto him: "Observe and mark everything that the shepherds will do to those sheep; for they will destroy more of them than I have commanded them. 62. And every excess and the destruction which will be wrought through the shepherds, record (namely) how many they destroy according to my command, and how many according to their own caprice: record against every individual shepherd all the destruction he effects. 63. And read out before me by number how many they destroy, and how many they deliver over for destruction, that I may have this as a testimony against them, and know every deed of the shepherds, that I may comprehend and see what they do, whether or

---

seventy shepherds is a development of the seventy years of Jeremiah, just as the writer of Daniel had seen in Jeremiah's seventy years seventy periods, and the four divisions into which the seventy shepherds fall correspond to the four world empires in Daniel. It is idle, however, to seek for chronological exactness in the four periods into which the writer of Enoch divides all history between the fall of Jerusalem and the Messianic kingdom. These four periods are thus divided: $12 + 23 + 23 + 12$. No system, whether of Hilgenfeld, Volkmar, or Wieseler, which attributes a like number of years to each shepherd, can arrive at any but a forced explanation of these numbers. As Schürer remarks, this division is merely intended to denote two longer periods coming between two shorter. The limits of these periods are on the whole not difficult to determine. The first period begins with the attack of Assyria on Israel, and ends with the return from the captivity under Cyrus, 89^{61-71}. The second extends from Cyrus to the conquests of Alexander, 332 B.C., 89^{72-77}. The third extends from this date to the transference of the supremacy over Israel from the Graeco-Egyptian to the Graeco-Syrian power, 90^{1-5}. The fourth extends from this date, about 200 B.C., to the establishment of the Messianic kingdom, 90^{6-17}. 60. **Duly numbered.** The number in each instance to be destroyed was a definite one. 61. **Another.** According to $90^{14, 22}$ this 'another' is an archangel and the guardian angel of Israel, and hence, probably, Michael. This task of the heavenly scribe was in the Babylonian religion performed by Nabû, in the Egyptian by Thot. Here it is Michael in all probability. But in $12^{3sq.}$ 15^1 92^1 it has devolved on Enoch, in 4 Ezra 14^{22-26} on Ezra, whereas in 2 Enoch $22^{11\,sqq.}$ on Vretil (? Dabriel as in Jellinc's *Beth ha-Midrasch*, p. 180, according to Kohler). See *K. A. T.*³ 400 sq. 63. **Destroy.** + 'of their own caprice' *bcefhnpx*. **Comprehend** = 'ĕmaṭṭĕnōmü. Emended from 'ĕwaṭṭĕnōmü

not they abide by my command which I have commanded them.
64. But they shall not know it, and thou shalt not declare it to them, nor admonish them, but only record against each individual all the destruction which the shepherds effect each in his time and lay it all before me." 65. And I saw till those shepherds pastured in their season, and they began to slay and to destroy more than they were bidden, and they delivered those sheep into the hand of the lions. 66. And the lions and tigers eat and devoured the greater part of those sheep, and the wild boars eat along with them; and they burnt that tower and demolished that house. 67. And I became exceedingly sorrowful over that tower because that house of the sheep was demolished, and afterwards I was unable to see if those sheep entered that house.

LXXXIX. 68-71. *First Period of the Angelic Rulers—from the Destruction of Jerusalem to the Return from the Captivity.*

68. And the shepherds and their associates delivered over those sheep to all the wild beasts, to devour them, and each one of them received in his time a definite number: it was written by the other in a book how many each one of them destroyed of them. 69. And each one slew and destroyed many more than was prescribed; and I began to weep and lament on account of those sheep. 70. And thus in the vision I saw that one who

(*yq*). *tnt*, β read 'ĕmattĕwŏmû (+ wa'ĕmanŏmû *m*). This emendation, suggested first in my edition of 1893, has since been accepted by Beer, Flemming, and Martin. 64. No remonstrance against or interference with the shepherds was to be made during their period of dominion, but all their deeds were to be recorded against the final judgement. 65. Into the hand of the lions. The lions appear to be the Assyrians, and the reign of the shepherds to begin contemporaneously with the final struggles of the northern kingdom; or possibly with a somewhat later date, as the former may come under the account given in vv. 55, 56. 66. The account in general terms of the destruction of the northern and southern kingdoms by the lions and tigers, i.e. the Assyrians and Babylonians. The wild boars: see ver. 12 (note). Cf. Obad. 10-12 Ezek. 25^{12} $35^{5\,sqq.}$ Is. 63^{1-4} Ps. 137^7. That tower ... that house: see ver. 50 (note). 68. Was written (*u*). So already Beer had conjectured. *g* 'should write', other MSS. 'wrote'. 69. Lament. + 'very much' β. 70. With the sealing of the book which recorded all the doings of these shepwrote how he wrote down every one that was destroyed by those shepherds, day by day, and carried up and laid down and showed actually the whole book to the Lord of the sheep—(even) everything that they had done, and all that each one of them had made away with, and all that they had given over to destruction. 71. And the book was read before the Lord of the sheep, and He took the book from his hand and read it and sealed it and laid it down.

LXXXIX. 72-77. *Second Period—from the time of Cyrus to that of Alexander the Great.*

72. And forthwith I saw how the shepherds pastured for twelve hours, and behold three of those sheep turned back and came and entered and began to build up all that had fallen down of that house; but the wild boars tried to hinder them, but they were not able. 73. And they began again to build as before, and they reared up that tower, and it was named the high tower; and they began again to place a table before the tower, but all the bread on it was polluted and not pure. 74. And as touching

herds it is implied that the first period has come to a close. 71. From his hand (ymt). β 'in His hand'. 72. At the close of the description of this period, the writer defines its duration exactly as twelve hours long, just as at the close of the third period described in 90$^{2-4}$ he defines its duration in 90^5. Further, we are to observe that the term 'hour' is to be taken in the same sense as 'time' in 90^5, since in the fifty-eight times there mentioned, the twelve hours are treated exactly as 'times'. In fact we may feel certain that the variation of expression 'hour' and 'time' originated with the Ethiopic translator as renderings of the same word ὥρα. Three of those sheep. Two of these were Zerubbabel and Joshua. If the text be correct, I see no objection to finding the third in Ezra or Nehemiah, notwithstanding the interval that separates these from the former. The account of the attempt of the Samaritans to prevent the rebuilding of the temple is as true of the latter as the former, Ezra 4-5; Neh. 4-6. In later times one of the two was at times mentioned without the other, Sir. 49$^{11-13}$ 2 Macc. 2^{13}. Büchler is of opinion that the three sheep here represent not individuals but the three tribes, Levi, Judah, and Benjamin. He compares T. Joseph 19^3. 73. Named. +'as before' q. The bread ... was polluted, i. e. the offerings were unclean; cf. Mal. 1^7, 'Ye offer polluted bread upon mine altar.' These words furnish no ground for supposing an Essene author of the Dream-visions: they are not stronger than Mal. 1, 2, and would only express the ordinary judgement of an old-fashioned Pharisee such as the all this the eyes of those sheep were blinded so that they saw not, and (the eyes of) their shepherds likewise; and they delivered them in large numbers to their shepherds for destruction, and they trampled the sheep with their feet and devoured them. 75. And the Lord of the sheep remained unmoved till all the sheep were dispersed over the field and mingled with them (i. e. the beasts), and they (i. e. the shepherds) did not save them out of the hand of the beasts.   76. And this one who wrote the book carried it up, and showed it and read it before the Lord of the sheep, and implored Him on their account, and besought Him on their account as he showed Him all the doings of the shepherds, and gave testimony before Him against all the shepherds.   77. And he took the actual book and laid it down beside Him and departed.

XC. 1-5. *Third Period—from Alexander the Great to the Graeco-Syrian Domination.*

XC. 1. And I saw till that in this manner thirty-five shepherds undertook the pasturing (of the sheep), and they

---

writer of this Section on the Persian period—a judgement certainly justified by the few details that survive of that period: see Ewald's *History of Israel*, v. 204-206. The author of the Assumption of Moses—a Pharisaic Quietist writing about the beginning of the Christian era—says that the two tribes grieved on their return 'because they could not offer sacrifices to the God of their fathers', 4⁵ (see my note *in loc.*)—the author therein implying that the sacrifices of the second temple were no true sacrifices because the nation was under the supremacy of the heathen, and its worship was conducted by an unworthy and heathenized hierarchy. 75. Israel sinned still further in mingling among the heathen nations. This is the beginning of the 'dispersion'. 76. Before the Lord (*g*). *mẹtu* 'in the mansions of the Lord', β 'in the mansions before the Lord'. The shepherds (*gmq*`. *t*, β 'their shepherds'. Gave testimony (*mt*, β). *gq* 'it was heard'. 77. Here the second period closes with the fall of the Persian power.

XC. 1. Thirty-five. All the MSS. are corrupt here. *gt*, β–*ky* read 'thirty-seven'. *qu* give further corruptions of 'thirty-seven'. The thirty-five gives the sum of the two periods already dealt with, i. e. 12 + 23, just as in 90⁵ at the close of the third period the three periods are summed together severally completed their periods as did the first; and others received them into their hands to pasture them for their period, each shepherd in his own period. 2. And after that I saw in my vision all the birds of heaven coming, the eagles, the vultures, the kites, the ravens; but the eagles led all the birds; and they began to devour those sheep, and to pick out their eyes and to devour their flesh. 3. And the sheep cried out because their flesh was being devoured by the birds, and as for me I looked and lamented in my sleep over that shepherd who pastured the sheep. 4. And I saw until those sheep were devoured by the dogs and eagles and kites, and they left neither flesh nor skin nor sinew remaining on them till only their bones stood there: and their bones too fell to the earth and the sheep became few. 5. And I saw until that twenty-three had undertaken the pasturing and completed in their several periods fifty-eight times.

$12 + 23 + 23 = 58$. **As did the first.** As the twelve had duly completed their times, so likewise did the rest of the thirty-five. **Others received them.** These words mark the transition to the Greek period. This period extends from the time of Alexander, 333, to the establishment of the Messianic kingdom. It falls into two divisions—the first constituted by the Graeco-Egyptian domination over Palestine, 333–200, during which twenty-three shepherds hold sway; and the second constituted by the Graeco-Syrian domination over Palestine from 200 till the establishment of the Messianic kingdom. During the fourth division twelve shepherds bear sway. 2. The new world-power—that of the Greeks, i.e. Graeco-Egyptian and Graeco-Syrian—is fittingly represented by a different order of the animal kingdom, namely, by birds of prey. The 'eagles' are the Greeks or Macedonians. The 'ravens', as we see from vv. 8, 9, 12, are the Syrians under the Seleucidae. The 'vultures' and 'kites' must stand for the Egyptians under the Ptolemies. Verses 2–4 deal with the Graeco-Egyptian domination. Yet the 'ravens', i.e. the Syrians, are mentioned once, and the reason is obvious, for the Syrians frequently contested the Egyptian supremacy over Palestine, and in all these struggles Palestine suffered severely. It was as Josephus says, 'like to a ship in a storm which is tossed by the waves on both sides,' *Ant.* xii. 3. 3. **My vision** ($a-m$). m, β 'the vision'. 3. **Was being devoured** ($a-u$). u, β 'was devoured'. **I looked** (gqu). m 'I saw', t, β 'I cried out'. 4. **The dogs.** According to $89^{42, 46, 47}$, these are the Philistines; cf. Sirach 50^{25}. **Neither flesh nor skin.** From Mic. $3^{2, 3}$. 5. See ver. 1 (note). **Twenty-three.**

XC. 6-12. *Fourth Period—from the Graeco-Syrian Domination to the Maccabean Revolt.*

6. But behold lambs were borne by those white sheep, and they began to open their eyes and to see, and to cry to the sheep.

+ 'shepherds' t, β.

6-17. The fourth and last period of the heathen supremacy. The beginning of this period synchronizes with the transference of the supremacy over Israel from the Graeco-Egyptian to the Graeco-Syrian power about 200 B.C. Though this is not stated in so many words, it is the only legitimate interpretation. For (1) the analogy of the three preceding periods points to this conclusion, as each is marked by a like transference of the supremacy over Israel from one heathen nation to another. (2) Not only does the analogy of the other periods lead to this conclusion, but also every subsequent statement in the text, and with its acceptance the traditional difficulties of interpretation vanish. (3) This period is marked by the rise of the Chasids. As these were already an organized party (see ver. 6 note) before the Maccabean rising, their first appearance must have been much earlier and possibly synchronizes with the beginning of this period. (4) There is absolutely no ground in the text for making this period begin with the reign of Antiochus Epiphanes, as all critics have done hitherto. This misconception has naturally made a right interpretation of the subsequent details impossible, and no two critics have been able to agree on their exegesis. 6. The beginning of this period is marked by the appearance of a new class or party in Israel. These were the Chasids or Asideans who existed as a party for some time before the Maccabean rising. Some have identified the Chasids with the followers of Judas Maccabeus, and have traced their origin to the efforts of that leader. But the separate mention of the Chasids as distinguished from the immediate followers of Judas, 1 Macc. 3[13], their leagued organization already existing before the Maccabean outbreak, as is clear from 1 Macc. 2[42] 3[13], and their action generally in support of Judas, but at times actually antagonistic to him, 1 Macc. 7[13], make it quite manifest that this theory is without foundation. In fact, so far from its being true that Judas founded this party, the only available evidence goes to prove that he was originally merely a member of it, as we shall see presently. The Chasids, while first appearing as the champions of the law against the Hellenizing Sadducees, were really the representatives of advanced forms of doctrine on the Messianic kingdom and the Resurrection. The Chasids possessed all the enthusiasm and religious faith of the nation, and though spiritual children of the Scribes, they drew within their membership the most zealous of the priestly as well as the non-priestly families. Hence our author represents (90[9]) the Maccabean family as belonging to the Chasids as well as the High-priest Onias III. Within this party, though a diversity of eschatological views was tolerated, the most strict observance of the law was enforced, and with its requirements no political aim was allowed to interfere. On the other hand, any movement that came forward as the champion of the law naturally commanded the adhesion of the Chasids, and so they cast in their lot with the

7. Yea, they cried to them, but they did not hearken to what they said to them, but were exceedingly deaf, and their eyes were very

Maccabean party—but that only after much indecision (1 Macc. 7¹³), because the Maccabean movement put them in strife with the high-priest of the time, the legitimate and religious head of the nation. By a member of this party the present Dream-visions were written. This is obvious from the doctrines of the Resurrection, the final judgement, and the kingdom of the Messiah which he teaches, but especially from his severe criticism on the moral and ceremonial irregularities in the services of the second temple (89⁷³). To remedy these abuses and defeat the schemes of Antiochus the Chasids were ready to sacrifice their lives, but all their efforts were directed to one end only—the reestablishment of the Theocracy and the preparation for the Messianic kingdom. To the writer of the Dream-visions all these hopes are bound up together with the success of the Maccabean leader. So long then as the Maccabean family fought for these objects, so long they carried with them the support of the Chasids; but the moment they laid hands on the high-priesthood, from that moment began the alienation of the Chasids, which afterwards developed into a deadly hostility. This hostility of the Pharisees to Hyrcanus is attested by their demand that the latter should resign the high-priesthood (*Ant.* xiii. 10. 5), and the same demand is practically made in the Pss. Sol. 17. The writer who so severely criticized the temple worship under the *legitimate* line of high-priests could not regard an *illegitimate* holder of that office as the champion of the Theocracy. On this ground, therefore, we hold that *chapters 83-90 must have been written before Jonathan's assumption of the high-priesthood*, 153 B.C. This in itself

makes it impossible to identify the 'great horn' with Hyrcanus—so Dillmann, Schürer, and others, or with Alex. Jannaeus—so Hilgenfeld, and we shall find that the natural and unforced interpretation of the text will confirm the conclusion we have thus arrived at. 6. Behold (*a*). β 'little'. 6-7. Lambs were borne by those white sheep, &c. The 'white sheep' are the faithful adherents of the Theocracy: the 'lambs' are the Chasids, a new and distinct party amongst the Jews, as we have above seen. Schürer thinks that it is only 'stubborn prejudice which can prevent any one from seeing that by the symbolism of the lambs the Maccabees are to be understood'. It seems, on the other hand, to be only 'stubborn prejudice' that can hold to such a view if the text is interpreted naturally. By taking the lambs in ver. 6 to symbolize the Chasids, every difficulty is removed. In vv. 6, 7 we have the unavailing appeals of the Chasids to the nation at large: in ver. 8 the destruction of one of them, Onias III, by the Syrians; and in ver. 9 the rise of the Maccabees—the horned or powerful lambs. If, with Schürer, the lambs in ver. 6 are the Maccabees, what is to be made of the horned lambs in ver. 9? Moreover, though the lambs or Chasids did appeal in vain to the nation, the Maccabees did not. 7. Yea, they cried to them (*q*). That is, the lambs cried to the sheep. *g* 'But they (i.e. the sheep) did not cry to them', *m* 'but they oppressed them', *t* 'but they did not hear them', β-*ino* 'but the sheep did not cry to them'. Only *q* has here preserved the text. Very exceedingly. The text, which varies in the different MSS., appears to be an exceedingly blinded. 8. And I saw in the vision how the ravens flew upon those lambs, and took one of those lambs, and dashed the sheep in pieces and devoured them. 9. And I saw till horns grew upon those lambs, and the ravens cast down their horns; and I saw till there sprouted a great horn of one of those sheep, and their eyes were opened. 10. And it †looked at† them [and their eyes opened], and it cried to the sheep, and the rams saw it and all ran to it. 11. And notwithstanding all

attempt to render σφόδρα σφόδρα: but the matter is doubtful. 8. The Syrians attack Israel and put Onias III to death, 171 B.C.: see 2 Macc. 4$^{33-36}$. We are still in the pre-Maccabean period. We should, perhaps, have expected Onias III to be symbolized by a white sheep rather than by a lamb. The writer may have gone back for a moment to the symbolic meaning of this term in 89^{45}; but it is more likely that it is used loosely as including Onias among the Chasids. In any case it cannot be interpreted of Jonathan who was chief of the nation, and would have been symbolized by *a horned lamb or a ram*; nor could it possibly be said, as in ver. 9, that the lambs did not become horned till after the death of Jonathan. 9. Of one (*g*). Other MSS. 'one'. The horned lambs, as we have seen, must be the Maccabees, and in the 'great horn' it is impossible to find any other than Judas Maccabeus. So Lücke, Schodde, and now Martin; but their interpretation could not be upheld against the objection that the period from Antiochus Epiphanes to Judas Maccabeus is far too short for the rule of the twelve last shepherds. Schodde indeed tries to show that the 'great horn' comes early in this period, and that it is not the 'great horn' but the Messianic kingdom which forms the *terminus ad quem*. But the text is against him. The 'great horn' is still warring in ver. 16, and the period of the twelve shepherds' rule is closed in ver. 17. But this objection does not hold against the true conception of the period, which dates its beginning about 200 B.C. Thus nearly forty years of this period would have elapsed before the writing of these chapters 83–90; for this Section must have been written before the death of Judas, 160 B.C. The author, therefore, must have expected the Messianic kingdom to appear within twenty years or more. This would allow sufficient time for the rule of the twelve shepherds, and also admit of the 'great horn' being represented as warring till God interposes in person and establishes the kingdom. The interpretation of Dillmann, Köstlin, Schürer, and others, which takes the 'great horn' to symbolize John Hyrcanus, does violence to the text, and meets with the insuperable objection that thus there would not be even the faintest reference to Judas, the greatest of all the Maccabees. Opened. + 'and their eyes saw' *gmt*. 10. And it †looked at†. For r'ĕja = 'looked at' read r'ĕja, 'pastured with.' It cried (*m*, β-*in*). *a–m* 'they cried. The eyes of the sheep are opened through the efforts of Judas Maccabeus. Rams. So I have rendered dâbêlât here and in the next verse in accordance with Dillmann's latest views: see Lex. col. 1101. The word

Sect. IV] *Chapter XC. 8–13* 209

this those eagles and vultures and ravens and kites still kept tearing the sheep and swooping down upon them and devouring them: still the sheep remained silent, but the rams lamented and cried out. 12. And those ravens fought and battled with it and sought to lay low its horn, but they had no power over it.

XC. 13–19. *The last Assault of the Gentiles on the Jews* (where vv. 13–15 and 16–18 are doublets).

13. And I saw till the

16. All the eagles and vul-

rendered 'ram' in 89^{42-44} is quite a different one, and has a technical meaning not found in this word. 11, 12. **Eagles and vultures and kites.** In the Syrian armies mercenaries were enrolled from the Greek and other nations; cf. 1 Macc. 5^{39} 6^{29}. Syria uses every effort against Judas, but in vain. 12. **With it.** g, eh read 'with them'. **Its horn.** q reads 'their horn'. 13. It would seem that the use of some of the symbols is not steady. The 'vultures' and the 'kites' in ver. 2 must mean the Graeco-Egyptians; but in this verse and in verse 11 it is doubtful who are to be understood by these. We have already observed that the writer uses the same brute symbol for different nations, i.e. the wild boars represent the Edomites in 89^{66}, but the Samaritans six verses later; see also ver. 16 (note). There may be a fresh change of symbols here, and the vultures and kites may stand for Ammon and Edom; cf. 1 Macc. 5. The struggle here depicted is a life and death one, and neither of Hyrcanus's wars against Antiochus Sidetes and Antiochus Cyzicenus can fairly be described as such. The latter, moreover, was conducted by Hyrcanus's sons while Hyrcanus himself was quietly discharging his priestly duties in Jerusalem; while the former occur-

ring during the first year of Hyrcanus could not be referred to in vv. 12, 13, as ver. 11 deals with the first attacks of the heathen on the 'great horn'. 13–19. *The criticism and reconstruction of this passage.* These verses as they stand in the text are unintelligible. In my edition of 1893 I observed in my notes that ver. 19 should be read before ver. 16, since the destruction of the Gentiles had already been accomplished in ver. 18. Next I bracketed ver. 15 as a doublet of ver. 18, as both deal with the coming of God for the help of Israel, and only the second coming was effectual. This criticism and reconstruction of the text are accepted by Martin, but he suggests that vv. 13–15 and vv. 16–18 are doublets. This suggestion is in the right direction, but it needs to be developed. It is true that vv. 13–15 correspond respectively to vv. 16–18, but it is further true that ver. 19 should be read immediately after ver. 13 (= ver. 16). In my translation I have rearranged the text as it stood at a very early date. By this reconstruction we are enabled to emend certain corruptions in the text. First of all in ver. 13 it is quite irregular if not impossible for 'the shepherds' to join in the fray. They are angels. If we compare ver. 16 we see no mention of them. This addition to the text has possibly arisen through

†shepherds and† eagles and those vultures and kites came, tures and ravens and kites were gathered together, and

a dittography in the Hebrew. 'Shepherds' = רעים corrupt for ערבים = 'ravens', which occurs later in the text. Next, it is absurd for the text to state that the eagles, vultures, and kites 'cried to the ravens' to help to break the horn of that ram, seeing that the ravens, i.e. the Syrians, had begun the fighting with the sheep, and the eagles, &c., only came to assist them. Now if we look at ver. 16 we see that 'the ravens' are enumerated along with the eagles, vultures, and kites, and no doubt this is the right text. How then are we to explain 'they cried to'? These words = ἐκραζον = יִזְעֲקוּ, but the word יזעקו should have been punctuated יִוָּעֲקוּ = 'were gathered together'; cf. Judg. 6²⁴, ³⁵ 18²² Jos. 8¹⁶ 1 Sam. 14²⁰, in all which passages the LXX (like the Greek translator of our text) mistranslates יִוָּעֲקוּ as if it were יִזְעֲקוּ. Or the confusion may have arisen similarly from a mistranslation of יָעַץ, which is rendered in the LXX as if it were יָעַץ except in Judg. 12¹. Hence ver. 13 is to be read as follows: 'And I saw till the ravens and eagles and vultures and kites were gathered together,' &c. Now if we compare ver. 16 we find that we have here recovered the original; for thus far the verses agree word for word. The above facts have a further value. They prove that *the doublet existed already* in Greek, and not only so but in the Hebrew. In ver. 19 there is no difficulty. The sword is given to Israel to resist the hosts of Gog and to avenge itself on its heathen oppressors. In ver. 14 the text is corrupt. The original is undoubtedly preserved with more faithfulness in ver. 17. Ver. 17 comes at the close of the victory of Israel over Gog and his hosts. It tells how the angel gives an account of the doings of the twelve last shepherds, just as in 89⁷⁰, ⁷⁷ he had given an account of the first two divisions of them. There is no real occasion here for his intervention in behalf of Israel. Israel is already victorious in ver. 19, which precedes ver. 14. Hence I bracket the words 'came and helped it and showed it everything: he had come down for the help of that ram'. But these words are full of interest. Before we deal further with them we must return to the first part of ver. 14. It is evidently imperfect. There is no object for the verb 'carried up'. This should evidently be 'the book' mentioned in ver. 17; cf. 89⁷⁰, ⁷¹, ⁷⁶, ⁷⁷. Corresponding to 'carried up' in ver. 14 we find 'opened' in ver. 17. It is probable that 'opened' was preceded by 'carried up' which we find in ver. 14. The usage of our author seems to require the presence of this phrase; cf. 89⁷⁰ 'carried up . . . and showed' and similarly in 89⁷⁶. Yet the opening of the books is not mentioned specifically till 90⁲⁰. This opening follows on the breaking of the seals. Hence there is just a bare possibility that ἕως τοῦ ἀνοῖξαι is corrupt for ἕως τοῦ ἀνοῖσαι (a form found in Philo i. 64). Hence ver. 14 so far as it survives would run: 'And I saw till that man, who wrote down the names of the shepherds, carried up (the book) into the presence of the Lord of the sheep.' And in ver. 17 we should read '(carried up) and opened' or only 'carried up' for 'opened'. Now we return to the addition in ver. 14: 'Came and helped it and showed it everything: he had come down for the help of that ram.' We have seen

[Sect. IV]   CHAPTER XC. 13-14

and †they cried to the ravens† that they should break the horn of that ram, and they battled and fought with it, and it battled with them and cried that its help might come.

there came with them all the sheep of the field, yea, they all came together, and helped each other to break that horn of the ram.

19. And I saw till a great sword was given to the sheep, and the sheep proceeded against all the beasts of the field to slay them, and all the beasts and the birds of the heaven fled before their face.

14. And I saw till that man, who wrote down the names of the shepherds [and] carried up into the presence of the Lord of the sheep [came and helped it and showed it everything: he had come down for the help of that ram].

17. And I saw that man, who wrote the book according to the command of the Lord, till he opened that book concerning the destruction which those twelve last shepherds had wrought, and showed that they had destroyed much more than their predecessors, before the Lord of the sheep.

---

above that the evidence points to these doublets having already existed in the Hebrew. It is uncertain whether this clause was added in the Hebrew or in the Greek. Its reference, however, is clear. The words speak of the help given by Michael to Judas Maccabaeus. According to 2 Macc. 11⁶ Judas and all the people prayed to God to send an angel to help them, and in 11⁸ it is recounted that 'there appeared at their head one on horseback in white apparel brandishing weapons of gold', i. e. Michael, the angelic patron of Israel, who is also the heavenly scribe in these chapters. In ver. 15 the words ' into His shadow ' can hardly be original. The corresponding phrase in ver. 13 ' from among the sheep '

seems [right. The former = בצלי which may be a corruption of מצאן = ' from among the sheep '. In ver. 18 the words 'staff' and 'smote the earth' recall Num. 20¹¹, while the phrase 'the earth clave asunder' recalls Num. 16³¹⁻³³. The text = ויך הארץ ותבקא הארץ ... ויבלעו בארץ ותבם עליהם. We should observe that the Ethiopic for 'the earth covered them', i. e. kadanat dibēhōmū, is not Ethiopic, but a literal reproduction of ἐκάλυψεν ἐπ' αὐτούς, which in turn is not Greek, but a literal reproduction of the Hebrew ותכם עליהם (Num. 16³³).
13. And eagles. *g* 'eagles'.   14. Helped it. + ' and saved it' *g*. For the help (*g*). Other MSS. 'a help'.

15. And I saw till the Lord of the sheep came unto them in wrath, and all who saw Him fled, and they all fell †into His shadow† from before His face.

18. And I saw till the Lord of the sheep came unto them and took in His hand the staff of His wrath, and smote the earth, and the earth clave asunder, and all the beasts and all the birds of the heaven fell from among those sheep, and were swallowed up in the earth and it covered them.

XC. 20-27. *Judgement of the Fallen Angels, the Shepherds, and the Apostates.*

20. And I saw till a throne was erected in the pleasant land, and the Lord of the sheep sat Himself thereon, and **the other** took the sealed books and opened those books before the Lord of the sheep. 21. And the Lord called those men the seven first

---

15. The Lord (a-*q*). *q*, β 'that Lord'. Into His shadow (*qlu*, β). *gm* 'into the shadow'. 16. All¹⁰. *u* reads 'and'. Ravens and kites. ∪ *m*. Came¹⁰ *gq*. *mtu*, β 'brought'. All the sheep (in the nom.) (*g*). In the acc. *mqt*, β. 17. Till he opened that book concerning the destruction. *y* reads 'for it was opened by the command of the Lord concerning the destruction'. · Before the Lord of the sheep (*mq*, β). *gtu* 'formerly. 18ª And the Lord of the sheep'. 18. God Himself destroys the last enemies of Israel after the manner of Korah and his followers, Num. 16³¹ ˢᵠᵠ. This is the first act of the final judgement; but the remaining acts are of a forensic nature. And I saw till the Lord of the sheep ('of the sheep' > *m*) came unto them (*m*, β). > *y* through hmt. *gt* 'and the Lord of the sheep I saw till He came to those sheep' ('till the Lord of the sheep came unto them' *t*), *u* 'and the Lord of the sheep came unto them'. Covered them (*mq*, *t*) = ἐκάλυψεν ἐπ' αὐτούς. *t*, β-*tl* = ἐκαλύφθη ἐπ' αὐτούς. *y* corrupt. > *u*. 20. The pleasant land: cf. 89⁴⁰, i.e. Palestine. Cf. Dan. 11¹⁶, ⁴¹, ⁴⁵. God's throne is set up in the immediate neighbourhood of Jerusalem (cf. ver. 29), the books are opened as in Dan. 7¹⁰; see 47³ (note). The Messiah does not appear till after the judgement in 83-90. The other. Here I read kāl'ū = 'other' instead of the MSS. reading kuellō = 'all'. 'The other' is the angel Michael. The Lord of the sheep does not Himself read the books. Cf. 89⁷⁰, ⁷¹, ⁷⁶, ⁷⁷ 90¹⁴, ¹⁷. The text reads 'and He took all the sealed books'. 21. Men (*a*). > β. The seven (*qlu*, β). > *g*. *m* 'and seven'. Seven first white ones. This order of seven archangels is derived from the Zoroastrian Amshaspands. They are spoken of in Tobit 12¹⁵; cf. Rev. 1⁴ 4⁵ 8⁲, ⁶. See Cheyne,

white ones, and commanded that they should bring before Him, beginning with the first star which led the way, all the stars whose privy members were like those of horses, and they brought them all before Him. 22. And He said to that man who wrote before Him, being one of those seven white ones, and said unto him: "Take those seventy shepherds to whom I delivered the sheep, and who taking them on their own authority slew more than I commanded them." 23. And behold they were all bound, I saw, and they all stood before Him. 24. And the judgement was held first over the stars, and they were judged and found guilty, and went to the place of condemnation, and they were cast into an abyss, full of fire and flaming, and full of pillars of fire. 25. And those seventy shepherds were judged and found guilty, and they were cast into that fiery abyss. 26. And I saw at that time how a like abyss was opened in the midst of the earth, full of fire, and they brought those blinded sheep, and they were all judged and found guilty and cast into this fiery abyss, and they burned; now this abyss was to the right of that house. 27. And I saw those sheep burning †and their bones burning†.

Origin of the Psalter, pp. 281, 282, 323-327, 334-337; *Jewish Encyc.* i. 590. **Bring** (*gm, β*). *q¹u* 'come'. **Before Him.** > *gu, d*. **Star**: see 86-88. **All the stars ... of horses.** So I render as in my edition of 1893, emending 'ĕmna zĕkû ('ĕlkû *m, β*) into laknĕllû with Dillmann. Furthermore in that edition I rejected as a dittograph the clause added after 'horses' in the MSS., 'and the first star which went out (*g*: other MSS. 'fell') first.' Subsequent translators have accepted both these suggestions. 22. The seventy angels who had charge of Israel are judged along with the fallen watchers. **Said unto him** (*mtu, β-hox ₁b*). *gq, hox ₁b* 'said unto them'. 23. This verse reads in *g* 'and behold they were all bound before Him'. Cf. 88³. 24. An abyss, full of fire. This final place of punishment is not to be confounded with the preliminary place of punishment in 18^{12-16} 19^{1-2} 21^{1-6}. It is that which is mentioned in 10^6 18^{11} 21^{7-10} 54^6. **Flaming, and full of.** *g* reads 'flaming with'. 25. The shepherds are cast into the same abyss; cf. 54^6 (note). 26. The apostates are cast into Gehenna. **In the midst of the earth**: cf. 26^1. **To the right of that house**, i. e. to the south of Jerusalem. 27. The apostates were punished in view of the blessed in Jerusalem; cf. Is. 66^{24} 1 En. 48^9 (note). This verse seems corrupt. It is absurd to speak of the bones burning as distinct from the men themselves. Hence I suggest that we have here a late Hebrew idiom. The verse would in Hebrew run וארא את־הצאן הואת בערת ועצמה בערת

XC. 28-38. *The New Jerusalem, the Conversion of the surviving Gentiles, the Resurrection of the Righteous, the Messiah.*

28. And I stood up to see till they folded up that old house; and carried off all the pillars, and all the beams and ornaments of the house were at the same time folded up with it, and they carried it off and laid it in a place in the south of the land. 29. And I saw till the Lord of the sheep brought a new house greater and loftier than that first, and set it up in the place of the first which had been folded up: all its pillars were new, and its ornaments were new and larger than those of the first, the old one which He had taken away, and all the sheep were within it.

30. And I saw all the sheep which had been left, and all the beasts on the earth, and all the birds of the heaven, falling down and doing homage to those sheep and making petition to and obeying them in every thing. 31. And thereafter those three who were clothed in white and had seized me by my hand [who

---

Here the second participle is probably a dittograph, and we might translate 'I saw those sheep burning, yea their very selves'. Or the original may have been וארא את־צאן עצמה בערת 'I saw the sheep themselves burning'. 28, 29. The removal of the old Jerusalem and the setting up of the New Jerusalem. This expectation is derived from O.T. prophecy: Ezek. 40-48 Is. 54[11, 12] 60 Hagg. 2[7-9] Zech. 2[4-13]. The idea of a new Jerusalem coming down from heaven was a familiar one in Jewish Apocalypses; cf. 4 Ezra 7[26] 13[36] Apoc. Bar. 32[2] Rev. 21[2, 10]. 28. Folded up (i.e. tawamū np). So practically y. gqtu, β-npy 'submerged'. Dillmann conjectured tômô = 'folded up'. But the forms in np occur. 29. And (>g) all the sheep were within it (a-m, acdiklo ₁a,b). m, befhnptx 'and (>m) the Lord of the sheep was within it'. The omission of the 'and' in gm, which are the chief representatives of the two readings, may point to the fact of 'which He had taken away ... within it' having originally constituted a single clause. Simply by reading 'abāg'a instead of 'abāg'ē and prefixing 'ē to ma'ēkalā we should have 'from which He had sent forth all the sheep'. 30. The conversion of the Gentiles— of those who took no part in the oppression of Israel; for the rest were destroyed in ver. 18—and their spontaneous submission to Israel; cf. Is. 14[2] 66[12, 19-21], and parallel passages. Later Judaism almost universally denied even this hope to the Gentiles; cf. Weber, *Jüd. Theol.* 384-387, 395. And obeying them (mt, β; >gqu. In every thing. The Ethiopic = 'in every word'. 'Word' here goes back to רבר, which here means 'matter', 'thing'. 31. Those three who had taken me up before], and the hand of that ram also seizing hold of me, they took me up and set me down in the midst of those sheep †before the judgement took place†.   32. And those sheep were all white, and their wool was abundant and clean.   33. And all that had been destroyed and dispersed, and all the beasts of the field, and all the birds of the heaven, assembled in that house, and the Lord of the sheep rejoiced with great joy because they were all good and had returned to His house.   34. And I saw till they laid down that sword, which had been given to the sheep, and they brought it back into the house, and it was sealed before the presence of the Lord, and all the sheep were invited into that house, but it held them not. 35. And the eyes of them all were opened, and they saw the good, and there was not one among them that did not see. 36. And I saw that that house was large and broad and very full.

37. And I saw that a white bull was born, with large horns,

were clothed in white: see 37³,³. That ram. Same word as used in vv. 10, 11. This ram is the sheep saved in 89²² from its enemies and brought up to live with Enoch. Paradise is only the temporary abode of Enoch and Elijah.   Before the judgement took place. These words are most confusing. If they are genuine it is hard to restore them to their place satisfactorily.   32. The righteousness of the members of the kingdom is expressed by the whiteness and cleanliness of the wool of the sheep; and the large measure of their righteousness by the abundance of the wool; cf. Is. 1²⁸ 4³ 60²¹.   33. The righteous dead will rise to share in the kingdom; cf. 51¹ (note). Likewise the dispersed of Israel will be gathered into it; cf. Mic. 4⁶,⁷.   Rejoiced: cf. Is. 62³⁻⁵ 65¹⁹.   34. The sword wherewith Israel had crushed its enemies is sealed and preserved as a memorial.   Into the house (g). *mṣt*, β 'into His house'.   Were invited (g). Other MSS. 'were enclosed'. It held them not: cf. Is. 49¹⁹⁻²¹ Zech. 2⁴ 10¹⁰.   37. A white bull, i.e. the Messiah. We have here the Messiah coming forth from the bosom of the community. He is a man only, but yet a glorified man; for he is described as a white bull to mark his superiority to the rest of the community of the righteous who are symbolized by sheep. So far as he is a man only, he may be regarded as the prophetic Messiah as opposed to the apocalyptic Messiah of the Parables; and yet he is not really the prophetic Messiah; for he has absolutely no function to perform, as he does not appear till the world's history is finally closed. Accordingly his presence here must be accounted for through literary reminiscence, and the Messiah-hope must be regarded as practically dead at this period. The nation, in fact, felt no need of such a personality so long as they had such and all the beasts of the field and all the birds of the air feared him and made petition to him all the time. 38. And I saw till all their generations were transformed, and they all became white bulls; and the first among them became a lamb, and that lamb became a great animal and had great black horns on

a chief as Judas. It was very different, however, in the following century, when the fondest enthusiast could no longer look to the Asmoneans, and the helpless degradation of this dynasty forced religious thinkers to give their hopes and aspirations a different direction. Of these some returned to a fresh study of the O.T. and revived the hopes of the Messianic Son of David as in the Pss. of Solomon (70–40 B.C.): others followed the bold and original thinker who conceived the Messiah as the supernatural Son of Man, who, possessing divine attributes, should give to every man his due and vindicate the entire earth for the possession of the righteous: so in the Parables (94–70 B.C.). 38. All the members of the kingdom are transformed: the white bull (i.e. the Messiah) into a great animal, and the sheep, beasts, and birds into white bulls or oxen. Thus mankind is restored to the primitive righteousness of Eden, i.e. Adam was symbolized by a white bull. A lamb. The text is corrupt and cannot be restored without the help of Test. Jos. 19$^{3-9}$. According to the Ethiopic it runs 'the first became among them (a-u, aikn: 'among them became' bcdlox $_1a_1b$) a word and that word became a great animal'. The term 'word' (nagar = $\dot{\rho}\hat{\eta}\mu\alpha$ not $\lambda\acute{o}\gamma os$) here is manifestly corrupt. Dillmann suggested that nagar (= 'word') is here a rendering of $\dot{\rho}\hat{\eta}\mu\alpha$, but that $\rho\eta\mu$ originally stood in the Greek version as a transliteration of רְאֵם = 'buffalo'. I adopted this suggestion in my first edition, but cannot any longer accept it.

The right reconstruction of the text was made by Goldschmidt in 1892, but I did not recognize its claims till I had edited the Testaments XII Patriarchs. Goldschmidt (*Das Buch Henoch*, p. 91) suggested that nagar here ultimately goes back to מָלָה, which was a corruption of טָלֶה = 'lamb'. Thus we recover the text 'and the first became among them a lamb, and the lamb became a great animal and had great black horns on its head'. This reconstruction is supported by Test. Jos. 19$^{3-9}$. In 19^{3,4} the three harts (= the three tribes of Levi, Judah, and Benjamin) become three lambs, and next these three with the remaining nine harts become twelve sheep. Again, in another vision beginning with 19^5, the twelve tribes are symbolized by twelve bulls, and in the third (?) tribe (i.e. Levi) there arose a bull calf (probably Judas the Maccabee) who helped the twelve bulls (19^7). Next in the midst of the horns of the tribe of Levi the bull calf (probably John Hyrcanus) became a lamb, and all the beasts and the reptiles rushed against him and the lamb overcame and destroyed them (19^8). Here we have a very close parallel to the symbolism and transformations in our text. 'The lamb' (= $\dot{\alpha}\mu\nu\acute{o}s$) or rather the horned lamb is clearly the head of the nation in the Testaments, and, what is more, the Messianic head. The same idea is, I think, clearly to be inferred from our text, on which the Testaments in this passage appear to be dependent. Great black horns (a). β 'great and black horns'. I cannot understand the its head; and the Lord of the sheep rejoiced over it and over all the oxen.   39. And I slept in their midst: and I awoke and saw everything.   40. This is the vision which I saw while I slept, and I awoke and blessed the Lord of righteousness and gave Him glory.   41. Then I wept with a great weeping, and my tears stayed not till I could no longer endure it: when I saw, they flowed on account of what I had seen; for everything shall come and be fulfilled, and all the deeds of men in their order were shown to me.   42. On that night I remembered the first dream, and because of it I wept and was troubled—because I had seen that vision.'

epithet 'black' here. It seems wrong. Over it. All MSS. read 'over them', but I have emended with Beer. But possibly the following 'and' is an intrusion. In that case we should simply render 'over all the oxen'. Though nothing is said as to the duration of the life of the individual in this section, the implication is that it is eternal. If Enoch and Elijah are transferred to the Messianic kingdom from Paradise, surely it is only reasonable to conclude that the new form of existence is an eternal one; for this new form of existence is more glorious than that enjoyed by Enoch and Elijah in Paradise. In Paradise Elijah was symbolized by a *ram*, but in the Messianic kingdom by a *bull*.   40. Cf. 22^{14}.   41, 42. Enoch weeps because of the woes that threaten mankind in his two visions.

SECTION V

(CHAPTERS XCI—CIV)

INTRODUCTION

A. *Critical Structure.* B. *Relation of* 91–104 *to* (a) 1–36; (b) 83–90. C. *Authorship and Date.* D. *The Problem and its Solution.*

A. Critical Structure. This section may be regarded as complete in the main and self-consistent. It has in some degree suffered at the hands of the final editor of the book, both in the way of direct interpolation and of severe dislocations of the text. The interpolations are—91^{11} 93^{11-14} 94^{7d} 96^2. The dislocations of the text are a more important feature of the book. They are confined (with the exception of 93^{13-14}, and of 106^{17a} which should be read immediately after 106^{14}) to 91–93. All critics are agreed as to the chief of these. 91^{12-17} should undoubtedly be read directly after 93. In 93 we have an account of the first seven weeks of the ten into which the world's history is divided, and in 91^{12-17} of the last three weeks. Taken together 93^{1-10} 91^{12-17} form an independent whole—the Apocalypse of Weeks—which has been incorporated in 91–104. See notes *in loc.* But this is far from a full account of the matter. The remaining dislocations only need to be pointed out in order to be acknowledged. On other grounds (pp. 65 sq., 219 sqq.) we find that 91–104 is a book of different authorship to the rest of the sections. Now this being so, this section obviously begins with 92—'Written by Enoch the scribe,' &c. On 92 follows $91^{1-10, 18-19}$ as a natural sequel, where Enoch summons his children to receive his parting words. Then comes the Apocalypse of Weeks, 93^{1-10} 91^{12-17}. The original order of the text, therefore, was: 92 $91^{1-10, 18-19}$ 93^{1-10} 91^{12-17} 94. These dislocations were the work of the editor, who put the different books of Enoch together and added 80 and 81.

B. (*a*) **Relation of 91–104 to 1–36.** Do these sections proceed from the same author? or if not, of what nature is the manifest relation between them? Let us proceed to weigh the evidence on the former question. At first sight, the evidence for unity of authorship seems overwhelming. (1) The phrase 'ye shall have no peace' is found in 91–104 and in 1–36, and in these sections only—94^6 $98^{11, 16}$ 99^{13} 101^3 102^3 103^8 5^4 12^5 13^1 16^4. 'Plant of righteousness,' $93^{2, 5, 10}$ 10^{16}. (2) Titles of God in common. 'Holy and Great One,' 'Holy Great One,' or 'Great Holy One,' 92^2 97^6 98^6 104^9 10^1 14^1 25^3. 'The Great One,' 103^4 104^1 14^2. 'The Great Glory,' 102^3 14^{20}. (3) References in each to the Law, 99^2 5^4; to the eating of blood, 98^{11} 7^5; to the regularity of nature, 101^{1-7} 2^1-5^4; to the hardheartedness of men, 98^{11} 5^4. (4) No hint of a Messiah in either. (5) The division of human history in the Apocalypse of Weeks into ten weeks, each apparently of seven generations, seems to agree with 10^{12}, where a period of seventy generations is given. (6) The date of the final judgement over the Watchers in 91^{15} at the close of the tenth week seems to agree with the date assigned to it in 10^{12}, i.e. at the end of seventy generations. (7) In both the resurrection is taught, 91^{10} 92^3 100^5 22. (8) In both the scene of the Messianic kingdom is the earth as it is.

There are thus many points of connexion, but as we proceed we shall see that these are mainly external. The points of divergence, on the other hand, are far more serious because internal. If we assume for the time being that the Apocalypse of Weeks, 93^{1-10} 91^{12-17}, forms a constituent part of 91–104, it follows that (1) in the first place, the last four points of agreement mentioned above are apparent, but not real. The seventh day of the tenth week in 91^{15} marks *the close of the Messianic kingdom*, which began in the eighth week: whereas the seventy generations in 10^{12} terminate with the *establishment of the Messianic kingdom*. Nor do these periods start from the same date: the Apocalypse of Weeks reckons from the creation of Adam: the seventy generations from the judgement of the angels. (2) The final judgement in 91^{15} is held at the close of the Messianic kingdom, but in 10^{12} 16^1 before its establishment. (3) Whereas the resurrection implied in 22 is only a resuscitation to a *temporary* blessedness, 5^9 10^{17} 25^6, the resurrection in 91–104 is not to the temporary Messianic kingdom spoken of in $91^{13, 14}$ 96^8, but to one of eternal blessedness subsequent to the final judgement. For, from $100^{4, 5}$ we see that the righteous do not rise till God has judged sinners and an end has been made of all sin. Thus the resurrection of the righteous in 91–104 follows the final judgement at the close of the temporary Messianic kingdom. Further evidence to this effect is to be found in $92^{3,\ 4}$, where the righteous are said to 'walk in eternal light'; in 104^6, where they are to become 'companions of the hosts of heaven'; in 104^2, where they are to 'shine as the lights', and have 'the portals of heaven open to them'. These statements could not possibly apply to the members of the temporary Messianic kingdom. (4) There is only a resurrection of the righteous in 91–104; cf. 91^{10} 92^3 100^5: whereas in 22 a general resurrection with the exception of one class of sinners is taught. (5) There is no resurrection of the body in 91–104: there is a resurrection of the body in 1–36. (6) Contrast the spiritual nature of the kingdom in 91–104 with the crass materialism of 1–36, where much of the bliss consists in good eating and drinking and the begetting of large families, and life itself depends on the external eating of the tree of life. (7) Finally, contrast the answers given by 1–36 and 91–104 to the question, 'why do the righteous suffer?' See pp. 3 sq., 222 sq.

The lines of thought, then, being so divergent in these two sections, there is no conclusion open to us other than that they proceed from different authors; whereas the obvious points of agreement necessitate the assumption that one of the two authors had the work of the other before him, and we need feel no hesitation in concluding that the author of 91–104 had 1–36 or some form of this section before him—some form of this section we repeat, for it is at the best fragmentary.

B. (b) **Relation of 91–104 to 83–90.** There are some points of resemblance between these sections. (1) Elijah's translation is referred to, 93^8 89^{52}. God rejoices over the destruction of the wicked, 94^{10} 89^{58}. (2) Titles of God in common: 'The Great King,' 91^{13} 84^5; 'the Holy and Great One,' 92^2 (note) 84^1.

But these and other superficial points of resemblance are far outweighed by the divergent lines of thought pursued in the two sections, which render the theory of one and undivided authorship impossible. . We should observe then, that—(1) the Messianic kingdom is finite in duration in 91–104, i.e. from the eighth to the tenth world-week inclusive; whereas in 83–90 it is eternal. In 91–104 the final judgement takes place at the close of the Messianic kingdom; in 83–90 it is consummated at the beginning of the Messianic kingdom. (2) There is a resurrection of the righteous only in 91–104; but in 83–90 a resurrection of apostate Jews also. (3) The period of the sword is differently dated and conceived in the two sections. In 91–104 it is separated from the final judgement by the whole period of the Messianic kingdom, see 91^{12}; in 83–90 it immediately precedes the final judgement, see 90^{19}; in 91–104 it is ethical and vindictive—the destruction of the wicked by the righteous; in 83–90 it is national and vindictive—the destruction of the hostile Gentiles by the Jews. (4) The building of the Temple precedes the final judgement in 91–104; in 83–90 it is subsequent to the final judgement. (5) The kingdom, to which the righteous rise, in 91–104 is apparently heaven; for in 91^{14-16} the former heaven and earth are destroyed and a new heaven created, but no new earth, and in 104^2 heaven is thrown open to the righteous.

We must therefore conclude that 91–104 and 83–90 proceed from different authors, and this conclusion is confirmed when we observe the forcible dislocations that 91–104 have undergone at the hands of the final editor. This section taken in the following order, 92 $91^{1-10, 18-19}$ 93^{1-10} 91^{12-17} 94 (see pp. 218, 224), forms a complete book in itself, and presents a world-view peculiarly its own. Why then was the original order departed from, unless in order to adapt it to a new context? On all sides, then, the conclusion is irresistible that 91–104 once formed an independent writing; that it was afterwards incorporated into a larger work, and underwent its present derangements in the process of incorporation.

On the other hand, there are good grounds for regarding 93^{1-10} 91^{12-17}—the Apocalypse of Weeks, and the rest of 91–104 as proceeding from different hands though agreeing in the main in their teaching.

C. **The Authorship and Date.** The author belongs to a clearly defined party. That this party is the Pharisees is obvious; for it is exclusive in an extreme degree, 97^4; it is an upholder of the law against an apostate hellenizing party, $99^{2, 14}$; it looks forward to a temporal triumph over its opponents, 91^{12}, &c.; it believes in a final judgement and resurrection of the righteou 91^{10} 92^3, and in Sheol as the place of eternal punishment for the wicked, 99^{11} $103^{7, 8}$.

The enemies of this party are rich and trust in their riches, 96^4 97^{8-10} 98^2; they oppress and rob the poor of their wages, 99^{13}; they have forsaken the law, 99^2, falsified the Old Testament writings, and led men astray through their heathen doctrines, 94^5 104^{10}; they are given up to superstition and idolatry, 99^{7-9}; they hold that God does not concern Himself with the doings of men,

$98^{6, 7}$ 104^7. As the former party are designated as the 'children of heaven', 101^1, these are called the 'children of earth', 100^6 102^3.

The date of this clearly defined and developed opposition of the two parties cannot have been pre-Maccabean, nor yet earlier than the breach between John Hyrcanus and the Pharisees. But a still later date must be assumed according to the literal interpretation of $103^{14, 15}$, where the rulers are said to uphold the Sadducean oppressors and to share in the murder of the righteous. This charge is not justified before 95 B.C. As for the later limit, the Herodian princes cannot be the rulers here mentioned, for the Sadducees were irreconcilably opposed to these, as aliens and usurpers. It appears, therefore, that this section should be assigned either to the years 95-79 B.C. or to 70-64 B.C., during which periods the Pharisees were oppressed by both rulers and Sadducees.

If, on the other hand, we might regard the word 'murder' as merely a strong expression for a severe persecution—and the silence elsewhere observed as to the rulers would point to this interpretation—then we should naturally refer this section to the years 107-95 B.C., i.e. after the breach between Hyrcanus and the Pharisees and before the savage destruction of the Pharisees by Jannaeus in 95. If the date of the book is subsequent to 95, the merely passing reference in 103^{15} to the cruelties of Jannaeus is hardly intelligible. We should expect rather the fierce indignation against 'the kings and the mighty', which we actually do find in 37-70, and which fittingly expresses the feelings of the Pharisees towards Jannaeus, 'the slayer of the pious.' We are inclined therefore to place 91-104 before 95 B.C., and if we may regard 100^2 as an historical reference, these chapters are to be assigned to the years 104-95 B.C.

The author is thus a Pharisee, writing between the years 104 and 95, or 95-79, or 70-64 B.C.

D. The Problem and its Solution. The author of 1-36 solves the problem of the righteous suffering by their resuscitation to a temporary blessedness in the Messianic kingdom: the wicked dead who *escaped punishment* in life, $22^{10, 11}$, rise also to receive requital for their sin. What becomes of the righteous after their second death is not so much as hinted at in that section. Thus in this respect the solution of the problem here presented has not advanced a single step beyond that given in Is. 65 and 66.

But this solution of the problem must have failed early to give satisfaction. In 91-104 we find another attempt to grapple with this difficulty, and in this an answer immeasurably more profound is achieved. The wicked are seemingly sinning with impunity; yet their evil deeds are recorded every day, 104^7; and for these they will suffer endless retribution in Sheol, 99^{11}; for Sheol is not a place such as the Old Testament writers conceived, but one in which men are requited according to their deserts, 102^4–104^5. From this hell of darkness and flame their souls will never escape, $98^{3, 10}$. But the time is coming when even on earth the wicked will perish and the righteous triumph over them, on the advent of the Messianic kingdom, at the beginning of the eighth world-week, 91^{12} 95^7 96^1 98^{12} $99^{4, 6}$. This kingdom will last till the close of the tenth world-week, and during it the righteous will enjoy peace and well-being, and see many good days on earth, $91^{13, 14}$ 96^3. Then will ensue the final judgement with the destruction of the former heaven and earth, and the creation of a new heaven, 91^{14-16}. And the righteous dead, who have been specially guarded by angels all the time hitherto, 100^5, will thereupon be raised, 91^{10} 92^3, as spirits only, $103^{3, 4}$, and the portals of the new heaven will be opened to them, 104^2, and they shall joy as the angels, 104^4, and become companions of the heavenly hosts, 104^6, and shine as the stars for ever, 104^2.

XCII. XCI. 1-10, 18-19. *Enoch's Book of Admonition for his Children.*

XCII. 1. The book written by Enoch—[Enoch indeed wrote this complete doctrine of wisdom, (which is) praised of all men and a judge of all the earth] for all my children who shall dwell on the earth. And for the future generations who shall observe uprightness and peace.

2. Let not your spirit be troubled on account of the times;
   For the Holy and Great One has appointed days for all things.

3. And the righteous one shall arise from sleep,
   [Shall arise] and walk in the paths of righteousness,
   And all his path and conversation shall be in eternal goodness and grace.

XCI—XCIV. In this edition I have rearranged these chapters in what I suggested was their original order in my first edition, i.e. 92 91$^{1-10, 18-19}$ 93$^{1-10}$ 91$^{12-17}$ 94, and have treated the Apocalypse of Weeks, i.e. 93$^{1-10}$ 91$^{12-17}$, as an earlier fragment incorporated by the author of 91-104 or the editor of the whole book in his work (as suggested in my first edition, p. 267). Of the extent of this Apocalypse I will treat *in loc.* The order of these chapters, which appears to be the original, and which is restored in this edition, is 92 (see p. 218) 91$^{1-10, 18-19}$ 93$^{1-10}$ 91$^{12-17}$ 94. Beer, on the other hand, takes 91$^{1-11, 18-19}$ as forming the introduction to the Apocalypse of Weeks, and thus arranges the text 91$^{1-11, 18-19}$ 93 91$^{12-17}$ 92 94. Martin follows Beer in this respect, though he admits that 92 should perhaps be placed before 91$^{1-11}$.

XCII. This chapter obviously forms the beginning of a new book just as 14^1 formed originally the beginning of the section 12-16; see p. 27. The words 'The book written', &c., evidently introduce a fresh collection of visions. 1. The book ... indeed wrote (g). Other MSS. 'written by Enoch the scribe'. [Enoch indeed ... all the earth]. I have, with some hesitation, bracketed these words as an interpolation. Enoch does not attempt a complete doctrine of wisdom, and seeing that it was for the chosen race only it could hardly be said to be 'praised of all men'. Wrote. Cf. 12^3, ^{4}. This complete doctrine of wisdom, (which is) praised ($a-t$ reading zakuëllô). t 'of the complete doctrine', &c., $\beta-y$ 'this complete doctrine of wisdom is praised'. A judge, &c. Wisdom is represented as the πάρεδρος or assessor of God in 84^3 (note). 2. The times are evil; but these too are the ordination of God. The Holy and Great One (gg, el_1a). ml, $\beta-el_1a$ 'the Holy Great One'; see 1^3 (note). 3. The righteous one. Used collectively as in 91^{10}. Instead of 'and the righteous ... from sleep, shall arise' g reads 'and wisdom shall arise'. Paths (m_1l. β 'path'. In eternal good-

4. He will be gracious to the righteous and give him eternal uprightness,
And He will give him power so that he shall be (endowed) with goodness and righteousness,
And he shall walk in eternal light.

5. And sin shall perish in darkness for ever,
And shall no more be seen from that day for evermore.

XCI. 1-11, 18-19. *Enoch's Admonition to his Children.*

XCI. 1. 'And now, my son Methuselah, call to me all thy brothers
And gather together to me all the sons of thy mother,
For the word calls me,
And the spirit is poured out upon me,
That I may show you everything
That shall befall you for ever.'

2. And thereupon Methuselah went and summoned to him all his brothers and assembled his relatives. 3. And he spake unto all the children of righteousness and said:

'Hear, ye sons of Enoch, all the words of your father,
And hearken aright to the voice of my mouth;
For I exhort you and say unto you, beloved:

Love uprightness and walk therein.

4. And draw not nigh to uprightness with a double heart,
And associate not with those of a double heart,

---

ness and grace. These words are further explained in ver. 4. **4. The righteous** (tu, β). gq 'righteousness'. **Power**. Uprightness and power will no longer be dissevered. **He shall** (mt, β). gq^u 'they shall'. **In eternal light**; see 38⁴ (note). 5. Cf. 10¹⁴, ²⁰.

XCI. 1. **All thy brothers... all the sons of thy mother**. ω g. According to 2 Enoch 1¹⁰ 57² the names of these sons are Methuselah, Regim, Riman, Ukhan, Khermion, Gaidal. 3. **Unto all the children of righteousness** (gq, $y_1 b$). $m t u$, β-$ełny_1 a_1 b$ 'to all ($> u$, + 'his children' t) concerning his ($> β$-$ełny_1 a_1 b$) righteousness'. **Beloved** (a-u). β 'my beloved'. **Love uprightness**, &c.: cf. 94¹. 4. **Draw not nigh to uprightness with a double heart**. This may be derived from Sir. 1²⁸ μὴ προσέλθῃς αὐτῷ (i.e. φόβῳ κυρίου) ἐν καρδίᾳ δισσῇ: cf. Ps. 12³ לֵב וָלֵב; Jas. 1⁸ δίψυχος. **Associate not**, &c.

But walk in righteousness, my sons.
And it shall guide you on good paths,
And righteousness shall be your companion.

5. For I know that violence must increase on the earth,
And a great chastisement be executed on the earth,
And all unrighteousness come to an end:

Yea, it shall be cut off from its roots,
And its whole structure be destroyed.

6. And unrighteousness shall again be consummated on the earth,
And all the deeds of unrighteousness and of violence
And transgression shall prevail in a twofold degree.

7. And when sin and unrighteousness and blasphemy
And violence in all kinds of deeds increase,
And apostasy and transgression and uncleanness increase,

A great chastisement shall come from heaven upon all these,
And the holy Lord will come forth with wrath and chastisement
To execute judgement on earth.

8. In those days violence shall be cut off from its roots,
And the roots of unrighteousness together with deceit,
And they shall be destroyed from under heaven.

> gu through hmt.; cf. 94², ³ 104⁶. In righteousness, my sons. g 'in uprightness and righteousness'. Good paths. There seems to be a reference here to the Two Ways. See ver. 19. 5. The Deluge. Violence must increase. The text reads 'the state (or 'essence') of violence shall increase'. But this is wholly unlikely. I have therefore emended hĕlâwŏ (= 'state') into halawŏ, i. e. the substantive verb with suffix. When we combine halawŏ with jĕṣan'ŏ the two = 'must increase'. Cut off from its roots: cf. vv. 8, 11. 6. The growth of wickedness after the Deluge. 7, 8. This fresh development of wickedness will call forth the final judgement. 7. In all (a–q). q, β 'and all'. And transgression. > gu. From heaven. > g. And. > mqt. Lord. + 'upon earth' g. 8. And the roots (mtu, β). > gq. Roots of unrighteousness: cf. vv. 5, 11. And (> u, $bcfhp$) they

9. And all the idols of the heathen shall be abandoned.
And the temples burned with fire,
And they shall remove them from the whole earth,

And they (i.e. the heathen) shall be cast into the judgement of fire,
And shall perish in wrath and in grievous judgement for ever.

10. And the righteous shall arise from their sleep,
And wisdom shall arise and be given unto them.

[11. And after that the roots of unrighteousness shall be cut off, and the sinners shall be destroyed by the sword ... shall be cut off from the blasphemers in every place, and those who plan violence and those who commit blasphemy shall perish by the sword.]

shall be destroyed (mtu, β). > gq.
9. The absolute rejection of the heathen seems to be taught here. This was a prevailing though not the universal belief of later Judaism; see Weber, *Jüd. Theol.* 386. Idolatry is reprobated in $99^{7-9, 18}$, as here. And ^{20} (gu, o_1b). > Other MSS. They shall be cast into the judgement of fire. This reprobation of the heathen does not appear to agree with the teaching of ver. 14 (see p. 233), where the conversion of the heathen is expected. That verse, however, belongs to the Apocalypse of Weeks which has all the appearance of an earlier fragment incorporated in his work by the original author of 91-104. 10. The righteous. The singular used collectively as in 92^3. Their sleep (gmq, x). $tu, \beta-x$ 'sleep'. In 91-104 only the righteous attain to the Resurrection; see 51^1 (note) for full discussion of the subject. Wisdom: see $42^{1, 2}$ (note). 11. As we have already seen (p. 224), 91^{12-17} originally stood after 93^{1-10}. As for this verse, we must regard it as an interpolation added by the final editor in order to introduce vv. 12-17 which he had torn from their original context. This verse is wholly out of place here. Judgement has already been consummated, all evil works destroyed, and all the wicked handed over to a judgement of fire (vv. 7-9). In ver. 10 the Resurrection ensues and judgement is now over. But in ver. 11 all this is ignored and a moral chaos is represented as still existing—a moral chaos of exactly the same nature as existed before the judgement of vv. 7-9. Moreover, the period of the Sword—man's part in the final judgement—precedes the Resurrection; cf. 90^{19} 91^{12}. The Resurrection follows upon the destruction of all evil and the final judgement, $100^{4, 5}$. Finally, this verse seems modelled partly on vv. 7 and 8, and partly on ver. 12, the expressions about blasphemers being drawn from ver. 7, the phrase 'roots of unrighteousness shall be cut off' from ver. 8, and the

18. And now I tell you, my sons, and show you
   The paths of righteousness and the paths of violence.
   Yea, I will show them to you again
   That ye may know what will come to pass.

19. And now, hearken unto me, my sons,
   And walk in the paths of righteousness,
   And walk not in the paths of violence;
   For all who walk in the paths of unrighteousness
      shall perish for ever.'

XCIII, XCI. 12-17. *The Apocalypse of Weeks.*

XCIII. 1. And after that Enoch both †gave† and began to recount from the books. 2. And Enoch said:

reference to the Sword from ver. 12 (see p. 232). 18. Will show (*m*, β). *gqt* 'have shown'. > *u*. 19. Hearken unto me (*g¹u*. β 'hearken'. > *g*. And²⁰. > *g*. Paths of righteousness . . . paths of violence. This theme is pressed home with great emphasis in 94¹⁻⁴ where we find the 'paths of righteousness' 94¹, 'paths of peace' 94⁴, 'paths of unrighteousness' 94¹, 'paths of violence and of death' 94², 'paths of wickedness' and 'paths of death' 94³. This is one of the earliest non-canonical references to the 'Two Ways'. See T. Ash. 1², ⁵ (note in my edition) 2 Enoch 30¹⁵ (note). Cf. Deut. 30¹⁵, ¹⁹ Jer. 21⁸ Ps. 1⁶.

XCIII. 1-10. In these verses we have an account of the great events of the world during the first seven weeks of its history. These seven belong to the past, the three last weeks described in 91¹²⁻¹⁷ belong to the future. As this Apocalypse of Weeks comes from a different author and date to the Dream-visions, 83-90, we are relieved of the task of harmonizing them, on which many critics have laboured and to no purpose. We are not to regard the ten weeks as being definite and equal periods of 700 years each, as Wieseler, Hoffmann, and others have done; for, not to press the fact that this reckoning would place the book after Christ, the facts recorded as occurring in the individual weeks would not fall within the limits assigned them by this theory. Dillmann's scheme of seventy generations of varying length, seven generations to each week, is still more unsatisfactory. In the first five weeks seven actual generations are taken for each week; but in the sixth and seventh weeks fourteen or more generations are compressed into the needful seven. Rather we are to regard the ten weeks as periods of varying length, each one of which is marked, especially towards its close, by some great event—the first by the birth of Enoch; the second by the corruption of primitive man and the Flood; the third by the call of Abraham; the fourth by the revelation of the law and the occupation of Palestine; the fifth by the building of the Temple; the sixth by the apostasy of Israel and the destruction of the Temple; the seventh by the publication of Enoch's writings. In the eighth

'Concerning the children of righteousness and concerning the elect of the world,

And concerning the plant of uprightness, I will speak these things,

Yea, I Enoch will declare (them) unto you, my sons:

According to that which appeared to me in the heavenly vision,

And which I have known through the word of the holy angels,

And have learnt from the heavenly tablets.'

3. And Enoch began to recount from the books and said:
'I was born the seventh in the first week,
While judgement and righteousness still endured.

4. And after me there shall arise in the second week great wickedness,

the Messianic kingdom is established and lasts to the close of the tenth week. The final judgement in 91¹⁵ is held at the close of the Messianic kingdom. Cf. also *Le Livre d'Henoch*, par T. G. Peter, Genève, 1890. **1.** †Gave† (a–mt). t, β 'was'. I do not see how the corruption can be explained. **And began.** > a–y. **From the books.** These were either written by Enoch, according to some Sections; or by the angel that accompanied him, according to others; cf. 33³, ⁴ 40⁸ 74³ 81¹, ². In the next verse Enoch appeals to visions, angels, and the heavenly tablets, as the source of his revelations. **2.** These disclosures are for the children of righteousness; cf. 92¹. **The elect of the world.** This designation of the elect is not found elsewhere in Enoch. **The plant of uprightness**: see 10¹⁶ (note). **Uprightness** (a–q). q 'righteousness', β 'righteousness and uprightness'. **Will declare** (gq. β). *mtu* 'have declared'. **Heavenly tablets**: see 47³ (note) for a complete account of this and similar expressions. **3. Enoch.** > mqt. **Seventh in the first week.** Ewald and Dillmann find in this expression the foundation of their theory that the reckoning here is according to generations. But this is to press the words too much. They mean nothing more than in Gen. 5³⁶, where he is the seventh of the patriarchs, or 'seventh from Adam', Jude 14. **Still endured.** The meaning is doubtful. 'Judgement' may be taken in a favourable sense. In that case Enoch was born before the demoralization of mankind. The next stanza appears to favour this view. On the other hand, the fact that the angels descended in the days of Jared, nearly sixty years before Enoch was born, Jubilees 4¹⁵⁻¹⁶, is against this view, and would favour such a rendering as 'were held back'. The righteous judgement of the Deluge had not yet come. **4. Great wickedness.** According to 6⁶ and

And deceit shall have sprung up;
And in it there shall be the first end.

And in it a man shall be saved;
And after it is ended unrighteousness shall grow up,
And a law shall be made for the sinners.

5. And after that in the third week at its close
A man shall be elected as the plant of righteous judgement,
And his posterity shall become the plant of righteousness for evermore.

6. And after that in the fourth week, at its close,
Visions of the holy and righteous shall be seen,
And a law for all generations and an enclosure shall be made for them.

7. And after that in the fifth week, at its close,
The house of glory and dominion shall be built for ever.

106¹³ this growth of wickedness should have been assigned to Jared's days, when the fall of the angels took place. This week includes the Deluge, and the Covenant made with Noah: Gen. 8²¹-9¹⁷. The time order in the close of this sentence is not observed. A law shall be made (*g*, *n*). Since *gms* read 'law' in the nom. I take it that jĕgabĕr is in them corrupt for jĕtgabar—the reading of *q*, *u*. Cf. ver. 6. *t*, β-א read 'He will make a law'. 5. Abraham and his seed chosen as the race in and through which God would reveal His righteous judgements—'the plant of righteous judgement'; cf. ver. 2; 10¹⁶ (note). His posterity. The text reads 'after him (or 'it') it shall come (or 'become') the plant of righteousness', &c. But, since this is unsatisfactory however we take it, I suggest that אחריו (= 'after him' or 'it') stood before the translator but was corrupt for אחריתו = 'his posterity'. 6. Visions of the holy and righteous (*mq*, β). So *u* but that it omits 'and righteous'. *g* reads 'visions of the holy and righteousness', *t* 'holy and righteous visions'. The divine manifestations in favour of Israel in Egypt. A law, &c. The law given on Sinai. This law is of eternal obligation; cf. 99². An enclosure. Dillmann thinks this refers to the Tabernacle and the hedging in of the national life by the law. It seems rather to refer to the occupation of Palestine; cf. 89². 7. The house. The Temple will, according to this author, stand 'for ever', though one form of it may give place to another. If this Apocalypse of Weeks was originally an integral part of 91-104 this 'for ever' means only an indefinitely long time; for though there is an eternal law, there appears to be no Temple after the final judgement, and the risen righteous enjoy a purely spiritual existence like the angels, as in the Book of Jubilees, and possibly

8. And after that in the sixth week all who live in it shall be blinded,

And the hearts of all of them shall godlessly forsake wisdom.

And in it a man shall ascend;

And at its close the house of dominion shall be burnt with fire,

And the whole race of the chosen root shall be dispersed.

9. And after that in the seventh week shall an apostate generation arise,

And many shall be its deeds,

And all its deeds shall be apostate.

10. And at its close shall be elected

The elect righteous of the eternal plant of righteousness,

To receive sevenfold instruction concerning all His creation.

[11. For who is there of all the children of men that is able to hear the voice of the Holy One without being troubled? And who can think His thoughts? and who is there that can behold all the works of heaven? 12. And how should there

in the Pss. of Solomon. 8. The time of the divided kingdom in Israel, of growing degeneracy and darkness. A man, i.e. Elijah; cf. 89^{52}. At the close of this week the Temple is destroyed and the nation carried into captivity. Chosen root (g, β). mqt 'root of might'. 9. This week embraces the period from the Captivity to the time of the author. It is an apostate period. The same judgement is passed upon it in 89^{73-75}. Apostate^{1e} > gm. 10. The writer here refers to his own disclosures which will be made known at the end of the seventh week. It might seem that it would be impossible for any writer to make such extravagant claims for his productions. We find some slight approach to these in Sir. 24^{23-32}. Shall be elected (a, $acfhikn$). $bdlopxy_1u_1b$

shall be recompensed'. The elect righteous (η, $abefhikx$). Cf. 1^1 Greek version. t supports this. g, $dloy_1a_1b$ read 'the elect of righteousness', m 'the righteous', u 'the elect'. The revelations are designed for the elect righteous, for only these will receive them; cf. 100^6 $104^{12, 13}$. 11-14. The verses are completely out of place in their present context, as Laurence, Hoffmann, and Schodde have already remarked, and subsequently Beer and Martin. They would belong rather to the Book of the Heavenly Luminaries, 72-79 82, but are foreign in character to the whole tone of this book, 91-104, and do not as a matter of fact rightly describe any one of the books of Enoch. 11. The voice of the Holy One, i.e. the thunder; cf. Job $37^{4, 5}$ Ps. 29. Think His be one who could behold the heaven, and who is there that could understand the things of heaven and see a soul or a spirit and could tell thereof, or ascend and see all their ends and think them or do like them? 13. And who is there of all men that could know what is the breadth and the length of the earth, and to whom has been shown the measure of all of them? 14. Or is there any one who could discern the length of the heaven and how great is its height, and upon what it is founded, and how great is the number of the stars, and where all the luminaries rest?]

XCI. 12-17. *The Last Three Weeks.*

12. And after that there shall be another, the eighth week, that of righteousness,
    And a sword shall be given to it that a righteous judgement may be executed on the oppressors,
    And sinners shall be delivered into the hands of the righteous.

13. And at its close they shall acquire houses through their righteousness,
    And a house shall be built for the Great King in glory for evermore,

14d. And all mankind shall look to the path of uprightness.

thoughts: cf. Job 5^9 9^{10} 38^{36} Pss. 40^1 92^5 Eccles. 11^5. 12. A soul (gmq, bxy). t, $β-bxy$ 'His breath'. A spirit (mtu, bxy). gq a corruption of text in mtu. $β-bxy$ 'His spirit'. These words would refer to Enoch's journey through heaven and Hades. Ascend: cf. Prov. 30^4. Their ends, i.e. of the things of heaven. But 'aknâfîhômû (= 'their ends') may be corrupt for meknjâtîhômû = 'their causes'. 13. Cf. Job $38^{4, 5}$. Not given in Enoch. 14. The length of the heaven, &c.: Jer. 31^{37} Job 11^8. Not given in Enoch. Founded: cf. $18^{2, 3}$. Number of the stars. This is nowhere found in Enoch.

XCI. 12-17. These verses giving an account of the last three weeks of the world's history are here restored to their place after 93^{1-10} (see p. 224), the account of the first seven weeks. 12. The eighth week sees the establishment of the Messianic kingdom. It likewise forms the first act of the final judgement, for it is the period of the Sword; cf. 90^{19}: and the wicked are given into the hands of the righteous cf. 95^7 96^1 98^{12} $99^{4, 6}$; also 38^5. 13 On the period of strife will follow that of rest and quiet possession of the earth; cf. Is. $60^{21, 22}$ 65^{20-23}. A house ... for the Great King ($a-g, β$). g 'the house of the Great King shall be built'.

14 *a*. And after that, in the ninth week, the righteous judgement shall be revealed to the whole world,
  b. And all the works of the godless shall vanish from all the earth,
  c. And the world shall be written down for destruction.

15. And after this, in the tenth week in the seventh part,
    There shall be the great eternal judgement,
    In which He will execute vengeance amongst the angels.

16. And the first heaven shall depart and pass away,
    And a new heaven shall appear,
    And all the powers of the heavens shall give sevenfold light.

17. And after that there will be many weeks without number for ever,

This means first of all the temple and in the next place Jerusalem. **14.** This stanza is difficult. It is too long by one line, whereas the preceding stanza is too short. Accordingly I have transposed 14 *d* to the close of the preceding stanza. The ninth week, as Dillmann supposes, may mean the period in which true religion will spread over the earth, and the judgement described in ver. 12, and executed by the righteous, will be made known to the neutral Gentile nations with a view to their conversion; cf. 50^{2-3} 90^{30}, ^{33}, ^{38}. With this view the concluding words of this verse would harmonize well. Yet see ver. 15 (note). **The works of the godless shall vanish**: cf. 10^{16}, ^{20}, ^{21}. **The world shall be written down for destruction** (*m*, β). *g* 'He shall write down (i.e. decree) the destruction of the world'. *t* 'He shall write down the world for destruction'. > *u*. *q* a corruption of *g* (?). The opposite phrase 'written down for life' is found in Is. 4^3 כתוב לחיים. This destination will take effect towards the close of the tenth week. **15.** The tenth week ends with the final judgement on the watchers. As there is no mention of the judgement of the wicked by God in person in this verse, the preceding verse may in some measure refer to it. **There shall be the great eternal judgement, In which ... amongst the angels** (*a–t*). The structure of the stanza supports this text. *t*, β–*in* insert a gloss and read

'There shall be the eternal judgement,
And it shall be executed on the watchers of the eternal heaven,
The great (judgement) in which He will execute vengeance amongst the angels.'

16. Observe that though there will be a new heaven, cf. Is. 65^{17} 66^{22} Ps. 102^{26}, there is no mention of a new earth, cf. 104^2 (note). For the idea of a new creation cf. 45^4 72^1 (note). **Sevenfold**: cf. Is. 30^{26} 60^{19}, ^{20}. *mqt*, β–*ahk* add 'for ever'. **17.** This verse

And all shall be in goodness and righteousness,
And sin shall no more be mentioned for ever.

XCIV. 1–5. *Admonitions to the Righteous.*

XCIV. 1. And now I say unto you, my sons, love righteousness and walk therein;
For the paths of righteousness are worthy of acceptance,
But the paths of unrighteousness shall suddenly be destroyed and vanish.

2. And to certain men of a generation shall the paths of violence and of death be revealed,
And they shall hold themselves afar from them,
And shall not follow them.

3. And now I say unto you the righteous:
Walk not in the paths of wickedness, nor on the paths of death,
And draw not nigh to them, lest ye be destroyed.

4. But seek and choose for yourselves righteousness and an elect life,
And walk in the paths of peace,
And ye shall live and prosper.

5. And hold fast my words in the thoughts of your hearts,
And suffer them not to be effaced from your hearts;
For know that sinners will tempt men to evilly-entreat wisdom,

---

closes the Apocalypse of Weeks. And all (*g*). > Other MSS.

XCIV. This chapter introduces the practical part of this Section. Though written for the righteous, it devotes as much attention to the woes awaiting the sinners. 1. Love righteousness, &c.: cf. 91³. Worthy of acceptation (*t*, β). *gmq* 'worthy and acceptable'. *u* 'worthy'. Cf. 1 Tim. 1¹⁵ ἀποδοχῆς ἄξιος. Paths of unrighteousness ... destroyed: cf. Ps. 1⁶. On the 'two paths' see 91¹⁹ note. 2. The revelations through Moses and the Prophets. Paths of... death: cf. Prov. 14¹² Jer. 21⁸. 3. Paths¹⁰ (*gml*, *bx*). β-*bx* 'path'. Wickedness. + 'and of violence' β. Draw not nigh: cf. 91⁴ 104⁶. 4. But seek. *g* reads 'as those who seek evil', and connects the words with the preceding verse. And ye shall (*gmq*). *t*, β 'that ye may'. 5. To evilly-entreat. The text = 'to

So that no place may be found for her,
And no manner of temptation may minish.

XCIV. 6-11. *Woes for the Sinners.*

6. Woe to those who build unrighteousness and oppression
   And lay deceit as a foundation;
   For they shall be suddenly overthrown,
   And they shall have no peace.

7. Woe to those who build their houses with sin;
   For from all their foundations shall they be overthrown,
   And by the sword shall they fall.

   [And those who acquire gold and silver in judgement
       suddenly shall perish.]

8. Woe to you, ye rich, for ye have trusted in your riches,
   And from your riches shall ye depart,
   Because ye have not remembered the Most High in the
       days of your riches.

9. Ye have committed blasphemy and unrighteousness,
   And have become ready for the day of slaughter,
   And the day of darkness and the day of the great judgement.

10. Thus I speak and declare unto you:
    He who hath created you will overthrow you,

make . . . evil', apparently a mis-rendering of κακοποιεῖν. No place may be found for her: cf. 42¹. 6. Some of the forms that wickedness will assume in those days. Build: cf. 91². Have no peace. This recurs in 98¹¹, ¹⁶ 99¹³ 101³ 102³ 103⁸. See also 5⁴ (note). 7. Build their houses with sin: from Jer. 22¹³ הוֹי בֹּנֶה בֵיתוֹ בְלֹא־צֶדֶק. They, i.e. the men who so build. [And those who acquire . . . perish.] I have bracketed this sentence as an interpolation. The subject of riches is not dealt with till the next woe in ver.

8. Our author does not condemn the acquisition of wealth in itself but its acquisition by wrong means. Cf. 97⁸, from which passage this interpolation may in part be drawn. The removal of this sentence sets the stanza right. 8. Trusted in your riches. This phrase is drawn from Prov. 11²⁸ בֹּטֵחַ בְּעָשְׁרוֹ. Cf. Pss. 49⁶ 52⁷. In Jer. 9²³ the rich man is bidden not to glory in his riches. Pss. 49⁶ 52⁷. Cf. also 1 En. 46⁷ 63¹⁰ 96⁴ 97⁸⁻¹⁰. 9. Through their sin and blasphemy they are now ripe for judgement. Day of slaughter, &c.: see 45² (note). And the day

And for your fall there shall be no compassion,
And your Creator will rejoice at your destruction.

11. And your righteous ones in those days shall be
A reproach to the sinners and the godless.

Enoch's Grief: fresh Woes against the Sinners.

XCV. 1. Oh that mine eyes were [a cloud of] waters
That I might weep over you,
And pour down my tears as a cloud † of † waters:
That so I might rest from my trouble of heart!

2. †Who has permitted you to practise reproaches and wickedness?
And so judgement shall overtake you, sinners.†

3. Fear not the sinners, ye righteous;
For again will the Lord deliver them into your hands,

---

of darkness. > *g, a*. **10. Your Creator will rejoice at your destruction.** This sentiment has its parallels in the O. T., cf. Pss. 2⁴,⁴ 37¹²,¹³, and in our text 89⁹⁶ and 97². **11. Your righteous ones**, i. e. the righteous among his children's descendants. This stanza is imperfect.

XCV. 1. Oh that mine eyes were [a cloud of] waters. 'Cloud' here is impossible, however it may be in the next line. Its genesis is, I think, clear. The text = מִי יִתֵּן עֵינַי עֲנַן מָיִם. Here the impossible עֲנַן is either a dittograph of עֵינַי: then we should have 'Oh that mine eyes were waters': or it is a corruption of עַיִן. In that case we should have 'Oh that mine eyes were a spring of waters'. In this latter case we might compare 2 Bar. 35² 'Become ye springs, O mine eyes, and ye, mine eyelids, a fount of tears'. Our text, of course, is based on Jer. 9¹ 'Oh that my head were waters, and mine eyes a fountain of tears'. **As a cloud of waters** = כַּעֲנַן מַיִם, which should probably have been translated 'as a cloud pours waters': or still better take מַיִם as corrupt for זְרַם: then we should have 'as a cloud (pours) rain'. **2. Who has permitted** (lit. 'given') **you** (*g β*(= מִי נְתַנְכֶם)). But *a-g*(= מִי יִתֶּנְכֶם) 'Who will give you' or 'Oh that ye were' is probably right. Then either omitting 'to practise' with *g*, or emending tĕgabĕrû into tĕtgabarû, we should have 'Oh that ye were become a reproach and wickedness'. In that case we should in the next line adopt the subjunctive with *β* and not the indicative in *a*. The couplet would then run:

'Oh that ye were become a reproach and an evil
And that so judgement might overtake you, sinners.'

3. Yet let not the righteous fear; for the period of their supremacy is at hand; cf. 91¹². **Again.** The writer may refer to the Maccabean victories; for

> That ye may execute judgement upon them according to your desires.

4. Woe to you who fulminate anathemas which cannot be reversed:
Healing shall therefore be far from you because of your sins.

5. Woe to you who requite your neighbour with evil;
For ye shall be requited according to your works.

6. Woe to you, lying witnesses,
And to those who weigh out injustice,
For suddenly shall ye perish.

7. Woe to you, sinners, for ye persecute the righteous;
For ye shall be delivered up and persecuted because of injustice,
And heavy shall its yoke be upon you.

Grounds of Hopefulness for the Righteous: Woes for the Wicked.

XCVI. 1. Be hopeful, ye righteous; for suddenly shall the sinners perish before you,
And ye shall have lordship over them according to your desires.

---

these were victories over Sadducean influences. Though the Maccabean princes are now Sadducees themselves, the period of the Sword, the time of the vengeance of the righteous, is coming. 4. Magical practices and incantations are here referred to. Which cannot ('can' gq) be reversed (gmq). t, β 'which you cannot reverse'. Cf. 8^3 on the reversing of incantation. 5. Requite... with evil. For like expressions cf. Prov. 17^{13} 'reward evil for good', 20^{22} 'Say not, I will recompense evil' אֲשַׁלְּמָה־רָע, 24^{29} Rom. 12^{17}. Requited according to your works: cf. 100^7 Judg. 1^7. 6. Weigh out injustice, i.e. are unjust judges, but the expression is strange. 7. Ye shall be delivered up (g). Other MSS. 'ye shall deliver up'. And persecuted (a–gt, β–a). gt, a 'and ye shall persecute'. Its yoke (gmq). t, β 'their yoke'.

XCVI. The righteous exhorted to hope in the coming Messianic kingdom, and fresh woes denounced against the sinners. 1. Lordship: cf. 91^{12} (note) $95^{3, 7}$ 98^{12}. 2. This verse

[2. And in the day of the tribulation of the sinners,
Your children shall mount and rise as eagles,
And higher than the vultures will be your nest,

And ye shall ascend and enter the crevices of the earth,
And the clefts of the rock for ever as coneys before the unrighteous,
And the sirens shall sigh because of you and weep.]

3. Wherefore fear not, ye that have suffered;
For healing shall be your portion,
And a bright light shall enlighten you,
And the voice of rest ye shall hear from heaven.

4. Woe unto you, ye sinners, for your riches make you appear like the righteous,
But your hearts convict you of being sinners,
And this fact shall be a testimony against you for a memorial of (your) evil deeds.

5. Woe to you who devour the finest of the wheat,
And drink wine in large bowls,
And tread under foot the lowly with your might.

must be an interpolation: it is foolish in itself and interrupts the context. It is the wicked who will flee to hide themselves in secret places, 97⁸ 100⁴ 102¹, and not the righteous: the latter will not have to conceal themselves on the day of judgement, 104⁵. Perhaps the first three lines may be original. In the day of the tribulation of the sinners. This would naturally mean when the sinners suffer tribulation; but it must mean here in the day when tribulation is caused by the sinners. Mount and rise, &c. From Is. 40³¹. Higher than the vultures: cf. Jer. 49¹⁶. Enter the crevices of the earth, &c. These words are taken from Is. 2¹⁰, ¹⁹, ²¹, and are used there of those who flee through fear from the presence of the Lord. Hence they are most inappropriate in their present connexion. Before the unrighteous. These words imply that the righteous go into the clefts of the rocks to escape the unrighteous. The sirens. Whether sirens (so the Ethiopic version renders σειρῆνες Is. 13²¹ Jer. 27³⁹) or satyrs, the meaning of the word is uncertain. *qt*, β read 'as the sirens' 3. A bright light: see 38⁴ (note). 4. Your riches make you appear like the righteous. Wealthy sinners could appeal to their riches as a proof of their righteousness; for according to the O.T. doctrine of retribution, prosperity was a mark of righteousness. This fact, i.e. that your riches prove you to be righteous. For a memorial, &c.: cf. ver. 7. 5. The finest of the wheat: Pss. 81¹⁷ (חֵלֶב חִטָּה) 147¹⁴. †Wine in large bowls†, i.e. not in wine cups. Like the magnates in Samaria,

Chapters XCVI. 2—XCVII. 2

6. Woe to you who drink water from every fountain,
   For suddenly shall ye be consumed and wither away,
   Because ye have forsaken the fountain of life.

7. Woe to you who work unrighteousness
   And deceit and blasphemy:
   It shall be a memorial against you for evil.

8. Woe to you, ye mighty,
   Who with might oppress the righteous;
   For the day of your destruction is coming.

   In those days many and good days shall come to the righteous—in the day of your judgement.

The Evils in Store for Sinners and the Possessors of unrighteous Wealth.

XCVII. 1. Believe, ye righteous, that the sinners will become a shame
   And perish in the day of unrighteousness.

2. Be it known unto you (ye sinners) that the Most High is mindful of your destruction,
   And the angels of heaven rejoice over your destruction.

Amos 6⁶, these wealthy sinners drank from flagons, not from cups. The text which is here corrupt = 'the strength of the root of the fountain' = ἰσχὺν ῥίζης πηγῆς = בֹּחַ עִיקַר עַיִן corrupt for בְּמִזְרְקֵי יַיִן—the actual phrase used of the drinking-vessels of the luxurious nobles in Samaria. 6. Drink water from every fountain. For 'from every fountain' the text reads literally 'at every time' = בְּכָל־עֵת corrupt for מִכָּל־עַיִן 'from every fountain'. The words are here used metaphorically as opposed to 'the fountain of life' used at the close of the stanza. Jer. 2¹³— 'they have forsaken Me the fountain of living waters'—was in the mind of our author. Cf. Ps. 36⁹. For suddenly shall ye be consumed (mqt). g, β 'for suddenly shall ye be requited and consumed'. u (defective) 'suddenly'. Forsaken, &c. See note on the first line of the stanza. 7. Cf. 91⁸ 94⁶,⁹. A memorial. Cf. ver. 4. 8. Many and good days. The reference here seems to be to the temporary Messianic kingdom in which the righteous who are living at the time will participate.

XCVII. This chapter mainly consists of threatenings against the wicked. 1. In the day of unrighteousness. A peculiar expression for the day appointed for the judgement of unrighteousness: see 45² (note). 2. Angels of heaven (a, n). β-n 'angels'. Cf.

3. What will ye do, ye sinners,
   And whither will ye flee on that day of judgement,
   When ye hear the voice of the prayer of the righteous?

4. Yea, ye shall fare like unto them,
   Against whom this word shall be a testimony:
   "Ye have been companions of sinners."

5. And in those days the prayer of the righteous shall reach unto the Lord,
   And for you the days of your judgement shall come.

6. And all the words of your unrighteousness shall be read out before the Great Holy One,
   And your faces shall be covered with shame,
   And He will reject every work which is grounded on unrighteousness.

7. Woe to you, ye sinners, who live on the mid ocean and on the dry land,
   Whose remembrance is evil against you.

8. Woe to you who acquire silver and gold in unrighteousness and say:
   "We have become rich with riches and have possessions;
   And have acquired everything we have desired.

94^{10} for a similar expression of religious hate contrasted with Luke 15^{10}.   3. **Whither will ye flee**: cf. 102^1. **The prayer of the righteous**: cf. ver. 5.   4. **Shall fare** (gqu). mt, β 'shall not fare'. **Against whom** (g). t 'for against you'. mq, β 'ye against whom'. **This word ... 'Ye have been companions of sinners.'** 96^4 may be taken in this sense. The Pharisaic duty of separation from the unrighteous could not be more strongly enforced.   5. **The prayer of the righteous**: cf. 47^2 97^2 99^3, ^{16} 104^3. This cry of the righteous for vengeance on their persecutors is found in Rev. 6^{10}. **Righteous** ($a-g$, $\beta-afhikpv$). g, $afhikpv$ 'holy'.   6. **All the words of** ($mqt, \beta-a$). g 'all'. **Shall be read out**, i.e. from the books of remembrance of evil deeds: see 47^3 (note). Cf. Matt. 12^{36} πᾶν ῥῆμα ἀργόν, ὃ ἐὰν λαλήσουσιν οἱ ἄνθρωποι, ἀποδώσουσιν περὶ αὐτοῦ λόγον ἐν ἡμέρᾳ κρίσεως— which seems a reminiscence of our text. **Great Holy One** (g_1gmq, n). $tu, \beta-n_1 a$ 'Great and Holy One': see 1^3 (note) 92^2 (note). **Covered with shame**: cf. 46^6 62^{10} 63^{11}. **He will reject every work** (gqt). mu, β 'every work shall be rejected'.   7. **On the mid ocean and on the dry land**, i.e. everywhere. **Remembrance**: cf. $100^{10, 11}$ 104^8.   8. Cf. $94^{7, 8}$ (note); also Sir. 11^{18} Luke 12^{19}. **With riches** (mqt, β). $> gu$. The words of the rich,

Sect. V]   *Chapters XCVII. 3—XCVIII. 2*   241

9. And now let us do what we purposed :
   For we have gathered silver,
   9ᵈ And many are the husbandmen in our houses,
   9ᵉ And our granaries are (brim)full as with water."

10. Yea and like water your lies shall flow away ;
    For your riches shall not abide
    But speedily ascend from you ;

    For ye have acquired it all in unrighteousness,
    And ye shall be given over to a great curse.

Self-indulgence of Sinners: Sin originated by Man: all Sin recorded in Heaven: Woes for the Sinners.

XCVIII. 1. And now I swear unto you, to the wise and to the foolish,
    For ye shall have manifold experiences on the earth.

2. For ye men shall put on more adornments than a woman,
   And coloured garments more than a virgin :
   In royalty and in grandeur and in power,
   And in silver and in gold and in purple,
   And in splendour and in food they shall be poured out as water.

when retranslated into Hebrew, rhyme as they do in Lamentations 5³ ׳׳׳ 'We have become rich with riches', &c. =

וְכֹל קָנִינוּ   עֹשֶׁר עָשַׁרְנוּ
אֲשֶׁר אִוִּינוּ   וּרְכֻשׁ לָנוּ

9.   וְנַעֲשֶׂה שֶׁחָשַׁבְנוּ
      כִּי כֶסֶף אָסֹף אָסַפְנוּ
9ᵈ.   וְרַבִּים אִכָּרֵי בָתֵּינוּ
9ᵉ.   וּמְלֵאִים כְּמַיִם אוֹצְרוֹתֵינוּ

9. And many (g_1g, $_1b$). qt, β–$_1b$ 'many'. As with water ($_1g$). Other MSS. 'and as with water'. 10. This verse is a rejoinder to the boasting of the sinners. The writer takes up the last words and gives them a different turn. Your lies: i.e. the false things in which you trust. Your riches

(u). a–u, β 'riches with you'. Riches shall ... speedily ascend: cf. Prov. 23⁵. All (gmt, β–n). > $_1gq\text{u}$, n.

XCVIII. This chapter introduces a fresh division in 91–104. This division, 98–102³, consists mainly of a denunciation of the sinners, of their errors in life and doctrine, and announces their coming judgement. 1. I swear unto you. This formula occurs here for the first time but recurs frequently; cf. vv. 4, 6 ; 99⁶, &c. To the wise and to the foolish. The foolish are addressed in 98–102³; the wise in 102⁴–104. To the foolish (mu, β). g_1gqt 'not to the foolish'. 2. Shall be poured out as water. Phrase from Ps. 22¹⁴. Their personality giving itself wholly to such external possessions will at last

3. Therefore they shall be wanting in doctrine and wisdom,
   And they shall perish thereby together with their possessions;
   And with all their glory and their splendour,
   And in shame and in slaughter and in great destitution,
   Their spirits shall be cast into the furnace of fire.

4. I have sworn unto you, ye sinners, as a mountain has not become a slave,
   And a hill does not become the handmaid of a woman,
   Even so sin has not been sent upon the earth,
   But man of himself has created it,
   And under a great curse shall they fall who commit it.

5. And barrenness has not been given to the woman,
   But on account of the deeds of her own hands she dies without children.

6. I have sworn unto you, ye sinners, by the Holy Great One,
   That all your evil deeds are revealed in the heavens,
   And that none of your deeds of oppression are covered and hidden.

7. And do not think in your spirit nor say in your heart that ye do not know and that ye do not see that every sin is

---

lose itself in them, as water is lost in the earth. **3. In great destitution.** In contrast to their wealth in this world. **Their spirits:** cf. ver. 10; 103⁸. **Into the furnace of fire** (g_1g, β). > *mqtu*. Cf. Matt. 13⁴², ⁵⁰. As incorporeal spirits the wicked are cast into hell. This 'furnace of fire' is the final place of punishment. **4.** The writer now proceeds to attack the immoral view that sin is something original and unavoidable. Sin was of man's own devising: see 69¹¹ (note). Yet the writer still ascribes the introduction of sin into the world to the fallen angels; cf. 100⁴. The contrast of mountain and slave and hill and handmaid is suggested by the fact that הר (= 'mountain') is masculine in Hebrew and נבעה (= 'hill') is feminine. In Aramaic we have טור and רמא. **5. And as a consequence of their sin men are punished just because sin is a voluntary thing.** The instance in the text is chosen as an illustration of this general law; cf. Hos. 9¹⁴. **Barrenness** (*tu, β-n¹*). *g₁y₁uq, n¹* 'simulation', or 'excuse'. **6–8.** The writer next deals with the view that God does not concern Himself with the world or the deeds of men, cf. Job 22¹³ Ps. 73¹¹, and declares that the deeds of men are recorded every day in heaven. **6. Holy Great One** (*g₁tu*).

every day recorded in heaven in the presence of the Most High. 8. From henceforth ye know that all your oppression wherewith ye oppress is written down every day till the day of your judgement.

9. Woe to you, ye fools, for through your folly shall ye perish: and ye transgress against the wise, and so good hap shall not be your portion. 10. And now, know ye that ye are prepared for the day of destruction: wherefore do not hope to live, ye sinners, but ye shall depart and die; for ye know no ransom; for ye are prepared for the day of the great judgement, for the day of tribulation and great shame for your spirits.

11. Woe to you, ye obstinate of heart, who work wickedness
    and eat blood:
    Whence have ye good things to eat and to drink and to be
        filled?
From all the good things which the Lord the Most High has placed in abundance on the earth; therefore ye shall have no peace. 12. Woe to you who love the deeds of unrighteousness: wherefore do ye hope for good hap unto yourselves? know that ye shall be delivered into the hands of the righteous, and they shall cut off your necks and slay you, and have no mercy upon you. 13. Woe to you who rejoice in the tribulation

---

ηm, β-n 'Holy and Great One'. 7. Recorded: cf. 97⁶ 98⁸ 100¹⁰ 104⁷,⁸. 8. From henceforth ye know, i.e. from the publication of Enoch's book in these later times. 9. This verse introduces a long succession of woes directed against the sinners. Transgress against (y₁g). m 'know not', q 'tend not', t, β 'hearken not to'. 10. Prepared: cf. 94⁹. Die. This refers not only to the loss of the life temporal but also of the life eternal. No ransom: Ps. 49⁷,⁸,⁹. For (y,β). y 'and'. > mq. Day of the great judgement, &c.: see 45² (note). For your spirits: see ver. 3 (note). 11. The denunciation of individual sinners. Obstinate of heart: cf. 100⁸. Who work (2nd sing. t, β). In 3rd sing. g ηmq. The next verb 'eat' is preserved only in β in the 2nd sing. Eat blood: cf. 7⁵. Not content with enjoying the best of everything that God gives, these sinners eat blood and break the divine law; cf. Book of Jubilees 7²⁸⁻³³ 21⁶ Acts 15²⁹. The Lord (a-m). m, β 'our Lord'. Have no peace: see 5⁴ note. 12. Delivered into of the righteous; for no grave shall be dug for you. 14. Woe to you who set at nought the words of the righteous; for ye shall have no hope of life. 15. Woe to you who write down lying and godless words; for they write down their lies that men may hear them and act godlessly towards (their) neighbour. 16. Therefore they shall have no peace but die a sudden death.

Woes pronounced on the Godless, the Lawbreakers: evil Plight of Sinners in the last Days: further Woes.

XCIX. 1. Woe to you who work godlessness,
And glory in lying, and extol them:
Ye shall perish, and no happy life shall be yours.

2. Woe to them who pervert the words of uprightness,
And transgress the eternal law,
And transform themselves into what they were not [into sinners]:
They shall be trodden under foot upon the earth.

3. In those days make ready, ye righteous, to raise your prayers as a memorial,

the hands of the righteous: see 91^{12} (note). 13. No grave shall be dug for you. gqg read 'no grave of yours shall be seen'. Cf. Jer. 8^2 22^{19}. 14. No hope of life, &c.: cf. 96^1 98^{10}. 15. Cf. 104^{10}. This verse attests the vigorous literary strife existing between the Sadducean or Hellenistic and the Pharisaic party. Act godlessly ($gqi'u. ra'sa = \dot{a}\sigma\epsilon\beta\epsilon\tilde{\iota}\nu$: cf. 1^9 5^8 8^2 &c.). β inserts a negative and changes ba'ĕd (= 'neighbour') into 'ĕbad = 'folly'. This necessitates a change of rendering 'not forget (their) folly'. Cf. ver. 9. 16. Have no peace: see 5^4 (note). A sudden death: cf. 94$^{1, 6, 7}$ 95^6 96$^{1, 6}$.

XCIX. 1. In 98^{15} the writers of the Hellenistic literature are denounced: here all those who sympathize with or praise them; cf. 94^6 98^{15} (note). To you ($a-gg$). gg, β 'to them'. There is a constant confusion of the second and third persons in the MSS.—in part owing no doubt to a not infrequent change in the original from the second person to the third or vice versa. I will notice only the most important. 2. To them (g_1gm). qtu, β 'to you'. Pervert the words of uprightness: cf. 94^9. The eternal law, i.e. the Mosaic law; 5^4 99^{14}. Transform themselves into what they were not. This may merely mean that they adopt generally the Hellenistic customs, as I thought in my first edition; but the reference is rather the medical operation undergone by many of the young Jews of noble birth, in order that they might appear like Greeks when they undressed for the Greek games in Jerusalem. Cf. Ass. Mos. 8^3; Jos. *Ant.* xii. 5. 1. By this operation the foreskin was brought forward. [Into sinners.] Bracketed as a gloss. 3. Your prayers: see 97^5 (note).

[Sect. V] *Chapters XCVIII. 14—XCIX. 7*

And place them as a testimony before the angels,
That they may place the sin of the sinners for a memorial before the Most High.

4. In those days the nations shall be stirred up,
And the families of the nations shall arise on the day of destruction.

5. And in those days the destitute shall go forth and carry off their children,
And they shall abandon them, so that their children shall perish through them:
Yea, they shall abandon their children (that are still) sucklings, and not return to them,
And shall have no pity on their beloved ones.

6. And again I swear to you, ye sinners, that sin is prepared for a day of unceasing bloodshed. 7. And they who worship stones, and grave images of gold and silver and wood (and stone)

Place them (*a.* β 'ye have placed them') ... **before the angels.** This mediatorial function of the angels (cf. 9⁹⁻¹¹ note) has its root in the O.T., cf. Job 5¹ 33²³ Zech. 1¹²; but has no place in the N.T., except in Rev. 8³,⁴. See my note on the mediation of angels in T. Lev. 3⁵ T. Dan. 6². **The Most High.** This title is found in all Sections of the book. The title 'Most High' appears in 9³ 10¹ 46⁷ 60¹, ¹² 62⁷ 77¹ 94⁸ 97² 98⁷, ¹¹ 99³, ¹⁰ 101¹, ⁶, ⁹. **4.** In the last times there will be wars and tumults among the nations of the earth. This will be the period of the Sword; cf. 90¹⁹ 91¹² 99⁴. **Shall be stirred up** (*t*, β). *a*₁*gt* 'are stirred up'. **Shall arise** (*t*, β). *a-mt* 'shall raise up'. **5.** The terrible results of famine are here depicted. There is no reference to miscarriages in the verse, as has generally been supposed and so rendered: nor to rending their children in pieces, as has been universally supposed and translated.

Abandon them (*a*). β 'abandon their children'. **6—C. 6.** Denunciation of the idolatry and superstition of the wicked. In this denunciation not only the apostates but also the actual heathen are included. **6. Day of unceasing bloodshed**, i. e. the judgement of the sword; see 91¹² (note) 45² (note). Quoted by Tertullian, *De Idol.* iv 'Et rursus iuro vobis, peccatores, quod in diem sanguinis perditionis poenitentia parata est'. It will be observed here that Tertullian's 'in diem sanguinis perditionis' = εἰς ἡμέραν αἵματος ἀπωλείας = ליום דם לאיד, where לאיד is corrupt for לעד = ἀδιαλείπτου as in our text. Symmachus so renders לעד in Job 16⁸ where the Mass. has לְעַד. Further 'poenitentia' in Tertullian appears to be corrupt for 'impenitentia' = ἀμετανοησία, of which the word 'sin' in our text may be a loose rendering. **7. Grave images of gold and silver and wood (and stone) ... worship ... demons**: cf.

and clay, and those who worship impure spirits and demons, and all kinds of idols not according to knowledge, shall get no manner of help from them.

8. And they shall become godless by reason of the folly of their hearts,

   And their eyes shall be blinded through the fear of their hearts

   And through visions in their dreams.

9. Through these they shall become godless and fearful;

   For they shall have wrought all their work in a lie,

   And shall have worshipped a stone:

   Therefore in an instant shall they perish.

10. But in those days blessed are all they who accept the words of wisdom, and understand them,

    And observe the paths of the Most High, and walk in the path of His righteousness,

    And become not godless with the godless;

    For they shall be saved.

11. Woe to you who spread evil to your neighbours;

    For you shall be slain in Sheol.

Rev. 9^{20}. I have added 'and stone' in accordance with Tertullian as quoted below. Impure (β, Tertullian 'infamibus'). a 'evil'. Corruption is native to the Ethiopic. Demons: cf. 16^1 19^1. Not according to knowledge: ዐቀተ (ጐኑ), Tert. 'non secundum scientiam'. β 'in idols' temples'. The passage in Tertullian, *De Idol.* iv, runs 'Qui servitis lapidibus, et qui imagines facitis aureas et argenteas et ligneas et lapideas et fictiles, et servitis phantasmatibus et daemoniis et spiritibus infamibus [MSS. give *infamis*] et omnibus erroribus *non secundum scientiam*, nullum ab iis invenietis auxilium'; cf. Book of Jubilees 1^{11} 11^4. 8. The victims of such superstition and idolatry will proceed from bad to worse; cf. Book of Wisdom $14^{12, 27}$ Rom. 1^{21}. Shall become godless: cf. 93^8 99^9. On the relation of dreams to superstition, cf. Sir. 31^{1-7}. 9. Through these, i.e. dreams, Sir. 40^6. 10. As sudden destruction will befall the idolaters, ver. 9, so salvation will be the recompense of those who accept the true wisdom. Of His righteousness ($a-u$). α, β 'of righteousness'. 11. Shall be slain: cf. 108^3. This is the extreme penalty of sin: a less severe punishment is eternal condemnation to Sheol, but that not attended by the 'slaying' of the soul; cf. 22^{13}. Sheol here means the eternal place of punishment; see 63^{10} (note) 103^7. 12. Prov. 11^1 Amos 8^5 Hos. 12^7.

12. Woe to you who make deceitful and false measures,
    And (to them) who cause bitterness on the earth;
    For they shall thereby be utterly consumed.

13. Woe to you who build your houses through the grievous toil of others,
    And all their building materials are the bricks and stones of sin;
    I tell you ye shall have no peace.

14. Woe to them who reject the measure and eternal heritage of their fathers
    And whose souls follow after idols;
    For they shall have no rest.

15. Woe to them who work unrighteousness and help oppression,
    And slay their neighbours until the day of the great judgement.

16. For He shall cast down your glory,
    And bring affliction on your hearts,
    And shall arouse His fierce indignation,
    And destroy you all with the sword;
    And all the holy and righteous shall remember your sins.

Measures ($a-mt$, i^1). t, $β-i$ 'foundations'. Cause bitterness (mt, $β$). gq 'know', $_1g$ 'tempt'. 13. Build ... through the grievous toil of others: cf. Jer. 22¹³; also 1 Enoch 94⁷ 97⁸. 14. The measure and eternal heritage, i.e. the Mosaic law; cf. ver. 2. The apostates as in that verse are here referred to. Whose souls follow after ($_1gm$). $gqtu$ 'and follow after the souls of'. $β$ 'who cause their souls to follow after'. Have no rest: see 94⁶ (note). 15. To them ($_1gu$, $β$). $gmqt$ 'to you'. Day of the great judgement: see 94⁹ 98¹⁰ 45² (note). 16. His fierce indignation. $_1gβ$ read 'the spirit of His indignation' רוח אפו = corrupt for חרן אפו 'His fierce indignation'. $gmqt$ read 'His indignation and His spirit'('His spirit' in nom. in qt). + 'into your heart' $_1g$. Holy and righteous (g_1gmq). ∾ t, $β$. Remember your sins. And accordingly pray for your destruction; see 97⁵ (note).

The Sinners destroy each other: Judgement of the fallen Angels: the Safety of the Righteous: further Woes for the Sinners.

C. 1. And in those days in one place the fathers together with their sons shall be smitten,
And brothers one with another shall fall in death
Till the streams flow with their blood.

2. For a man shall not withhold his hand from slaying his sons and his sons' sons,
And the sinner shall not withhold his hand from his honoured brother:
From dawn till sunset they shall slay one another.

3. And the horse shall walk up to the breast in the blood of sinners,
And the chariot shall be submerged to its height.

4. In those days the angels shall descend into the secret places
And gather together into one place all those who brought down sin,

C. 1. The thought in 99⁶ is here expanded. Brothers one with another shall fall (β). α 'brothers one with another and shall fall'. Suggested by Ezek. 38²¹ 'Every man's sword shall be against his brother'; Hagg. 2²². Cf. second line of the next stanza. Streams flow with their blood: cf. Is. 34³,⁷ Ps. 58¹⁰. 2. His sons' sons (β). gmt 'his son's son', ₁gq corrupt. + 'in compassion' t, β. The sinner (t, β). g₁gmq 'as for the sinner, he'. From his honoured brother. It is very probable that we have here a reference to the murder of Antigonus by his brother Aristobulus I. Josephus (Ant. xiii. 11. 1, 2) tells us that Aristobulus specially loved Antigonus, but moved by calumnies put him to death, and afterward died of remorse for this deed. On the internecine strife that was to initiate the kingdom, cf. 56⁷ 99⁵, ⁶ Zech. 14¹³ Ezek. 38²¹ Hagg. 2²² Mic. 7⁶ 'A man's enemies are the men of his own house'. In N.T. cf. Mt. 10²¹, ³⁴, ³⁵ 24¹⁰ Mk. 13¹² Luke 21¹⁶. 3. Up to the breast. This phraseology reappears later in Talmudic writings; cf. Midrash Ech. Rabb. ii 'Nor shall they cease slaying till the horse is submerged in blood to the mouth'. Cf. Jer. Taanith 69ᵃ; cf. Schürer, i. 695 note; Lightfoot, *Opera*, ii. 127; Rev. 14²⁰. To its height (m, β). g₁gq 'to the day of its (>₁g) height' (through a dittograph), t 'for it shall be filled to its height'. 4. The angels shall descend . . . and gather. So in Matt. 13³⁹, ⁴¹, ⁴⁹. Brought down sin (a-t). t, β 'helped sin'. The reference

> And the Most High will arise on that day of judgement
> To execute great judgement amongst sinners.

5. And over all the righteous and holy He will appoint guardians from amongst the holy angels
  To guard them as the apple of an eye,
  Until He makes an end of all wickedness and all sin,
  And though the righteous sleep a long sleep, they have nought to fear.

6. And (then) the children of the earth shall see the wise in security,

in this verse can only be to the fallen angels who are here described as having 'brought down sin'. These fallen angels were temporarily buried in abysses of the earth, i.e. 'the secret places'. See note on 98⁴. **Day of judgement** (a-tu). tu, β 'day'. **Amongst** ($_1gmq u$). g 'and amongst', t, β 'on all the'. **5.** This verse has always been interpreted of the righteous on earth, but wrongly. The righteous here spoken of are not the living, but are righteous souls in the place of the departed. This place was afterwards called the chambers or promptuaries, as in 4 Ezra 7⁸⁵ 'videntes aliorum habitacula ab angelis conservari cum silentio magno'; and again in 7⁹⁵ the souls in their promptuaries 'requiescent cum silentio multo ab angelis conservati'; cf. also 4 Ezra 4³⁷ 7³³ 2 Bar. 30². **All**¹⁰. > $_1gu$. **The apple of an eye**: cf. Deut. 32¹⁰ Ps. 17⁸. **He makes an end of all** ($g _1gmq^2$). q^1tu, β 'all — has been made an end of'. **The righteous sleep a long sleep**. The writer of 91–104 did not expect the resurrection at the beginning of the temporary Messianic kingdom. The words 'sleep a long sleep' could not be said with reference to this kingdom; for the writer living at the close of the seventh week expects its advent immediately at the beginning of the eighth week. The 'long sleep' extends from his time till the close of the tenth week, when the righteous rise. Again, from vv. 4, 5 we see that the righteous do not rise till God has judged sinners and an end is made of all sin. Thus the resurrection of the righteous in 91–104 follows the final judgement at the close of the Messianic kingdom. **6. And (then) the children of the earth**, &c. I have here transposed the words 'the children of the earth' from the second line to the first, and with $_1gq$ taken 'the wise' in the acc. and not in the nom. as in gmt, β. Further, for the phrase 'in security' we find 'ĕmûna (in t, β) = πιστόν or πεποιθότα (cf. Prov. 10⁹), 'emani (in g_1gm) corrupt. 'ĕmûna could mean also τὸ πιστόν, and accordingly all translators in the past have followed the reading of gmt, β, and taken 'the righteous' in the nom. Thus they rendered:—

> 'And the wise shall see what is to be believed,
> And the children of earth shall understand,' &c.

But there is no question here as to the wise seeing *in the future* what is to be believed. The judgement has

And shall understand all the words of this book,
And recognize that their riches shall not be able to save them
In the overthrow of their sins.

7. Woe to you, sinners, on the day of strong anguish,
Ye who afflict the righteous and burn them with fire:
Ye shall be requited according to your works.

8. Woe to you, ye obstinate of heart,
Who watch in order to devise wickedness:
Therefore shall fear come upon you
And there shall be none to help you.

9. Woe to you, ye sinners, on account of the words of your mouth,
And on account of the deeds of your hands which your godlessness has wrought,
In blazing flames burning worse than fire shall ye burn.

come, and whilst the righteous are secure (100⁶) nothing can save the wicked (100⁷⁻¹³). Moreover, the lot of the wicked is aggravated by seeing the righteous in security, just as in 4 Ezra 7⁸⁵ (quoted above), while the same thought reappears in Wisdom 4¹⁷ 5¹, ²⁻⁵. Hence the stanza is to be taken as dealing with the children of the earth. Next 'ĕmûna is here a rendering of πεποιθότα(ς) as in Prov. 10⁹, which in turn goes back to בֶּטַח (adv.) = 'in security', but used frequently = 'dwelling in security' as in Gen. 34²⁵ Ezek. 30⁹. Children of the earth. This title belongs to the Sadducees, sinners, apostates, paganizers, 102²; cf. the Hebrew phrase עַם הָאָרֶץ: the righteous are designated as the 'children of heaven', 101¹. Shall understand. The sinners shall not understand till the judgement has already come upon them. The same idea is in Wisdom 5³ sqq. Riches shall not be able to save them: cf. Zeph. 1¹⁸.

7. The righteous underwent such persecution under Antiochus Epiphanes; cf. 2 Macc. 7, if we may trust the latter. On the day of strong anguish. The MSS. have wrongly transposed this phrase into the next clause. I have restored it as suggested in my edition of 1893. Ye who. The MSS. read sôba (= 'when') corrupt for 'ěllā (i.e. ሶበ፡ corrupt for እለ፡). The text as it stands is very unsatisfactory: 'Woe to you sinners when ye afflict ... on the day of strong anguish.' The woe is not felt till the judgement-day: then they shall be requited according to their works; cf. 45² (note). Otherwise they must be taken of the time of the persecution of the righteous. Requited according to your works: cf. 95⁵. 8. Obstinate of heart (a). β 'perverse of heart'; cf. 98¹¹. Watch: cf. Is. 29²⁰. 9. The wicked will suffer in the flames of hell for their godless words and deeds. Sinners. + 'for' ₁g, β. Which your godlessness has wrought (gmu). t 'because of the work of your godless-

10. And now, know ye that from the angels He will inquire as to your deeds in heaven, from the sun and from the moon and from the stars in reference to your sins because upon the earth ye execute judgement on the righteous. 11. And He will summon to testify against you every cloud and mist and dew and rain; for they shall all be withheld because of you from descending upon you, and they shall be mindful of your sins. 12. And now give presents to the rain that it be not withheld from descending upon you, nor yet the dew, when it has received gold and silver from you that it may descend. 13. When the hoar-frost and snow with their chilliness, and all the snow-storms with all their plagues fall upon you, in those days ye shall not be able to stand before them.

Exhortation to the Fear of God: all Nature fears Him but not the Sinners.

CI. 1. Observe the heaven, ye children of heaven, and every work of the Most High, and fear ye Him and work no evil in

ness', q 'which are the work of your godlessness', β 'which as a work ye have godlessly committed'. In blasing flames burning worse than fire shall ye burn. Here $a-g$ > 'shall ye burn', and $_1g$, β > 'burning'. The two texts appear to be complementary. 10. All the heavenly powers which have witnessed the sins of the wicked will testify against them; cf. 98^{6-8}; also 97^7 104^8. In Hab. 2^{11} this testimony is given by the stones and beams of the dwelling of the wicked. In heaven. g 'from heaven'. + 'and' $a-u$. Execute judgement on = ποιεῖτε κρίσιν μετά (so $gmqt, \beta$)—a Hebraism. 11. All the natural powers which minister to the fruitfulness of the earth will testify against sinners, as they have been withholden on account of their sins. This is exactly in keeping with 80, one of the chapters interpolated in 72–82; cf. Jer. 3^3. And they shall be mindful $(a-mt)$. mt, β 'and shall they not be mindful' (t, β 'watchful'). 12. Spoken ironically. That it may descend (g_1gt, $bilofxy_1a_1b$). mq 'that it should not descend'. > u, β-$bilopxy_1a_1b$. 13. Even the lesser punishments of the elements are irresistible.

CI. 1. The same subject pursued; but the writer turns aside for a moment to address the righteous who are here called 'children of heaven', as elsewhere sinners are called 'children of earth'; cf. 106^6 102^3. The phrase 'children of heaven' (cf. Pirke Aboth, iii. 22 בָּנִים לַמָּקוֹם) is the equivalent of 'sons of God'. The designation is here limited to the righteous Israelites. For the view that the individual Israelite was regarded as a son of God already in the second century B.C. see Test. Lev. 4^2 (note) Wisd. $2^{13, 18}$. Ye children

His presence. 2. If He closes the windows of heaven, and withholds the rain and the dew from descending on the earth on your account, what will ye do then? 3. And if He sends His anger upon you because of your deeds, ye cannot petition Him; for ye spake proud and insolent words against His righteousness: therefore ye shall have no peace. 4. And see ye not the sailors of the ships, how their ships are tossed to and fro by the waves, and are shaken by the winds, and are in sore trouble? 5. And therefore do they fear because all their goodly possessions go upon the sea with them, and they have evil forebodings of heart that the sea will swallow them and they will perish therein.

6. Are not the entire sea and all its waters, and all its movements, the work of the Most High, and has He not set limits to its doings, and confined it throughout by the sand? 7. And at His reproof it is afraid and dries up, and all its fish die and all that is in it; but ye sinners that are on the earth fear Him not. 8. Has He not made the heaven and the earth, and all that is therein? Who has given understanding and wisdom to

(a). t^2, β 'all ye children'. 2, 3. The writer resumes his address to the wicked and recurs to the subject; cf. $100^{11, 12}$. 2. If (gt, β–enx). $_1g\varkappa$, ax 'for', mq, א 'when'. Windows of heaven: Gen. 7^{11}. 3. If (g_1gtu, β). mq 'when'. Because of (+ 'all' $_1g$) your deeds ($_1gm$). t, β 'and upon (+ 'all' β) your deeds'. gq 'your deeds'. Proud and insolent words: 5^4 (note) 27^2. As instances of such insolent speech cf. $98^{7, 8}$ 102^6. 4–7. They who go down to the sea in ships are filled with fear at the might of the sea: how much more should not men fear God by whom the sea has been made and of whom it is sore afraid? 4. And ^{10} (q, β). > a–q. Sailors of the ships. Text = 'kings of the ships' = מַלְכֵי הָאֳנִיּוֹת corrupt, as Halévy pointed out, for מַלָּחֵי הָאֳ = 'sailors of the ships'. For the thought of the verse cf. Ps. 107^{23-27}. 6, 7. The sea can do nothing save according to divine command. 6. Has He not set limits to its doings (e, though by a slip reading 'aqama for 'aqama). The verb is rightly preserved in y though otherwise corrupt. In β–y this verb is changed into hatama = 'has sealed'. gmqt 'its doings and waters', where wamàjà (= 'its waters') may be corrupt for 'aqama. With this passage cf. Jer. 5^{22} Job 26^{10} 38^{8-11} Ps. 89^9 104^9 Prov. 8^{29}. 7. At His reproof it ... dries up. From Is. 50^2. Is afraid and dries up (a–$_1g$, x). β–x 'dries up and is afraid'. 8. God has not only made the sea, but also heaven and earth and all that in them is. He too has given instinct to animals and every thing that moves on the earth and in the sea? 9. Do not the sailors of the ships fear the sea? Yet sinners fear not the Most High.

Terrors of the Day of Judgement: the adverse Fortunes of the Righteous on the Earth.

CII. 1. In those days when He hath brought a grievous fire upon you,
Whither will ye flee, and where will ye find deliverance?
And when He launches forth His word against you,
Will you not be affrighted and fear?

2. And all the luminaries shall be affrighted with great fear,
And all the earth shall be affrighted and tremble and be alarmed.

3. And all the †angels shall execute their commands†
And shall seek to hide themselves from the presence of the Great Glory,
And the children of earth shall tremble and quake;
And ye sinners shall be accursed for ever,
And ye shall have no peace.

4. Fear ye not, ye souls of the righteous,
And be hopeful ye that have died in righteousness.

reason to man. 9. The whole argument of the chapter summed up in a few pregnant words. Sailors of the ships: see note on ver. 4.

CII. 1-3. If they now refuse to fear God, the day will come when they will be terrified before the awful day of the Lord—a day so terrible that heaven and earth will be affrighted, and even the holy angels will seek to hide themselves from it. What then will become sinners? 1. A grievous fire, i.e. the fire of hell; cf. 99¹¹. His word, i.e. word of judgement. 3. The †angels shall execute their commands†. The text is against the parallelism and is clearly here corrupt. It is not good angels that will seek to hide themselves. 'Angels'= מלאכים corrupt for מלכים = 'kings'. We have then a parallel here to Rev. 6¹⁵. But what is the original text behind 'execute their commands' I cannot see. The Great Glory (a). β 'the Great in glory'; cf. 14²⁰. Children of earth: cf. 100⁶ 101¹ (note). Have no peace: cf. 94⁶ (note). 4—CIV. 9. The discussion and condemnation of the Sadducean views of the future life. 4, 5. The righteous are bidden to be of good cheer though their life be such as only sinners deserved, and their latter end be full of grief (vv. 4, 5). 4. Ye that have died (*m, cſhiklu* ₁*a*).

5. And grieve not if your soul into Sheol has descended in grief,
   And that in your life your body fared not according to your goodness,
   But wait for the day of the judgement of sinners
   And for the day of cursing and chastisement.

6. And yet when ye die the sinners speak over you:
   "As we die, so die the righteous,
   And what benefit do they reap for their deeds?

7. Behold, even as we, so do they die in grief and darkness,
   And what have they more than we?
   From henceforth we are equal.

8. And what will they receive and what will they see for ever?
   Behold, they too have died,
   And henceforth for ever shall they see no light."

9. I tell you, ye sinners, ye are content to eat and drink, and

gqʹu 'they who have died', abdeoɛ₁b 'the day of your death', g 'the souls of those who have died'. q adds 'ye who have died in righteousness' after 'grieve not' in the next line. **5.** The author, given the standpoint of belief in a blessed future for the righteous, can readily concede that there is often no difference in the outward lot of the righteous and the wicked either in life or death. Such a concession according to the O.T. doctrine of retribution was impossible. **If** (g_1g). Other MSS. 'that' or 'because'. **Soul.** + 'into great tribulation and wailing and sorrow and grief' $t_1\beta$. **Sheol**: see 63¹⁰ (note). **Wait for.** Here I emend 'ĕnka ba (= 'moreover on' which is here unmeaning) into ṣenḥû la = 'wait for' in 108³, where this verb occurs in a like context: 'wait for those days', i.e. the days of judgement. **Judgement of sinners.** Here the text has 'ye became sinners', i.e. kônkemmû ḫaṭeâna (ḫaṭeân g_1g, a), which I have emended into kuenané ḫaṭeân = 'judgement of sinners'. The next line shows that it is the judgement day to which this line must refer. The parallelism is thus restored. **Day of ... chastisement.** From Hos. 5⁹ יוֹם תּוֹכֵחָה. **6-8.** The sinners—the Sadducean opponents—start from the O.T. doctrine of retribution which taught the prosperity of the righteous in this life, and argue that as there is no difference in the lot of the righteous and the wicked in this life—a point just conceded by the author in ver. 5—so there is none in an existence beyond this life; cf. Book of Wisdom 2¹⁻⁶ 3¹⁻⁴ Eccles. 2¹⁴⁻¹⁶ 3¹⁹⁻²¹, &c. **7. In grief and darkness.** This refers to the O.T. conception of Sheol, 63¹⁰ (note). **8. What will they receive** (mt, β). g_1gq 'how will they rise'. **Behold** ($a_{-1}g$). ₁g, β 'for behold'. **9, 10.** The answer of the rob and sin, and strip men naked, and acquire wealth and see good days. 10. Have ye seen the righteous how their end falls out, that no manner of violence is found in them till their death? 11. "Nevertheless they perished and became as though they had not been, and their spirits descended into Sheol in tribulation."

Different Destinies of the Righteous and the Sinners: fresh Objections of the Sinners.

CIII. 1. Now, therefore, I swear to you, the righteous, by the glory of the Great and Honoured and Mighty One in dominion, and by His greatness I swear to you.

2. I know a mystery
 And have read the heavenly tablets,
 And have seen the holy books,
 And have found written therein and inscribed regarding them:

author. The life of the wicked is fashioned by material and temporal aims only, and so all their desires find satisfaction in this world; but the life of the righteous, as is manifest from first to last, is moulded by spiritual and eternal aims. 9. See good days. So LXX of Ps. 34^{12}, which implies a slightly different reading. 10. How their end falls out (a). β 'how their end is peace'. Again, as in ver. 5, the author concedes that there is no outward distinction between the righteous and the wicked in this life, but that there is a religious and ethical distinction. Death (a–$_1g$). $_1g$, β 'day of their death'. 11. The wicked rejoin: this difference in character is of no advantage—the same lot awaits good and bad alike. Spirits (a–$_1g$). $_1g$, β 'souls'.

CIII. 1–4. The author, instead of replying directly to the wicked, turns to the righteous, and solemnly assures them that every good thing is in store for them; for so he has read in the heavenly tablets and in the holy books. Hence they were not to regard the contumely of the wicked. 1. The oath is more solemn here than in 98^{1,6} 99^6 104^1. By the glory ... dominion (y and practically $_1y$). mq^1 'by His great glory ('by the glory of the Great One' qt) and by His honoured kingdom'. β–y 'by His great glory and honour and by His honoured kingdom'. 2. The writer bases his knowledge on the heavenly tablets which he has read. A mystery (a–t). t, β 'this mystery'. Read the heavenly tablets (gqu). ml, β 'read in the heavenly tablets'. The holy books (gq^1). $_1gm$, β 'books of the holy ones', i.e. of the angels; cf. 108^7. See 47^3 (note). Dillmann comparing 108^3 takes the holy ones here to mean the saints or righteous. 3, 4. The blessings here depicted will be enjoyed by the righteous, both in Sheol and in the spiritual theocracy established after the final judgement. The words here are vague and might apply

3. That all goodness and joy and glory are prepared for them,
   And written down for the spirits of those who have died in righteousness,

   And that manifold good shall be given to you in recompense for your labours,
   And that your lot is abundantly beyond the lot of the living.

4. And the spirits of you who have died in righteousness shall live and rejoice,
   And their spirits shall not perish, nor their memorial from before the face of the Great One
   Unto all the generations of the world: wherefore no longer fear their contumely.

5. Woe to you, ye sinners, when ye have died,
   If ye die in the wealth of your sins,
   And those who are like you say regarding you:

   "Blessed are the sinners: they have seen all their days.

6. And now they have died in prosperity and in wealth,
   And have not seen tribulation or murder in their life;
   And they have died in honour,
   And judgement has not been executed on them during their life."

7. Know ye, that their souls will be made to descend into Sheol
   And they shall be wretched in their great tribulation.

to either. There is apparently only a resurrection of the spirit. **3.** For them ($_1g$, $β$). > $a-_1g$. The spirits of those who (mt, $β$). gq 'your spirits which'. Manifold good ($_1gmq$). gt 'things manifold and good', $β$ 'with manifold good'. **4.** Spirits of you (g_1gq, $β$). mt 'spirits of them'. Who have died (2nd sing. $_1g$, $t^2β$). $a-_1g$ 'who have died' (3rd sing.). Rejoice. + 'and be glad' (g_1gm, $β$). And their spirits shall not perish, nor (a). $β$ 'their spirits and'. **5-8.** A different fate awaits the wicked. These have enjoyed all the blessings which according to the O.T. belonged to the righteous. Hence they vaunt themselves on their prosperity and immunity from punishment; but a sure doom awaits them in Sheol—darkness and chains and a burning flame. **5.** When ye have died ($a-u$). > $β$. The wealth of ($a-q$). > $q, β$. The phrase 'wealth of wickedness' הון הרשע is found in the Zadokite Fragment 8¹². **7.** Sheol: see 63¹⁰ (note). Sheol here is the final place of punishment. Our text here appears to be dependent on and to be a development of Jub. 7²⁹:

'For into Sheol shall they go
  And into the place of condemnation shall they descend.'

8. And into darkness and chains and a burning flame where there is grievous judgement shall your spirits enter;
And the great judgement shall be for all the generations of the world.
Woe to you, for ye shall have no peace.

9. Say not in regard to the righteous and good who are in life:
"In our troubled days we have toiled laboriously and experienced every trouble,
And met with much evil and been consumed,
And have become few and our spirit small.

In Jubilees Sheol is not yet associated with fire and burning, but this stage is reached in our text. It has assumed thus one of the characteristics of Gehenna; and become a place of flaming fire. See ver. 8ᵃ. Cf. the different significations it has in 102⁵,¹¹.   8. Of the world (a). β 'unto eternity'. Have no peace: see 5⁴ (note) 94⁶ (note). 9-15. These verses are in the mouth of the wicked an ironical description of the lot of the righteous. For the time being they speak in the person of the righteous. From this verse to the end of this chapter ₉g stands alone frequently, exhibiting nearly sixty variations, but these are mainly between the 1st and 3rd plurals in the verbs and the corresponding suffixes, verbal and substantival. ₉g favours throughout the 3rd pl., whereas g in the main agrees with the rest of the MSS. in giving the 1st plural. The question arises on which person, the 1st or 3rd, are we to decide. The evidence of the MSS. goes to prove that the *1st person was the original*. For, whereas ₉g gives the 3rd person in all, except seven instances, confined to vv. 14 and 15, all other MSS., with few exceptions, give the 1st person. The exclusive use of the 3rd person would make the sense of the text clearer. But the evidence of the MSS. is irresistible. The wicked assume the rôle of the righteous and speak in their person. 103⁹⁻¹⁵ are pronounced derisively by the sinners of the righteous. For in 102⁶⁻⁸, when the sinners declare that the righteous live in trouble and darkness and have no advantage over the wicked beyond the grave, the author (102¹⁰) in reply points to the nature of their death and the purity of their life. To this the sinners rejoin (102¹¹), 'despite all that they go down to Sheol in woe as we.' The author now addresses himself first to the righteous (103¹⁻⁴) and then to the sinners. In the case of the latter he gives their glorification of their own life (103⁵⁻⁸) and their depreciation of the life of the righteous (103⁹⁻¹⁵). In these verses the wicked describe the wretchedness and helplessness of the present life of the righteous, just as in 102⁶,⁷ they had described the wretchedness of the future of the righteous. At the close of these words the author addresses his reply (104¹⁻⁶) not directly to the sinners who have just spoken but to the righteous, just as in the opening of 103, and returns to the sinners in vv. 7-9.   9. Our troubled days (tᵃβ). gqt¹ᵤ 'their troubled days', ₉g 'the days of their life with their troublous toil'. We have toiled. ₉g 'they have toiled', and so on in the 3rd person except in vv. 14-15. I will not record these variations so far as they

10. And we have been destroyed and have not found any to
     help us even with a word:
   We have been tortured [and destroyed], and not hoped to
     see life from day to day.

11. We hoped to be the head and have become the tail:
   We have toiled laboriously and had no satisfaction in our
     toil;
   And we have become the food of the sinners and the
     unrighteous,
   And they have laid their yoke heavily upon us.

12. They have had dominion over us that hated us †and smote us;
   And to those that hated us † we have bowed our necks
   But they pitied us not.

13. We desired to get away from them that we might escape
     and be at rest,
   But found no place whereunto we should flee and be safe
     from them.

14. And we complained to the rulers in our tribulation,
   And cried out against those who devoured us,
   But they did not attend to our cries
   And would not hearken to our voice.

---

consist only in a change of the person of the verb or suffix. **Been consumed.** $_1g$ 'they have suffered from disease'. **Become few.** Cf. Deut. 28⁶³ Ps. 107³⁹. **Our spirit small.** Not 'humble' but 'poor spirited' ($\mu\kappa\rho\delta\psi\nu\chi\sigma s$). 10. Cf. Deut. 26³⁹, ⁶⁴, ⁶⁷. **We ... have not found any to help us even with a word** ($a-_1gt$). So $_1g$ but with a change of persons. t, β 'there has been none to help us in word or deed: we are powerless and have found nothing'. 11. **We hoped** (a). β 'and we hoped'. **To be the head, &c.** From Deut. 28¹³. **Laid their yoke ... upon us.** From Deut. 28⁴⁸. 12. **They have had** ($a-t$, $deloy$ $_1a_1b$). $t, \beta - deloy$ $_1a_1b$ 'and they have had'. **They have had dominion ... that hated us.** For diction cf. Esther 9¹. **To those that hated us.** I think that this is a dittograph from the preceding line, and that the clause which should be here has been transposed into that line. Hence I suggest that we should read:

'They have had dominion over us that hated us,
And to those that smote us we have bowed our necks,
But they pitied us not.'

13. **We desired** ($a-_1g$). $_1g, \beta$ prefix 'and'. 14. **Cried out.** + 'and made lamentation' g. $_1g$ inserts this clause before

15. And they helped those who robbed us and devoured us and those who made us few; and they concealed their oppression, and they did not remove from us the yoke of those that devoured us and dispersed us and murdered us, and they concealed their murder, and remembered not that they had lifted up their hands against us."

Assurances given to the Righteous: Admonitions to Sinners and the Falsifiers of the Words of Uprightness.

CIV. 1. I swear unto you, that in heaven the angels

'in our tribulation'. 14, 15. These verses furnish materials towards determining the date of 91-104. In 83-90 the rulers are regarded as the divinely appointed leaders of the righteous. In this section, on the other hand, the rulers appear as the aiders and abettors of the enemies of the righteous. These enemies are the Sadducees, sinners, apostates, and paganizers, while the righteous are the Pharisaic party. The issues between these parties as they appear in this book could not have been so clearly defined before the Maccabean times. Nor again could this book have been written before the breach between John Hyrcanus and the Pharisees. But the date must be brought down still further, if we are to explain literally such statements as 'dispersed us and murdered us', and 'their murder', where the murder of the righteous is meant; for there was no blood spilt between the parties till the reign of Jannaeus, 94 B.C. The later limit is not hard to determine. The close confederacy which here prevails between the Sadducees and the rulers did not exist under the Herodian princes, but only under the later Maccabean princes. Hence this section was written before 64 B.C., and may be assigned either to the years 94-79 B.C. or 70-64 B.C., during which periods the Pharisees were oppressed by the rulers and Sadducees. But the rest of the section is against taking the words 'murder', &c. literally. We should probably regard them merely as the description of a severe but not murderous persecution; see Special Introd. (pp. 221, 222). 15. They helped ($_1g, \beta$). *gmt* 'you have helped', *q* 'thou hast helped'. The yoke of those that (g, gm, fo_1b). *qt*, β-fo_1b 'their yoke but'. Dispersed us and murdered us. These words taken literally would apply well to the actual destruction and dispersion of the Pharisaic families under Jannaeus.

CIV. 1-6. Instead of answering directly the wicked who have thus derisively described the lot of the righteous in this life, the author turns to the righteous and addresses them. This is exactly what he did in the opening of 103. He returns to the sinners in 104$^{7-9}$. In these verses the author practically concedes that the wicked have rightly described the lot of the righteous in this life; but he holds out a sure hope, a hope however not to be fulfilled in the transitory Messianic kingdom on earth, but to be directed to the blessed future that is awaiting them in heaven: the angels are mindful of them for good even now, and in due time they will become 'companions of the hosts of heaven'. 1. Unto you. + 'ye righteous' $t^2\beta$. The angels remember you for good before the glory of the Great One: and your names are written before the glory of the Great One. 2. Be hopeful; for aforetime ye were put to shame through ill and affliction; but now ye shall shine as the lights of heaven, ye shall shine and ye shall be seen, and the portals of heaven shall be opened to you. 3. And in your cry, cry for judgement, and it shall appear to you; for all your tribulation shall be visited on the rulers, and on all who helped those who plundered you. 4. Be hopeful, and cast not away your hope; for ye shall have great joy as the angels of heaven. 5. What shall ye be obliged to do? Ye shall not have to hide on the day of the great judgement and ye shall not be found as sinners, and the eternal judgement shall be far from you for all the generations of the world. 6. And now fear not, ye righteous, when ye see the sinners growing strong and prospering in their ways: be not companions with them, but keep afar

remember you. Though apparently forgotten on earth, the righteous are not forgotten before God by the angels. On the intercession of the angels cf. 15³ (note) 40⁵⁻⁷ 47² 89⁷⁶. And (a, i). > β–ei. Names are written: see 47³ (note). The Great One; cf. 14³ 103⁴. 2. Now. This word (= עַתָּה) is used here not of the immediate present but of the impending future. Shine as the lights: cf. Dan. 12³ 4 Ezra 7⁹⁷, ¹²⁵. Ye shall shine ²⁰ (a). > β. Portals of heaven shall be opened to you, i.e. heaven will become their dwelling-place, for they will 'shine as the lights of heaven', have 'joy as the angels', and be 'companions of the hosts of heaven'. The author does not hope for a new earth; cf. 91¹⁶ (note). 3. Their demand for justice which they make in vain on earth, 103¹⁴, ¹⁵ will one day be satisfied: wherefore let them continue to make it; cf. 97³, ⁵ (note) 99³, ¹⁶. The rulers. These are brought forward very prominently here; cf. 103¹⁴, ¹⁵ (note). 4. As the angels of heaven: cf. Matt. 22³⁰ Mark 12²⁵; also 1 En. 104⁶. 5. What shall ye ... do (a–t, e). t, β–e 'as for what ye shall ... do'. Day of the great judgement: cf. 19¹ 84⁴ 94⁹ 98¹⁰ 99¹⁵. The eternal judgement: cf. 91¹⁵ 'great eternal judgement': also 45² (note). There appears to be no judgement for the righteous according to this verse. Contrast the teaching of 37–70: see 62³. 6. Prospering in their ways: gigmqt. β 'prospering in their lusts'. Cf. Jer. 12¹. The Pharisaic exclusiveness is clearly defined here; cf. 91³,⁴. Observe that the righteous are not bidden to hope for blessedness on earth through the overthrow of the sinners. No doubt the sinners will be cut off in the period of the Sword, but the author sets little store by the temporary Messianic kingdom thereby established on earth. The hopes of the righteous can be realized in heaven alone. Be not companions, &c.: cf. 104², ⁴. The righteous will be companions of the heavenly hosts, 104⁶, and rejoice as from their violence; for ye shall become companions of the hosts of heaven. 7. And, although ye sinners say: "All our sins shall not be searched out and written down," nevertheless they shall write down all your sins every day. 8. And now I show unto you that light and darkness, day and night, see all your sins. 9. Be not godless in your hearts, and lie not and alter not the words of uprightness, nor charge with lying the words of the Holy Great One, nor take account of your idols; for all your lying and all your godlessness issue not in righteousness but in great sin. 10. And now I know this mystery, that sinners will alter and pervert the words of righteousness in many ways, and will speak wicked words, and lie, and practise great deceits, and write books concerning their words. 11. But when they write down truthfully all my

---

the angels in heaven, 104⁴. The idea is further developed in 2 Bar.; the righteous will be transformed into the glory of the angels, 51⁵, and be made like unto them, 51¹⁰, and their surpassing splendour will exceed that of the angels, 51¹². This, too, is the teaching of the Talmud. Be not (α). β 'and be not'. Hosts. So β reading ḥarà. Cf. Luke 2¹³ Rev. 19¹⁴. gmqt read ḥerāna = τῶν ἀγαθῶν, which Flemming takes to be a corruption of τῶν ἀγγέλων. This is possible. 7–8. After showing the blessed destiny of the righteous in the future life, he turns finally to the wicked, and declares that, though they prosper and are strong, and for that reason conceive that no account is taken of their sin, nevertheless all their sins are recorded, and recorded daily. 7. All our sins shall not be searched out. Here I read jĕthaḥaś with n. So Beer emended in 1900 without a knowledge of n. Other MSS. read 'ye shall not search out (tĕḥĕśśū) all our sins' —which is clearly corrupt. t, β give 'all our sins' in the nom. g₁gmq in the acc. Written down (t,β). g 'they shall write', nu 'ye shall write', uyq

'he shall write'. 8. Even the natural powers will give witness against them; cf. 100¹⁰ (note). 9–13. From a reproof of the life and the attitude of the wicked towards the O. T. revelation, the author passes on to certain disclosures and directions regarding his own book. 9. The wicked are admonished not to alter or misinterpret the O. T.; cf. 94⁶ 98¹⁴ 99². Holy Great One: see 1³ (note). Take account of (g₁yq). mt, β 'praise'. Your idols: cf. 99⁷⁻⁹, ¹⁴. 10. A time will come when the words of revelation will be perverted, and books be written enforcing wicked and heathen doctrine. Sinners . . . pervert . . . in many ways (g yjmt). q, β 'many sinners . . . pervert'. Books (t, β). g₁gmq 'my books'. 11. But the writings of Enoch will counteract these heathen teachings, and these writings will be handed down from generation to generation and through various languages, and in the course of transmission be exposed to voluntary and involuntary perversions and changes. The author speaks here from the standpoint of Enoch. My words (tu, β). g₁gmq 'words'. In their words in their languages, and do not change or minish ought from my words but write them all down truthfully—all that I first testified concerning them, 12. Then, I know another mystery, that books shall be given to the righteous and the wise to become a cause of joy and uprightness and much wisdom. 13. And to them shall the books be given, and they shall believe in them and rejoice over them, and then shall all the righteous who have learnt therefrom all the paths of uprightness be recompensed.'

God and the Messiah to dwell with Man.

CV. 1. In those days the Lord bade (them) to summon and testify to the children of earth concerning their wisdom: Show (it) unto them; for ye are their guides, and a recompense over the whole earth. 2. For I and My Son will be united with

---

languages. The O.T. was already translated into Greek. It is probable that Aramaic and Greek are the languages here referred to. 12. At last in the course of transmission these books will reach the generation for whom they were designed—a 'righteous' and 'wise' generation, and this generation will be the first to understand their worth. For this idea cf. Dan. $12^{4, 9, 10}$. 13. The righteous and the wise will recognize and believe in these books; cf. Dan. 12^{10} 'None of the wicked shall understand, but the wise shall understand'. *Recompensed.* The gift of these books with their revelations and wisdom seems to be the recompense of the righteous. This is certainly the view of the writer of 105^1; cf. 93^{10} 100^6 $104^{12, 13}$. Or is it meant that soon after their reception the Messianic kingdom will appear?

CV. This chapter does not seem to belong to 91-104. For (1) the phrase 'children of earth', which in 91-104 is a synonym for the sinners or heathen, has here a good ethical signification: see 100^6 (note) 101^1 (note). (2) The Messiah is introduced in 105^2, to whom there is not the faintest allusion throughout 91-104. (3) The finite duration of the lives of the saints seems to be implied in 105^2. This is the doctrine in 1-36, but not in 91-104. (4) The emphasis is laid in 105 on the finite life on earth: in 91-104 on the immortal life in heaven. This chapter, like 56^5-$57^{3 a}$, is a literary revival of O.T. thoughts and ideals. 1. *In those* (a-m). m, β 'and in those'. *And testify.* $> m$. *Children of earth.* This phrase has a good signification here; for the books of Enoch, which only 'the righteous and the wise' will receive, are the guides of those designated 'children of earth'. Contrast with this the technical meaning of this phrase in 100^6 102^3. *Recompense:* cf. 104^{13}. 2. *I and My Son.* There is no difficulty about the phrase 'My Son' as applied them for ever in the paths of uprightness in their lives; and ye shall have peace: rejoice, ye children of uprightness. Amen.

to the Messiah by the Jews; cf. 4 Ezra $7^{28, 29}$ 14^9. If the righteous are called 'God's children' in 62^{11}, the Messiah was pre-eminently the Son of God. Moreover, the early Messianic interpretation of Ps. 2 would naturally lead to such an expression. In 62^{14} above we have practically the same thought expressed; cf. John 14^{23}. In their lives: see introduction to this chapter. Ye shall have peace. This was the special blessing of the righteous, as its loss was the curse entailed on the wicked; cf. 94^6 (note).

FRAGMENT OF THE BOOK OF NOAH

LATIN FRAGMENT

CVI. 1. And after some days my son Methuselah took a wife for his son Lamech, and she became pregnant by him and bore a son. 2. And his body was white as snow and red as the blooming of a rose, and the hair of his head †and his long locks were white as wool, and his eyes beautiful†. And when he opened his eyes, he lighted up the whole house like the sun, and the whole house was very bright. 3. And thereupon he arose in the hands of the midwife, opened his mouth, and †conversed with† the Lord of

CVI. 1. Factum est autem [cum esset Lamech annorum tricentorum quinquaginta] natus est ei filiu(s)

2. Cui oculi sunt sicut radi solis capilli autem ei*us* candi⟨di⟩ores in septies niue, corpori autem eius nemo hominum potest intueri.

3. et surexit int*er* man*us* obstetricis suae et adorauit do*minum* uiuentem in secula [laudauit].

CVI-CVII. We have here again a fragment of a Noah Apocalypse. Part of this section has been preserved in a Latin version which I print side by side with the translation of the Ethiopic.
2. †And his long locks ... beautiful†. It is rather astonishing that the new-born infant should have 'long locks'. Since there is no mention of these in the Latin, and since it is possible that dĕ.udĕmâhû ... ěanâj 'a'ĕjentî:û (= 'his long locks ... and (> *199*) his eyes beautiful') is corrupt for 'ĕgarîhû laḍaḥâj 'a'ĕjentîhû. If this is right we should have 'was white ... and his eyes were like the rays of the

sun'. This restoration is supported by the Ethiopic version in ver. 5 'his eyes are as the rays of the sun': also 'septies' (ver. 10) or 'in septies' (ver. 2) seems corrupt for 'capitis', which depends on 'capilli'. See ver. 10 (note).
3. And thereupon (*ɯj*). Other MSS. 'and when'. Opened his mouth. This phrase recurs in ver. 11. The Latin is defective here. †Conversed with†. Here tanâgara = 'conversed with' is corrupt for tagânaja = προσεκύνησε or ἐξωμολογήσατο. Hence render 'praised'. Cf. 'laudavit' in the Latin. But adoravit' occurs there also and = προσεκύνησε. In ver. 11, where the substance of ver. 3

righteousness. 4. And his father Lamech was afraid of him and fled, and came to his father Methuselah. 5. And he said unto him: 'I have begotten a strange son, diverse from and unlike man, and resembling the sons of the God of heaven; and his nature is different and he is not like us, and his eyes are as the rays of the sun, and his countenance is glorious. 6. And it seems to me that he is not sprung from me but from the angels, and I fear that in his days a wonder may be wrought on the earth. 7. And now, my father, I am here to petition thee and implore thee that thou mayest go to Enoch, our father, and learn from him the truth, for his dwelling-place is amongst the angels.' 8. And when Methuselah heard the words of his son, he came to me to the ends of the earth; for he had heard that I was

et timuit Lamech. 6. ne non ex eo natus esset nisi nontius dei. 4, 5. et uenit ad patrem suum Mathusalem et narrauit illi omnia.

7. dixit Mathusalem: Ego autem non possum scire nisi eamus ad patrem nostrum Enoc.

8. quum autem uidit Enoc filium suum Mathusalem uenientem ad se [et] ait. quid est quod uenisti ad me nate?

---

recurs, the Ethiopic = εὐλόγησε and the Latin 'orauit'—evidently a corruption for 'adorauit'. Thus the Ethiopic = ἐξωμολογήσατο (or προσεκύνησε) (ver. 3) and εὐλόγησε (ver. 11) and the Latin εὐλόγησε (ver. 3) and προσεκύνησε (vv. 3, 11). From this it is clear that the Latin and the Ethiopic presuppose different words in the Greek version before them. Lord of Righteousness: cf. 22¹⁴ 90⁴⁰. 5. And²⁰ (g, y). > Other MSS. Sons of the God of heaven: cf. 69⁴,⁵; also 71¹ (note). 6. But from the angels. The Latin gives a somewhat different idea. 'Nuntius' = ἄγγελος. 7. Latin corrupt. Observe 'eamus'. Amongst the angels, i.e. at the ends of the earth, as in 65² there, and he cried aloud, and I heard his voice and I came to him. And I said unto him: 'Behold, here am I, my son, wherefore hast thou come to me?' 9. And he answered and said: 'Because of a great cause of anxiety have I come to thee, and because of a disturbing vision have I approached. 10. And now, my father, hear me: unto Lamech my son there hath been born a son, the like of whom there is none, and his nature is not like man's nature, and the colour of his body is whiter than snow and redder than the bloom of a rose, and the hair of his head is whiter than white wool, and his eyes are like the rays of the sun, and he opened his eyes and thereupon lighted up the whole house. 11. And he arose in the hands of the midwife, and opened his mouth and blessed the Lord of heaven. 12. And his father Lamech became afraid

9. Dix*it*:

10. q*uo*d natus e*st* filio suo [no*mine*] Lamech cui oculi sunt sicut radi solis capilli[s] eius candidiores septies niue, corpori au*tem* eius nemo hominum potest intueri,

11. et surexit inter manus obstetricis suae eadem hora qua p*r*ocidit de utero matris suae. orauit d*omi*n*u*m uiuente*m* in secula et laudauit.

66³. 8. **Wherefore.** So Latin 'quid est quod' = διὰ τί. But the Ethiopic = διότι, a corruption of the former. 9. **Cause of anxiety** (*g*₁*gmt*). β 'matter'. 10. **And now.** + 'hear me' ₁*gm*. **Colour of his body** (₁*g*). Other MSS. 'his colour'. But the presence of 'corpori' in the Latin and of σώματα in the following quotation appear to support ₁*g*. **The colour ... rose.** Borrowed by Apoc. Petri: τὰ μὲν γὰρ σώματα αὐτῶν ἦν λευκότερα πάσης χιόνος καὶ ἐρυθρότερα παντὸς ῥόδου. **Eyes ... sun:** cf. Apoc. Petri: ἀπὸ τῆς ὄψεως αὐτῶν ἀκτὶν ὡς ἡλίου. 11. **Lord of heaven.** Here only in Enoch. But compare the Latin 'dominum viventem in secula',

Sect. V] *Chapter CVI.* 9-15 267

and fled to me, and did not believe that he was sprung from him, but that he was in the likeness of the angels of heaven; and behold I have come to thee that thou mayest make known to me the truth.' 13. And I, Enoch, answered and said unto him: 'The Lord will do a new thing on the earth, and this I have already seen in a vision, and make known to thee that in the generation of my father Jared some of the angels of heaven transgressed the word of the Lord. 14. And behold they commit sin and transgress the law, and have united themselves with women and commit sin with them, and have married some of them, and have begot children by them. 17. And they shall produce on the earth giants not according to the spirit, but according to the flesh, and there shall be a great punishment on the earth, and the earth shall be cleansed from all impurity. 15. Yea, there

12. et timuit Lamech.

13. et dixit Enoc: nontiatum *est* mihi fili q*uia* post quingentos annos

15. mitt*et* de*u*s cataclismu*m*

and 5^1. 13. Do a new thing. For this phrase cf. Num. 16^{30} Is. 43^{19}. In the generation of . . . Jared: cf. 6^6. Some of the angels. Here I emend 'ĕmmal'ĕlta (= 'some from the heights') of a, β–*ehkn* into emmalā'ĕkta = 'some of the angels'. *n* reads 'angels'. I question whether the rendering 'some from the heights' is possible. 14. The law, i.e. the law appointed to them as spiritual beings; cf. 15. 17. I have restored this verse to its original place. And (qt, x). $>m$, β-x. g_1g are here defective shall come a great destruction over the whole earth, and there shall be a deluge and a great destruction for one year. 16. And this son who has been born unto you shall be left on the earth, and his three children shall be saved with him: when all mankind that are on the earth shall die [he and his sons shall be saved]. 18. And now make known to thy son Lamech that he who has been born is in truth his son, and call his name Noah; for he shall be left to you, and he and his sons shall be saved from the destruction, which shall come upon the earth on account of all the sin and all the unrighteousness, which shall be consummated on the earth in his days. 19. And after that there shall be still more unrighteousness than that which was first consummated on the earth; for I know the mysteries of the holy ones; for He, the Lord, has showed me and informed me, and I have read (them) in the heavenly tablets.

aquae ut deleat omnem creaturam [XL.] ostendit oculis nostris.

16. et erunt illi ·iii.· filii [et erunt nomina filiorum eius ·Sem · Cham · Iafeth]

18. et ipse uocabitur Noe qui interpretatur requies quia requiem prestabit in archam.

owing to an hmt. 15. One year: cf. Gen. 7¹¹ and 8¹⁴. 16. And ¹⁰ (g_1gq). > Other MSS. [He and his sons shall be saved.] > g_1gq. A repetition of the clause in ver. 18. 18. Unrighteousness, which shall (mt, β).

g_1g_1l read ' unrighteousness of apostasy (which) shall '. 19. The mysteries of the holy ones. Either the secrets known to the angels, or the secrets relating to the righteous in the future. Heavenly tablets: see 47³ (note).

CVII. 1. And I saw written on them that generation upon generation shall transgress, till a generation of righteousness arises, and transgression is destroyed and sin passes away from the earth, and all manner of good comes upon it. 2. And now, my son, go and make known to thy son Lamech that this son, which has been born, is in truth his son, and that (this) is no lie.' 3. And when Methuselah had heard the words of his father Enoch—for he had shown to him everything in secret—he returned and showed (them) to him and called the name of that son Noah; for he will comfort the earth after all the destruction.

CVIII. 1. Another book which Enoch wrote for his son Methuselah and for those who will come after him, and keep the law in the last days. 2. Ye who have done good shall wait for those days till an end is made of those who work evil, and an end of the might of the transgressors. 3. And wait ye indeed till sin has passed away, for their names shall be blotted out of the book of life and out of the holy books,

---

CVII. 1. The fresh growth of sin after the Deluge: its destruction and the advent of the Messianic kingdom. Till (t, β). g_1gmq 'that'. 3. The derivation of Noah given in Gen. 5^{29} is here repeated. Everything in secret (a). β 'every secret thing'. Returned and showed. So g save that it omits two letters by hmt. t, $abcdloxy_1b$ 'returned after having seen'. $> {}_1gqu$.

CVIII. This final chapter forms an independent addition. Its writer was acquainted with sections 1–36 and 91–104, or at all events with parts of them. But his acquaintance with 1–36 is very inaccurate. In vv. 3–6 what was originally the place of punishment for the disobedient stars in chapters 18 and 21 becomes in his hands practically Gehenna. The writer is Essene in tone. Observe the high honour paid to asceticism, the scorn of gold and silver in vv. 8–10, the blessed immortality of the spirit, but apparently not of the body, as well as the dualism of light and darkness so prominent in vv. 11–14. 108 is more nearly akin to 91–104 than any other section in the book. The object of this chapter is to encourage the righteous still to hope on despite the long delay of the advent of the kingdom. 1. Keep the law, as opposed to 'fall away from the law', 99^2. 2. The faithful are exhorted to further patience. Good (g_1g). > Other MSS. Shall wait (g_1gmq). t, β 'and are waiting'. 3. And 1° (a). > β. Blotted out of the book of life: from Ps. 69^{28}: cf. 47^3 (note). Out of the book of life and (g_1g). q, z 'out of the books of the living', mt 'out of the book and'. Holy books (mqt, e_1b, cf. 103^2). g 'book of the Holy One', β-ex_1b 'books of the holy ones'.

and their seed shall be destroyed for ever, and their spirits shall be slain, and they shall cry and make lamentation in a place that is a chaotic wilderness, and in the fire shall they burn; for there is no earth there. 4. And I saw there something like an invisible cloud; for by reason of its depth I could not †look over†, and I saw a flame of fire blazing brightly, and things like shining mountains circling and sweeping to and fro. 5. And I asked one of the holy angels who was with me and said unto him: 'What is this shining thing? for it is not a heaven but only the flame of a blazing fire, and the voice of weeping and crying and lamentation and strong pain.' 6. And he said unto me: 'This place which thou seest—here are cast the spirits of sinners and blasphemers, and of those who work wickedness, and of those who pervert every thing that the Lord hath spoken through the mouth of the prophets—(even) the things that shall be. 7. For some of them are written and inscribed above in the heaven, in order that the angels may

These contain the roll of the members of the kingdom; cf. $103^{2, 3}$. **Spirits shall be slain**: cf. 22^{13} 99^{11} (note). Though the extreme penalty of sin, it does not imply annihilation, for the victims of it 'cry and make lamentation'. **In a place**, &c. This chaotic flaming hell beyond the limits of the earth is the place of punishment of the angels in 18^{12-16} 21^{1-7}. **Chaotic**. Eth. = ἀόρατος, which is the LXX rendering of תהו in Gen. 1^2. The rendering of בהו (Gen. 1^2) is found twice in $21^{1, 2}$, i.e. ἀκατασκεύαστος. **In the fire shall they burn** = ba'ĕsât jĕnaddû. So I emend ba'ĕsât naddû (g_1gmqt, β—abcx) = 'in the fire they have burnt'. abcx emend into ba'ĕsât jĕnadĕdû 'in fire they shall burn'. But 21^3 ba'ĕsât ... jĕnaddû supports my emendation. 4. This hell and its inhabitants further described, in terms borrowed from 18^{13} 21^3. **†Look over†.** We might emend la'ĕla (= 'over') into lĕ'ĕlnâhû and render 'behold its height' or emend both words into behil haserô 'tell its circuit' (or 'size'). But the text is uncertain. **Of fire** (g_1gu). Other MSS. 'of its fire'. 5. **One of the holy angels**, &c. This phrase is borrowed from 1–36; cf 27^2. **Voice**, &c.: cf. 18^{13}. **Weeping and crying** (a¹. ∞ β. 6. This hell which is outside the earth is the final place of punishment of sinners and blasphemers and perverters of God's revelation and action through the prophets. In verses 3–6 the writer of this chapter has confounded places, i.e. Gehenna and the hell of the disobedient stars, that are most carefully distinguished in 1–36, and yet borrowed the phraseology of that section. **Blasphemers**: cf. 91^7. **Spoken** (*mtu*, β). g_1gq 'done'. **The prophets**. Here only mentioned expressly in Enoch. 7. **Written and inscribed**. This refers to the heavenly tablet; cf. 47^3. These records read them and know that which shall befall the sinners, and the spirits of the humble, and of those who have afflicted their bodies, and been recompensed by God; and of those who have been put to shame by wicked men: 8. Who love God and loved neither gold nor silver nor any of the good things which are in the world, but gave over their bodies to torture. 9. Who, since they came into being, longed not after earthly food, but regarded everything as a passing breath, and lived accordingly, and the Lord tried them much, and their spirits were found pure so that they should bless His name. 10. And all the blessings destined for them I have recounted in the books. And He hath assigned them their recompense, because they have been found to be such as loved heaven more than their life in the world, and though they were trodden under foot of wicked men, and experienced abuse and reviling from them and were put to shame, yet they blessed Me. 11. And now I will summon the spirits of the good who belong to the generation of light, and

are also called the book of the holy ones, for their purpose is to acquaint the angels with the future: cf. 103^2. See also Asc. Is. 7^{27}. 7-9. The humble. These are the עֲנִיִּים and עֲנָוִים so often referred to in the Psalms. They constitute the true Israel as opposed to the proud, the selfish, and the paganizers; see Cheyne on Ps. 9^{13}. Those who have afflicted their bodies, loved neither gold nor silver, longed not after earthly food. These phrases would apply well to the Essene party; cf. 48^7 102^6. These characteristics of the righteous have their counterpart in those of the wicked; cf. 96$^{5-7}$ 97$^{8-10}$ 98^2. 7. Read (mt, β). g_1gqu 'place'. 8. Loved (a, β-$alnoy_1b$). $_1g$, $alnoy_1b$ 'love'. 9. Who ($_1gq$ reading 'ålla). Of this g gives a corruption 'allå and mt^1 'ållå. u reads 'and' and β 'and who'. Everything (u), i.e. everything in this world. $_1g$ reads 'their bodies'. But to compare their bodies to 'a passing breath' would be rather inapt. gmq^t, β read 'themselves'. But the righteous could not rightly regard themselves as a 'passing breath'. Yet see James 4^{14} ἀτμὶς γάρ ἐστε. Such language would more rightly befit the sinners, as in Wisdom 2$^{2-4}$, where the sinners declare that their 'spirit shall be dispersed as thin air' and their 'life shall pass away as the traces of a cloud' and 'scattered as is a mist'. Similarly in Job 7$^{7, 8}$ 'O remember that my life is wind ... as the cloud ... vanisheth away so he that goeth down to Sheol shall come up no more'. How the various readings in the text arose I cannot explain. The Lord tried them much, &c. Cf. Wisd. 3^5 ὁ θεὸς ἐπείρασεν αὐτοὺς καὶ εὗρεν αὐτοὺς ἀξίους ἑαυτοῦ. 10. Enoch speaks, and refers his hearers and readers to his books. Their life in the world: cf. 48^7. 11. Verses 11 and 12 are represented as being spoken by God. Generation of light: cf. 61^{12} (note)

I will transform those who were born in darkness, who in the flesh were not recompensed with such honour as their faithfulness deserved. 12. And I will bring forth in shining light those who have loved My holy name, and I will seat each on the throne of his honour. 13. And they shall be resplendent for times without number; for righteousness is the judgement of God; for to the faithful He will give faithfulness in the habitation of upright paths. 14. And they shall see those who were born in darkness led into darkness, while the righteous shall be resplendent. 15. And the sinners shall cry aloud and see them resplendent, and they indeed shall go where days and seasons are prescribed for them.'

38⁴ (note). **Who were born in darkness.** Of those who were born in darkness, i.e. in heathenism, such as were faithful and were not recompensed in the body will be transformed, but those who remain in their darkness are cast into darkness; cf. ver. 14. **Were not recompensed with** ($a-gu$, β). g 'did not seek'. 12. **In shining light**, i.e. clad in shining light. The same idiomatic use of ba is found in Matt. 7¹⁵. The statement in the next verse 'they shall be resplendent' calls for this translation. Otherwise the text could mean 'into shining light'. Cf. 2 Enoch 22⁸⁻¹⁰, where the garments of the blessed are said to be composed of God's glory. These garments are according to our text 62¹⁶ (see note) 'garments of life'. They are really the spiritual bodies of the blessed; cf. Rev. 3⁴, ⁵, ¹⁸ 4⁴ 6¹¹ 7⁹, ¹³, ¹⁴ 4 Ezra 2³⁹, ⁴⁵ Asc. Is. 4¹⁶ 7²² 8¹⁴, ²⁶. **Throne of his honour** (a, n). β-n 'throne of honour, of his honour'. Cf. Matt. 19²⁸ Rev. 3²¹ 4⁴ Asc. Is. 9¹⁰, ¹⁸. 13. **Resplendent**, &c.: cf. 39⁷ 104² 108¹⁴. **The habitation of upright paths** (t, β). gq 'the habitation and ($>q$) upright paths', m 'the habitation and uprightness', u 'the upright paths'. 14. **Led** (gmq). t, β 'cast'. 103⁸ favours the former reading. 15. **Resplendent** (a). β 'shining'. Cf. Dan. 12², ³.

APPENDIX I

THE GIZEH GREEK FRAGMENT OF ENOCH

Λόγος εὐλογίας Ἐνώχ, καθὼς εὐλόγησεν ἐκλεκτοὺς δικαίους
ὁι ἔσονται εἰς ἡμέραν ἀνάγκης ἐξᾶραι¹ πάντας τοὺς ἐχθρούς², καὶ ὠθήσονται δίκαιοι⌐³.

Καὶ ἀναλαβὼν τὴν παραβολὴν αὐτοῦ εἶπεν· Ἐνώχ, ἄνθρωπος
...ς, ἔστιν⁴ ὅρασις⁵ ἐκ θεοῦ αὐτῷ ἀνεῳγμένη, ἣν⁶ †⁷ ἔχων † ⁷ τὴν
...ιν τοῦ ἁγίου *καὶ τοῦ οὐρανοῦ⁸, † ἔδειξέν μοι⁹ ⌐καὶ ἁγιολόγων⌐
ἤκουσα ἐγώ⌐, καὶ ⌐ὡς⌐ ἤκουσα παρ᾽ αὐτῶν πάντα καὶ ἔγνων
ἐωρῶν¹⁰· καὶ οὐκ ἐς τὴν νῦν γενεὰν ⌐διενοούμην⌐, ἀλλὰ ἐπὶ
...οῦσαν ⌐ἐγὼ λαλῶ⌐¹¹. 3. ⌐Καὶ⌐ περὶ τῶν ἐκλεκτῶν ⌐νῦν⌐
καὶ περὶ αὐτῶν ἀνέλαβον τὴν παραβολήν ⌐μου⌐.

[Καὶ] ἐξελεύσεται ὁ ἅγιός † μου † ¹² ὁ μέγας ἐκ τῆς κατοική-
σεως αὐτοῦ,

καὶ ὁ θεὸς τοῦ αἰῶνος ἐπὶ γῆν¹³ πατήσει ἐπὶ τὸ Σεινὰ ὄρος,

[καὶ φανήσεται *ἐκ τῆς παρενβολῆς αὐτοῦ¹⁴]

καὶ φανήσεται ἐν τῇ δυνάμει τῆς ἰσχύος αὐτοῦ ἀπὸ τοῦ οὐρανοῦ
⌐τῶν οὐρανῶν⌐

καὶ φοβηθήσονται πάντες

καὶ † πιστεύσουσιν †¹⁵ οἱ ἐγρήγοροι

...ς. ἐξάρῃ. ² E adds καὶ τοὺς
...
³ Though E omits, the
...may be genuine. ⁴ To be taken
...ἀνεῳγμένη or omitted. ⁵ E =
...αὐτοῦ which gives better sense,
...rees with Num. 24⁴. בְּלוּי עֵינָיִם
...ust either be written ἦν or ᾖν.
...e context is against the former,
...is quite intelligible. It is to
...ken with †ἔχων† as forming
...phrastic conjugation = 'he was
...ᾳτ†. ⁷ = יֵשׁ אֶת, ἔχειν is found
...endering of אֵת in Job 17⁹ 18²⁰
...Is. 12⁸, and it may be so here.

It is corrupt for יהיה = ὁρῶν. The
passage in E = Ἐνώχ, ἄνθρωπος δίκαιος
οὗ ἐκ θεοῦ ὀφθαλμοὶ αὐτοῦ ἀνεῳγμένοι
καὶ ἑώρα τὴν ὅρασιν τοῦ ἁγίου. ⁸ Corrupt (?) for κατὰ τὸν οὐρανόν as in E.
⁹ Text corrupt. E = ἦν ἔδειξάν μοι οἱ
ἄγγελοι. ¹⁰ MS. θεορων. ¹¹ So
Swete emends from εγω αλλω. ¹² Can
hardly be right: unexampled in Enoch;
E = καί. ¹³ E corrupt = ἐκεῖθεν.
¹⁴ E = σὺν or ἐν τῇ παρενβολῇ. ¹⁵ E
= σαλευθήσονται. Flemming suggests
πτήξουσιν. ¹⁶ This clause, which E
omits, I have removed to the margin

After ἐγρή-
γοροι the fol-
lowing words
are interpo-
lated : καὶ
ᾄσουσιν ἀπό-
κρυφα ἐν πᾶσιν
τοῖς ἄκροις τῆς
καὶ σισθήσον-
ται πάντα τὰ
ἄκρα τῆς γῆς¹⁶

καὶ λήμψεται αὐτοὺς τρόμος καὶ φόβος μέγας μέχρι τῶν περάτων τῆς γῆς

6. καὶ σεισθήσονται [καὶ πεσοῦνται καὶ διαλυθήσονται] ὄρη ὑψηλὰ
καὶ ταπεινωθήσονται βουνοὶ ὑψηλοὶ [τοῦ διαρυῆναι ὄρη]²
καὶ τακήσονται ὡς κηρὸς ἀπὸ προσώπου πυρὸς [ἐν φλογί]³

7. καὶ διασχισθήσεται ἡ γῆ ⌜σχίσμα [ῥαγάδι]⌝⁴,
καὶ πάντα ὅσα ἐστὶν ἐπὶ τῆς γῆς ἀπολεῖται
καὶ κρίσις ἔσται κατὰ πάντων.

8. καὶ μετὰ⁵ τῶν δικαίων τὴν εἰρήνην ποιήσει,
καὶ ἐπὶ τοὺς ἐκλεκτοὺς ἔσται συντήρησις ⌜καὶ εἰρήνη⌝,
καὶ ἐπ' αὐτοὺς γενήσεται⁶ ἔλεος.

καὶ ἔσονται πάντες τοῦ θεοῦ,
καὶ τὴν †εὐδοκίαν†⁷ δώσει αὐτοῖς,
καὶ πάντας εὐλογήσει.

⌜καὶ πάντων ἀντιλήμψεται⌝⁸, [καὶ βοηθήσει ἡμῖν]⁹
καὶ φανήσεται αὐτοῖς φῶς
[καὶ ποιήσει ἐπ' αὐτοὺς εἰρήνην]⁸.

9. †Ὅτι†⁹ ἔρχεται σὺν ταῖς¹⁰
μυριάσιν [αὐτοῦ καὶ τοῖς]¹¹ ἁγίοις
αὐτοῦ,

(a) ποιῆσαι κρίσιν κατὰ
πάντων,

JUDE 14, 15.
Ἰδοὺ ἦλθεν Κύριος ἐν ἁγίαις
μυριάσιν αὐτοῦ

(a) ποιῆσαι κρίσιν κατὰ
πάντων

as an interpolation at variance with the closing genuine words of this verse, and with all that follows on the fate of the Watchers who were imprisoned beneath the hills. The scribe who added it was possibly thinking of 2 En. 18, where the singing of the Watchers is mentioned. ¹. These words are omitted by E and against the parallelism. ² Bracketed because omitted by E and against sense. ³ A duplicate rendering. ⁴ These two words look like two renderings of the same Hebrew word. ⁵ MS. μέγα. ⁶ MS. γενηται. ⁷ Corrupt for εὐοδίαν. G thus = בחרצ in the active, while E gives the passive form. ⁸ This verse though omitted by E is probably genuine, being supported by the parallelism. ⁹ E = καὶ ἰδού: Jude, Pseudo-Cypr. and Pseudo-Vig. ἰδού. ¹⁰ MS. τοῖς. ¹¹ Interpolated against E and all other authorities. Read

(b) καὶ ἀπολέσαι¹ ⌜πάντας⌝ τοὺς ἀσεβεῖς,

(c) καὶ (ἐ)λέγξαι² πᾶσαν σάρκα

(α) περὶ πάντων ἔργων ⌜τῆς ἀσεβείας αὐτῶν⌝ ὧν ἠσέβησαν

(β) ⌜καὶ σκληρῶν ὧν ἐλάλησαν λόγων⌝³ κατ' αὐτοῦ ἁμαρτωλοὶ ἀσεβεῖς.

(bc) καὶ ἐλέγξαι πάντας τοὺς ἀσεβεῖς

(α) περὶ πάντων τῶν ἔργων ἀσεβείας αὐτῶν ὧν ἠσέβησαν

(β) καὶ περὶ πάντων τῶν σκληρῶν ὧν ἐλάλησαν κατ' αὐτοῦ ἁμαρτωλοὶ ἀσεβεῖς.

PSEUDO-CYPRIAN: *Ad Novatianum*
(Hartel's Cyprian, iii. 67).

Ecce venit cum multis milibus nuntiorum suorum
(a) facere iudicium de omnibus
(b) Et perdere omnes impios
(c) Et arguere omnem carnem
(α) de omnibus factis impiorum quae fecerunt impie
(β) et de omnibus verbis impiis quae de † Deo † locuti sunt peccatores.

PSEUDO-VIGILIUS (Migne 62, col. 363)
Et in epistola Iudae apostoli:

Ecce veniet Dominus in millibus
(a) facere iudicium
(b) Et perdere omnes impios
(c) Et arguere omnem carnem
(α) de omnibus operibus impietatis eorum

II. Κατανοήσατε πάντα τὰ ἔργα ἐν τῷ οὐρανῷ, πῶς οὐκ ἠλλοίωσαν τὰς ὁδοὺς αὐτῶν, ⌜καὶ⌝ τοὺς φωστῆρας τοὺς ἐν τῷ οὐρανῷ, ὡς τὰ πάντα ἀνατέλλει καὶ δύνει, τεταγμένος ἕκαστος ἐν τῷ ⌜τεταγμένῳ⌝ καιρῷ, ⌜καὶ ταῖς ἑορταῖς αὐτῶν φαίνονται,⌝ καὶ οὐ παραβαίνουσιν τὴν ἰδίαν τάξιν. 2. ἴδετε τὴν γῆν καὶ διανοήθητε περὶ

ἁγίαις instead of ἁγίοις to agree with μυριάσιν. ¹ MS. απολεσει, but the parallelism, Pseudo-Cypr. and Pseudo-Vig. and E require ἀπολέσαι. Other edd. ἀπολέσαι. ² MS. λενξει. Parallelism and Jude, Ps.-Cypr. and Ps.-Vig. require ἐλέγξαι. ³ Undoubtedly genuine though omitted by E. G adds τῶν ἔργων τῶν ἐν αὐτῇ γινομένων ἀπ' ἀρχῆς μέχρι τελειώσεως, ⌜ὥς⌝¹ εἰσιν φθαρτά,⌝² ὡς οὐκ ἀλλοιοῦται³ ⌜οὐδὲν τῶν ἐπὶ γῆς, ἀλλὰ⌝ πάντα ἔργα θεοῦ ⌜ὑμῖν⌝ φαίνεται. 3. ἴδετε τὴν θερείαν καὶ τὸν χειμῶνα .... III. καταμάθετε καὶ ἴδετε πάντα τὰ δένδρα⁴,

V. ... πῶς τὰ φύλλα χλωρὰ ἐν αὐτοῖς σκέποντα τὰ δένδρα⁵ καὶ [πᾶς]* ὁ καρπὸς αὐτῶν⁶ [εἰς τιμὴν καὶ δόξαν.] διανοήθητε ⌜καὶ γνῶτε⌝ περὶ πάντων ⌜τῶν ἔργων⌝ αὐτοῦ, καὶ νοήσατε ὅτι [θεὸς ζῶν] ἐποίησεν αὐτὰ οὕτως⁷, * καὶ ζῇ⁸ εἰς πάντας τοὺς αἰῶνας· 2. καὶ τὰ ἔργα αὐτοῦ ⌜πάντα [ὅσα ἐποίησεν], εἰς τοὺς αἰῶνας⌝ ἀπὸ ἐνιαυτοῦ εἰς ἐνιαυτὸν γινόμενα ⌜πάντα οὕτως,⌝ καὶ πάντα ὅσα ἀποτελοῦσιν αὐτῷ τὰ ἔργα, καὶ οὐκ ἀλλοιοῦνται ⌜αὐτῶν τὰ ἔργα,⌝ ἀλλ' ὡσπερεὶ κατὰ ἐπιταγὴν⁹ τὰ πάντα γίνεται. 3. ἴδετε πῶς ἡ θάλασσα καὶ οἱ ποταμοὶ ὡς ὁμοίως ἀποτελοῦσιν, ⌜καὶ οὐκ ἀλλοιοῦσιν⌝ αὐτῶν τὰ ἔργα ⌜ἀπὸ τῶν λόγων αὐτοῦ⌝.

4. Ὑμεῖς δὲ οὐκ ἐνεμείνατε οὐδὲ ἐποιήσατε κατὰ τὰς ἐντολὰς αὐτοῦ¹⁰

ἀλλὰ ἀπέστητε, καὶ κατελαλήσατε μεγάλους καὶ σκληροὺς λόγους ἐν στόματι ἀκαθαρσίας ὑμῶν κατὰ τῆς μεγαλοσύνης αὐτοῦ. [ὅτι κατελαλήσατε ἐν τοῖς ψεύμασιν ὑμῶν]

σκληροκάρδιοι, οὐκ ἔστ' εἰρήνη ὑμῖν.

5. τοιγὰρ τὰς ἡμέρας ὑμῶν ὑμεῖς καταράσεσθε¹¹

*καὶ τὰ ἔτη¹² τῆς ζωῆς ὑμῶν ἀπολεῖται

καὶ ⌜τὰ ἔτη τῆς ἀπωλείας ὑμῶν⌝ πληθυνθήσεται ἐν κατάρᾳ αἰώνων,

καὶ οὐκ ἔσται ὑμῖν ἔλεος [καὶ εἰρήνη]¹³

6 α. Τότε ἔσται¹⁴ τὰ ὀνόματα ὑμῶν εἰς κατάραν αἰώνιον πᾶσιν τοῖς δικαίοις,

---

dittographic clauses καὶ περὶ πάντων ὧν κατελάλησαν. ¹ Supplied by Swete. ² φθαρτά = נבלים corrupt for נכנים = 'steadfast'. ³ So Dillmann and Radermacher from αλλυουνται. Cf. ηλλυοσαν iu ver. 1 for ἠλλοίωσαν. ⁴ III. 1ᵇ–V. 1ᵃ lost through hmt. ⁵ E = τὰ δένδρα ἐν φύλλοις χλωροῖς σκέπονται. ⁶ E = καρποφοροῦσι. ⁷ = ḫasyu: of which ḫaḥasu: may be a corruption. ⁸ E = ὁ ζῶν. ⁹ E adds θεοῦ. ¹⁰ E = τοῦ Κυρίου. ¹¹ MS. κατηρασασθαι. ¹² Em. by Dillmann and Lods from κατα. ¹³ An interpolation, E omits. εἰρήνη forms end of ver. 4. ¹⁴ E = δώσετε. ἔσται corrupt.

Appendix I

b. καὶ ἐν ὑμῖν καταράσονται¹ ⌜πάντες⌝ οἱ καταρώμενοι,

c. ⌜καὶ πάντες⌝ οἱ ἁμαρτωλοὶ ⌜καὶ ἀσεβεῖς⌝ ἐν ὑμῖν ὀμοῦνται,

7 c. ὑμῖν δὲ τοῖς ἀσεβέσιν ἔσται κατάρα.

6 d. ⌜καὶ πάντες οἱ † ἁμαρτοι² † χαρήσονται,

e. καὶ ἔσται [αὐτοῖς] λύσις ἁμαρτιῶν,

f. καὶ πᾶν ἔλεος καὶ εἰρήνη καὶ ἐπιείκεια,

g. ἔσται αὐτοῖς σωτηρία, φῶς ἀγαθόν.

h. [καὶ αὐτοὶ κληρονομήσουσιν τὴν γῆν]³.

i. καὶ πᾶσιν ὑμῖν τοῖς ἁμαρτωλοῖς οὐχ ὑπάρξει σωτηρία

j. ἀλλ' ἐπὶ πάντας ὑμᾶς καταλύσει κατάρα⌝⁴

7 a. καὶ τοῖς ἐκλεκτοῖς ἔσται φῶς καὶ χάρις καὶ εἰρήνη,

b. καὶ αὐτοὶ κληρονομήσουσιν τὴν γῆν.

8. τότε δοθήσεται τοῖς ἐκλεκτοῖς⁵ σοφία,

καὶ πάντες οὗτοι ζήσονται καὶ οὐ μὴ ἁμαρτήσονται ἔτι

οὐ κατ' ἀσέβειαν⁶ οὔτε ὑπερηφανίαν,

⌜καὶ ἔσται ἐν ἀνθρώπῳ πεφωτισμένῳ φῶς καὶ ἀνθρώπῳ ἐπιστήμονι νόημα⌝⁷.

9. καὶ οὐ μὴ πλημμελήσουσιν

οὐδὲ μὴ ἁμάρτωσιν πάσας τὰς ἡμέρας τῆς ζωῆς αὐτῶν,

καὶ οὐ μὴ ἀποθάνωσιν ἐν ὀργῇ θυμοῦ⁸,

ἀλλὰ τὸν ἀριθμὸν αὐτῶν ζωῆς ἡμερῶν πληρώσουσιν,

καὶ ἡ ζωὴ⁹ αὐτῶν αὐξηθήσεται ἐν εἰρήνῃ,

καὶ τὰ ἔτη τῆς χαρᾶς αὐτῶν πληθυνθήσεται

ἐν ἀγαλλιάσει καὶ εἰρήνῃ αἰῶνος

ἐν πάσαις ταῖς ἡμέραις τῆς ζωῆς αὐτῶν.

G^g	G^s
VI. Καὶ ἐγένετο ὅταν ἐπληθύνθησαν οἱ υἱοὶ τῶν ἀνθρώπων,	VI. Καὶ ἐγένετο ὅτε ἐπληθύνθησαν οἱ υἱοὶ τῶν ἀνθρώπων,

---

¹ G preserves Hebrew idiom. G wrongly = ὑμᾶς καταράσονται. ² Perhaps corrupt for ἀναμάρτητοι. ³ A doublet of 7 b. ⁴ Emended by Radermacher. MS. reads καταλυσιν καταραν. E omits 6 d–j. ⁵ Here there is a doublet of 7 a b and 8 a [φῶς καὶ χάρις, καὶ αὐτοὶ κληρονομήσουσιν τὴν γῆν. τότε δοθήσεται πᾶσιν τοῖς ἐκλεκτοῖς]. ⁶ Emended from ἀλήθειαν with E. ⁷ E = οἱ δὲ τὴν σοφίαν ἔχοντες πραεῖς ἔσονται. ⁸ E = ὀργῇ καὶ θυμῷ. ⁹ E = plural.

Gg

ἐν ἐκείναις ταῖς ἡμέραις ἐγεννήθησαν[1] θυγατέρες ὡραῖαι ⌜καὶ
καλαί. 2. καὶ ἐθεάσαντο⌝
αὐτὰς οἱ ἄγγελοι υἱοὶ οὐρανοῦ
καὶ ἐπεθύμησαν αὐτάς, καὶ εἶπαν
πρὸς ἀλλήλους Δεῦτε ἐκλεξώμεθα
ἑαυτοῖς γυναῖκας ἀπὸ τῶν ἀνθρώπων[2], καὶ γεννήσομεν ἑαυτοῖς
τέκνα. 3. καὶ εἶπεν Σεμειαζᾶς
πρὸς αὐτούς, ὃς ἦν ἄρχων αὐτῶν,
Φοβοῦμαι μὴ οὐ θελήσετε ποιῆσαι τὸ πρᾶγμα τοῦτο, καὶ ἔσομαι
ἐγὼ μόνος ὀφειλέτης ἁμαρ-
τίας μεγάλης. 4. ἀπεκρίθησαν οὖν αὐτῷ πάντες Ὁμόσωμεν
ὅρκῳ πάντες καὶ ἀναθεματίσωμεν
πάντες ἀλλήλους μὴ ἀποστρέψαι
τὴν γνώμην ταύτην, μέχρις οὗ ἂν
[τελέσωμεν αὐτὴν καὶ][3] ποιήσω-
μεν τὸ πρᾶγμα τοῦτο. 5. τότε
ὤμοσαν πάντες ὁμοῦ καὶ ἀνεθεμάτισαν ἀλλήλους ἐν αὐτῷ....

7. Καὶ ταῦτα τὰ ὀνόματα[5] τῶν
ἀρχόντων αὐτῶν· Σεμιαζά, οὗτος
ἦν ἄρχων αὐτῶν· Ἀραθάκ, Κιμ-
βρά, Σαμμανή, Δονεϊήλ, Ἀρεαρώς,
Σεμιήλ, Ἰωμειήλ, Χωχαριήλ,
Ἐζεκιήλ, Βατριήλ, Σαθιήλ, Ἀτ-
ριήλ, Ταμιήλ, Βαρακιήλ, Ἀνανθάν,

Gs

ἐγεννήθησαν αὐτοῖς θυγατέρες
ὡραῖαι. 2. καὶ ἐπεθύμησαν
αὐτὰς οἱ ἐγρήγοροι ⌜καὶ ἀπεπλανήθησαν ὀπίσω αὐτῶν,⌝ καὶ εἶπον
πρὸς ἀλλήλους Ἐκλεξώμεθα
ἑαυτοῖς γυναῖκας ἀπὸ τῶν θυγατέρων τῶν ἀνθρώπων τῆς γῆς.
3. καὶ εἶπε Σεμιαζᾶς ὁ ἄρχων
αὐτῶν πρὸς αὐτούς Φοβοῦμαι μὴ
οὐ θελήσητε ποιῆσαι τὸ πρᾶγμα
τοῦτο, καὶ ἔσομαι ἐγὼ μόνος
ὀφειλέτης ἁμαρτίας μεγάλης.
4. καὶ ἀπεκρίθησαν αὐτῷ πάντες
⌜καὶ εἶπον⌝ Ὁμόσωμεν ἅπαντες
ὅρκῳ καὶ ἀναθεματίσωμεν ἀλλήλους τοῦ μὴ ἀποστρέψαι τὴν
γνώμην ταύτην, μέχρις οὗ ἀποτε-
λέσωμεν αὐτήν. 5. τότε πάντες ὤμοσαν ὁμοῦ καὶ ἀνεθεμάτισαν ἀλλήλους. 6. ἦσαν δὲ
οὗτοι διακόσιοι οἱ καταβάντες ἐν
ταῖς ἡμέραις Ἰάρεδ εἰς τὴν κορυφὴν τοῦ Ἑρμονιεὶμ ὄρους, καὶ
ἐκάλεσαν τὸ ὄρος Ἑρμών, κα-
θότι ὤμοσαν καὶ ἀνεθεμάτισαν
ἀλλήλους ἐν αὐτῷ[4].

7. Καὶ ταῦτα τὰ ὀνόματα τῶν
ἀρχόντων αὐτῶν· α΄ Σεμιαζᾶς, ὁ
ἄρχων αὐτῶν, β΄ Ἀταρκούφ, γ΄
Ἀρακιήλ, δ΄ Χωβαβιήλ, ε΄ Ὀραμ-
μαμή, ς΄ Ῥαμιήλ, ζ΄ Σαμψίχ, η΄
Ζακιήλ, θ΄ Βαλκιήλ, ι΄ Ἀζαλζήλ,
ια΄ Φαρμορός, ιβ΄ Ἀμαριήλ, ιγ΄

[1] E Gs add αὐτοῖς. [2] E = υἱῶν τῶν ἀνθρώπων. [3] Bracketed as a doublet. [4] Gs omit. [4] Gs omits ver. 6 through homoioteleuton. [5] On these names

Appendix I

G^g

Θωνιήλ, Ῥαμιήλ, Ἀσεάλ, Ῥακειήλ, Τουριήλ. 8. οὗτοί εἰσιν ἀρχαὶ αὐτῶν οἱ δέκα.[1]

VII. Καὶ[2] ἔλαβον ἑαυτοῖς γυναῖκας· ἕκαστος αὐτῶν ἐξελέξαντο ἑαυτοῖς γυναῖκας[3], καὶ ἤρξαντο εἰσπορεύεσθαι πρὸς αὐτὰς καὶ μιαίνεσθαι[6] ἐν αὐταῖς· καὶ ἐδίδαξαν αὐτὰς φαρμακείας καὶ ἐπαοιδὰς καὶ ῥιζοτομίας, καὶ τὰς βοτάνας ἐδήλωσαν αὐταῖς. 2. Αἱ[8] δὲ ἐν γαστρὶ λαβοῦσαι ἐτέκοσαν γίγαντας μεγάλους ἐκ πηχῶν τρισχιλίων, 3. οἵτινες κατέσθοσαν τοὺς κόπους τῶν ἀνθρώπων. ὡς δὲ[11] οὐκ ἐδυνήθησαν αὐτοῖς οἱ ἄνθρωποι ἐπιχορηγεῖν, 4. οἱ γίγαντες ἐτόλμησαν[12] ἐπ' αὐτούς, καὶ κατεσθίοσαν τοὺς ἀνθρώπους. 5. καὶ ἤρξαντο ἁμαρτάνειν ἐν τοῖς πετεινοῖς καὶ τοῖς (θ)ηρίοις καὶ ἑρπετοῖς καὶ τοῖς (ἰ)χθύσιν, καὶ ἀλλήλων τὰς (σ)άρκας κατεσθίειν, καὶ τὸ αἷμα (ἔ)πινον. 6. τότε ἡ γῆ ἐνέτυχεν κατὰ τῶν ἀνόμων.

G^s

Ἀναγημάς, ιδ΄ Θαυσαήλ, ιε΄ Σαμιήλ, ιϛ΄ Σαριναᾶς, ιζ΄ Εὐμιήλ, ιη΄ Τυριήλ, ιθ΄ Ἰουμιήλ, κ΄ Σαριήλ.

VII. *Οὗτοι καὶ οἱ λοιποὶ πάντες[4] [ἐν τῷ χιλιοστῷ ἑκατοστῷ ἑβδομηκοστῷ ἔτει τοῦ κόσμου[5]] ἔλαβον ἑαυτοῖς γυναῖκας, καὶ ἤρξαντο μιαίνεσθαι ἐν αὐταῖς [ἕως τοῦ κατακλυσμοῦ].[7] 2. καὶ ἔτεκον ⌜αὐτοῖς γένη τρία· πρῶτον⌝[9] γίγαντας μεγάλους, ⌜οἱ δὲ Γίγαντες † ἐτέκνωσαν †[10] Ναφηλείμ, καὶ τοῖς Ναφηλεὶμ † ἐγεννήθησαν †[10] Ἐλιούδ. καὶ ἦσαν αὐξανόμενοι κατὰ τὴν μεγαλειότητα αὐτῶν.⌝[9] καὶ ἐδίδαξαν [ἑαυτοὺς καὶ] τὰς γυναῖκας ἑαυτῶν φαρμακείας καὶ ἐπαοιδάς.

VIII. ⌜Πρῶτος⌝ Ἀζαὴλ ⌜ὁ δέκατος τῶν ἀρχόντων⌝ ἐδίδαξε

---

see pp. 16, 17.   [1] The manuscript reading seems corrupt for ἀρχαὶ αὐτῶν τῶν δεκάδων, a literal rendering of ראשׁי עשׂרתיהון. We have an undoubted case of this in 19[2] αἱ γυναῖκες αὐτῶν τῶν ... ἀγγέλων. Radermacher proposes ἀρχαὶ αὐτῶν οἱ (ἐπὶ) δέκα, but this would mean 'their chiefs over ten (angels)'.   [2] See note 4.   [3] E = ἐξελέξατο ἕκαστος ἑαυτῷ μίαν.   [4] E = καὶ οἱ λοιποὶ πάντες μετ' αὐτῶν καί, where the final καί is an intrusion.   [5] Addition of Syncellus.   [6] E = μίγνυσθαι.   [7] Addition of Syncellus.   [8] MS. reads ἐν.   [9] These clauses, though omitted by E and G^s, go back to the original.   [10] ἐτέκνωσαν and τοῖς Ν"· ἐγεννήθησαν may be corrupt. We should expect according to Jub. 7[22] ἔκτειναν and οἱ Ν"· ἔκτειναν.   [11] E = ὥστε.   [12] E = ἐτράπησαν, of which ἐτόλμησαν seems a corruption.

G^g

VIII. Ἐδίδαξεν τοὺς ἀνθρώπους Ἀζαὴλ μαχαίρας ποιεῖν καὶ ὅπλα καὶ ἀσπίδας καὶ θώρακας [διδάγματα ἀγγέλων], καὶ ὑπέδειξεν αὐτοῖς τὰ μέταλλα¹ καὶ τὴν ἐργασίαν αὐτῶν, καὶ ψέλια καὶ κόσμους καὶ στίβεις² καὶ τὸ καλλιβλέφαρον³ καὶ παντοίους λίθους ἐκλεκτοὺς καὶ τὰ βαφικά⁴. 2. καὶ ἐγένετο ἀσέβεια πολλή, καὶ ἐπόρνευσαν καὶ ἀπεπλανήθησαν καὶ ἠφανίσθησαν ἐν πάσαις ταῖς ὁδοῖς αὐτῶν. 3. Σεμιαζᾶς ἐδίδαξεν ἐπα(οι)δὰς καὶ ῥιζοτομίας⁵. Ἀρμαρὼς *ἐπαοιδῶν λυτήριον· (Βα)ρακιὴλ⁷ ἀστρολογίας⁸. Χωχιὴλ⁷ τὰ σημειωτικά· Σαθ(ι)ὴλ⁷ ἀστεροσκοπίαν⁹. Σεριὴ(λ)⁷ σεληναγωγίας¹⁰.

G^s

ποιεῖν μαχαίρας καὶ θώρακας καὶ ⌜πᾶν⌝ σκεῦος πολεμικόν, καὶ τὰ μέταλλα τῆς γῆς ⌜καὶ τὸ χρυσίον⌝ πῶς ἐργάσωνται καὶ ⌜ποιήσωσιν αὐτὰ⌝ κόσμια ⌜ταῖς γυναιξί, καὶ τὸν ἄργυρον ἔδειξε δὲ αὐτοῖς⌝ καὶ τὸ †στίλβειν†² καὶ τὸ καλλωπίζειν καὶ τοὺς ἐκλεκτοὺς λίθους καὶ τὰ βαφικά· ⌜καὶ ἐποίησαν ἑαυτοῖς οἱ υἱοὶ τῶν ἀνθρώπων καὶ ταῖς θυγατράσιν αὐτῶν, καὶ παρέβησαν καὶ ἐπλάνησαν τοὺς ἁγίους⌝. 2. καὶ ἐγένετο ἀσέβεια πολλὴ ⌜ἐπὶ τῆς γῆς,⌝ καὶ ἠφάνισαν τὰς ὁδοὺς αὐτῶν. 3. ⌜ἔτι δὲ καὶ ὁ πρώταρχος αὐτῶν⌝ Σεμιαζᾶς ἐδίδαξεν †εἶναι ὀργὰς⁶ ⌜κατὰ τοῦ νοός,⌝ καὶ ῥίζας βοτανῶν ⌜τῆς γῆς⌝. ⌜ὁ δὲ ἑνδέκατος⌝ Φαρμαρὼς ἐδίδαξε ⌜φαρμακείας, ἐπαοιδάς, σοφίας, καὶ⌝ ἐπαοιδῶν λυτήρια· ὁ ἔνατος ⌜ἐδίδαξεν⌝ ἀστροσκοπίαν· ὁ δὲ τέταρτος ⌜ἐδίδαξεν⌝ ἀστρολογίαν· ὁ δὲ ὄγδοος ἐδίδαξεν ἀεροσκοπίαν· ⌜ὁ δὲ τρίτος ἐδίδαξε τὰ σημεῖα τῆς γῆς· ὁ δὲ ἕβδομος ἐδίδαξε τὰ σημεῖα τοῦ ἡλίου⌝· ὁ δὲ εἰκοστὸς ἐδίδαξε τὰ σημεῖα τῆς σελήνης. ⌜πάντες οὗτοι ἤρξαντο ἀνακαλύπτειν τὰ μυστήρια ταῖς

---

¹ MS. μεγαλα. ² G^s has στίλβειν which is corrupt; Diels emends to στιβίζειν. ³ Since G^s has τὸ καλλωπίζειν the Aram. may have been simply מכחל. ⁴ E adds τὰ μέταλλα τῆς γῆς—a doublet. ⁵ E=ἐπαοιδοὺς καὶ ῥιζοτόμους. ⁶ Corrupt for ἐπαοιδάς (Raderm.). ⁷ See notes on pp. 16, 17. ⁸ E=ἀστρολόγους. ⁹ This word (which E translates) is corrupt for ἀεροσκοπίαν as in G^s. ¹⁰ MS.

Appendix I

G^g

G^s

γυναιξὶν αὐτῶν καὶ τοῖς τέκνοις αὐτῶν. μετὰ δὲ ταῦτα⌐ [VII. 4–5] ἤρξαντο οἱ γίγαντες κατεσθίειν ⌐τὰς σάρκας⌐ τῶν ἀνθρώπων¹.

G^g

4. τῶν οὖν² ἀνθρώπων ἀπολλυμένων ἡ βο(ὴ) εἰς οὐρανοὺς ἀνέβη.

G^s1

4. καὶ ἤρξαντο οἱ ἄνθρωποι ἐλαττοῦσθαι ⌐ἐπὶ τῆς γῆς. οἱ δὲ λοιποὶ⌐ ἐβόησαν εἰς τὸν οὐρανὸν ⌐περὶ τῆς κακώσεως αὐτῶν, λέγοντες εἰσενεχθῆναι τὸ μνημόσυνον αὐτῶν ἐνώπιον Κυρίου⌐.

G^s2 (G. Syncellus I. 42 sqq.)

4. ⌐Τότε⌐ ἐβόησαν οἱ ἄνθρωποι εἰς τὸν οὐρανὸν ⌐λέγοντες Εἰσαγάγετε τὴν κρίσιν ἡμῶν πρὸς τὸν ὕψιστον, καὶ τὴν ἀπώλειαν ἡμῶν ἐνώπιον τῆς δόξης τῆς μεγάλης, ἐνώπιον τοῦ κυρίου τῶν κυρίων πάντων τῇ μεγαλωσύνῃ⌐.

IX. Τότε παρ(α)κύψαντες Μιχαὴλ καὶ Οὐ(ρι)ὴλ καὶ Ῥαφαὴλ καὶ Γαβριή(λ), ⌐οὗτοι⌐ ἐκ τοῦ οὐρανοῦ ἐθεάσα(ν)το αἷμα πολὺ ἐκχυννόμεν(ον) ἐπὶ τῆς γῆς⌐. 2. καὶ εἶπαν πρὸ(ς) ἀλλήλους Φωνὴ βοώντω(ν) ἐπὶ τῆς γῆς· μέχρι πυλῶ(ν) τοῦ οὐρανοῦ⁴ 3. ἐντυγχάνου-

IX. Καὶ ⌐ἀκούσαντες οἱ τέσσαρες μεγάλοι ἀρχάγγελοι⌐, Μιχαὴλ καὶ Οὐριὴλ καὶ Ῥαφαὴλ καὶ Γαβριὴλ παρέκυψαν ⌐ἐπὶ τὴν γῆν⌐ ἐκ ⌐τῶν ἁγίων⌐ τοῦ οὐρανοῦ· καὶ θεασάμενοι αἷμα πολὺ ἐκκεχυμένον ἐπὶ τῆς γῆς ⌐καὶ πᾶσαν ⌐ἀσέβειαν καὶ⌐ ἀνομίαν ⌐γενομένην ἐπ' αὐτῆς,⌐

IX. Καὶ ⌐ἀκούσαντες οἱ τέσσαρες μεγάλοι ἀρχάγγελοι⌐, Μιχαὴλ καὶ Οὐριὴλ καὶ Ῥαφαὴλ καὶ Γαβριὴλ παρέκυψαν ⌐ἐπὶ τὴν γῆν⌐ ἐκ ⌐τῶν ἁγίων⌐ τοῦ οὐρανοῦ· καὶ θεασάμενοι αἷμα πολὺ ἐκκεχυμένον ἐπὶ τῆς γῆς καὶ πᾶσαν ἀνομίαν καὶ ⌐ἀσέβειαν⌐ γινομένην ἐπ' αὐτῆς,⌐

σεληνοναγιας. ¹ This sentence summarizes 7⁴, ⁵ of G^s. The order of narration in G^s is better than in G^g. ² MS. τον νουν. ³ G^s omits through hmt. καὶ πᾶσαν ἀσέβειαν γινομένην ἐπ τῆς γῆς against EG^s1, ². ⁴ E adds καὶ νῦν πρὸς ὑμᾶς τοὺς ἁγίους τοῦ οὐρανοῦ. The words μέχρι πυλῶν τ. οὐρ.

G{sup}g{/sup}

σιν οἱ ψυχαὶ τῶν ἀνθρώπων λεγόντων Εἰσαγάγετε τὴν κρίσιν ἡμῶν πρὸς τὸν ὕψιστ(ον). 4. Καὶ εἶπα(ν) τῷ κυρίῳ[1] Σὺ εἶ κύριος τῶν κυρίων καὶ ὁ θεὸς τῶν θεῶν καὶ βασιλεὺς †τῶν αἰώνων†[3]. ὁ θρόνος τῆς δόξης σου εἰς πάσας τὰς γενεὰς τοῦ αἰῶνος, καὶ τὸ ὄνομά σου τὸ ἅγιον καὶ μέγα[5] καὶ εὐλογητὸν εἰς πάντας τοὺς αἰῶνας.

G{sup}s1{/sup}

2. ⌜εἰσελθόντες⌝ εἶπον πρὸς ἀλλήλους ⌜ὅτι 3. Τὰ πνεύματα καὶ⌝ αἱ ψυχαὶ τῶν ἀνθρώπων ⌜στενάζουσιν⌝ ἐντυγχάνοντα καὶ λέγοντα ὅτι Εἰσαγάγετε τὴν κρίσιν ἡμῶν πρὸς τὸν ὕψιστον, ⌜καὶ τὴν ἀπώλειαν ἡμῶν ἐνώπιον τῆς δόξης τῆς μεγαλωσύνης, ἐνώπιον τοῦ κυρίου τῶν κυρίων πάντων τῇ μεγαλωσύνῃ⌝. 4. Καὶ εἶπον τῷ κυρίῳ ⌜τῶν αἰώνων⌝[2] Σὺ εἶ ὁ θεὸς τῶν θεῶν καὶ κύριος τῶν κυρίων καὶ ὁ βασιλεὺς τῶν βασιλευόντων ⌜καὶ θεὸς τῶν αἰώνων⌝[4], καὶ ὁ θρόνος τῆς δόξης σου εἰς πάσας τὰς γενεὰς τῶν αἰώνων, καὶ τὸ ὄνομά σου ἅγιον[5] καὶ εὐλογημένον εἰς πάντας τοὺς αἰῶνας[6].

G{sup}s2{/sup}

2. ⌜εἰσελθόντες⌝ εἶπον πρὸς ἀλλήλους ⌜ὅτι 3. Τὰ πνεύματα καὶ⌝ αἱ ψυχαὶ τῶν ἀνθρώπων ἐντυγχάνουσι ⌜στενάζοντα καὶ⌝ λέγοντα Εἰσαγάγετε τὴν ⌜δέησιν⌝ ἡμῶν πρὸς τὸν ὕψιστον. 4. Καὶ ⌜προσελθόντες οἱ τέσσαρες ἀρχάγγελοι⌝ εἶπον τῷ κυρίῳ[1] Σὺ εἶ θεὸς τῶν θεῶν καὶ κύριος τῶν κυρίων καὶ βασιλεὺς τῶν βασιλευόντων ⌜καὶ θεὸς τῶν ἀνθρώπων⌝, καὶ ὁ θρόνος τῆς δόξης σου εἰς πάσας τὰς γενεὰς τῶν αἰώνων, καὶ τὸ ὄνομά σου ἅγιον[5] καὶ εὐλογημένον εἰς πάντας τοὺς αἰῶνας.

---

must be taken with ἐντυγχάνουσιν as in 9¹⁰ G{sup}g{/sup}. [1] E adds τῶν βασιλέων. G{sup}s1{/sup} has τῶν αἰώνων. [2] E = τῶν βασιλέων = מלכיא corrupt (?) for עלמיא. Hence 'Lord of the ages'. [3] Corrupt. E G{sup}s{/sup} = τῶν βασιλέων or βασιλευόντων. If this corruption is not native to G{sup}g{/sup} then we must assume a corruption in the Aramaic, the converse of that in note 2. [4] G{sup}s2{/sup} has ἀνθρώπων, i.e. ἀντων, corrupt for αἰώνων. Converse corruption in 11². [5] E G{sup}g{/sup} add καὶ μέγα (or δεδοξασμένον). [6] Here G{sup}s1{/sup} adds καὶ τὰ ἑξῆς. τότε ὁ ὕψιστος ἐκέλευσε

Appendix I

G^g

5. Σὺ γὰρ ἐποίησας τὰ πάντα, καὶ πᾶσαν¹ τὴν ἐξουσίαν ἔχων, καὶ πάντα ἐνώπιόν σου φανερὰ καὶ ἀκάλυπτα, καὶ πάντα σὺ ὁρᾷς²

... 6. ἃ ἐποίησεν Ἀζαήλ, ὃς ἐδίδαξεν πάσας τὰς ἀδικίας ἐπὶ τῆς γῆς καὶ ἐδήλωσεν τὰ μυστήρια τοῦ αἰῶνος τὰ ἐν τῷ οὐρανῷ ἃ ἐπιτηδεύουσιν †ἔγνωσαν† ἄνθρωποι⁴.

7. καὶ Σεμιαζᾶς, ᾧ τὴν ἐξουσίαν ἔδωκας ἄρχειν τῶν σὺν αὐτῷ ἅμα ὄιτων. 8. καὶ ἐπορεύθησαν πρὸς τὰς θυγατέρας τῶν ἀνθρώπων⁷ τῆς γῆς καὶ συνεκοιμήθησαν αὐταῖς καὶ⁸ ... ἐμιάνθησαν, καὶ ἐδήλωσαν αὐταῖς πάσας τὰς ἁμαρτίας. 9. καὶ αἱ γυναῖκες ἐγέννησαν Τιτᾶνας, *ὑφ' ὧν⁹ ὅλη ἡ γῆ ἐπλήσθη αἵματος καὶ ἀδικίας. 10. καὶ νῦν ἰδοὺ βοῶσιν αἱ ψυχαὶ τῶν τετελευτηκότων καὶ ἐντυγχάνουσιν μέχρι τῶν πυλῶν τοῦ οὐρανοῦ, καὶ

G^s (Syncellus I. 43)

5. Σὺ γὰρ εἶ ὁ ποιήσας τὰ πάντα καὶ πάντων¹ τὴν ἐξουσίαν ἔχων, καὶ πάντα ἐνώπιόν σου φανερὰ καὶ ἀκάλυπτα· καὶ πάντα ὁρᾷς, καὶ οὐκ ἔστιν ὃ κρυβῆναί σε δύναται. 6. ὁρᾷς ὅσα ἐποίησεν Ἀζαὴλ ⌜καὶ ὅσα εἰσήνεγκεν⌝, ὅσα ἐδίδαξεν, ἀδικίας ⌜καὶ ἁμαρτίας⌝ ἐπὶ τῆς γῆς καὶ ⌜πάντα δόλον ἐπὶ τῆς ξηρᾶς. ἐδίδαξε γὰρ⌝ *τὰ μυστήρια καὶ ἀπεκάλυψε τῷ αἰῶνι³ τὰ ἐν οὐρανῷ. * ἐπιτηδεύουσι δὲ ⌜τὰ ἐπιτηδεύματα αὐτοῦ,⌝ εἰδέναι ⌜τὰ μυστήρια,⌝⁴ οἱ υἱοὶ τῶν ἀνθρώπων. 7. *τῷ Σεμιαζᾷ⁵ τὴν ἐξουσίαν ἔδωκας †ἔχειν⁶ τῶν σὺν αὐτῷ ἅμα ὄντων. 8. καὶ ἐπορεύθησαν πρὸς τὰς θυγατέρας τῶν ἀνθρώπων⁷ τῆς γῆς καὶ συνεκοιμήθησαν μετ' αὐτῶν καὶ ἐν ταῖς θηλείαις ἐμιάνθησαν, καὶ ἐδήλωσαν αὐταῖς πάσας τὰς ἁμαρτίας, ⌜καὶ ἐδίδαξαν αὐτὰς μίσητρα ποιεῖν⌝. 9. καὶ ⌜νῦν ἰδοὺ αἱ θυγατέρες τῶν ἀνθώπων⌝ ἔτεκον ⌜ἐξ αὐτῶν υἱοὺς⌝ γίγαντας· ⌜κίβδηλα ἐπὶ τῆς γῆς τῶν ἀνθρώπων ἐκκέχυται,⌝ καὶ ὅλη ἡ γῆ ἐπλήσθη

τοῖς ἁγίοις ἀρχαγγέλοις, καὶ ἔθηκαν τοὺς ἐξάρχους αὐτῶν καὶ ἔβαλον αὐτοὺς εἰς τὴν ἄβυσσον ἕως τῆς κρίσεως, καὶ τὰ ἑξῆς. Here Syncellus summarizes 10⁴ ¹². Cf. end of 8⁸ G⁸.   ¹ E G⁸ = πάντων. ² G⁸ omits through hmt. καὶ οὐκ ἔστιν ὁ κρυβῆναί σε δύναται. ὁρᾷς against E G⁸.

³ E G⁸ = καὶ ἐδήλωσεν τὰ μυστήρια τοῦ αἰῶνος. ⁴ See note on p. 21. ⁵ Corrupt. E G⁸ = καὶ Σεμιαζᾶς. ⁶ Corrupt for ἄρχειν (Raderm.). ⁷ E adds ἐπί. ⁸ Add ἐν ταῖς θηλείαις with E G⁸. ⁹ G⁸ = καί.

Gg

ἀνέβη ὁ στεναγμὸς αὐτῶν καὶ οὐ δύναται ἐξελθεῖν ἀπὸ προσώπου τῶν ἐπὶ τῆς γῆς γινομένων ἀνομημάτων. 11. καὶ σὺ πάντα οἶδας πρὸ τοῦ αὐτὰ γενέσθαι, καὶ σὺ ὁρᾷς ταῦτα καὶ * ἐᾷς αὐτούς[1], καὶ οὐδὲ ⌜ἡμῖν⌝ λέγεις τί δεῖ ποιεῖν αὐτοὺς περὶ τούτων.

X. Τότε Ὕψιστος εἶπεν[4] ⌜περὶ τούτων⌝, * ὁ μέγας Ἅγιος, καὶ[5] ἐλάλησεν * καὶ εἶπεν[6] καὶ ἔπεμψεν Ἰστραὴλ πρὸς τὸν υἱὸν Λάμεχ 2. Εἰπὸν αὐτῷ ἐπὶ τῷ ἐμῷ ὀνόματι Κρύψον σεαυτόν, καὶ δήλωσον αὐτῷ τέλος ἐπερχόμενον, ὅτι ἡ γῆ ἀπόλλυται πᾶσα, καὶ κατακλυσμὸς μέλλει γίνεσθαι πάσης τῆς γῆς καὶ ἀπολέσει πάντα ὅσα ἔστ᾽ ἐν[7] αὐτῇ. 3. ⌜καὶ⌝ δίδαξον αὐτὸν ὅπως ἐκφύγῃ, καὶ μενεῖ τὸ σπέρμα αὐτοῦ εἰς πάσας τὰς γενεὰς τοῦ αἰῶνος.

Gs

ἀδικίας. 10. καὶ νῦν ἰδοὺ ⌜τὰ πνεύματα⌝ τῶν ψυχῶν[2] τῶν ἀποθανόντων ἀνθρώπων ἐντυγχάνουσι, καὶ μέχρι τῶν πυλῶν τοῦ οὐρανοῦ ἀνέβη ὁ στεναγμὸς αὐτῶν καὶ οὐ δύναται ἐξελθεῖν ἀπὸ προσώπου τῶν ἐπὶ τῆς γῆς γινομένων ἀδικημάτων. 11. καὶ σὺ αὐτὰ οἶδας πρὸ τοῦ[3] αὐτὰ γενέσθαι καὶ ὁρᾷς αὐτοὺς καὶ ἐᾷς αὐτούς, καὶ οὐδὲν λέγεις, τί δεῖ ποιῆσαι αὐτοὺς περὶ τούτου.

X. Τότε ὁ Ὕψιστος εἶπε καὶ ὁ ἅγιος ὁ μέγας ἐλάλησε, καὶ ἔπεμψε τὸν Οὐριὴλ πρὸς τὸν υἱὸν Λάμεχ λέγων 2. ⌜Πορεύου πρὸς τὸν Νῶε καὶ⌝ εἰπὸν αὐτῷ τῷ ἐμῷ ὀνόματι Κρύψον σεαυτόν, καὶ δήλωσον αὐτῷ τέλος ἐπερχόμενον, ὅτι ἡ γῆ ἀπόλλυται πᾶσα· καὶ ⌜εἰπὸν αὐτῷ ὅτι⌝ κατακλυσμὸς μέλλει γίνεσθαι πάσης τῆς γῆς, ἀπολέσαι πάντα ⌜ἀπὸ προσώπου τῆς γῆς⌝. 3. δίδαξον ⌜τὸν δίκαιον⌝[8] τί ⌜ποιήσει, τὸν υἱὸν Λάμεχ, καὶ τὴν ψυχὴν αὐτοῦ εἰς ζωὴν συντηρήσει, καὶ⌝ ἐκφεύξεται ⌜δι᾽ αἰῶνος⌝, καὶ ἐξ αὐτοῦ ⌜φυτευθήσεται⌝ φύτευμα ⌜καὶ⌝ σταθήσεται πάσας τὰς γενεὰς τοῦ αἰῶνος.

---

[1] Gg E = αἱ ψυχαί. [2] MS. has αιας. E = τὰ εἰς αὐτούς—a corruption. [3] Emended by Raderm. from τῶν. [4] E omits wrongly. [5] E = ὁ μέγας καὶ ὁ ἅγιος. [6] These words should with Gs E be placed after Λάμεχ. E = καὶ εἶπε πρὸς αὐτόν. Gs λέγων. [7] Emended by Raderm. from εστιν [8] Gg E = αὐ-

G^g

4. Καὶ¹ τῷ Ῥαφαὴλ εἶπεν Δῆσον τὸν Ἀζαὴλ ποσὶν καὶ χερσίν, καὶ βάλε αὐτὸν εἰς τὸ σκότος, καὶ ἄνοιξον τὴν ἔρημον τὴν οὖσαν ἐν τῷ Δαδουὴλ κἀκεῖ βάλε αὐτόν, 5. καὶ ὑπόθες² αὐτῷ λίθους τραχεῖς καὶ ὀξεῖς καὶ ἐπικάλυψον αὐτῷ τὸ σκότος, καὶ οἰκησάτω ἐκεῖ εἰς τοὺς αἰῶνας, καὶ τὴν ὄψιν αὐτοῦ πώμασον καὶ φῶς μὴ θεωρείτω· 6. καὶ ἐν τῇ ἡμέρᾳ ⌜τῆς μεγάλης⌝ τῆς κρίσεως ἀπαχθήσεται εἰς τὸν ἐνπυρισμόν. 7. καὶ ἰαθήσεται ἡ γῆ, ἣν ἠφάνισαν οἱ ἄγγελοι, καὶ τὴν ἴασιν τῆς γῆς⁴ δήλωσον, ἵνα ἰάσωνται⁵ τὴν πληγήν⁶, ἵνα μὴ⁷ ἀπόλωνται πάντες οἱ υἱοὶ τῶν ἀνθρώπων ἐν τῷ μυστηρίῳ ⌜ὅλῳ⌝ ᾧ † ⁸ οἱ ἐγρήγοροι καὶ ἐδί(δα)ξαν τοὺς υἱοὺς αὐτῶν, 8. καὶ ἠρημώθη πᾶσα ἡ γῆ [ἀφανισθεῖσα]⁹ ἐν *τοῖς ἔργοις τῆς διδασκαλίας¹⁰ Ἀζαήλ· καὶ ἐπ' αὐτῷ γράψον τὰς ἁμαρτίας πάσας. 9. Καὶ τῷ Γαβριὴλ εἶπεν ὁ κύριος· Πορεύου ἐπὶ τοὺς μαζηρέους, ἐπὶ τοὺς κιβδήλους¹² καὶ τοὺς υἱοὺς τῆς πορνείας¹³, καὶ ἀπόλεσον¹⁴

G^s

4. Καὶ τῷ Ῥαφαὴλ εἶπε ⌜Πορεύου, Ῥαφαήλ, καὶ⌝ δῆσον τὸν Ἀζαὴλ χερσὶ καὶ ποσὶ [συμπόδισον αὐτόν], καὶ ἔμβαλε αὐτὸν εἰς τὸ σκότος, καὶ ἄνοιξον τὴν ἔρημον τὴν οὖσαν ἐν τῇ [ἐρήμῳ] Δουδαήλ, καὶ ἐκεῖ ⌜πορευθεὶς⌝ βάλε αὐτόν· 5. καὶ ὑπόθες αὐτῷ λίθους ὀξεῖς καὶ ⌜λίθους⌝ τραχεῖς καὶ ἐπικάλυψον αὐτῷ σκότος, καὶ οἰκησάτω ἐκεῖ εἰς τὸν αἰῶνα· καὶ τὴν ὄψιν αὐτοῦ πώμασον καὶ φῶς μὴ θεωρείτω· 6. καὶ ἐν τῇ ἡμέρᾳ τῆς κρίσεως ἀπαχθήσεται εἰς τὸν ἐμπυρισμὸν ⌜τοῦ πυρός⌝. 7. καὶ ἴασαι τὴν γῆν ἣν ἠφάνισαν οἱ ἐγρήγοροι³, καὶ τὴν ἴασιν τῆς πληγῆς⁴ δήλωσον, ἵνα *ἰάσωνται τὴν πληγὴν⁶ καὶ μὴ ἀπόλωνται πάντες οἱ υἱοὶ τῶν ἀνθρώπων ἐν τῷ μυστηρίῳ ὃ εἶπον οἱ ἐγρήγοροι καὶ ἐδίδαξαν τοὺς υἱοὺς αὐτῶν, 8. καὶ ἠρημώθη πᾶσα ἡ γῆ ἐν τοῖς ἔργοις τῆς διδασκαλίας Ἀζαήλ· καὶ ἐπ' αὐτῇ¹¹ γράψον πάσας τὰς ἁμαρτίας. 9. Καὶ τῷ Γαβριὴλ εἶπε Πορεύου, ⌜Γαβριήλ⌝, ἐπὶ τοὺς γίγαντας, ἐπὶ τοὺς κιβδήλους, ἐπὶ τοὺς υἱοὺς τῆς πορνείας, καὶ

τόν. ¹ E adds πάλιν ὁ κύριος. ² E = ἐπίθες. ³ G^g E = ἄγγελοι. ⁴ = E. G^g πληγῆς. ⁵ MS. ιασονται. ⁶ E = τὴν γῆν. ⁷ MS. μην. ⁸ Here ἐπάταξαν = אבדו corrupt for אמרו = εἶπον as we have in G^s. ⁹ G^g E omit. ¹⁰ E = τῇ διδασκαλίᾳ τῶν ἔργων. ¹¹ G^g αὐτῷ. ¹² κίβδηλος here seems to represent שעטנז (cf. Lev. 19¹⁹ Deut. 22¹¹) or some derivative of it as representing beings who are derived from two distinct classes of creatures. E took it as = ἀδόκιμος. ¹³ E = πόρνης, corrupt for πορνείας. ¹⁴ E adds τοὺς

Gg

τοὺς υἱοὺς τῶν ἐγρηγόρων ἀπὸ τῶν ἀνθρώπων·¹ πέμψον αὐτοὺς² ἐν πολέμῳ ἀπωλείας. μακρότης γὰρ ἡμερῶν οὐκ ἔστιν αὐτῶν, 10. καὶ πᾶσα ἐρώτησις⁴ (οὐκ) ἔσται τοῖς πατράσιν αὐτῶν [καὶ] ⸢περὶ αὐτῶν⸣, ὅτι ἐλπίζουσιν ζῆσαι ζωὴν αἰώνιον, καὶ ὅτι ζήσεται ἕκαστος αὐτῶν ἔτη πεντακόσια. 11. Καὶ εἶπεν (τῷ) Μιχαὴλ Πορεύου καὶ †δήλωσον†⁵ Σεμιαζᾷ καὶ τοῖς λοιποῖς τοῖς σὺν αὐτῷ ταῖς γυναιξὶν μιγέντας, μιανθῆναι ἐν αὐταῖς ἐν⁶ τῇ ἀκαθαρσίᾳ αὐτῶν· 12. καὶ ὅταν κατασφαγῶσιν οἱ υἱοὶ αὐτῶν καὶ ἴδωσιν τὴν ἀπώλειαν τῶν ἀγαπητῶν, [καὶ] δῆσον αὐτοὺς ἑβδομήκοντα γενεὰς εἰς τὰς νάπας τῆς γῆς μέχρι ἡμέρας κρίσεως αὐτῶν καὶ συντελεσμοῦ, ἕως τελεσθῇ τὸ κρίμα τοῦ αἰῶνος τῶν αἰώνων. 13. τότε ἀπαχθήσονται εἰς τὸ χάος τοῦ πυρὸς καὶ⁷ εἰς τὴν βάσανον καὶ εἰς τὸ δεσμωτήριον * συνκλείσεως αἰῶνος⁸. 14. καὶ * ὃς ἂν⁹ †κατακαυσθῇ†¹⁰ καὶ ἀφανισθῇ, ἀπὸ τοῦ νῦν μετ' αὐτῶν ὁμοῦ δεθήσονται μέχρι τελειώσεως γενεᾶς.¹¹

Gs

ἀπόλεσον τοὺς υἱοὺς τῶν ἐγρηγόρων ἀπὸ τῶν υἱῶν τῶν ἀνθρώπων· πέμψον αὐτοὺς * εἰς ἀλλήλους, ἐξ αὐτῶν εἰς αὐτούς³, ἐν πολέμῳ καὶ ἐν ἀπωλείᾳ. καὶ μακρότης ἡμερῶν οὐκ ἔσται αὐτοῖς, 10. καὶ πᾶσα ἐρώτησις οὐκ ἔστι τοῖς πατράσιν αὐτῶν, ὅτι ἐλπίζουσι ζῆσαι ζωὴν αἰώνιον, καὶ ὅτι ζήσεται ἕκαστος αὐτῶν ἔτη πεντακόσια. 11. Καὶ τῷ Μιχαὴλ εἶπε· Πορεύου, ⸢Μιχαήλ⸣, δῆσον⁵ Σεμιαζᾶν καὶ τοὺς ἄλλους. σὺν αὐτῷ τοὺς συμμιγέντας ταῖς θυγατράσι τῶν ἀνθρώπων τοῦ μιανθῆναι ἐν αὐταῖς ἐν⁶ τῇ ἀκαθαρσίᾳ αὐτῶν. 12. καὶ ὅταν κατασφαγῶσιν οἱ υἱοὶ αὐτῶν καὶ ἴδωσι τὴν ἀπώλειαν τῶν ἀγαπητῶν αὐτῶν, δῆσον αὐτοὺς ἐπὶ ἑβδομήκοντα γενεὰς εἰς τὰς νάπας τῆς γῆς μέχρι ἡμέρας κρίσεως αὐτῶν, μέχρι ἡμέρας τελειώσεως [τελεσμοῦ], ἕως συντελεσθῇ κρίμα τοῦ αἰῶνος τῶν αἰώνων. 13. τότε ἀπενεχθήσονται εἰς τὸ χάος τοῦ πυρὸς καὶ⁷ εἰς τὴν βάσανον καὶ εἰς τὸ δεσμωτήριον τῆς συγκλείσεως τοῦ αἰῶνος⁸. 14. καὶ ὃς ἂν κατακριθῇ καὶ ἀφανισθῇ,

υἱοὺς τῆς πόρνης καί. ¹ E adds ἐξαπόστειλον αὐτοὺς καί—a dittographic rendering. ² Add εἰς ἀλλήλους with Gg E. ³ So also E. Gs omits. ⁴ MS. εργεσις. Em. by Lods. ⁵ Gg = E. Gs is right. ⁶ E adds πάσῃ. ⁷ E omits. ⁸ E = καὶ συγκλειθήσονται εἰς τοὺς αἰῶνας—a free rendering of the text. ⁹ Em. with Gs from οταν: E = ὅταν. ¹⁰ = E. Corrupt for

G^g   G^a
ἀπὸ τοῦ νῦν μετ' αὐτῶν δεθήσεται
μέχρι τελειώσεως γενεᾶς αὐτῶν[11].

15. Ἀπόλεσον πάντα τὰ πνεύματα τῶν κιβδήλων καὶ τοὺς υἱοὺς τῶν ἐγρηγόρων διὰ τὸ ἀδικῆσαι τοὺς ἀνθρώπους. 16. καὶ ἀπόλεσον τὴν ἀδικίαν πᾶσαν ἀπὸ τῆς γῆς, καὶ πᾶν ἔργον πονηρίας ἐκλειπέτω, καὶ ἀναφανήτω τὸ φυτὸν τῆς δικαιοσύνης καὶ τῆς ἀληθείας[1] εἰς τοὺς αἰῶνας .... μετὰ χαρᾶς φυτευ(θή)σεται.

17. Καὶ νῦν πάντες οἱ δίκαιοι ἐκφεύξονται,
καὶ ἔσονται ζῶντες ἕως γεννήσωσιν χιλιάδας,
καὶ πᾶσαι αἱ ἡμέραι νεότητος αὐτῶν, καὶ † τὰ σάββατα αὐτῶν[2]
μετὰ εἰρήνης πληρώσουσιν[3].

18. τότε ἐργασθήσεται πᾶσα ἡ γῆ ἐν δικαιοσύνῃ καὶ καταφυτευθήσεται[4] δένδρον ἐν αὐτῇ[4], καὶ πλησθήσεται εὐλογίας. 19. καὶ πάντα τὰ δένδρα τῆς †γῆς ἀγαλλιάσονται †[5] φυτευθήσεται, καὶ ἔσονται φυτεύοντες ἀμπέλους, (κ)αὶ ἡ ἄμπελος ἣν ἂν φυτεύσωσιν, ποιήσουσιν προχοὺς οἴνου· * χιλιάδας καὶ σπόρου ποιήσει καθ' ἕκαστον μέτρον[6], ἐλαίας ποιήσει ἀνὰ βάτους δέκα. 20. καὶ σὺ καθάρισον τὴν γῆν ἀπὸ πάσης ἀκαθαρσίας[7] καὶ ἀπὸ πάσης ἀδικίας καὶ ἀπὸ (πά)σης ἁμαρτίας καὶ[8] ἀσεβείας, καὶ πάσας τὰς ἀκαθαρσίας τὰς γινομένας ἐπὶ τῆς γῆς ἐξάλειψον[9]. 21. καὶ ἔσονται πάντες λατρεύοντες οἱ λαοὶ καὶ εὐλογοῦντες πάντες ἐμοὶ καὶ προσκυνοῦντες. 22. καὶ καθαρισθήσεται ⌈πᾶσα⌉ ἡ γῆ ἀπὸ παντὸς μιάσματος καὶ ἀπὸ πάσης ἀκαθαρσίας καὶ ὀργῆς καὶ μάστιγος, καὶ οὐκέτι πέμψω ἐπ' αὐτοὺς εἰς πάσας τὰς γενεὰς τοῦ αἰῶνος. XI. καὶ τότε ἀνοίξω τὰ ταμεῖα τῆς εὐλογίας τὰ ὄντα ἐν τῷ οὐρανῷ, καὶ κατενεγκεῖν αὐτὰ[10] ἐπὶ

κατακριθῇ as in G^a. [11] E = πασῶν γενεῶν. [1] Add with E καὶ ἔσται εὐλογία· τὰ ἔργα τῆς δικαιοσύνης καὶ τῆς ἀληθείας lost through hmt. [2] = שַׁבַּתְהוֹן in which the word is wrongly vocalized for שִׂבְתְהוֹן = 'their old age.' The error is explicable in Heb. also i. e. שַׁבָּתָם instead of שִׂבְתָם. Hence read τὸ γῆρας αὐτῶν. [3] Appears to be intransitive here. E renders it transitively and puts the preceding nominatives in the accusative. [4] E = πᾶσα δένδροις. [5] Corrupt. E = 'and all desirable trees.' [6] Text is translateable but seems corrupt. E = καὶ πᾶς ὁ σπόρος ὁ σπαρεὶς ἐν αὐτῇ ἕκαστον μέτρον ποιήσει χιλιάδας καὶ ἕκαστον μέτρον. Here πᾶς ... αὐτῇ is a nominativus pendens. [7] E = 'oppression.' [8] E adds πάσης. [9] E adds ἀπὸ τῆς γῆς. 21. καὶ ἔσονται πάντες οἱ υἱοὶ τῶν ἀνθρώπων δίκαιοι. [10] E adds ἐπὶ τὴν γῆν.

τὰ ἔργα, ἐπὶ τὸν κόπον τῶν υἱῶν τῶν ἀνθρώπων. 2. καὶ ⸢τότε⸣
* ἀλήθεια καὶ εἰρήνη ¹ κοινωνήσουσιν ὁμοῦ εἰς πάσας τὰς ἡμέρας τοῦ
αἰῶνος καὶ εἰς πάσας τὰς γενεὰς τῶν ἀνθρώπων ².

XII. Πρὸ τούτων τῶν λόγων ἐλήμφθη Ἐνώχ, καὶ οὐδεὶς ³ τῶν
ἀνθρώπων ἔγνω ποῦ ἐλήμφθη καὶ ποῦ ἐστιν καὶ τί ἐγένετο αὐτῷ.
2. καὶ τὰ ἔργα αὐτοῦ ⁴ μετὰ τῶν ἐγρηγόρων, καὶ μετὰ τῶν ἁγίων * αἱ
ἡμέραι ⁵ αὐτοῦ. 3. Καὶ ⸢ἑστὼς⸣ ἤμην Ἐνώχ εὐλογῶν τῷ κυρίῳ⁶ τῆς
μεγαλοσύνης, τῷ βασιλεῖ τῶν αἰώνων. καὶ ἰδοὺ οἱ ἐγρήγοροι ⸢τοῦ
ἁγίου τοῦ μεγάλου⸣ ἐκάλουν με Ἐνώχ ⁷, ... 4. ὁ γραμματεὺς τῆς
δικαιοσύνης Πορεύου καὶ εἰπὲ τοῖς ἐγρηγόροις τοῦ οὐρανοῦ οἵτινες
ἀπολιπόντες τὸν οὐρανὸν τὸν ὑψηλόν, τὸ ἁγίασμα τῆς στάσεως τοῦ
αἰῶνος, μετὰ τῶν γυναικῶν ἐμιάνθησαν, καὶ ὥσπερ οἱ υἱοὶ τῆς γῆς
ποιοῦσιν, οὕτως καὶ αὐτοὶ ποιοῦσιν ⁸, καὶ ἔλαβον ἑαυτοῖς γυναῖκας·
ἀφανισμὸν μέγαν †κατηφανίσατε⁹ τὴν γῆν, 5. καὶ οὐκ ἔσται ὑμῖν ¹⁰
εἰρήνη οὔτε ἄφεσις. καὶ περὶ ὧν χαίρουσιν τῶν υἱῶν αὐτῶν ¹¹, 6. τὸν
φόνον τῶν ἀγαπητῶν αὐτῶν ὄψονται, καὶ ἐπὶ τῇ ἀπωλείᾳ τῶν υἱῶν
αὐτῶν στενάξουσιν καὶ δεηθήσονται εἰς τὸν αἰῶνα, καὶ οὐκ ἔσται
αὐτοῖς εἰς ἔλεον καὶ εἰρήνην ¹².

XIII. Ὁ δὲ Ἐνὼχ †τῷ Ἀζαὴλ εἶπεν Πορεύου·† ¹³ οὐκ ἔσται σοι
εἰρήνη. κρίμα μέγα ἐξῆλθεν κατὰ σοῦ δῆσαί σε, 2. καὶ ἀνοχὴ καὶ
ἐρώτησίς σοι οὐκ ἔσται περὶ ὧν ἔδειξας ἀδικημάτων καὶ περὶ πάντων
τῶν ἔργων τῶν ἀσεβειῶν καὶ τῆς ἀδικίας καὶ τῆς ἁμαρτίας, ὅσα
ὑπέδειξας τοῖς ἀνθρώποις.

3. Τότε πορευθεὶς εἴρηκα πᾶσιν αὐτοῖς, καὶ αὐτοὶ πάντες ἐφοβή-
θησαν, καὶ ἔλαβεν αὐτοὺς τρόμος καὶ φόβος. 4. καὶ ἠρώτησαν ¹⁴

---

¹ E trans. ² E = αἰώνων a wrong expansion of αὐτῶν which appears in G. ³ E adds τῶν υἱῶν. ⁴ MS. αὐτῶν. ⁵ E corrupt = ἐν ταῖς ἡμέραις. ⁶ Εὐλογεῖν used with dat. in Sir. 50²², 51¹² &c. ⁷ Add with E τὸν γραμματέα καὶ εἶπον ἐμοί Ἐνώχ lost through hmt. ⁸ E = ἐποίησαν or πεποιήκεσαν. ⁹ MS. καιηφανίσατε. E = καὶ ἀφ. μέγ. ἠφανίσθησαν. ¹⁰ E = αὐτοῖς which appears wrong. ¹¹ Read ὑμῶν and ὑμῖν for αὐτῶν and αὐτοῖς here and in the next verse. ¹² A strange construction. ¹³ Corrupt for πορευθεὶς εἶπεν Ἀζαὴλ as is shown by E, and G 13³. The corruption in G may have originated in the Aram. G = אזל אל corrupt for אל אזל. Here we may conclude either to a happy emendation of the Ethiopic translator of G or of the scribe of the Greek MS. used by E or to the existence in the Aramaic of both forms, the corrupt in the text and the true reading in the margin. ¹⁴ E adds

ὅπως γράψω αὐτοῖς ὑπομνήματα ἐρωτήσεως, ἵνα γένηται[1] αὐτοῖς ἄφεσις, καὶ ἵνα ἐγὼ ἀναγνῶ[2] αὐτοῖς τὸ ὑπόμνημα τῆς ἐρωτήσεως ἐνώπιον Κυρίου τοῦ οὐρανοῦ, 5. ὅτι αὐτοὶ οὐκέτι δύνανται λαλῆσαι, οὐδὲ ἐπᾶραι αὐτῶν τοὺς ὀφθαλμοὺς εἰς τὸν οὐρανὸν ἀπὸ αἰσχύνης * περὶ ὧν ἡμαρτήκεισαν καὶ κατεκρίθησαν[3]. 6. Τότε ἔγραψα τὸ ὑπόμνημα τῆς ἐρωτήσεως αὐτῶν καὶ τὰς δεήσεις περὶ τῶν πνευμάτων αὐτῶν[4] καὶ περὶ ὧν δέονται, ὅπως αὐτῶν γένωνται ἄφεσις καὶ μακρότης. 7. καὶ πορευθεὶς ἐκάθισα ἐπὶ τῶν ὑδάτων Δὰν ἐν γῇ[5] Δάν, ἥτις ἐστὶν ἐκ * δεξιῶν Ἑρμωνειεὶμ δύσεως[6]· ἀνεγίνωσκον τὸ ὑπόμνημα τῶν δεήσεων αὐτῶν ἕως[7] ἐκοιμήθην. 8. καὶ ἰδοὺ ὄνειροι ἐπ' ἐμὲ ἦλθον καὶ ὁράσεις ἐπ' ἐμὲ ἐπέπιπτον, καὶ ἰδὸν ὁράσεις ὀργῆς, ⌜καὶ ἦλθεν φωνὴ λέγουσα⌝ Εἰπὸν[8] τοῖς υἱοῖς τοῦ οὐρανοῦ * τοῦ ἐλέγξαι[9] αὐτούς. 9. καὶ ἔξυπνος γενόμενος ἦλθον πρὸς αὐτούς, καὶ πάντες συνηγμένοι ἐκάθηντο πενθοῦντες [σ]ἐν Ἐβελσατά[10], ἥτις ἐστὶν ἀνὰ μέσον τοῦ Λιβάνου καὶ Σενισήλ[11], περικεκαλυμμένοι τὴν ὄψιν. 10. ἐνώπιον αὐτῶν καὶ[12] ἀνήγγειλα αὐτοῖς πάσας τὰς ὁράσεις ἃς εἶδον κατὰ τοὺς ὕπνους, καὶ ἠρξάμην λαλεῖν τοὺς λόγους τῆς δικαιοσύνης, ἐλέγχων[13] τοὺς ἐγρηγόρους τοῦ οὐρανοῦ.

XIV. Βίβλος λόγων δικαιοσύνης καὶ ἐλέγξεως ἐγρηγόρων τῶν ἀπὸ τοῦ αἰῶνος, κατὰ τὴν ἐντολὴν τοῦ ἁγίου[14] τοῦ μεγάλου ἐν ταύτῃ τῇ ὁράσει. 2. Ἐγὼ εἶδον κατὰ τοὺς ὕπνους μου ὃ[15] νῦν λέγω ἐν γλώσσῃ σαρκίνῃ * ἐν τῷ πνεύματι τοῦ στόματός μου, ὃ ἔδωκεν ὁ μέγας[16] τοῖς ἀνθρώποις λαλεῖν ἐν αὐτοῖς καὶ * νοήσει καρδίας[17]· 3. ὃς[18] ἔκτισεν καὶ ἔδωκεν[19] ἐλέγξασθαι[20] ἐγρηγόρους τοὺς υἱοὺς τοῦ οὐρανοῦ. 4. Ἐγὼ τὴν ἐρώτησιν ὑμῶν [τῶν ἀγγέλων][21] ἔγραψα, καὶ

ἐμέ. [1] MS. γενωνται. [2] MS. αναγνοι. E = ἀνάγω corrupt for ἀναγνῶ. [3] E = περὶ τῶν ἁμαρτιῶν αὐτῶν περὶ ὧν κατεκρίθησαν. [4] E adds 'and their deeds individually'. [5] E wrongly omits. [6] E gives the right order = δεξιῶν δύσεως Ἑρ. [7] Em. with E from ὅτ. [8] E = ἵνα εἴπω. [9] E = καὶ ἐλέγξω. [10] E = Ἀβελσιαήλ. [11] E = Sénêêr = the O.T. Senir, a name of Hermon (Deut. 3⁹) or of a part of it (Cant. 4⁸). [12] Trans. before ἐνώπιον with E. [13] E = καὶ ἐλέγχειν. [14] E adds καί. [15] MS. ων. [16] E = καὶ ἐν τῷ πνεύματί μου ὃ ἔδωκεν ὁ μέγας εἰς τὸ στόμα, but is easily emended. [17] If the text were right νοήσει should be taken as under the same government as γλώσσῃ. E = νοῆσαι καρδίᾳ. [18] Read ὃς with E. [19] Add with E the following words which have been lost through hmt.: νοεῖν τοὺς λόγους τῆς γνώσεως, καὶ ἐμὲ ἔκτισεν καὶ ἔδωκεν. [20] MS. εκλεξασθαι. [21] A gloss. E omits.

ἐν τῇ ὁράσει μου τοῦτο[1] ἐδείχθη· *καὶ οὔτε[2] ἡ ἐρώτησις ὑμῶν παρεδέχθη[3], 5. *ἵνα μηκέτι[4] εἰς τὸν οὐρανὸν ἀναβῆτε ἐπὶ πάντας τοὺς αἰῶνας, καὶ *ἐν τοῖς †δεσμοῖς† τῆς γῆς[5] ἐρρέθη δῆσαι ὑμᾶς εἰς πάσας τὰς γενεὰς[6] τοῦ αἰῶνος, 6. καὶ ⌈ἵνα⌉ πρὸ[7] τούτων ἴδητε τὴν ἀπώλειαν τῶν υἱῶν ὑμῶν τῶν ἀγαπητῶν, καὶ ὅτι οὐκ ἔσται ὑμῖν ὄνησις αὐτῶν, ἀλλὰ πεσοῦνται ἐνώπιον ὑμῶν ἐν μαχαίρᾳ. 7. καὶ ἡ ἐρώτησις ὑμῶν περὶ αὐτῶν οὐκ ἔσται οὐδὲ περὶ ὑμῶν· *καὶ ὑμεῖς κλαίοντες[8] καὶ δεόμενοι καὶ μὴν[9] λαλοῦντες πᾶν ῥῆμα ἀπὸ τῆς γραφῆς ἧς ἔγραψα. 8. Καὶ ἐμοὶ *ἐφ᾽ ὁράσει[10] οὕτως ἐδείχθη· ἰδοὺ νεφέλαι ἐν τῇ ὁράσει ἐκάλουν καὶ ὁμίχλαι με ἐφώνουν, καὶ διαδρομαὶ τῶν ἀστέρων καὶ διαστραπαί με κατεσπούδαζον καὶ †ἐθορύβαζόν†[11] με, καὶ ἄνεμοι ἐν τῇ ὁράσει μου †ἐξεπέτασάν†[12] με καὶ ἐπῆράν[13] με ἄνω[14] καὶ εἰσήνεγκάν με εἰς τὸν οὐρανόν. 9. καὶ εἰσῆλθον μέχρις ἤγγισα τείχους οἰκοδομῆς[15] ἐν λίθοις χαλάζης καὶ γλώσσαις[16] πυρὸς κύκλῳ αὐτῶν· καὶ ἤρξαντο ἐκφοβεῖν με. 10. Καὶ εἰσῆλθον εἰς τὰς γλώσσας τοῦ πυρός, καὶ ἤγγισα εἰς οἶκον μέγαν οἰκοδομημένον ἐν λίθοις χαλάζης, καὶ οἱ τοῖχοι τοῦ οἴκου ὡς λιθόπλακες, καὶ πᾶσαι ἦσαν ἐκ χιόνος[17], καὶ ἐδάφη χιονικά, 11. καὶ αἱ στέγαι ὡς διαδρομαὶ ἀστέρων καὶ ἀστραπαί, καὶ μεταξὺ αὐτῶν χερουβὶν πύρινα, καὶ οὐρανὸς αὐτῶν ὕδωρ, 12. καὶ πῦρ φλεγόμενον κύκλῳ τῶν τοίχων, καὶ θύραι πυρὶ καιόμεναι. 13. εἰσῆλθον[18] εἰς τὸν οἶκον ἐκεῖνον, θερμὸν[18] ὡς πῦρ καὶ ψυχρὸν ὡς χιών[19], καὶ πᾶσα τροφὴ[20] ζωῆς οὐκ ἦν ἐν αὐτῷ· φόβος με ἐκάλυψεν καὶ τρόμος με ἔλαβεν. 14. καὶ ἤμην σειόμενος καὶ τρέμων, καὶ ἔπεσον *ἐπὶ πρόσωπόν μου καὶ[21] ἐθεώρουν *ἐν τῇ ὁράσει ⌈μου⌉[22], 15. καὶ ἰδοὺ *ἄλλην θύραν ἀνεῳγμένην κατέναντί μου,

---

[1] E = κατὰ τοῦτο. [2] E = ὅτι. [3] E = οὐκ ἔσται ὑμῖν, and adds εἰς πάσας τὰς ἡμέρας τοῦ αἰῶνος καὶ ἡ κρίσις ἐτελειώθη ἐφ᾽ ὑμᾶς καὶ οὐκ ἔσται ὑμῖν. [4] E = καὶ ἀπὸ τοῦ νῦν. [5] For δεσμοῖς τῆς γῆς we should probably read δεσμοῖς ἐν τῇ γῇ. E has ἐν τῇ γῇ only. [6] E = ἡμέρας. [7] MS. περί. [8] We should expect καὶ κλαιόντων. [9] Em. from MS. μη, which E follows. [10] E = ὅρασις. [11] This word (= perturbabant, and so E) cannot be right. We require a synonym οἱ κατεσπούδαζον. [12] This may be an attempt to render אפרח = 'caused to fly'. E = ἀνεπτέρωσαν. Or rather it may be corrupt for ἐξεπέρασαν (Lods). [13] E = κατεσπούδαζον, or possibly ἔναιρον. [14] E wrongly trans. into next clause. [15] E = οἰκοδομημένον. [16] MS. γλωσσης. [17] E = ἐν λίθοις τοῖς ἐκ χιόνος. [18] E prefixes καί. [19] E = κρύσταλλος. [20] E = τρυφή. These words are frequently confused. [21] Added from E. [22] E = ὅρασιν.

Appendix I

καὶ ὁ οἶκος μείζων τούτου, καὶ ὅλος [1] οἰκοδομημένος ἐν γλώσσαις πυρός, 16. καὶ ὅλος διαφέρων ἐν δόξῃ καὶ ἐν τιμῇ καὶ ἐν μεγαλοσύνῃ, ὥστε μὴ δύνασθαί με ἐξειπεῖν ὑμῖν περὶ τῆς δόξης καὶ περὶ τῆς μεγαλοσύνης αὐτοῦ. 17. τὸ [2] ἔδαφος αὐτοῦ ἦν πυρός, τὸ δὲ ἀνώτερον αὐτοῦ ἦσαν ἀστραπαὶ καὶ διαδρομαὶ ἀστέρων, καὶ ἡ στέγη αὐτοῦ ἦν πῦρ φλέγον. 18. Ἐθεώρουν δὲ καὶ εἶδον [3] θρόνον ὑψηλόν [4], καὶ τὸ εἶδος αὐτοῦ ὡσεὶ κρυστάλλινον, καὶ *τροχὸς ὡς ἡλίου λάμποντος [5] καὶ †ὅρος† [6] χερουβίν. 19. καὶ ὑποκάτω τοῦ θρόνου ἐξεπορεύοντο ποταμοὶ πυρὸς φλεγόμενοι [7], καὶ οὐκ ἐδυνάσθην ἰδεῖν. 20. καὶ ἡ δόξα ἡ μεγάλη ἐκάθητο ἐπ' αὐτῷ· τὸ περιβόλαιον αὐτοῦ [ὡς εἶδος] [8] ἡλίου λαμπρότερον καὶ λευκότερον πάσης χιόνος. 21. καὶ οὐκ ἐδύνατο πᾶς ἄγγελος παρελθεῖν ⌜εἰς τὸν οἶκον τοῦτον⌝ καὶ ἰδεῖν τὸ πρόσωπον αὐτοῦ *διὰ τὸ ἔντιμον καὶ ἔνδοξον [9], καὶ οὐκ ἐδύνατο πᾶσα σὰρξ ἰδεῖν αὐτόν. 22. τὸ πῦρ φλεγόμενον κύκλῳ· καὶ πῦρ μέγα παρειστήκει αὐτῷ, καὶ οὐδεὶς ἐγγίζει αὐτῷ (τῶν) [10] κύκλῳ, μυρίαι μυριάδες ἐστήκασιν ἐνώπιον αὐτοῦ, *καὶ πᾶς λόγος αὐτοῦ ἔργον [11]. 23. καὶ οἱ ἅγιοι τῶν ἀγγέλων [12] οἱ ἐγγίζοντες αὐτῷ οὐκ ἀποχωροῦσιν νυκτὸς οὔτε ἀφίστανται αὐτοῦ. 24. Κἀγὼ ἤμην ἕως τούτου ἐπὶ πρόσωπόν μου βεβλημένος [13] καὶ τρέμων, καὶ ὁ κύριος τῷ στόματι αὐτοῦ ἐκάλεσέν με καὶ εἶπέν μοι Πρόσελθε ὧδε, Ἐνώχ, καὶ τὸν λόγον μου ἄκουσον [14]. 25. ⌜καὶ προσελθών μοι εἷς τῶν ἁγίων ἤγειρέν με⌝ καὶ ἔστησέν με, καὶ προσήγαγέν με μέχρι τῆς θύρας· ἐγὼ δὲ τὸ πρόσωπόν μου κάτω ἔκυφον.

XV. Καὶ ἀποκριθεὶς εἶπέν μοι [Ὁ ἄνθρωπος ὁ ἀληθινός, ἄνθρωπος τῆς ἀληθείας ὁ γραμματεύς] [15] καὶ τῆς φωνῆς αὐτοῦ ἤκουσα· μὴ

---

[1] Seems corrupt. E which gives good sense = ἄλλος οἶκος μείζων τούτου καὶ ὅλη ἡ θύρα αὐτοῦ ἀνεῳγμένη κατέναντί μου καί. G⁵ appears to be a dislocated form of E.   [2] E = καὶ τό.   [3] E adds ἐν αὐτῷ.   [4] g m q of E = ὑψηλοῦ.   [5] E = τροχὸς αὐτοῦ ὡς ἥλιος λάμπων.   [6] Corrupt for ὅρασις. E seems to have had ορος before it and emended it into ὀπός (from ὄψ) 'the voice'.   [7] Better read φλεγομένου with E: cf. Dan. 7¹⁰.   [8] Bracketed as an interpolation.   [9] E = τοῦ ἐντίμου, καὶ ἐνδόξου.   [10] τῶν supplied from E. So Diels and Flemming. κύκλῳ cannot be connected with the next clause owing to the words ἐνώπιον αὐτοῦ.   [11] E = οὐδὲ προσδεῖται οὐδεμιᾶς συμβουλῆς. It is probable that this clause, or some equivalent, is lost in G.   [12] E = ἁγίων.   [13] E = περίβλημα which is corrupt.   [14] E = ἅγιον corrupt.   [15] Bracketed as an interpolation. They occur in their correct form and place two lines later. If they are in any sense authentic the second ἄνθρωπος must be

φοβηθῆς, Ἐνώχ, ἄνθρωπος ἀληθινὸς καὶ γραμματεὺς τῆς ἀληθείας·
πρόσελθε ὧδε, καὶ τῆς φωνῆς μου ἄκουσον.   2. πορεύθητι[1] καὶ[1]
εἰπὲ[2] τοῖς πέμψασίν σε[3] .... Ἐρωτῆσαι ὑμᾶς ἔδει περὶ τῶν
ἀνθρώπων, καὶ μὴ τοὺς ἀνθρώπους περὶ ὑμῶν.   3. διὰ τί ἀπελίπετε
τὸν οὐρανὸν τὸν ὑψηλὸν τὸν ἅγιον τοῦ αἰῶνος, καὶ μετὰ τῶν γυναικῶν
ἐκοιμήθητε καὶ μετὰ τῶν θυγατέρων τῶν ἀνθρώπων ἐμιάνθητε καὶ
ἐλάβετε ἑαυτοῖς γυναῖκας;[4] ὥσπερ υἱοὶ τῆς γῆς ἐποιήσατε καὶ ἐγεννήσατε ἑαυτοῖς [τέκνα][5] υἱοὺς γίγαντας.   4. καὶ ὑμεῖς ἦτε ἅγιοι
*καὶ πνεύμα(τα)[6] ζῶντα αἰώνια· ἐν τῷ αἵματι τῶν γυναικῶν ἐμιάνθητε,
καὶ ἐν αἵματι σαρκὸς ἐγεννήσατε καὶ † ἐν αἵματι ἀνθρώπων ἐπεθυμήσατε[7], καθὼς καὶ αὐτοὶ ποιοῦσιν, σάρκα καὶ αἷμα, οἵτινες ἀποθνή-
σκουσιν καὶ ἀπόλλυνται.   5. διὰ τοῦτο ἔδωκα αὐτοῖς θηλείας, ἵνα
σπερματίσουσιν[8] εἰς αὐτὰς καὶ τεκνώσουσιν ἐν αὐταῖς[9] τέκνα οὕτως,
ἵνα μὴ ἐκλείπῃ[10] αὐτοῖς[11] πᾶν ἔργον ἐπὶ τῆς γῆς.   6. ὑμεῖς δὲ
ὑπήρχετε πνεύμα(τα)[12] ζῶντα αἰώνια καὶ[13] οὐκ ἀποθνήσκοντα εἰς
πάσας τὰς γενεὰς τοῦ αἰῶνος.   7. καὶ διὰ τοῦτο οὐκ ἐποίησα ἐν
ὑμῖν θηλείας· τὰ[14] πνεύμα(τα)[12] τοῦ οὐρανοῦ, ἐν τῷ οὐρανῷ ἡ κατοίκησις αὐτῶν.

G^g

8. καὶ νῦν οἱ γίγαντες οἱ γεν-
νηθέντες ἀπὸ τῶν πνευμάτων καὶ
σαρκὸς πνεύμα(τα) † ἰσχυρὰ †[15]
⟨κληθήσονται⟩[16] ἐπὶ τῆς γῆς καὶ ἐν
τῇ γῇ ἡ κατοίκησις αὐτῶν ἔσται.
9. πνεύμα(τα) πονηρὰ ἐξῆλθον
ἀπὸ τοῦ σώματος αὐτῶν, διότι
ἀπὸ τῶν † ἀνωτέρων †[17] ἐγένοντο,

G^s

8. Καὶ νῦν οἱ γίγαντες οἱ γεν-
νηθέντες ἀπὸ πνευμάτων καὶ
σαρκὸς πνεύματα πονηρὰ ἐπὶ τῆς
γῆς καλέσουσιν αὐτούς[16], ὅτι ἡ
κατοίκησις αὐτῶν ἔσται ἐπὶ τῆς
γῆς.   9. πνεύματα πονηρὰ
⌜ἔσονται, τὰ πνεύματα⌝ ἐξεληλυ-
θότα ἀπὸ τοῦ σώματος ⌜τῆς σαρ-

---

regarded as an intrusion.   [1] E trans.
[2] E adds τοῖς ἐγρηγόροις τοῦ οὐρανοῦ.
[3] Add with E the following words
lost through hmt.: ἐρωτῆσαι περὶ αὐτῶν.
[4] E adds καί.   [5] Bracketed as a
dittographic rendering.   [6] E = πνευ-
ματικοί.   [7] The error appears to lie
in ἐν αἵματι ἀνθρώπων. This = בדם
אנשא which may be corrupt (?) for
כבני נשא = ὥσπερ υἱοὶ τῶν ἀνθρώπων.
In that case the object of ἐπεθυμήσατε
is σάρκα καὶ αἷμα.   [8] MS. σπερματί-
ζουσιν.   [9] MS. αυτοις.   [10] MS.
εκλειπει.   [11] E = ἐν αὐταῖς.   [12] E =
πνευματικά.   [13] E = τά.   [14] E prefixes διότι.   [15] May be corrupt for
σκληρά: see ver. 11. EG^s = πονηρά.
[16] Added with E. G^s has καλέσουσιν
αὐτούς.   [17] So also E.   Corrupt for
ἀνθρώπων as in G^s.

Appendix I

G^g

καὶ ἐκ τῶν ἁγίων ἐγρηγόρων ἡ ἀρχὴ *τῆς κτίσεως¹ αὐτῶν *καὶ ἀρχὴ θεμελίου². *πνεύματα πονηρὰ κληθήσεται³. [10. πνεύμα(τα) οὐρανοῦ, ἐν τῷ οὐρανῷ ἡ κατοίκησις αὐτῶν ἔσται· καὶ τὰ πνεύματα ἐπὶ τῆς γῆς τὰ γεννηθέντα, ἐπὶ τῆς γῆς ἡ κατοίκησις αὐτῶν ἔσται.⁴] 11. καὶ τὰ πνεύματα τῶν γιγάντων † νεφέλας †⁵ ἀδικοῦντα, ἀφανίζοντα καὶ ἐνπίπτοντα καὶ συνπαλαίοντα καὶ συνρίπτοντα ἐπὶ τῆς γῆς [πνεύματα σκληρὰ γιγάντων]⁶ καὶ δρόμους⁷ ποιοῦντα καὶ μηδὲν ἐσθίοντα, ⌜ἀλλ' ἀσιτοῦντα⌝⁸ καὶ διψῶντα καὶ προσκόπτοντα⁹. 12. καὶ ἐξαναστήσει ταῦτα (τὰ) πνεύμα(τα)¹⁰ εἰς τοὺς υἱοὺς τῶν ἀνθρώπων καὶ *τῶν γυναικῶν¹¹, ὅτι ἐξεληλύθασιν ⌜ἀπ' αὐτῶν⌝, XVI. ἀπὸ ἡμέρας σφαγῆς καὶ ἀπωλείας καὶ θανάτου¹², ἀφ' ὧν¹³ τὰ πνεύματα ἐκπορευόμενα ἐκ τῆς ψυχῆς τῆς σαρκὸς αὐτῶν

G^s

κὸς¹ αὐτῶν, διότι ἀπὸ τῶν ἀνθρώπων ἐγένοντο, καὶ ἐκ τῶν ἁγίων τῶν ἐγρηγόρων ἡ ἀρχὴ *τῆς κτίσεως¹ αὐτῶν καὶ ἀρχὴ θεμελίου²· πνεύματα πονηρὰ ἐπὶ τῆς γῆς ἔσονται³. 11. τὰ πνεύματα τῶν γιγάντων νεμόμενα, ἀδικοῦντα, ἀφανίζοντα, ἐμπίπτοντα καὶ συμπαλαίοντα καὶ ῥιπτοῦντα ἐπὶ τῆς γῆς καὶ δρόμους ποιοῦντα, καὶ μηδὲν ἐσθίοντα, ⌜ἀλλ' ἀσιτοῦντα⌝⁸ *καὶ φάσματα ποιοῦντα⌝ καὶ διψῶντα καὶ προσκόπτοντα⁹. 12. καὶ ἐξαναστήσονται τὰ πνεύματα ἐπὶ τοὺς υἱοὺς τῶν ἀνθρώπων καὶ *τῶν γυναικῶν¹¹, ὅτι ἐξ αὐτῶν ἐξεληλύθασι, XVI. καὶ ἀπὸ ἡμέρας ⌜καιροῦ⌝ σφαγῆς καὶ ἀπωλείας καὶ θανάτου τῶν γιγάντων [Ναφηλείμ, οἱ ἰσχυροὶ τῆς γῆς, οἱ μεγάλοι ὀνομαστοί,] τὰ πνεύματα τὰ ἐκπορευόμενα ἀπὸ τῆς ψυχῆς αὐτῶν, ⌜ὡς ἐκ⌝ τῆς σαρκὸς ἔσονται ἀφανίζοντα χωρὶς κρίσεως· οὕτως ἀφανίσουσι μέ-

---

¹ E omits. ² The phrase is possibly a dittography. ἀρχὴ τῆς κτίσεως = ראש מולדת which could easily be corrupted into ר = מוסדה = ἀρχὴ θεμελίου. In Aram. we may suppose ראש ילדותא corrupted into יסודא ר. ³ E = πνεύματα πονηρὰ ἔσονται ἐπὶ τῆς γῆς καὶ πνεύματα πονηρὰ κληθήσεται. Add with G^s E καὶ πνεύματα πονηρὰ κληθήσεται. ⁴ This verse is merely a repetition of phrases in verses 7, 8. G^s rightly omits. ⁵ So also E = ענני. G^s has νεμόμενα, which in the sense of 'laying waste' may = רעין which was corrupted into ענני. ⁶ A gloss. G^s E omit. ⁷ E = τρόμους. ⁸ So also G^s: E omits. It may be a doublet of μηδὲν ἐσθίοντα. ⁹ E corrupt = ἀόρατα. ¹⁰ MS. wrongly trans. before καὶ ἐξαναστήσει. ¹¹ E = εἰς τὰς γυναῖκας. ¹² Add τῶν γιγάντων with G^s E. It is required by ἀφ' ὧν. ¹³ ἀφ' ὧν must be taken with ἐκ τῆς ψυχῆς τῆς σαρκὸς αὐτῶν. It is the Semitic idiom די מנפש בסרהון = 'from

294 *The Book of Enoch*

Gg
ἔσται ἀφανίζοντα χωρὶς κρίσεως· οὕτως ἀφανίσουσιν μέχρις ἡμέρας τελειώσεως, *τῆς κρίσεως¹ τῆς μεγάλης, ἐν ᾗ ὁ αἰὼν *ὁ μέγας¹ τελεσθήσεται².

Gs
χρις ἡμέρας τῆς τελειώσεως, ἕως τῆς κρίσεως τῆς μεγάλης, ἐν ᾗ ὁ αἰὼν *ὁ μέγας¹ τελεσθήσεται· ἐφάπαξ ὁμοῦ τελεσθήσεται.

2. Καὶ νῦν ἐγρηγόροις τοῖς πέμψασίν σε ἐρωτῆσαι περὶ αὐτῶν, οἵτινες³ ἐν οὐρανῷ ἦσαν. 3. Ὑμεῖς ἐν τῷ οὐρανῷ ἦτε, καὶ πᾶν μυστήριον [ὃ]⁴ οὐκ ἀνεκαλύφθη ὑμῖν καὶ μυστήριον* τὸ ἐκ τοῦ θεοῦ γεγενημένον⁵ ἔγνωτε, καὶ τοῦτο ἐμηνύσατε ταῖς γυναιξὶν ἐν ταῖς σκληροκαρδίαις ὑμῶν, καὶ ἐν τῷ μυστηρίῳ τούτῳ πληθύνουσιν αἱ θήλειαι καὶ οἱ ἄνθρωποι τὰ κακὰ ἐπὶ τῆς γῆς. 4. εἰπὸν οὖν αὐτοῖς⁶ Οὐκ ἔστιν εἰρήνη.

XVII. Καὶ παραλαβόντες με εἰς τινα τόπον ⌈ἀπήγαγον⌉, ἐν ᾧ οἱ ὄντες ἐκεῖ γίνονται ὡς πῦρ φλέγον καί, ὅταν θέλωσιν, φαίνονται ὡσεὶ ἄνθρωποι. 2. Καὶ ἀπήγαγόν με εἰς ζοφώδη⁷ τόπον καὶ εἰς ὄρος οὗ *ἡ κεφαλὴ⁸ ἀφικνεῖτο εἰς τὸν οὐρανόν. 3. καὶ ἴδον τόπον τῶν φωστήρων ⌈καὶ τοὺς θησαυροὺς τῶν ἀστέρων⌉ καὶ τῶν βροντῶν, ⌈καὶ⌉ εἰς τὰ ἀεροβαθῆ⁹, ὅπου τόξον πυρὸς καὶ τὰ βέλη καὶ αἱ θῆκαι αὐτῶν¹⁰ καὶ αἱ ἀστραπαὶ πᾶσαι. 4. Καὶ ἀπήγαγόν με μέχρι ὑδάτων ζώντων καὶ μέχρι πυρὸς δύσεως, ὅ ἐστιν καὶ παρέχον¹¹ πάσας τὰς δύσεις τοῦ ἡλίου. 5. καὶ ἦλθο[με]ν μέχρι ποταμοῦ πυρός, ἐν ᾧ κατατρέχει τὸ πῦρ ὡς ὕδωρ καὶ ῥέει εἰς θάλασσαν μεγάλην δύσεως. 6. ἴδον¹² τοὺς μεγάλους ποταμού(s), καὶ μέχρι τοῦ ⌈ποταμοῦ καὶ μέχρι τοῦ μεγάλου⌉¹³ σκότους κατήντησα, καὶ ἀπῆλθον ὅπου πᾶσα σὰρξ ⌈οὐ⌉ περιπατεῖ. 7. ἴδον τοὺς ἀνέμους τῶν γνόφων †¹⁴ τοὺς χειμερινοὺς καὶ τὴν ἔκχυσιν* τῆς ἀβύσσου πάντων ὑδάτων¹⁵. 8. ἴδον¹² τὸ στόμα τῆς γῆς πάντων τῶν ποταμῶν καὶ τὸ

---

the souls of whose flesh'. ¹ E wrongly omits. ² Add with E ἐπὶ τοῖς ἐγρηγόροις καὶ τοῖς ἀσεβέσιν ὅλως τελεσθήσεται. ³ E adds πρότερον. ⁴ Interpolated (?). E omits. ⁵ E = ἐξουθενημένα. ⁶ E adds Ὑμῖν. ⁷ E = γνοφώδη taking γνόφος in the sense of 'whirlwind' or 'tempest', as in Job 27²⁰ (LXX). ⁸ E = ἡ κορυφὴ τῆς κεφαλῆς. ⁹ E seems corrupt, but may point back to ἄκρα βάθη. ¹⁰ E adds καὶ μάχαιραν πυρός. ¹¹ E = παραδεχόμενον. I don't understand παρέχον in this clause. ¹² E = καὶ ἴδον. ¹³ E omits through hmt. ¹⁴ E = τὰ ὄρη τῶν γνόφων. ¹⁵ E = ὑδάτων τῆς στόμα τῆς ἀβύσσου. XVIII. ἴδον¹ τοὺς θησαυροὺς τῶν ἀνέμων πάντων, ἴδον¹ ὅτι ἐν αὐτοῖς ἐκόσμησεν πάσας τὰς κτίσεις καὶ τὸν θεμέλιον τῆς γῆς, 2. καὶ τὸν λίθον ἴδον τῆς γωνίας τῆς γῆς. ἴδον τοὺς τέσσαρας ἀνέμους [τὴν γῆν]² βαστάζοντας, καὶ τὸ στερέωμα τοῦ οὐρανοῦ, 3. καὶ³ αὐτοὶ ἱστᾶσιν μεταξὺ γῆς καὶ οὐρανοῦ⁴. 4. ἴδον¹ ἀνέμους *τῶν οὐρανῶν⁵ στρέφοντας καὶ †διανεύοντας†⁶ τὸν τροχὸν τοῦ ἡλίου, καὶ πάντας τοὺς ἀστέρας. 5. ἴδον τοὺς ἐπὶ τῆς γῆς ἀνέμους βαστάζοντας †ἐν νεφέλῃ†⁷. ἴδον⁸ ⟨παρὰ⟩⁹ πέρατα τῆς γῆς, τὸ στήριγμα τοῦ οὐρανοῦ ἐπάνω. 6. Παρῆλθον¹⁰ ⌜καὶ ἴδον τόπον⌝ καιόμενον νυκτὸς καὶ ἡμέρας, ὅπου τὰ ἑπτὰ ὄρη ἀπὸ λίθων πολυτελῶν, ⟨τρία⟩¹¹ εἰς ἀνατολὰς καὶ τρία¹¹ εἰς νότον ⌜βάλλοντα.⌝¹² 7. καὶ τὰ μὲν πρὸς ἀνατολὰς¹³ ἀπὸ λίθου χρώματος, τὸ δὲ ἦν ἀπὸ λίθου μαργαρίτου, καὶ τὸ ἀπὸ λίθου †ταθέν†¹⁴, τὰ¹⁵ δὲ κατὰ νότον ἀπὸ λίθου πυρροῦ· 8. τὸ δὲ μέσον αὐτῶν ἦν εἰς οὐρανόν, ὥσπερ θρόνος θεοῦ ἀπὸ λίθου φουκά¹⁶, καὶ ἡ κορυφὴ τοῦ θρόνου ἀπὸ λίθου σαπφείρου· 9. καὶ πῦρ καιόμενον ἴδον. κἀ(πέ)κεινα τῶν ὀρέων τούτων 10. τόπος ἐστὶν πέρας¹⁷ τῆς μεγάλης γῆς· ἐκεῖ συντελεσθήσονται¹⁸ οἱ οὐρανοί. 11. καὶ ἴδον χάσμα μέγα ἐν τοῖς στύλοις¹⁹ τοῦ πυρὸς καταβαίνοντας καὶ οὐκ ἦν μέτρον οὔτε εἰς βάθος οὔτε εἰς ὕψος. 12. καὶ ἐπέκεινα τοῦ χάσματος τούτου²⁰ ἴδον τόπον ὅπου οὐδὲ στερέωμα οὐρανοῦ ἐπάνω, οὔτε γῆ²¹ ἡ²¹ τεθεμελιωμένη²¹ ὑποκάτω αὐτοῦ οὔτε ὕδωρ ἦν ὑπὸ αὐτῷ²² οὔτε πετεινόν, ἀλλὰ τόπος ἦν ἔρημος καὶ φοβερός. 13. ἐκεῖ ἴδον ἑπτὰ ἀστέρας ὡς ὄρη μεγάλα καιόμενα, *περὶ ὧν πυνθανομένῳ μοι²³ 14. εἶπεν ὁ ἄγγελος Οὗτός ἐστιν ὁ τόπος τὸ τέλος τοῦ οὐρανοῦ καὶ γῆς· δεσμω-

---

ἀβύσσου πάσης. ¹ E = καὶ ἴδον. ² So also E, corruptly. ³ Before καὶ E adds καὶ ἴδον ὡς οἱ ἄνεμοι ἐξέτεινον τὸ ὕψος τοῦ οὐρανοῦ—lost through hmt. ⁴ Add with E καὶ οὗτοί εἰσιν οἱ στῦλοι τοῦ οὐρανοῦ—lost through hmt. ⁵ We should probably emend into τὸν οὐρανόν with E. ⁶ E = δύνοντας in an active sense, and this is probably the right reading here. ⁷ So also gmqu of E. t, β = τὰς νεφέλας. ⁸ Add with E τὰς ὁδοὺς τῶν ἀγγέλων ἴδον—lost through hmt. ⁹ Added with E. Lost before πέρατα. Radermacher and Diels add περὶ τά. ¹⁰ E adds πρὸς νότον. ¹¹ MS. τρις. ¹² MS. βαλλοντας. ¹³ Add τὸ μέν (Radermacher). ¹⁴ E = ιασεως corrupt for ἰάσπιδος. ¹⁵ MS. το. ¹⁶ An Aramaic form of פוך. ¹⁷ E = πέρατ. ¹⁸ E = συνετελέσθησαν. ¹⁹ MS. εἰς τοὺς στύλους. Add with E τοῦ πυρὸς τοῦ οὐρανοῦ καὶ ἴδον ἐν αὐτοῖς στύλους—lost through hmt. ²⁰ E = ἐκείνου. ²¹ MS. puts in acc. ²² MS. αυτο. ²³ MS. πυθανομαιον μοι. E corrupt = καὶ ὡς πνεύματα πυνθανόμενά

τήριον τοῦτο ἐγένετο τοῖς ἄστροις καὶ *ταῖς δυνάμεσιν τοῦ οὐρανοῦ[1].
15. καὶ οἱ ἀστέρες οἱ κυλιόμενοι *ἐν τῷ πυρί[2], οὗτοί εἰσιν οἱ παραβάντες πρόσταγμα Κυρίου[3] ἐν ἀρχῇ τῆς ἀνατολῆς αὐτῶν [ὅτι τόπος ἔξω τοῦ οὐρανοῦ κενός ἐστιν][4], ὅτι οὐκ ἐξῆλθαν ἐν τοῖς καιροῖς αὐτῶν· 16. καὶ ὀργίσθη αὐτοῖς καὶ ἔδησεν αὐτοὺς μέχρι καιροῦ τελειώσεως [αὐτῶν] ἁμαρτίας αὐτῶν, *ἐνιαυτῶν μυρίων[5].

XIX. καὶ εἶπέν μοι Οὐριὴλ Ἐνθάδε οἱ μιγέντες ἄγγελοι ταῖς γυναιξὶν στήσονται, καὶ τὰ πνεύματα αὐτῶν πολύμορφα γενόμενα λυμαίνεται τοὺς ἀνθρώπους καὶ πλανήσει αὐτοὺς ἐπιθύειν τοῖς δαιμονίοις[6] μέχρι[7] τῆς μεγάλης κρίσεως, ἐν ᾗ κριθήσονται εἰς ἀποτελείωσιν. 2. *καὶ αἱ γυναῖκες αὐτῶν τῶν παραβάντων ἀγγέλων[8] εἰς σειρῆνας γενήσονται.

G^g1

3. κἀγὼ Ἐνὼχ ἴδον τὰ θεωρήματα μόνος, τὰ πέρατα πάντων, καὶ οὐ μὴ ἴδῃ οὐδὲ εἷς ἀνθρώπων ὡς ἐγὼ ἴδον.

XX. Ἄγγελοι τῶν δυνάμεων[9]. 2. Οὐριήλ, ὁ εἷς τῶν ἁγίων ἀγγέλων ὁ ἐπὶ τοῦ κόσμου[10] καὶ τοῦ ταρτάρου[11]. 3. Ῥαφαήλ, ὁ εἷς τῶν ἁγίων ἀγγέλων ὁ ἐπὶ τῶν πνευμάτων τῶν ἀνθρώπων. 4. Ῥαγουήλ, ὁ εἷς τῶν ἁγίων ἀγγέλων ὁ ἐκδικῶν[13] τὸν κόσμον *τῶν φωστήρων[15]. 5. Μιχαήλ,

G^g2

3. ...... ἀνθρώπων ὡς ἐγὼ εἶδον.

XX. ...... 2. ὁ εἷς τῶν ἁγίων ἀγγέλων ὁ ἐπὶ τοῦ κόσμου καὶ τοῦ ταρτάρου. 3. Ῥαφαὴλ ὁ εἷς τῶν ἁγίων ἀγγέλων ὁ ἐπὶ τῶν πνευμάτων τῶν ἀνθρώπων. 4. Ῥαγουὴλ ὁ εἷς τῶν[12] ἁγίων ἀγγέλων ὁ ἐκδικῶν[14] τὸν κόσμον τῶν φωστήρων. 5. Μιχαήλ, *ὁ εἷς τῶν[16] ἁγίων ἀγγέλων ὃς ἐπὶ

---

[1] = צְבָא הַשָּׁמַיִם מου. [2] E = ὑπὲρ τοῦ πυρός. [3] E = θεοῦ. [4] A gloss in G^g. [5] E corrupt = ἐνιαυτῷ μυστηρίου. Cf. 21⁶. [6] E adds ὡς θεοῖς. [7] E adds τῆς ἡμέρας. [8] This phrase reproduces literally an Aramaic idiom. [9] This verse is defective. Its complement is found at the close of the chapter: G^g1 ἀρχαγγέλων ὀνόματα ἑπτά which should, however, be read as in G^g2 ὀνόματα ζ´ ἀρχαγγέλων. Taken together these point to ὀνόματα τῶν ἑπτὰ ἀρχαγγέλων τῶν δυνάμεων. E = καὶ ταῦτά ἐστιν ὀνόματα τῶν ἐγρηγόρων τῶν ἁγίων ἀγγέλων. [10] If the original were Hebrew we might with Lods take κόσμος here to be a rendering of צְבָא as in LXX, Gen. 2¹ Deut. 4¹⁹ 17³ Isa. 24²¹. [11] E corrupt = τρόμου. [12] MS. τον. [13] MS. εκδικων I have emended in accordance with E. [14] MS. εκεκων. [15] E = καὶ τοὺς φωστῆρας, but G is right. [16] MS. ο εις τον.

Appendix I

G⁵¹

ὁ εἷς τῶν ἁγίων ἀγγέλων ὁ ἐπὶ τῶν τοῦ λαοῦ ἀγαθῶν τεταγμένος καὶ¹ ἐπὶ τῷ χάῳ². 6. Σαριήλ, ὁ εἷς τῶν ἁγίων ἀγγέλων ὁ ἐπὶ τῶν πνευμάτων οἵτινες *ἐπὶ τῷ πνεύματι³ ἁμαρτάνουσιν. 7. Γαβριήλ, ὁ εἷς τῶν ἁγίων ἀγγέλων ὃς ἐπὶ τοῦ παραδείσου καὶ τῶν δρακόντων καὶ χερουβείν⁴. *ἀρχαγγέλων ὀνόματα ἑπτά⁵.

XXI. Καὶ ἐφώδευσα ἕως τῆς ἀκατασκευάστου. 2. κἀκεῖ ἐθεασάμην ἔργον φοβερόν· ἑώρακα οὔτε οὐρανὸν ἐπάνω, οὔτε γῆν τεθέαμαι τεθεμελιωμένην, ἀλλὰ τόπον ἀκατασκεύαστον καὶ φοβερόν. 3. καὶ ἐκεῖ τεθέαμαι ἐπτὰ τῶν ἀστέρων τοῦ οὐρανοῦ δεδεμένους καὶ ἐρριμμένους⁶ ἐν αὐτῷ⁷, ὁμοίους ὄρεσιν μεγάλοις καὶ ἐν πυρὶ καιομένους. 4. τότε εἶπον Διὰ ποίαν αἰτίαν ἐπεδέθησαν, καὶ διὰ τί ὧδε ἐρίφησαν; 5. τότε εἶπέν μοι Οὐριήλ, ὁ εἷς τῶν ἁγίων ἀγγέλων ὃς μετ' ἐμοῦ ἦν καὶ αὐτὸς ἡγεῖτο αὐτῶν, καὶ εἶπέν ⌜μοι⌝ Ἐνώχ, περὶ τίνος ἐρωτᾷς, ἢ περὶ

G⁵²

τῶν τοῦ λαοῦ ἀγαθῶν τέτακται καὶ ἐπὶ τῷ χάῳ¹. 6. Σαριήλ, ὁ εἷς τῶν ἁγίων ἀγγέλων ὁ ἐπὶ τῶν πνευμάτων οἵτινες ἐπὶ τῷ πνεύματι ἁμαρτάνουσιν. 7. Γαβριήλ, ὁ εἷς τῶν ἁγίων ἀγγέλων ὁ ἐπὶ τοῦ παραδείσου καὶ τῶν δρακόντων καὶ χερουβίν. 8. ⌜Ρεμειήλ, ὁ εἷς τῶν ἁγίων ἀγγέλων ὃν ἔταξεν ὁ θεὸς ἐπὶ τῶν ἀνισταμένων.⌝ *ὀνόματα ζ´ ἀρχαγγέλων.

XXI. Καὶ ἐφώδευσα μέχρι τῆς ἀκατασκευάστου. 2. καὶ ἐκεῖ ἐθεασάμην ἔργον φοβερόν· ἑώρακα οὔτε οὐρανὸν ἐπάνω οὔτε γῆν τεθεμελιωμένην, ἀλλὰ τόπον ἀκατασκεύαστον καὶ φοβερόν. 3. καὶ ἐκεῖ τεθέαμαι ζ´ ἀστέρας τοῦ οὐρανοῦ δεδεμένους καὶ ἐρριμμένους ἐν αὐτῷ⁷, ὁμοίους †ὁράσει μεγάλῃ⁸ καὶ ἐν πυρὶ καιομένους. 4. τότε εἶπον Διὰ ποίαν αἰτίαν ἐπεδέθησαν, καὶ *διὰ ποίαν αἰτίαν⁹ ἐρίφησαν ὧδε; 5. καὶ¹⁰ εἶπέν μοι Οὐριήλ, ὁ εἷς τῶν ἁγίων ἀγγέλων ὁ μετ' ἐμοῦ ὢν καὶ αὐτὸς αὐτῶν ἡγεῖτο, καὶ εἶπέν ⌜μοι⌝ Ἐνώχ, περὶ τίνος ἐρωτᾷς, ἢ περὶ

---

¹ E wrongly omits. ² Though E = λαῷ, the above is right. Uriel presides over Chaos: see 21¹,² (18¹²). The καί which G⁵ preserves before ἐπὶ τῷ λαῷ supports this view. ³ E gives acc. of limitation. ⁴ See G⁵² for ver. 8 omitted here and in E. ⁵ On these words see note on verse 1 above. ⁶ This phrase goes badly with τεθέαμαι. E omits it. Is it a gloss due to ver 4? ⁷ E adds ὁμοῦ, which goes well with δεδεμένους, and could easily fall out before ὁμοίους. ⁸ Corrupt. ⁹ G⁵¹ E = διὰ τί. ¹⁰ G⁵¹ E = τότε.

Gg¹

τίνος *τὴν ἀλήθειαν φιλοσπουδεῖς¹; 6. οὗτοί εἰσιν τῶν ἀστέρων ⌜τοῦ οὐρανοῦ⌝ οἱ παραβάντες τὴν ἐπιταγὴν τοῦ κυρίου², καὶ ἐδέθησαν ὧδε μέχρι τοῦ πληρῶσαι³ μύρια ἔτη, τὸν χρόνον⁴ τῶν ἁμαρτημάτων αὐτῶν.

7. Κἀκεῖθεν ἐφώδευσα εἰς ἄλλον τόπον τούτου φοβερώτερον, καὶ τεθέαμαι ἔργα φοβερώτερα⁵, πῦρ μέγα ἐκεῖ καιόμενον καὶ φλεγόμενον, καὶ διακοπὴν εἶχεν ὁ τόπος ἕως τῆς ἀβύσσου, πλήρης στύλων πυρὸς μεγάλου⁶ καταφερομένων· οὔτε μέτρον οὔτε πλάτος⁷ ἠδυνήθην ἰδεῖν οὐδὲ εἰκάσαι. 8. τότε εἶπον Ὡς φοβερὸς ὁ⁸ τόπος⁹ καὶ ὡς δεινὸς¹⁰ τῇ ὁράσει. 9. τότε ἀπεκρίθη μοι¹¹ ὁ εἷς τῶν ἁγίων ἀγγέλων ὃς μετ᾽ ἐμοῦ ἦν, καὶ εἶπέν μοι ⌜Ἐνώχ⌝, διὰ τί ἐφοβήθης οὕτως καὶ ἐπτοήθης; * καὶ ἀπεκρίθη(ν)¹² Περὶ τούτου τοῦ φοβεροῦ (τόπου) καὶ περὶ τῆς προσόψεως *τῆς δεινῆς¹³. 10. καὶ εἶπεν Οὗτος ὁ τόπος δεσμωτήριον ἀγγέλων· ὧδε¹⁴ συνσχεθήσονται [μέχρι ἑνὸς]¹⁵ εἰς τὸν αἰῶνα.

XXII. Κἀκεῖθεν ἐφόδευσα εἰς ἄλλον τόπον, καὶ ἔδειξέν μοι πρὸς δυσμὰς ⌜ἄλλο⌝ ὄρος μέγα καὶ ὑψηλὸν¹⁶ πέτρας στερεᾶς¹⁷. 2. καὶ

Gg²

τίνος τὴν ἀλήθειαν φιλοσπουδεῖς¹; 6. οὗτοί εἰσιν τῶν ἀστέρων ⌜τοῦ οὐρανοῦ⌝ οἱ παραβάντες τὴν ἐπιταγὴν τοῦ κυρίου², καὶ ἐδέθησαν ὧδε μέχρι πληρωθῆναι μύρια ἔτη, τὸν χρόνον τῶν ἁμαρτημάτων αὐτῶν.

7. Κἀκεῖθεν ἐφώδευσα εἰς ἄλλον τόπον τούτου φοβερώτερον, καὶ τεθέαμαι ἔργα φοβερά· πῦρ μέγα ἐκεῖ καιόμενον καὶ φλεγόμενον, καὶ διακοπὴν εἶχεν ὁ τόπος ἕως τῆς ἀβύσσου, πλήρης στύλων πυρὸς μεγάλου⁶ καταφερομένων· οὔτε μέτρον οὔτε μέγεθος ἠδυνήθην ἰδεῖν οὔτε εἰκάσαι. 8. τότε εἶπον Ὡς φοβερὸς ὁ τόπος οὗτος καὶ ὡς δεινὸς τῇ ὁράσει. 9. τότε ἀπεκρίθη μοι καὶ εἶπεν....

---

¹ = אֲשֶׁר חֲטַאּ Cf. Dan. 7¹⁶, ¹⁹. ² E = θεοῦ. ³ Gg² E = πληρωθῆναι. ⁴ E = τὸν ἀριθμὸν τῶν ἡμερῶν. ⁵ Gg² E = φοβερά. ⁶ Read μεγάλων with E. ⁷ Gg² E = μέγεθος which is better than πλάτος as is clear from μέτρον which precedes. ⁸ E gives הָיָה; and thus agrees with Gg². ⁹ E Gg² add οὗτος. ¹⁰ E = ὀδυνηρός. ¹¹ E adds Οὐριήλ. ¹² E wrongly trans. before καὶ εἶπέν μοι and changes into 3rd sing. ¹³ E = τῆς ὀδύνης. ¹⁴ E = καὶ ὧδε. ¹⁵ This phrase forms a doublet with εἰς τὸν αἰῶνα. Here ἑνὸς is a corruption of αἰῶνος. ¹⁶ E adds καί. ¹⁷ Here in genitive. But if we follow E we must

Appendix I

†τέσσαρες†[1] τόποι ἐν αὐτῷ κοῖλοι, βάθος[2] ἔχοντες καὶ λίαν λεῖοι, ⌜τρεῖς αὐτῶν σκοτεινοὶ καὶ εἷς φωτεινός, καὶ πηγὴ ὕδατος ἀνὰ μέσον αὐτοῦ. καὶ εἶπον⌝[3] †Πῶς†[1] λεῖα τὰ κοιλώματα[1] ταῦτα καὶ ὁλοβαθῆ καὶ σκοτεινὰ τῇ ὁράσει. 3. τότε ἀπεκρίθη Ῥαφαήλ, ὁ εἷς τῶν ἁγίων ἀγγέλων ὃς μετ᾽ ἐμοῦ ἦν, καὶ εἶπέν μοι Οὗτοι οἱ τόποι οἱ κοῖλοι, ἵνα ἐπισυνάγωνται εἰς αὐτοὺς τὰ πνεύματα τῶν ψυχῶν τῶν νεκρῶν, εἰς αὐτὸ τοῦτο ἐκρίθησαν, ὧδε ἐπισυνάγεσθαι πάσας τὰς ψυχὰς[4] τῶν ἀνθρώπων. 4. καὶ οὗτοι οἱ τόποι εἰς ἐπισύνσχεσι(ν) αὐτῶν ἐποι(ήθ)ησαν[5] μέχρι τῆς ἡμέρας τῆς κρίσεως αὐτῶν καὶ μέχρι τοῦ διορισμοῦ[6] [καὶ διορισμένου χρόνου,] ἐν ᾧ ἡ κρίσις ἡ μεγάλη ἔσται ἐν αὐτοῖς. 5. Τεθέαμαι †ἀνθρώπους νεκροὺς ⌜ἐντυγχάνοντος⌝, καὶ ἡ φωνὴ αὐτοῦ†[7] μέχρι τοῦ οὐρανοῦ προέβαινεν καὶ ἐνετύγχανεν. 6. καὶ[8] ἠρώτησα[9] Ῥαφαὴλ τὸν ἄγγελον ὃς μετ᾽ ἐμοῦ ἦν, καὶ εἶπα αὐτῷ Τοῦτο τὸ πνεῦμα ⌜τὸ ἐντυγχάνον⌝ τίνος ἐστίν, οὗ[10] οὕτως[11] ἡ φωνὴ αὐτοῦ προβαίνει καὶ ἐντυγχάνει ⌜ἕως τοῦ οὐρανοῦ⌝; 7. καὶ ἀπεκρίθη μοι λέγων Τοῦτο τὸ πνεῦμά ἐστιν τὸ ἐξελθὸν ἀπὸ Ἄβελ ὃν ἐφόνευσεν Κάειν ὁ ἀδελφός, καὶ ⌜Ἄβελ⌝ ἐντυγχάνει περὶ αὐτοῦ μέχρι τοῦ ἀπολέσαι τὸ σπέρμα αὐτοῦ ἀπὸ προσώπου τῆς γῆς, καὶ ἀπὸ τοῦ σπέρματος τῶν ἀνθρώπων ἀφανισθῇ τὸ σπέρμα αὐτοῦ. 8. Τότε ἠρώτησα[12] περὶ τῶν κοιλωμάτων[13] πάντων, διὰ τί ἐχωρίσθησαν *ἐν ἀπὸ τοῦ ἑνός[14]. 9. καὶ ἀπεκρίθη μοι λέγων Οὗτοι οἱ τρὶς ἐποιήθησαν χωρίζεσθαι τὰ πνεύματα τῶν νεκρῶν· καὶ οὕτως[15] (ἐ)χωρίσθη εἰς τὰ πνεύματα τῶν δικαίων, οὗ[16] ἡ πηγὴ τοῦ ὕδατος ἐν αὐτῷ[16]

---

read στερεάς in acc. MS. εισтερεας. [1] See notes in text. [2] E adds καὶ πλάτος. [3] E omits. For σκοτεινοί MS. gives εισκοτινοι. [4] E adds τῶν υἱῶν. [5] The impossible εποιησαν is accurately reproduced by E. The οὗτοι οἱ τόποι (also in nominative in E) may of course be a nominativus pendens. [6] E adds αὐτῶν. [7] Text corrupt: also that of E which = τὰ πνεύματα ἀνθρώπων νεκρῶν καὶ ἡ φωνὴ αὐτῶν. As Lods has pointed out, vers. 5 b and 6 of G show that only a single spirit is referred to. Moreover G has lost πνεῦμα which is preserved by E. Hence read πνεῦμα ἀνθρώπου νεκροῦ ἐντυγχάνοντος καὶ ἡ φωνὴ αὐτοῦ. [8] E = τότε. [9] MS. ηρωτησεν. [10] Em. with E from διο. Thus in οὗ ... ἡ φωνὴ αὐτοῦ we have the Semitic idiom אֲשֶׁר ... ד. [11] E omits. [12] E adds περὶ αὐτοῦ καὶ but wrongly, apparently. [13] Em. from κυκλωμάτων. The translator of E found κυκλώματα in ver. 2 for a corruption of κοιλώματα preserved in G, and here κριμάτων another corruption of κοιλωμάτων. [14] Em. by Dillmann and Lods from ην απο του αιωνος. [15] Corrupt for οὗτος. See note in text. [16] Semitic idiom = בו ... אֲשֶׁר or בה ... ד.

φωτινή¹.   10. καὶ οὕτως ἐκτίσθη *τοῖς ἁμαρτωλοῖς², ὅταν ἀποθάνωσιν καὶ ταφῶσιν εἰς τὴν γῆν, καὶ κρίσις οὐκ ἐγενήθη ἐπ' αὐτῶν ἐν τῇ ζωῇ αὐτῶν.   11. ὧδε χωρίζεται τὰ πνεύματα αὐτῶν εἰς τὴν μεγάλην βάσανον ταύτην, μέχρι τῆς μεγάλης ἡμέρας τῆς κρίσεως, τῶν μαστίγων καὶ τῶν βασάνων τῶν κατηραμένων³ *μέχρι αἰῶνος⁴ *ἵν' ἀνταπόδοσις⁵ τῶν πνευμάτων· ἐκεῖ δήσει αὐτοὺς μέχρις αἰῶνος.   12. καὶ οὕτως ἐχωρίσθη τοῖς πνεύμασιν τῶν ἐντυγχανόντων, οἵτινες ἐνφανίζουσιν περὶ τῆς ἀπωλείας, ὅταν φονευθῶσιν ἐν ταῖς ἡμέραις τῶν ἁμαρτωλῶν.   13. καὶ οὕτως ἐκτίσθη τοῖς πνεύμασιν τῶν ἀνθρώπων, ὅσοι οὐκ ἔσονται⁶ ὅσιοι ἀλλὰ ἁμαρτωλοί, ὅσοι⁷ ἀσεβεῖς, καὶ μετὰ τῶν ἀνόμων ἔσονται μέτοχοι. τὰ δὲ πνεύματα [ὅτι οἱ ἐνθάδε θλιβέντες ἔλαττον κολάζονται]⁸ αὐτῶν, οὐ τιμωρηθήσονται⁹ ἐν ἡμέρᾳ τῆς κρίσεως, οὐδὲ μὴ μετεγερθῶσιν ἐντεῦθεν.   14. Τότε ηὐλόγησα τὸν κύριον τῆς δόξης, καὶ εἶπα Εὐλογητὸς *εἶ, Κύριε ὁ τῆς δικαιοσύνης¹⁰, κυριεύων *τοῦ αἰῶνος¹¹.

XXIII. Κἀκεῖθεν ἐφώδευσα εἰς ἄλλον τόπον πρὸς δυσμὰς¹² τῶν περάτων τῆς γῆς.   2. καὶ ἐθεασάμην πῦρ¹³ διατρέχον καὶ οὐκ ἀναπαυόμενον οὐδὲ ἐνλεῖπον τοῦ δρόμου, ἡμέρας καὶ νυκτὸς †ἅμα†¹⁴ διαμένον.   3. καὶ ἠρώτησα λέγων Τί ἐστιν τὸ μὴ ἔχον ἀνάπαυσιν; 4. τότε ἀπεκρίθη μοι Ῥαγουήλ, ὁ εἷς τῶν ἁγίων ἀγγέλων ὃς μετ' ἐμοῦ ἦν¹⁵ Οὗτος ὁ δρόμος τοῦ πυρός¹⁶ τὸ πρὸς δυσμὰς πῦρ τὸ ἐκδιῶκόν ἐστιν πάντας τοὺς φωστῆρας τοῦ οὐρανοῦ.   XXIV. Καὶ¹⁷ ἔδειξέν μοι ὄρη πυρὸς καιόμενα¹⁸ . . . . νυκτός.   2. καὶ ἐπέκεινα αὐτῶν ἐπορεύθην καὶ ἐθεασάμην ἑπτὰ ὄρη ἔνδοξα, πάντα ἑκάτερα τοῦ ἑκατέρου διαλλάσσοντα, *ὧν οἱ λίθοι ἔντιμοι τῇ καλλονῇ¹⁹, καὶ πάντα ἔντιμα καὶ ἔνδοξα καὶ εὐειδῆ, ⟨τρία ἐπ'⟩ ἀνατολὰς ἐστηριγμένα ⟨ἓν⟩ ἐν τῷ ἑνί, καὶ τρία ἐπὶ νότον ⟨ἓν⟩ ἐν τῷ ἑνί. καὶ φάραγγες βαθεῖαι καὶ τραχεῖαι²⁰, μία τῇ μιᾷ οὐκ ἐγγίζουσαι,   3. καὶ [τῷ ὄρει]²¹

---

[1] E = 'brightness'.   [2] Em. with E from τῶν ἁμαρτωλῶ.   [3] E takes this transitively: but it is to be taken passively.   [4] E = μέχρι αἰῶνος καί.   [5] So Radermacher emends from ἦν ἀνταποδώσεις. E = καὶ τῆς ἀνταποδόσεως.   [6] E = ἦσαν.   [7] Add ὅλοι with E.   [8] An explanatory gloss.   [9] E = ἀναιρεθήσονται or ἀποθανοῦνται.   [10] E = κύριός μου, ὁ κύριος τῆς δικαιοσύνης.   [11] = 'the world'. E = μέχρι τοῦ αἰῶνος.   [12] E adds μέχρι.   [13] E adds φλεγόμενον.   [14] Read ἀλλά with E.   [15] E adds καὶ εἶπέν μοι.   [16] E adds ὃν εἶδες.   [17] Before καί insert with E κἀκεῖθεν ἐφώδευσα εἰς ἄλλον τόπον τῆς γῆς.   [18] E adds ἡμέρας καί.   [19] E = καὶ τοὺς λίθους ἐντίμους καὶ καλούς or by a slight change the nom. can be read.   [20] E = σκολιαί.   [21] An intrusion.

Appendix I

ἕβδομον ὄρος ἀνὰ μέσον τούτων, καὶ *ὑπερεῖχεν τῷ ὕψει, ὅμοιον¹ καθέδρᾳ θρόνου, καὶ περιεκύκλου δένδρα αὐτὸ² εὐειδῆ³. 4. καὶ ἦν ἐν αὐτοῖς δένδρον ὃ οὐδέποτε ὠσφράνμαι καὶ οὐδεὶς ἕτερος αὐτῶν ⌜εὐφράνθη⌝, καὶ οὐδὲν ἕτερον ὅμοιον αὐτῷ⁴· ὀσμὴν εἶχεν εὐωδεστέραν πάντων ἀρωμάτων, καὶ τὰ φύλλα αὐτοῦ καὶ τὸ ἄνθος καὶ τὸ δένδρον οὐ φθίνει⁵ εἰς τὸν αἰῶνα· *οἱ δὲ περὶ τὸν καρπὸν⁶ ὡσεὶ βότρυες φοινίκων.   5. τότε εἶπον ⌜Ὡς⌝ καλὸν τὸ δένδρον τοῦτό ἐστιν καὶ εὐῶδες⁷, καὶ ὡραῖα τὰ φύλλα, καὶ τὰ ἄνθη αὐτοῦ ὡραῖα⁸ τῇ ὁράσει. 6. τότε ἀπεκρίθη μοι Μιχαήλ, εἷς τῶν ἁγίων⁹ ἀγγέλων ὃς μετ' ἐμοῦ ἦν καὶ αὐτὸς αὐτῶν ἡγεῖτο,   XXV. καὶ εἶπέν μοι Ἐνώχ, τί ἐρωτᾷς¹⁰ ⌜καὶ τί ἐθαύμασας⌝ ἐν τῇ ὀσμῇ τοῦ δένδρου, καὶ ⌜διὰ τί⌝ *θέλεις τὴν ἀλήθειαν μαθεῖν; 2. τότε ἀπεκρίθην¹¹ αὐτῷ¹² Περὶ πάντων εἰδέναι θέλω, μάλιστα δὲ περὶ τοῦ δένδρου τούτου σφόδρα. 3. καὶ ἀπεκρίθη λέγων Τοῦτο τὸ ὄρος τὸ ὑψηλόν¹³, οὗ ἡ κορυφὴ ὁμοία θρόνου θεοῦ, καθέδρα¹⁴ ἐστὶν οὗ καθίζει¹⁵ *ὁ μέγας κύριος, ὁ ἅγιος τῆς δόξης¹⁶, ὁ βασιλεὺς *τοῦ αἰῶνος¹⁷, ὅταν καταβῇ ἐπισκέψασθαι τὴν γῆν ἐπ' ἀγαθῷ. 4. καὶ τοῦτο τὸ δένδρον εὐωδίας, καὶ οὐδεμία σὰρξ ἐξουσίαν ἔχει ἅψασθαι αὐτοῦ μέχρι τῆς μεγάλης κρίσεως, ἐν¹⁸ ᾗ ἐκδίκησις πάντων καὶ τελείωσις μέχρις αἰῶνος· τότε¹⁹ δικαίοις καὶ ὁσίοις δοθήσεται. 5. *ὁ καρπὸς αὐτοῦ τοῖς ἐκλεκτοῖς †εἰς ζωήν† εἰς βοράν, καὶ²⁰ μεταφυτευθήσεται ἐν τόπῳ ἁγίῳ παρὰ τὸν οἶκον τοῦ θεοῦ²¹ βασιλέως²² *τοῦ αἰῶνος²³.

6. τότε εὐφρανθήσονται εὐφραινόμενοι καὶ χαρήσονται
   καὶ²⁴ *εἰς τὸ ἅγιον εἰσελεύσονται·
   αἱ ὀσμαὶ αὐτοῦ²⁵ ἐν τοῖς ὀστέοις αὐτῶν,
   καὶ ζωὴν πλείονα²⁶ ζήσονται ἐπὶ γῆς

---

¹ E (i.e. h o, b) = ὑπερεῖχεν (a, β-h o, b = καὶ τὸ ὕψος) αὐτῶν ἦσαν ὅμοια πάντα, but πάντα is an intrusion.   ² MS. αυτα.   ³ E = εὐώδη which is right. Cf. vers. 4, 5, 25⁴.   ⁴ For οὐδεὶς ... αὐτῷ E gives οὐδὲν (or οὐδεὶς) αὐτῶν καὶ οὐδὲν ἕτερον ὅμοιον αὐτῷ ἦν.   ⁵ MS. φθειυι.   ⁶ E = ὁ δὲ καρπὸς καλὸς καὶ ὁ καρπός.   ⁷ E = εὐειδές but text is better.   ⁸ E adds σφόδρα.   ⁹ E adds καὶ ἐντίμων.   ¹⁰ E adds με.   ¹¹ MS. απεκρειθη.   ¹² E adds λέγων.   ¹³ E adds ὁ εἶδες.   ¹⁴ E adds αὐτοῦ.   ¹⁵ E = καθίσει.   ¹⁶ Text confused. E = ὁ ἅγιος καὶ ὁ μέγας ὁ κύριος τῆς δόξης. ὁ κύριος τῆς δόξης is supported by 27⁵.   ¹⁷ E = αἰώνιος.   ¹⁸ MS. ει.   ¹⁹ E = τόδε.   ²⁰ This text seems right save the phrase εἰς ζωήν = לחיים or possibly לחיה corrupt for להיה = ἔσται.   ²¹ E = κυρίου.   ²² MS. βασιλεύς.   ²³ E = αἰωνίου.   ²⁴ E trans. after ἅγιον and perhaps rightly.   ²⁵ See notes on text, pp. 53, 54.   ²⁶ This seems to

ἣν ἔζησαν οἱ πατέρες σου,
καὶ ἐν ταῖς ἡμέραις αὐτῶν[1] καὶ βάσανοι
καὶ πληγαὶ καὶ μάστιγες οὐχ ἅψονται αὐτῶν.

7. Τότε ηὐλόγησα[2] τὸν θεὸν τῆς δόξης, τὸν βασιλέα *τοῦ αἰῶνος[3], ὃς ἡτοίμασεν *ἀνθρώποις τὰ τοιαῦτα δικαίοις[4], καὶ αὐτὰ ἔκτισεν καὶ εἶπεν δοῦναι αὐτοῖς.

XXVI. Καὶ ἐκεῖθεν ἐφώδευσα εἰς τὸ μέσον τῆς γῆς, καὶ ἴδον τόπον ηὐλογημένον, ἐν ᾧ ⌜δένδρα ἔχοντα⌝ παραφυάδας μενούσας καὶ βλαστούσας [τοῦ δένδρου ἐκκοπέντος]. 2. κἀκεῖ τεθέαμαι ὄρος ἅγιον[5]. ὑποκάτω τοῦ ὄρους ὕδωρ ἐξ ἀνατολῶν, καὶ τὴν † δύσιν †[6] εἶχεν πρὸς νότον. 3. καὶ ἴδον πρὸς ἀνατολὰς ἄλλο ὄρος ὑψηλότερον τούτου, καὶ ἀνὰ μέσον αὐτοῦ[7] φάραγγα βαθεῖαν, οὐκ ἔχουσαν πλάτος, καὶ δι' αὐτῆς ὕδωρ πορεύεται ⌜ὑποκάτω⌝ ὑπὸ τὸ ὄρος. 4. καὶ πρὸς δυσμὰς τούτου ἄλλο ὄρος ταπεινότερον αὐτοῦ καὶ οὐκ ἔχον ὕψος, καὶ φάραγγα ⌜βαθεῖαν καὶ ξηρὰν⌝[8] ἀνὰ μέσον αὐτῶν, καὶ ἄλλην φάραγγα βαθεῖαν καὶ ξηρὰν ἐπ' ἄκρων τῶν τριῶν ⌜ὀρέων.⌝ 5. καὶ *πᾶσαι φάραγγές[9] εἰσιν βαθεῖαι[10] ἐκ πέτρας στερεᾶς, καὶ δένδρον οὐκ ἐφυτεύετο ἐπ' αὐτάς. 6. καὶ ἐθαύμασα[11] περὶ τῆς φάραγγος, καὶ λίαν ἐθαύμασα. XXVII. καὶ[12] εἶπον Διὰ τί ἡ γῆ αὕτη ἡ εὐλογημένη καὶ πᾶσα πλήρης δένδρων, αὕτη δὲ ἡ φάραγξ κεκατηραμένη ἐστίν[13]; . . . . . 2. γῆ[14] κατάρατος τοῖς κεκαταραμένοις ἐστὶν μέχρι αἰῶνος. ὧδε ἐπισυναχθήσονται πάντες ⌜οἱ κεκατηραμένοι⌝ οἵτινες[15] ἐροῦσιν τῷ στόματι αὐτῶν κατὰ Κυρίου φωνὴν ἀπρεπῆ, καὶ περὶ τῆς δόξης αὐτοῦ σκληρὰ λαλήσουσιν. ὧδε ἐπισυναχθήσονται, καὶ ὧδε ἔσται τὸ οἰκητήριον[16], 3. ἐπ' ἐσχάτοις αἰῶσιν, *ἐν ταῖς ἡμέραις[17] τῆς κρίσεως τῆς ἀληθινῆς ἐναντίον τῶν

---

[1] E adds καὶ λύπη. [2] MS. ηυλογησαν. [3] E = αἰώνιον. [4] This order is preserved in E. [5] E adds καί. [6] Corrupt. E = ῥύσιν which is right. [7] Better αὐτῶν with E. [8] Instead of this phrase E reads ὑποκάτω. [9] MS. ποσε φαραγγες. [10] E adds καὶ οὐκ ἔχουσαι πλάτος. [11] Add with E περὶ τῶν πετρῶν καὶ ἐθαύμασα—lost through hmt. [12] E = τότε. [13] Add with E ἐν μέσῳ; τότε ἀπεκρίθη Οὐριήλ, ὁ εἷς τῶν ἁγίων ἀγγέλων ὃς μετ' ἐμοῦ ἦν, καὶ εἶπεν. [14] A transliteration of אלה. The translator of E understood it rightly as = φάραγξ. Before γῆ add with E αὕτη ἡ. [15] MS. τινες. [16] E = κριτήριον αὐτῶν. E is corrupt. [17] E = ἔσται ἡ ὅρασις. Thus E makes the sentence begin with this verse, whereas G makes the first half of this verse part of the sentence which immediately precedes.

δικαίων εἰς τὸν ἄπαντα χρόνον. ὧδε εὐλογήσουσιν οἱ εὐσεβεῖς[1] τὸν κύριον τῆς δόξης, τὸν βασιλέα *τοῦ αἰῶνος[2], 4. ἐν ταῖς ἡμέραις τῆς κρίσεως αὐτῶν εὐλογήσουσιν ἐν ἐλέει[3], ὡς ἐμέρισεν αὐτοῖς. 5. Τότε ηὐλόγησα τὸν κύριον τῆς δόξης, καὶ ⌈τὴν δόξαν⌉ αὐτοῦ ἐδήλωσα καὶ ὕμνησα μεγαλοπρεπῶς.

XXVIII. Καὶ ἐκεῖθεν ἐπορεύθην[4] εἰς τὸ μέσον[5], Μανδοβαρά[6], καὶ ἴδον αὐτὸ[7] ἔρημον καὶ αὐτὸ μόνον, πλήρης δένδρων· † καὶ ἀπὸ τῶν σπερμάτων †[8] 2. ὕδωρ[9] ἀνομβροῦν[10], ἄνωθεν 3. φερόμενον[11] ὡς ὑδραγωγὸς δαψιλὴς[12] ὡς[13] *πρὸς βορρᾶν ἐπὶ δυσμῶν[14] πάντοθεν *ἀνάγει †ὕδωρ† καὶ δρόσον[15]. XXIX. *Ἔτι ἐκεῖθεν[16] ἐπορεύθην εἰς ἄλλον τόπον *ἐν τῷ[17] Βαβδηρά[18], καὶ[19] πρὸς ἀνατολὰς τοῦ ὄρους τούτου ᾠχόμην, 2. καὶ[20] ἴδον κρίσεως[21] δένδρα πνέοντα[22] ἀρωμάτων λιβάνων καὶ ζμύρνης[23], καὶ τὰ δένδρα αὐτῶν ὅμοια καρύαις[24]. XXX. Καὶ *ἐπέκεινα[25] τούτων ᾠχόμην[26] πρὸς ἀνατολὰς[27] μακράν, καὶ ἴδον τόπον ἄλλον ⌈μέγαν⌉, φάραγγα ὕδατος[28], 2. *ἐν ᾧ καὶ δένδρον[29] χρόα[30] ἀρωμάτων ὁμοίων σχίνῳ, 3. καὶ τὰ παρὰ τὰ χείλη τῶν φαράγγων τούτων ἴδον *κιννάμωμον ἀρωμάτων·[31] καὶ *ἐπέκεινα[25] τούτων ᾠχόμην πρὸς ἀνατολάς. XXXI. καὶ ἴδον ἄλλα ὄρη καὶ ἐν αὐτοῖς ⌈ἄλση⌉ δένδρων, καὶ ἐκ-

---

[1] MS. ασεβεις. [2] E = αἰώνιον. [3] E = ὑπὲρ ἐλέους. [4] E adds πρὸς ἀνατολάς. [5] E adds τοῦ ὄρους, which G wrongly omits. [6] A faulty transliteration of מדברא, more faulty as Βαβδηρά in 29¹. Though מדברא is Aramaic it does not prove that the original was Aramaic; for ᴍᴀᴅʙᴀʀᴀ̈ (= madbarā), which is an Ethiopic transliteration of the same Hebrew word מדבר in Jos. 5⁶, implies an Aramaic form. For other forms see Jos. 5⁶ 18¹² μαδβαρῖτις or μαβδαρῖτις. The Greek translators were often Aramaic-speaking Jews, and introduced Aramaisms probably unconsciously. [7] E omits αὐτό rightly. [8] E = ἀπὸ τῶν σπερμάτων καί. [9] E adds ἐν αὐτῷ. [10] Em. with E from ανομβρον which gives no good sense. [11] E = φαινόμενον, but G is right. MS. φαιρομενον. [12] E adds ὡς ὑδραγωγεῖ. [13] ὡς is redundant. [14] North-West. A Semitic idiom. Cf. Hebrew צפונה מערבה or צפונית מערבית in this sense. [15] E = ἀνάγεται ὕδωρ καὶ δρόσον, but by a slight change in vocalization becomes = G. [16] E = καὶ ἐκεῖθεν which it has trans. into previous verse. [17] E = ἀπὸ τοῦ. [18] See note on 28¹. [19] E corrupt. [20] E adds ἐκεῖ. [21] Here we should have εὐώδη instead of κρίσεως. [22] E corrupt. [23] = מר. MS. Ζμυρνα. [24] E omits, but see note on p. 58. MS. Καροης. [25] E misrenders by ἐπὶ ἐκείνων, cf. 18⁹. [26] E = ὄρη. [27] E adds οὐ. [28] E adds ἀσπάον, a gloss. [29] E = καὶ ἴδον δένδρον καλόν. [30] E = ὅμοιον. χρόα may be corrupt for χλόᾳ (Radermacher). [31] See

πορευόμενον ἐξ αὐτῶν¹ νέκταρ τὸ καλούμενον σαρρὰν² καὶ χαλβάνη³. 2. καὶ ἐπέκεινα⁴ τῶν ὀρέων τούτων⁵ ἴδον ἄλλο ὄρος ⌜πρὸς ἀνατολὰς τῶν περάτων τῆς γῆς⌝⁶, καὶ πάντα τὰ δένδρα πλήρης⁷ στακτῆς⁸ ἐν ὁμοιώματι ἀμυγδάλων. 3. ὅταν τρίβωσιν⁹, διὸ¹⁰ εὐωδέστερον ὑπὲρ πᾶν ἀρωμά[των]...... XXXII. *εἰς βορρᾶν¹¹ ⌜πρὸς ἀνατολὰς⌝ τεθέαμαι ἑπτὰ ὄρη πλήρη νάρδου χρηστοῦ καὶ * σχίνου¹² καὶ κινναμώμου καὶ πιπέρεως.

2. Καὶ ἐκεῖθεν ἐφόδευσα ἐπὶ¹³ τὰς ἀρχὰς ⌜πάντων⌝ τῶν ὀρέων τούτων, μακρὰν ἀπέχων πρὸς ἀνατολὰς ⌜τῆς γῆς⌝, καὶ διέβην ἐπάνω τῆς ἐρυθρᾶς θαλάσσης, καὶ ᾠχόμην *ἐπ᾽ Ἄκρων, καὶ ἀπὸ τούτου¹⁴ διέβην ἐπάνω¹⁵ τοῦ Ζωτιήλ. 3. καὶ ἦλθον¹⁶ πρὸς τὸν παράδεισον τῆς δικαιοσύνης, καὶ ἴδον *μακρόθεν τῶν δένδρων τούτων¹⁷ δένδρα πλείονα¹⁸ καὶ μεγάλα * δύω μὲν¹⁹ ἐκεῖ²⁰, μεγάλα σφόδρα καλὰ καὶ ἔνδοξα ⌜καὶ μεγαλοπρεπῆ²¹⌝, καὶ τὸ δένδρον τῆς φρονήσεως, οὗ²² ἐσθίουσιν ⌜ἁγίων τοῦ καρποῦ αὐτοῦ⌝²² καὶ ἐπίστανται φρόνησιν μεγάλην. 4. ὅμοιον ⌜τὸ δένδρον ἐκεῖνο στροβιλέᾳ τὸ ὕψος, τὰ δὲ φύλλα αὐτοῦ⌝²³ κερατίᾳ²⁴ ὅμοια, ὁ δὲ καρπὸς αὐτοῦ ὡσεὶ βότρυες ἀμπέλου ἱλαροὶ λίαν, ἡ δὲ ὀσμὴ αὐτοῦ διέτρεχεν πόρρω ἀπὸ τοῦ δένδρου. 5. τότε²⁵ εἶπον ⌜Ὡς⌝ καλὸν τὸ δένδρον, καὶ ὡς ἐπίχαρι²⁶ τῇ ὁράσει. 6. τότε ἀπεκρίθη Ῥαφαήλ, ὁ ἅγιος ἄγγελος ὁ μετ᾽ ἐμοῦ ὤν, Τοῦτο τὸ δένδρον φρονήσεως, ἐξ οὗ ἔφαγεν ὁ πατήρ σου.

note on p. 58. ¹ E adds ὅτι. ² = עֲרִי. ³ = חלבנה. ⁴ E misrenders by ἐπὶ ἐκείνων, cf. 18⁹. ⁵ E = ἐκείνων. ⁶ This clause defines the habitat of the tree. E omits this, but gives the name καὶ ἐν αὐτῷ δένδρα ἀλόης. ⁷ Indeclinable as in 28¹. ⁸ Em. from ἐξάντης. E corrupt = στερεύς. στακτή = נטף Gen. 37²⁵ 43¹¹. It also translates חלבנה, לט, נכאת, צרי in the LXX. ⁹ E = λάβωσιν, and adds ἐκεῖνον τὸν καρπόν, and connects this clause with what follows. For τρίβωσιν we should read καύσωσιν. ¹⁰ E omits. ¹¹ E = καὶ μετὰ ταῦτα τὰ ἀρώματα εἰς βορρᾶν ὁρῶν ὑπὲρ τὰ ὄρη the first five words of which were lost through hmt. ¹² E = δένδρων εὐωδῶν a free rendering. ¹³ E = ὑπέρ. ¹⁴ E = μακρὰν ἀπὸ τούτου καί. ¹⁵ E adds τοῦ ἀγγέλου. ¹⁶ MS. ελθων. ¹⁷ E takes μακρόθεν as = μακρὰν governing the following words in the genitive. ¹⁸ E = πολλά. ¹⁹ E = φυόμενα. ²⁰ E adds εὐώδη. ²¹ Can the Greek before the translator of E have been εὐειδή? If so, it is a corruption of the εὐώδη found in E after ἐκεῖ. ²² = the Aramaic idiom פִּירֵיהּ...דְּ. See also 16¹ 22⁴,⁹. ²³ This clause is lost in E through hmt., though the order such a loss presumes must have been different such as: ὅμοιον ⌜τὸ δένδρον ἐκεῖνο...ὅμοια⌝ κερατίᾳ. ²⁴ MS. κερατι. ²⁵ E = καί. ²⁶ E adds καλὸν καί before this word.

ADDITIONAL FRAGMENT PRESERVED IN SYNCELLUS' CHRONOGRAPHIA

(ed. Dindorf, 1829, vol. i. p. 47.)

Καὶ αὖθις· παρὰ δὲ τοῦ ὅρους ἐν ᾧ ὤμοσαν καὶ ὀνεθεμάτισαν πρὸς τὸν πλησίον αὐτῶν, ὅτι εἰς τὸν αἰῶνα οὐ μὴ ἀποστῇ ἀπ' αὐτοῦ ψῦχος καὶ χιὼν καὶ πάχνη καὶ δρόσος οὐ μὴ καταβῇ εἰς αὐτό, εἰ μὴ εἰς κατάραν καταβήσεται ἐπ' αὐτό, μέχρις ἡμέρας κρίσεως τῆς μεγάλης. ἐν τῷ καιρῷ ἐκείνῳ κατακαυθήσεται καὶ ταπεινωθήσεται καὶ ἔσται κατακαιόμενον καὶ τηκόμενον ὡς κηρὸς ἀπὸ πυρός, οὕτως κατακαήσεται περὶ πάντων τῶν ἔργων αὐτοῦ. καὶ νῦν ἐγὼ λέγω ὑμῖν υἱοῖς ἀνθρώπων, ὀργὴ μεγάλη καθ' ὑμῶν, κατὰ τῶν υἱῶν ὑμῶν, καὶ οὐ παύσεται ἡ ὀργὴ αὕτη ἀφ' ὑμῶν, μέχρι καιροῦ σφαγῆς τῶν υἱῶν ὑμῶν. καὶ ἀπολοῦνται οἱ ἀγαπητοὶ ὑμῶν καὶ ἀποθανοῦνται οἱ ἔντιμοι ὑμῶν ἀπὸ πάσης τῆς γῆς, ὅτι πᾶσαι αἱ ἡμέραι τῆς ζωῆς αὐτῶν ἀπὸ τοῦ νῦν οὐ μὴ ἔσονται πλείω τῶν ἑκατὸν εἴκοσιν ἐτῶν. καὶ μὴ δόξητε ἔτι ζῆσαι ἐπὶ πλείονα ἔτη· οὐ γάρ ἐστιν ἐπ' αὐτοῖς πᾶσα ὁδὸς ἐκφεύξεως ἀπὸ τοῦ νῦν διὰ τὴν ὀργὴν ἣν ὠργίσθη ὑμῖν ὁ βασιλεὺς πάντων τῶν αἰώνων· μὴ νομίσητε ὅτι ἐκφεύξεσθε ταῦτα.

Καὶ ταῦτα μὲν ἐκ τοῦ πρώτου βιβλίου Ἐνὼχ περὶ τῶν ἐγρηγόρων.

APPENDIX II

THE SON OF MAN: ITS MEANING IN JEWISH APOCALYPTIC AND THE NEW TESTAMENT

WITHIN the last eighteen years a vast literature[1] has been written on the above Messianic title, which started with the publication of the first edition of the present work. I have followed with much interest the various attempts to explain the origin and meaning of this title or else to prove that it had no part originally in 1 Enoch or in the N.T. Into a discussion of these hypotheses I cannot enter here, and will only state my present position on the question, and this position is the same as regards the meaning of the title in 1 Enoch and the N.T. as in 1893. However scholars may differ as to the origin of the title, its meaning in the N.T. is to my mind free from such ambiguities. If the title has a long history behind it, it does not in the least follow that what was its meaning in O.T. times persisted in later Judaism or Christianity. In fact every analogy teaches us to expect an entire transformation. I will here republish with a few verbal corrections what I wrote in 1892.

The true interpretation of the N.T. title 'Son of Man' will, we believe, be found *if we start with the conception as found in 1 Enoch and trace its enlargement and essential transformation in the usage of our Lord. In this transformation it is reconciled to and takes over into itself its apparent antithesis, the conception of the Servant of Jehovah, while it betrays occasional reminiscences of Dan. 7, the ultimate source of this designation.*

First, shortly, as to the facts of the problem. The expression is found in St. Matthew thirty times, in St. Mark fourteen, in

---

[1] See the Articles in the Encyc. Bib. and Hastings, *B. D.* for the fairly exhaustive bibliography on this question.

St. Luke twenty-five, in St. John twelve. Outside the Gospels, in Acts 7⁵⁶ Rev. 1¹³ 14¹⁴. In all these cases we find ὁ υἱὸς τοῦ ἀνθρώπου, except in St. John 5²⁷ and Rev. 1¹³ 14¹⁴. The two passages in Rev. may be disregarded, since the phrase is different, i.e. ὅμοιον υἱὸν ἀνθρώπου. Even there they are real designations of the Messiah. As for St. John 5²⁷ I can find no satisfactory explanation of the absence of the article.

Our interpretation of this title is as follows: (1) *Its source in Daniel and its differentiation therefrom.* The title 'Son of Man' in Enoch was undoubtedly derived from Dan. 7, but a whole world of thought lies between the suggestive words in Daniel and the definite rounded conception as it appears in Enoch. In Daniel the phrase seems merely symbolical of Israel, but in Enoch it denotes a supernatural person. In the former, moreover, the title is indefinite, 'like a son of man,' but in Enoch it is perfectly definite and distinctive, 'the Son of Man.'

(2) *The first occasion of its use.* As the Parables are pre-Christian, they furnish the first instance in which the definite personal title appears in literature.

(3) *Its supernatural import in Enoch.* The Son of Man as portrayed in the Parables is a supernatural being and not a mere man. He is not even conceived as being of human descent, as the Messiah in 1 En. 90³⁷. He sits on God's throne, 51³, which is likewise His own throne, 62³, ⁵ 69²⁷, ²⁹, possesses universal dominion, 62⁶, and all judgement is committed unto Him, 41⁹ 69²⁷.

(4) *Its import in the New Testament.* This title, with its supernatural attributes of superhuman glory, of universal dominion and supreme judicial powers, was adopted by our Lord. The Son of Man has come down from heaven, St. John 3¹³ (cf. 1 En. 48² note); He is Lord of the Sabbath, St. Matt. 12⁸;[1] can forgive sins, St. Matt. 9⁶; and all judgement is committed unto Him, St. John 5²², ²⁷ (cf. 1 En. 69²⁷). But while retaining its supernatural associations, this title underwent transformation

---

[1] The text in St. Matt. here is doubtful. Originally it may only have meant that 'man was Lord of the Sabbath'.

in our Lord's use of it, a transformation that all Pharisaic ideas, so far as He adopted them, likewise underwent. And just as His kingdom in general formed a standing protest against the prevailing Messianic ideas of temporal glory and dominion, so the title 'the Son of Man' assumed a deeper spiritual significance; and this change we shall best apprehend if we introduce into the Enoch conception of the Son of Man the Isaiah conception of the Servant of Jehovah. *These two conceptions, though outwardly antithetic, are through the transformation of the former reconciled and fulfilled in a deeper unity—in the New Testament Son of Man.* This transformation flowed naturally from the object of Jesus' coming, the revelation of the Father. The Father could be revealed not through the self-assertion of the Son, not through His grasping at self-display in the exhibition of superhuman majesty and power, but through His self-emptying, self-renunciation and service (Phil. 2⁶). Whilst, therefore, in adopting the title 'the Son of Man' from Enoch, Jesus made from the outset supernatural claims, yet these supernatural claims were to be vindicated not after the external Judaistic conceptions of the Book of Enoch, but in a revelation of the Father in a sinless and redemptive life, death, and resurrection. Thus in the life of the actual Son of Man the Father was revealed in the Son, and supernatural greatness in universal service. He that was greatest was likewise Servant of all. This transformed conception of the Son of Man is thus permeated throughout by the Isaiah conception of the Servant of Jehovah; but though the Enochic conception is fundamentally transformed, the transcendant claims underlying it are not for a moment foregone. *If then we bear in mind the inward synthesis of these two ideas of the past in an ideal, nay in a Personality transcending them both, we shall find little difficulty in understanding the startling contrasts that present themselves in the New Testament in connexion with this designation.* We can understand how on the one hand the Son of Man hath not where to lay His head (St. Matt. 8[20]) and yet release men from their sins (St. Matt. 9⁶); how He is to be despised and rejected of the elders and chief priests and scribes and be put to death (St. Luke 9^{22}), and yet be the Judge of all mankind (St. John 5^{27}).

It has been objected that St. Matt. 16^{13} St. John 12^{34} prove that the Son of Man was not a current designation of the Messiah in the time of Christ; but no such conclusion can be drawn from these passages; for in the older form of the question given in St. Matt. 16^{13} the words 'the Son of Man' are not found: see St. Mark 8^{27} St. Luke 9^{18}. In St. John 12^{34} it is just the strangeness of this *new* conception of this current phrase of a Messiah who was to suffer death, that makes the people ask ' Who is this Son of Man? we have heard of the law that the Christ abideth for ever'.

On the other hand, though the phrase was to some extent a current one,[1] our Lord's use of it must have been an enigma, not only to the people generally, but also to His immediate disciples, so much so that they shrank from using it; for, as we know, it is used in the Gospels only by our Lord in speaking of Himself.

---

[1] On the survival of its use as a Messianic designation see Jer. Taanith ii. 1: 'R. Abbahu said, If a man says to thee—I am God, he lies; I am the Son of Man, he will at last repent it: I ascend to heaven, if he said it he will not prove it.'

INDEX I

PASSAGES FROM THE SCRIPTURES AND OTHER ANCIENT BOOKS DIRECTLY CONNECTED OR CLOSELY PARALLEL WITH THE TEXT

(a) THE OLD TESTAMENT

Gen. 4^{16}	1 En. 22^6	Job 28^{25}	1 En. 60^{12}
4^{16}	60^8	28^{26}	60^{22}
5^{29}	107^3	36^{31}	59^1
$6^{1,2}$	$6^{1,2}$	$37^{3,4}$	60^{13-15}
6^4	7^2	$37^{4,5}$	93^{11}
6^9	67^1	37^{13}	59^1
7^{11}	60^7	38^5	93^{13}
7^{11}	89^3	38^6	$18^{1,2}$
7^{11}	101^2	38^7	69^4
7^{16}	89^1	38^{24-27}	59^3
15^{14}	84^3	35^{27}	60^{22}
Exod. 15^{10}	48^{9c}	38^{33}	93^{12}
Num. 16^{30}	106^{13}	$40^{15 \text{sqq.}}$	60^{8-10}
$16^{31,33}$	90^{18}	41	60^7
20^{11}	90^{18}	Ps. 1^5	38^1
$23^{7,18}$	$1^2 \, 37^5$	1^6	94^1
$24^{3,4,15}$	1^2	7^{12}	17^3
Deut. 10^{17}	9^4	12^2	91^4
28^{12}	11^1	$14^{1,3}$	81^5
28^{13}	103^{11}	14^2	91
28^{46}	103^{10}	17^8	100^5
28^{48}	103^{11}	19^{10}	82^3
28^{63}	103^9	22^{14}	98^2
30^{15-19}	$91^{18,19}$	24^2	69^{17}
32^{10}	100^5	34^{12} (LXX)	102^9
32^{17}	$19^1 \, 99^7$	36^{12}	48^{10}
33^1	1^1	37^{11}	5^{7b}
33^2	1^4	49^6	94^8
33^2	1^{9a}	$49^{7,8,9}$	98^{10}
33^{28}	65^{12d}	52^7	94^6
Judges 1^7	95^5	58^{10}	100^1
$5^{4,5}$	$1^{3,6}$	66^{17}	1^4
1 Sam. 29^9	46^{1d}	68^{23}	65^{12d}
2 Kings 2^{11}	70^2	69^{23}	60^{30}
Esther 9^1	103^{12}	69^{28}	$47^3 \, 108^3$
Job 7^7	108^9	72^{11}	48^5
14^2	49^{2bc}	74^1	89^{12}
26^{10}	$69^{13} \, 101^6$	75^4	62^1

Ps. 79^{13}	1 En. 89^{12}	Isa. 49$^{19,\,20}$	1 En. 9^{4}
80^{13}	89^{66}	52^{7}	71^{15}
81^{16}	96^{5}	56^{9}	89$^{55,\,56}$
85^{10}	11^{2}	57^{1}	81^{9}
89^{9}	101^{6}	61^{2}	48^{46}
89^{14}	84^{3}	64$^{1-3}$	1^{6}
97^{5}	1^{6} 52^{6}	65^{16}	5^{64}
100^{3}	89^{12}	65^{17}	45^{4} 91^{16}
104$^{5,\,10,\,13}$	69^{17}	65^{19}	96^{33}
104^{9}	69^{15} 101^{6}	65^{20}	10^{17}
106^{37}	19^{1} 99^{7}	66^{22}	45^{4} 91^{16}
107$^{23-27}$	101^{4}	66^{24}	90^{27}
107^{39}	103^{9}	Jer. 2^{13}	96^{6}
114$^{4,\,6}$	51^{4}	3^{3}	80^{2}
135^{7}	28^{3}	5^{22}	69^{15} 101^{6}
136^{6}	69^{17}	5^{25}	80^{2}
147^{4}	43^{1}	8^{2}	98^{13}
147^{14}	96^{6}	9^{1}	95^{1}
Prov. 5^{1}	85^{3}	10^{13}	28^{3}
8^{22}	69^{19}	12^{9}	89$^{55,\,56}$
8^{29}	101^{6}	21^{8}	91^{15} 94^{2}
8^{30}	84^{3}	22^{13}	94^{7} 99^{13}
11^{1}	99^{12}	23^{1}	89^{13}
11^{28}	94^{8}	31^{37}	93^{14}
14^{12}	94^{2}	32$^{17,\,27}$	84^{3}
17^{13}	95^{5}	49^{16}	96^{2}
20^{22}	95^{5}	51^{16}	28^{3}
Eccles. 11^{5}	93$^{11,\,12}$	Ezek. 26$^{13,\,14}$	18$^{7-9}$
Isa. 2$^{10,\,19,\,21}$	96^{2}	34$^{5,\,8}$	89$^{55,\,56}$
4^{3}	91^{14c}	36^{31}	100^{1}
5^{14}	56^{8}	47^{12}	24^{4}
5^{24}	48^{9}	Dan. 4^{10}	85^{3}
13^{8}	62^{4}	5^{12}	8^{3}
14^{11}	46^{6}	7^{8}	90^{9}
14^{14}	68^{4}	7$^{8,\,11,\,20}$	5^{4}
21^{3}	62^{4}	7^{9}	14^{18}
21^{10}	56^{6}	7^{9}	46^{1} 71^{10}
26^{17}	62^{4}	7^{10}	14$^{19,\,22}$
26^{21}	1^{3}	7^{10}	47^{3} 90^{20}
27^{1}	60^{7}	7^{10}	71^{2}
29^{20}	100^{2b}	7^{13}	46$^{1,\,2}$
33^{7}	40^{8a}	7^{16}	21^{5}
34^{6}	62^{12d}	8^{10}	46^{7}
40^{26}	43^{1}	8^{17}	14^{14}
40^{31}	96^{2}	8^{18}	60^{4}
42^{1}	39^{6}	9^{4}	60^{6}
42^{6}	48^{4b}	10$^{10,\,19}$	60^{4}
43$^{5,\,6}$	57^{1}	10^{20}	56^{5}
43^{19}	106^{13}	11$^{16,\,41}$	89^{40}
45^{1}	60^{3a}	12^{1}	90^{14}
49^{12}	57^{1}	12^{3}	39^{7b}

Index I. Parallel Passages and Phrases

Dan. 12^8	1 En. 104^2	Micah $4^6, 7$	1 En. 90^{33}
Hos. 5^9	102^6	6^{10}	97^8
12^7	99^{12}	Zeph. 1^{18}	100^6
Joel 2^{10}	$80^{6, 7}$	Haggai 2^{22}	100^1
Amos 5^{24}	39^{64}	Zech. $2^{1, 2}$	$61^{1, 2}$
6^6	96^5	9^{10}	71^{15}
8^8	99^{12}	16^{10}	90^{34}
Micah 1^3	$1^{3, 4}$	Mal. 1^7	89^{73}
1^4	$1^6 52^6$	4^1	48^9
$3^2, 3$	96^4		

(b) THE APOCRYPHA AND PSEUDEPIGRAPHA

Sirach 1^{28}	1 En. 91^4	Wisdom 3^5	1 En. 108^9
42^{21}	14^{22}	4^{15}	1^{8b}
Jubilees 4^7	85^6	Pss. Sol. 4^9	1^1
4^{15}	6^6	18^{12-14}	2^1
4^{19}	83^2	Ass. Mos. 10^3	1^3
$4^{21, 23}$	$12^{1, 2}$	10^4	1^4
4^{22}	$10^{11} 12^4$	10^7	1^4
5^9	10^9	2 Enoch $19^6 20^1$	$61^{10} 71^7$
6^{32-36}	74^{12}	21^2	$14^{14, 24}$
$7^{21, 22}$	$7^2 (G^s)$	30^{15}	91^{18}
7^{24}	$7^3 (E G^s)$	33^4	14^{22}
7^{29}	103^7	41^2	38^2
7^{39}	60^8	47^3	37^4
8^{29}	77^6	2 Baruch 10^6	38^2
21^4	63^{6cd}	29^4	60^{7-10}
Test. XII Patr.		29^5	10^{19}
T. Dan. 6^6	40^2	35^2	95^1
T. Naph. $3^2, 3$	91^{14}	4 Ezra 4^{12}	38^2
T. Ash. $1^3, 8$	91^{18}	4^{35}	22^6
6^6	40^2	5^4	80^4
T. Benj. 6^1	40^8	6^{49-52}	60^{7-10}
Tobit 12^{12}	99^3	$7^{28, 29}$	105^2
1 Baruch 3^{34}	43^1	7^{32}	51^1
2 Macc. $11^{6, 8}$	$90^{13, 14}$	$7^{33, 30}$	100^5
Wisdom 2^{2-4}	108^9	$7^{97, 125}$	104^2
$2^{13, 18}$	101^1	14^9	105^2

(c) THE NEW TESTAMENT

Matt. 5^{11}	1 En. 108^{10}	Luke 2^{13}	1 En. 104^6
$10^{21, 34, 35}$	100^2	2^{32}	48^{4b}
12^{36}	97^6	10^{20}	108^7
$13^{39, 41, 49}$	100^4	21^{16}	100^2
$13^{42, 50}$	98^3	John 5^{22}	69^{27}
13^{43}	108^{14}	Acts 4^{12}	48^{7c}
19^{28}	108^{12}	Rom. 8^{38}	61^{10}
22^{30}	104^4	12^{17}	95^5
26^{24}	38^2	1 Cor. 6^{11}	48^{7c}
Mark 13^{12}	100^2	Eph. 1^{21}	61^{10}

Phil. 4^3	1 En. 47^3	Jude 14, 15	1 En. 1^9 5^4
Col. 1^{16}	61^{10}	Rev. 3^d &c.	62^{16}
1 Tim. 1^{15}	94^{1b}	3^5	47^3
6^{16}	14^{21}	9^{20}	99^7
Jas. 1^5	91^4	13^8	5^4
2 Pet. 3^{13}	45^4 91^{16}	14^6	37^5
Jude 4	38^2	14^{20}	100^3
6	10^{12}	20^{12}	47^3
14	60^8	21^1	45^4 91^{16}

INDEX II

NAMES AND SUBJECTS

Aaron, 89$^{16, 31, 37}$.
Abel, 22$^{4, 7}$ 85$^{3, 4, 6}$.
'Abelsjail, 13^9.
Abraham = a white bull, 89^{10}; = the plant of righteous judgement, 93^5.
Abyss, earth swallowed up in a great, 83$^{4, 7}$; place cleft as far as the, 21^7; of complete condemnation, 54^6; of fire, 10^{13}; a deep a. with columns of heavenly fire, 18$^{11, 12}$; full of fire and flaming and full of pillars of fire, 90^{24}; of the earth, 88^3; in the midst of the earth, 90^{26}, cf. 26^1; deep, horrible, and dark, 88^1.
Abyss, of fire, 10^{13} 18^{11} 21^7 54^5 90$^{22-26}$. of the earth, 88^3. Cf. 89^7. See 'Gehenna', 'Punishment'.
Abysses, 77^3; of the earth, 89^7; of the ocean, 60^7; of the sea, 60^9.
See also 'Chasm', 'Deep', 'Depth', 'Ravine', 'Valley'.
Accursed, the, 22^{11} 27^2. See 'Valley'.
Acheron, 17^6 (n.).
Adam, 37^1 32^6 85$^{3-7}$.
Adam and Eve, Book of, xciv, xcv.
Adnar'el, 82^{14}.
Affliction. See 'Day'.
Age, 16^1.
Ages, 9^4 12^3. See 'God'.
Akae, 69^{15}.
Alexander the Great, 89^{50} (n.) 90^1 (n.).
Alexander Jannaeus, 38^5 (n.) 103$^{14, 15}$ (n.).
Alexandra, 38^5 (n.), p. 67.
Aloe-trees, 31^2.
Ammonites = foxes in 89$^{42, 55}$.
Ananel, 6^7.
Anathema, 93^4.
Anatolius of Laodicea, lxxxvii.
Angelology, cv.

Angels:
Cherubim, 14$^{11, 18}$ 20^7 61^{10} 71^7.
Seraphim, 61^{10} 71^7.
Ophannim, 61^{10} 71^7.
the seven, 20$^{1-8}$; holy ones, 81^5; first white ones, 90$^{21, 22}$.
the four, 40$^{2-10}$ 87^2 88^1. Cf. 9^1 10^1, $^{4, 9, 11}$; Michael, Uriel, Raphael, Gabriel, 9^1; Uriel, Raphael, Gabriel, Michael, 10^1, $^{4, 9, 11}$; Michael, Raphael, Gabriel, Phanuel, 40^9.
the three, 87^3; who were clothed in white, 90^{31}.
the Watchers. See 'Watchers'.
symbolized by shepherds, 39^{89}-90^{25}; stars, 86$^{1, 3}$, 88^1; white men, 87^2. Cf. 90$^{21, 22}$.
of natural phenomena, powers on the earth, 61^{10}; over the water, 61^{10}; of the hail, 60^{17}; of the hoar-frost, 60^{17}; of lead and tin, 65^8; of the mist, 60^{19}; angels of the rain, 60^{21}.
of power, 61^{10}.
of principalities, 61^{10}.
intercede for men, 9$^{3-11}$ 15^2 40^6 47^2 99^3 104^1.
of punishment, 40^7 (n.) 53^3 56^1 62^{11} 63^1. Cf. 100^4. See also 'Satans'.
the holy ones (or 'the holy') 9^3 12^2 14^{23} 39^5 47^2 57^2 60^4 61^5, $^{10, 12}$ 65^{12} 69^{13} 71^8 81^5 106^{19}.
holy ones of heaven, 9^3. Cf. 57^2 61^{12}.
holy angels, 20$^{1-8}$ 21$^{5, 9}$ 22^3 24^6 27^2 32^6 71^8 93^2.
children of (the) heaven, 6^2 14^3.
elect and holy children ... from the high heaven, 39^1.
sons of heaven, 13^8.
sons of God, 69$^{4, 5}$; sons of the God of heaven, 106^5; holy sons of God, 71^1.

Angels:
: spiritual ones of the heaven, 15^7.
: spirits of the heaven, 15^{10}.
: who fell, 6^{1-6} (n.) 15^3 $60^{4, 5}$ $86^{1, 3}$ 106^{13}.
: punishment of, 10^{4-15} 12^{4-6} 14^{4-6} 19^1 21^{7-10} 55^4 $67^{4, 6, 7, 11, 12}$ 90^{21-24} 91^{15}.
: See also 'Gabriel', 'Michael', 'Phanuel', 'Raguel', 'Raphael', 'Remiel', 'Saraqael', 'Uriel'; 'Spirits'.

Anger. See 'Wrath'.
Anguish. See 'Day'.
Antigonus, 100^3 (n.).
Antiochus Cyzicenus, 90^{13} (n.).
Antiochus Epiphanes, 46^6 (n.) 90^9 (n.) 100^7 (n.).
Antiochus Sidetes, 90^{13} (n.).
Apostasy, 91^7. See 'Sin'.
Apostate deeds, 93^9.
: generation, 93^9.
Apostolic Constitutions, xcii.
Arakiba, 6^7.
Aramaic original of 1 Enoch, lvii–lxx.
Araqiel, 8^3.
Archelaus, Disputation of, with Manes, xciii.
Aristobulus I, 38^5 (n.) 100^3 (n.).
Aristobulus II, 38^5 (n.).
Armaros, 6^7 8^3 69^2.
Armen, 69^2.
Artaqifa, 69^2.
Asael, 6^7.
Asbeel, 69^2.
Asfa'el, 82^{20}.
Asonja, 78^2.
Ass, wild = Ishmael, 89^{11}.
Asses = a species of giants, 86^4.
: wild = Midianites, $89^{11, 13, 16}$.
Assyrians = tigers in $89^{55, 66}$.
Athenagoras, lxxxii–lxxxiii, 13^6 (n.).
Augustine, xcii, 6^2 (n.).
Azazel, 6^6 (n.) $8^{1, 2}$ 8^3 (G^5) 9^6 $10^{4, 8}$ 13^1 54^5 55^4 69^2 86^1 (n.) 88^1 (n.); all sin ascribed to, 10^8; bound in desert of Dudael, 10^4; hosts of, judged, 54^5 55^4.
†Azazel†, 69^2 6^7 (n.).

Babylonians = lions in $89^{55, 56, 65, 66}$.
Baraqel, 69^2.
Baraqijal, 6^7 8^3.

Bardesanes (?), lxxxv.
Barnabas, Epistle of, lxxxi, 89^{56} (n.).
Baruch, Apocalypse of, influence of 1 Enoch on, lxxvii–lxxviii.
Batarel, 6^7.
Batarjal, 69^2.
Beasts, wild = Gentiles, 85–90 (n.).
Behemoth and Leviathan, $60^{7, 8, 24}$.
Benase, 78^2.
Berka'el, 82^{17}.
Biqa, 69^{13}.
Blasphemy, $91^{7, 11}$ 94^9 96^7. See 'Sin'.
Blessing, $10^{16, 18}$ 41^8 $45^{4, 5}$ $59^{1, 2, 3}$ $76^{4, 13}$.
Blood, $9^{1, 9}$ 15^4 100^1.
: of flesh, 15^4.
: righteous, $47^{2, 4}$.
: sinners, 100^3.
: women, 15^4.
: drink, 7^5.
: eat, 98^{11}.
: shed, 9^1 96^6.
Boar, black wild = Esau, 89^{12}.
Boars, wild = Edomites, 89^{12} (n.) $^{42, 43, 49, 66}$; = Samaritans, 89^{72} 90^{13} (n.).
Book, the (of the Seventy Shepherds), $89^{68, 70, 71, 76, 77}$ $90^{17, 19}$.
Book, sealed, $89^{70, 71}$.
Book of life, 108^3.
: of the words of righteousness, 14^1.
: of unrighteousness, 81^4. Cf. $98^{7, 8}$ 104^7.
: of zeal and wrath, disquiet and expulsion, 39^1.
Books, of heathen writers, 104^{10}; the holy, 103^2 108^3. See also 'heavenly tablets', and cf. 108^7.
Books of the living, 47^3. Cf. 104^1.
Books, opened, 90^{20}.
Bull, symbolically used, 85^{3-9} 86^3 $89^{1, 9-12}$.
: white = Messiah, 90^{37}.
†Busasejal†, 69^2.

Cain, 22^7 85^{3-6}.
Cainan, 37^1.
Camels = a class of giants, 86^4.
Carob tree, 32^4.
Cassianus, xci.
Chambers, $41^{4, 5}$ $60^{12, 13}$.
Chaos, 18^{12} 20^5 $21^{1, 2}$ 108^3.
Chasids, existed as a party before the

Index II. Names and Subjects

Maccabean rising, 90^{6-17} (n.), xi, liii, liv; symbolized by 'lambs', 90^{6-9}.
Chasm, of the abyss of the valley, $56^{3, 4}$.
Chasms, of the earth levelled up, 69^7.
  See also 'Abyss', 'Ravine', 'Valley'.
Chastisement, great, $91^{5, 7}$.
  day of, 102^5.
  visions of, 13^8.
Cherubim. See 'Angels'.
Children, 82^2; slay with mothers, &c., 60^{23}.
  elect and holy, 39^1.
  of destitute, 99^5.
  of earth, 12^4 15^3 86^6 105^1; = sinners, 100^6 102^3.
  of fornication, 10^9.
  of heaven, = Watchers, 6^2 14^3; = righteous, 101^1 (n.).
  of men, $6^{1, 2}$ $10^{7, 21}$ 12^1 $15^{4, 12}$ $22^{3, 5}$ (E) 39^1 40^9 42^2 64^2 69^{4-14}.
  of righteousness, 91^3 93^2.
  of uprightness, 105^2.
  of Watchers, 10^{9-12} 12^4, cf. 14^6.
  See 'Sons'.
Chrysostom, xci.
Clement of Alexandria, lxxxiv, lxxxv, 8^3 16^2 19^3 (notes).
Clementine Homilies, lxxxvii–lxxxix.
Clementine Recognitions, lxxxix.
Cocytus, 17^6 (n.).
Commodianus, lxxxvi.
Compassion, 50^3.
Congregation, of the righteous, 38^1; of the Righteous and Elect One, 53^6; of the elect and holy, 62^8.
Consummation. See 'Day', and cf. 19^1 'made an end of'.
Creation, New, $45^{4, 5}$ (n.) $51^{4, 5}$ 72^1 $91^{15, 16}$.
Cyprian, lxxxvi, lxxxvii.
Cyrus, 89^{40} (n.).

Dan, land of, 13^7; waters of, 13^7.
Danel, 6^7.
Danjal, 69^2.
Darkness, $10^{4, 5}$ $17^{4, 7}$ 41^3 46^6 58^6 60^{19} 62^{10} $63^{6, 11}$ 74^3 77^3 $89^{4, 8}$ 92^5 94^9 102^7 103^8 104^8 $108^{11, 14}$.
David = a lamb, raised to being a ram, 89^{45-46}.

Day, that great, 54^6.
  of ... judgement, $22^{4, 13}$ 97^3 100^4.
  of judgement and ... consummation, 10^{12}.
  of the great judgement, 10^6 19^1 94^9 98^{10} 99^{15} 104^5.
  of judgement, the great, 22^{11} 84^4.
  of affliction, 48^{10} 50^2.
  of anguish and affliction, 48^8.
  of the consummation, 16^1.
  of cursing and chastisement, 102^3.
  of darkness, 94^9.
  of death of the giants, 16^1.
  of destruction, 16^1 98^{10}.
  of slaughter. 16^1 94^9.
  of suffering and tribulation, 45^2 63^8.
  of tribulation, 1^1 96^2.
  of t. and pain, 55^3.
  of t. and great shame, 98^{10}.
  of unceasing bloodshed, 99^6.
  of unrighteousness, 97^1.
Death, $94^{2, 3}$ 98^{16} 102^{10}; due to sin or rather to unrighteous knowledge, 69^{11}.
  a long sleep (for the righteous), 100^5.
Deceit, 91^8 93^8 94^6 104^{10}.
Deep, mouth of, 17^6.
Deluge, 10^2 54^{7-10} 65^1 89^{3-6} 91^5 106^{15}.
  foretold to Noah, 65^1; held in check, 66^2.
Demonology, cv.
  fallen Watchers, 6 69^2, ^{3} 86 $106^{13, 14}$.
  Demons proper, $15^{8, 9, 11}$ 16^1 19 69^{12} 99^7.
Demons = evil spirits, spirits of the giants, $15^{8, 9, 11}$ 16^1; impure spirits, 99^7.
  destroy without incurring judgement until the day of the consummation, 16^1.
  men sacrifice to as gods, 19^1 99^7.
  See 'Angels of punishment', 'Satans'.
Deny. See 'Name'.
Depth, 60^{11}; depths made fast, 69^{19}.
  uttermost, 17^3.
  See also 'Abyss'.
Dogs = Philistines, $89^{42, 44, 47, 49}$.
Dominion. See 'Power'.
Doxologies, Enochic, 22^{14} 25^7 27^5 36^4 39^{9-13} 48^{10} 81^3 83^{11} 84 90^{40}.
Dream-Visions, the, 83–90.
  first, 83^2.

Dream-Visions, second, 85¹.
Dudael, 10⁴.
Duidain, 60⁸.
Dwell on the earth, those that, 37⁵ (n.).
   in good sense, 37², 40⁶, ⁷ 48⁵.
   in bad sense, 54⁹ 55¹ 60⁵ 65⁶, ¹² 66¹ 67⁸.
   merely geographical, 43⁶ 46⁷ 53¹ 54⁶ 55³ 67⁷ 69¹, ⁷ 70¹.
Dwelling-place of the Elect One, 39⁷; of the holy, 39⁴ (n.) ⁷, ⁸ 71¹⁶. See 'Mansions'.

Eagles = Greeks or Macedonians, 90², ⁴, ¹², ¹⁶.
Earth, ends of, 33¹, ² 34¹ 35¹ 36¹ 65² 76¹ 106⁹. See 'Ends'.
   middle of = Jerusalem, 26¹.
   abyss in midst of = Gehenna, 90²⁶.
   pillars of, 57².
   cleanse, 10²⁰, ²² ; heal, 10⁷.
   shall rejoice, 51⁵.
   God will transform, 45⁵.
   elect shall inherit, 5⁷.
   elect shall walk thereon, 51⁵.
   righteous shall dwell upon it, 51⁵.
Ebla, 78².
Edna, wife of Enoch, 85³. Cf. 83².
Edomites = wild boars in 89¹² (n.) ⁴², ⁴³, ⁶⁶, ⁷² 90¹³ (n.); = (?) Kites, 90¹¹.
Egypt, Exodus from, 89²²⁻²⁷.
   Plagues of, 89²⁰.
Egyptians = wolves in 89¹³⁻²⁷, ⁵⁵.
Elect, the, 1¹, ⁸ 5⁷ 25⁵ 40⁵ 41³ 48¹ 51⁵ 56⁶ 58¹⁻³ 61⁴, ¹² 62², ⁸ 93².
   and beloved ones, their, 56², ⁴.
   and holy, 62⁵.
   and holy children (= angels), 39¹.
   and righteous, 1¹ 60⁸.
   covenant for, 60⁶.
   dwell in garden of life, 61¹².
   dwell with elect, 61⁴.
   God will protect, 1⁸.
   in the light of eternal life, 58³.
   inherit the earth, 5⁷.
   light, grace, and peace shall be to, 5⁷ᵃ.
   live and never again sin, 5⁹.
   mansions of, 41².
   of the world, 93¹.
   One, the, 40⁵ (n.) 49², ⁴ 51³, ⁵ 52⁶, ⁹ 53⁶ 61⁵, ⁸, ¹⁰ 62¹.

Elect One, Mine, 45³, ⁴ 55⁴.
   One of righteousness and faith, 39⁶.
   ones, His, 56⁶ 62¹¹, ¹².
   ones, Mine, 45⁵, ⁵ 48⁹.
   Son of Man revealed to, 62⁷.
   stand before Son of Man, 62⁸.
   tree of life, its fruit food for, 25⁵.
   walk on renewed earth, 51⁵.
   who hang upon Lord of Spirits, 40⁵. Cf. 38².
   wisdom bestowed upon, 5⁸.
   works (of righteous), 38².
   See also 'Righteous' and 'Holy'.
Elephants = a class of giants, 86⁴.
Elijah, 89⁵² (n.) 93⁸.
'Elome'el, 82¹⁴.
Enchantments, 7¹ 8³. Cf. 65⁶.
End (destruction of the world), 10² 65⁶; first, 93⁴.
   of all generations, 10¹⁵.
   of the righteous, 102¹⁰.
   of heavens, 39³.
   of heaven and earth, 18¹⁴.
Ends, of all, 19³.
   of earth, 1⁵ 18⁵ 23¹ 33¹, ² 34¹ 35¹ 36¹ 65² 76¹ 106⁹.
   of heaven, 36² 54⁹ 57² 60¹¹, ²⁰ 71⁴ 93¹².

Enoch, the First Book of. See Introduction, ix sqq.
   Account of (short), ix–xii.
   Canonicity, xiii–xiv.
   Critical inquiries, xxx–xlvi.
   Elements (different) in 1 Enoch, xi, xlvi–lii; characteristics and dates of, lii–lvi.
   Element (poetical) in 1 Enoch, lvi.
   Influence on Jewish Literature, New Testament, Patristic Literature. See under 'Jewish Literature', 'New Testament', and 'Patristic Literature'.
   Language, original, of, 1–5, lvii–lviii; 6–36, lviii–lxi; 37–71, lxi–lxviii; 72–82, lxviii–lxix; 83–90, lxix; 91–104, lxix–lxx.
   Noachic fragments in, xlvi–xlvii.
   Title, xii, xiii.
   Translations, xxix, xxx.

Index II. Names and Subjects

Enoch:
  Versions, Greek, editions of, xiv–xvi; relations of, to each other, and to E., xvi–xix.
    Latin, and Quotations, xix, xx.
    Ethiopic, xx, xxi; MSS. of, xxi–xxiv; MSS. relations of, xxiv–xxvii; editions of, xxvii–xxix.
Enoch, the Second Book of. See Index I. The Hebrew Book of, lxxix–lxxxi.
Enoch, $1^{1, 2}$ $12^{1, 3}$ 13^1 14^{24} 15^1 19^3 $21^{5, 9}$ 25^1 37^1 39^2 †60^1† $65^{2, 5, 9}$ 66^3 67^4 68^1 69^{29} 80^1 81^1 85^2 91^3 92^1 $93^{1, 2, 3}$ $106^{7, 13}$ 107^3 108^1.
  the scribe, 12^3.
  scribe of righteousness, 12^4 15^1.
  translation of, in a vision, $14^{8, 9}$; in sleep, $13^{7, 10}$ 14^2; a real, 39^3 52^1. Cf. 'hidden', 12^1; final (name raised aloft), 70^1; in spirit, $71^{1, 5, 6}$.
Enos, 37^1.
Erae, 78^2.
Erythraean Sea, 32^2.
Esau = black wild boar, 89^{12}.
Essenes, 89^{73} (n.) 108 (n.), ciii, civ.
Eternal destruction, 84^5.
  goodness and grace, 92^3.
  judgement, 91^{15}. Cf. 91^9.
  King. See 'God'.
  law, 99^2.
  life, 10^{10} $15^{4, 6}$ 37^4 40^9 58^3. Cf. 5^1. See 'Life'.
  light, 92^4.
  plant, 93^{10}. See 'Plant'.
  seed, 84^6.
  uprightness, 92^4.
Eternity, 69^{18} 72^1.
  For ever(more), $10^{5, 16, 22}$ 22^{11} 24^4 25^4 $27^{2, 3}$ 36^4 39^{10-12} 40^4 46^3 47^2 48^6 58^6 $65^{11, 12}$ 67^{13} 69^{16} 77^1 84^2 92^5 91^1 93^7 $91^{13, 17}$ $102^{2, 8}$.
  For ever and ever, 39^6 53^2 $61^{3, 11}$ $67^{3, 9}$ $71^{15, 16, 17}$ 84^2.
Ethiopians = hyenas in 89^{55}.
Euphrates, 77^6 (n.).
Eve, led astray by a Satan, 69^6.
  history of, $85^{3–7}$.
Evil, 10^{16} $15^{2, 9}$ 16^3 69^{29} 94^5 99^{11} 101^1 103^9 108^2.
  origin of, civ, cv.
Exodus. See 'Egypt'.

Ezeqeel, 6^7 8^3.
Ezra, 89^{73} (n.).
Ezra, Fourth Book of, influence of 1 Enoch on, lxxviii–lxxix.

Face, of Elect One, unrighteous destroyed from before, 62^3; lifted up His countenance to judge, 61^9.
  of God, no angel could behold, 14^{21}.
    Elect One shall appear before, 52^9.
    sinners destroyed before, 53^2.
    we pass away from before, 63^9.
    hide not Thy face, 84^6.
    dazzling and glorious and terrible to behold, 89^{22}, cf. 89^{30}.
    flee before, 89^{28}.
    afraid before, 89^{30}.
    their memorial before, 103^4.
    Cf. 'presence', 84^3 90^{34}, 'appearance', 89^{30}.
Faces of angels, 51^4 71^1.
Faith, 39^6 (n.) 43^4 58^5 $61^{4, 11}$.
  Elect One of, 39^6.
  heritage of, 58^5.
  measures given to, 61^4.
  spirit of, 61^{11}.
  See 'Messiah', 'Salvation'.
Faithful, 46^{8n}, cvi.
Fire, 10^6 $14^{12, 17, 19, 22}$ $17^{1, 5}$ 21^7 39^7 54^1 71^{3-6} 72^4 $90^{24, 26}$ 91^9 100^9 108^3.
  abyss of, 10^{13} &c. See 'Abyss'.
  ever burning, 67^{13}.
  grievous, 102^1.
  of West, 17^4 23^2.
  columns of, 18^{11} 21^7 90^{24}.
  flames of, 71^1 72^7 103^8 $105^{4, 5}$.
  furnace of, 98^3.
  mountain range of, 24^1.
  river of, 17^5.
  streams of, 14^{19} 17^5 67^7 $71^{2, 6}$.
Firmament, $18^2, ^{12}$.
Flesh, 1^9 7^5 14^{21} 15^8 16^1 17^6 61^{12} 84^6 106^{17} 108^{11}.
  and blood, 15^4.
  of man, $84^{4, 5}$.
  of righteousness, 84^6.
Forgiveness, 5^6 12^6 $13^{4, 6}$.
Fountain beneath the earth, 54^7.
  opened, 89^2.
  produces lead and tin, 65^8.
  of life, 96^6.

Fountain:
  of the righteous and holy, 65^{12}.
  of righteousness, 48^1.
  of wisdom, 48^1.
  See 'Spring'.
Foxes = Ammonites, $89^{42, 55}$.

Gabriel, 9^1 10^9 20^7 40^9 54^6.
Gadreel, 69^6.
Garden of life, 61^{12}.
  of Righteousness, 32^3 77^3.
  of the Righteous, 60^{23}.
  where the elect and righteous dwell, 60^8 61^{12}. Cf. the place for the elect and righteous, 70^3. Cf. 65^2 89^{52}. See also 'Paradise'.
Garments of glory, 62^{16}.
  of life, 62^{16}. Cf. 108^{12}.
  white, 71^1.
Gehenna:
  (1) place of corporal and spiritual punishment—in the presence of the righteous for ever, 27^2, 3 $90^{26, 27}$; in the presence of the righteous for a time only, 48^9 $62^{12, 13}$, i.e. in 37–70.
  (2) place of spiritual punishment only, 98^3. Cf. 103^8, i.e. in 91–104. See also 'Punishment', 'Sheol', 'Valley'.
Gentiles, conversion of, 50^{2-5} 90^{30} (n.) 91^{14}, cix.
  the Son of Man, the light of, 48^4.
Giants, $7^{2, 4}$ 9^9 15^3, ^{11} 16^1. Cf. 86^4 88^2.
Gida'ijal, 82^{20}.
Glory, 9^4 $14^{20, 21}$ 25^7 39^{12} 47^3 $49^{1, 2}$ 50^1 55^4 60^2 61^8 $62^{2, 3, 5, 16}$ $63^{2, 7}$ $69^{13, 27, 29}$ 71^7 81^3 91^{13} 96^3 99^{16} 102^3 $103^{1, 3}$ 104^1. Cf. 'splendour', 14^{16}; 'grandeur and splendour', 96^3.
  the Great, 14^{20} 102^3. See 'God'.
  of the Great One, 104^1.
Gnostic Literature, influence of 1 Enoch on, xcii–xcv.
God, titles of:
  Blessed for ever, He who is, 77^1.
  Creator, 81^5 94^{10}.
  Eternal God, 1^4.
  Eternal King, $25^{3, 5, 7}$ 27^3.
  Eternal Lord, 58^4.

God, titles of:
  God of glory, 25^7.
  God of gods, 9^4.
  God of heaven, 106^5.
  God of the ages, 9^4.
  God of the whole world, 84^2.
  Glory, the Great, 14^{20} 102^3.
  Great One, the, 14^2 $103^{1, 4}$ 104^1 (twice).
  Great Holy One, the, 97^6.
  Head of days, One who had a, 46^1.
  Head of days, the, 46^2 47^3 48^2 55^1 60^2 $71^{10, 12, 13, 14}$.
  Holy One, the, 1^2 37^2 93^{11}.
  Holy (and) Great One, 1^3 10^1 14^1 25^3 84^1 92^2 98^6 104^9.
  Honoured (One), the, 103^1.
  King, 84^2.
  King, great, 84^5 91^{13}.
  King of the ages, 12^3.
  King of glory for ever, 81^3.
  King of kings, 9^4 84^2. Cf. 63^4.
  Liveth for ever, He that, 5^1 $106^{3, 11}$ (Lat. Frag.).
  Lord, My, 22^{14} 84^6.
  Lord, the Great, 81^3.
  Lord the Most High, the, 98^{11}.
  Lord of the ages, 9^4.
  Lord of glory, 22^{14} 25^3 $27^{3, 5}$ 36^4 40^3 63^2 75^3 83^8.
  Lord of heaven, 106^{11}.
  Lord of judgement, 83^{11}.
  Lord of kings, $63^{3, 4}$.
  Lord of lords, 9^4.
  Lord of majesty, 12^3.
  Lord of the mighty, 63^2.
  Lord of the rich, 63^2.
  Lord of righteousness, 22^{14} 90^{40} 106^3.
  Lord of Spirits, 37^2 (n.) ^{4} $38^{2, 4, 6}$ $39^{2, 7, 8, 9, 12}$ $40^{1, 2, 4, 5, 6, 7, 10}$ $41^{2, 6, 7}$ 43^4 $45^{1, 2}$ $46^{3, 4, 7, 8}$ $47^{1, 2, 4}$ $48^{2, 3, 5, 7, 10}$ $49^{2, 4}$ $50^{2, 3, 5}$ 51^3 52^5, ^{9} 53^6 $54^{5, 7}$ $55^{3, 4}$ 57^3 $58^{4, 6}$ $59^{1, 2}$ $60^{6, 8, 24, 25}$ $61^{3, 5, 8, 9, 11, 13}$ $62^{2, 10, 12, 14, 16}$ $63^{1, 2, 7, 12}$ 65^9, ^{11} 66^2 $67^{8, 9}$ 68^4 $69^{24, 29}$ 70^1 $71^{2, 17}$.
  Lord of the sheep, $89^{16, 22, 26, 29, 33, 36, 42, 45, 50, 51, 52, 54, 57, 70, 71, 75, 76}$, $90^{14-20, 29, 33}$.
  Lord of the whole creation of the heaven, 84^2.
  Lord of wisdom, 63^2.

God, titles of:
- Lord of the world, 81¹⁰.
- Mighty One in dominion, 103¹.
- Most High, 9⁸ 10¹ 46⁷ 60¹, ²² 62⁷ 77¹ 94⁸ 97² 98⁷, ¹¹ 99³, ¹⁰ 106⁴ 101¹, ⁴, ⁹.
- Ruleth for ever, Who, 22¹⁴ (E).
- Rulest over the world, Who, 22¹⁴ (Gˢ).

Godless, 1¹ 5⁷ 16¹ 38³ 81⁹ 91¹⁴ 94¹¹ 98¹³ 99⁸, ¹⁰.

Godlessness, 10²⁰ 104⁹.

Graeco-Egyptians = vultures and kites in 90². Cf. 90¹¹, ¹³ (n.).

Greeks or Macedonians = eagles, 90², ⁴, ¹³, ¹⁶.

Hananel, 69².
Head of Days. See 'God'.
Head to be, 103¹¹.
Healing, 95⁴; of the body, 67⁸.
  of the earth, 10⁷.
Heart, 14² 47⁴ 48⁴ 68⁸ 93⁵ 94⁵ 95¹ 96⁴ 98⁷ 99⁸, ¹⁶ 104⁹.
  double, 91⁴.
Heaven, 6² 14⁵, ¹¹ 15³ 21², ³ 33² 45⁴ 47³ 55² 57² 61⁶, ¹² 69¹⁶ 75¹⁷ 79¹ 80¹, ² 83³ 83¹¹ 86¹, ³ 93¹², ¹⁴ 101¹, ⁸ 104², ⁶ 108⁸, ¹⁰.
  of heavens, 1⁴ 60¹ 71⁵.
  children of = angels, 6² 14³ ; = righteous, 101¹.
  end of, 18¹⁴. See 'Ends'.
  first, 91¹⁶.
  high, 12⁴ 39¹.
  high, holy, and eternal, 15³.
  host of, 104⁶.
  new, 91¹⁶.
  See 'Angels', 'God'.
Heavenly. See 'Luminaries', 'Tablets', 'Visions'.
Heavens, 1² 18¹⁰ 39³ 41¹ 42¹ 47² 61¹⁰ 71¹, ⁸ 84³ 91¹⁶ 98⁶.
  host of, 61¹⁰.
  powers of, 91¹⁶.
Hebrew, original, of 1 Enoch. See lvii-lxx.
He'el, 82²⁰.
Hel'emmelek, 82¹³, ¹⁸.
Hell, 51¹ (n.).
Hermon, 6⁶ (n.) 13⁷.
Herod, 67⁸ (n.).
Herodian princes, p. 67.

Hilary, xci 6⁶ (n.).
Hilujaseph, 82¹⁷.
Hinnom, valley of (see Gehenna), 26⁴, ⁶.
Hippolytus, lxxxvii.
Hollow places (= Sheol), 22², ³, ⁸.
Holy, 1⁹ 9³ 12² 38⁵ 39¹, ⁴, ⁵ 41² 43⁴ 45¹ 47², ⁴ 48¹, ⁹ 50¹ 51² 57² 58³, ⁵ 60⁴ 61⁸, ¹⁰, ¹² 62⁶ 65¹² 103² 106¹⁹.
  heaven, 15³.
  Holy, holy, holy, 39¹².
  Lord, 91⁷.
  name (of God) 9⁴ 108¹².
  One. See 'God'.
  ones. See 'Angels'.
  place, 25⁵.
  eternal place, 12⁴.
  righteous and elect, 38⁴; and elect, 50¹.
  Watchers, 15⁴, ⁹.
  See 'Elect', 'God', 'Righteous'.
Honour, 50¹ 103⁶ 108¹¹, ¹².
Horn, the great = Judas Maccabaeus, 90⁹ (n.).
Host of the heavens, 61¹⁰, 104⁶. Cf. 1⁹ 60¹.
Hosts of Azazel, 54⁵ 55⁴.
Hours, 89⁷² (n.). Cf. 'periods', 90¹; 'times', 90⁵.
House, for the Great King, 91¹³.
  for the Lord of the sheep, 89³⁴, ⁴⁰.
  of dominion, 93⁸.
  of glory and dominion, 93⁷.
  of the sheep, 89²⁰, ⁵¹, ⁵⁶ 90²⁹.
  a new, 90²⁹.
Hyenas = Ethiopians, or (?) Syrians, 89⁵⁵ (n.).
Hyrcanus, John, 38⁵ (n.) 90⁹ (n.) ¹³ (n.) 103¹⁴, ¹⁵ (n.), p. 222.
Hyrcanus II, 38⁵ (n.).

Ijasusa'el, 82¹⁴.
Images, 65⁶ 99⁷.
Indus, 77⁷ (n.).
Innumerable places of rest, 45³.
  secrets of God, 63³.
  See 'Number'.
Inquiries, critical. See under 'First Book of Enoch'.
Intercession, by angels for men, 9², ³ 15². See 'Angels'.
Irenaeus, lxxxiii-lxxxiv, 13⁶ (n.).

Isaac = 'a white bull', 89¹¹.
Ishmael = 'a wild ass', 89¹¹.
Islands, the Seven Great, 77⁸.

Jacob = 'a white sheep', 89¹².
Jared, 6⁶ 37¹ 106¹³.
Jaxartes, 77⁷ (n.).
Jehoshaphat, valley of, 26³ 53¹ (n.).
Jeqon, 69⁴.
Jerome, xci.
Jerusalem = 'the holy place', 25⁵ (n.).
  'the city of my righteous', 56⁷.
  'the house' (of the sheep), 89⁵⁰, ⁵¹, ⁵⁶ 90³⁶.
  New Jerusalem, symbolized by 'a new house', 90²⁹.
Jetrel, 69².
Jewish Literature, influence of 1 Enoch on, lxx-lxxxi.
Jomjael, 6⁷.
Jonathan Maccabaeus, 90⁶ (n.).
Jordan = 'a stream of water', 89³⁷ (n.).
Joseph = 'one of them' (the twelve sheep), 89¹³.
Joseph of Arimathaea, Narrative of, xciii, xciv.
Joshua, the high priest, 89⁷² (n.).
Joshua and the Judges, the time of, 89³⁹ (n.).
Joy, 10¹⁶ 47⁴ 51⁵ 69²⁶ 103³ 104⁴.
Jubilees, Book of, lxx-lxxv, 7², ⁸ 16¹ 98¹¹ (notes).
Judaism and apocalyptic, ix, ciii.
  religious development of, x.
Judas Maccabaeus, 90⁹ (n.) ¹⁰⁻¹².
Judgement, cix, cx, 45² (n.) 17⁷, ⁹ 14⁴ 22¹⁰, ¹¹, ¹³ 45⁶ 47² 50⁴ 60⁴, ²⁵ 63⁴, ¹² 65¹⁰ 66¹ 67¹⁰, ¹², ¹³ 68², ³, ⁵ 69¹, ²⁷ 81⁴ 83¹¹ 84⁴ 90⁴, ³¹ 91⁷ 93³, ⁵ 91¹⁴, ¹⁵ 95², ³ 96⁵ 97³, ⁵ 98², ¹⁰ 99¹⁵ 100¹⁰ 103⁴, ⁸ 104³.
  eternal, 91¹⁵ 104⁵, cf. 10¹².
  great, 16¹ 22⁴ 25⁴ 91¹⁵ 94⁹ 98¹⁰ 100⁴ 103⁸ 104⁵.
  grievous, 91⁹.
  righteous, 27³ 60⁶ 61⁹ 91¹⁴.
  true, 27³.
  of angels, 68².
  of fire, 91⁹.
  of God, 108¹³.
  of secrets, 68².

Judgement:
  Differing conceptions of:
  (1) First World Judgement—over men = Deluge, 54⁷⁻¹⁰; 'a great chastisement', 91⁵; 'the first end', 93⁴; when the earth and those who dwell on it will be destroyed, 10² 106¹⁵; over fallen angels and giants, 10⁴, ⁶, ¹², ¹⁵.
  (2) Judgement of the Sword at the *beginning* of the Messianic kingdom, when the righteous are victorious and slay the wicked, 50² 90¹⁹ 91¹² 95⁷ 96¹ 98¹².
  (3) Final World Judgement at the beginning of the Messianic kingdom, 'the great judgement', 10⁶ 16¹ 19¹ 22⁴; 'the great day', 22¹¹ 54⁶; 'the judgement that is for ever and ever', 10¹²ᶜ—over Azazel and his hosts, 54⁵ 55⁴; over their elect and beloved children, 56³; over the fallen stars, the seventy shepherds, and the blinded sheep, 90²⁰⁻²⁷.
  (4) Final World Judgement at the *close* of the Messianic kingdom —'great judgement', 94⁹ 98¹⁰ 100⁴ 103⁸ 104⁵.
  (2) and (3) are combined in 48⁸⁻¹⁰.
  (2) and (4) are combined in 99⁹, ¹⁵.
  See also 'Day', 'Messianic Kingdom', 'Punishment'.
Julius Africanus, lxxxv.
Justin Martyr, lxxxii, 8⁸, ⁹ (n.) 15⁸ (n.).

Kasbeel, 69¹³.
Kasdeja, 69¹².
Kedron, 26² (n.).
Ke'el, 82²⁰.
Kingdom. See 'Messianic Kingdom'.
Kings and the mighty, 38⁵ 62¹, ³, ⁴, ⁹ 63¹, ², ¹² 67⁸, ¹².
Kites = Egyptians under the Ptolemies, 90² (n.).
  = (?) Edomites, 90¹³ (n.).
Kokabel, 8² 69².
Kokabiel, 6⁷.

Lactantius, lxxxix-xci.
Lambs = Chasids, 90⁶⁻¹⁷ (n.) ⁸, ⁹.

Index II. Names and Subjects

Lamb = Samuel, David, 89^{45}.
Lamech, 10^1 $106^{1, 4, 10, 13, 18}$.
Land (= Palestine), blessed, 27^1.
   of His elect ones, 56^6.
   a pleasant and glorious, 89^{40}.
Law, 93^6 106^{14} 108^1, cf. 5^4 99^{14}.
   eternal, 99^2.
   of luminaries, $72^{1, 2}$.
     moon, 73^1 74^1.
     stars, 79^1.
     sun, 72^{35}.
     twelve portals, 76^{14}.
   for sinners, 93^4.
Law and Prophecy, x.
Leader, 82^{20}.
   of day and night, 75^3.
   of sheep, 89^{48}.
   of stars, 72^3 74^2 80^1 $82^{10, 11}$.
Lebanon, 13^9.
Length, of days, 10^9 71^{17}. Cf. 13^6.
Leviathan, 60^7.
Life, $5^{4, 9}$ 14^{13} 22^{10} 38^4 48^7 56^4 58^3
   $61^{7, 12}$ 62^{16} 67^2 96^6 98^{14} 103^9 108^{10}.
   elect, 94^4.
   eternal (= everlasting), $15^{4, 6}$ 37^4 40^9
     58^3 ; (= 500 years) 10^{10}.
   long, 25^6.
   to see, 103^{10}.
Live, 10^{17} 98^{10}.
Living, 47^2.
Light, eternal, 45^4 92^4 ; generation of,
   108^{11}.
   spirit of, 61^{12} $(n.)$.
   shall appear to the righteous and
     elect, $38^{2, 4}$ $(n.)$ 1^8 5^7 50^1 $58^{3, 4, 6}$.
   righteous (clad) in shining, 108^{12} ;
     shall walk in eternal, 92^4 ; shine
     as the lights of heaven, 104^2.
   (of the Lord of Spirits), 38^4 $(n.)$.
   of days shall abide upon the holy and
     elect, 50^1.
   of the sun, the righteous shall be in,
     58^3.
   of eternal life, the elect shall be in,
     58^3.
   of uprightness established for ever,
     58^4.
   of the Gentiles, 48^4.
Lights, of heaven, righteous shine as,
   104^2.
Lights, $59^{1, 3}$.

Lightning, $14^{11, 17}$ 17^3 41^3 43^{1-2} 44
   $59^{1, 3}$ 60^{13-15}.
Lions = Babylonians, 89^{68} $(n.)$.
Long-suffering, 60^5 61^{13}.
Lordship. See 'Power'.
Luminaries, 17^3 ; world of the, 20^4.
   of heaven, 23^4 $72^{1, 2}$ 79^6 82^7.
Luminary, the great, named the sun,
   $72^{4, 35, 36}$.
   the smaller, named the moon, 73^1.
Lunar Year, 74.

Maccabean princes, p. 67.
Maccabees, rise of, p. 67, 90^{6-17} $(n.)$.
Macedonians. See 'Greeks'.
Mahalel, 37^1 $83^{3, 4}$.
Man, 7^3 8^4 10^9 13^2 $14^{2, 3}$ 15^2 17^1 $19^{1, 3}$
   $20^{3, 5}$ $22^{7, 13}$ 36^4 $41^{1, 8}$ 57^1 67^4
   $69^{9, 10, 11}$ 75^2 81^2 82^5 84^1 91^{14} 94^5
   98^4 106^{16} 105^{10}.
   white men, 87^2.
Man, Son of. See 'Son'.
Mankind, 19^1 20^5 67^6 81^2 91^{14} 106^{16}.
Mansions, 41^2. See 'Dwelling-places'.
Marriage, ciii-civ, 83^2 $(n.)$.
Mel'ejal, 82^{13}.
Melkejal, 82^{13}.
Memorial, 103^4. See 'Testimony'.
Merciful, 60^5.
Mercy, 61^{13} ; no, 5^6 50^3.
Messiah, 38^2 $(n.)$ $46^{2, 3}$ $(n.)$ 48^{10} $(n.)$
   90^{37} $(n.)$.
Messiah, variously conceived by the
   different authors, liv-lvi, cix.
   titles of :
     Anointed (God's), 52^4.
     Elect One, Mine, $45^{3, 4}$ 55^4.
     Elect One, the, $49^{2, 4}$ $51^{5, 3}$ $52^{6, 9}$
       $61^{5, 8, 10}$ 62^1.
     Elect One of righteousness and faith,
       39^6.
     Righteous One, 38^2.
     Righteous and Elect One, 53^6.
     Son of Man, $46^{2, 3, 4}$ 48^2 $62^{5, 7, 9, 14}$
       63^{11} $69^{26, 27, 29}$ 70^1 $71^{14, 17}$. See
       'Son'.
     Son, My (God's), 105^2.
Messianic Kingdom, liv-lvi, cviii-cix,
   5^{6-9} $10^{16}-11^2$ 27^{4-6} 38^1-39^2 45^{3-6}
   46^4-52^5 $53^{6, 7}$ 58 61 62 69^{26-29}
   71^{14-17} 90^{38} 91^{12-15}.

Messianic Kingdom:
   eternal, on earth, after final judgement, 1-36.
   temporary, on earth, followed by final judgement, 91-104.
   eternal, on earth and in heaven, initiated by final judgement, 37-71.

Methuselah, 76^{14} 81^5 82^1 $83^{1,9}$ 85^2 $91^{1,2}$ $106^{4,8}$ 107^3.

Michael, 9^1 10^{11} 20^5 24^6 40^9 54^6 $60^{4,5}$ 67^{12} $68^{2,3,4}$ $69^{14,15}$ $71^{3,8,9,13}$.

Midianites = the asses in $89^{13,16}$.

Might. See 'Power'.

Milki'el, 82^{13}.

Minucius Felix, lxxxiii.

Month, $74^{4,5}$.

Moon, 8^3 $41^{6,7}$ 60^{12} 69^{20} 72^{3} 72^{37}–74^{17} $75^{3,6}$ $78^{3,4,6}$ $80^{1,4}$ 82^6 83^{11} 100^{10}.
   names of, 78^3.

Moses, $89^{16-18, 29-38}$.

Moses, Assumption of, influence of 1 Enoch on, lxxvi-lxxvii.

Mountain, 1^4 29^1 $31^{1,2}$ $32^{1,3}$ 51^4 53^7 60^{16} 69^{17} 83^4 98^4.
   great and high, of hard rock, in which is Sheol), 22^1.
   God's throne, 25^3.
   whose summit reached to heaven, 17^2.
   of fire, 24^1.
   (Zion), 26^2.
   (Mount of Olives), 26^3.
   (Mount of Evil Counsel), 26^4.

Mountains, great burning, 18^{13} 21^3.
   Seven, $18^{4,9}$ 24^2 32^1.
   seven high, 77^4.
   shining, 108^4.
   of darkness of winter, 17^7.
   of iron, copper, &c., $52^{2,6}$ 67^4.

Myrrh, 29^2.

Mysteries, 7^1 $8^{1,3}$ 16^3 106^{19}.

Mystery, 103^2 104^{10}.

Name, 9^4 $39^{7,9,13}$ $41^{2,6}$ 43^4 45^2 $46^{6,7,8}$ 47^2 $61^{11,12}$ 63^7 $67^{3,8}$ 69^{24} 108^9.
   in the name, 10^3 40^6 41^8 48^7 $50^{2,3}$ 55^4 58^6 61^{13} $67^{3,8}$.
   blessed, 9^4 61^{12}.
   glorious, 9^4 45^3.
   great, 55^3.
   holy, 9^4 108^{12}.

Name:
   of dwelling of the holy, 45^1.
   Enoch (= his person), 65^{12} $70^{1,2}$.
   His righteousness, 41^6.
   the holy, 43^4.
   the Lord of Spirits, 40^6 43^4 $46^{6,8}$ 47^2 48^7 $50^{2,3}$ 55^4 61^{13} 63^7 69^{24}; those who deny the, 41^2 45^2 46^7. Cf. 38^2 (n.); not glorified, 63^7; be blessed, 39^{13} 48^{10} 61^{11}; righteous saved in, 48^7.
   Son of Man, $48^{2,3}$ 69^{26}.
   world to come, 71^{15}.

Names, 5^6.
   blotted out of book of life, 108^3.
   call by, 43^1 69^{21}.
   written, 104^1.

Narel, 82^{13}.

Nectar, 31^1.

Nehemiah, 89^{72} (n.).

†Neqael†, 69^2.

New. See 'Creation', 'Heaven'.

New Testament, influence of 1 Enoch on, xcv-ciii.
   meaning of 'Son of Man' in, p. 307.

Noah, 10^2 $65^{1,2}$ 67^1 106^{18} 107^3.
   Book of. See 'Enoch, First Book of'.

North, 61^1 70^3.

Number of Kasbeel, 69^{13}.
   of righteous, 47^4.
   of stars, 93^{14}.
   no number of corpses, 56^7.
   beyond number, 40^1.
   without number, angels, 71^8, cf. 71^8; days of holy, 58^3; fountain of righteous, 65^{12}; times, 108^{13}; weeks, 91^{17}.
   See 'Innumerable'.

Oath, $69^{13-21, 25}$.

Ocean stream, 17^5 (n.).

Onias III, 90^{6-17} (n.) $^{6-7}$ (n.).

Ophannim. See 'Angels'.

Oppression, 94^6 $98^{4,8}$ 99^{15}. See 'Sin'.

Oppressors, 91^{12}.

Origen, lxxxv, 16^3 19^3 (notes).

Orjares, 78^1.

Oxus, 77^1 (n.).

Palestine. See 'Land'.

Parable, $1^{2,3}$ 38^1 43^4 45^1 57^3 58^1 60^1 68^1 69^{29}.

Index II. Names and Subjects

Parables, the = 37-71.
  First, 38^1.
  Second, 45^1.
  Third, 58^1.
  the Book of, 68^1.
Paradise, 20^7.
Parthians and Medes, 56^5.
Paths, good, 91^4.
  of death, 94^4.
    peace, 94^4.
    righteousness, 92^3 $91^{18, 19}$ 94^1 99^{10}.
    unrighteousness, 91^{19} 94^1.
    uprightness, 91^{14} 104^{13} 105^2.
    violence, $91^{18, 19}$.
    wickedness, 94^3.
Patience, 60^{25}. See 'Spirit'.
Patristic literature, influence of 1 Enoch on, lxxxi-xcv.
Paul, Apocalypse of, xciv.
Peace, $5^{7, 9}$ 10^{17} 11^2 58^4 $71^{15, 17}$ 92^1.
  no, 1^8 5^4 11^2 12^6 13^1 16^4 94^6 $98^{11, 15}$ 99^{13} 101^3 102^3 103^8.
Penemue, 69^8.
Periods. See 'Hours'.
Perpetua and Felicitas, Acts of, lxxxvi.
Peter, Apocalypse of, lxxxi-lxxxii, 106^{10}.
Petition, of the Watchers, $13^{4, 6}$ $14^{4, 7}$.
Phanuel (only in the Parables), 40^9 54^6 $71^{8, 9, 13}$.
Pharisaic exclusiveness, 97^4 104^6.
Pharisees, religious and literary strife with the Sadducees or Hellenistic party, 98^{15} (n.) 102^4-104^{13}.
  their varying relations with the Maccabees, liii, liv.
  — 'the children of heaven', 101^1.
Philistines = dogs in $89^{42, 46, 47, 49}$.
Pistis Sophia, xcii, xciii.
Plant, of righteousness and truth, 10^{16} (n.).
  of righteousness, 93^5.
  of righteousness, the eternal, 93^{10}.
  of righteous judgement, 93^5.
  of uprightness, 93^2.
  of the eternal seed, 84^6.
Power, 9^5 41^9 46^7 $60^{6, 12, 15}$ $61^{6, 10}$ 63^3 65^6 68^2 $69^{11, 13}$ 71^{11} 82^9 92^4 98^2.
  angels of, 61^{10}.
  powers of heaven, 82^8.
    on earth, 61^{10}.
    over water, 61^{10}.

Power:
  Dominion, 52^4 84^2 93^8.
  Lordship, 96^1.
  Might, 49^3 62^7 108^2.
Prayer, of righteous, $47^{1, 2, 4}$ $97^{3, 5}$ 99^3.
Presences, the four, 40^{1-8}. See 'Angels'.
Priscillian, xci.
Prophecy and Law, x.
Prophets, 108^6.
Pseudo-Cyprian, lxxxvii, 1^9 (n.).
Pseudonymity, x.
Pseudo-Tertullian, lxxxvi.
Punishment, 41^2 (n.) 80^8 106^{17}.
  day, power, p., judgement, 60^6.
  earth cleansed from all defilement, sin, p., 10^{22}.
  of kings, 56^7.
  of Lord of Spirits, 60^{25}.
  from Lord of Spirits, 54^7.
  great, on the earth, 106^{17}.
  See also 'Angels', 'Chastisement', 'Judgement', 'Wrath'.

Quarters, the Four, 77^{1-3}.

Raguel, 20^4 23^4.
Ram = Chasids, $90^{10, 11}$.
  David, 89^{43-49}.
  Elijah, 90^{31}.
  Judas Maccabaeus, $90^{13, 14, 16}$.
  Saul, 89^{42-47}.
Rameel, 6^7.
Ramiel, 6^7.
Raphael, 9^1 10^4 20^3 $22^{3, 6}$ 32^6 40^9 54^6 $68^{2, 3, 4}$ $71^{8, 9, 13}$.
Ravens = Syrians, $90^{8, 9, 12}$.
Ravine, deep and narrow (= Kedron or valley of Jehoshaphat) 26^3; deep and dry (= valley of Hinnom), $26^{4, 6}$.
  See also 'Abyss', 'Chasm', 'Valley'.
Remiel, 20^8.
Repent, 50^2 55^1.
Repentance unto hope, 40^9. Contrast 'no place of repentance', 65^{11}, and 63^{1-11}.
Resurrection, cx, 5^7 22^{13} 51^1 61^5 90^{33} 91^{10} 100^5.
  to earthly Messianic kingdom of eternal duration, of soul (spirit) and body, 6-36, 83-90.

Resurrection:
: to spiritual kingdom, in which the righteous have a spiritual body, 37-71.
: resurrection of spirit only, 91-104. Cf. 91^{10} 100^5.

Retribution, national and individual, cvii-cviii.

Reveal, everything revealed by Enoch, 82^1; to Enoch, 52^5; to righteous and elect, 61^{13}.
: evil deeds revealed in the heavens, 98^6.
: mysteries not all revealed to Watchers, 16^3.
: name of Son of Man revealed, 69^{26}.
: righteous judgement, 91^{14}.
: secrets (by angels), 9^6 10^7 64^2.
: treasures of that which is hidden (by Son of Man), 46^3.

Riches, 46^7 94^8 96^4 97^{10} 100^6. Cf. 98^3 103^5. See 'Wealth'.

Righteous, 1^2 (n.) 5^6 $10^{17, 21}$ 25^4 $38^{3, 4, 5}$ 39^4 43^4 45^6 $47^{1, 2, 4}$ $48^{1, 7, 9}$ 50^2 53^7 56^7 $58^{3, 5}$ 60^2 61^3 62^3 82^4 91^{10} $94^{3, 11}$ $95^{3, 7}$ $96^{1, 8}$ $97^{1, 3, 5}$ 98^{12-14} 99^3 $100^{5, 7, 10}$ $102^{4, 10}$ 103^1 $104^{1, 6, 12, 13}$.
: Righteous and Elect One, 53^6. See 'Messiah'.
: righteous and elect, $38^{2, 3}$ $39^{6, 7}$ $58^{1, 2}$ 61^{13} $62^{12, 13, 15}$; righteous and holy, 25^4; righteous, holy, and elect, 48^1.

Righteousness, acquire houses through their, 91^{13}.
: earth tilled in, 10^{18}.
: Enoch lifted up hands in, 84^1.
: of the Elect One, 53^7 61^4 62^3.
: flowed like water, 39^5.
: of God, 41^8 63^3 99^{10} 101^3.
: is the judgement of God, 108^{13}.
: issue not in, 104^9.
: love and walk in, 94^1.
: man who dies in, 81^4.
: never forsaketh the Son of Man, 71^{16}.
: prevails in Elect One's days, 39^6.
: seek and choose, 94^4.
: Son of Man born unto, 71^{14}.
: Son of Man who hath, 46^3; ... with whom dwelleth r., 46^3.
: those who have died in, 103^3.
: who have fallen asleep in, 49^3.
: those who practise, 81^9.
: walk in, 91^4.

Righteousness:
: week of, 91^{12}.
: weeks without number in, 91^{17}.
: ye that have died in, 102^4.
: See also 'Children', 'Elect One', 'Flesh', 'Fountain', 'Garden', 'Lord', 'Path', 'Plant', 'Scribe', 'Secret', 'Spirit', 'Way', 'Word', 'Work'.

Rivers, seven, 77^{5-7}.
†Rumael†, 69^2.
Rumjal, 69^2.

Sacrifice, civ.
Sadducees, 38^5 94^8 95^3 98^{15} $103^{14, 15}$.
: support O.T. view of Sheol, 102^4-104^9.
: = 'children of earth', 100^6.

Salvation by works and yet by grace, cv, cvi.
Samaritans, 90^{72} (n.).
Samjaza, 69^2. See also 'Semjaza'.
Samsapeel, 6^7. See also 'Shamsiel' and 'Simapesiel'.
Samuel, $89^{42, 44}$ (n.).
Saraqael, 20^6.
Sariel, 6^7 8^3.
Satan, 54^6.
Satans, 65^6.
: accuse as in O.T., 40^7.
: tempt, 69^4 sqq.
: punish, 53^3 56^1 62^{11} 63^1.

Satarel, 6^7.
Saul, 89^{42} (n.).
Save, 48^7 50^3 51^2 62^{13} 63^8 99^{10} $106^{14, 16}$.
Scribe. See 'Enoch'.
Sea, the Great = the Mediterranean, $77^{5, 7, 8}$.
Secrets, 41^3 65^{11} $68^{1, 2}$ 71^3. Cf. 40^2 46^2.
: (evil), 69^8.

Secret(s) of angels, $65^{6, 11}$.
: clouds, 41^3.
: depths, 61^5.
: eternal... in heaven, 9^6. Cf. 10^7 16^3.
: God, 63^3.
: the heavens, 41^1.
: ends of heaven, 71^4.
: the holy, 106^{19}. See 'Mysteries'.
: lightning, 59^2. See 'Thunder'.
: the righteous, 38^3.
: righteousness, 49^2 58^5 71^3.

Secret(s):
  sin, 83⁷.
  thunder and lightning, 41³ 59¹,²,³.
  winds, 41³.
  wisdom, 51³ 69⁸.
Seleucidae, 90³ (n.).
Semiazaz, 6⁷.
Semjaza, 6⁸ 6³ 9⁷ 10¹¹. See also 6⁷ 69².
Seneser, 13⁹.
Seraphim. See 'Angels'.
Serpents, the, 20⁷.
Seth, 37¹; = 'a great white bull', 85⁹.
Seven, 18⁶ (n.) 24² 32¹ 61¹¹ (n.) 72³⁷ 77⁴,⁵,⁸ (n.) 78⁴ 91¹⁶ 93¹⁰.
Shamsiel, 8⁸.
Sheep, blinded, 90²⁶.
Sheep, white (= Jacob), 89¹².
  Lord of. See 'God, titles of'.
Sheol, 22 (n.) 51 56⁸ 63¹⁰ (n.) 99¹¹ (n.) 102⁴ (n.)-104⁵ (n.), cx.
  O. T. conception of, the goal of all, and involving social not moral distinctions, 63¹⁰ (n.) 102¹¹.
  the intermediate state of the righteous and the wicked involving moral distinctions, 22 51¹ 63¹⁰ (n.) 102⁵. Cf. 100⁵.
  three hollow places in, 22.
  the intermediate state of the wicked, 63¹⁰ (n.).
  the final abode of the wicked = hell, 63¹⁰ (n.) 99¹¹ (n.) 103⁷ (n.). See also 'Gehenna'.
Shepherds, the seventy, 89⁵⁹ (n.)-90¹ 90¹³,¹⁷,²⁵.
Sign, 55².
  (of Zodiac), 72¹³,¹⁹.
  of the days, 82¹⁶,¹⁹.
Signs (of Zodiac), 48³ 75³.
Siloah, 26².
Simapesiel, 69².
Sin, due to the fall of the angels, and the knowledge they imparted to mankind, civ-cvi, 7⁵ 9¹,⁶,⁸ 10⁸ (n.) 16³. Cf. 69¹¹.
  due to demons, 15⁸,⁹,¹¹ 16¹.
  due to Satans, 40⁷.
  due to man, 98⁴.
  of Adam, 32⁶.
  of Eve attributed to a Satan, Gadreel, 69⁶.

Sin:
  man of himself has created, 98⁴⁴, cvi.
Sinai, 1⁴ 89²⁹,³²,³³ (n.).
Sins, penalty of a great sin, 6³.
  revealed to them (women) all kinds of sin, 9⁸.
  to him (Azazel) ascribe all sin, 10⁸.
  cleanse earth from all oppression, all unrighteousness, sin, godlessness, 10²⁰.
  earth cleansed from all defilement, sin, punishment, torment, 10²².
  no forgiveness of, 12⁵.
  works of godlessness, unrighteousness, and sin shown to men, 13².
  for what sin are they bound, 21⁴.
  the time entailed by their sins, 21⁶. Cf. 18¹⁶.
  sinners judged for their sins, 38¹.
  kings and mighty confess their sins, 63¹.
  all our sins are reckoned up in righteousness, 63⁹.
  angels seduced the children of men into committing, 64².
  sin, unrighteousness, blasphemy, violence increase, 91⁷.
  sin shall perish in darkness ... no more seen from that day, 92⁵.
  sin no more mentioned for ever, 91¹⁷.
  build houses with sin, 94⁷.
  healing far from you because of your sins, 95⁴.
  has not been sent upon the earth ... man of himself hath created it ... under a great curse shall they fall who commit it, 98⁴.
  every sin is every day recorded in heaven, 98⁷.
  place the sin of the sinners for a memorial before the Most High, 99³.
  sin is prepared for a day of unceasing bloodshed, 99⁶.
  the bricks and stones of sin, 99¹³.
  the holy and righteous shall remember your sins, 99¹⁶.
  those who brought down sin, 100⁴.
  an end of all wickedness and sin, 100⁵.
  the overthrow of their sins, 100⁶.
  inquire of sun and moon in reference to sins, 100¹⁰.

Sins:
:   mist, dew, and rain mindful of sins, 100^{11}.
    wealth of sins, 103^5. Cf. 'unrighteous gains', 63^{10}.
    sins not searched out or written down ... they shall write down your sins every day, 104^7.
    light and darkness, day and night, see all your sins, 104^8.
    lying and godlessness issue in great sin, 104^9.
    commit sin (with the women), 106^{14}.
    all the sin consummated, 106^{18}.
    till sin passes away from the earth, 107^1.
    till sin has passed away, 108^3.
    See also 'Apostasy', 'Blasphemy', 'Deceit', 'Godlessness', 'Oppression', 'Transgression', 'Uncleanness', 'Unrighteousness', 'Violence', 'Wickedness'.

Sinners, 5^6 $22^{10, 13}$ 38^{1-3} 41^2 $45^{2, 5, 6}$ 50^2 $53^{2, 7}$ $62^2, ^{13}$ 69^{27}.
:   caused to pass away, 69^{27}.
    destroyed by the sword, 91^{11}.
    judged for their sins, 38^1.
    judgement impending for, 45^6.
    shall not set foot on new earth, 45^5.
    tempt men to evilly-entreat wisdom, 94^5.

Sirens, 19^2.
Slay, 60^{25} 62^2 98^{12} 99^{15}.
:   spirits not slain, 22^{13}.
    slain in Sheol, 99^{11}.
    spirits slain, 108^3.

Sleep not, those who. See 'Watchers'.
Solar Year, 74.
Son of Man, 46^2 (n.) 48^2 (n.). See lxiii–lxvi, also Appendix II, pp. 306–309.
:   meaning of title, p. 307.
    all judgement committed to, 69^{27}.
    pre-existence of the, 48^2 (n.).
    universal dominion of, 62^6.
    to sit on God's throne, 51^3.
    Son of man = Enoch, 60^{10}.
    See also 'Messiah'.

Son, My (God's), 105^2.
:   of serpent, 69^{12}.

Sons, of God, $69^{4, 5}$. See 'Angels'.

Sons, of the God of heaven, 106^5.
:   holy, of God, 71^1.
    of heaven, 13^8.
    of Watchers, 10^{12} 14^6.
    See 'Children'.

Soul, Who could see a, 93^{12}.
Souls, of dead, 22^3.
:   of those who have died, 9^{10}.
    of flesh, 16^1.
    of men, 9^3.
    of righteous, 102^4. Cf. 102^{11}.
    See 'Spirit'.

Soul and spirit, cv.
Spectacle, 21^9 27^3 62^{12}. Cf. 48^9.
Spirit, 13^6 15^{10} $22^{6, 7, 9-13}$ $39^{8, 12}$ $60^{4, 14, 15, 17}$ $67^{8, 9}$ 68^2 70^2 $71^{1, 5, 11}$ 92^2 91^1 93^{12} $98^{3, 7, 10}$ 102^{11} $103^{8, 9}$ 106^{17} $108^{3, 7}$.
:   (evil), 15^{12} 16^1 20^6 69^{12}.
    evil, $15^{8, 9}$. See 'Demons'.
    of Abel, 22^7.
    angels, 19^1.
    dead, $22^{5, 9}$.
    dew, 60^{20} 75^5.
    earth, 15^{10}.
    faith, 61^{11}.
    giants, $15^{11, 12}$ 16^1.
    good, 108^{11}.
    goodness, 61^{11}.
    hail, 60^{17}.
    heaven, 15^{10}.
    hoar-frost, 60^{17}.
    insight, 49^3.
    judgement, 61^{11}.
    life, 61^7.
    light, 61^{12}.
    lightning and thunder, $60^{14, 15}$.
    Lord, 67^{10}.
    man, 98^7.
    men, 20^3 22^5 41^8.
    mercy, 61^{11}.
    mist, 60^{19}.
    patience, 61^{11}.
    peace, 61^{11}.
    power, 71^{11}.
    rain, 60^{21}.
    reprobate, 10^{15}.
    righteous, 22^9 41^8.
    righteousness, 62^2.
    sea, 60^{16}.
    sinners, 22^{13} 108^6.

Spirit:
   of snow, 60^{17}.
      souls of dead, 22^3.
      those who died in righteousness, 49^3 $103^{3, 4}$.
      thunder. See 'Lightning'.
      understanding and might, 49^3.
      water, 69^{22}.
      winds and zephyrs, 69^{22}.
      wisdom, 49^3 61^{11}.
   Lord of Spirits. See 'God'.
   punishment of, 67^8.
   slain. See 'Slay'.
   See 'Soul'.
Spirits over natural phenomena, 60^{12} (n.).
Spring, bright, of water, 22^9.
Stars, conscious existence of, 41^5 (n.).
   punished (the seven), 18^{13-16} 21^{1-6}.
   shooting, 44 (n.).
   symbolize angels, $86^{1, 3}$; men, 43^4 46^7.
Styx, 17^6 (n.).
Sun, 4^1 $41^{5, 6, 8}$ 43^3 58^3 69^{20} 72^1-73^4 $75^{3, 6}$ $78^{1, 4, 10}$ 79^5 80^1 $82^{4, 8, 13, 16}$ 83^{11} $100^{2, 10}$.
   names of, 78^1.
Sword, period of, 38^5 98^{12} $99^{4, 6}$.
   given to the sheep, 90^{19} 91^{12}.
   used figuratively, 62^{12} 63^{11}.
Synagogues. See 'Congregation'.
Syncellus, xiv, xcii, 6^3 (n.), p. 305.
Syrians = ravens in $90^{8, 9, 12}$.

Taba'et, 69^{12}.
Tablets, heavenly, $81^{1, 2}$ 93^2 103^2 106^{19}. Cf. 47^3 (n.).
†Tam'aini†, 82^{15}.
Tamiel, 6^7.
Tartarus, 20^2.
Tatian, lxxxii.
Temple. See 'Holy Place', 'Tower'.
Ten thousand, 14^{22} 40^1.
Tertullian, lxxxiv, 8^1 $15^{8, 9}$ 19^1 $99^{6, 7}$ (notes).
Testaments of the Twelve Patriarchs, influence of 1 Enoch on, lxxv-lxxvi.
Testimony, 67^{12} $89^{63, 76}$ 96^4 97^4 99^3. Cf. 89^{53} 103^4.
Thomas, Acts of, xiii.

Throne, of God, 25^3.
   of glory, the Elect One sits on, 45^3 55^4 $62^{3, 5}$.
Thrones, of the elect, 108^{12}.
Thunder. See 'Lightning', 59^2.
Tigers = Assyrians, 89^{55} (n.).
Tigris, 77^6 (n.).
Times. See 'Hours'.
Tomas, 78^1.
Tongue, 14^2.
Tower = Temple, 89^{50} (n.) $^{54, 56, 67, 73}$.
Transgression, 22^{13} $91^{6, 7}$ 107^1. See 'Sin'.
Transgressors, 22^{13}.
Translation. See 'Enoch'.
Treasuries, of the stars, 17^1.
   of the winds, 18^1.
Trees, desirable, 10^{19}.
   fourteen evergreen, 3.
   fragrant, 24^3 29^2 30^3 32^1.
   with branches abiding and blooming, 26^1.
Tree of life, 24^4 25^{4-6}.
   of wisdom, 32^{3-6} (n.).
   dismembered = Israel, 26^1.
Tumael, 69^2.
†Turael†, 69^2.
Turel, 6^7 69^2.
†Turel†, 69^2.

Uncleanness, $10^{11, 20}$ 91^7. Cf. 106^{17}. See 'Sin'.
Ungodly, ungodliness, 1^9.
Unrepentant, 50^4.
Unrighteous, $62^{2, 13}$ 96^2 103^{11}. See 'Sinners', 'Wicked'.
Unrighteous gains, 63^{10}. See 'Wealth'.
Unrighteousness, taught u. on earth, 9^6.
   cleanse earth from all u., 10^{20}.
   u. went forth, whom she sought not she found, 42^3.
   their deeds manifest u., 46^7.
   this world of u., 48^7.
   shall disappear as a shadow, 49^2.
   shall not maintain itself, 50^4.
   u. in becoming subject to Satan, 54^6.
   because of their u. their judgement has been determined upon, 65^{10}.
   angels who have shown u., 67^4.
   no book of u. written, 81^4.
   all u. come to an end, 91^5.

Unrighteousness:
u. shall again be consummated ... ... deeds of u. prevail, 91^6.
sin, u., blasphemy, violence increase, 91^7.
roots of u., 91^8.
roots of u. ... cut off, 91^{11}.
walk in paths of u., 91^{19}.
u. shall grow up, 93^4.
paths of u., 94^1.
those who build u. and oppression, 94^6.
commit blasphemy and u., 94^9.
work u., deceit, blasphemy, 96^7.
the day of u., 97^1.
words of your u. ... read out, 97^6.
work u. and help oppression, 99^{13}.
u. consummated on the earth, 106^{18}.
still more u. consummated, 106^{19}.
See 'Sin'.

Uprightness, 58^6 67^1 84^6 $92^{1,4}$ $91^{3,4}$ 93^2 91^{14} $104^{12,13}$ 105^2.
children of, 105^2.
paths of, 105^2. Cf. 105^{13}.
plant of, 93^2.
See 'Righteousness'.

Uriel, 9^1 10^1 19^1 20^2 (over Tartarus), $21^{5,9}$ 27^2 33^4 72^1 74^2 $75^{3,4}$ 78^{10} 79^6 80^1 82^7.

Valley, accursed (= Gehenna), 27^2.
burning, among metal mountains, 67^4. Cf. 67^7. See 54^7-55 (n.).
deep, with burning fire, $54^{1,2}$.
deep, with open mouths, 53^1.
full of water, 30^1.
Valleys, cinnamon, 30^3.
of the earth, 10^{12}.
See 'Abyss', 'Chasm', 'Deep', 'Depth', 'Gehenna', 'Ravine'.
Violence, 65^6 91^3 $91^{4,8,11,13,19}$ 94^2 102^{10} 104^9. See 'Oppression', 'Sin'.
Vision, of the Holy One, 1^2.
of chastisement, 13^8.
of cherubim, 14^{18}.
of wisdom, 37^1.
heavenly, 93^2.
Visions, 13^8 $14^{4,8,14}$ 19^3 37^1 $83^{1,2,3,7}$ $85^{2,3}$ 87^2 88^3 $89^{7,70}$ $90^{2,8,40,42}$ 93^2 106^{13}.
Vultures = Graeco-Egyptians, 90^2. Cf. $90^{11,13}$ (n.).

Watchers = archangels, $12^{2,3}$. Cf. 20^1 ('who watch'), also $39^{12,13}$ 40^2 61^{12} 71^7 ('who sleep not').
— fallen angels, 1^5 $10^{9,15}$ 12^4 13^{10} $14^{1,3}$ 15^2 $16^{1,2}$ 91^{15}.
Water, 18^{12} $28^{2,3}$ 39^5 52^8 $60^{7,21}$ 61^{10} 66^1 $67^{5,6,8,11,13}$ 69^{17} 76^4 89^3.
of the deep, 17^7.
of judgement, 67^{13}.
above the heavens, $54^{7,8}$.
beneath the earth, 54^8 66^1.
earth upon, 69^{17}.
See also 10^2 26^2 30^1 53^7 $89^{2,7,23,24}$ 96^6.
See 'Fountain', 'Spring'.
Waters, living, 17^4. Cf. 22^9.
Way, 61^9; of righteousness, 82^4. See 'Paths'.
Ways, the Two, 91^4 (n.) ^{19} (n.).
Wealth, of sins, 103^5. See 'Unrighteous'.
Week, 93 91^{12-17}.
Weighing, 41^1 43^2 60^{12} 61^8.
West, 67^4 70^3.
White, symbolizes righteousness, 83^2 (n.).
Wicked, 1^1 104^{10} 108^{10}. See 'Unrighteous'.
Wickedness, 93^4 95^2 98^{11} $100^{5,8}$. See 'Sin'.
Windows, 72^3, ^{7} 75^7 83^{11} 101^2.
Winds, 18^{1-5} 34–36 41^4 60^{12} 76.
the twelve, 76^1; portals of, 76^1. See 'Chambers', 'Treasuries'.
Wisdom, 5^8 $32^{3,4}$ $37^{1,2,3,4}$ $42^{1,3}$ 48^1 49^1 51^3 $61^{7,11}$ 63^2 69^8 $82^{2,3}$ 84^3 91^{10} 93^8 94^5 98^3 99^{10} 101^8 104^{12} 105^1.
Wisdom, assessor of God, 84^3.
allegory concerning, $42^{1,2}$.
beginning of, 37^2.
bestowed on the elect, 5^8 91^{10}. Cf. 37^4.
claimed for Enochic revelations, 37^4 82^2 92^1 93^{10}.
Lord of, 63^2.
fountains of, 48^1.
poured out as water before the Messiah, 49^1 51^3.
secrets of, 69^8.
sinners evilly-entreat, 94^5.
spirit of, 61^{11}.
tree of, 32^3.
vision of, 37^1.
words of, 37^2 99^{10}.

Index II. Names and Subjects

Witchcraft, 65^6.
Wolves = Egyptians, $89^{13-27, 38}$.
Woman, 62^4 98^4.
Women, 6^1 7^1 9^8, 9 10^{11} 12^4 $15^{3, 4, 12}$ 16^3 $19^{1, 2}$ 106^{14}.
Word, $14^{1, 3, 24}$, 59^2 61^9 62^3 68^3 69^{29} 102^1 $104^{9, 10}$ 106^{13}.
Words, 5^4 13^{10} 27^2 37^2 61^6 98^{14} $99^{2, 10}$.
   of the holy angels, 93^2.
   of the Holy One, 37^2 104^9.
   of righteousness, 13^{10} 14^1 104^{10}.
   of wisdom, 14^3 37^2 99^{10}.
Works, 11^1 38^2 61^8 81^3.
   of righteousness and truth, 10^{16}.
   Salvation by. See 'Salvation'.
World, $75^{2, 8, 9}$.
   creation of, 48^6 69^{16}.
   days of, 11^2.
   elect of, 93^1.
   generations of, 15^6 82^1 $103^{4, 8}$ 104^5.
   God of. See 'God'.
   good things in, 108^8.
   led astray, 69^{27}.
   life in, 108^{10}.
   Lord of. See 'God'.
   quarters of, 77^1.
   works of, 81^3.
   whole, 84^3 91^{14}.
   years of, 72^1.

World:
   of luminaries, 20^4.
   to come, 71^{15}.
   of unrighteousness, 48^7.
   world-stations, 74^{17} 75^2.
   See 'Age', 'Earth'.
Wrath (of God), 55^3 62^{12} 84^4 90^{18} $91^{7, 9}$; anger, 5^9 101^3. Cf. 18^{16} 99^{16}.
Write down (sins), 89^{70} 98^8 104^7.
   for destruction, 91^{14}.
   Cf. 'record', $89^{62, 64}$.
   See 'Name'.

Year, 74^{10} 82^6.
   four parts of, $82^{4, 6, 11, 13}$.
Years, 5^{00}, 10^{10}.
   of destruction, 5^5.
   joy, 5^9.
   life, 5^8.
   of world, 72^1.
   reckoning of, 82^6.

Zaqiel, 6^7.
Zeleba'el, 82^{17}.
Zerubbabel, 90^{72} (n.).
Zion, 26^2 (n.).
Zodiac. See 'Signs'.
Zosimus of Panopolis, lxxxvii.
Zotiel (the angel), 32^2.

CPSIA information can be obtained at www.ICGtesting.com
Printed in the USA
BVOW09*0719040216
435438BV00020B/49/P